BIOGRAPHICAL DICTIONARY
OF MODERN EGYPT

BIOGRAPHICAL DICTIONARY OF MODERN EGYPT

ARTHUR GOLDSCHMIDT JR.

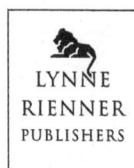

LYNNE
RIENNER
PUBLISHERS

BOULDER
LONDON

Published in the United States of America in 2000 by
Lynne Rienner Publishers, Inc.
1800 30th Street, Boulder, Colorado 80301
www.rienner.com

and in the United Kingdom by
Lynne Rienner Publishers, Inc.
3 Henrietta Street, Covent Garden, London WC2E 8LU

Library of Congress Cataloging-in-Publication Data
Goldschmidt, Arthur, 1938–
   Biographical dictionary of modern Egypt / Arthur Goldschmidt Jr.
     p.   cm.
   Includes bibliographical references (p.   ) and index.
   ISBN 1-55587-229-8 (hc)
    1. Egypt—History—1517–1882 Biography Dictionaries.   2. Egypt—
History—1798– Biography Dictionaries.   I. Title.
DT97.G65   2000
920.062—dc21

99-33550
CIP

British Cataloguing in Publication Data
A Cataloguing in Publication record for this book
is available from the British Library.

Printed and bound in the United States of America

5   4   3   2

To the People in and of Egypt

Let us now praise famous men,
And our fathers that begot us.
The Lord hath wrought great glory by them
Through his great power from the beginning.
Such as did bear rule in their kingdoms,
Men renowned for their power,
Giving counsel by their understanding,
And declaring prophecies:
Leaders of the people by their counsels,
And by their knowledge meet for the people,
Wise and eloquent in their instructions:
Such as found out musical tunes,
And recited verses in writing:
Rich men furnished with ability,
Living peaceably in their habitations:
All these were honored in their generations,
And were the glory of their times.
There be of them, that have left a name behind them,
That their praises might be reported.
And some there be, which have no memorial,
Who are perished, as though they had never been;
And are as though they had never been;
And their children after them.
But these were merciful men,
Whose righteousness has not been forgotten.
With their seed shall continually remain a good inheritance,
And their children for their sakes.
Their seed shall remain for ever,
And their glory shall not be blotted out.
Their bodies are buried in peace;
But their name liveth for evermore.
The people will tell of their wisdom,
And the congregation will show forth their praise.

—Ecclesiasticus (King James Version)

CONTENTS

PREFACE

Egypt ranks first among the Arab countries in population, popular culture, and historical documentation. Its people have a durable sense of national identity. Both Egyptians and foreigners have written numerous scholarly studies and popular accounts of modern Egypt's foreign relations, domestic politics, commerce and industry, religions, prose and poetry, visual arts, entertainment, and intellectual life. Specialized works of collective biography also abound, and in Arabic at least, there are individual biographies for most of Egypt's intellectual and political leaders, past and present. Up to now, however, researchers in Egypt's modern history have not had an organized and accessible reference tool, comparable to the *American National Biography*, with concise accounts of the lives of the country's leaders. Nor could they find bibliographic aids that could point them to source materials published in Arabic and in European languages. This work fills that void.

For more than thirty years I have wanted to assemble, or to persuade others to assemble, a biographical dictionary of Egypt that could later serve as a working model for volumes covering other Arab countries, as well as Israel, Turkey, Iran, and Afghanistan. The development of the computer's word-processing capabilities has made what was a utopian vision seem attainable.

I made some debatable decisions in producing this biographical dictionary. The work takes "Egypt" to be the region or country ruled from Cairo by Mamluks, Ottoman governors or khedives, British consuls or high commissioners, kings, and presidents; but it excludes Sudan. There is no consensus on when "modern" Egypt begins; Egyptian historians often debate whether Napoleon's invasion in 1798 or Muhammad

'Ali's seizure of power in 1805 marks the onset of modernity. I think that an ambitious effort was made to strengthen Egypt during the reigns of 'Ali Bey and Muhammad Bey Abu al-Dhahab in the late eighteenth century and that the first signs of intellectual revival can be seen in the work of Murtada al-Zabidi and 'Abd al-Rahman al-Jabarti. Therefore, these leaders and a few of their contemporaries are the earliest figures dealt with in the dictionary.

Almost everyone asks about the criteria for inclusion. Many worthy generals, admirals, poets, novelists, journalists, lawyers, doctors, and parliamentarians failed to make the cut; some readers may gasp at the inclusion of a few men and women who did. The primary criterion was, "Is the inclusion of person X needed to give a representative picture of modern Egypt's history?" Traditional biographical dictionaries in the West stress generals, politicians, and diplomats; those of the Muslim world emphasize religious leaders, scholars, and poets. All deserve attention, but so, too, do founders of newspapers, department stores, theatrical troupes, and innovative techniques of visual representation. There are some regrettable omissions: farmers and laborers, athletes and guides, and some Egyptians now at the leading edge of the arts and sciences. I deliberately omitted Egyptians whose historically significant activities took place in other countries. I included some non-Egyptians, especially French and British nationals, who did play a prominent role in Egypt's modern history.

The entries vary in length according to my judgment of the importance of the people covered. Exact birth and death dates are usually supplied, to facilitate future analysis of age cohorts and access to obituaries, but they were not always attainable. Arabic personal names are transliterated in the style prescribed by the *International Journal of Middle East Studies*, which in some cases will jar eyes attuned to journalistic or to Gallo-Egyptian conventions.

Each entry is followed by a list of sources that will provide further information. Within each entry, the first mention of any name that has its own entry in the dictionary appears in small capital letters. A list of abbreviations used in the work, a complete bibliography, and a subject index appear at the end of the dictionary.

*   *   *

A work of this magnitude could not have been created without access to many libraries and archives outside my home institution. The one that proved superb for contemporary Egypt was the archives of *al-Ahram*, with its dossiers and folders of clippings about hundreds of men and women. Collections at the American Research Center in Egypt, the American University in Cairo, the Bibliothèque Nationale, the British Library (old and new), Dar al-Kutub, the École des Langues Orientales Vivantes, the Library of Congress, the New York Public Library, and the University of California yielded treasures for this study. Penn State's Inter-Library Loan Office obtained Arabic materials from various U.S. research libraries.

Among the individuals who advised me on key issues were Margot Badran, Indira Gesink, Robert Johnston, and Caroline Williams (1997–1998 research fellows at the American Research Center in Egypt); Professors Joel Gordon of the University of Arkansas, Peter Gran of Temple University, Donald M. Reid of Georgia State University, and Jason Thompson of the American University in Cairo; and correspondents with related projects, Wolfgang Behn in Berlin and Dennis Walker in Melbourne.

I received invaluable advice from Yunan Labib Rizq, professor of modern Egyptian history at Ain Shams University's Women's College: Rizq arranged my access to *al-Ahram*'s archives and invited me to speak to the Egyptian historians' *nadwa* (club), where 'Abd al-Khaliq Lashin and others gave me much advice and encouragement. Many other Egyptians shared their knowledge about significant figures in their history; among them were Samir Raafat, Ibrahim Sadek, and Sayyid Karim. Indeed, almost every cabdriver in Cairo acquainted me with modern Egypt's musical heritage, and staff members at the Hotel Cosmopolitan proffered their advice on performers and poets. I learned much from such old Cairo hands as Chris Langtvet and Raymond Stock. Above all, I thank Sa'd Zinnari for supplying me with his books, advice, and friendship for thirty years.

At Lynne Rienner Publishers, I thank Lynne Rienner herself, Sally Glover, and Shena Redmond; I thank copyeditor Marian Safran as well as proofreader Rich Kalmanash and indexer Kate Bowman. I also appreciated the anonymous reader's helpful comments. I take full responsibility, however, for my choice of biographical entries (to quote Ecclesiasticus: some there be who have no memorial) and for any errors that I may have committed.

Financial support for my research came from the United States Information Service via the American Research Center in Egypt, a timely sabbatical leave from the Pennsylvania State University, and a special gift from my late mother-in-law, Dorothy Robb. Another kind of material support was the hospitality offered by our daughter-in-law's parents, Norman and Easter Goldstein, in Berkeley; by my sister and brother-in-law, Ann and Raymond Richardson, who let us stay in their apartment while I was doing research in Paris; and by my father, Arthur "Tex" Goldschmidt, who, in addition to hosting us in Haverford, listened to weekly reports of my progress from Cairo.

Anyone who has written a book or lived with an author knows the toll that writing takes on his or her significant other. My wife, Louise, gets a special note of thanks for her patience at times when I was absent, preoccupied, or unable to fulfill my domestic duties.

—*Arthur Goldschmidt Jr.*

A

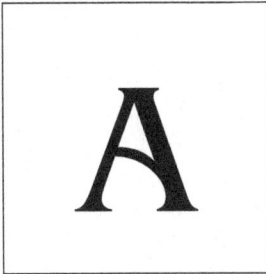

Abaza, [Muhammad] Fikri

(1897–14 February 1979)

Writer, lawyer, politician, and long-time editor of *al-Musawwar*, often called the Dean of Journalists. Fikri was born in Abu Shahata, near Minya al-Qamh. His father, Shaykh Husayn Abaza, hoped that Fikri might follow in his footsteps and study at al-Azhar. Instead, Fikri attended the Sa'idiyya School in Cairo, where he began his journalistic career by writing for *al-Muayyad*. He graduated from the government Law School in 1917 and worked for a while as a lawyer in Asyut, then moved his office to Zaqaziq and finally to Cairo. He was an active orator and writer during the 1919 Revolution, writing fiery articles in *al-Ahram* against the British protectorate. He even composed a national anthem, sung at the time by Copts and Muslims together. Joining the National Party, he was first elected to the Chamber of Deputies in 1926. Thrice asked to become a minister, he always refused on the Nationalist principle against serving in a cabinet while British troops occupied Egypt.

As he became more politically active, he committed himself to a journalistic career. In 1924 he began writing for *al-Musawwar*, becoming its editor-in-chief in 1926, and in 1949 he founded its entertainment magazine. In 1944 he became head of the Journalists' Syndicate and was reelected four times to that position. He was also elected honorary president of the Ahli Sporting Club and a member of the supervisory committee of Dar al-Kutub. He wrote books, of which the best-known is *al-Dahik al-baki* [The Weeping Laugher], produced plays, and composed songs for the mandolin and the flute. In 1961 he was dismissed as editor of *al-Mu-sawwar*, at Nasir's insistence, for writing a veiled suggestion of peace with Israel, but he was reinstated after publishing an apology in *al-Ahram*. Although Fikri was notorious for publicly criticizing anyone in power, Sadat awarded him an honorary doctorate in 1976.

Bibliographic Sources
Abaza, Faruq, *Fikri Abaza.*
'Abd al-Hayy, *'Asir hayati,* 100–109.
Abu al-Majd, *Fikri Abaza.*
al-Ahram Archives, file 421.
Amin, Mustafa, *Shakhsiyat,* II, 87–104.
Bishri, 'Abd al-'Aziz, *Fi al-mirah,* 83–88.
Fahmi, Zaki, *Safwat al-'asr,* 681–685.
Fuda, *Nujum Shari' al-Sihafa,* 26–32.
Jindi, Anwar, *al-Sihafa al-siyasiyya,* 412–419.
Khidr, *Suhufiyyun mu'asirun,* 79–98.
Muti'i, *Haula al-rijal min Misr,* III, 227–238.
———, *Mawsu'a,* 411–417.
Rizq, Fathi, *Khamsa wa sab'una najman,* 179–187.
Tamawi, *"al-Hilal" miat 'am min tarikh.*
Tawfiq, Najib, *Ashhar al-usrat,* 96–115.
Taymur, Mahmud, *al-Shakhsiyyat al-'ishrun,* 108–115.

Abaza, Tharwat

(28 June 1927–)

Writer of plays, film scenarios, and short stories. He was born in Cairo's Munira district, the son of lawyer-politician Ibrahim Disuqi Abaza and a cousin of FIKRI. Educated in government schools, Abaza published his first article (under a pen name) when he was sixteen, criticizing his Arabic teacher. Upon receiving his *license* from Cairo University's Law Faculty in 1950, he married his cousin, the daughter of poet 'Aziz Abaza, and began writing plays and short stories for Egyptian State Broadcasting. He received a state encouragement award in 1959 and became a member of the international writers' union in London in 1971. Upon being dropped from membership in the ASU in 1973, he became treasurer of the Society to Protect the Rights of Writers. He then became a literary adviser for the state-run Cinema, Stage, and Music Organization, and in 1975 he joined the administrative board of *al-Idha'a wa al-tilvizyun*, of which he also became the editor-in-chief. A year later he became an editor for *al-Ahram*. Abaza also became secretary-general of the Egyptian Writers Union and in 1980 was elected its president. He served five terms but resigned his membership

1

in April 1997 right after having been reelected to a sixth term. He was also elected vice president of the Egyptian Senate. He has written frequently about his family, which is famous for its landholdings and dominant role in Sharqiyya province, and has publicly attacked Nasirism as well as Marxism.

Bibliographic Sources
Abaza, Tharwat. *Dhikrayat la mudhakkirat.*
————, "Lamahat min hayati."
al-Ahram Archives, file 22407.
EAL, I, 2.
Najib, *A'lam Misr,* 151.
Shalabi, Muhammad, *Ma'a ruwwad al-fikr.*

'Abbas Hilmi I

(1 July 1812–13 July 1854)
Egypt's viceroy from 1848 to 1854. The son of Tusun, who predeceased his father, MUHAMMAD 'ALI, 'Abbas was born in Jidda and reared in Cairo. He succeeded IBRAHIM upon his death in November 1848. Often labeled a reactionary for dismantling some of his grandfather's westernizing reforms, he did indeed dismiss many of Muhammad 'Ali's European advisers. Although 'Abbas was motivated by parsimony and paranoia, peasant taxpayers benefited from his reduced imposts and rates. During his reign an English company, headed by Robert Stephenson, won a concession to build the first railroad between Cairo and Alexandria. The route from Cairo to Suez was also improved. In 1853 'Abbas sent 20,000 troops to fight for the Ottoman Empire against the Russians in the Crimean War, in which his soldiers suffered heavy casualties. The cause of his death in Benha has never been explained, but it is thought that he was murdered by two mamluks sent to him from Istanbul by his aunt, who sought revenge because of a dispute over his heirs' inheritance.

Bibliographic Sources
'Abd al-Karim, Ahmad 'Izzat, *Tarikh al-ta'lim fi Misr,* I, 3–165.
Asaf, *Dalil,* I, 151–152.
Durri [al-Hakim], *al-Nukhba al-durriyya,* 18.
EI2, I, 13, article by Marcel Colombe.
Fahmi, Zaki, *Safwat al-'asr,* 40–41.
Fuad, Faraj Sulayman, *al-Kanz al-thamin,* 46–48.
Heyworth-Dunne, J., *Introduction,* 285–312.
Nubar, *Mémoires,* 78–124.
Rafi'i, 'Abd al-Rahman, *'Asr Isma'il,* I, 10–22.
Sammarco, *Les règnes de 'Abbas, de Sa'id, et d'Isma'il.*
Times (London) (28 July 1854): 7c; (31 July 1854): 8f, 9e.
Toledano, *State and Society,* 7–8 et passim.
Tugay, *Three Centuries,* 97–100.
Tusun, *al-Jaysh al-misri fi Harb al-Krim.*
Zakhura, *Mirat al-'asr,* I, 29–30.
Zaki, 'Abd al-Rahman, "Le journal manuscrit d'Abbas Bey."
Zaydan, Jurji, *Mashahir al-sharq,* 30–31.
Zirikli, *al-A'lam,* III, 261.

'Abbas Hilmi II

(14 August 1874–21 December 1944)
Egypt's khedive from 1892 to 1914. Born in Cairo, he was educated by tutors, at the Princes' School, the Thudicum in Geneva, and the Theresianum Military Academy in Vienna. Because his father, Khedive TAWFIQ, died unexpectedly in January 1892, when 'Abbas was still a cadet, his reign began when he was barely eighteen years old by the Muslim calendar. High-spirited and nationalistic, he soon replaced some of his palace staff, and in January 1893 he clashed with the British diplomatic agent, Lord CROMER, when 'Abbas tried to replace his pro-British premier, MUSTAFA FAHMI, with HUSAYN FAKHRI and a new cabinet without first securing Cromer's consent. Cromer, backed by his government, told the khedive that he could not change his ministers without prior British permission. 'Abbas again challenged the British, in particular Sir Herbert (later Lord) KITCHENER, the head of the Egyptian army, a year later while reviewing the troops near Egypt's southern border. Unable after 1894 to oppose British rule openly, 'Abbas formed a secret group composed of Europeans and nationalistic Egyptians, the Society for the Revival of the Nation, which later became the nucleus of MUSTAFA KAMIL's National Party. He subsidized Mustafa's anti-British propaganda in Europe and the publication of *al-Muayyad* at home.

As the Nationalists' hopes for French aid against the British occupation waned after the Fashoda Incident (the military encounter in 1898 between the Anglo-Egyptian army and a French expeditionary force), 'Abbas made peace with Britain, partly due to his friendship with the Prince of Wales, later King Edward VII. He distanced himself from the National Party after the Entente Cordiale, although he briefly made peace with Mustafa Kamil and MUHAMMAD FARID following the Dinshaway Incident (a British atrocity in 1906 against Egyptian peasants, which led to widespread protests against the British occupation in both Europe and Egypt) and subsidized the publication of British and French editions of al-Liwa. He expressed his moral support for constitutional rule, one of the National Party's desiderata, but abandoned anti-British nationalism because of Cromer's retirement and the *politique d'entente* pursued by Cromer's successor, Sir ELDON GORST. To signal this new policy in 1908, 'Abbas replaced Mustafa Fahmi's cabinet with a new one headed by BUTRUS GHALI, who opposed the Nationalists. 'Abbas turned against the National Party and its newspapers, approving the 1881 Press Law revival, Shaykh JAWISH's trials, and the promulgation of the 1910 Exceptional Laws, partly owing to his friendship with Gorst, which he affirmed by calling on the ailing British agent shortly before his death in 1911. When Kitchener, 'Abbas's nemesis, took charge, the khedive resumed his old hostility to the British, but the National Party had lost much of its power, and its newspapers were muzzled during 1912. The elections for the Legislative Assembly set up under the 1913 Organic Law opened new opportunities to seek political support, but much of its leadership came from the traditionally hostile Umma Party, notably SA'D ZAGHLUL. Kitchener now hoped to replace 'Abbas by a more pliable relative.

While 'Abbas was in Istanbul in July 1914, he was shot by a deranged Egyptian student thought to be an agent of the ruling Committee of Union and Progress. Before 'Abbas was well enough to leave, however, World War I broke out, and Britain's ambassador in Turkey warned him that he would not be readmitted to Egypt until the war ended. The khedive decided to make peace with the CUP through War Minister Enver and with the exiled Egyptian Nationalists, notably Muhammad Farid and Shaykh Jawish. After the Ottoman Empire joined the Central Powers, 'Abbas issued manifestos "dismissing" his ministers, granting a constitution to the Egyptian people, and calling on them to revolt against the British. But his ties with the CUP and the Ottoman government remained troubled, and he left Istanbul for Vienna in December 1914. Soon afterward the British officially deposed him in favor of his uncle, HUSAYN KAMIL, severing Egypt's vestigial Ottoman ties. The ex-khedive stayed away from Istanbul for three years, during which he intrigued with Germany to obtain funds, ostensibly to buy shares to subvert Paris newspapers (known as the Bolo Affair), and with Britain to ensure himself an income from his properties in Egypt and to secure recognition of his son, 'Abd al-Mun'im, as heir to Egypt's throne. Discredited by the Bolo Affair and unable to settle with the British, 'Abbas returned to Istanbul late in 1917 and backed the Central Powers for the rest of the war. After the Armistice, he moved from one European city to another, and until 1922 he sought to recover control of his property in Egypt. Formally renouncing his family's claim to the throne in 1931, he invested in real estate and various business enterprises and still engaged in politics, notably trying to resolve the Palestine question, but never returned to Egypt. He backed the Axis Powers in World War II and died in Geneva. Energetic and patriotic, 'Abbas failed as khedive to stem the entrenchment of the British occupation.

Bibliographic Sources
'Abbas Hilmi, *'Ahdi*.
————, *Last Khedive of Egypt*.
Anis, *Safahat majhula*.
————, *Safahat matwiya*.
Antaki, *al-Nujum*, 4–7.
Asaf, *Dalil*, 190–193.
'Awad, Ahmad Hafiz, in *al-Hilal*.
'Azmi, "'Abbas Hilmi al-Thani."
Beaman, *Dethronement of the Khedive*.
Berque, *Egypt*, 164–169, 248–250.
Cromer, *Abbas II*.
EI2, I, 13, article by Marcel Colombe.
Fahmi, Zaki, *Safwat al-'asr*, 70–71.
Fuad, Faraj Sulayman, *al-Kanz al-thamin*, 68–70.
Hirszowicz, "The Sultan and the Khedive."
Jami'i, *al-Khidiwi 'Abbas Hilmi*.
Kilani, Muhammad Sayyid, *'Abbas Hilmi al-Thani*.
Mujahid, *al-A'lam al-sharqiyya*, I, 27–28.
New York Times (22 Dec. 1944): 17.
Qadi, Shukri, *Khamsun shakhsiyya*, 23–26.
Shafiq, *Mudhakkirati*, II, i–ii.
Tugay, *Three Centuries*, 151–155.
Zakhura, *Mirat al-'asr*, I, 7–16.
Zaydan, Jurji, *Mashahir al-sharq*, I, 50.
Zirikli, *al-A'lam*, III, 260–261.

al-'Abbasi, Shaykh Muhammad al-Mahdi

(1827–7 December 1897)
Chief Hanafi mufti of Egypt and rector of al-Azhar. Born in Alexandria, he was the son and grandson of Azharite shaykhs. His father, Muhammad Amin, was mufti of Egypt until his death in 1831/32. After his father died, 'Abbasi's family lived in dire poverty until he moved to Cairo at the age of twelve and entered al-Azhar, where some of the shaykhs intervened to give his mother a pension. He was named mufti in 1848 because of his father's excellent reputation, but in his youth he relied heavily on another shaykh as his secretary. SA'ID was especially fond of him. 'Abbasi became the rector of al-Azhar in 1870 but lost his post during the 'URABI Revolution when he refused to sign an order to depose TAWFIQ. The khedive restored 'Abbasi to the rectorship after the revolution ended, but when Tawfiq heard rumors that a group of notables and merchants were meeting in 'Abbasi's house and denouncing the British occupation, 'Abbasi again resigned as rector and devoted the rest of his life to his work as a mufti. He was stricken with epilepsy and died four years later. A collection of his verdicts was published in al-Waqai' al-misriyya.

Bibliographic Sources
Amin, 'Uthman, *Muhammad 'Abduh.*
Fikri, 'Ali, *Subul al-najah*, II, 60–65.
al-Hilal 8:17–18 (15 June 1900): 519–523.
Kahhala, *Mu'jam*, XI, 193–194.
al-Muayyad, 8, 9 Dec. 1897, 3.
Mubarak, 'Ali, *Khitat*, XVII, 12.
Mujahid, *al-A'lam al-sharqiyya*, I, 404–405.
Rafi'i, 'Abd al-Rahman, *'Asr Isma'il*, I, 279–282.
Schölch, *Egypt for the Egyptians!* 350.
Taymur, Ahmad, *A'lam al-fikr al-islami*, 62–72.
———, *Tarajim*, 67–80.
Walili, *Mafakhir al-ajyal*, 63–64.
Zakhura, *Mirat al-'asr*, II, 225.
Zaydan, Jurji, *Mashahir al-sharq*, II, 1st ed., 173–176; II, 2nd ed., 210–213.
Zayyati, *Kanz al-jawhar*, 147–150.
Zirikli, *al-A'lam*, VII, 75–76.

'Abbud, [Muhammad] Ahmad

(2 May 1889–28 December 1963)
Wealthy industrialist. Born in Cairo, he attended the Tawfiqiyya Secondary School, the School of Engineering, and the University of Glasgow, where he was trained as a civil engineer. After starting his career as an engineer for a British company, he worked on an irrigation scheme in Iraq and for the Palestinian and Syrian railway system. Upon returning to Egypt in 1922, 'Abbud worked on the enlargement of the Aswan Dam, became a supply contractor for the British troops, and was elected to the Chamber of Deputies in 1926. He was made a pasha for supervising construction of the Fuadiyya Canal in 1931. He managed the Khedivial Mail Line, held a near monopoly on sugar refining in Egypt, owned paper mills and fertilizer and chemical plants, represented many British firms in Egypt, had a controlling interest in several Egyptian banks (eighty thousand shares in Bank Misr alone), and served on the board of the Suez Canal Company before it was nationalized. All his enterprises, valued at more than $100 million, were nationalized in July 1961, and he was offered a government pension of £E 50 monthly. In that December he was tried for smuggling $660,000 out of Egypt, a charge that the government dropped in 1962, whereupon he left for Switzerland and continued to make money there. Rated as one of the world's ten richest men, he died in London at Claridge's Hotel.

Bibliographic Sources
al-Ahram Archives, file 282.
Mutawalli, *Dirasat fi tarikh Misr*, 372–382.
New York Times (30 Dec. 1963): 21.
Times (London) (30 Dec. 1963): 12.
Vitalis, "On the Theory and Practice of Compradors."

'Abd al-Hadi, Ibrahim

(1899–18 February 1981)
Cabinet minister, premier, and Sa'dist Party leader. Born in al-Zarqa (Daqahliyya), 'Abd al-Hadi was a student leader in the 1919 Revolution and spent four years in prison. He received his *license* from the government Law School in 1925. He served in the Chamber of Deputies, representing al-Zarqa in the 1929, 1936, and 1938 sessions, then became minister of state for parliamentary affairs (1939–1940), minister of commerce (1940), public works (1941–1942), public health (1944–1946), foreign affairs (1946), finance twice (1946–1947 and 1948–1949), chief of the royal cabinet (1947–1948), and prime minister and interior (1948–1949). Keeping Egypt under

martial law, he managed to restore order following the political crisis engendered by the 1948 Palestine War and the assassination of his predecessor, MAHMUD FAHMI AL-NUQRASHI. After the 1952 Revolution 'Abd al-Hadi was tried for his repressive policies, or, as his indictment read, for "corruption, terrorism, graft, and treason." Although he was condemned to death, his sentence was later commuted to life imprisonment, but his property was confiscated. He was released in 1954 for health reasons, and his property was restored in 1975, but he played no further role in politics. After his death in Ma'adi, his memoirs were serialized in *Ruz al-Yusuf*.

Bibliographic Sources
al-Ahram Archives, file 510.
Mahmud, Hafiz, "Ibrahim 'Abd al-Hadi."
Najib, *A'lam Misr*, 76.
Shimoni, *BDME*, 12.

'Abd al-Halim, Muhammad
(15 July 1831–4 June 1894)
Pretender to Egypt's khedivate, often called Prince Halim. He was educated at the Princes' School and then at a military school in France. Upon returning to Egypt, he rose through the Egyptian army to the rank of lieutenant general. He became its commander-in-chief, director of the War Department, military commander of the Sudan, and then member of the Ottoman council of state in Istanbul. When Khedive ISMA'IL changed the succession system, Prince Halim lost his primary claim to the khedivate. Accordingly, he opposed Isma'il and his successor, TAWFIQ, and probably backed 'URABI's movement in 1881–1882. 'Abd al-Halim died in Istanbul. His son, Mehmet Said Halim, joined the Committee of Union and Progress and became Ottoman grand vizir from 1913 to 1917, claiming Egypt's throne against the British-appointed Sultan HUSAYN KAMIL and the deposed Khedive 'ABBAS II.

Bibliographic Sources
Blunt, *Gordon at Khartoum*, 311–313, 337.
de Leon, *Khedive's Egypt*, 155, 252–261.
Fairman, *Prince Halim Pacha of Egypt*.
al-Hilal, 2:20 (15 June 1894): 637–638.
Jami'i, "al-Tanafus 'ala al-khidiwiyya."
Jerrold, *Egypt Under Ismail-Pacha*, 83–102.
Landau, *Middle Eastern Themes*, 23–30.
———, *Parliaments and Parties*, 77–80, 94–96.

Mujahid, *al-A'lam al-sharqiyya*, I, 25.
Tugay, *Three Centuries*, 103.
Tusun, *al-Ba'that al-'ilmiyya*, 317–319.
Zakhura, *Mirat al-'asr*, I, 53–54.

'Abd al-Majid, Dr. Ahmad 'Ismat
(10 March 1924–)
Diplomat. Born in Alexandria, he earned a *license* from Alexandria University's Law Faculty in 1944 and his doctorate from the Sorbonne in 1947. Upon joining Egypt's foreign service in 1950, he was posted to London. He took part in the Anglo-Egyptian negotiations in 1954, served in the delegation to the United Nations in 1955, and negotiated with France after the 1956 Suez War. Counselor to Egypt's permanent mission to the UN in Geneva from 1958 to 1961, he returned to work in Egypt's foreign office, becoming head of its information bureau in 1969 and ambassador to France in 1970. 'Abd al-Majid became deputy foreign minister in 1970 and Egypt's chief delegate to the UN from 1972 to 1983. He served as foreign minister and deputy premier from 1984 to 1991, when he was elected secretary-general of the Arab League. He tried to resolve the 1998 Iraqi arms crisis. An advocate of Arab unity, he was a disciple of MAHMUD RIYAD, whom he long served.

Bibliographic Sources
al-Ahram Archives, file 7970.
Egypt, Ministry of Information, *al-Mawsu'a al-qawmiyya*, I, 114–115.
"Interview with Esmat Abdul Magid."
Nisf al-dunya (8 Sept. 1997): 89–92.
Shimoni, *BDME*, 16.
WWAW, 1997–1998, 37.

'Abd al-Nur, Fakhri
(15 June 1881–9 December 1942)
Wafdist deputy, a Copt. Born in Jirja to a landowning family, from which he would inherit some 600 *feddan*s, Fakhri was educated at Cairo's Jesuit School. In 1904 he became the director of the Upper Egyptian branch of the Egyptian Bank. He joined the Umma Party in 1907 and was one of the founders of it daily, *al-Jarida*. Visited by Khedive 'ABBAS in 1909, he was made a Bey. He was one of three Copts who spoke to SA'D ZAGHLUL in 1918 about including Christians in the Wafd, to which Sa'd agreed,

and Fakhri subsequently persuaded other Copts to join. He was tried and imprisoned for his participation in the secret revolutionary society involved in the 1919 Revolution. Elected to represent Jirja in the Chamber of Deputies in 1924, he remained a deputy throughout his life, and he died while addressing the Chamber. He had left the Wafd when NAHHAS refused to cooperate with the other parties against SIDQI. His memoirs are a major source on the 1919 Revolution; as they focus almost entirely on the period from 1918 to 1923 and were dated November 1942, he may well have intended to write a sequel.

Bibliographic Sources

'Abd al-Nur, *Mudhakkirat Fakhri.*
al-Ahram Archives, file 6686.
al-Ahram Weekly, 12 May 1993.
Antaki, *al-Nujum,* 157–158.
Bowie, "The Copts, the Wafd, and Religious Issues," 107, 111–116.
Deeb, *Party Politics,* 108 n, et passim.
Fuad, Faraj Sulayman, *al-Kanz al-thamin,* 408–411.
Muti'i, *Mawsu'a,* 404–410.
QTQ, 167–168.
Tadrus, *al-Aqbat,* III, 83–85.
Zakhura, *Mirat al-'asr,* II, 447–449.

'Abd al-Quddus, Ihsan

(1 January 1919–11 January 1990)
Journalist, novelist, and playwright. Born in Kafr al-Mamuna (near Zifta), he was the son of the actress and pioneer woman journalist, FATIMA [RUZ] AL-YUSUF, and of an engineer-turned-artist, Muhammad 'Abd al-Quddus, but his parents divorced and he was reared by his mother. After attending Khalil Agha and Fuad I Schools in Cairo, he earned his law *license* from Cairo University in 1942 and worked for a year in a law office before becoming a journalist. He began writing for the popular weekly magazine that bears his mother's name, serving as an editor from 1945 to 1960. One of his first articles was an attack on the British ambassador, Lord KILLEARN. Ihsan predicted the Arab defeat in Palestine after a visit there in 1946. He won early fame by writing articles exposing the government's role in providing the troops with defective arms during the Palestine War, for which he was imprisoned. He came to know NASIR before the 1952 Revolution, thus emerging as one of the journalists close to the Revolutionary Command Council, but he was jailed again in 1954 after writing an article, "al-Jam'iyya al-sirriyya al-lati tahkum Misr," revealing Nasir's machinations in the March Crisis.

He also began writing fiction, including the script for a popular film, *Ana hurr* [I Am Free], directed by SALAH ABU SAYF. It was Ihsan who proposed forming the Supreme Council for the Arts, Letters, and Social Sciences, of which he became a member. He directed *Ruz al-Yusuf* from 1960 until he was appointed to manage *Akhbar al-Yawm* in 1971 and *al-Ahram* in 1974. He wrote at least sixty novels and six hundred short stories, mainly psychological studies of political and social behavior, some of which became films. In later years he wrote a syndicated column called "At a Cafe on Politics Street." Passionately devoted to press freedom, Ihsan 'Abd al-Quddus received a state prize in 1989. Since his death in Cairo, annual prizes have been awarded in his name for the best novel and short story.

Bibliographic Sources

Abu al-Futuh, *Ihsan 'Abd al-Quddus yatadhakkir.*
al-Ahram Archives, file 909.
'Ali, *Ihsan 'Abd al-Quddus fi arba'in 'aman.*
"Crisis of the Intellectuals."
EAL, I, 17–18.
Fuda, *Nujum Shari' al-Sihafa,* 47–52.
al-Hawadith (19 Feb. 1990): 52–59.
Khidr, *Suhufiyyun mu'asirun,* 17–39.
New York Times (16 Jan. 1990): D26.
Quwaysni, *Ihsan 'Abd al-Quddus.*
Rizq, Fathi, *Khamsa wa sab'una najman,* 359–368.
Shukri, Ghali, weekly articles in *al-Ahram,* Jan. 1990.
Ya'qub, Lusi, *Ihsan 'Abd al-Quddus.*

'Abd al-Rahman, Dr. 'Aisha

(6 November 1913–1 December 1998)
Writer and literary scholar, usually called *Bint al-Shati* (Daughter of the Shore), a pen name she adopted to respect her family's customs. Born in Damietta, 'Aisha was educated by her father, an Azharite, in a *kuttab* (primary school teaching the Quran) and later at Cairo University, where she earned a B.A. in Arabic in 1939, an M.A. in 1941, and a Ph.D. in 1950. She began teaching at Ain Shams University in 1952 and was professor of Arabic Literature and director of its Women's College from 1962, also teaching in the Sudan, Algeria, Morocco, Lebanon, the United Arab

Emirates, and Saudi Arabia. She became the first woman to lecture at al-Azhar.

Bint al-Shati began contributing articles and poetry to women's magazines in 1933 and wrote both novels and academic studies. Her first book, on the problems of Egypt's countryside, won a social sciences award in 1936. The next year she began writing for *al-Ahram* and published articles in that paper for more than sixty years. Although she did not write as a feminist, her best-known books were about women related to Muhammad. She also wrote on Quranic interpretation, the Arabic language, and the Islamic heritage, as well as an autobiography. She died in Heliopolis.

Bibliographic Sources
'Abd al-Hayy, *'Asir hayati*, 119–125.
al-Ahram, 1 Dec. 1998.
al-Ahram Archives, file 852.
Bint al-Shati, *'Ala al-jisr*.
————, *Sirr al-shati*.
Boullata, "Modern Quran Exegesis."
Brockelmann, *GAL*, S III, 262–263.
Hoffman-Ladd, "Polemics."
Jansen, *Interpretation of the Koran*, 68–76.
Jawadi, *Mudhakkirat al-mara*, 9–16.
Jindi, Anwar, *al-Muhafaza wa al-tajdid*, 810–815.
Kahhala, *Mu'jam*, II, 334.
Kooij, C., "Bint al-Shati," 67–72.
OEMIW, I, 4–5, article by Valerie J. Hoffman-Ladd.
Rooke, *In My Childhood*, 261–268 et passim.
WWAW, 1997–1998, 40.
Zeidan, *Arab Women Novelists*, 79–81.

'Abd al-Rahman, Shaykh 'Umar [Ahmad]

(3 May 1938–)
Expatriate Islamist leader. Born to a poor family in al-Jamaliyya (Daqahliyya) and blind since infancy stemming from diabetes, 'Umar was educated in his local *kuttab*, government schools, and at al-Azhar, receiving his *license* in religious fundamentals in 1965, his M.A. in *tafsir* (Quranic interpretation) in 1967, and his doctorate in 1972. He began his career as a preacher in a village in the Fayyum in 1967. His denunciations of NASIR as an infidel in the sermons that he preached in various Fayyum mosques led to his arrest in 1970, eight months' imprisonment, and temporary exile in Saudi Arabia, which was financing a campaign against communism and

atheism in Egypt. 'Umar soon returned to Egypt, preached in Fayyum, then in Minya, and became a professor in al-Azhar's Asyut branch in 1973. Propagating the teachings of SAYYID QUTB and Pakistan's Abul Ala al-Mawdudi, Shaykh 'Umar joined *al-Jihad al-Jadid* and other militant *jama'at* (Islamic societies). In 1977 he went to teach at the Women's College in Saudi Arabia, where he met Hasan al-Turabi, a Sudanese Islamist, and spent three years preaching in various parts of the Arab world before returning to resume teaching in Asyut. He was one of the political activists arrested on SADAT's orders in the massive sweep of September 1981 and released by MUBARAK two months later. Accused of plotting Sadat's assassination, 'Umar was detained and tried with KHALID AL-ISLAMBULI but was acquitted. He was jailed again in 1985 for forming a secret society and the next year for preaching in an Aswan mosque without permission. In 1988 'Umar went to Peshawar to aid the Afghan *mujahidin* against the Soviet occupation; he was funded by the Saudis in that endeavor and probably worked with Pakistani and U.S. intelligence. He left Egypt in 1990 for Saudi Arabia, the Sudan, and, finally, the United States (aided inadvertently or perhaps deliberately by the U.S. embassy in Khartum). He settled in Jersey City, supported by expatriate Egyptian Muslims in greater New York. Accused of inciting militant Muslims to blow up the World Trade Center in February 1993, Shaykh 'Umar was arrested by U.S. authorities in July, tried, convicted of conspiracy in October 1995, and given a life sentence at Springfield (Missouri) Federal Penitentiary.

Bibliographic Sources
al-Ahram Archives, file 8858.
al-'Arabi, 12 May 1997.
Fawzi, Muhammad, *'Umar 'Abd al-Rahman*.
New Republic (29 Mar. 1993): 18–20.
Newsmaker 3 (1993): 100–103.
OEMIW, I, 10–11, article by Gehad Auda.
Weaver, "The Trail of the Sheikh."
Zeghal, "Religion and Politics in Egypt."

'Abd al-Raziq, 'Ali

(1888–23 September 1966)
Islamic judge, writer, and minister. 'Ali was born in Abi Jurj (Minya province) to an Upper Egyptian family that owned about 7,000 *fed-*

*dan*s; he was educated at al-Azhar and Oxford. He became a Shari'a Court judge in Mansura. In 1925 he published a controversial book, *al-Islam wa usul al-hukm* [Islam and the Principles of Rule], in which he argued that the caliphate as a political institution was a post-Quranic innovation not essential to Islam. Many Egyptians opposed his book because Mustafa Kemal [Atatürk] had just abolished the caliphate unilaterally, some Muslims hoped to name a new caliph in a country other than Turkey, and King FUAD was seeking the office for himself. The Azharite ulama (religious scholars) accused 'Ali of promoting atheism, took away his title of "shaykh," and had him removed from his judgeship. Many liberals, including TAHA HUSAYN and MUHAMMAD HUSAYN HAYKAL, backed him. He defended his ideas in articles written for *al-Siyasa al-usbu'iyya* and in lectures delivered in Cairo University's Faculties of Law and of Letters. He later was elected to the Chamber of Deputies and the Senate, served as *awqaf* (pious endowments) minister, and was named to the Arabic Language Academy.

Bibliographic Sources

Abdel-Malek, Anouar, *Arab Political Thought*, 41–45.
Adams, *Islam and Modernism*, 251–253, 259–268.
al-Ahram (24 Sept. 1966): 9.
'Alim, "Thawra fikriyya."
'Allam, *Majma'iyyun*, 215–217.
Baha al-Din, *Ayyam laha tarikh*, 121–137.
Bakhit, *Haqiqat "al-Islam wa usul al-hukm."*
Berque, *Egypt*, 358–361.
Binder, "Ali Abd al-Raziq and Islamic Liberalism."
——, *Islamic Liberalism*, 170–205.
Brockelmann, *GAL*, S III, 329–330.
Haqqi, Mamduh, *al-Islam wa usul al-hukm.*
Hourani, *Arabic Thought*, 183–191.
'Imara, *Ma'rakat "al-Islam wa usul al-hukm."*
Kawtharani, *al-Dawla wa al-khilafa fi al-khitab al-'arabi.*
Khemiri and Kampffmeyer, *Leaders*, I, 9–10.
Kishk, *Jahalat 'asr al-tanwir.*
Morabia, "Des rapports entre religion et état."
Musa, Salama [S], "Sa'a ma'a al-Shaykh 'Ali 'Abd al-Raziq."
OEMIW, I, 5–7, article by Eric Davis.
Radwan, Fathi, *Mashhurun*, 97–113.
Rosenthal, *Islam in the Modern Nation State*, 85–102.
al-Tali'a (Nov. 1971): 90–160.
Wielandt, *Offenbarung.*
Zirikli, *al-A'lam*, IV, 276.

'Abd al-Raziq, Shaykh Mustafa
(1885–15 February 1947)

Islamic philosopher, teacher, writer, and cabinet minister. Born to Hasan Ahmad Abd al-Raziq, who was prominent in the Minya village of Abu Jirj, Mustafa began his schooling in the village *kuttab* and studied from about 1895 to 1908 at al-Azhar, where he was a disciple of MUHAMMAD 'ABDUH. He taught briefly at the Shari'a Judges School and the Egyptian University. In 1909 he was sent to Paris and Lyons, having been charged with teaching Islamic philosophy. He submitted his thesis to the Sorbonne on al-Shafi'i. He returned briefly to Cairo in 1912, then went back to France to spend two years in a sanatorium, writing intermittently for *al-Jarida*. When that paper folded in 1915, he founded a liberal weekly called *al-Sufur*. In that year he also became secretary-general to the Azhar Council, then to the Islamic Benevolent Society in 1916, inspector in the Shari'a Courts in 1920, and professor of philosophy in Cairo University's Faculty of Arts in 1927 and at al-Azhar in 1928. Mustafa became minister of *awqaf* in 1937 and again in 1940 and rector of al-Azhar in 1945, a post that he held until his death, forgoing his title of "pasha" because he felt it unsuitable to his new role. Calm and deliberate in his manners, he was an enlightened scholar. His books include a history of Islamic philosophy; biographies of al-Kindi, al-Farabi, and Muhammad 'Abduh; and a collaborative translation of 'Abduh's *Risalat al-tawhid* [Treatise on (God's) Unity]. He wrote unpublished studies on logic and Sufism and "Daily Memoirs," of which portions appeared in the press. Some of Mustafa's writings were published by his brother posthumously. In 1940 he became a member of the Arabic Language Academy. Politically liberal and devoted to the pursuit of knowledge, he was an avid reader and a masterful writer.

Bibliographic Sources

'Abd al-Raziq, 'Ali, *Min athar Mustafa 'Abd al-Raziq.*
'Abd al-Raziq, Mustafa, "al-Hadith al-ladhi athara fi hayati."
Abu-Rabi', "al-Azhar and Islamic Rationalism in Modern Egypt."
Adams, *Islam and Modernism*, 251–253.
——, "Shaykh Mustafa 'Abd al-Razik."
al-Ahram Archives, file 8735.

'Allam, *Majma'iyyun*, 355.
Amin, Ahmad, *Fayd al-khatir*, VII, 312–318.
Amin, Osman, "Moustafa Abdel Raziq."
Anawati, "Une figure de proue."
'Aqqad, 'Abbas Mahmud, "Mustafa 'Abd al-Raziq."
Brockelmann, *GAL*, S III, 329.
Daghir, *Masadir*, II, i, 588–590.
EAL, I, 18–19.
Fuad, Faraj Sulayman, *al-Kanz al-thamin*, 170.
Gharaba, *Shakhsiyyat*, 195–197.
Hilmi, "Mustafa 'Abd al-Raziq."
Husayn, Taha, "Mustafa 'Abd al-Raziq."
Kahhala, *Mu'jam*, XII, 245–246.
Khafaji, *al-Azhar fi alf 'am*, II, 181–188.
Khemiri and Kampffmeyer, *Leaders*, 10–11.
Kurd 'Ali, *Mu'asirun*, 434–439.
———, *Mudhakkirat*, II, 452, 560.
Madkur, Ibrahim Bayumi, et al., *al-Shaykh al-akbar Mustafa 'Abd al-Raziq*.
Musa, Salama [S], "Sa'a ma'a al-Shaykh Mustafa 'Abd al-Raziq."
Muti'i, *Haula al-rijal min al-Azhar*, 259–274.
———, *Mawsu'a*, 586–592.
New York Times (16 Feb. 1947): 57.
Ramadi, *Adab wa tarab*, 132–138.
Sharif, M.M., *Muslim Philosophy*, II, 1510–1512.
Zirikli, *al-A'lam*, VII, 231.

memoirs: *'Ala masharif al-khamsin* and *Hayati fi al-shi'r*. He was memorialized by a festival in Minya (1989) and a writers' conference in Asyut (1995).

Bibliographic Sources
al-Ahram, 15 Aug. 1981.
al-Ahram Archives, file 6185.
Allen, *Modern Arabic Literature,* 5–11.
Badawi, M.M., *Modern Arabic Drama*, 220–228.
Becka, *DOL*, 2.
EAL, I, 19–20.
EI2, VIII, 909–910, article by S. Moreh.
Faraj, Nabil, *Salah 'Abd al-Sabur*.
al-Fusul: majallat al-naqd al-adabi 2:1 (Oct. 1981).
Jayyusi, Salma Khadra, "Modernist Poetry in Arabic," in *CHAL*, 160–177.
Khurshid, Faruq, articles in *al-Musawwar* (15 July 1986; 5 Sept. 1986) and in *al-Ahram al-masai* (Aug.–Sept. 1992).
Misri, Nashat, *Salah 'Abd al-Sabur*.
Muti'i, *Haula al-rijal min Misr*, III, 111–118.
Ra'i, Ali, "Arabic Drama Since the Thirties," in *CHAL*, 361–365.
Ruz al-Yusuf (24 Aug. 1981): 47–52.
Snir, "Human Existence."
Yusuf, Majid, in *Majallat al-Kuwayt*.

'Abd al-Sabur, Salah
(3 May 1931–14 August 1981)

Journalist, free-verse poet, and playwright. Born in Zaqaziq, Salah earned his bachelor's degree in Arabic literature from Cairo University in 1951. After briefly teaching in a state secondary school, he began writing for *Ruz al-Yusuf* and *Sabah al-khayr*, became literary editor of *al-Ahram*, served briefly as press counselor in India in 1977, and then headed the General Egyptian Book Organization until his death. He received state prizes in 1965 and in 1981 and was invited in that year to serve on the Supreme Press Council. Salah was one of modern Egypt's most innovative writers: his poetic *diwan*s (collections) included *al-Nas fi biladi* [The People in My Country], 1957; *Aqulu lakum* [I Am Telling You], 1961; and *Ahlam al-faris al-qadim* [Dreams of the Old Knight], 1964. He wrote many plays, including one drawn from the tragedy of al-Hallaj and one based on the Majnun Layla theme. In addition, he translated T.S. Eliot's *The Cocktail Party* and Ibsen's *The Master Builder*. After Salah's sudden death in Cairo, two books were published containing partial

'Abd al-Wahhab, Muhammad
(13 March 1900–3 May 1991)

Actor, singer, and composer of popular music. 'Abd al-Wahhab was born to a religious family in Bab al-Sha'riyya, Cairo; his father was a muezzin and mosque preacher who hoped that his son would graduate from al-Azhar. Fascinated by music from an early age, 'Abd al-Wahhab was taught the Quran at the local *kuttab* and apprenticed to a tailor, as his family would have been embarrassed for him to become a professional singer. However, the tailor had a brother singing in the chorus of Muhammad al-Jazayirli, a popular Cairo musician. Recognizing the boy's talent, the tailor's brother arranged to bring him into Jazayirli's troupe in 1917. Advancing to better-known groups, notably those of NAJIB AL-RIHANI and SAYYID DARWISH, 'Abd al-Wahhab learned to play the *'ud* (short-necked lute) and studied Western musical theory at Guerin Music Academy in Cairo. He taught music in Egyptian public schools until 1952, even as he was performing on the stage.

In 1930 he met AHMAD SHAWQI, who brought him into Egypt's nascent state broadcasting system, and soon 'Abd al-Wahhab (featured as "the singer for important men, kings, and princes") gained much wider recognition than he could ever have achieved in a musical troupe. Enabled to study music theory in the Italian Institute, he pioneered the development of modern Arabic music. He sang and wrote hundreds of songs, composing for such major singers as UMM KULTHUM and his ex-pupil, 'ABD AL-HALIM HAFIZ. He also made seven musical films, including *Rasasa fi al-qalb* [A Bullet in the Heart]. He was elected head of the Musicians' Syndicate in 1953 and of the Union of Syndicates in 1955, and he became a member of the Supreme Council for Arts and Letters and of the Egyptian Senate. 'Abd al-Wahhab received an honorary doctorate from the Academy of Music and the Nile Medal in 1937, the Libyan Independence Award in 1955, the Gold Medal from the Moscow Music Festival in 1957, the Gold Medal from the Toulouse Institute in 1962, the Independence Medal from Syria in 1970, the Egyptian State Achievement Award in 1971, the title of "First Arab Musician" from the Arab Society in 1975, and the "World Artist" title from the Society of Writers and Composers in France in 1983, as well as a platinum disk for his record sales. He has been memorialized by a broadcasting studio bearing his name in Cairo, a Beirut street, and a cultural center in the village of Abu Kabir.

Bibliographic Sources
'Abd Allah, 'Abd Allah Ahmad, *'Abd al-Wahhab.*
'Abd al-Wahhab, *Mudhakkirat Muhammad 'Abd al-Wahhab.*
al-Ahram Archives, file 109.
Amin, Mustafa, *Shakhsiyyat,* II, 305–332.
Armbrust, *Mass Culture,* 63–93.
Butrus, *A'lam al-musiqa,* 248–251.
Danielson, *Voice of Egypt,* 171–177.
Darwish, Mustafa, *Dream Makers,* 18.
EAL, I, 20.
Hafiz, Ahmad, *Ayyam min shababihim,* 181–188.
Hifni, R., *Muhammad 'Abd al-Wahhab.*
Naqqash, Raja, *Lughz Umm Kulthum.*
Radwan, Lutfi, *Muhammad 'Abd al-Wahhab.*
Ramadi, *Adab wa tarab,* 215–219.
Sadoul, *Cinema,* 49–51 et passim.
Sultan, *'Abd al-Wahhab.*
Wahba, *Muhammad 'Abd al-Wahhab.*
Zaki, 'Abd al-Hamid Tawfiq, *al-Mu'asirun min ruwwad al-musiqa al-'arabiyya,* 45–48.

'Abduh, Shaykh Muhammad
(1849–11 July 1905)

Islamic reformer, author and editor, chief Maliki mufti (jurisconsult), and professor at al-Azhar. Born in Shanra (Gharbiyya) to a peasant family of Kurdish and Turkic origin, 'Abduh grew up in Mahallat Nasr (Buhayra) and studied at his village *kuttab,* the Ahmadi Mosque in Tanta, and al-Azhar, where he was drawn to philosophy and to Sufism (of the Shadhiliyya *tariqa* [order]). He also came to know JAMAL AL-DIN AL-AFGHANI and became his most devoted disciple. He taught for a while at Dar al-'Ulum and the School of Languages and worked in journalism, editing *al-Waqai' al-misriyya* in 1880–1882. After being jailed for three months for having backed URABI's movement, he was exiled to Syria. He later went to Paris and joined Afghani in editing an influential pan-Islamic fortnightly, *al-'Urwa al-wuthqa* [The Strongest Link], in 1884. After it was banned, 'Abduh returned to Beirut to teach and write. In 1888 he was readmitted to Egypt, where he became a judge and a chancellor in the National Court of Appeals, and in 1899 he became the country's chief mufti. He had a far-reaching influence on such younger thinkers as QASIM AMIN, AHMAD LUTFI AL-SAYYID, and SA'D ZAGHLUL. 'Abduh's publications include an incomplete interpretation of the Quran, *Risalat al-tawhid* (translated by Kenneth Cragg as *The Theology of Unity*), and a translation of Afghani's *al-Radd 'ala al-dahriyin* [Refutation of the Materialists] from Persian. He had many disciples, both religious and secular, and the Umma Party is sometimes called *Hizb al-Imam* (Imam 'Abduh's party). His work of Islamic reinterpretation was carried on by MUHAMMAD RASHID RIDA. Although his efforts to reconcile Islam with modernism have not fully stood the test of time, and his ties with the British consul general, Lord CROMER, made him suspect in the eyes of Khedive 'ABBAS HILMI II and the National Party, Egyptians now respect 'Abduh as a towering figure in their intellectual history.

Bibliographic Sources
'Abd al-Rahman, 'Abd al-Ghaffar, *al-Imam Muhammad 'Abduh.*
'Abd al-Raziq, 'Ali, "al-Shaykh Muhammad 'Abduh."
'Abd al-Raziq, Mustafa, *Muhammad 'Abduh.*
Abdel-Malek, *Idéologie,* 371–405.

'Abduh, Ibrahim, *A'lam al-sihafa*, 68–79.
Adams, *Islam and Modernism*, 18–176.
Ahmad, *al-Imam Muhammad 'Abduh*.
Ahmed, J.M., *Intellectual Origins*, 35–52.
Amin, 'Uthman, "Muhammad 'Abduh."
———, *Muhammad 'Abduh*.
'Aqqad, 'Abbas Mahmud, *Muhammad 'Abduh*.
'Ashur, Nu'man, *Butulat misriyya*, 139–151.
Ayyub, "Islam and Christianity."
Badawi, Zaki, *Reformers of Egypt*, 35–95.
Bayyumi, Zakariyya Sulayman, *al-Tayyarat al-siyasiyya*.
Becka, *DOL*, III, 2–3.
Blunt, *Gordon at Khartoum*, 270–286.
Brugman, *Introduction*, 214–215.
Carra de Vaux, *Penseurs*, V, 254–267.
Dayf, *al-Adab al-'arabi*, 218–227.
Dunya, Sulayman, *al-Shaykh Muhammad 'Abduh*.
EAL, I, 20–21.
*EI*2, VII, 418–420, article by Joseph Schacht.
———, IV, 141–163, article on "Islah" by A. Merad.
Fahmi, Zaki, *Safwat al-'asr*, 517–519.
Flores, "Reform, Islam, and Secularism."
Gharaba, *Shakhsiyyat*, 177–183.
Gibb, *Modern Trends*.
Goldziher, *Richtungen*, 320–370.
Hamada, 'Abd al-Mun'im, *Imam Muhammad 'Abduh*.
Hamza, *Adab al-maqala*, II, 62–113.
Hijazi, Anwar, *'Amaliqa*, 127–132.
Hourani, *Arabic Thought*, 130–160.
Ibrahim, Shihata 'Isa, *'Uzama al-wataniyya*, 139–172.
'Imara, *al-Imam Muhammad 'Abduh*.
'Iraqi, *al-Shaykh Muhammad 'Abduh*.
Jindi, Anwar, *Adwa*, 125–126, 258–260.
———, *A'lam wa ashab aqlam*, 381–399.
Jum'a, Muhammad Lutfi, in *al-Balagh al-usbu'i*, no. 121 (6 July 1929).
Jundi, 'Abd al-Halim, *al-Imam Muhammad 'Abduh*.
———, *A'lam al-adab*, II, 443–446.
Kedourie, *Afghani and 'Abduh*.
Khafaji, *Qissat al-adab*, IV, 145–164.
Kurd 'Ali, *al-Mu'asirun*, 343–366.
Livingston, "Muhammad 'Abduh on Science."
Michel and Abdel-Raziq, *Risalat al-tawhid*.
Mujahid, *al-A'lam al-sharqiyya*, II, 512–515.
Muqbil, *Ruwwad al-islah*.
al-Muqtataf 30:8 (Aug. 1905): 593–596; 11 (Nov. 1905): 909–922; 12 (Dec. 1905): 985–991.
Muti'i, *Haula al-rijal min al-Azhar*, 217–239.
———, *Haula al-rijal min Misr*, I, 159–173.
———, *Mawsu'a*, 461–470.
OEMIW, I, 11–12, article by Kenneth Cragg.
Qal'aji, *Muhammad 'Abduh*.
Radwan, Fathi, *Dawr al-'amaim*, 49–77.
Rahman, *Islam and Modernity*.
Rida, Muhammad Rashid, *Tarikh al-Ustadh al-Imam*.
Rizq, Fathi, *Khamsa wa sab'una najman*, 39–48.
Safran, *Egypt in Search*, 62–75.
Sa'idi, *al-Mujaddidun*, 530–538.
Shayib, *Muhammad 'Abduh*.
Shaykha, *Aqlam thaira*, 70–100.
Sulayman, 'Abd al-Jawad, *al-Shaykh Muhammad 'Abduh*.
Tanahi, Tahir, *'Ala firash al-mawt*, 55–64.
Tarrazi, *Tarikh al-sihafa*, II, 287–293.
Taymur, Ahmad, *A'lam al-fikr al-islami*, 143–165.
Walili, *Mafakhir al-ajyal*, 69–71.
Zaki, Muhammad Amin, *Mashahir al-Kurd*, II, 157–159.
Zaydan, Jurji, *Mashahir al-sharq*, 2nd ed., I, 300–309.
Zirikli, *al-A'lam*, VI, 252–253.

Abu al-Dhahab, Muhammad
(1745?–1775)

Mamluk successor and brother-in-law of 'ALI BEY AL-KABIR. Circassian in origin, he was purchased by 'Ali Bey around 1760, surnamed Abu al-Dhahab (Father of Gold) for passing out gold—instead of silver—coins among the Cairo populace upon his elevation to the rank of bey following his pilgrimage with his master to Mecca and Medina in 1764. In 1769 he undertook a punitive expedition on behalf of 'Ali Bey against rebellious mamluks in Upper Egypt. The next year he was sent to extend 'Ali's control over the Hijaz, while 'Ali was invading Palestine and Syria. In 1771 Abu al-Dhahab led an expedition that took Damascus, but he inexplicably withdrew after ten days. The two leaders became estranged during that year, ostensibly due to Abu al-Dhahab's reluctance to remain in Syria, but also to their contest for supremacy, and 'Ali exiled Abu al-Dhahab to Upper Egypt. There he organized his mamluks to rebel against 'Ali while he was on campaign in Syria in 1772 and Abu al-Dhahab managed to take control of Cairo. 'Ali tried and failed to dislodge him in May 1773, dying soon afterward. During his short reign, Abu Dhahab continued 'Ali's expansionist policies in Palestine and Syria and tried to loosen Egypt's Ottoman ties. He cultivated commercial relations with the British East India Company, hoping to revive the overland trade between the Red Sea and the Mediterranean. Like his prede-

cessor, he pursued policies later developed by
MUHAMMAD 'ALI.

Bibliographic Sources
Crecelius, *Roots of Modern Egypt,* 42–46.
———, "The Waqfiyah of Muhammad Bey Abu
   al-Dhahab."
EI2, VII, 420; S, 21, articles by P.M. Holt.
Jabarti, *'Ajaib al-athar,* I, 252–259, 413–420.
Volney, *Voyage en Égypte,* "État politique," chap.
   4.

Abu al-Fath, Mahmud

(15 August 1885–16 August 1958)
Wafdist journalist and editor of *al-Misri.* The
son of Shaykh Hasan Abu al-Fath, a professor of
Shari'a jurisprudence, Mahmud was born in Zaqaziq. He entered the government Law School in
1906, but his interests gradually shifted from
law to journalism. In 1914 he became a reporter
for *Wadi al-Nil* at a monthly salary of P.T. 150
but soon became an editor. He was an editor of
al-Afkar (1920) and of *al-Ahram* (1921–1928).
He wrote two of the earliest accounts of the 1919
Revolution, *Ma'a al-Wafd al-Misri* [With the
Egyptian Delegation] and *al-Masala al-misriyya
wa al-Wafd* [The Egyptian Question and the Del-
egation]. Starting in 1928 he worked for Wafdist
newspapers and then in 1936 founded *al-Misri,*
which became the leading Wafd Party organ. He
became the first head of the Journalists' Syndicate, which was founded in 1941 in his apartment, its first headquarters. He was first elected
to the Chamber of Deputies in 1938 and later he
was elected to the Senate. He was a member of
Egypt's delegation to the UN in 1950. Mahmud
and his brother Ahmad (who was briefly close to
NASIR) at first supported the 1952 Revolution
but broke with the new regime because of its authoritarian policies. After an acrimonious trial,
they went into exile in 1954, initially going to
Iraq, which offered them citizenship, but finally
settled in Tunis. Meanwhile they were sentenced
in absentia for fifteen years. *Al-Misri* was closed
by the government and has never been allowed
to reopen. In 1958, when De Gaulle came to
power in France, he gave the Abu al-Fath brothers the radio transmitter once used by the French
resistance to serve as the "Voice of Free Egypt."
Mahmud died soon afterward in Paris and was
buried in Tunis. His brother published a memoir,
L'Affaire Nasser, in 1962 and returned to Egypt

under SADAT. MUBARAK has restored some of the
family's seized assets to them.

Bibliographic Sources
Abbas Hilmi papers, Durham University, Box
   129/1–185.
al-Ahram Archives, file 707.
Muti'i, *Haula al-rijal min Misr,* II, 223–236.
———, *Mawsu'a,* 564–571.
Najib, *A'lam Misr,* 350.
New York Times (17 Aug. 1958): 86.
Rizq, Fathi, *Khamsa wa sab'una najman,* 311–314.
Zirikli, *al-A'lam,* VII, 165.

Abu Hadid, Muhammad Farid

(1 July 1893–18 May 1967)
Writer, poet, and historian. Born in Cairo, he
was reared and given his primary education in
Damanhur, attended the 'Abbasiyya Secondary
School in Alexandria, and went on to the Higher
Teachers College in Cairo, receiving his diploma
in literature and education in 1914. In that same
year, he became a board member of AHMAD
AMIN'S *Lajnat al-talif wa al-tarjama wa al-
nashr* (Committee for Writing, Translation, and
Publication). He contributed articles on blank
verse to *al-Sufur* and also wrote for *al-Siyasa al-
usbu'iyya* and for *al-Hilal.* While teaching, Abu
Hadid obtained his *license* from the government
Law School in 1924. In 1937 he was one of the
founders of the Egyptian Society for the Social
Sciences. He then entered the civil service, serving as secretary to the University of Alexandria
(1942), vice president of Dar al-Kutub (1943),
principal of the higher Teachers College (1945),
and cultural affairs director (1947) and then undersecretary (1950) of the Education Ministry.
He briefly edited a revival of *al-Thaqafa* in
1963, also serving as an adviser to Libya's Education Ministry. He wrote historical novels;
among the best-known are *Antara ibn Shaddad*
and several featuring Juha, the Arab folk hero.
Admitted to the Arabic Language Academy in
1946, he received state prizes for literature in
1959 and 1964 and was named to the Supreme
Council for the Arts, Letters, and Social Sciences in 1965. Abu Hadid died suddenly in
Cairo.

Bibliographic Sources
al-Ahram (19 May 1967): 8.
al-Ahram Archives, file 1990.
'Allam, *Majma'iyyun,* 305–307.

Brockelmann, *GAL*, S III, 227.
Brugman, *Introduction*, 310–313.
Daghir, *Masadir*, III, ii, 968–970.
EAL, I, 33.
Fuad, Ni'mat Ahmad, *Qimam adabiyya*, 281–326.
Qadi, Shukri, in *al-Jumhuriyya*, 26 May 1986, 22 May 1989.
Sakkut, *Egyptian Novel*, 48–59.
Shawkat, *al-Fann al-qasasi fi Misr*, 150–165.
Zayyat, Ahmad Hasan, "Muhammad Farid Abu Hadid."
Zirikli, *al-A'lam*, VI, 328.

Abu Sayf, Salah

(10 May 1915–22 June 1996)
Film director, sometimes called *Faris al-Waqi'a* (Champion of Realism). Born in Bulaq, Abu Sayf earned his *license* in commerce from Cairo University in 1932, after which he worked in a Bank Misr textile mill, where he got his start in cinematography by filming a documentary on its operation. The bank sent him to Paris in 1939, where he spent a year at the Studio Éclair. He then worked until 1945 at Studio Misr's montage section. In 1939 he produced his first independent documentary, *al-Muwasalat fi al-Iskandariyya* [Communications in Alexandria], and his first creative film, *Dayman fi qalbi* [Always in My Heart], came out in 1946. He taught for a time at the Higher Cinema Institute. His prizewinning films included *al-Wahsh* [The Beast] in 1954, *Shabab imra'a* [A Woman's Youth] in 1956, *Ana hurr* [I Am Free] in 1959, *al-Saqqa mat* [The Water Carrier Died] in 1977, and *al-Bidaya* [Beginning] in 1986. He was a member of the Supreme Council for Arts and Letters, headed the Filmontage Company in 1963, and in that year founded the Higher Cinema Institute, serving as its dean until 1966. He chaired the Carthage Film Festival in 1975. He wrote *al-Sinima fann* [Cinema Is an Art Form] and *Kayfa tuktab al-sinariyu* [How the Scenario Is Written] and received numerous prizes and film awards. He was famous for his sensitivity to the lives of humble people and their struggle for a better life, usually in the setting of Cairo. He produced at least thirty-six films, but his last, *al-Sayyid Kaf* [Mr. K], intended for television, was banned by the censors, and he resolved never to write another scenario. He died in Ma'adi after spending two weeks in a coma following an operation. His son, Muhammad, is also a filmmaker.

Bibliographic Sources
al-Ahram, 23, 24, 28 June 1996; 2 July 1996; 12 Sept. 1997.
al-Ahram Archives, file 1593.
al-Ahram Weekly, 27 June 1996.
Berrah, Levy, and Cluny, *Cinémas arabes*, 172–173.
Darwish, Mustafa, *Dream Makers*, 36.
Khayati, *Cinémas arabes*.
Sadoul, *Dictionary of Film Makers*, 1.
Shiri, *Directory of African Film-Makers*, 5–6.
Tawfiq, Sa'd al-Din, *Salah Abu Sayf*.
Thoraval, *Le cinéma égyptien*, 57–70.

Abu Shadi, Dr. Ahmad Zaki

(9 February 1892–12 April 1955)
Physician and poet. Ahmad was born in Cairo. His father, Muhammad Abu Shadi, was a Wafdist who became head of the Lawyers' Syndicate and hosted a literary salon. Ahmad went to school in Cairo, including two years at Qasr al-'Ayni, but received most of his medical education in London, where he married an English woman. He became increasingly involved with literature, English as well as Arabic. Upon returning to Egypt, he worked for the Health Ministry and later did bacteriological research, finally becoming associate dean of the Faculty of Medicine. During his lifetime he published several *diwan*s of his poetry, the first when he was only eighteen. He also wrote scripts for operas, translated books, and was an accomplished painter. His interests also included bee-keeping and chicken raising; he founded organizations and journals for both of these avocations. He is best known for having founded the Apollo Club in 1932 and for editing its monthly magazine, *Apollo*, which encouraged many young writers and poets (among them IBRAHIM NAJI and 'ALI MAHMUD TAHA) and served as a forum for intellectual discussion. After the magazine was closed for lack of funds, Abu Shadi withdrew from Egyptian society, and eventually, after his wife died, he emigrated in 1946 to the United States, where he taught Arabic at New York's Asia Institute, organized a literary and artistic society called Minerva, and published his final *diwan*. He died suddenly in Washington. He condemned the separation between letters and sciences and acknowledged a strong literary debt to KHALIL MUTRAN. So numerous were his interests and activities that one wonders what he might

have achieved if he had concentrated on one of his talents.

Bibliographic Sources
'Abd al-Ghafur, *Abu Shadi.*
Abu Shadi, *Yawmiyyat al-Duktur Ahmad Abu Shadi.*
al-Ahram Archives, file 7171.
Allen, *Modern Arabic Literature*, 21–29.
'Ashur, 'Abd al-Ghaffar, and Fuad, *al-Muntakhab min shi'r Abi Shadi.*
Badawi, M.M., *CHAL*, 110–115.
Brockelmann, *GAL*, S III, 96–125.
Daghir, *Masadir*, II, i, 55–64.
Dayf, *al-Adab al-'arabi*, 145–153.
Disuqi, 'Abd al-'Aziz, *Jama'at Apollo.*
EAL, I, 45.
*EI*2, S, 34–35.
Gharaba, *Shakhsiyyat*, 173–176.
Habib, *Hawamish*, 10–12.
Ibrahim, Muhammad 'Abd al-Fattah, *Ahmad Zaki Abu Shadi.*
Jawdat, *Balabil*, 39–46.
Jayyusi, *Trends*, 370–384.
Jiddawi, *Nazarat naqdiyya fi al-shi'r Abi Shadi.*
Joynboll, "Ismail Ahmad Adham (1911–1940)."
Jundi, *A'lam al-adab*, II, 477.
Kahhala, *Mu'jam*, I, 226.
Khafaji, *Ahmad Zaki Abu Shadi.*
Khalili, *Mu'jam al-udaba al-atibba*, 56–59.
Misri, Ibrahim, "Sha'iriyyat Abi Shadi," 178–194.
Moreh, "Free Verse in Modern Arabic Literature."
Nashat, *Abu Shadi.*
Ostle, "Modern Egyptian Renaissance Man."
———, "The Romantic Poets," in *CHAL*, 110–115.
Rafi'i, 'Abd al-Rahman, *Shu'ara al-wataniyya*, 1st ed., 270–288; 2nd ed., 326–353.
Ramadi, *Min a'lam al-adab*, 259–264.
Saharti, Mustafa 'Abd al-Latif, *Adab al-tabi'a*, 99–104.
Shinnawi, Kamil, in *al-Akhbar*, 18 Apr. 1955.
'Uwayda, Kamil Muhammad Muhammad, *Ahmad Zaki Abu Shadi.*
Wakil, Mukhtar, *Ruwwad al-shi'r al-hadith*, 48–64.
Yusuf, Niqula, *A'lam min al-Iskandariyya*, 498.
Zahlawi, *Udaba mu'asirun*, 51–55.
Zirikli, *al-A'lam*, I, 127–128.

Abu Zayd, Dr. Hikmat

(1922–)

Egypt's first woman cabinet minister. She was born in the village of Shaykh Daud near al-Qusiyya (Asyut). Her father, a Nationalist, worked for the Egyptian State Railways and was assigned to many stations, moving often. Al-

though her mother was illiterate, her father encouraged her to read books from his large library. She received her secondary education at the Helwan Girls School. She earned her *license* in history at Cairo University in 1940, a teaching certificate in 1941, an M.A. in education in 1950, and a doctorate in educational psychology from the University of London in 1957. She taught in the Women's College from 1955 to 1964, then became a professor at Cairo University in 1965. NASIR named her social affairs minister in 1962. She became coordinator for women's activities within the ASU in 1963 and received the Lenin Prize in 1970. Abu Zayd's career stalled under SADAT, and in 1974 she and her husband, Chancellor Muhammad al-Sayyad, moved to Libya, where she wrote articles and made speeches attacking the Egyptian government. Accused of involvement in the plot on Sadat's life, she was deprived of her Egyptian passport by the interior minister, causing a long legal struggle. Late in 1991 a judge ruled that she and her husband were entitled to their passports, and they returned to Egypt in March 1992. An avowed Nasirite, she has denounced the Gulf War, the Madrid Peace Conference, and U.S. and Israeli imperialism. In 1998 she wrote articles for *al-Usbu'* about Western imperialism and Arab unity.

Bibliographic Sources
al-Ahram Archives, file 5135.
al-Ahrar, 20 Apr. 1994; 7, 14 June 1994.
al-'Arabi, 25 Sept. 1995, 4 Aug. 1997.
Najib, *A'lam Misr*, 192–193.
Nisf al-dunya, 6, 13 Oct. 1996.
WWAW, 1997–1998, 56–57.

Abyad, Jurj

(5 May 1880–21 May 1959)

Actor, director, and playwright. Born and educated in Beirut, Abyad moved in 1898 to Egypt, where he was exposed to the theater. He secured a stipend from Khedive 'Abbas to study acting at the Paris Conservatoire from 1904 to 1910. After returning to Egypt, he commissioned the translation of several plays into literary Arabic and assembled a troupe to perform them before large audiences, soon going on tours throughout Egypt and other Arab countries. He acted in some of these plays himself. He also acted in radio plays, starting in 1927, and began to teach acting and diction at the Institute of Dramatic Arts in 1930. He had a part in the first talking Arabic film in 1931–1932. The first president of the Egyptian Actors' Union, organized in 1943, Abyad did much to win public support for the Arabic theater and to establish the respectability of the acting profession in Egypt.

Bibliographic Sources

'Abd al-Hayy, *'Asir hayati*, 194–201.
Abyad, *Ayyam lan yusdal 'alayha al-sattar*.
———, *al-masrah al-misri fi miat 'am*.
Barbour, "Arabic Theatre in Egypt."
Brockelmann, *GAL*, S III, 273–274.
Daghir, *Masadir*, III, i, 101–103.
EI2, supp. I, 39–40, article by J.M. Landau.
al-Hilal 20:8 (Apr. 1912): 436–438.
——— 33:9 (June 1925): 906–909.
Hajjaji, *al-Adab wa fann al-masrah*, 85–87.
Jundi, *A'lam al-adab*, II, 576–577.
Kamal al-Din, *Ruwwad al-masrah al-misri*, 81–91, 106.
Landau, *Studies in the Arab Theater*, 75–85 et passim.
Mandur, *al-Masrah*, 40–42.
Najm, *al-Masrahiyya*, 152–167 et passim.
Rushdi, *Kifahi fi al-masrah wa al-sinima*, 28–30.
Taymur, Mahmud, *Talai' al-masrah al-'arabi*.
———, *Hayatuna al-tamthiliyya*, 136–143.
Tulaymat, "Jurj Abyad al-raid wa al-fannan."
Yusuf, Fatima, *Dhikrayat*, 27–31, 36–37.
Zirikli, *al-A'lam*, II, 144–145.

al-Afghani, Jamal al-Din

(1838–10 March 1897)
Pan-Islamic agitator, philosopher, teacher, and the major instigator of early nationalism in Egypt and other Muslim countries. Born Muhammad ibn Safdar in As'adabad (Persia), he later claimed to have come from a village having the same name in Afghanistan and to have been educated in Kabul, probably to disguise his Shi'i origins, and hence also changed his name. Afghani was actually educated in As'adabad, Qazvin, Tehran, and the Shi'i shrine cities of al-Najaf and Karbala. After traveling to India during the 1857 Mutiny, he made the hajj, passed through Persia, and settled in Kabul and served in Dost Muhammad Khan's government. Expelled for his anti-British views in 1868, he spent forty days in Egypt and settled in Istanbul, where he joined the Education Council in 1869. Exiled two years later, he was invited by RIYAD to Egypt with the offer of a P.T. 1,000

monthly salary. After teaching briefly at al-Azhar, he rented rooms nearby, established a salon, and began attracting disciples who shared his views on religious reform and national resistance, notably MUHAMMAD 'ABDUH and journalists ADIB ISHAQ, editor of *Misr*, for which Afghani wrote, and YA'QUB SANNU'.

Early in 1879 he helped to found a secret political society, one of whose members was Prince TAWFIQ. However, when Tawfiq became khedive later in that year, he fell under influences hostile to Afghani, whom he banished from Egypt. Afghani went to Hyderabad (India), where he wrote his treatise, known as *al-Radd 'ala al-dahriyin* [Refutation of the Materialists], and later to Paris, where he and 'Abduh published *al-'Urwa al-wuthqa* in 1884. After that magazine was banned, he lived in Tehran, St. Petersburg, and then Munich, where he met Nasir al-Din Shah of Persia, who invited him back. He inspired the Persian Tobacco Boycott of 1891–1892 and is suspected of instigating the shah's subsequent assassination in 1896, but by then he had moved to Istanbul as the guest of Sultan 'Abdulhamid, who soon quarreled with him for hosting Khedive 'ABBAS. Afghani's death was officially ascribed to cancer; some think he was poisoned by the sultan's agents. His fiery speeches and newspaper articles were his main legacy; some have been translated in *An Islamic Response to Imperialism*. Preaching rationalist philosophy to the enlightened, and orthodox Islam to the masses, while opposing British imperialism, he inspired the modern revival of Islamic power.

Bibliographic Sources

'Abd al-Fattah, Muhammad, *Ashhar mashahir*, II, 34–80.
'Abduh, Muhammad, *Jamal al-Din al-Afghani*.
Abu Rayya, *Jamal al-Din al-Afghani*.
Adams, *Islam and Modernism*, 4–17.
Afghani and 'Abd al-Majid, *Nabighat al-sharq*.
Ahmed, J.M. *Intellectual Origins*, 15–17.
Amin, Ahmad, *Zu'ama al-islah*, 59–120.
Amin, al-Sayyid Muhsin, *A'yan al-Shi'a*, XVI, 336–380.
Amin, 'Uthman, *Ruwwad al-wa'y*.
'Ashur, Nu'man, *Butulat Misriyya*, 57–70.
Badawi, Zaki, *Reformers of Egypt*, 19–34.
Becka, *DOL*, III, 92.
Brockelmann, *GAL*, S III, 311–315.
Browne, Edward G., *Persian Revolution*, 1–45.
Cole, *Colonialism and Revolution*, 138–153.

Daghir, *Masadir*, II, i, 126–131.
EAL, I, 59–60.
*EI*1, I, 1008–1011, article by Ignaz Goldziher.
*EI*2, II, 416–419, article by Ignaz Goldziher and Jacques Jomier.
Fikri, 'Ali, *Subul al-najah*, II, 320–323.
Habib, *Hawamish*, 61–66.
Hairi, "Afghani on the Decline of Islam."
Harris, Christina Phelps, *Nationalism and Revolution*, 115–127.
Hijazi, Anwar, *'Amaliqa*, 110–117.
al-Hilal 5:14 (15 Mar. 1897): 533–534; 5:15 (1 Apr. 1897): 561–571.
Hourani, *Arabic Thought*, 103–129.
'Imara, *Jamal al-Din al-Afghani al-muftari 'alayhi*.
Ishaq, *al-Durar*, 220–223.
Jabalawi, *Jamal al-Din al-Afghani*.
Jindi, Anwar, *A'lam wa ashab aqlam*, 101–125.
————, *al-Muhafaza wa al-tajdid*, 29–37.
————, *al-Sharq fi fajr al-yaqza*, 13–35.
Jundi, *A'lam al-adab*, II, 432–434.
Kahhala, *Mu'jam*, X, 92.
Keddie, *An Islamic Response to Imperialism*.
————, *Sayyid Jamal al-Din "al-Afghani."*
Kedourie, *Afghani and 'Abduh*.
Khafaji, *Qissat al-adab*, III, 56–61.
Kudsi-Zadeh, "Afghani and Freemasonry in Egypt."
————, "al-Afghani and the National Awakening of Egypt."
————, "Islamic Reform in Egypt."
————, *Sayyid Jamal al-Din al-Afghani*.
Landau, "al-Afghani's pan-Islamic Project."
Lutfullah, *Jamal al-Din al-Asad Abadi*.
Madkur, Muhammad Salam, *al-Hakim al-thair Jamal al-Din al-Afghani*.
Madlaji, *Jamal al-Din al-Afghani*.
Maghribi, 'Abd al-Qadir, *Jamal al-Din al-Afghani*.
Mahdavi and Afshar, *Documents inédits*.
Makhzumi, *Khatirat Jamal al-Din al-Afghani*.
Matthee, "al-Afghani and the Egyptian National Debate."
Milson, "The Elusive Jamal al-Din al-Afghani."
Moazzam, "Jamal al-Din al-Afghani."
Muqbil, *Ruwwad al-islah*.
Mustafa, Ahmad 'Abd al-Rahim, "Afkar Jamal al-Din al-Afghani."
————, "Nazra jadida ila Jamal al-Din al-Afghani."
OEMIW, I, 23–27, article by Nikki R. Keddie.
Pakdaman, *Djamal al-Din Assad Abadi dit Afghani*.
Qal'aji, *Jamal al-Din al-Afghani*.
Qarni, "al-'Adala."
Qasim, *Jamal al-Din al-Afghani*.
Rafi'i, 'Abd al-Rahman, *'Asr Isma'il*, II, 125–148.
————, *Jamal al-Din al-Afghani*.
Ramadi, *Adab wa tarab*, 102–107.
Ramli, *Jamal al-Din al-Afghani*.

Rida, Muhammad Rashid, *Tarikh al-Ustadh al-Imam*, I, 27–102.
Rizq, Fathi, *Khamsa wa sab'una najman*, 27–38.
Safran, *Egypt in Search*, 43–46.
Sa'idi, *al-Mujaddidun*, 490–495.
Shamis, *Safir Allah*.
Shaykha, *Aqlam thaira*, 30–44.
Shayyal, *al-Tarikh wa al-muarrikhun*, 164–165.
Tarrazi, *Tarikh al-sihafa*, II, 293–299.
'Umar, Mahmud Fathi, *Abtal al-hurriyya*, 29–34.
Walili, *Mafakhir al-ajyal*, 65–69.
Zaydan, Jurji, *Mashahir al-sharq*, 1st ed., II, 54–66.
Zirikli, *al-A'lam*, under Muhammad b. Safdar, VI, 168–169.

'Afifi, Dr. Hafiz

(9 November 1886–1 June 1961)

Physician and politician. Born in Cairo, where he got his medical diploma in 1907 from Qasr al-'Ayni, he undertook specialized training and practice in pediatrics in Ireland and France. A member of the National Party, he headed a Red Crescent mission to the Ottoman Empire during the Libyan War, spending about a year in Barqa. He later became director of the Infants' Hospital in Cairo and joined the Wafd (as a Nationalist sympathizer) in 1919 but resigned in 1921 to help form the Constitutional Liberal Party, of which he became vice president. He later became a regular writer for its newspaper, *al-Siyasa*. Elected to Parliament in 1926, 'Afifi served as foreign minister under MUHAMMAD MAHMUD and ISMA'IL SIDQI. He was part of the national bloc that negotiated the 1936 Anglo-Egyptian Treaty, then served from 1936 to 1938 as Egypt's first ambassador to Britain. Among his published writings are *al-Ingliz fi biladihim* [The British in Their Country] and *'Ala hamish al-siyasa: ba'd masailina al-qawmiyya* [On the Margin of Politics: Some of Our National Issues]. He was president of Bank Misr in 1939–1951, serving on the boards of forty-three companies, drawing an annual income of £E 132,000. In December 1951 he became FARUQ's *chef du cabinet*. Retiring after the 1952 Revolution, he died in Cairo.

Bibliographic Sources
al-Ahram, 25 Dec. 1951; 2 June 1961; 1, 12 Feb. 1970.
al-Ahram Archives, file 5065.
Deeb, *Party Politics*, 43, 97 n, et passim.
Mutawalli, "Shakhsiyyat rasmaliyya," 35–36.
Muti'i, *Haula al-rijal min Misr*, III, 83–95.

———, *Mawsu'a*, 128–134.
Najib, *A'lam Misr*, 170.
Zirikli, *al-A'lam*, VI, 77.

Aflatun, Inji

(16 April 1924–17 April 1989)
Artist, political leftist, and writer. The daughter
of Muhammad (a member of the Arabic Language Academy) and Salha Aflatun (a French-
trained dress designer who served in the Red
Crescent Society's women's committee), Inji
was born in Cairo and educated at the French
Lycée and Cairo University. She began painting
at an early age and studied with the Egyptian-
born Swiss artist Margo Veillon. Soon after her
first exhibition in 1942, Inji joined *Iskra*, a Communist youth group, and represented Egypt at
the 1945 Paris meeting of the World Congress of
Women sponsored by the Communist Democratic Federation of Women. She helped found the
University and Institutes Youth League and became a member of the National Executive of
Workers and Students and the National Women's
Committee. She wrote an anti-imperialist and
feminist manifesto, *Thamanun milyun imraa
ma'ana* [Eighty Million Women Are with Us] in
1948 and *Nahnu al-nisa al-misriyyat* [We the
Egyptian Women] in 1949. She joined the
Movement of the Friends of Peace in 1950 and
also the Egyptian Feminist Union's youth group.
She also backed the resistance to the British occupation of the Suez Canal in 1951, helping to
organize the Women's Committee for Popular
Resistance. Both before and after the 1952 Revolution she wrote for *al-Misri*. Inji was arrested
and imprisoned during NASIR's roundup of Communists in 1959; the paintings that she made
during her incarceration are a visual record of al-
Qanatir Women's Prison. Released in 1963, she
then devoted most of her time to painting, ex-
hibiting her work in Cairo, Paris, Venice, Germany, Poland, Bulgaria, and Kuwait. She helped
set up a large exhibition, "Women Painters over
Half a Century" in 1975, and was elected vice
president of the Society of Writers and Artists.
Her work purported to represent Egyptian society and women's struggle for political equality.
Some of her paintings of rural people are now in
Egypt's Modern Art Museum, and some writers
have called for a museum dedicated entirely to
her works.

Bibliographic Sources
Aflatun, *Mudhakkirat Inji Aflatun*.
al-Ahram Archives, file 10036.
Badran, *Feminists*, 152, 157.
Badran and Cooke, *Opening the Gates*, 343–351.
Iskandar, *Khamsun sana min al-fann*, 40.
Jawadi, *Mudhakkirat al-mara*, 47–70.
Karnouk, *Contemporary Egyptian Art*, 12–13, 33.
Shafiq, Samira, in *al-Musawwar*, 28 Apr. 1989.
WWAW, 1997–1998, 219.

Ahmad, Zakariyya

(6 January 1896–15 February 1961)
Singer and composer. Born in Cairo to an Egyptian father and a Turkish mother, he was educated
at al-Azhar, except for an interlude at the Khalil
Agha Elementary School. He developed an early
love for music, as his parents used to sing Arabic,
Turkish, and desert songs. Entranced by the
melody of the *adhan* (call to Muslim worship),
he learned Quran recitation. As a young man he
heard the singing of 'ABDUH AL-HAMULI and
SALAMA AL-HIJAZI (among others) and committed their songs to memory. He sang mainly religious songs as a member of several groups from
1919 to 1929 but later expanded his repertory,
based on his excellent command of popular
melodies. Starting in 1931, Zakariyya composed
some of the sentimental and patriotic songs sung
by UMM KULTHUM. He also began writing operettas in 1924, eventually producing (by his own
count) 56 operettas and 1,070 songs, a figure often cited in press articles about his life.

Bibliographic Sources
Abu al-Majd, *Zakariyya Ahmad*.
al-Ahram, 16–17 Feb. 1961, 28 Feb. 1969, 12 Mar.
   1982, 15 Feb. 1997.
al-Ahram Archives, file 730.
Butrus, *A'lam al-musiqa*, 207–219.
al-Hilal 61:9 (Sept. 1953): 68–69.
al-Kawakib, 23 Feb. 1993.
Najib, *A'lam Misr*, 223.
Zaki, 'Abd al-Hamid Tawfiq, *A'lam al-musiqa*, 43–
   50.

Alfi Bey

(1751?–28 or 30 January 1807)
Mamluk leader, originally the protégé of MURAD
BEY, who had paid 1,000 *ardabs* of wheat for
him (hence the name Alfi—1,000). Alfi emerged
as a leader following the French occupation. His

zeal in collecting taxes from Upper Egyptians made him a byword for cruelty, and they were greatly relieved when the British took him to England for a year to represent the mamluks, whom the British and Ottomans were backing against the French. Upon his return, he began collecting taxes in the Delta. After MUHAMMAD 'ALI and the Cairo ulama engineered the deposition of KHURSHID, the Ottoman governor, Alfi tried to make peace with Muhammad 'Ali, but his claims for tax farms exceeded what the new governor was prepared to grant, and he suspected Alfi of having British support. Alfi died, presumably of cholera, soon after he allegedly poisoned his rival, BARDISI. Irascible and ruthless toward bedouin and peasants, he was the last obstacle to Muhammad 'Ali's taking full control of Egypt.

Bibliographic Sources
Ghorbal, *Beginnings,* 216–232.
Hanotaux, *Histoire,* VI, 27–30.
Marlowe, *Perfidious Albion*, 96–111.
Rafi'i, 'Abd al-Rahman, *'Asr Muhammad 'Ali,* 43.

'Ali Bey al-Kabir

(1728–8 May 1773)
Mamluk soldier and Egypt's de facto ruler from 1760 to 1772. Originally from the Abkhazian region of the Caucasus Mountains, 'Ali was brought as a boy slave to Egypt. In 1743 he was presented to Ibrahim Katkhuda, then Egypt's Mamluk leader, and given the rank of *kashif* (local governor). In 1753/54 he was given command of the official pilgrimage caravan from Cairo to Mecca and, for his victories over the bedouin tribes, earned the nicknames *Bulut Kapan* (Cloud Catcher) and *Jinn 'Ali* (Ali the Genie). In 1755 he became a Bey and in 1760 was named *shaykh al-balad*, or virtual leader of Egypt's mamluks. Thereupon he admitted into his service a young mamluk named Muhammad, later surnamed ABU AL-DHAHAB. Muhammad Abu al-Dhahab married 'Ali's sister and became his trusted lieutenant in later military campaigns. 'Ali Bey managed to weaken the rival mamluk factions by playing them off against one another and by poisoning or exiling their leaders. At first he was backed by Egypt's Ottoman governor, but in 1769 'Ali deposed him and began building an independent Egyptian sultanate. Acting on

'Ali's orders, Abu al-Dhahab occupied Mecca and Jidda in 1770. Aided by mercenary troops from the republic of Venice and the Knights of Malta, he then invaded Ottoman Palestine and Syria. 'Ali Bey and Abu al-Dhahab became estranged after the latter took Damascus, only to withdraw ten days later, hastening back to Cairo. When 'Ali Bey tried to exile his brother-in-law in 1772, the latter won the support of 'Ali's commanding officer and most of his troops. 'Ali fled to Jaffa and waged an inconclusive campaign against the Ottoman Empire. Having returned in an attempt to resume control in Cairo, he was defeated by Abu al-Dhahab's superior forces. He was captured and wounded while trying to resist; he died of his wounds a week later.

'Ali's reign marked a transition between medieval and modern Egypt, for he tried to strengthen his government by taking control of the country's trade, reduced his dependence on his fellow mamluks, and made Egypt briefly independent of the Ottoman Empire. Although his expensive military campaigns led to high taxes, which alienated the Egyptian people at the time, he is now viewed as a precursor to the better-known and more successful MUHAMMAD 'ALI.

Bibliographic Sources
Abu Hadid, Muhammad Farid, in *al-Hilal* 47:1 (Nov. 1938): 21–27.
An Account of the Revolt of Aly Bey.
Anis, *al-Dawla al-'Uthmaniyya wa al-sharq al-'arabi.*
Bruce, *Travels,* I, 83–105.
Crecelius, *Roots of Modern Egypt*, 37–42.
Dehérain, *L'Egypte turque.*
EI2, I, 391–392, article by Gaston Wiet.
Gran, *Islamic Roots,* 12–18.
Holt, P.M. "'The Cloud Catcher.'"
Jabarti, *Ajaib al-athar*, I: 250–259, 380–383; II: 415–429, 636–642.
Livingstone, "Ali Bey al-Kabir."
———, "The Rise of Shaykh al-Balad Ali Bey al-Kabir."
Lusignan, *Revolt of Ali Bey.*
Ramadan, Muhammad Rif'at, *'Ali Bey al-Kabir.*
Volney, *Voyage en Égypte*, "État politique," chap. 3.
Wiet, "L'agonie."

'Ali, Kamal Hasan

(18 September 1921–27 March 1993)
Army officer and politician. He had originally planned to study medicine but changed his mind

after admission to the cadet corps was opened to competitive examination. He graduated from the Military Academy in 1942 and Staff College in 1946 and served as a battalion commander in the Palestine War. He then spent 1949–1950 in Britain, served on the general staff during the 1956 Suez War, and completed more-advanced military courses in the USSR in 1958–1959. He led Egypt's expeditionary force during the Yemen Civil War, fought in both the June 1967 War and the War of Attrition, and commanded an armored brigade in the October War. 'Ali was deputy defense minister under JAMASI in 1975–1977 and replaced him in 1978 as minister and commander-in-chief. He took part in the peace talks with Israel, becoming foreign minister and deputy prime minister in 1980 and premier in 1984. Ill health forced him to retire in 1985, but he served for a time as administrative president of the Egyptian Gulf Bank. His memoirs were serialized in *al-Sharq al-awsat* immediately after his death.

Bibliographic Sources
al-Ahram Archives, file 34135.
'Ali, Kamal Hasan, *Muhariban wa mufawidan.*
Najib, *A'lam Misr*, 378.
Shimoni, *BDME*, 25.
WWAW, 1993–1994, 74.

Allenby, Edmund Henry, Viscount

(23 April 1861–14 May 1936)
English military leader and colonial administrator. Educated at Haileybury and Sandhurst, Allenby chose a military career after twice failing to pass the examination for the Indian Civil Service. Before World War I, he saw service in South Africa, Ireland, and France. Because of his victories over the Ottoman and German armies in Palestine and Syria, he was offered "a special high commission with supreme and military control" in Egypt and the Sudan following the outbreak of the 1919 Revolution, becoming high commissioner when WINGATE, who was recalled to London, resigned. Allenby restored order in Egypt, in part by allowing SA'D ZAGHLUL and his companions, who had been interned in Malta, to go to the Paris Peace Conference in April 1919. He later issued the unilateral declaration of Egypt's independence on 28 February 1922 and encouraged the drafting of the 1923 Constitution, which became the basis of parlia-

mentary government, though often honored in the breach, until the 1952 Revolution. He was deeply angered by the assassination of his close friend, Sir Lee Stack, the commander-in-chief of the Egyptian army, in 1924. Holding Premier Zaghlul and his cabinet responsible for the murder, he submitted an ultimatum demanding a large indemnity from the Egyptian government and imposing other penalties on the country, causing the premier to resign. The terms of Allenby's ultimatum were sterner than his government had intended. Estranged from the Foreign Office, he resigned his post in 1925 and retired from government service. A man of great courage and integrity, he could become irate when provoked. Some of his private papers are now at St. Antony's College, Oxford.

Bibliographic Sources
Assali, *al-Marishal Allinbi.*
DNB (1931–1940), 7–12.
EMME, I, 109–110, article by Jon Jucovy.
Gardner, *Allenby of Arabia.*
Grafftey-Smith, *Bright Levant*, 66–79.
James, *Imperial Warrior.*
New York Times (15 May 1936): 25.
Parker, *Famous British Generals*, 119–139.
Times (London), 15 May 1936.
Wavell, *Allenby: Study.*
———, *Allenby in Egypt.*
———, *Allinbi fi Misr.*

'Alluba, Muhammad 'Ali

(November 1875 or 1878–25 March 1956)
Lawyer, early Arab nationalist, and diplomat. Born in Asyut to a flour mill owner originally from Juhayna, he graduated from the Khedivial Law School in 1899 and opened his first office in Asyut. He served on the administrative board of the National Party from 1907 to 1914, and was elected to the 1914 Legislative Assembly. Although he joined the Wafd in 1918, he became one of the organizers of the Constitutional Liberal Party and was elected its first secretary. He was minister of *awqaf* (1925), education (1936), and parliamentary affairs (1939 and 1946). Among the first Egyptians to take an interest in Arab and Islamic affairs, he helped to mediate the dispute between Saudi Arabia and Yemen, attended the Arab Congress in Jerusalem, and defended Muslim interests in the *Buraq* (Wailing Wall) dispute. He headed the Egyptian Lawyers' Syndicate in

1937 and became Egypt's first ambassador to Pakistan in 1948. He also wrote *Mabadi al-siyasa al-misriyya* [Principles of Egyptian Politics], several law books, and a critique of the 1936 Anglo-Egyptian Treaty. His book *Filastin wa al-damir al-insani* [Palestine and the Human Conscience] influenced NASIR's views on the Palestine question. 'Alluba died in Cairo.

Bibliographic Sources
al-Ahram, 26 Mar. 1956.
al-Ahram Archives, file 1485.
'Alluba, *Dhikrayat ijtima'iyya wa siyasiyya.*
———, "al-Hadith al-ladhi la ansah."
———, *Mabadi al-siyasa al-misriyya.*
Deeb, *Party Politics.*
Kahhala, *Mu'jam,* XI, 29.
Mazini, Ahmad Fathi, *Qudat,* 137–139.
Muti'i, *Haula al-rijal min Misr,* II, 151–162.
———, *Mawsu'a,* 478–484.
Rifa'i, *Rijal wa mawaqif,* I.
Sayigh, Anis, *al-Fikra al-'arabiyya fi Misr,* 235.
Tawfiq, 'Awad, and Hasan Sabri, *Wuzara al-ta'lim,* 90–91.
Ziadeh, *Lawyers,* 131–134.
Zirikli, *al-A'lam,* VI, 307.

Amin, Ahmad

(1 October 1886–30 May 1954)
Arabic scholar, teacher, and editor. Ahmad was born in Cairo; his father was an Azhari shaykh from a peasant background. Ahmad received most of his education in *kuttab*s (but briefly attended the 'Abbas School) and at al-Azhar. He began his career as an Arabic teacher at state primary schools in Alexandria and Cairo, then studied at the Shari'a Judges School, where he was a teaching assistant after his graduation in 1911. Serving a brief stint as a judge in the Kharja oasis, he returned to the school as a teacher of ethics. He also learned English from a private tutor and formed a literary study group with some friends, who combined to set up the Committee on Authorship, Translation, and Publication. This group printed hundreds of original and translated books and published a literary magazine, *al-Thaqafa,* of which Amin was to serve as editor from 1939 to 1953 (his articles were later reissued as *Fayd al-khatir*). In 1918 he began his literary career by publishing an Arabic translation from the English version of a German philosophy textbook and in the following year entered the world of journalism with a report on the pro-Wafd women's

demonstration. He lost his position at the Shari'a Judges School because of his support for SA'D ZAGHLUL, whose kinsman, 'Atif Barakat, was removed from its directorship, but Amin rejoined the Shar'i judiciary in 1922, serving for two years in the country and two years in Cairo.

In 1926, at TAHA HUSAYN's invitation, Amin became a lecturer in Arabic language and literature at Cairo University and gave a series of courses on the intellectual history of early Islam. He was removed from his teaching position in 1932 because of his opposition to SIDQI's government, but he continued to write and eventually was allowed to return to Cairo University, becoming dean of its Arts Faculty in 1939. Amin continued to teach full-time until 1946 and part-time until 1949. He was elected to the Arabic Language Academy in 1940 and also belonged to the Damascus and Baghdad academies. Working closely with Taha Husayn and other humanists, Amin began writing the series of volumes on Islamic history that have won him fame in the Arab world, starting with *Fajr al-Islam* [The Dawn of Islam], followed by *Duha al-Islam* [The Forenoon of Islam]. He visited Turkey in 1928, Syria and Palestine in 1930, Iraq in 1931, and he represented Egypt at the International Congress of Orientalists in Leiden in 1931 and Brussels in 1938, also making the pilgrimage to Mecca in 1937. He helped represent Egypt at the 1946 London Conference on Palestine and then became director of the Arab League Cultural Bureau. He was awarded an honorary doctorate in 1948 and also the FUAD I Prize for *Zuhr al-Islam* [The Midday of Islam]. Reformist in his approach, he remained profoundly Muslim and critical of Western imperialism and materialism. Hardworking but intensely shy, Ahmad Amin was an exemplar of Arabic scholarship in a time of rapid flux in Egyptian society.

Bibliographic Sources
al-Ahram, 31 May 1954.
al-Ahram Archives, file 3060.
al-Ahram Weekly, 30 May 1991.
'Allam, *Majma'iyyun,* 30–32.
Amin, Ahmad, *Hayati.* Eng. trans. Boulatta, *My Life.*
———, *al-Sharq wa al-Gharb.* Eng. trans. Behn, *Orient and Occident.*
Ahmad Amin bi-qalamihi wa qalam asdiqaihi.
Amin, Husayn Ahmad, *Fi bayt Ahmad Amin.*
'Aqqad, Amir, *Ahmad Amin.*
'Atiyya, Ahmad 'Abd al-Halim, *Ahmad Amin.*

Boulatta, "Early Schooling."
Brockelmann, *GAL*, S III, 305.
Caspar, "Le renouveau du Mo'tazilisme."
Cragg, "Then and Now in Egypt."
Daghir, *Masadir*, II, i, 132–137.
Danasuri, *Ahmad Amin.*
EAL, I, 86.
EI2 I, 279, article by H.A.R. Gibb.
Hijazi, Anwar, *'Amaliqa,* 257–259.
al-Hilal 62:7 (July 1954): 6–7.
'Id, Muhammad al-Sayyid, *Ahmad Amin.*
Jindi, Anwar, *al-Muhafaza wa al-tajdid*, 673–681.
Kahhala, *Mu'jam,* I, 168–170.
Khaki, *Ahmad Amin.*
Khalid, "Legacy of Muhammad 'Abduh."
———, "Modern Interpretations of Muslim Universalism."
———, "Some Aspects of Neo-Mu'tazilism."
Khurays, *Jinayat Ahmad Amin.*
Mahasini, *Muhadarat 'an Ahmad Amin.*
MMIA 29 (1954): 440.
Mandur, "al-Adab surat al-nafs."
Matar, 'Abd al-'Aziz, in *al-Ahram*, 2 June 1954.
Mazyad, *Ahmad Amin.*
Muti'i, *Haula al-rijal min al-Azhar*, 13–29.
———, *Mawsu'a,* 9–15.
Radwan, Fathi, *'Asr wa rijal,* 599–654.
Rizzitano, "Lo scrittore arabo-agiziano Ahmad Amin."
Sa'b, Hasan, *Shakhsiyyat 'araftuha,* 31–34.
Safran, *Egypt in Search*, 138–139, 226–228.
Sakkut and Jones, *Ahmad Amin.*
Shaybub, Siddiq, *Shakhsiyyat 'arabiyya,* 129–138.
Shepard, "The Dilemma of a Liberal."
———, *Faith of a Modern Muslim Intellectual.*
———, "Modernist View of Islam."
Tarabishi, Mata', *Ahmad Amin.*
Taymur, Mahmud, *al-Shakhsiyyat al-'ishrun,* 36–42.
'Uwayda, Kamil Muhammad Muhammad, *Ahmad Amin.*
Zayn al-Din, Muhammad Amin, *Ma'a al-Duktur Ahmad Amin.*
Zirikli, *al-A'lam*, I, 101.

Amin, 'Ali

(21 February 1914–3 April 1976)
Prominent journalist. The son of Amin Yusuf, 'Ali was born in the Cairo house called *Bayt al-Umma* (House of the Nation), belonging to his maternal uncle, SA'D ZAGHLUL. There 'Ali and his twin brother, MUSTAFA, issued their first magazines, *al-Huquq* and *al-Asad*, written in pencil, in 1922. 'Ali studied at the Royal Awqaf School from 1926 to 1928, when he was expelled for taking part in a demonstration against MUHAMMAD MAHMUD's government. After en-

tering the preparatory section of the American University at Cairo, he tried to publish a magazine called *al-Tilmidh*, but it was suppressed. He briefly studied at the Khedivial Secondary School and again at AUC before going to study engineering at Sheffield (England) in 1931. Upon returning in 1937, he worked as an engineer at various government offices until 1945. He and his brother Mustafa founded a popular weekly, *Akhbar al-Yawm*, in November 1944. Nominally independent but anti-Wafd, the magazine was popularly believed to be close to King FARUQ. In 1952 they founded *al-Akhbar*, which became Egypt's largest daily newspaper, with a circulation of over 700,000 during the 1950s. They briefly published an Arabic version of the *Reader's Digest*. Their newspapers were nationalized in 1960, but the brothers were reappointed as editors and board chairmen in 1962. In 1964 'Ali proposed founding a Higher Institute for Secretarial Studies. Owing to his clashes with NASIR's government and MUHAMMAD HASANAYN HAYKAL's allegations that he was in the pay of British and Saudi intelligence, 'Ali went into exile in 1965, serving briefly as a London-based correspondent for *al-Ahram*. SADAT invited him back to Egypt in 1974 to replace Haykal as editor of *al-Ahram*. 'Ali later rejoined his brother at *al-Akhbar*, but they soon quarreled with Sadat and in 1976 they were dismissed. 'Ali died of cancer two weeks later.

Bibliographic Sources
Abaza, Fikri, in *al-Akhbar*, 15 Apr. 1976.
al-Ahram Archives, file 1519.
al-Akhbar, 11 Apr. 1976.
Akhir sa'a, 10 Apr. 1976.
Amin, Mustafa, *Shakhsiyyat*, II, 136–148.
Baha al-Din, Ahmad, in *al-Ahram*, 11 Apr. 1976.
Haykal, Muhammad Hasanayn, *Bayn al-sihafa wa al-siyasa.*
Khidr, *Suhufiyyun mu'asirun*, 57–77.
Labban, "*Akhbar al-Yawm*": *masira suhufiyya fi nisf qarn.*
New York Times (4 Apr. 1976): 63.
Rizq, Fathi, *Khamsa wa sab'una najman*, 277–286.
Shusha, *Asrar 'Ali Amin wa Mustafa Amin.*
Zalata, *Ali Amin.*

Amin, Mustafa

(21 February 1914–13 April 1997)
Influential editor of *al-Akhbar*. A native of Cairo and 'ALI AMIN's twin brother, Mustafa began his

journalistic efforts within *Bayt al-Umma*, SAʿD ZAGHLUL's home. He entered the Khedive Ismaʿil School but was expelled for demonstrating against the government in 1928 and soon afterward, because of his opposition to King FUAD, Mustafa was barred permanently from government schools. His articles against the king, published anonymously in several journals, were suppressed while he was studying at the American University at Cairo. Mustafa also held unpaid editorial positions at *al-Sarkha* and *Akhir Saʿa* during the early 1930s. In 1935 he went to Georgetown University; he served as Washington correspondent for *al-Misri* and in 1938 earned an M.A. in political science. He wrote his first signed article for *Akhir Saʿa* in 1939, causing both its editor, Muhammad al-Tabiʿi, and himself to be jailed for six months. Upon his release, he became a news editor at *al-Ahram*, and from 1941 to 1944 editor-in-chief of *al-Ithnayn*. He and his brother ʿAli founded *Akhbar al-Yawm* as a weekly magazine in 1944, followed by *Akhir Lakhza* in 1948 and *al-Jil* in 1951. In 1952, shortly before the 23 July Revolution, they founded *al-Ahkbar* as a popular daily. Although it was put under the control of the National Union in 1960, the Amin brothers continued to manage it and were reappointed as editors in 1962. In defying NASIR's efforts to muzzle the press, they lost their positions. Mustafa was arrested in 1965 on charges of spying for the United States and smuggling money out of Egypt. In 1966 he was tried, convicted, and sentenced to life imprisonment at hard labor. Continuing to write articles in prison, he managed to have some of them smuggled out and published under a pseudonym in a Beirut newspaper. Pardoned by SADAT in 1974 and released, Mustafa was reinstated as editor of *al-Akhbar* but was again dismissed in 1976. Working as a freelance journalist, he published *al-Kitab al-mamnuʿ* [The Forbidden Book] on his prison experiences, as well as other books on politics and personalities. Always controversial, he antagonized every political leader from King FARUQ to Sadat by his advocacy of liberal democracy, capitalism, and a free press. He was elected to the Arabic Language Academy in 1990.

Bibliographic Sources

al-Ahram Archives, file 1493.
Akhir saʿa (24 Apr. 1997): 4–62.
Amin, Mustafa, *Li-kull maqal azma.*
al-Jadid 3:17 (Apr. 1997): 2.
Egypt, Ministry of Information, *al-Mawsuʿa al-qawmiyya*, II, 1191.
Najib, *Aʿlam Misr*, 468.
New York Times (16 Apr. 1997): D22.
Rizq, Fathi, *Khamsa wa sabʿuna najman*, 287–300.
Uktubir, no. 1070 (27 Apr. 1997): 14–18.
WWAW, 1997–1998, 89.

Amin, Qasim

(1 December 1863–22 April 1908)
Lawyer, writer, and pioneer of Egyptian feminism. Son of a Kurdish amir who became a general in ISMAʿIL's army, Qasim was born in Tura, near Cairo, where he was educated. He earned his *license* from the Khedivial School of Administration (later the Khedivial Law School), later going on to Montpellier for legal studies. Returning to Egypt in 1885, he held various judicial posts, rising to that of chancellor of the Cairo National Court of Appeals. He wrote *Les Égyptiens*, a work defending Egypt and Islam against a critical book by a French writer, but then was convinced, some say by Princess NAZLI, others by MUHAMMAD ʿABDUH, that he had erred in defending the traditional female role in Islam. He proceeded to publish two books advocating greater rights for women, *Tahrir al-mara* [The Liberation of Woman] and *al-Mara al-jadida* [The New Woman]. He argued that it was not Islam, but the way in which Muslims had interpreted it, that had led to women's seclusion, veiling, early marriage, and lack of education. His views were attacked by many contemporaries, including TALʿAT HARB and MUSTAFA KAMIL, but inspired later Egyptian feminists, although some now argue that his influence has been exaggerated. A patriotic Egyptian, disciple of Muhammad ʿAbduh and friend of LUTFI AL-SAYYID and SAʿD ZAGHLUL, he helped to found the Islamic Benevolent Society, the Higher Schools Club, and the Egyptian University.

Bibliographic Sources

ʿAbbud, Marun, *Ruwwad al-nahda*, 266–268.
Ahmed, J.M., *Intellectual Origins*, 47–51.
Ahmed, Leila, *Women and Gender in Islam*, 144–168.
Amin, Ahmad, "Bayna Qasim Amin wa Duq Darkur."
Ata, "The Impact of Westernising."
Badran, "Dual Liberation."

————, *Feminists*, 18–19.
Baron, *Women's Awakening in Egypt*, 4–5.
Brockelmann, *GAL*, S III, 330–331.
Cole, "Feminism, Class, and Islam," 387–407.
Daghir, *Masadir*, II, i, 138–140.
Eliraz, "Egyptian Intellectuals and Women's Emancipation."
EAL, I, 86–87.
EI2, IV, 721–722, article by U. Rizzitano.
Fahmi, Mahir Hasan, *Qasim Amin*.
Gharaba, *Shakhsiyyat*, 85–92.
Hourani, *Arabic Thought*, 164–170.
'Imara, *Qasim Amin*.
Jindi, Anwar, *a'lam wa ashab aqlam*, 326–334.
Jundi, *A'lam al-adab*, II, 454–455.
Khaki, *Qasim Amin*.
Kurd 'Ali, *Mu'asirun*, 290–297.
Mujahid, *al-A'lam al-sharqiyya*, II, 489–490.
Muti'i, *Haula al-rijal min Misr*, III, 239–251.
————, *Mawsu'a*, 418–424.
Paret, *Zur Frauenfrage*.
Philipp, "Feminism and Nationalist Politics."
Ragai [Shafiq], *La femme et le droit religieux*, 97–112.
Sakakini, *Qasim Amin*.
Shamis, *'Uzama*, 131–136.
Subki, *al-Haraka al-nisaiyya*.
'Umar, Mahmud Fathi, *Abtal al-hurriyya*, 41–45.
Walili, *Mafakhir al-ajyal*, 99–100.
Zaki, Muhammad Amin, *Mashahir al-Kurd*, II, 114.
Zaydan, Jurji, *Bunat al-nahda al-'arabiyya*, 101–118.
Zeidan, *Arab Women Novelists*, 15–20.
Zirikli, *al-A'lam*, V, 184.

'Amir, 'Abd al-Hakim

(11 December 1919–14 September 1967)
Army officer and politician. He graduated from the Military Academy in 1938 and served in the Palestine War. One of the founders of the Free Officers, he subsequently became a member of the Revolutionary Command Council, commander-in-chief of Egypt's armed forces in June 1953, and war minister in 1954. Promoted to the rank of field marshal in 1958, he became vice president and war minister of the United Arab Republic in 1958. When opposition to NASIR grew in Syria, he went there as special commissioner to preserve the union. After Syria seceded in 1961, he became Egypt's defense minister and also a member of the Presidential Council. He was appointed first vice president and deputy commander-in-chief of the Egyptian armed forces under the 1964 Constitution. He is said to

have ordered the troops to launch a preemptive attack on Israel in late May 1967, an order countermanded by Nasir, who feared that such a strike would lead to U.S. intervention on Israel's side. Generally blamed for Egypt's defeat in the ensuing June War, 'Amir was subsequently dismissed from all his positions. Accused of plotting a military coup, he was put under house arrest in August 1967. In the following month 'Amir committed suicide by taking poison, but some Egyptians believe he was murdered by the intelligence service, the *Mukhabarat* (the investigation was kept secret). Regarded by the Free Officers as right-wing, in his later years he enriched himself from questionable land deals. These may have resulted from his affair with a film star, whose apartment allegedly served as a den of spies. He opposed the government's growing populism and pro-Soviet ties, but personally loyal to Nasir, he never differed with him publicly.

Bibliographic Sources

'Abd al-Hamid, Birlanti, *al-Mushir wa ana*.
al-Ahram Archives, file 4.
Amir, "Intihar am ightiyal al-Mushir Amir!"
al-Anba, 19 Sept.–9 Nov. 1993.
Beattie, *Nasser Years*, 124–127, 159–162.
Imam, 'Abd Allah, *'Amir wa Birlanti*.
Najib, *A'lam Misr*, 292.
Shimoni, *BDME*, 27.

Antun, Farah

(1874–6 June 1922)
Playwright, journalist, and radical westernizer. Born in Tripoli, the son of a Greek Orthodox lumber dealer, Antun graduated from the Kaftin School and worked briefly for his father but chose to devote his time to study rather than to business. He later became the headmaster of an Orthodox school in his village. Moving to Egypt in 1897, he soon founded *al-Jami'a al-'Uthmaniyya*, a monthly magazine so radical that it angered readers by its attacks on the views of MUHAMMAD 'ABDUH. Antun moved briefly in 1906 to New York, where he tried, unsuccessfully, to publish *al-Jami'a* as a daily. Returning to Cairo, he wrote for other papers, including *al-Ahali* and *al-Mahrusa*. He translated and adapted plays for JURJ ABYAD, writing some dramas of his own and translating into Arabic Nietsche's *Also sprach Zarathustra* and Renan's *La*

vie de Jésus. His best-known work is a historical novel about the Arab conquest of Jerusalem, *Ur-ishalim al-jadida aw fath al-'Arab bayt al-maqdis* [New Jerusalem, or How the Arabs Captured the Holy City]. He died in Cairo.

Bibliographic Sources
'Abbud, Marun, "Farah Antun," *al-Kitab.*
———, "Farah Antun," *al-Hilal.*
———, *Judud wa qudama,* 17–66.
———, *Ruwwad al-nahda,* 268–273.
Aqqad, 'Abbas Mahmud, "Farah Antun."
———, *Mutala'at fi al-kutub wa al-hayat,* 61–66.
———, *Rijal 'araftuhum,* 199–206.
Badawi, M.M., "Arabic Drama: Early Developments," *CHAL,* 343–344.
Brockelmann, *GAL,* S III, 192–194.
Brugman, *Introduction,* 224–228.
Daghir, *Masadir,* II, i, 147–152.
EAL, I, 96.
EI2, II, 782–783, article by Moshe Perlmann.
EMME, I, 163–164, article by Zachary Karabell.
Haddad, Niqula, in *al-Muqtataf* 61:3 (Aug. 1922): 261–265.
———, in *al-Sayyidat* 3 (1922): 565–571.
Haddad and Dumit, *Farah Antun.*
Hourani, *Arabic Thought,* 253–259.
Isma'il, *Farah Antun.*
Jindi, Anwar, *al-Muhafaza wa al-tajdid,* 264–269.
Jum'a, Muhammad Lutfi, in *al-Sayyidat* 3 (1922): 625–632.
Kahhala, *Mu'jam,* VIII, 59–60.
Mansi, *Farah Antun.*
Mumin and Manhal, *Min talai' yaqzat al-umma al-'arabiyya,* 55–90.
Nawfal, 'Abdallah Habib, *Tarajim 'ulama Tarablus,* 227–230.
Reid, *Farah Antun.*
Sa'id, *Thalathat Lubnaniyyin.*
Sarkis, *Mu'jam al-matbu'at,* II, 1440–1441.
Taymur, Muhammad, *Hayatuna al-tamthiliyya,* 75–84.
UNESCO, *A'lam al-Lubnaniyyin,* 199.
Zirikli, *al-A'lam,* V, 141.

al-'Aqqad, 'Abbas Mahmud

(28 June 1889–12 March 1964)

Journalist, poet, and writer. Born in a village near Aswan to a man from Damietta who had become a money-changer in Esna and a woman of Kurdish origin, al-'Aqqad graduated from a state primary school in 1903 but, because of his family's modest means, was mainly self-educated. He worked for the Egyptian State Railways and the *awqaf* ministry, taught school, studied at the School of Arts and Crafts, and worked six months in a telegraph office before going into journalism. He wrote cultural and literary articles for *al-Dustur* between 1907 and 1909 and also talked with SA'D ZAGHLUL, the first time an Egyptian minister was interviewed by the press. He contributed poetry to *al-'Ukaz* and edited successively *al-Bayan, al-Muayyad, al-Ahali,* and *al-Ahram.* He worked briefly for the press censorship office during World War I and in 1919 translated the MIL-NER Commission's report into Arabic. In 1921 he became the editor of the Wafd's newspaper, *al-Balagh,* and joined the Black Hand Society, for which he wrote some tracts.

During the 1920s 'Aqqad became prominent as an innovative poet and writer, issuing a manifesto in 1921 with IBRAHIM 'ABD AL-QADIR AL-MAZINI that challenged the classical canon of Arabic poetry, founding what is called the Diwan Group, and publishing together with Mazini the two-volume *al-Diwan.* 'Aqqad was elected as a Wafdist to the Chamber of Deputies in 1930, then was imprisoned by the SIDQI government, allegedly for his threats against King FUAD inspired by his loyalty to the 1923 Constitution. 'Aqqad used his nine months in jail to learn French. After breaking with NAHHAS in 1935, he joined the Sa'dist Party in 1937, edited its newspaper, *al-Asas,* and was reelected as a deputy in 1938 and named a senator in 1944. Antifascist during World War II, he would later oppose communism under NASIR. He chaired the poetry committee of the Supreme Council for Arts, Literature, and Social Sciences, and in 1959 he received a state prize for literature. 'Aqqad wrote poems about nature, love, his own feelings, and children, but also memoirs about such public figures as Sa'd Zaghlul, who was also the subject of one of his biographies. He also wrote biographies of the Prophet Muhammad and the first four caliphs, studies of Arab poets, and many sketches about incidents and personalities in Egypt's modern history. One of his novels, *Sara* (1938), has been translated into English, and his literary study of Ibn al-Rumi was translated in *Four Egyptian Literary Critics.* He was elected to the Arabic Language Academy in 1940 and also became a corresponding member of the Damascus and Baghdad academies. He died in Cairo. Individualistic, opinionated (if at times not fully informed) on many subjects, he held a Friday morning salon at his Heliopolis home for admirers and curious visitors. He is memorialized by a statue and a library in Aswan, and the main commercial street in Victory City (Madinat Nasr), near Cairo, bears his name.

Bibliographic Sources

'Abd al-Hamid, Isma'il, *al-Udaba al-khamas*, 109–175.

'Abd al-Haqq, *'Abbas Mahmud al-'Aqqad.*

'Abd al-Muttalib, Rif'at Fawzi, *'Abqariyyat al-'Aqqad.*

Abu Hadid, Muhammad Farid, in *MMLA* 17 (1965): 165–174.

al-Ahram (13 Mar. 1964): 1, 10.

al-Ahram Archives, file 121.

'Allam, *Majma'iyyun*, 137–140.

Allen, *Modern Arabic Literature*, 49–55.

Amin, Mustafa, *Shakhsiyyat*, II, 20–39.

Amin, 'Uthman, *Nazarat fi fikr al-'Aqqad.*

'Aqqad, 'Abbas Mahmud, "Ahamm hadith fi majra hayati."

———, *Ana.*

'Aqqad, Amir, *al-'Aqqad: ma'arikuhu fi al-siyasa wa al-adab.*

———, *Gharamiyyat al-'Aqqad.*

———, *Lamahat min hayat al-'Aqqad.*

———, *Safahat min ma'arik al-'Aqqad al-siyasiyya.*

Baqari, *al-'Aqqad wa al-mara.*

Becka, *DOL*, III, 17–18.

Berque, *Egypt*, 353–354.

Brockelmann, *GAL*, S III, 139–156, 253–255.

Daghir, "'Abbas Mahmud al-'Aqqad."

Dayf, *al-Adab al-'arabi*, 136–144.

———, *Ma'a al-'Aqqad.*

Didi, *'Abqariyyat al-'Aqqad.*

———, *al-Falsafa wa al-ijtima' 'ind al-'Aqqad.*

———, *al-Naqd wa al-jamal 'ind al-'Aqqad.*

Diyab, 'Abd al-Hayy, *'Abbas Mahmud al-'Aqqad.*

———, *al-'Aqqad wa tatawwuruhu al-fikri.*

———, *al-Mara fi hayat al-'Aqqad.*

———, *al-Nuzha al-insaniyya fi shi'r al-'Aqqad.*

———, *Sha'iriyyat al-'Aqqad fi mizan al-naqd al-hadith.*

Elbarbary, "al-Aqqad's Hardy."

EAL, I, 97–99.

EI2, supp. I, 57–58, article by Roger Allen.

Fahmi, Zaki, *Safwat al-'asr*, 666–671.

Fuad, Ni'mat Ahmad, *al-Jamal wa al-hurriyya.*

———, *Qimam adabiyya*, 65–108.

Hafiz, Ahmad, *Ayyam min shababihim*, 27–35.

Hall, *Egypt in Silhouette*, 244–252.

Halwaji, *'Abbas Mahmud al-'Aqqad.*

Hijazi, Anwar, *'Amaliqa*, 303–315.

al-Hilal 75:4 (Apr. 1967), special issue.

Hufi, Ahmad, *al-Ittijah al-nafsi.*

Jabalawi, *Dhikrayati ma'a 'Abbas al-'Aqqad.*

Jawdat, *Balabil*, 134–150.

Jayyusi, *Trends*, I, 153–154, 163–175.

Jindi, Anwar, *al-Muhafaza wa al-tajdid*, 311–315, 429–441.

———, *al-Sihafa al-siyasiyya*, 363–377.

Khafaji, *'Abbas Mahmud al-'Aqqad.*

Khemiri and Kampffmeyer, *Leaders*, I, 12–16.

Kilpatrick, *Modern Egyptian Novel*, 30–35.

Maqalih, *'Amaliqa.*

Moreh, *Modern Arabic Poetry.*

Musa, Salama, "'Abbas Mahmud al-'Aqqad."

Radwan, Fathi, *'Asr wa rijal*, 200–248.

Ramadi, *Min a'lam al-adab*, 15–39, 231–236.

Safran, *Egypt in Search*, 135–137, 150–158, 210–226.

Saharti, Mustafa 'Abd al-Latif, *Adab al-tabi'a*, 104–106.

Sakkut, *'Abbas Mahmud al-'Aqqad.*

Schoonover, "Tawfiq al-Hakim and al-'Aqqad."

Semah, *Four Egyptian Literary Critics*, 3–65.

Sharaf, 'Abd al-'Aziz, *'Asr al-'Aqqad.*

Shihabi, "'Abbas Mahmud al-'Aqqad."

Sidqi, 'Abd al-Rahman, "al-'Aqqad kama 'arif-tuhu."

Strika, "Filosofia a religione."

Taymur, Mahmud, *al-Shakhsiyyat al-'ishrun*, 43–49.

Tawil, *al-Maqala fi adab al-'Aqqad.*

Tunisi, *Fusul min al-naqd 'ind al-'Aqqad.*

'Ubayd, Ahmad, *Mashahir shu'ara*, I, 224–248.

'Uthman, Muhammad Salih, *al-'Aqqad fi nad-watihi.*

Vial, "al-'Aqqad (1888–1964)."

Wakil, al-'Awadi, *al-'Aqqad wa al-tajdid fi al-shi'r.*

———, *Qadiyyat al-saffud bayn al-'Aqqad wa khusumihi.*

Wakil, Mukhtar, *Ruwwad al-shi'r al-hadith*, 65–82.

Wielandt, *Offenbarung.*

Zaki al-Din, *al-Kuttab al-thalatha*, 130–235.

Zirikli, *al-A'lam*, III, 266–267.

Zubaydi, "The Diwan School."

Artin, Ya'qub

(15 April 1842–21 January 1919)

Armenian educator and scholar. The son of MUHAMMAD 'ALI's foreign minister, Artin Bey, Ya'qub was born in Cairo. Educated in Istanbul and in Europe, he was appointed tutor for ISMA'IL's children. In 1879 he became the khedive's secretary for European affairs and in 1884 undersecretary for the education ministry. He was a member of the Institut Égyptien and then its honorary president. Ya'qub represented the Egyptian government on the Suez Canal Company board. He wrote articles for the *Bulletin de l'Institut d'Égypte* and two books, *L'instruction publique en Egypte* (1890) and *La propriété fon-cière en Égypte* (1908), both of which were translated into Arabic.

Bibliographic Sources
Artin, *Artin Bey.*
Crabbs, *Writing of History,* 186–187.
Davidian, *Généalogie.*
Kahhala, *Mu'jam,* XIII, 242.
Lüthi, *Français en Égypte,* 86–87.
———. *Introduction,* 269.
Piot Bey, "Discours sur la tombe de Yacoub Artin Pacha."
Times (London) (27 Jan. 1919): 7d.

al-Ashmawi, Muhammad Sa'id

(1932–)

Secularist judge and former head of the State Security Tribunal. Born in Giza province, Ashmawi received his law degree from Cairo University in 1954 and did advanced studies at Harvard University. He began his legal career in the *Niyaba,* moving up through the judiciary until he was appointed undersecretary for general administration in the department of legislation in 1978. The author of several general and specialized works on legislation, he took part in the Paris Conference on the Laws of Authorship in 1977. More recently, as a writer for *Uktubir* and *Ruz al-Yusuf,* he has played a major role in opposing the political claims of the Islamist *jama'at,* reportedly placing his own life in danger.

Bibliographic Sources
al-Ahram Archives, file 33140.
Mussad, "Debate on the Adoption of the Shari'a."
Najib, *A'lam Misr,* 413.
WWAW, 1993–1994, 95.

'Atiyya, Rawiya

(19 April 1926–9 May 1997)

First woman in Egypt's parliament. 'Atiyya was originally from Giza province; her father was secretary-general for the Wafd Party in Gharbiyya. Among her childhood memories was one of visiting her father while he was in prison. While taking part in the 1939 anti-imperialist demonstrations, she was wounded by a stray bullet and was taken home by HUDA SHA'RAWI for medical treatment. She earned her *license* in letters from Cairo University in 1947 and a diploma in education and psychology, a mas-

ter's degree in journalism, and another diploma in Islamic studies. She worked as a teacher for fifteen years and as a journalist for six, also taking part in numerous volunteer activities. 'Atiyya was the first woman to be commissioned as an officer in the Liberation Army in 1956 and helped train 4,000 women in first aid and nursing during the Suez War. She chaired the Society of Women Mobilized for Social Service in 1957 and the Society of Families of Martyrs and Soldiers in 1973. Elected to the Chamber of Deputies in June 1957, she was the first woman deputy in the Arab world, but she lost her bid for reelection two years later. She served on the boards of the Red Crescent and the Huda Sha'rawi Society. She was awarded the badge of the Third Army, the Medallion of 6 October, and the medal of the armed forces. Chosen as the Exemplar of 1976, 'Atiyya was elected to the People's Assembly in 1984 as a member of the National Democratic Party and later headed the Population and Family Council for Giza in 1993.

Bibliographic Sources
al-Ahram, 5 June 1997.
al-Ahram Archives, file 154.
al-Ahram Weekly, 1 June 1995.
Mayu, 28 July 1987.
Najib, *A'lam Misr,* 212.
Nisf al-dunya, 18 May 1997.
al-Siyasa, 28 July 1984, 26 Sept. 1990, 28 May 1994.
Sullivan, Earl L., *Women in Egyptian Public Life,* 39–40.

al-Atrash, Farid

(21 April 1915?–26 December 1974)

Composer, singer, and actor. Farid was born in Suwayda (Jabal al-Duruz) and descended from Druze princes. His mother brought him with his brother and sister (later known as Asmahan, the film singer) to Egypt during the Druze uprising against the French in 1925. He studied at the College des Frères and later enrolled in the Institute of Arabic Music and studied the *'ud* with RIYAD AL-SUNBATI. He performed publicly for the first time in Mary Mansur's troupe on Cairo's Shari' 'Imad al-Din, singing with Asmahan, but his better-known debut was in 1931 with BADI'A MASABNI, who paid him £E 5 monthly. He became known through his performances on Egyptian State Radio and on the screen. In 1941 he and Asmahan produced and costarred in a highly successful film, *Intisar al-shabab* [The Triumph of Youth]. The songs that he wrote incorporated Western rhythms and genres while preserving their essential Arabic character, using both classical and colloquial language. He went on to compose the music for and star in at least thirty Arabic films, winning widespread acclaim throughout the Arab world for his expressive manner. He received fifteen awards and decorations, notable among which was winning the first international *'ud* competition in Turkey in 1962. Atrash died in Beirut. His songs remain popular among most Arabs.

Bibliographic Sources
al-Ahram Archives, file 112.
Atrash, *Mudhakkirat.*
Butrus, *A'lam al-musiqa,* 259–261.
Darwish, Mustafa, *Dream Makers,* 26.
EMME, I, 256–257, article by Virginia Danielson.
Jundi, *A'lam al-adab,* I, 302.
Mallakh, Kamal, in *al-Ahram,* 27–30 Dec. 1974.
Najmi, *al-Ghina al-misri.*
al-Qabas, 17 Nov. 1983, article by Sa'id Mustafa.
Ramzi, *Nujum al-sinima,* 207–218.
Zaki, 'Abd al-Hamid Tawfiq, *A'lam al-musiqa,* 109–112.
Zirikli, *al-A'lam,* V, 143–144.

al-'Attar, Shaykh Hasan

(1766–1835)
Islamic scholar, reformer, and rector of al-Azhar. Born in Cairo to a family of North African origin, he was educated at al-Azhar. During NAPOLEON's occupation, he observed some of the research being done by French scholars. He then fled to Damascus and Albania, later returning to Egypt. As a teacher at al-Azhar, he introduced new teaching methods, stressing analysis instead of rote learning. His interests were wide-ranging; his essays, *al-Rasail* (first published in 1866), covered law, grammar, logic, medicine, and other sciences. In 1828 MUHAMMAD 'ALI named him the first editor of Egypt's official journal, *al-Waqai' al-misriyya,* and in 1830 rector of al-Azhar. One of his disciples was RIFA'A RAFI' AL-TAHTAWI, an early reformer. Al-'Attar died in Cairo.

Bibliographic Sources
Brugman, *Introduction,* 15–16.
Cheikho, *al-Adab al-'arabiyya,* I, 51–53.

De Jong, "The Itinerary of Hasan al-'Attar."
Delanoue, *Moralistes,* II, 344–357.
EAL, I, 111.
*EI*2, I, 755, article by H.A.R. Gibb.
Gran, *Islamic Roots,* 75–110.
Hasan, Muhammad 'Abd al-Ghani, *Hasan al-'Attar.*
Jundi, *A'lam al-adab,* II, 424–425.
Shamis, *'Uzama,* 45–52.
Taymur, *A'lam al-fikr al-islami,* 19–38.
Zayyati, *Kanz al-jawhar,* 138–141.
Zirikli, *al-A'lam,* II, 220.

'Awad, Ahmad Hafiz

(1874–29 December 1950)
Journalist and historian. He was born in Damanhur and educated in a local *kuttab,* al-Azhar, and at the Higher Teachers College in Cairo. Together with two fellow Damanhuri students at the Teachers College, he organized the first Accession Day fete for Khedive 'ABBAS, with MUSTAFA KAMIL as the main speaker. He worked as an English translator and clerk for *al-Muayyad* from 1898 to 1906 and published the magazine *al-Adab.* He became the khedive's secretary and was privy to many of his political activities. After leaving the Palace, 'Awad resumed work at *al-Muayyad* but was unemployed during World War I. He joined the 1919 Revolution and published *Kawkab al-Sharq* as a Wafdist daily for twenty years. He was elected three times to the Chamber of Deputies, served a term in the Egyptian Senate, and became a member of the Arabic Language Academy in 1942. After a long illness, he died in Cairo. His books include *Fath Misr al-hadith, aw Nabulyun Bunabart fi Misr* [The Modern Conquest of Egypt, or Napoleon Bonaparte in Egypt].

Bibliographic Sources
al-Ahram, 30 Dec. 1950, 9.
'Allam, *Majma'iyyun,* 38.
'Awad, Ahmad Hafiz, "Ahamm hadith fi majra hayati."
———, "Dhikrayat Ahmad Hafiz 'Awad."
———, "Khamas shakhsiyyat misriyya atharat fi hayati."
Daghir, *Masadir,* III, ii, 887–889.
Jindi, Anwar, *al-Muhafaza wa al-tajdid,* 290–296.
———, *al-Sihafa al-siyasiyya,* 288–291.
Kahhala, *Mu'jam,* I, 186–187.
Najib, *A'lam Misr,* 87–88.
Tarrazi, *Tarikh al-sihafa,* IV, 204.
Zirikli, *al-A'lam,* I, 109.

'Awad, Dr. Louis

(21 December 1914–9 September 1990)
Essayist, literary critic, and novelist. Born in Sharuma (Minya province), 'Awad spent his early years in the Sudan, where his father was working for the government. He attended the École des Frères and the Amiriyya Elementary School and Secondary School in Minya and graduated from Cairo University with a degree in English literature in 1937. He was sent on an educational mission to King's College, Cambridge, to study for a doctorate in English, but his studies were interrupted by the outbreak of World War II. While he was there, he wrote his first *diwan* of poems, called *Plutoland*, and in 1942 would write an account of his experiences abroad, *Mudhakkirat talib ba'tha* [Memoirs of a Government Scholarship Student]. He earned his M.A. from Cairo University while serving as an assistant instructor and proceeded to work his way up the ladder, publishing books on Horace, Shelley, and modern English literature generally, and he became the first Egyptian to head Cairo University's English Department. Aided by a Rockefeller Foundation grant, he earned another M.A. and his doctorate in English and French literature from Princeton University in 1953. He worked briefly for the United Nations and then was director of the cultural affairs bureau in Egypt's Ministry of Culture and National Guidance in 1958, also editing the literary section of *al-Jumhuriyya* (1953–1954) and later of *al-Sha'b* (1957–1959). He then served as cultural adviser to Dar al-Tahrir Publishers (1959–1961) and to *al-Ahram* (1962–1982). He was Visiting Professor of Comparative Literature at the University of California in 1974. 'Awad participated in numerous conferences in Egypt and abroad and was the author of more than forty books in literature, criticism, and cultural history, including studies on the Orestes trilogy and on Shakespeare. He received a state prize in 1988. As the standard-bearer for a secular Egyptian culture open to the world generally and to the West in particular, he was attacked in later years by both the Muslim establishment and the rising Islamist wave.

Bibliographic Sources
al-Ahram (10 Sept. 1990): 1, 12, articles by Mustafa Bahjat Badawi, Salah al-Din Hafiz, Mustafa 'Abd al-Ghani, and others.
al-Ahram Archives, file 1663.
'Awad, Louis, Awraq al-'umr.
———, Mudhakkirat talib ba'tha.
———, "Problems of the Egyptian Theatre," 179–193.
EAL, I, 113–114.
Khouri, "Lewis 'Awad."
Kilpatrick, Modern Egyptian Novel, 65–71.
QTQ, 200.
Raghib, A'lam al-tanwir, 63–79.
Vatikiotis, Middle East, 206–207.
WWAW, 1997–1998, 110.

'Azmi, Dr. Mahmud

(5 May 1889–3 November 1954)
Writer, journalist, and lawyer. Born in Shibat Qush, near Minya al-Qamh (Sharqiyya), Mahmud 'Azmi was educated there and in Cairo, earning his *license* from the Khedivial Law School in 1909. He was sent on an educational mission to Paris, where he earned a doctorate of laws in 1912, whereupon he was appointed to teach political economy at the Higher School of Commerce in Cairo. After editing several Egyptian newspapers, such as *al-Mahrusa* (1919), he founded *al-Istiqlal*, a daily, in 1921, followed by a magazine, *al-Jadid*, in 1925. Becoming editor-in-chief of *al-Siyasa al-usbu'iyya* in 1922, he pioneered in reporting on the sessions of the new Egyptian Parliament. He also edited at various times *al-Jihad, Ruz al-Yusuf*, and *Akhbar al-Yawm*. At a time when Kemal Atatürk had outlawed the fez in Turkey, 'Azmi proposed replacing that head covering in Egypt with the beret, a proposal that was opposed by MANFALUTI and other Muslim traditionalists. He was appointed professor and then dean of the Law College in Baghdad in 1936, but after a student tried to kill him, he returned to Egypt. In 1940 'Azmi was named director of Cairo University's Institute for Editing, Translation, and Journalism. He helped draft the bylaws for the press syndicate in 1941 and was the first journalist to publicly oppose the 1936 Anglo-Egyptian Treaty and to support Egypt's Arab mission. He eventually became head of Egypt's delegation to the United Nations, where he chaired the Human Rights Commission in 1954. He died suddenly while addressing the Security Council in response to allegations made by Israel.

Bibliographic Sources
al-Ahram (4 Nov. 1954): 1, 5; (26 Nov. 1989).
al-Ahram Archives, file 397.
Najib, *A'lam Misr*, 459.
Le Progrès égyptien, Almanach, 189.
Qadi, Shukri, *Miat shakhsiyya,* 286–288.
Rizq, Fathi, *Khamsa wa sab'una najman,* 120–125.
Tarrazi, *Tarikh al-sihafa,* IV, 200, 214.
Zirikli, *al-A'lam,* VII, 177.

'Azzam, 'Abd al-Rahman

(8 March 1893–2 June 1976)
Pan-Arab advocate and first secretary-general of the Arab League. Born in Shubak al-Gharbi, near Ayyat (Giza province), 'Azzam was from a family of Arab background; his grandfather had served as governor of Giza but was exiled when the British occupied Egypt. A supporter of the National Party in his youth, he received his primary and secondary education in Helwan and then studied medicine in London but left his studies to serve as a volunteer paramedic for the Ottoman army during the first Balkan War. In World War I he joined the Libyan guerrillas against the Italians in Cyrenaica, returning to Egypt in 1923. He joined the Wafd when SA'D ZAGHLUL was prime minister and he became a member of Parliament, but later left the party and sided with 'ALI MAHIR. 'Azzam was Egypt's minister to Iraq, Iran, and Saudi Arabia, served as counselor to the Arab delegations at the 1939 London Conference on Palestine, and became minister of *awqaf* and of social affairs in 'Ali Mahir's cabinet in 1939–1940. A leading advocate of Arab unity from the early 1930s on, 'Azzam took part in several all-Arab congresses. In 1945 he was chosen to be the first secretary-general of the Arab League but resigned (partly due to pressure from the Free Officers) after the 1952 Revolution. He stayed away from Egypt for twenty years, during which time he represented Saudi Arabia in its Buraymi dispute with Britain and wrote his book, *The Eternal Message of Muhammad,* but returned in 1972. Portions of his Arabic memoirs, dictated to Jamil Arif, were published serially in Egypt and Lebanon, then in book form in 1977 as *Safahat min al-mudhakkirat al-sirriyya li awwal amin 'amm li al-Jami'a al-Arabiyya* [Pages from the Secret Memoirs of the First Secretary-General of the Arab League]. He be-

lieved that Arab unity should be achieved on the foundation of firm Islamic principles, a stand that has gained wider acceptance since his death.

Bibliographic Sources
Abdel-Malek, *Arab Political Thought,* 142–145.
al-Ahram, 3 June 1976; 6 June article by Zakariyya Nil; 22 June article by Ahmad Husayn.
al-Ahram Archives, file 211.
'Azzam, 'Abd al-'Aziz, *al-Islam wa al-fikr al-'alami.*
Arab Report and Record, 1–15 June 1976, 366.
Bishri, Tariq, *al-Haraka al-siyasiyya fi Misr.*
Coury, *Making of an Arab Nationalist.*
Current Biography (Apr. 1947): 26–28.
Dali, *Asrar al-jami'a al-'arabiyya.*
EMME, I, 273, article by Mahmoud Haddad.
Gershoni and Jankowski, *Redefining the Egyptian Nation.*
Gomaa, *League of Arab States.*
Heyworth-Dunne, James, "Egypt Discovers Arabism."
Jindi, Anwar, *al-Muhafaza wa al-tajdid,* 573–579.
———, *al-Sihafa al-siyasiyya,* 378–386.
al-Jumhuriyya, 16 June to 24 Nov. 1977, 'Azzam's memoirs.
Porath, *In Search of Arab Unity.*
Times (London) (4 June 1976): 18g–h.
Zawi, Ahmad Tahir, *Jihad al-abtal fi Tarabulus al-Gharb.*

'Azzam, Dr. 'Abd al-Wahhab

(1 August 1895–18 January 1959)
Writer and Islamic scholar. Born in 'Ayyat (Giza province) to a family of Arab origin, he graduated from the Shari'a Judges School in 1920, earned a *license* in humanities from the Egyptian University in 1923, received an M.A. in Oriental languages from London's School of Oriental Studies in 1928, and earned his doctorate in Arabic literature from Cairo University in 1932. 'Azzam then rose through the ranks of its Faculty of Arts, becoming dean in 1945. He was elected to the Arabic Language Academy in 1946 and was delegated to teach in Baghdad. Appointed Egypt's ambassador to Pakistan in 1950 and to Saudi Arabia in 1954, he founded King Saud University in Riyadh and in 1957 became its first director. He wrote books about the Indian Muslim poet, Mohammed Iqbal, and was awarded an honorary degree by the University of Dacca. Admitted to the Arabic language acade-

mies of Cairo, Damascus, Baghdad, and Tehran, he died in Saudi Arabia. 'Azzam was Egypt's foremost pan-Arab intellectual and was the nephew of 'ABD AL-RAHMAN 'AZZAM.

Bibliographic Sources
al-Ahram Archives, file 592.
Coury, *Making of an Arab Nationalist,* 349–352.

Fuad, Ni'mat Ahmad, in *al-Ahram,* 21 Apr. 1996.
———, *Qimam adabiyya,* 233–254.
Husayn, Taha, "al-Duktur 'Abd al-Wahhab 'Azzam."
Jindi, Anwar, *A'lam wa ashab aqlam,* 268–274.
Mahasini, *'Abd al-Wahhab 'Azzam.*
Muti'i, *Mawsu'a,* 310–316.
Qadi, Shukri, *Miat shakhsiyya,* 178–183.
Zirikli, *al-A'lam,* IV, 186.

B

Bibliographic Sources
al-Ahram Archives, file 203.
Akhar sa'a, 18 Aug. 1965.
'Allam, *Majma'iyyun*, 149–151.
Badawi, Mustafa Bahjat, "al-Janib al-akhar."
————, in *al-Jumhuriyya*, 9 Aug. 1965.
Baligh, 'Ali, in *al-Jumhuriyya*, 6 Aug. 1965.
Hijazi, Anwar, *'Amaliqa*, 265–268.
New York Times (6 Aug. 1965): 7.
Qadi, Shukri, *Miat shakhsiyya*, 142–144.
Rifa'i, 'Abd al-Hakim, "Abd al-Hamid Badawi."
Sanhuri, 'Abd al-Razzaq, "al-Duktur 'Abd al-Hamid Badawi."
Sarahan, *Musahamat al-qadi 'Abd al-Hamid Badawi*.
Zirikli, *al-A'lam*, III, 285.

Badawi, Dr. 'Abd al-Hamid
(13 March 1887–4 August 1965)

Judge and legal expert. 'Abd al-Hamid was born in Alexandria; his father, a farmer, moved to Mansura soon after his son's birth. 'Abd al-Hamid was educated in one of the schools of al-'Urwa al-Wuthqa Society, the Ras al-Tin School (graduating in 1904), and the Khedivial Law School, earning his *license* in 1908. After serving briefly in the Tanta *Niyaba* (public prosecutor's office) and the Cairo Court of Appeals, he went to France, where in 1912 he earned a doctorate from the University of Grenoble, presenting as his thesis *La développement de la notion de privilège*. For two years he taught at the Khedivial Law School and then served as THARWAT's *chef du cabinet*. During the 1919 Revolution he was elected to the government employees' committee and named adviser to the government cases division. After he accompanied 'ADLI to London for his 1921 talks with Curzon, he served as secretary-general to the cabinet and royal adviser. He helped draft the 1923 Constitution and later became a member of the Senate. 'Abd al-Hamid headed the government cases division in 1926–1940, chaired the conference that abolished the Capitulations in 1937, and drafted much of the Montreux Treaty. He held the portfolios for finance in 1940 and foreign affairs in 1945, serving on Egypt's delegation to the UN San Francisco Conference. He was elected to the Arabic Language Academy in that year. Named in 1946 to the International Court of Justice, he served as vice president in 1955–1958, remaining there until he died.

al-Baghdadi, 'Abd al-Latif
(20 September 1917–8 January 1999)

Air force officer and politician. 'Abd al-Latif was born in Mansura and attended its elementary and secondary schools. A 1938 graduate of the Military Academy, he also attended flight school, then worked in the administration of several Cairo military airports and fought in the Palestine War. He became a leading member of the Free Officers and the Revolutionary Command Council, president of the court that tried prerevolutionary political figures, and inspector-general of the Liberation Rally. Defense minister under NAJIB in 1953–1954, he was moved to municipal affairs when NASIR took power in 1954; Baghdadi later assumed control of planning. He is famous for having arranged the construction of the Nile Corniche. He became president of the National Assembly in 1957 and, following the creation of the UAR, became its vice president for economic affairs and minister of planning. After Syria seceded from the UAR, he served as Egyptian minister of finance and economic planning. In 1962 Baghdadi became one of Egypt's five vice presidents and resumed the presidency of the National Assembly, also serving on the Arab Socialist Union's executive board and Presidential Council. Dropped as vice president in 1964 because of differences with the cabinet over the Yemen War, he quit the National Assembly and held no other political post, although he claimed that Nasir intended to name him vice president in 1970 to prevent the succession of SADAT. The press interviewed Baghdadi often on political issues and he published mem-

31

oirs. He assailed the 1971 Egyptian-Soviet Friendship Treaty and later the Camp David Accord. He died in Heliopolis from complications caused by liver cancer.

Bibliographic Sources
al-Ahram Archives, file 313.
al-Anba, 26 Nov. 1988.
Baghdadi, *Mudhakkirat 'Abd al-Latif al-Baghdadi*.
Najib, *A'lam Misr*, 315.
New York Times (11 Jan. 1999): A15.
al-Shabab (1 Feb. 1989): 6–10, 82.
Uktubir, 3, 10 July 1988; 4 June 1993–13 Feb. 1994.
WWAW, 1997–1998, 169.

Baha al-Din, Ahmad

(11 February 1927–24 August 1996)
Journalist, author, and editor. Born in Alexandria, Baha al-Din attended Sa'idiyya Secondary School and earned his law *license* from Alexandria University in 1946, when he was too young to practice, so he became a writer and editor for *al-Fusul*. He got a temporary position in the *Niyaba* in 1947, serving until 1954. In 1951 he went to work for Ruz al-Yusuf Publishing House, for which he founded a magazine, *Sabah al-khayr*, serving as its editor from 1956 to 1958. After that he took charge of editing *al-Sha'b*. He became editor of *Akhbar al-Yawm* in 1959 and of *Akhir sa'a* in 1962, board chairman of Dar al-Hilal Publishing House in 1964, editor-in-chief of *al-Musawwar* in 1965, leader of the Press Syndicate in 1967–1969, member of the Supreme Council of the ASU in 1968, chairman of Ruz al-Yusuf in 1971, and editor-in-chief of *al-Ahram* in 1974–1975. He was elected in 1972 to the vice presidency of the International Union of Journalists for a four-year term. He was one of the hundred journalists briefly barred by SADAT from practicing their profession; they were pardoned shortly before the October War. Baha al-Din edited Kuwait's monthly magazine, *al-Arabi*, from 1976 to 1981, then wrote a column, "al-Yawmiyyat," in *al-Ahram* until 1990.

Just after the July Revolution Baha al-Din wrote an exposé of FARUQ, called *Faruq malikan* [Faruq as King]. Other works included *Ayyam laha tarikh* [Days Having a History], *Yawmiyyat hadha al-zaman* [Diaries of This Time], and *Israil wa al-dawla al-filistiniyya* [Israel and the Palestinian State]. He supported the Afro-Asian Peoples' Solidarity Organization, opposed U.S. military presence in the Persian Gulf, and viewed Israel as an outpost of U.S. power in the Middle East. Regarded by Egyptians as an expert on Israel, he actually learned Hebrew. As Baha al-Din was one of Egypt's most respected commentators, a collection of his best articles was published posthumously by the Supreme Council for the Press. A prize was established in his name for the best essay written by an Arab under forty.

Bibliographic Sources
'Abd al-Ghani, Mustafa, *Ahmad Baha al-Din*.
al-Ahram Archives, file 1862.
al-Bayan, no. 5916 (26 Aug. 1996).
Fuda, *Nujum Shari' al-Sihafa*, 140–145.
Maraghi, "Ayyam laha tarikh."
al-Musawwar (30 Aug. 1996): 17–67.
Rizq, Fathi, *Khamsa wa sab'una najman*, 525–530.
Segev, *Fundamentalism*, 71–72.
Vatikiotis, *Middle East*, 20–21.
WWAW, 1997–1998, 126.

Bahjat, 'Ali

(1858–17 March 1924)
Archaeologist, Islamic art historian, and leading excavator of Fustat, Egypt's first Arab capital. Of Turkish extraction (both of his grandfathers had served in MUHAMMAD 'ALI's administration), he was born in the village of Bahat al-'Ajuz (in Beni Suef province). He attended Cairo's Nasiriyya and Tajhiziyya Schools, followed by the School of Languages, where one of his professors was Shaykh HASUNA AL-NAWAWI. He graduated in 1882, having learned French, German, Persian, and Turkish. He then was appointed an assistant instructor at that school and later also at the Institut Français d'Archéologie Orientale. He developed a passion for archaeology, got to know French Orientalist scholars at the institute, and then took charge of the Education Ministry's translation bureau, also serving as an inspector of elementary schools supported by *awqaf*. In 1899 he represented Egypt at the International Congress of Orientalists in Rome. Shortly after that he quarreled with DUNLOP and published anonymous articles against the British adviser in *al-Muayyad*, so he left the Education Department and became assistant curator of the Museum of Arab [now Islamic] Art, later becoming head curator and finally director. He was

the first Egyptian to enter a scholarly field hitherto restricted to foreigners. Elected a member in the Institut d'Égypte in 1900, he attended scholarly conferences in Europe and published his research findings in newspapers and magazines as well as scholarly journals, sometimes in languages other than Arabic. Among his writings are *Fouilles d'al Foustat* (Paris, 1921) and a translated guide to the contents of the Islamic Art Museum. He died in Matariyya.

Bibliographic Sources
'Abd al-Raziq, Mustafa, "Ali Bey Bahgat."
Iskarus, Tawfiq, in *al-Hilal* 33:8 (May 1924): 856–861.
Jindi, Anwar, *A'lam wa ashab aqlam*, 292–299.
Reid, "Cultural Nationalism and Imperialism."
Shayyal, *al-Tarikh wa al-muarrikhun*, 152–155.
Zirikli, *al-A'lam*, IV, 268.

Bajuri, Shaykh Ibrahim
(1784–10 June 1860)
Shafi'i scholar, theologian, teacher, and rector of al-Azhar. Bajuri was born and raised in the Minufiyya village of Bajur (which some call "Bijur," in which case his name would be "al-Bijuri"); he enrolled at al-Azhar in 1798 and later taught there. 'ABBAS I attended his lectures. Bajuri wrote commentaries in logic, religious duties, theology, and grammar. A statement attributed to him, that *ijtihad* (judicial interpretation) ceased to be practiced after about A.H. 300, quoted by Snouck Hurgronje, began the debate in Western Orientalist discourse about closing the gate of *ijtihad* and led later to discussion among Muslim reformers about reopening it. In 1847/48 he was named shaykh of al-Azhar for life, although he was senile in his last year. A committee was formed in 1860 to take over his administrative duties and continued to function for the next four years, long after his death.

Bibliographic Sources
Berque, *Egypt*, 78.
Brockelmann, *GAL*, II, 639; S II, 741.
Cheikho, *al-Adab al-'arabiyya*, I, 87.
*EI*2, I, 867.
Fikri, 'Ali, *Subul al-najah*, II, 57–60.
Kahhala, *Mu'jam*, I, 84.
Mardam, *A'yan al-qarn al-thalith 'ashr*, 122.
Mubarak, 'Ali, *Khitat*, II, 2–3; IV, 30.
Sarkis, *Mu'jam al-matbu'at*, I, 507–508.
Zaydan, Jurji, *Tarikh adab al-lugha*, IV, 304.

Zayyati, *Kanz al-jawhar*, 143–146.
Zirikli, *al-A'lam*, I, 71.

Bakhit [al-Muti'i al-Hanafi], Shaykh Muhammad
(24 September 1854–18 October 1935)
Judge in the Shari'a Courts, rector of al-Azhar, and chief mufti of Egypt. Born in al-Muti'ah (near Asyut), Bakhit studied at al-Azhar and taught there from 1875 to 1880, when he was appointed qadi (Muslim judge) of Qalyubiyya, after which he served as a judge in various provincial centers, Alexandria, and Cairo. He was appointed Egypt's chief mufti on 21 December 1914, serving until 1921. He opposed MUHAMMAD 'ABDUH's reforms at al-Azhar, issued a *fatwa* (Muslim legal opinion) to warn Muslims against bolshevism (presumably meaning politically inspired violence) in the midst of the 1919 Revolution, and took conservative stands on such issues as the translation of the Quran, women's rights, and the abolition of family *awqaf*. After he ceased to be the chief mufti, he attacked severely 'ALI 'ABD AL-RAZIQ's *al-Islam wa usul al-hukm*. Bakhit published numerous treatises on Islamic law and theology.

Bibliographic Sources
al-Ahram, 19, 27 Oct. 1935.
*EI*2 Supp., 121, article by Fred de Jong.
Fahmi, Zaki, *Safwat al-'asr*, 501–504.
Fuad, Faraj Sulayman, *al-Kanz al-thamin*, 118–120.
al-Islam 4 (1935): 30, 38–39.
Kahhala, *Mu'jam*, IX, 98–99.
McIntyre, *Boycott of the Milner Mission*, 87–91.
Mujahid, *al-A'lam al-sharqiyya*, II, 497–499.
Zakhura, *Mirat al-'asr*, II, 467.
Zayyati, *Kanz al-jawhar*, 172–174.
Zirikli, *al-A'lam*, VI, 50.

al-Bakri, Muhammad Tawfiq
(24 September 1870–14 August 1932)
Muslim dignitary and classical poet. Born in Cairo, he was educated at the Princes' School and at home by private tutors. In 1892 he succeeded his brother as *naqib al-ashraf* (leader of the Sufi orders) and head of al-Bakriyya (the families descended from Abu Bakr). He wrote (or, more accurately, authorized) the regulations for Egypt's Sufi orders in 1895. 'ABBAS II obliged him to abdicate as *naqib* in that year because of his opposi-

tion to the khedive's pro-Ottoman policy. The two men later became reconciled, however, and Bakri was reappointed in 1903. They collaborated against the policies and ideas of MUHAMMAD 'ABDUH, thought to be pro-British. Bakri called for parliamentary government in Egypt and for Islamic unity. Again estranged from the khedive, he abdicated as *naqib* late in 1911 and, afflicted with paranoia, was confined to the Asfuriyya (Beirut) mental hospital from 1912 to 1928. He took no further part in politics but published books on Islam and the Sufi orders.

Bibliographic Sources
Antaki, *al-Nujum*, 57–59.
'Aqqad, 'Abbas Mahmud, *Shu'ara Misr,* 53–75.
Bakri, Muhammad Tawfiq, *Bayt al-Siddiq,* 11–26.
Brockelmann, *GAL,* S III, 81–82.
Brugman, *Introduction,* 80–82.
Daghir, *Masadir,* II, i, 207–208.
de Jong, *Turuq,* 125–140, 182–186.
EAL, I, 131.
EI2, Supp. I, 122–123.
Fahmi, Mahir Hasan, *Muhammad Tawfiq al-Bakri.*
Jindi, Anwar, *A'lam wa ashab aqlam,* 86–93.
Jundi, *A'lam al-adab,* II, 450.
Louca, *Voyageurs,* 221–225.
Kahhala, *Mu'jam,* IX, 141.
Kurd 'Ali, *Mudhakkirat,* I, 34–35.
Mikhail, Sa'd, *Adab al-'asr,* 225–231.
Mujahid, *al-A'lam al-sharqiyya,* II, 549–550.
Sabri, Muhammad, *Shu'ara al-'asr,* I, 194–208.
Shaybub, Siddiq, *Shakhsiyyat 'arabiyya,* 93–106.
Tanahi, Tahir, *'Ala firash al-mawt,* 139–150.
Taqwim "al-Hilal" (1933): 37.
'Ubayd, Ahmad, *Mashahir shu'ara,* I, 168–190.
Wright, *Twentieth Century Impressions of Egypt,* 198–199.
Zakhura, *Mirat al-'asr,* I, 217–224, and insert on Bakri family.
Zirikli, *al-A'lam,* VI, 65–66.

al-Banna, Hasan

(October 1906–12 February 1949)
Founder and Supreme Guide of the Society of Muslim Brothers. Hasan was born in Mahmudiyya, near Alexandria, the son of a devout watchmaker. Hasan was educated in his village *kuttab,* a primary school in Damanhur, and at Dar al-'Ulum. As a youth he participated in the 1919 Revolution and took part in Hasafiyya Sufism. Following at first the teachings of Muslim reformer RASHID RIDA, Banna taught principles of Islam in various cities, especially Ismailia where, in 1928, he founded the Society of Muslim Brothers as an association for religious teaching. Branches soon sprang up in other Canal cities. When the headquarters moved from Ismailia to Cairo in 1932, the Brothers evolved into a political society aiming at purifying Islam and calling for transforming Egypt into an Islamic state. Banna's simple doctrine won widespread support among urban workers and some younger intellectuals. His charisma (and devotion to the Palestinian cause) won him sympathy among Muslims in many Arab countries. He founded a daily newspaper, *al-Ikhwan al-Muslimun,* which became the mouthpiece for his ideas, and he tried to run candidates for election to the Chamber of Deputies. After the UN decision to partition Palestine, the Brothers took the lead in advocating a policy of active resistance and forming volunteer brigades to fight against the Zionists. As his society grew more radical and prone to terrorism, the government tried to suppress it, confiscating its funds, closing its branches, and interning some of its leaders under the state of martial law that had been declared during the Palestine War. Two months after Prime Minister NUQRASHI was assassinated in December 1948 by a student attached to the Brotherhood, Banna was murdered by government agents as he was leaving the Cairo headquarters of the Muslim Youth Association. Several collections of Banna's speeches and articles have been published, as have his memoirs, *Mudhakkirat al-da'wa wa al-di'aya.* An articulate speaker and writer, committed to social justice and resistance to imperialism, Banna was personally incorruptible in an era dominated by politicians, but his ideological rigidity blunted his political impact.

Bibliographic Sources
'Abd al-Jawad, Muhammad, *Taqwim Dar al-'Ulum,* 470.
Abdel-Malek, *Arab Political Thought,* 45–50.
Abdel Nasser, *The Islamic Movement in Egypt,* 117–187.
al-Ahram Archives, file 359.
al-Ahrar, 12 Apr. 1998.
'Assaf, *Ma'a al-imam al-shahid Hasan al-Banna.*
Banna, Hasan, *Majmu 'at rasail.*
Carré, Olivier, and Michaud, *Les Frères Musulmans.*
Colombe, *L'évolution de l'Égypte,* 141, 264–269.
Daghir, *Masadir,* II, i, 209–212.

EAL, I, 132.
EI2, I, 1018–1019, article by J.M.B. Jones.
———, III, 1068–1071, article by Gilbert Delanoue.
Gershoni, "Emergence of Pan-Nationalism."
Harris, Christina Phelps, *Nationalism and Revolution,* 143–185.
Heyworth-Dunne, Jamal al-Din, *Religious and Political Trends.*
Husayni, *al-Ikhwan al-Muslimin.*
Imam, 'Abd Allah, *'Abd al-Nasir wa al-Ikhwan. al-Imam al-shahid Hasan al-Banna.*
Kahhala, *Mu'jam,* III, 200.
Khadduri, *Political Trends,* 73–85.
Lia, *Society of the Muslim Brothers in Egypt.*
Marel, "L'Association des Frères musulmans."
Mitchell, *Muslim Brothers,* 1–71.
Muhammad, Muhsin, *Man qatala Hasan al-Banna?*
Muti'i, *Haula al-rijal min al-Azhar,* 65–68.
———, *Mawsu'a,* 135–141.
OEMIW, I, 195–198, article by Olivier Carré.
Qadi, Shukri, *Khamsun shakhsiyya,* 87–91.
Sa'id, Rif'at, *Hasan al-Banna.*
Shaikh, *Memoirs of Hassan al-Banna Shaheed.*
Shalabi, Muhammad, *Hasan al-Banna imam wa qaid.*
Shalabi, Rauf, *al-Shaykh Hasan al-Banna.*
Sonbol, Amira El Azhary, "Hassan al-Banna."
Stewart, *Middle East: Temple of Janus,* 294–298.
Times (London) (14 Feb. 1949): 3d.
Wendell, *Five Tracts of Hasan al-Banna.*
Yusuf, al-Sayyid, *al-Ikhwan al-Muslimun,* I.
Zaki, Muhammad Shawqi, *al-Ikhwan al-Muslimin.*
Zirikli, *al-A'lam,* II, 183–184.

al-Baqli, Dr. Muhammad 'Ali
(1815–1876)

Physician and surgeon. Born in Zawiyat al-Baqli (Minufiyya), he attended the local *kuttab,* where he memorized the Quran and received his basic education. At age nine he was enrolled by his father in the new preparatory school at Abu Za'bal. After graduation he went on to the medical college recently founded by Clot Bey; the latter recommended him for the first educational mission to Paris, where he studied until he obtained his doctorate. Returning to Egypt in 1838, he was named instructor of surgery and anatomy at the medical college and quickly became a leading surgeon at Qasr al-'Ayni, where his success brought about the jealousy of the less competent and less scrupulous foreign doctors. After MUHAMMAD 'ALI died, Baqli was dismissed from Qasr al-'Ayni but opened his own clinic in Cairo and soon attracted a large clientele. He was later reinstated in his position and eventually made a pasha by Khedive ISMA'IL. He wrote a number of useful treatises, including *Rawdat al-najah al-kubra fi al-'amaliyyat al-jarahiyya al-sughra* [The Garden of Greatest Success in Performing Small Surgical Operations], *Ghurar al-najah fi a'mal al-jarrah* [The Utmost Success in the Actions of the Surgeon], and *Ghayat al-falah fi a'mal al-jarrah* [Highlights of Success in Surgical Operations]. He also coauthored several medical books. Together with another Egyptian physician, he published *al-Ya'sub fi al-tibb,* Egypt's first medical periodical, in 1865. He was hoping to accompany the military expedition to Ethiopia at the time that he died.

Bibliographic Sources
'Isa, *Mu'jam al-atibba,* 471–474.
Mubarak, 'Ali, *Khitat,* XI, 85.
Rafi'i, 'Abd al-Rahman, *'Asr Muhammad 'Ali,* 551–553.
Shamis, *'Uzama,* 107–112.
Tusun, *al-Ba'that al-'ilmiyya,* 131–133.
Zaydan, Jurji, *Tarajim mashahir al-sharq,* 1st ed., II, 113–116.
Zirikli, *al-A'lam,* VI, 300.

Barakat, Daud
(1870–4 November 1933)

Journalist and editor of *al-Ahram.* Born in Yahshush (in the Kisrawan district of present-day Lebanon), he was educated in Arabic and French schools in Beirut. He moved to Egypt in 1890, taught in Zifta and Tanta, then became a writer for *al-Mahrusa* in 1894. Together with Shaykh Yusuf al-Khazin he helped to put out *al-Akhbar* and in 1899 became an editor of *al-Ahram,* taking charge of the paper after the death of its founder, BISHARA TAQLA, in 1901. A four-page daily when he took over, it had become the Arab world's largest newspaper by the time he died. He also wrote books, including one on the Sudan and British imperial ambitions in Egypt, and a series of articles about IBRAHIM Pasha.

Bibliographic Sources
al-Ahram (5 Nov. 1933): 1–2, articles by 'Abd al-Rahman 'Azzam, Ahmad Wafiq, and Salih al-Bahnasawi.
———, 11 Feb. 1932, article by Tawfiq Habib.

Daghir, *Masadir*, II, i, 177–179.
Fahmi, Zaki, *Safwat al-'asr*, 650–652.
Ghanim, "Daud Barakat."
Jindi, Anwar, *al-Muhafaza wa al-tajdid*, 249–253.
———, *al-Sihafa al-siyasiyya*, 91–95.
Kahhala, *Mu'jam*, IV, 135–136.
Kull shay wa al-dunya, no. 419 (15 Nov. 1933): 4–5, 44.
Ma'luf, 'Isa Iskandar, in *MMIA* 13 (Nov.–Dec. 1933): 495–497.
Musa, Salama [S], "Sa'a ma'a shaykh al-sihafa."
Mutran, Khalil, in *al-Hilal* 42:2 (Dec. 1933): 136–137.
Naththar al-afkar, I, 126, Daud Barakat's autobiography.
Tanahi, Tahir, *'Ala firash al-mawt*, 158–162.
Taqwim "al-Hilal" (1933): 38.
Zakhura, *Mirat al-'asr*, III, 34–35.
———, *al-Suriyyun fi Misr*, 89–93.
Zirikli, *al-A'lam*, II, 331.

al-Bardisi, 'Uthman

(1758–19 November 1806)

Mamluk factional leader after the French occupation. Initially acting as a surrogate for the aging IBRAHIM BEY, Bardisi was a rival to the ALFI BEY faction and a temporary ally of MUHAMMAD 'ALI, who in 1802 was just taking charge of his Albanian regiment that made up the bulk of the Ottoman army in Egypt. Bardisi and Muhammad 'Ali besieged the Ottoman governor, KHUSRAW PASHA, in Damietta, devastating the city in the process of capturing him. Bardisi's mamluk factions took charge of Cairo, where the population's reaction to the high tax levies worked to Muhammad 'Ali's advantage. Arrears in pay led to soldiers' demonstrations in Cairo, and new levies were imposed on the civilian population. Bardisi scolded the Cairo ulama for allowing this revolt, but Muhammad 'Ali openly supported the demonstrators. His forces drove Bardisi's mamluks out of Cairo, to the delight of the ulama and the merchant guilds. Bardisi's death was popularly ascribed to poisoning by Alfi Bey, who survived him by only two months.

Bibliographic Sources

Ghorbal, *Beginnings*, 208–231.
Hanotaux, *Histoire*, VI, 20–33.
Herold, *Bonaparte in Egypt*, 255–259.
Marlowe, *Perfidious Albion*, 81–111.
Rafi'i, 'Abd al-Rahman, *'Asr Muhammad Ali*, 40.

al-Barudi, Mahmud Sami

(6 October 1839–12 December 1904)

Army officer, cabinet minister, prime minister, and neoclassical Arabic poet. A native of Cairo, he claimed descent from the brother of a Circassian Mamluk sultan and from a family of Buhayra tax farmers. His father was an artillery officer under MUHAMMAD 'ALI; Mahmud was educated in one of Muhammad 'Ali's military schools, graduating in 1854. He worked for the Ottoman government while SA'ID was governor of Egypt. When ISMA'IL went to Istanbul upon his succession in 1863, he brought Barudi back to command his viceregal guard and later to serve as his private secretary, and Barudi went on missions to Paris, London, and Istanbul. He also served in the Egyptian corps that aided the Ottoman army in Crete in 1865 and in the war against Russia in 1877–1878, attaining the rank of brigadier general. He was named governor of Sharqiyya province in 1878 and then *awqaf* minister. The nationalist officers around 'URABI demanded Barudi's appointment as war minister in 1881 and as premier in 1882. He sided with the 'Urabist officers against the British expeditionary force. After the 'Urabists' defeat at Tel al-Kabir, Barudi was tried, exiled to Ceylon, and not readmitted to Egypt until 1900. Blind and saddened by the news that most of his relatives had died, he played no further role in public life. He wrote patriotic poetry, published in his lifetime and reissued in many anthologies since his death; his poetry is still read and admired for its classical Arabic allusions and motifs. Egyptians respect him as a leader of their literary renaissance.

Bibliographic Sources

'Abbud, Marun, *Ruwwad al-nahda*, 141–147.
'Aqqad, 'Abbas Mahmud, *Shu'ara Misr*, 120–148.
'Ashur, Nu'man, *Butulat misriyya*, 119–138.
Badawi, M.M., "al-Barudi."
Badrawi, Sami, *Awraq al-Barudi*.
Becka, *DOL*, III, 30.
Brockelmann, *GAL*, S III, 7–18.
Brugman, *Introduction*, 28–33.
Daghir, *Masadir*, II, ii, 159–162.
Dayf, *al-Barudi*.
———, *al-Adab al-'arabi*, 83–91.
Disuqi, 'Umar, *Mahmud Sami al-Barudi*.
EAL, I, 137–138.
EI2, I, 1069–1070, article by Henri Pérès.
Fikri, 'Ali, *Subul al-Najah*, II, 191–194.
Gharaba, *Shakhsiyyat*, 97–103.

Hadidi, 'Ali, *Mahmud Sami al-Barudi.*
Hamuda, 'Abd al-Wahhab, *al-Tajdid fi al-adab,* 89–94.
Haykal, Muhammad Husayn, *al-Adab wa al-hayat,* 27–68.
Hijazi, Anwar, *'Amaliqa,* 105–109.
al-Hilal 13:5 (1 Feb. 1905): 258–264.
al-Hilal 81:3 (Mar. 1972), special issue.
Ibrahim, 'Abd al-Fattah, in *al-Hilal* 42:10 (Aug. 1934): 1212–1217.
———, *Shu'arauna al-dubbat,* 17.
Jayyusi, *Trends,* I, 37–39.
Jindi, Anwar, *Adwa,* 260–262.
Jundi, *A'lam al-adab,* II, 434–435.
Kahhala, *Mu'jam,* XII, 165–167.
Khafaji, *Qissat al-adab,* V, 98–125.
Khattab, Sadiq Ibrahim, *al-Shi'r fi al-'asr al-hadir.*
Khouri, *Poetry,* 13–36.
Kurd 'Ali, *Mu'asirun,* 389–426.
Mikhail, Sa'd, *Adab al-'asr,* 216–224.
al-Muayyad (13 Dec. 1904): 5–6.
Mujahid, *al-A'lam al-sharqiyya,* I, 166–668.
al-Muqtataf 30:1 (Jan. 1905): 6–8; 30:2 (Feb. 1905): 92–96.
Qadi, Shukri, *Khamsun shakhsiyya,* 53–56.
Rafi'i, 'Abd al-Rahman, *Shu'ara al-wataniyya,* 18–29.
———, *al-Thawra al-'urabiyya,* 562–567.
Rafi'i, Mustafa Sadiq, "Shi'r al-Barudi."
Ramadi, *Min a'lam al-adab,* 183–190.
Rizq, Yunan Labib, *Tarikh al-wizarat,* 97–103.
Sabri, Muhammad, *Adab wa tarikh,* 41–42.
———, *Mahmud Sami al-Barudi.*
———, *Shu'ara al-'asr,* I, 17–47.
Salih, 'Izz al-Din, *Mahmud Sami al-Barudi.*
Sayrafi, Hasan Kamil, "Mahmud Sami al-Barudi."
UAR, *Mahrajan Mahmud Sami al-Barudi.*
Walili, *Mafakhir al-ajyal,* 54–57.
Zaki, 'Abd al-Rahman, *A'lam al-jaysh,* 181–183.
Zaydan, Jurji, *Mashahir al-sharq,* 2nd ed., II, 333–340.
———, *Tarikh adab al-lugha,* IV, 224–225.
Zirikli, *al-A'lam,* VII, 171.

al-Bishri, Shaykh 'Abd al-'Aziz

(1886–26 March 1943)

Shari'a judge and humorous writer. 'Abd al-'Aziz was born in the Hayy al-Baghala quarter of Cairo, the son of Shaykh SALIM AL-BISHRI, rector of al-Azhar, and studied there himself. After graduation he took a secretarial post in the *awqaf* bureau in 1911, later working in the Education Ministry before taking various judicial posts in the Shari'a Courts in Giza, Asyut, Zaqaziq, and Isna. He then became general supervisor of the Arabic Language Academy. Besides articles for *al-Kashkul* and *al-Siyasa al-usbu'iyya,* Bishri wrote several books, including *Fi al-mirat* and *al-Mukhtar.* He died in Cairo.

Bibliographic Sources
al-Ahram, 9 May 1997.
al-Ahram Archives, file 4013.
Jindi, Anwar, *al-Muhafaza wa al-tajdid,* 415–420.
Jundi, *A'lam al-adab,* II, 462–463.
Khafaji, *Qissat al-adab,* V, 38–61.
Mahmud, Hafiz, in *al-Jumhuriyya,* 19 May 1968.
Ramadi, *'Abd al-'Aziz al-Bishri.*
———, *Min a'lam al-adab,* 64–72.
———, *Sihafat al-fukaha,* 32–38, 73–75.
Rizq, Fathi, *Khamsa wa sab'una najman,* 115–119.
Zirikli, *al-A'lam,* IV, 18.

al-Bishri, Shaykh Salim

(1832–21 September 1917)

Chief Maliki mufti and rector of al-Azhar. Son of Sayyid Abu al-Faraj, he was born in Bishr, near Shubra al-Khit, in Buhayra province. When Salim was seven years old, his father died. He memorized the Quran in his native village and, at the age of nine, went to Cairo and lived with his maternal uncle, who also taught Salim various Islamic subjects. While enrolled at al-Azhar, he studied with some of the major scholars of his day, including 'ILLAYSH and AL-BAJURI, and became a specialist in the Prophet's sunnah and hadith. After completing his studies, Salim was appointed shaykh of the Sayyida Zaynab Mosque in Cairo. He later taught at al-Azhar, where he produced many illustrious scholars and was twice appointed rector: in 1899 and 1909. He is generally seen as a conservative, although in fact many reforms to the administration and physical plant of al-Azhar were implemented during his second term in office. Salim died in Cairo and is buried in the Maliki cemetery near al-Sayyida al-Nafisa. All of his six sons became shaykhs.

Bibliographic Sources
Abu al-'Uyun, *al-Jami' al-Azhar.*
Eccel, *Egypt, Islam, and Social Change.*
Fuad, Faraj Sulayman, *al-Kanz al-thamin,* 106–109.
al-Hilal 26:2 (Nov. 1917): 206–207.
Mujahid, *al-A'lam al-sharqiyya,* I, 313–314.
Rida, Muhammad Rashid, *Tarikh al-Ustadh al-Imam,* I, 464.
Salman, 'Abd al-Karim, *A'mal majlis idarat al-Azhar.*
Shafiq, *Mudhakkirati,* II, ii, 182.

Zakhura, *Mirat al-'asr*, II, 465–467.
Zayyati, *Kanz al-jawhar.*
Zirikli, *al-Alam*, III, 119.

Blunt, Wilfrid Scawen

(17 August 1840–10 September 1922)
English poet, Orientalist, horse breeder, and advocate of Muslim causes. Blunt worked for ten years in the British foreign service, but after his marriage to Anne, Lord Byron's granddaughter, he left the service and spent several years exploring the Arabian desert. He is best known for his involvement in the 'URABI Revolution in 1881–1882, on which he later wrote a memoir, *The Secret History of the English Occupation of Egypt* (1907). After 'Urabi's defeat, Blunt hired a British barrister to defend the colonel at his treason trial and helped get the death sentences imposed by the Egyptian courts reduced to exile or imprisonment. He went on using his official connections to press for an early withdrawal of British forces from Egypt, about which he wrote in *Gordon at Khartoum* (1912). He also aided the later National Party of MUSTAFA KAMIL, whom he greatly admired, and the 1919 Revolution. From 1911 to 1913 Blunt financed a monthly magazine, *Egypt*, in which he and others attacked the British occupation and backed the Nationalists. A wealthy Sussex landowner and minor poet, Blunt may have misled Egyptians by overstating his influence with British politicians. He published *My Diaries* (1921), a bowdlerized version of his notes (the Fitzwilliam Museum, Cambridge, has the original notes), commenting freely on politics in Egypt and elsewhere between 1888 and 1914. Some of his diaries and correspondence are at Reading University; there are also papers in the West Sussex County and Diocesan Record Office in Chichester.

Bibliographic Sources
'Aqiqi, *al-Mustashriqun*, II, 498.
Assad, *Three Victorian Travelers.*
DNB (1922–1930): 34–36, article by P.G. Elgood.
Finch, *Wilfrid Scawen Blunt.*
Foreign Office List, 1921, 249.
Forster, *Abinger Harvest.*
Hourani, *Europe and the Middle East.*
Khaki, "Sadiq al-'urabiyyin."
Kramer, Martin, "Pen and Purse."
Leslie, *Men Were Different*, 229–288.
Longford, *Pilgrimage of Passion.*
Lytton, *Wilfrid Scawen Blunt.*
Times (London) (12 Sept. 1922): 15c.
Tidrick, *Heart-Beguiling Araby.*
Wentworth, *Authentic Arabian Horse.*
Who Was Who (1916–1928), 101–102.

Bonaparte. *See* NAPOLEON BONAPARTE.

Boutros-Ghali, Dr. Boutros

(14 November 1922–)
United Nations secretary-general, professor, and editor. He was born in Cairo and received his *license en droit* from Cairo University in 1946, a *diplome* in law (1947) and in economics (1948) and a doctorate in international law (1949), all from the University of Paris. He briefly taught political science at the School of Commerce in 1945 and in 1949 began teaching at Cairo University, serving for many years as head of the Department of Political Science and Economics. In 1954–1955 he was a Fulbright research scholar at Columbia University. He edited *al-Ahram al-iqtisadi* and *al-Siyasa al-dawliyya* from 1959 to 1967. In 1967–1969 he directed the research center of The Hague Academy of International Law. He lectured on law and international relations at Columbia, Princeton, New Delhi, Warsaw, Geneva, Algiers, Dakar, Dar as Salam, and Nairobi Universities, among others; took part in various international conferences; and produced more than a hundred books, chapters, and articles in French, English, and Arabic. Boutros-Ghali headed *al-Ahram*'s Center for Strategic Studies in 1975. Secretary of state for foreign affairs from November 1977 until 1991, he accompanied SADAT on his peace mission to Jerusalem and played a key role in the Camp David summit. He also played a key peacemaking role within the Organization of African Unity. He was heading Egypt's delegation to the Francophone Union in Paris at the time he was elected UN secretary-general in November 1991. Boutros-Ghali served from 1992 to 1996, mediating the Cambodian crisis, the India-Pakistan dispute, and civil wars in Bosnia and Somalia, among other issues. His quest for a second term was vetoed by the United States. In 1997 he was elected to chair the Francophone Union at its meeting in Hanoi. He received the Egyptian state award for his peacemaking efforts

in 1979 but is widely thought to have been excluded from a higher government post because of his being a Copt and because of his grandfather's reputation for collaborating with the British.

Bibliographic Sources
al-Ahram Archives, file 330.
Boutros-Ghali, *Egypt's Journey to Jerusalem.*
———, *Unvanquished.*
Egypt, Ministry of Information, *al-Mawsu'a al-qawmiyya*, I, 212.
EMME, I, 395–396, article by Bryan Daves.
Goldschmidt, "Butrus Ghali Family," 183, 188.
Ignatieff, "Alone with the Secretary General."
Lemsine, "Outspoken Emissary for Peace."
QTQ, 48.
Spencer, "A Francophone at the Helm."
Times (London) (22 Nov. 1991): 14.
Watani (16 Aug. 1992): 7.
West Africa, no. 3873 (2–8 Dec. 1991): 2002.
WWAW, 1997–1998, 176–177.

Boyle, Harry

(5 July 1863–6 April 1937)
Interpreter, diplomat, and first oriental secretary of the British Agency. Harry's father, Henry Boyle, was a man of letters and an amateur inventor who gave his son access to his library but no formal schooling. Nevertheless, Harry took the highly competitive examination for the Consular Service, finishing third, and in 1883 became a student interpreter in Istanbul, where he also was attached to the International Lifeboat Service on the Black Sea and briefly with its coastal antismuggling cavalry squadron. He went to Egypt in 1885, initially with an appointment as vice-consul in Massowa, but instead, having learned to speak Arabic after five weeks working for an Egyptian *makwagi* (ironing man), he became the right-hand man of the British agent and consul general in Cairo, Sir Evelyn Baring, later Lord CROMER. Boyle's ability to gather information from both Egyptians and foreigners in Cairo was legendary, and Cromer came to rely so heavily on his advice that Boyle was nicknamed Enoch, because he "walked daily with the Lord" and bore the title of oriental secretary.

Although Cromer retired in 1907, Boyle remained in Cairo until 1909 but disliked serving under GORST and sought a transfer. Regrettably, the Foreign Office could not find him a suitable

post in the Near East, naming him Britain's first *consul de carrière* in Berlin, a post hitherto held by a German banker in an honorary capacity. Although Boyle retired on pension on 1 July 1914, he served during World War I in the Foreign Office and then in the Intelligence Division of the War Office. He returned to Egypt in 1921 at the behest of the Foreign Office to study the political situation. While there, he met SA'D ZAGHLUL, who reportedly confided that, if the British appointed Boyle as their new representative in Cairo, he would personally "go with England instead of against her—I will work *for you*." Sa'd's rival, 'ADLI YAKAN, expressed similar feelings. Boyle had to cut short his visit because he was besieged by callers who remembered him as Cromer's secretary and who sought his influence on their behalf. In a private memorandum, he wrote that no Egyptian wanted to see the protectorate maintained. He continued to perform missions for the Foreign Office until he retired to his native Cornwall, where he died. Except for the Coronation Medal that he received in 1911, he received no official recognition for his services to British imperialism.

Bibliographic Sources
Boyle, *Boyle of Cairo.*
———, *A Servant of the Empire.*
Foreign Office List, 1921, 253–254.
Marlowe, *Cromer in Egypt*, 232–234, 262.
Sayyid, Afaf Lutfi, *Egypt and Cromer*, 95, 143, 177.
Stewart, *Middle East: Temple of Janus*, 174–176.
Times (London) (8 Apr. 1937): 18b, article by Philip Graves; 10, 19e.
Who Was Who (1929–1940), 148.

Brunyate, Sir William

(12 September 1867–29 August 1943)
British administrator. Brunyate began his Egyptian service in 1898. He was judicial adviser from 1916 to 1919 and acting financial adviser from 1917 to 1919. He helped to draft the text of Britain's protectorate over Egypt in 1914 and is well known for his memorandum suggesting the termination in Egypt of the Capitulations and the establishment of a bicameral legislature giving foreigners predominance in its upper house, a plan energetically opposed by nearly all Egyptians. Brunyate also wanted to become the Egyptian government's permanent financial ad-

viser, an appointment that the Foreign Office opposed. His British contemporaries viewed him as hardworking, ambitious, stubborn, and tactless.

Bibliographic Sources
Lévi, "La note de Sir William Brunyate."
Times (London) (31 Aug. 1943): 6e.
Who Was Who (1941–1950), 154.

Bughus, Yusuf

(1768–9 January 1844)

MUHAMMAD 'ALI's chief translator and commerce and foreign minister, sometimes called Boghos Yusufian. Born to an Armenian merchant family in Izmir, he learned Armenian, Turkish, Greek, Italian, and French in school and became a Customs official and trader in Cyprus, Syria, and Egypt. He became a British consul in 1790 because of his language skills and aided his patrons in their campaign against the French. He then backed Muhammad 'Ali, soon becoming his personal secretary, first in Cairo and later in Alexandria, where he managed the Customs House from 1810 to 1813. Briefly imprisoned and threatened with execution on the accusation of mismanaging the accounts, he was soon set free and recalled to reform Egypt's financial administration; he served as commerce and foreign minister from 1826 until about 1843. Ousted from power by European intriguers seeking the viceroy's patronage, he retreated to his home in Alexandria and starved himself to death. Muhammad 'Ali grieved for him and ordered him buried, at government expense, in the Armenian cemetery in Alexandria. Bughus brought many Armenians to Egypt to serve in Muhammad 'Ali's government. He was NUBAR's uncle.

Bibliographic Sources
Adalian, "The Armenian Colony of Egypt."
Archarouni, *Nubar Pacha,* 9–17.
EMME, IV, 1943, article by Rouben P. Adalian.
al-Hilal 7:9 (1 Feb. 1899): 262–265.
Rivlin, *Agricultural Policy,* 179–180.
Sabri, M., *L'Empire égyptien,* 121–124 et passim.
Sayyid-Marsot, *Egypt in the Reign,* 76.
Walili, *Mafakhir al-ajyal,* 28–29.
Zaydan, Jurji, *Mashahir al-sharq,* 1st ed., I, 211–215.

C

world's seventh best. Although viewed as cold and rigid, Cerisy was capable of solving difficult engineering problems.

Bibliographic Sources
Clot-Bey, *Aperçu général,* I, 192.
Durand-Viel, *Les campagnes navales.*
Hanotaux, *Histoire,* VI, 84–85.
Mubarak, 'Ali, *Khitat,* VII, 52.
Rafi'i, 'Abd al-Rahman, *'Asr Muhammad 'Ali,* 428–440.
Tusun, *al-Sanai' wa al-madaris al-harbiyah.*
Vivielle, "Cerisy Bey."
Weygand, *Histoire militaire de Mohammed Aly.*
Wiet, *Mohammed 'Ali et les beaux-arts,* 19, 195–200.

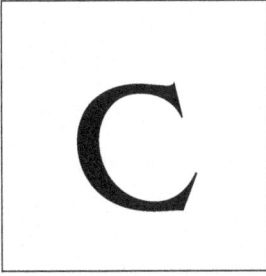

Cerisy, Louis-Charles Lefebure de
(15 September 1789–15 December 1864)
French naval engineer, developer of MUHAMMAD 'ALI's fleet and the Alexandria arsenal, and first commander of Egypt's naval war college. Son of the mayor of d'Abbeville, where Louis-Charles was born, he received his primary education at the communal school and then went on to the École Centrale of Caen. Cerisy was admitted to the École Polytechnique in 1807 and graduated in 1809. He worked at the Toulon military shipyards from 1809 to 1813 and was officially licensed as a *sous-ingénieur* in 1812; soon after that he was transferred to the naval arsenal at Civita-Vecchia, but he found little to do as the Napoleonic Wars were drawing to a close. He returned to Toulon in 1817 and studied naval architecture in England from 1822 to 1825. He supervised the construction at Brest of some frigates for the Egyptian navy. Soon after most of that fleet was destroyed in the Battle of Navarino, Muhammad 'Ali sought a French engineer to supervise the construction of a new one, and Cerisy was chosen in 1828. After reporting for duty in April 1829, one of his first tasks was to arrange for the transport of an obelisk from Luxor to Paris, where it still stands. He also built the Jabbari Palace and gardens for Muhammad 'Ali. He proceeded to modernize the naval arsenal in Alexandria and turned out numerous frigates, corvettes, "bricks" (brigs), and a *goélette* (schooner). One of his design innovations was to have all the guns on a given ship be of the same caliber, simplifying the storage and distribution of ammunition. At the time of his return to France (following a quarrel with Muhammad 'Ali), Egypt's fleet was rated as the

Chahine, Youssef. *See* SHAHIN, YUSUF

Champollion, Jean François
(23 December 1790–4 March 1832)
French Oriental scholar and the father of modern Egyptology. Born in Figeac, he was educated at home by his elder brother, at the Lycée in Grenoble, and at the Collège de France and the École Spéciale des Langues Orientales Vivantes in Paris. He taught history and politics in Grenoble (1809–1816). As occupant of a professorial chair at the Royal College, Grenoble (1818–1821), and later as conservator of the Louvre's Egyptian collections, he was able to use his knowledge of Greek, Coptic, and other ancient languages to devise a system for translating the demotic and hieroglyphic versions of the Rosetta stone, which had been found by Napoleon's troops. He thus laid the groundwork for all later studies of ancient Egyptian inscriptions. His elder brother, Jacques Joseph, helped prepare and edit his work; they may deserve joint credit for the discoveries attributed to Jean François.

Bibliographic Sources
A'lam "al-Muqtataf," I, 92–95.
'Aqiqi, *al-Mustashriqun,* I, 331.
Carré, Jean-Marie, *Voyageurs,* I, 223–245.
Champollion-Figeac, *Les deux Champollion.*
Dawson, *Egyptology,* 58–60.
DBF, VIII, 349–351, article by P. Hamon.
Dewachter, *Champollion.*
EMME, I, 465, article by Donald M. Reid.
Erman, "Die Entzifferung der Hieroglyphen."
Gabra, *À la mémoire de Champollion.*
Hartleben, *Champollion, sein Leben.*

————, *Lettres de Champollion.*
Journal of Egyptian Archaeology 37 (1950): 38–
46.
Kettel, Jeannot, *Jean-François Champollion le Jeune.*
Porterfield, *The Allure of Empire.*
Pourpoint, *Champollion.*
Recueil d'études égyptologiques.
Renouf, "Young and Champollion."
Sorokine, *Champollion et les secrets de l'Égypte.*
Textes et langues de l'Égypte pharaonique.

Cheetham, Sir Milne
(9 July 1869–6 January 1938)
British diplomat at the British Agency from 1910 to 1919 who took charge when the consuls general were absent. Born in Preston, England, he studied classics at Christ Church College, Oxford, after which he entered the diplomatic service. He was posted to Madrid, Paris, Tokyo, Berlin, Rome, and Rio de Janeiro before he went to Cairo as first secretary in January 1910, becoming counselor the following year. He took charge of the British Agency for GORST in the summers of 1910 and 1911 and also for KITCHENER in subsequent summers. When World War I began, he led Britain's diplomatic mission through a difficult six months of imperial mobilization while Egypt was still legally a privileged province of the Ottoman Empire. The latter declared war on Britain in November 1914. When the British government declared its protectorate over Egypt the following month, Cheetham became acting high commissioner, pending the arrival of Sir HENRY MCMAHON. He took charge of the Residency in the fall of 1915 and again during the spring and fall of 1919; hence he had to confront the political crisis caused by the 1919 Revolution. He also advised the MILNER Mission during its visit to Egypt in 1919–1920 and influenced ALLENBY's early policies as high commissioner. Cheetham later served in the British embassy in Paris and was minister in Berne, Athens, and Copenhagen, retiring in 1928. He was remembered as a well-mannered, loyal, and hardworking diplomat. His unpublished memoir, "British Policy, 1910–1945," is held by the Middle East Centre, St. Antony's College, Oxford. He received the Coronation Medal in 1911 and was made a Knight Commander of the Order of Saints Michael and George in 1915.

Bibliographic Sources
Foreign Office List, 1928, 196.
Times (London) (7 Jan. 1938): 14b.
Who Was Who (1929–1940), 244.

Cicurel, Salvator Moreno
(14 October 1894–?)
Jewish leader, sportsman, and department store owner. He was of Sephardic background; his father had come to Egypt from Smyrna (Izmir) in 1870 and started out as a textile merchant in Cairo's Mousky district before opening Au Petit Bazaar, a department store that evolved during World War I into Les Grands Magazins Cicurel et Oreco, located in central Cairo. Salvator received his training at the Haut École du Commerce in Paris. An enthusiastic athlete, Salvator captained Egypt's Olympic fencing team in 1928, became a champion golfer, and chaired Cairo's Maccabi Sports Club. A leading member of the Sephardic Jewish community, he was elected its vice president in 1943 and served as president from 1946 to 1957. He was also a member of the Egyptian Chamber of Commerce until the late 1950s. After his store was destroyed in the Cairo fire of January 1952, it was rebuilt on a grander scale with assistance from the Free Officers (some of whom knew Salvator as a sportsman), but as a consequence of the Anglo-French attack during the 1956 Suez Crisis, he had to sell his store to an Egyptian citizen (it was later nationalized). Salvator left Egypt for France in 1957, never to return.

Bibliographic Sources
Beinin, *Dispersion of Egyptian Jewry*, 47–49.
Najib, *A'lam Misr*, 239.
Raafat, "The House of Cicurel."
Who's Who in Egypt and the Near East, 293.

Clot, Dr. Antoine Barthélemy
(9 November 1793–28 August 1868)
French physician. Born in Grenoble to a poor family, he was educated at the Hospice de la Charité, Marseilles, and in Montpellier. He started a surgical practice in Marseilles; then in 1825 MUHAMMAD 'ALI invited him to become his chief surgeon in Egypt, a post that Clot held officially from 1828 to 1838. He organized the public health service and medical school. He and his European staff trained many Turks and Egyptians

in Cairo to become army surgeons, sending some of his best pupils to France for specialized training there. Muhammad 'Ali sent him to France in 1839. After getting married and publishing his two-volume work, *Aperçu générale sur l'Égypte,* in France, Clot again joined the Egyptian service in 1840. Although dismissed by 'ABBAS I in 1849, he was able to return to Egypt in 1856 and retired the following year. He was an outstanding example of a French citizen who devoted himself wholeheartedly to Egypt's modernization. He died in Marseilles. Streets in Grenoble and Cairo bear his name.

Bibliographic Sources
'Abd al-Karim, Ahmad 'Izzat, *Tarikh al-ta'lim fi 'asr Muhammad 'Ali,* 251–260 et passim.
A'lam "al-Muqtataf," I, 105–109.
Batatuni, *Tarikh al-Duktur Klut Bey.*
Carré, Jean-Marie, *Voyageurs,* I, 286–290.
Charles-Roux, François, "Clot Bey et le consul-general."
Clot-Bey, *À Son Altesse Ismail-Pacha.*
———, *Documents concernant le Dr. Clot-Bey.*
———, *Le Dr Clot-Bey et sa conduite en Egypte.*
———, *Mémoires.*
———, *Position officielle de Clot-Bey.*
Dawson, *Egyptology,* 36–37.
DBF, IX, 30, article by P. Hamon.
Euzière, *Petite histoire.*
al-Hilal 2:11 (1 Feb. 1894): 321–328.
'Isa, Ahmad, *Mu'jam al-atibba,* 349–352.
Kuhnke, *Lives at Risk,* 33–34.
al-Muqtataf 18:4 (1 Jan. 1894): 220–224.
Rafi'i, 'Abd al-Rahman, *'Asr Muhammad 'Ali,* 468–471 et passim.
Thiers, *Le Docteur Clot Bey.*
Walili, *Mafakhir al-ajyal,* 35–37.
Zaydan, Jurji, *Mashahir al-sharq,* II, 1–8.
———, *Tarikh adab al-lugha,* IV, 30, 168–169.
Zayn al-Din, Isma'il Muhammad, *al-Ajanib,* 94–100.

Colvin, Sir Auckland

(8 March 1838–24 March 1908)
Financial superintendent. Born in India, where his father was in the Indian Civil Service, Colvin was educated at Eton and the East India College of Haileybury. He, too, entered the Indian Civil Service, holding various secretaryships before being appointed in 1880 to the International Commission for Egyptian [Debt] Liquidation. During the 'URABI Revolution Colvin served as British representative on the Dual Financial Control and counselor to Khedive TAWFIQ. When the British occupied Egypt, he became the first financial adviser to the khedive. He returned to India in 1883. After retiring from the civil service, he served on the boards of the Egyptian Delta Light Railways and the Khedivial Steamship Company, among others.

Bibliographic Sources
Colvin, *Making of Modern Egypt.*
Cromer, *Modern Egypt,* I, 206–208.
DNB (1901–1911), 395–396.
Times (London) (26 Mar. 1908): 4b.
Who Was Who (1897–1915), 151.
Wills and Barrett, *Anglo-African Who's Who,* I, 31–32.

Cromer, Sir Evelyn Baring, Earl of

(26 February 1841–29 January 1917)
Britain's agent and consul general in Cairo from 1883 to 1907. Born in Norfolk, he came from the well-known English banking family of Baring, of German origin. Trained as an army officer at Woolwich Academy, Evelyn was commissioned in the Royal Artillery in 1858. Named secretary to the viceroy of India in 1872, he first came to Egypt in 1877 as Britain's public debt commissioner, returned in 1879 to India, and was named British agent in Cairo in 1883, with instructions to prepare for the evacuation of the British forces that had defeated 'URABI in 1882. The Mahdi's revolt in the Sudan against Egyptian rule obliged the British to delay withdrawing from Egypt, and Baring (as he was then known) undertook to reform the finances of Egypt's government. In his early years in the British Agency, he had a daunting mission because state revenues did not suffice to pay for needed reforms and the Egyptian government could not float any new loans without the approval of the European powers represented on the Caisse de la Dette Publique. Baring, working closely with the British financial adviser, managed to balance the state budget and then, by well-chosen reforms in irrigation, to increase agricultural output and hence land-tax revenues. Istanbul's rejection of the Drummond-Wolff Convention prolonged the British occupation. As French naval power in the Mediterranean increased and as Britain distanced itself from the Ottoman Empire, the British navy came to need a base at Alexandria. Baring, never eager to withdraw from Egypt, be-

gan instituting the financial reforms that he believed the country needed, attaching British advisers to as many government ministries as possible and exercising discreet influence over the khedive.

This "veiled protectorate" worked well under Khedive TAWFIQ, but less well when his son, 'ABBAS II, succeeded him. Soon after Baring was elevated to the peerage with the title of Lord Cromer in 1892, the new khedive and the old consul clashed over the choice of a prime minister to replace the ailing MUSTAFA FAHMI and later over control of the Egyptian army. The British government, although still opposed in principle to a prolonged occupation of Egypt, supported Cromer against the khedive and left him free to pursue the policies by which he hoped to regenerate Egypt.

In the areas of state finance and irrigation, Cromer's reforms succeeded, but his long tenure as consul general made him increasingly impervious to criticism either from his subordinates in the British Agency or from the Egyptian bureaucracy, to which Cromer gradually added young Englishmen from Oxford and Cambridge. His annual reports on conditions in Egypt (and, after 1898, the Sudan) were published—and even translated into Arabic by *al-Muqattam*—and became in practice the official version of Egypt's recent history. As his financial successes led to Egypt's economic regeneration, European opposition to the British occupation waned and British determination to remain grew. Rising Egyptian resistance, as expressed by MUSTAFA KAMIL or by more moderate nationalists, such as AHMAD LUTFI AL-SAYYID, did not impress Cromer, who dismissed their opposition as inspired by pan-Islam. As the British distanced themselves from the Egyptian people, mutual incomprehension spread, causing such events as the 1906 Dinshaway Incident, which occasioned so much criticism of the British occupation in both Egypt and Europe that he decided to resign. Cromer believed that the only true Egyptian nationality must include all the Europeans and other minorities living in Egypt and that his veiled protectorate had benefited all classes of Egyptian society, especially the peasants. Early financial stringencies made him cut expenditures on public health and education. Neither he nor his successors ever made up for this neglect, and

Egypt eventually paid a high price for their failure to invest generously in its human resources. The British honored him with a knighthood, elevation to the peerage in June 1892, an honorary doctorate from Cambridge in 1905, a parliamentary grant of £10,000 after he resigned, and burial in Westminster Abbey.

Bibliographic Sources
Berque, *Egypt*, 146–150.
Blunt, *Gordon at Khartoum*.
Boyle, *Servant of the Empire*, vii–xxvi, 40–112.
Cromer [Baring], *Internal Administration of Egypt*.
———, *Memorandum*.
———, *The Situation in Egypt*.
DNB (1912–1921), 20–28.
EMME, I, 319–321, article by Robert L. Tignor.
Foreign Office List, 1917, 245–246.
al-Hilal 15:8 (May 1907): 451–465.
Marlowe, *Cromer in Egypt*.
Mera, *Une page de politique coloniale*.
Owen, "Influence of Lord Cromer's Indian Experience."
Reid, "Cromer and the Classics."
Sanderson, "Evelyn Earl of Cromer."
Sayyid, Afaf Lutfi, *Egypt and Cromer*, 54–55, 196–197.
Stewart, *Middle East: Temple of Janus*, 171–176.
Tignor, *Modernization*, 57–63, 368–374.
Wills and Barrett, *Anglo-African Who's Who*, 34–35.
Zetland, *Lord Cromer*.

Cyril [Kyrillos] IV, Abuna Daud Tumas Bashut

(1816–31 January 1861)
Reforming Coptic patriarch. Cyril entered St. Anthony's monastery at Bush when he was twenty-three and became its head within two years, after which he set up a new school for monks. Consecrated metropolitan of Cairo in 1853, he was chosen the next year by the Coptic bishops to become their patriarch despite his youth and reformist zeal. He set up new schools for boys and girls in Cairo, Mansura, and Bush, and purchased the first printing press for the patriarchate. He built churches and restored the Coptic cathedral in Cairo. SA'ID sent him in 1856 to negotiate with Ethiopia over its border with Egypt. The cause of his death was never explained (some say Sa'id had him poisoned). Cyril IV is considered one of the greatest Coptic patriarchs.

Bibliographic Sources
Atiya, *Eastern Christianity*, 104–107.
'Awad, Jirjos Philuthawus, *Dhikra muslih 'azim*.
Butcher, *Story of the Church*, II, 397–404.
CE, III, 677–679, article by Mounir Shoucri.
Cramer, *Das christlich-koptische Ägypten*, 93.
Evetts, "Un prélat reformateur."
Fowler, *Christian Egypt*, 131–133.
Heyworth-Dunne, J., "Education in Egypt and the Copts."
al-Hilal 1:11 (July 1893): 481–492.
Iskarus, *Nawabigh al-aqbat*, II, 83–197.
Meinardus, *Christian Egypt: Faith and Life*, 19–20.
Nakhla, *Tarikh al-umma al-qibtiyya*.
Seikaly, "Coptic Communal Reform," 248–250.
Strothmann, *Die koptische Kirche*.
Watani, 1 May 1993.

Atiya, *Eastern Christianity*, 107–112.
Butcher, *Story of the Church*, II, 404–411.
CE, III, 679, article by Mounir Shoucri.
Fahmi, Zaki, *Safwat al-'asr*, 533–540.
Fowler, *Christian Egypt*, 135–143.
Fuad, Faraj Sulayman, *al-Kanz al-thamin*, 147–150.
al-Hilal 24:5 (Feb. 1916): 422–423.
Meinardus, *Christian Egypt*, 23–25.
Muti'i, *Mawsu'a*, 425–431.
QTQ, 191.
Times (London) (9 Aug. 1927): 9b.
Seikaly, "Coptic Communal Reform," 251–265.
Wakin, *Lonely Minority*, 106–107, 150.
Walili, *Mafakhir al-ajyal*, 149–150.
Zakhura, *Mirat al-'asr*, I, 241–245; II, 88.

Cyril [Kyrillos] V, Yuhanna al-Nasikh

(1831–7 August 1927)

Coptic patriarch from 1874 to 1927. Cyril was born in Beni Suef. After an abortive attempt to enter the monastery at Dayr al-Suryan, he managed to join that of St. Thomas in Wadi al-Natrun in 1845. He later directed the monastery of St. Baramus in Buhayra. Although he founded churches, hospitals, benevolent societies, and schools, notably the Clerical College in Cairo (1894), he is best remembered for quarreling with successive lay-led Coptic Community Councils, often enjoying the support of Muslims (Khedive TAWFIQ, for example), as well as conservative Copts and Muslims, because of his great spirituality. He permitted women to remove their veils forty years before Muslim women unveiled but maintained strict standards of modesty within the church. He supported 'URABI's movement, opposed what he viewed as CROMER's attempt to divide Copts from Muslims, urged Copts to subscribe funds for the Egyptian University in 1908, and cooperated with the shaykh of al-Azhar and other Muslim leaders in promoting patriotism during the 1919 Revolution. He remained firm in his support of SA'D ZAGHLUL even when other politicians sought his patriarchal blessing. Cyril V's funeral occasioned a large-scale public demonstration by both Christians and Muslims.

Bibliographic Sources
Antaki, *al-Nujum*, 60–62.

Cyril [Kyrillos] VI, 'Adhir Yusuf 'Ata

(8 August 1902–9 March 1971)

Influential Coptic patriarch from 1959 to 1971. He was born in Damanhur and educated at St. Thomas's monastery in Wadi al-Natrun, the Helwan ecclesiastical school, and in Alexandria. From 1924 to 1927 he worked for Thomas Cook Travel Agency in Alexandria. After his ordination as Mina al-Mutawahhid in 1931, Cyril spent four years at Deir Baramus, then worked in Old Cairo from 1936 to 1942 and for the next two years at Babiliyun, where he built a new church. Upon his election as patriarch in 1959, he developed close ties with NASIR, with Ethiopian Emperor Haile Selassie, and with leaders of Eastern Orthodox churches. During his patriarchate, the Egyptian government contributed £E 100,000 toward building the new cathedral. He also called for the return of St. Mark's remains from Venice to Egypt. He chaired the 1965 Oriental Orthodox Conference in Addis Ababa, hosted the 1968 celebration of the nineteen-hundredth anniversary of the Martyrdom of St. Mark, and won membership in the World Council of Churches for the Coptic church. He also made Maryut a major center of Coptic scholarship. He promoted Coptic education at both the elementary and the advanced levels, set up an ecclesiastical press, opened thirty-three churches in Cairo and ten in Alexandria, and extended the church's mission to serve the needs of the growing Coptic diaspora in Kuwait, North America, and Australia. A loyal Egyptian, he issued various anti-Zionist proclamations before and during the June War, tried to promote Christian-Muslim unity, and verified the apparition of the Virgin Mary in Zaytun on 4 May 1968.

Bibliographic Sources
al-Ahram Archives, file 2427.

CE, III, 679–681, article by Mounir Shoucri.
EMME, I, 520–521, article by Donald Spanel.
Meinardus, *Christian Egypt,* 43–45.
QTQ, 342–343.
Wakin, *Lonely Minority,* 103–118.
Watani, 2 Jan. 1994.

D

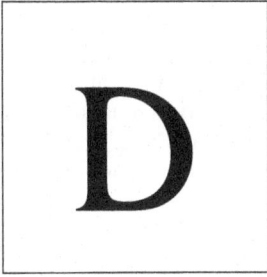

Darwish, Sayyid
(17 March 1892–15 September 1923)
Prominent composer and performing singer. Born in Kum al-Dikka, Alexandria, and educated at Shams al-Madaris, he memorized the Quran and mastered its cantillation (*tartil*), then went on to reciting postclassical Arabic poetry. Because his father had abandoned his family, Sayyid in his youth reportedly had to recite at people's homes, cafes, and bars for food. During the 1907 economic crisis he worked as a hod carrier for a contractor, enabling him to learn some of the builders' work songs. He traveled with a theatrical troupe to Syria from 1909 to 1913, learning the art of poetry recitation from experts. Returning to Egypt, he took to playing the *'ud*, developing a new style of performance. He organized his own theatrical troupe and later worked for JURJ ABYAD. SALAMA HIJAZI gave him his debut on the Cairo stage in 1916. Sayyid Darwish organized another troupe in 1921. He freed Arabic music from its dependence on Turkish and Western modes. He produced hundreds of Arabic songs for public performance, writing for such actors as NAJIB AL-RIHANI and MUNIRA AL-MAHDIYYA. Because of his poor memory, he was one of the first Arab musicians to take up sound recording. He wrote music for such plays as *Shahrazad, al-'Ashara al-tayyiba,* and *Cleopatra*. Sometimes he wrote music for five plays within one month. Profoundly moved by the nationalist speeches of MUSTAFA KAMIL, MUHAMMAD FARID, and SA'D ZAGHLUL, he wrote the patriotic song "Biladi, biladi" [My Country, O My Country], now Egypt's national anthem. Darwish lived among poor people, and his compositions reflected their musical traditions. Ad-dicted to cocaine, he died of a heart attack in Alexandria, impoverished and largely forgotten.

Bibliographic Sources
al-Ahram, 15 Sept. 1938.
'Ashur, Nu'man, *Suwar min al-butula*, 81–88.
Bishri, 'Abd al-'Aziz, *al-Mukhtar,* II, 95–105.
Butrus, *A'lam al-musiqa*, 195–206.
Darwish, Hasan, *Min ajl abi Sayyid Darwish.*
Dawwara, Muhammad Mahmud, *Sawt al-thawra aw qissat Sayyid Darwish.*
———, *Sayyid Darwish al-fannan wa al-insan.*
Dickie, "Sayyid Darwish."
Kholy, "Musical Life in Egypt."
EMME, II, 538, article by Virginia Danielson.
Farhat, Muhiyy al-Din, in *al-Misri*, 14 Oct. 1937.
Hammad, *Sayyid Darwish.*
Hifni, Mahmud Ahmad, *Sayyid Darwish.*
Husami, "Sayyid Darwish."
Ibrahim, Muhammad, *al-Musiqar Sayyid Darwish.*
'Izz al-Din, *Shakhsiyyat wa marahil 'ummaliyya*, 38–54.
Jam'iyyat Asdiqa Musiqa al-Sayyid Darwish, *Fannan al-sha'b: Sayyid Darwish.*
Jundi, *A'lam al-adab*, II, 578–581.
Kamil, Mahmud, *Tazawwuq al-musiqa al-arabiyya,* 105–107.
Ramadi, *Adab wa tarab*, 193–205.
Sahhab, *al-Sab'a al-kibar.*
Tantawi, *Sayyid Darwish.*
Yusuf, Niqula, *A'lam min al-Iskandariyya*, 433–439.
Zaki, 'Abd al-Hamid Tawfiq, *A'lam al-musiqa*, 153–160.
Zirikli, *al-A'lam*, III, 146–147.

Drovetti, Bernardino
(7 January 1776–5 March 1852)
Italian politician, antiquities collector, and France's consul general in Egypt during the First Empire and from 1820 to 1829. He was born in a village near Leghorn and is well known for finding the Turin Canon of Kings, which was badly damaged during shipment to Italy. He sold his first collection to the king of Sardinia, his second to King Charles X of France, and his third to the Berlin Museum. He also exercised great influence over MUHAMMAD 'ALI and is reported to have aided his rise to power and suggested many of his reforms.

Bibliographic Sources
Carré, Jean-Marie, *Voyageurs,* I, 176 et passim.
Dawson, *Egyptology*, 90.
DBF, XI, 836–837, entry by Roman d'Amat.

Drovetti, *Il corpo epistolare*.
Douin, *Mohamed Aly, pacha du Caire*, v–vii et passim.
Marro, *La personalita di Bernardino Drovetti*.
Wiet, *Mohammed Ali et les beaux-arts*.

Dunlop, Douglas

(1861–9 October 1937)
British undersecretary and adviser to the Ministry of Public Instruction. A Scot who came to Egypt as a missionary, Dunlop was appointed by CROMER to direct the government school system. Dunlop was notorious among Egyptians for his parsimonious and rigid education policies. He had contempt for the intellectual abilities of the people and frequently antagonized Egyptian nationalists, but he was not dismissed until after 1920.

Bibliographic Sources
'Aqqad, 'Abbas Mahmud, *Sa'd Zaghlul*, 106–107.
Bowman, *Middle-East Window*, 41–44.
Kinsey, "Egyptian Education Under Cromer," 244–262 et passim.
Mid-Devon Advertiser, 9 Oct. 1937.
Salama, Jirjis, *Athar al-ihtilal al-baritani fi al-ta'lim*.
Tignor, *Modernization*, 328–329.
Weinthal, *Anglo-African Who's Who*.
Zakhura, *Mirat al-'asr*, II, 245.

Dus, Layla Tawfiq

(1916–)
Pioneer social worker and feminist, usually known as Lily Doss. Born in Asyut, Dus was educated in the American mission school there and at French schools in Cairo. After passing her general secondary examination, she volunteered for work at the Red Crescent Society in 1933. Three years later she hosted the meeting of upper-class young women who formed *al-Jam'iyya al-nisaiyya li-tahsin al-sihha* (Women's Society for the Improvement of Health) to combat the scourges of tuberculosis and diabetes among the poor. The organization started with a working capital of seventy piasters and raised money for its projects, initially modest but eventually nationwide in scope, from private donations. She served as a board member for forty years and attended international conferences in China, Kenya, and the United States. Resuming her education at age sixty-four, she got her General Certificate of Education diploma in 1980 and earned an M.A. in English and comparative literature from the American University in Cairo in 1991.

Bibliographic Sources
AUC Today (fall 1998): 7.
Badran, *Feminists*, 114–116.
Najib, *A'lam Misr*, 389.
QTQ, 202–203.

F

Fahmi, 'Abd al-'Aziz

(23 December 1870–3 March 1951)
Liberal politician, jurist, and intellectual. Born in the Minufiyya village of Kafr al-Musayliha, Fahmi came from a long line of *'umda*s (village headmen). He began his education at the village *kuttab*, went on to Tanta's Ahmadi Mosque, and then to al-Azhar. Changing to the government system, he attended Tanta elementary and secondary schools, graduated in 1885 from the Khedivial Secondary School in Cairo, and earned his *license* from the School of Administration in 1890. He worked for several years in the *Niyaba* in Daqahliyya, Tanta, Qina, Naj' Hamadi, and Beni Suef. In 1897–1903 he was a deputy counselor in the *awqaf* administration. He resigned in 1903 to open his own law office. He served on the board of the Egyptian University and the Supreme Hisbi Council. He was elected in 1913 to the Legislative Assembly and headed the Egyptian Bar Association three times, beginning in 1914. A friend of Ahmad Lutfi al-Sayyid, Fahmi helped found the Wafd in November 1918. The Wafd asked him to debate the Milner proposals in 1920. Later, in Paris, he broke with Sa'd Zaghlul. He served on the committee that drafted the 1923 Constitution and is said to have proposed adopting the Belgian model. A founder of the Constitutional Liberal Party, he became its president in 1924. He served as justice minister (1925), president of the High Court of Appeals (1928), and head of the Court of Cassation (1931). Even though he advocated writing Arabic in the Roman alphabet, he became a member of the Arabic Language Academy in 1940. Fahmi's statue was erected at the preparatory school of his native village in 1960.

Bibliographic Sources
Abaza, Tharwat, article in *al-Ahram*, 25 May 1978.
al-Ahram, 3 Mar. 1951.
al-Ahram Archives, file 1985.
'Allam, *Majma'iyyun*, 168–170.
Fahmi, 'Abd al-'Aziz, *Hadhihi hayati*.
Hasan, Muhammad 'Abd al-Ghani, in *al-Kitab* 10:4 (Apr. 1951): 383–384.
Hijazi, Anwar, *'Amaliqa*, 198–205.
Mahmud, Hafiz, *Asrar al-madi*.
———, in *al-Jumhuriyya*, 28 Dec. 1989.
Marshall, *Egyptian Enigma*, 66–71.
Mazini, Ahmad Fathi, *Qudat*, I, 21–22.
al-Musawwar, no. 853 (14 Feb. 1941): 12.
Muti'i, *Haula al-rijal min Misr*, III, 162–173.
———, *Mawsu'a*, 275–281.
New York Times (5 Mar. 1951): 21.
Qadi, Shukri, *Miat shakhsiyya*, 169–171.
Reid, "National Bar Association," 614–615.
Taymur, Mahmud, *al-Shakhsiyyat al-'ishrun*, 23–35.
Ziadeh, *Lawyers*, 93–96.
Zirikli, *al-A'lam*, IV, 25.

Fahmi, 'Abd al-Rahman

(3 March 1870–July 1946)
Pioneer labor union leader. Reared by his elder brother, Muhammad Mahir (the father of 'Ali and Ahmad Mahir), 'Abd al-Rahman attended the Military Academy, graduating in 1888. After serving briefly under Kitchener, he entered the entourage of Khedive 'Abbas II and in 1896 he was aide-de-camp to Mustafa Fahmi and thus became acquainted with his son-in-law, Sa'd Zaghlul. Fahmi later held a number of police and administrative posts, eventually becoming governor of Beni Suef and then of Giza (where he quarreled with the British adviser to the Interior Ministry). From 1911 to 1913 he was deputy director of *awqaf*. As general secretary of the Wafd's Central Committee and head of its secret branch during the 1919 Revolution, he brought National Party members into the organization, organized the highly effective boycott of the Milner Mission, and sought to politicize Egyptian workers by encouraging them to form unions. Arrested by the British in 1920 and accused of conspiracy, he was tried in a military court, convicted, and sentenced to death. The sentence was commuted to fifteen years' imprisonment, and he was released in 1924. Soon after his release, four labor unions asked him to become their leader. He encouraged them to form the General Federation of Labor Unions in the

Nile Valley. Elected its president, he directed the workers' activities paternalistically, trying to counter the Communists. He once reminded the workers that he would defend capitalists' rights as much as he would theirs. He was elected as a Wafdist to the Chamber of Deputies in 1924, representing Sayyida Zaynab, and as a Sa'dist in 1938, representing Kirdasa. He briefly edited *Ruz al-Yusuf* in 1936. Portions of his memoirs were published in *al-Dunya al-musawwara* and *Kull shay wa al-dunya*; the full text is in Dar al-Kutub.

Bibliographic Sources
Anis, *Dirasat*, I, 7–33 et passim.
Beinin and Lockman, *Workers on the Nile,* 104, 157–161, 168–169.
Deeb, *Party Politics.*
Jindi, Anwar, *Min a'lam al-hurriyya,* 109–118.
Kull shay wa al-dunya, 17 Mar.–14 Apr. 1935, memoirs.
McIntyre, *Boycott of the Milner Mission,* 42–45.
Mujahid, *al-A'lam al-sharqiyya,* I, 152.
Radwan, Fathi, *Mashhurun,* 55–76.
Wright, *Twentieth Century Impressions of Egypt,* 385.

Fahmi, Isma'il

(20 October 1922–22 November 1997)
Foreign minister and deputy premier under SA-DAT. The son of a public prosecutor in Cairo, he earned his *license* in political science from Cairo University in 1945. He joined the Egyptian foreign service in 1946 and served in Egypt's delegation to the United Nations from 1949 to 1957 and then for three years on the International Atomic Energy Agency. In 1959 he returned to Cairo as a counselor in the Foreign Office, then as head of its UN desk. He was elected in 1965 to the General Assembly's First Committee, becoming its elected chair in 1967, and he headed Egypt's delegation to the annual meeting of the International Atomic Energy Commission. He was Egypt's minister to Austria in 1968 and to France in 1969–1970, deputy foreign minister from 1971 to November 1973, and foreign minister for the next four years, resigning in protest against Sadat's decision to go to Jerusalem. He gave many press interviews in later years, explaining his opposition to NASIR's pro-Soviet leanings, Sadat's lurch to the right, and the Camp David Accords, and ran unsuccessfully as a Wafdist in the 1984 parliamentary elections. He died in Cairo.

Bibliographic Sources
al-Ahram Archives, file 3131.
Fahmi, Isma'il, *Negotiating for Peace.*
Fawzi, Mahmud, in *Uktubir,* no. 1101 (30 Nov. 1997).
Frankel, "Interview with Isma'il Fahmy."
New York Times (24 Nov. 1997): B7.
al-Siyasa, 23 Mar. 1994.
U.S. News and World Report 78:16 (21 Apr. 1975): 23–24, interview.
Washington Post (23 Nov. 1997): B8.
al-Watan al-'Arabi, no. 314 (18 June 1993): 3–13.
WWAW, 1997–1998, 225.

Fahmi, Mahmud

(1839–17 June 1894)
Army officer and engineer. Originally from Shantur (Beni Suef), he attended a state provincial school and the Polytechnic in Bulaq. He worked as an engineering instructor in the military schools and as a military engineer, building seventeen fortresses along the Mediterranean coast. He served in the Ottoman army during the war against Serbia and Montenegro (1875–1876), attaining the rank of colonel. He supported the 'URABI Revolution, serving as public works minister in the BARUDI cabinet. When the British attacked, he was chief of staff of the Egyptian army. Taken prisoner after a courageous defense, he was put on trial with the 'Urabist leaders and sentenced to death, but his sentence was commuted to exile to Ceylon, where he died. Mahmud Fahmi wrote a general history of the world and a military textbook. Egyptians and Europeans admired his engineering talents and moral and patriotic principles.

Bibliographic Sources
Broadley, *How We Defended Arabi,* 318–320.
Brockelmann, *GAL,* S II, 734–735.
Chaillé-Long, *Three Prophets,* 98.
Dep, *Egyptian Exiles in Ceylon,* 25–26.
Fahmi, Mahmud, *al-Bahr al-zakhir,* 211–212.
———, *Mudhakkirat Mahmud Basha Fahmi.*
Kahhala, *Mu'jam,* XII, 189–190.
Mujahid, *al-A'lam al-sharqiyya,* I, 121–122.
Rafi'i, *'Asr Isma'il,* I, 282–283.
———, *al-Thawra al-'Urabiyya,* 567–568.
Schölch, *Egypt for the Egyptians!* 346.
Shamis, *'Uzama,* 123–130.
Shayyal, *al-Tarikh wa al-muarrikhun,* 173–174.
Zaki, 'Abd al-Rahman, *A'lam al-jaysh,* 183–185.
Zirikli, *al-A'lam,* VII, 180.

Fahmi, Dr. Mansur

(1886–27 March 1959)
Writer, philosopher, and scholar on women's issues. Mansur was the son of 'Ali Fahmi 'Abd al-Mut'al; the family originated from Tilimsan (Tlemcen) in Morocco and claimed descent from Muhammad via al-Husayn. Mansur was born in Shanqas (near Talkha, Daqahliyya) and was educated in Mansura and at a French secondary school in Cairo, graduating in 1906. He briefly studied law, then was sent on an educational mission to study philosophy in Paris, receiving his doctorate in 1913 for a dissertation on the role of women in Islam. He taught at the University of Cairo, eventually becoming dean of the Faculty of Arts, then director of Dar al-Kutub, and then head of the University of Alexandria in 1946. He was a founding member and the secretary of the Arabic Language Academy from 1934 until his death, belonging also to the language academies of Damascus, Baghdad, and Tehran. He was also active in *al-Rabita al-Sharqiyya* (The Eastern League). He wrote *Khatirat nafs* [Thoughts of a Soul] and *Muhadarat 'an Mayy Ziyada* [Lectures on Mayy Ziyada].

Bibliographic Sources
Adams, *Islam and Modernism*, 251–252.
'Allam, *Majma'iyyin*, 362–365.
Brockelmann, *GAL*, S III, 211–212.
Daghir, *Masadir*, III, ii, 1295–1298.
Fahmi, Mansur, "Ahamm hadith aththara fi majra hayati."
———, "Limadha darastu al-falsafa."
Jindi, Anwar, *A'lam wa ashab aqlam*, 443–449.
Kahhala, *Mu'jam*, 16–17.
Khemiri and Kampffmeyer, *Leaders*, 16.
Liwa al-Islam 13 (9 Apr. 1959): 107.
Madkur, Ibrahim, and Muhammad Diyab, "al-Marhum al-Duktur Mansur Fahmi."
Ramadi, Muhammad Jamal al-Din, in *Qafilat al-zayt*, Jan. 1964.
Shihabi, Mustafa, in *MMIA* 34 (1954): 531–534.
Taymur, Mahmud, *al-Shakhsiyyat al-'ishrun*, 50–57.
Zirikli, *al-A'lam*, VII, 302.

Fahmi, Mustafa

(1840–13 September 1914)
Politician, cabinet minister, and twice premier. He was born in Crete to a Turkish family that had earlier settled in Algeria. His father, Husayn Efendi, a colonel, died in the Crimean War, and Mustafa Fahmi was adopted by an uncle, Muhammad Zaki, director of the Public Works Department. Fahmi was educated at the Military Academy and, upon being commissioned, rose through the Egyptian army to the rank of lieutenant general. He then was appointed governor of Minufiyya, then of Cairo, and, finally, of Port Said. He later became director of the khedivial estates and then master of ceremonies. Prefect of the Cairo police in 1876, he was widely suspected of murdering the *Mufattish*, ISMA'IL SIDDIQ. He served as minister of public works (1879), foreign affairs (1879–1882), justice (1882), finance (1884–1887), interior three times (1887–1888, 1891–1893, and 1895–1908), and war and marine twice (1887–1891 and 1894–1895). He was prime minister from 1891 to 1893 and again from 1895 to 1908. His illness early in 1893 caused a crisis between Lord CROMER and Khedive 'ABBAS, who tried to replace his cabinet with one headed by HUSAYN FAKHRI without consulting the British consul. Fahmi was allowed to leave the government for a while to recover his health, but returned under NUBAR and soon afterward took charge of what would be Egypt's longest-lasting cabinet, one in which the power of the British advisers far outweighed that of the ministers. He was pro-British for most of his active career, deferring repeatedly to Lord Cromer, but after he left office, he fell under the influence of SA'D ZAGHLUL, who was married to one of Fahmi's daughters. It was rumored that Fahmi might head a cabinet in 1914 after MUHAMMAD SA'ID's resignation, but he was in poor health and died shortly afterward in Cairo. Most Egyptians regard him as having been too complaisant toward the British.

Bibliographic Sources
Antaki, *al-Nujum*, 23–24.
Cromer, *Modern Egypt*, II, 346.
Egyptian Gazette (14 Sept. 1914): 3a.
Fuad, Faraj Sulayman, *al-Kanz al-thamin*, I, 71.
al-Hilal 23:1 (Oct. 1914): 77–78.
Mujahid, *al-A'lam al-sharqiyya*, I, 125–126.
Ninet, *Arabi Pacha*, 8.
Rafi'i, *al-Thawra al-'urabiyya*, 149.
Sayyid, Afaf Lutfi, *Egypt and Cromer*, 77–78.
Schölch, *Egypt for the Egyptians!* 332.
Walili, *Mafakhir al-ajyal*, 105–106.
Zakhura, *Mirat al-'asr*, I, 80–82.

Fahmi, Mustafa
(1886–1972)

Architect and cabinet minister. The son of Mahmud Fahmi, the first modern Egyptian architect, Mustafa graduated from the École des Ponts et Chaussées in Paris and returned to become the first Egyptian employee in the Department of Architecture and Design in the Public Buildings Service, rising through its ranks until he became director in 1921–1929, later serving as the Palace architect. He helped design several of the modern palaces and also lectured in the Engineering Faculty. He had a solid grounding in the principles of Islamic architecture, which he admired, and many of his buildings reflect this neo-Islamic tendency, among them the Engineers' Society, the Agricultural Society, the HUDA SHA'RAWI Women's Society, and the Doctors' Syndicate. He also designed SA'D ZAGHLUL's mausoleum, which combines pharaonic and Islamic themes. He served as minister of works in 1949–1950. He also taught in the Engineering Faculty at Cairo University and founded its Architecture Department. Sent temporarily to Saudi Arabia, he designed King Faysal's palace in Riyad and the reconfiguration of the sacred enclosure to the Ka'ba in Mecca.

Bibliographic Sources

'Abd al-Jawad, Tawfiq, *'Amaliqat al-'imara fi al-qarn al-'ishrin*, 148.
Najib, *A'lam Misr*, 473.
Sakr, *Early Twentieth Century Islamic Architecture*, 13–14.

Fakhri, Husayn
(25 September 1843–23 December 1910)

Politician, cabinet minister, and controversial premier appointed by Khedive 'ABBAS II against CROMER's wishes in January 1893. Born in Cairo to a family of Circassian background, Fakhri was educated in the princely schools. In 1863 he was appointed as a *mu'awin* (assistant) in the governorate and then transferred to foreign affairs. Sent to Paris by the Egyptian government for the 1867 exposition, he stayed there to study administrative law. After returning to Egypt in 1874, he worked in the Justice Ministry and in the *Niyaba* of the Mixed Courts. Fakhri became justice minister, serving in 1879–1881 under MUSTAFA RIYAD, in 1882–1884 under MUHAMMAD SHARIF, and in 1888–1891 under Riyad

again; interior minister under MUSTAFA FAHMI; and after serving for three days as the khedive's prime minister, he would serve as minister of works and education under NUBAR and Fahmi. Although he could do little as a minister under British control, he did set up the first women's teachers college at the Saniyya Girls School in 1900. Khedive 'Abbas considered naming him premier again in 1908 but decided to appoint BUTRUS GHALI instead. An amateur of science, he belonged to the Institut d'Égypte, the Geographical Society, and the Committee for the Preservation of Arab Monuments. His son, Mahmud, married Princess Fawqiyya, one of King FARUQ's sisters. Because of the public controversy over his khedivial appointment against Cromer's wishes, Fakhri earned an undeserved reputation as a nationalist.

Bibliographic Sources

Antaki, *al-Nujum*, 25–27.
Asaf, *Dalil*, I, 222–227.
Bell, *Khedives and Pashas*, 196–199.
Fahmi, Zaki, *Safwat al-'asr*, 226–231.
Fakhri, "Mudhakkirat Husayn Basha Fakhri," I, 107–115.
al-Muayyad (24 Dec. 1910): 6.
Mujahid, *al-A'lam al-sharqiyya*, I, 76–77.
Tawfiq and Sabri, *Wuzara al-ta'lim*, 49–50.
Walili, *Mafakhir al-ajyal*, 108–110.
Zakhura, *Mirat al-'asr*, I, 83–85; II, 126–127.
Zaki, Ahmad, in *al-Muqtataf* 38 (1911): 105.

al-Falaki, Isma'il Mustafa
(1825–27 July 1901)

Astronomer and mathematician. Of Turkish origin, he was born and reared in Cairo. He completed his education in Paris. Recognizing his mathematical ability, Khedive ISMA'IL charged him with setting up the 'Abbasiyya observatory and reorganizing the School of Engineering. He wrote textbooks and scientific treatises in astronomy and also an almanac, which he published annually in French and Arabic.

Bibliographic Sources

Brockelmann, *GAL*, S II, 642.
Fikri, 'Ali, *Subul al-najah*, III, 122–124.
Hasan, Muhammad 'Abd al-Ghani, and 'Abd al-'Aziz Disuqi, *Rawdat al-madaris*, 403–404.
Hijazi, Anwar, *'Amaliqa*, 82–85.
Kahhala, *Mu'jam*, II, 296.
Mas'ud, Muhammad, in *Taqwim "al-Muayyad"* 5 (1902): 101.

Mujahid, *al-A'lam al-sharqiyya*, II, 862–863.
al-Muqtataf 26:8 (Aug. 1901): 766–767.
Rafi'i, *'Asr Isma'il*, I, 264–269.
Tusun, *al-Ba'that al-'ilmiyya*, 455–457.
Zaki, Ahmad, *Isma'il Pasha al-Falaki*.
Zaydan, Jurji, *Mashahir al-sharq*, 2nd ed., II, 169–172.
———, *Tarikh adab al-lugha*, IV, 192–193.
Zirikli, *al-A'lam*, I, 327.

al-Falaki, Mahmud Ahmad Hamdi

(1815–19 July 1885)
Engineer, mathematician, and scientist. Mahmud was born in the village of al-Hissa (Gharbiyya province); his father died early, and he was reared by a brother and sent to MUHAMMAD 'ALI's Polytechnic School in the Citadel. He later taught mathematics and astronomy at that school. Chosen to be a part of 'ABBAS I's student mission to Europe in 1851, he spent nine years in Paris. Upon his return to Cairo, SA'ID charged him with drawing maps, among them the first complete topographical map of Egypt. He held several important government posts, including public works minister, and became the president of the Khedivial Geographic Society. He represented Egypt at the International Congress of Geographers in Venice in 1881 and in Paris in 1885. As minister of public instruction (1884–1885) he instituted several important educational reforms, one of which was to require that the foreign schools receiving subsidies from the Egyptian government undergo regular inspections. In his published writings, he tried to prove that the Giza Pyramids were built for astronomical purposes; he also established the exact birth and death dates for the prophet Muhammad. He directed the Education Ministry and the Geographical Society until his death in Cairo.

Bibliographic Sources
'Abd al-Rahman, Ibrahim Hilmi, "Mahmud al-Falaki."
'Aqqad, 'Abbas Mahmud, "Mahmud Basha al-Falaki."
Brockelmann, *GAL*, S II, 642–3; III, 747.
Cheikho, *al-Adab al-'arabiyya*, II, 103.
Dimirdash, *Mahmud Hamdi al-Falaki*.
EI2, II, 764, article by Jacques Jomier.
Fikri, 'Ali, *Subul al-najah*, III, 115–117.
Hijazi, Anwar, *'Amaliqa*, 82–85.
al-Hilal 5:8 (15 Dec. 1896): 282–285.
Kahhala, *Mu'jam*, XII, 145–146.
Maspéro, "Éloge de Mahmoud Pacha al-Falaki."

Mujahid, *al-A'lam al-sharqiyya*, I, 118–119.
al-Muqtataf 10:8 (Nov. 1886): 510.
Mustafa, Ismail, and Mukhtar, *Notice nécrologique*.
Muti'i, *Haula al-rijal min Misr*, II, 237–247.
———, *Mawsu'a*, 557–563.
Qadi, Shukri, *Miat shakhsiyya*, 277–279.
Rafi'i, *'Asr Isma'il*, I, 264–269.
Shayyal, *al-Tarikh wa al-muarrikhun*, 113–120.
Shamis, *'Uzama*, 85–91.
Tawfiq, 'Awad, and Hasan Sabri, *Wuzara al-ta'lim*, 46–47.
Tusun, *al-Ba'that al-'ilmiyya*, 450–455.
Walili, *Mafakhir al-ajyal*, 41–42.
Zakhura, *Mirat al-'asr*, II, 436–437.
Zaydan, Jurji, *Mashahir al-sharq*, II, 1st ed., 132–135; 2nd ed., 169–172.
———, *Tarikh adab al-lugha*, IV, 190–191.
Zirikli, *al-A'lam*, VII, 164.

Farid, Muhammad

(20 January 1868–15 November 1919)
Nationalist leader, writer, and lawyer. Farid came from a landowning family of Turkish origin; his father was the director of *al-Daira al-Saniyya* (state domains administration). Born in Cairo and educated in the Khalil Agha School, l'École des Frères, and at the School of Administration, Muhammad Farid worked as a lawyer for the government and the *Niyaba*. Following his dismissal in 1896 because of his support for Shaykh 'ALI YUSUF, who was accused of publishing secret telegrams taken from the Defense Ministry, Farid opened his own law office, one of the first Egyptians to do so. Close to MUSTAFA KAMIL, Farid became one of his main political and financial backers and, after Mustafa's premature death in 1908, was elected second president of the National Party. Farid led the party in Egypt until March 1912 and then in exile until his death. He adhered to the principle that the British had to withdraw their forces from Egypt and that only the khedive could grant constitutional government to his subjects. Farid called for the spread of education and economic and social reforms. At times he sought the help of Egypt's suzerain, the Ottoman Empire, especially while in exile during World War I, but he often suspected the Turks of not backing Egyptian national aims. He sometimes espoused pan-Islam, thus alienating the Copts. Although the National Party became divided during his presidency, Egyptians respect Farid for his patriotic

courage and self-sacrifice. He wrote histories of the MUHAMMAD 'ALI dynasty, the Romans, and the Ottoman Empire. His memoirs have been published as *Mudhakkirat Muhammad Farid: al-qism al-awwal, tarikh Misr min ibtida sanat 1891* [Muhammad Farid's Memoirs, Part I: Egypt's History Beginning in 1891] (1975) and *Awraq Muhammad Farid: Mudhakkirati ba'd al-hijra (1904–1919)* [Muhammad Farid's Papers: My Memoirs After My Emigration, 1904–1919] (1978). He died in Berlin and is now buried beside Mustafa Kamil and 'ABD AL-RAHMAN RAFI'I in Cairo. Many streets and schools bear his name, and his statue stands in Cairo's Ezbekiyya Gardens.

Bibliographic Sources
Abu al-Majd, *Muhammad Farid.*
African Times and Orient Review, N.S. 1:18 (21 July 1914): 411.
al-Ahram, 25 Aug.–Sept. 1972, memoirs of Aziza de Rochebrune.
'Ashur, Nu'man, *Butulat misriyya,* 163–177.
Bayyumi, Zakariyya Sulayman, *al-Hizb al-Watani.*
Campagne de Mohamed Bey Farid.
Crabbs, *Writing of History,* 167–184.
EAL, I, 221.
EI2, VII, 439, article by C.E. Bosworth.
Farid, Muhammad, *Memoirs and Diaries.*
Fikri, 'Ali, *Subul al-najah,* III, 264–271.
Gharaba, *Shakhsiyyat,* 41–46.
Goldschmidt, *al-Hizb al-watani al-misri.*
———, "Egyptian Nationalist Party," 308–333.
Ibrahim, Shihata 'Isa, *'Uzama al-wataniyya,* 209–245.
Jindi, Anwar, *A'lam wa ashab aqlam,* 369–380.
Mujahid, *al-A'lam al-sharqiyya,* I, 164–165.
Murqus, *Sihafat al-Hizb al-Watani.*
Muti'i, *Haula al-rijal min Misr,* III, 279–292.
———, *Mawsu'a,* 498–503.
Qadi, Shukri, *Khamsun shakhsiyya,* 39–43.
Radwan, Fathi, *Mashhurun,* 11–24.
Rafi'i, 'Abd al-Rahman, "Durus li al-shabab fi hayat Muhammad Farid."
———, *Muhammad Farid.*
Rathmann, "Ägypten in Exil (1914–1918)."
Rida, Muhyi al-Din, *Abtal al-wataniyya,* chapter by Amin al-Rafi'i.
Sa'id, Rif'at, *Muhammad Farid.*
Saghir, *al-Hizb al-Watani wa al-nidal al-sirri.*
Taymur, Mahmud, *Malamih wa ghudun,* 149–155.
Trefzger, *Die nationale Bewegung Ägyptens.*
'Umar, Mahmud Fathi, *Abtal al-hurriyya,* 57–62.
Walili, *Mafakhir al-ajyal,* 86–88.
Zirikli, *al-A'lam,* VI, 327–328.

Faruq

(11 February 1920–18 March 1965)

Egypt's last king, reigning from 1936 (under a regency until his eighteenth birthday) until he abdicated in 1952. Born in Cairo, Faruq was educated by tutors and briefly attended the Royal Military Academy in Woolwich, England. Initially charismatic and popular, he was the first member of his family who could make a formal speech in Arabic. He occasionally led Friday congregational worship at mosques, traditionally a caliph's prerogative. Some Egyptians, notably MUSTAFA AL-MARAGHI, hoped to revive the caliphate, which had been abolished by Mustafa Kemal (Atatürk) in 1924, so that Faruq could be given the position. His marriage to Safinaz Zulfiqar, whom he renamed Farida, was popular. He competed with the Wafd, which controlled the cabinet until December 1937, when he dismissed it for sponsoring a popular demonstration near 'Abdin Palace and appointed a ministry made up of politicians from other parties. A rigged election, boycotted by the Wafd, gave these parties control of Parliament in 1938.

When the British declared war on Germany in 1939, they asked Egypt to follow their example and sent additional troops to defend the Suez Canal. King Faruq and his ministers opposed fighting against Germany, which many Egyptians viewed as a potential liberator of their country from Britain. While the Allies seemed to be losing the war in 1940–1942, Britain's ambassador to Egypt, Sir MILES LAMPSON, wanted to depose Faruq and to install a cabinet headed by MUSTAFA AL-NAHHAS that would uphold the 1936 Anglo-Egyptian Treaty. Faruq hoped to unite Egypt's leading politicians in opposition to British interference, with 'ALI MAHIR as his prime minister. Needing to secure British control over Egypt, Lampson told Faruq he was obliged either to appoint Nahhas to head a Wafdist cabinet or to abdicate. Faruq gave in and then withdrew from politics, devoting himself to gambling and sexual adventures. He had a car accident in 1943. Many Egyptians think that during his prolonged convalescence in a British army hospital, medical maltreatment affected his glands, causing his eccentric behavior, although his confrontation with Lampson is the more likely cause.

After Faruq dismissed the Wafdist cabinet in October 1944, he reentered the political fray with a succession of Palace-dominated governments. Discontent spread after World War II, as popular pressure mounted to renounce the 1936 Anglo-Egyptian Treaty, force the British troops to evacuate Egypt, and annex the Anglo-Egyptian Sudan. Although sympathetic to these aims, Faruq could only distract the public with an enhanced enthusiasm for Arab unity. After the United Nations General Assembly accepted the 1947 Partition Plan for Palestine, all the Arab governments vied to show support for the Palestinian Arabs and defiance of the UN decision. Even though Faruq's ministers and his generals privately advised him that the Egyptian army was unready for war, he committed Egypt to fight in Palestine. Ill equipped and badly led, the Egyptians were soon thrown back. In February 1949 Egypt signed an armistice with Israel, the first Arab state to do so. At the height of the war, Faruq divorced the popular Queen Farida, and his picture was publicly hissed for the first time at a Cairo cinema.

Late in 1949 Faruq finally agreed to allow free parliamentary elections, and the Wafd returned to power. As Nahhas and his cabinet proceeded to institute some reforms, Faruq came to be seen as marginal, although the Wafd changed his title to "king of Egypt and the Sudan" upon abrogating the 1936 treaty. His second marriage, in 1951, to sixteen-year-old Narriman Sadiq, followed by a three-month honeymoon cruise, appalled Egyptians. During the burning of Cairo on 26 January 1952, Faruq was hosting a luncheon to celebrate the birth of his first son. After the fire, he dismissed the Wafdist cabinet and appointed a series of governments but could not restore political control. His attempt to rig the elections for the Officers Club presidency alienated the Egyptian army, traditionally royalist, and his appointment of his brother-in-law, Isma'il Shirrin, as war minister proved to be the last straw. On 22–23 July 1952 the Free Officers seized control and decided to depose Faruq. Denied support by the British and the U.S. ambassador, he abdicated in favor of his infant son and left Egypt. He spent the rest of his life in Europe. His death in a Rome nightclub may have been caused by NASIR's secret service. Although bright and charming, Faruq lacked education and mental discipline. Unable to discriminate among his would-be advisers, he failed to lead his people. When he returned from England to succeed his father as king, Faruq had no enemies; when he left Egypt, he had no friends.

Bibliographic Sources

'Abd al-Karim, Lotus, *al-Malika Farida*.
Abu al-Majd, *Ayyam Faruq*.
al-Ahram Archives, file 139.
Anis, *4 Fibrayir 1942*.
Bernard-Derosne, *Farouk*.
Burke's Royal Families, II, 37.
Current Biography (Oct. 1942): 258–261.
Douglas, *Years of Command*.
EI2, S, 299–302, article by P.J. Vatikiotis.
Evans, *Killearn Diaries*.
Farraj, *al-Malika Nazli*.
Grafftey-Smith, *Bright Levant*, 230–236.
McBride, *Farouk of Egypt*.
McLeave, *Last Pharaoh*.
Morsi, "Britain's Wartime Policy in Egypt."
———, "Farouk in British Policy."
———, "Indicative Cases."
New York Times (18 Mar. 1965): 1.
Ramadan, 'Abd al-'Azim, *al-Sira' bayn al-Wafd wa al-'arsh*.
Sabet, *A King Betrayed*.
Salim, Jamal, *Qiraa jadida*.
Salim, Latifa Muhammad, *Faruq*.
Sallam, *Ayyamuhu al-akhira*.
Samakuri, *Asrar hukm al-qusur*, 23–53.
Skelton, *Tears Before Bedtime*.
Smith, Charles D., "4 February 1942."
Stadiem, *Too Rich*.
Stewart, *Middle East: Temple of Janus*, 219–221, 265–266, 321–341.
Tanahi, Tahir Ahmad, *Faruq al-awwal*.
Warburg, "Lampson's Ultimatum to Faruq."
Yusuf, Hasan, *al-Qasr wa dawruhu fi al-siyasa*.
Zirikli, *al-A'lam*, V, 128–129.

Fath Allah, Shaykh Hamza

(1849–19 January 1918)

Azharite scholar, editor of *al-I'tidal* and *al-Burhan*, and writer on linguistic and religious topics. Born in Alexandria, he went to Cairo and was educated at al-Azhar. He then moved to Tunis, where he created the official newspaper, *al-Raid*, and spent eight years there. Returning to Alexandria, he edited *al-Burhan*, followed by *al-I'tidal*. He then became an inspector of Arabic language instruction in the Education Ministry, working there for the last thirty years of his life, but he continued to write. Fath Allah maintained Arabic classical style and imagery in his numerous poems, some of which he read at meetings of the International Congresses of Orientalists in

Vienna (1886) and Stockholm (1889), at which he represented the Egyptian government. He published treatises on women's rights in Islam, translations into Arabic, Arab drawings of horses and camels, and the Islamic calendar.

Bibliographic Sources
Brockelmann, *GAL*, II, 627; S II, 724–725.
Brugman, *Introduction*, 323–324.
Cheikho, *al-Adab al-'arabiyya*, II, 24–25.
Daghir, *Masadir*, III, i, 339–340.
Fikri, 'Ali, *Subul al-najah*, 194–196.
Fuad, Faraj Sulayman, *al-Kanz al-thamin*, 165–166.
Hasan, Muhammad 'Abd al-Ghani, and 'Abd al-'Aziz Disuqi, *Rawdat al-madaris*, 355–356.
International Congress of Orientalists 7, I, 55.
Jindi, Anwar, *A'lam wa ashab aqlam*, 147–152.
Kahhala, *Mu'jam*, IV, 80.
Khafaji, *Qissat al-adab*, IV, 46–48.
Louca, *Voyageurs*, 203–206.
Mardam, *A'lam al-qarn al-thalith 'ashr*, 244–245.
Mujahid, *al-A'lam al-sharqiyya*, II, 706–707.
Tajir, *Harakat al-tarjama*, 10.
Yusuf, Niqula, *A'lam min al-Iskandariyya*, 277.
Zirikli, *al-A'lam*, II, 280.

Fathi, Hasan

(23 March 1900–30 November 1989)
Architect who championed traditional peasant designs. Born in Alexandria to a landowning family, Hasan studied architecture at Cairo University, receiving his *license* in 1925 (he later earned a diploma from the École des Beaux Arts in Paris). Although trained in European architectural methods, upon visiting his family's Upper Egyptian estates for the first time in 1927, he was struck by the simplicity and rightness of the local building traditions and dedicated himself to making their principles more systematic and more suitable to the housing needs of other poor people. Meanwhile, he taught at Cairo University and worked in the architectural section of the Municipal Affairs Department, but later went into private practice. In 1940 he got his first chance to test his ideas when the Royal Agriculture Society asked him to design an experimental farm at Bahtim. He investigated and revived Nubian techniques of building arches and domes with mud brick, also using these techniques in constructing some private homes. His main achievement was the design and construction, begun in 1945 and only partly implemented, of the village of New Qurna

("Gourna") in Qina province, across the Nile from Luxor. In 1969 he described his work in *Gourna, a Tale of Two Villages*, later republished as *Architecture for the Poor* and since translated into twenty-two other languages. He argued that a community's collective wisdom about its use of space should guide architectural design and town planning, although he could not actually persuade Qurna's inhabitants to move into the houses he had designed for them.

He also served as director of school buildings for the Education Ministry from 1949 to 1952, head of the Architecture Department of the Fine Arts Faculty at Cairo University from 1953 to 1957, and a member of the UN Committee for Housing in South Arabia. He designed a village in the New Valley in 1963, but his plans lay dormant for twenty years, then were reexamined but are still unimplemented. He designed an adobe village, "Dar al-Salam," in New Mexico, completed in 1980. He was awarded several Egyptian state prizes, the Agha Khan Prize for Islamic Architecture and a Swedish prize in 1980, a gold medal awarded by the International Association of Architects in Paris in 1984, and the Louis Sullivan Award in 1987. An outstanding teacher, better on general principles than on details, Fathi drew young architects and students from many parts of the world to his reconditioned Mamluk palace in Dar al-Labban, near the Citadel, to learn his techniques. An international architecture award has been set up in his memory, but his work has had little influence in Egypt.

Bibliographic Sources
al-Ahram, 1 Dec. 1989.
al-Ahram Archives, file 3534.
Andrews, *Annual Obituary 1989*, 700–702.
Architectural Review 187 (Jan. 1990): 9.
Daud, "Hasan Fathi."
DePopolo and Goethert, *Hassan Fathy, Architect*.
Doumato, *Hassan Fathy*.
Holod and Rastorfer, "Hassan Fathy, Chairman's Award."
Karnouk, *Modern Egyptian Art*, 79–84.
al-Musawwar (1 Dec. 1989): 28.
New York Times (2 Dec. 1989): 15.
OEMIW, II, 5–7, article by Yasir M. Saqr.
Richards, *Hassan Fathy*.
Said, *Contemporary Art in Egypt*, x–xi, 20–34.
Schleifer, "Hassan Fathi."
Steele, *Architecture for the People*.
———, *Hassan Fathy*.
Steele, comp., *Hassan Fathy Collection*.

Fawwaz, Zaynab

(1860?–19 January 1914)
Pioneer feminist essayist, poet, and novelist. Born in Tibnin in the Jabal 'Amil region of what is now Lebanon, Fawwaz was a Shi'i Muslim who moved to Beirut and immigrated to Egypt in 1870 with the As'ad family for whom she was working. Educated in Alexandria, she began to write in 1891 as an apprentice for the poet Hasan Husni al-Tuwayrani, publisher of *al-Nil*. As she became established, her articles appeared also in *al-Muayyad, al-Fatah,* and *al-Anis al-jalis*. She published one of the first biographical dictionaries devoted to famous women: *al-Durr al-manthur fi tabaqat al-khudur* [Pearls Strewn in Women's Quarters] in 1894, with the aid of her brother. She also wrote three novels and published a collection of her essays and articles, *al-rasail al-Zaynabiyya* [Zaynab's Letters], in 1897. She argued cogently that women should be accorded the same political rights as men and refuted the notion, common then to both sexes, that women's lives should be limited to the household sphere. She also wrote a four-act play about love and family honor and was writing a biographical dictionary of famous men at the time of her death. At least three of her works remain unpublished.

Bibliographic Sources
Badran, *Feminists,* 14–15, 64–66.
Badran and Cooke, *Opening the Gates,* 220–226.
Baron, *Women's Awakening in Egypt,* 21, 54.
Booth, "Exemplary Lives, Feminist Aspirations." *EAL,* I, 226.
Fawwaz, *al-Rasail al-Zaynabiyya.*
Hashim, "al-Sayyida Zaynab Fawwaz."
Kahhala, *A'lam al-nisa,* II, 82.
Maskuni, *Min 'abqariyyat nisa,* 223–240.
Muhammad, Fathiyya, *Balaghat al-nisa,* I, 115–160.
Nimnim, *al-Raida al-majhula.*
Zirikli, *al-A'lam,* III, 67.

Fawzi [al-Najjar], Dr. Husayn

(11 July 1900–20 August 1988)
Artist, musician, and writer. The son of an engineer, Husayn was born in the Husayniyya quarter of Cairo. He got his primary education at the Muhammad 'Ali School and went on to the Sa'idiyya Secondary School, after which he went to medical school and earned a medical degree, with a specialty in ophthalmology, in

Cairo. He went on for further scientific training in Paris, meanwhile studying music as well. His interest in music had begun when he first heard a symphony orchestra play Beethoven's Seventh Symphony while a student in Cairo; he started to take violin lessons from a German music teacher. He gradually shifted his interest to Eastern music, for which the violin has largely replaced the ancient *rababa.* When Fathi Radwan named him permanent undersecretary of the Culture Ministry, Husayn Fawzi gave special attention to the National Institute of Music (the "Conservatoire") and set up the Second (i.e., cultural) Program on the Egyptian broadcasting service. He left the ministry in 1959 after a quarrel with THARWAT 'UKASHA. Fawzi wrote various books on music, his travels, and his theory of the "Egyptian personality." He received state prizes in 1963 and 1988 for his writing and music. Passionately devoted to Egypt and its culture, he wrote essays and biographies in his later years.

Bibliographic Sources
Abdel-Malek, *Arab Political Thought,* 32–34.
de Moor, "Husayn Fawzi and 'The New School.'" *EAL,* I, 226.
Hafiz, Ahmad, *Ayyam min shababihim,* 93–96.
Hafiz, S., "The Maturation of a New Literary Genre."
Muti'i, *Haula al-rijal min Misr,* II, 54–56.
———, *Mawsu'a,* 142–149.
Najib, *A'lam Misr,* 189–190.
Segev, *Fundamentalism,* 78–79.
Somekh, "Husayn Fawzi."
Zaki, 'Abd al-Rahman, *A'lam al-musiqa al-misriyya,* 279–282.

Fawzi, Dr. Mahmud

(19 September 1900–12 June 1981)
Diplomat, cabinet minister, and premier. His father was one of the first graduates of Dar al-'Ulum and the Shari'a Judges School. Born in a village near Quwaysina (Minufiyya), Fawzi attended local schools, earned his *license* from the government Law School in 1923, and did graduate work in political science and history at the Universities of Liverpool, Columbia, and Rome; the last awarded him a doctorate in criminal law in 1926. After joining the Egyptian Foreign Service, he helped to organize the ministry and held posts in the United States, Japan, and France. He headed Egypt's delegation to the United Nations from 1945 to 1951, was ambassador to Great

Britain in 1952 for the first three months after the revolution, and then served as foreign minister from December 1952 until 1964 (tutoring NASIR on diplomacy); he was deputy premier in 1964–1967 and Nasir's special adviser on foreign affairs in 1967–1970. From 1968 to 1970 Fawzi sat on the executive board of the Arab Socialist Union and reorganized it, at Nasir's behest, even though he had never been active in internal politics. He served as SADAT's prime minister, a post he did not seek or enjoy, from October 1970 to January 1972, then resumed serving as vice president and special adviser to the president on foreign affairs until he retired in September 1974. His greatest achievements were negotiating the 1954 Anglo-Egyptian Treaty and dealing with the 1956 Suez Crisis. Sometimes called the Sindbad of Egyptian Diplomacy, he received state awards from various Latin American and African countries, as well as from the Egyptian government. Although he served Nasir and Sadat as a spokesman respected by the outside world, he remained a diplomat-technician without any political influence at home. His *Suez 1956: An Egyptian Perspective* was published in London after his death; only much later did it appear in an Arabic translation.

Bibliographic Sources
al-Ahram Archives, file 14.
Akhir sa'a (18 Dec. 1946): 5.
Fuad, Ni'mat Ahmad, in *al-Ahram*, 14 June 1981.
New York Times Biographical Service 12 (June 1981): 809.
Podell, *Annual Obituary 1981*, 384–385.
Qadi, Shukri, *Khamsun shakhsiyya*, 71–74.
Shimoni, *BDME*, 80–81.

Fawzi, Muhammad

(5 March 1915–)
Army officer and politician. Born in Abbasiyya (Cairo), he graduated from the Military Academy in 1936, earned an M.A. in military sciences at the same place in 1952, and taught there briefly in 1953, having fought and been wounded in the Palestine War. He later headed Egypt's military mission to the UN forces in the Congo in 1961. He fought in the June War, after which he succeeded 'ABD AL-HAKIM AMIR as commander-in-chief of the armed forces; he served as Egypt's defense minister from 1968 to 1971. A political ally of 'ALI SABRI, Fawzi be-

longed to the leftist faction that was purged in the Corrective Revolution, in part because he was not trusted by his chief of staff, let alone by SADAT. Given a fifteen-year prison sentence with hard labor, he was pardoned in 1974 because of his health and his military record. Politically inactive for a time, he later became a founding member of the Nasirite Arab Democratic Party, has written memoirs, and gives frequent press interviews about the June War, the War of Attrition, and the deterioration of relations between NASIR and 'Abd al-Hakim 'Amir.

Bibliographic Sources
al-Ahram Archives, file 5589.
al-Ahrar, 31 July 1997, detailed interview.
Egypt, Ministry of Information, *al-Mawsu'a al-qawmiyya*, II, 881–882.
Fawzi, Muhammad, *Harb al-thalath sanawat*.
International Who's Who of the Arab World, 182.
Najib, *A'lam Misr*, 436.
al-Siyasa al-Misriyya, June–July 1997.
al-Wasat, nos. 18–19 (1, 8 June 1992).

Fikri, 'Abd Allah

(July 1834–27 July 1890)
Poet and travel writer. He was born in Mecca, where his father, Muhammad Baligh, an Egyptian army officer, was stationed, having served as an engineer in MUHAMMAD 'ALI's Hijaz campaign. After Baligh's death in 1845, 'Abd Allah returned to Cairo and studied (as had his father and grandfather) at al-Azhar, where he learned Turkish and Persian. He worked for a while as a tutor to the princes, including TAWFIQ, and was regarded as Egypt's leading poet under ISMA'IL. He served the Egyptian government in its Turkish chancery, *Diwan al-Muhafaza*, the Ministries of Interior and Finance, and was in the cabinet as deputy minister of education (1876) and briefly as minister (February–May 1882). He was especially interested in a project to set up an elementary school in every town and village. Accused of backing the 'URABI Revolution, he was cleared in the trial. A panegyric poem redeemed him in the eyes of Khedive Tawfiq, who restored his pension, but he never again held an important post. He made trips to Istanbul, Syria and Lebanon, Mecca (in 1885), and headed Egypt's delegation to the 1889 International Congress of Orientalists in Stockholm, where he presented two papers. His son, AMIN, published many of his works

posthumously as *al-Athar al-fikriyya*. AHMAD AMIN ranked 'Abd Allah Fikri, 'ALI MUBARAK, and RIFA'A AL-TAHTAWI as the three "knights" of the Egyptian literary renaissance, and his poetic abilities are still widely respected by Egyptians.

Bibliographic Sources
'Abd al-Fattah, Muhammad, *Ashhar mashahir*, II, 1–31.
Amin, Ahmad, in *al-Hilal* 55:7 (July 1947): 44–49.
———, *Fayd al-khatir*, V, 204–210.
'Aqqad, 'Abbas Mahmud, *Shu'ara Misr*, 77–86.
Asaf, *Dalil*, 239–244.
Bitar, 'Abd al-Raziq, *Hilyat al-bashr fi tarikh al-qarn al-thalith 'ashr*.
Brockelmann, *GAL*, S II, 625.
Brugman, *Introduction*, 77–80.
Cheikho, *al-Adab al-'arabiyya*, II, 95–96.
Daghir, *Masadir*, III, ii, 976–979.
EAL, I, 233–234.
EI2, II, 892, entry by Jacques Jomier.
Fikri, 'Abd Allah, and Amin Fikri, *Irshad al-al-ibba*.
Fikri, 'Ali, *Subul al-najah*, II, 182–187.
Fikri, Amin, *al-Athar al-fikriyya*, 4–12.
Hasan, Muhammad 'Abd al-Ghani, *'Abd Allah Fikri: 'asruhu, hayatuhu, adabuhu*.
———, *'Abd Allah Fikri*.
Hijazi, Anwar, *'Amaliqa*, 96–99.
al-Hilal 3:18 (15 May 1895): 681–687.
'Inani, Sayyid, *'Abd Allah Basha Fikri*.
Kahhala, *Mu'jam*, VI, 102–103.
Khafaji, *Qissat al-adab*, III, 102–113.
Louca, *Voyageurs*, 197–203.
Mubarak, 'Ali, *Khitat*, II, 46–57.
Mujahid, *al-A'lam al-sharqiyya*, I, 92–94.
al-Muqtataf 15:1 (Oct. 1890): 9–16; 15:2 (Nov. 1890): 81–89.
Rafi'i, 'Abd al-Rahman, *'Asr Isma'il*, I, 278–279.
Sabri, Muhammad, *Shu'ara al-'asr*, 188–194.
Tawfiq, 'Awad, and Hasan Sabri, *Wuzara al-ta'lim*, 43–44.
Walili, *Mafakhir al-ajyal*, 62–63.
Zaydan, Jurji, *Mashahir al-sharq*, II, 1st ed., 216–221; 2nd ed., 305–310.
Zirikli, *al-A'lam*, IV, 113.

Fikri, Muhammad Amin

(1856–17 January 1899)
Writer and legal expert. Son of 'ABD ALLAH FIKRI, Muhammad Amin was born in Cairo, educated at the royal schools there, and studied law in Aix-en-Provence. He was appointed a judge in the National Appeals Court, then governor of Minufiyya and of Alexandria, and in 1895 director of *al-Daira al-Saniyya*. He wrote books

about his travels to Europe and about Egypt's geography and published some of his father's poetry. He died in Cairo.

Bibliographic Sources
Asaf, *Dalil*, 302–303.
Brockelmann, *GAL*, II, 642; S II, 749–750.
Cheikho, *al-Adab al-'arabiyya*, II, 96–97.
Fikri, 'Ali, *Subul al-najah*, III, 196–198.
al-Hilal 7:9 (1 Feb. 1899): 281–282.
Kahhala, *Mu'jam*, III, 9.
Louca, *Voyageurs*, 197–203.
Mujahid, *al-A'lam al-sharqiyya*, II, 452–453.
al-Muqtataf 23:2 (Feb. 1899): 120.
Zakhura, *Mirat al-'asr*, I, 505–506.
Zaydan, Jurji, *Mashahir al-sharq*, II, 1st ed., 177–178; 2nd ed., 214.
———, *Tarikh adab al-lugha*, IV, 264.
Zirikli, *al-A'lam*, VI, 43.

Fuad I, Ahmad

(26 March 1868–28 April 1936)
Prince, university head, and sultan (later king) of Egypt from 1917 to 1936. As the youngest son of Khedive ISMA'IL, he spent most of his youth with his exiled father in Naples and was educated in Geneva and at the military academy in Turin. When he returned to Egypt after his father's death, he led a dissolute life for a time. His first marriage, to Princess Chivékiar, failed, and he was shot (and narrowly escaped being killed) by her deranged brother. Fuad served for a time as a military attaché in Vienna and as aide-de-camp to Khedive 'ABBAS. The nominal rector of the Egyptian University, 1908–1913, he lectured only on marksmanship and horsemanship, at which he excelled. Considered in 1914 for Albania's throne, Albanian nationalists and the European powers both preferred a Christian ruler instead.

The British chose him for the Egyptian sultanate in 1917, succeeding HUSAYN KAMIL, whose son was viewed as anti-British. Fuad secretly encouraged the agitation that led to the 1919 Revolution. In April 1919 he married Nazli Sabri so that he could beget an heir and thus forestall the return of ex-Khedive 'ABBAS or his son, 'Abd al-Mun'im. He outwardly tolerated but privately loathed the 1923 Constitution, the Wafd Party, and SA'D ZAGHLUL and yearned to replace them with institutions and politicians more amenable to Palace control. Fuad feared assassination and once told English historian H.A.L. Fisher that he had ordered the construction of his coffin upon ascending the Egyptian throne. In 1930, aided by ISMA'IL SIDQI, he suspended the 1923 Constitution and promulgated one that increased his powers to the detriment of Parliament's. Five years later, he acceded to popular demands for the restoration of the earlier constitution and the return of the Wafd Party to power. He appointed Egypt's all-party delegation to negotiate with Britain to settle the Egyptian question but died before the Anglo-Egyptian Treaty was signed. Autocratic and avaricious, Fuad did not like his subjects or their leaders and preferred authoritarian government.

Bibliographic Sources

'Abd al-Fattah, Ahmad, *al-Amir Ahmad Fuad*.
Anis, *Safahat majhula*.
Bakr, "al-'Alaqat al-sirriyya."
Burke's Royal Families, II, 36.
*EI*2, II, 934, article by J. Jomier.
EMME, II, 683–684, article by Robert L. Tignor.
Fahmi, Zaki, *Safwat al-'asr*, 1–16.
Fisher, H.A.L., private papers, Bodleian Library, Oxford University.
Fuad, Faraj Sulayman, *al-Kanz al-thamin*, alif–jim.
Hanotaux, *Histoire,* VII, iii–xxxii (chapter by Henri Dehérain).
al-Hilal 26:2 (Nov. 1917): 150–152.
——— 44:8 (June 1936): 853–856, article by al-'Aqqad; 887–889, article by Zaki Mubarak.
Jami'i, *al-Jami'a al-misriyya al-qadima*.
Luhayta, *Tarikh Fuad al-awwal al-iqtisadi*.
Mahallawi, *al-Malika Nazli*, 77–136.
Mujahid, *al-A'lam al-sharqiyya*, I, 15–17.
New York Times (29 Apr. 1936): 8.
Reid, *Cairo University,* 28.
Salim, 'Abd al-Hamid, *al-Malik Fuad al-Awwal*.
Sayyid-Marsot, *Egypt's Liberal Experiment,* 59–60 et passim.
Shah, *King Fuad of Egypt*.
Stadiem, *Too Rich*, 103–108.
Tanahi, Tahir, *'Ala firash al-mawt*, 50–54.
Thabit, Karim, *al-Malik Fuad*.
Times (London) (29 Apr. 1936): 14c.
Tugay, *Three Centuries*, 159–163.
Wingate papers, Durham University, Boxes 298/2, 153–154.
Yeghen, *L'Égypte sous le regne de Fouad Ier*.
Zakhura, *Mirat al-'asr*, I, 62–64; II, 58–59.
Zirikli, *al-A'lam*, I, 196.

G

Garstin, Sir William Edmund

(29 January 1849–8 January 1925)
Irrigation engineer. He was the son of Charles
Garstin, a civil engineer who served in India,
where William was born; he was educated at
Cheltenham College and King's College, London. William Garstin entered the Indian Public
Works Department in 1872 and was sent to service in Egypt in 1885. He was appointed Egypt's
inspector general of irrigation in May 1892,
soon thereafter becoming undersecretary of state
for public works, in which capacity he helped to
plan and build the first Aswan Dam. He became
adviser to the ministry in 1904. After his retirement in 1908 he became one of the directors of
the Suez Canal Company. He surveyed many of
the maps of Upper Egypt and the Sudan that are
still in use. CROMER wrote that Garstin had
"raised himself to the rank of the greatest hy-
draulic engineer in this or any other country,"
and on his retirement a nationalist newspaper
wrote: "No dweller in Egypt, be he fellah, merchant, or capitalist, but mentions Garstin's name
with esteem, respect, and thankfulness for the
services he has rendered." He received the grand
cordons of the Osmanieh and Mejidieh.

Bibliographic Sources
Cromer, *Modern Egypt*, I, 686.
DNB (1922–1930), 328–330, article by E.I. Car-
    lyle.
Garstin, *Administration of the Irrigation Services*.
Journal of the Royal Geographical Society 65
    (1925): 279.
Nature, 17 Jan. 1925.
Times (London) (9 Jan. 1925): 14a.
Who Was Who (1916–1928), 394.
Wills and Barrett, *Anglo-African Who's Who*, 58.

Ghali, Butrus

(1846 or 11 May 1849–21 February 1910)
Diplomat and cabinet minister. Born in a village
near Beni Suef, Butrus was educated in the reformist Coptic school at Harat al-Saqqayin and
then at the school of Prince Mustafa Fadil. Although he later studied at the School of Languages, he never earned a higher degree. He
learned Arabic, French, English, Persian, Turkish, and Coptic. After being a clerk for the
Alexandria Commercial Court, he was appointed by MUHAMMAD SHARIF to the head
clerkship of the Justice Ministry in 1873. He
also helped at this time to organize the Coptic
(lay) Council and later the Coptic Benevolent
Society. When the Mixed Courts were being set
up, he helped the justice minister prepare an
Arabic translation of their law code, although he
lacked any legal training. Ghali's work brought
him to the attention of Prime Minister NUBAR,
who appointed him to represent Egypt on the
Caisse de la Dette Publique; he thus became an
intermediary between the Egyptian government
and its European creditors. In 1877 he became
the secretary-general of the Justice Ministry. He
became secretary to the cabinet in 1881 and then
deputy justice minister later in the same year.
Following the 'URABI Revolution he mediated
between Khedive TAWFIQ and the Nationalists,
securing trials that saved many of them from execution.

Butrus Ghali's first ministerial appointment
was within the 1893 HUSAYN FAKHRI cabinet that
pitted Khedive 'ABBAS against Lord CROMER,
but he was able to retain the finance portfolio in
MUSTAFA RIYAD's compromise ministry. Ghali
served as foreign minister from 1894 to 1910 under Nubar and MUSTAFA FAHMI, and then in his
own cabinet. He continued to play a mediating
role between power centers, signing the 1899
Sudan Convention. He represented the cabinet
on the bench in the 1906 Dinshaway trial, con-
curring in the death sentences that angered the
National Party, although he reportedly sought to
reduce the number of the accused and to mitigate
the harsh sentences. 'Abbas recommended him
(over Husayn Fakhri) to replace Fahmi as prime
minister in 1908, overriding GORST's concerns
about letting a Copt head Egypt's government.
As premier he further angered many Egyptians
by reviving the Press Law and publicly advocating the extension of the Suez Canal Company's

concession, policies that he is said to have privately opposed. When he was assassinated by a Nationalist pharmacist on the steps of the Justice Ministry, a wave of Muslim-Christian polemics ensued as well as more government repression against the National Party. A subtle and conciliatory politician who stayed in office to uphold unpopular policies, Ghali believed that he served Egypt's best interests and fell victim to others who were less willing to compromise than he.

Bibliographic Sources
'Arusi, *Ashhar qadaya al-ightiyalat*, 15–151.
CE, II, 415–416, article by Doris Behrens-Abuseif.
Ghali, Ibrahim Amin, *L'Égypte nationaliste*, 85–110.
Goldschmidt, "Butrus Ghali Family," 183–187.
Haykal, Muhammad Husayn, *Tarajim misriyya*, 110–128.
Mujahid, *al-A'lam al-sharqiyya*, I, 75–76.
al-Muqtataf 36 (1910): 313–318.
QTQ, 49–51.
Seikaly, "Prime Minister and Assassin."
Tadrus, *al-Aqbat*, II, 62–142.
Walili, *Mafakhir al-ajyal*, 106–108.
Wright, *Twentieth Century Impressions of Egypt*, 91–92.
Zaydan, Jurji, *Mashahir al-sharq*, 2nd ed., I, 267–270.
Zirikli, *al-A'lam*, II, 59.

Ghali, Butrus Butrus. *See* BOUTROS-GHALI, BOUTROS.

Ghali, Mu'allim

(1776–May 1822)
MUHAMMAD 'ALI's finance and foreign minister. He began his career as a clerk for ALFI BEY but left him to serve Muhammad 'Ali. He knew Turkish well and organized the government departments and the country's provinces. He ordered a cadastral survey to make sure that all landowners actually paid their taxes, thus increasing state revenues, and divided the country into provinces and districts (most of which are still in effect). He is credited with being the first to propose that Egypt manufacture its own armaments, both to save import costs and to provide well-paid jobs for Egyptians. When the French ambassador urged Muhammad 'Ali to make the Copts accept papal supremacy over their church, Mu'allim Ghali and his family became Roman Catholics. Court jealousy against Ghali increased with his influence, and he was jailed and then killed in Zifta on orders from IBRAHIM Pasha.

Bibliographic Sources
CE, IV, 1141, article by Mounir Shoucri.
Chaleur, *Histoire des Coptes d'Egypte*, 164–165.
Fuad, Faraj Sulayman, *al-Kanz al-thamin*, 227–230.
Nakhla, *Tarikh al-umma al-qibtiyya*.
Tadrus, *al-Aqbat*, II, 42–48; III, 57.
Walili, *Mafakhir al-ajyal*, 31–32.
Zaydan, Jurji, *Mashahir al-sharq*, 1st ed., I, 193–195.

Ghali, Wasif Butrus

(14 April 1878–8 January 1958)
Diplomat, scholar, and writer. Born in Cairo, a son of cabinet minister BUTRUS GHALI, Wasif Butrus Ghali was educated by the Jesuits there and at the University of Paris, where he received his *license en droit* in 1904. He opened a law practice in Cairo and then worked for Khedive 'ABBAS, leaving the country soon after his father was assassinated in 1910. While living in Paris during World War I, he gave a series of lectures on Arabic literature, resulting in two of his books, *Le jardin des fleurs* and *La tradition chevaleresque chez les arabes*. He resumed his career in Cairo in 1919, becoming minister of foreign affairs in SA'D ZAGHLUL's 1924 cabinet. He held that portfolio in NAHHAS's early ministries and played a leading role in negotiating the 1936 Anglo-Egyptian Treaty. Married to a French woman, he lived in France during World War II. In 1950 Wasif Ghali was named to the Administrative Board of the Suez Canal Company and to the Egyptian Senate, but he resigned in 1952 due to poor health. He then devoted his time to literary pursuits, supported by his substantial landholdings in Beni Suef. He died in Cairo after a long illness. He strongly influenced his nephew, BOUTROS BOUTROS-GHALI.

Bibliographic Sources
'Abd al-Hadi, Amin, *al-Sihafa al-tahira*, 12.
Deeb, *Party Politics*, 108 n, et passim.
Goldschmidt, "Butrus Ghali Family," 187.
Kamil, Raouf, *Waçif Ghali*.
Lüthi, *Les français en Égypte*, 99–100.
———, *Introduction*, 277–278.
Muti'i, *Mawsu'a*, 638–643.

Najib, A'lam Misr, 502.
QTQ, 259.
Tadrus, al-Aqbat, III, 117–118.
Who's Who in Egypt and the Near East, 1953, 366.

Ghalib, Dr. 'Uthman
(16 February 1845–28 January 1920)
Physician, biologist, and medical researcher. Originally from a peasant family in al-Talibiyya (Giza), he attended his village school, then the Military Academy, and graduated from Qasr al-'Ayni Medical School in 1868. He was sent to Paris for further medical studies, but his interests shifted to the natural sciences, and he received his license there in 1879. He discovered four new species of parasites and published a book on the cotton boll weevil; the Egyptian government distributed the book without giving Ghalib proper credit. He also wrote the first Arabic book on the modern principles of zoology. He taught natural history and then became deputy director of Qasr al-'Ayni but resigned when DUNLOP sought to replace him with an Englishman. He left Egypt for Paris, where he formed close ties with the Egyptian students. Initially a Nationalist and a close friend of WISA WASIF, he later broke with the party and especially with MUHAMMAD FARID. Ghalib died in Switzerland.

Bibliographic Sources
'Azmi, Mahmud, in al-Siyasa al-usbu'iyya 2 (29 Oct. 1927): 15–16.
'Isa, Ahmad, Mu'jam al-atibba, 288–289.
Jindi, Anwar, A'lam wa ashab aqlam, 275–284.
Kahhala, Mu'jam, VI, 267.
Zirikli, al-A'lam, IV, 212.

Ghanim, Fathi
(24 March 1924–2 February 1999)
Journalist and novelist. The son of a teacher, Fathi was born in Cairo and educated at the Ibrahimiyya Secondary School and Cairo University's Law Faculty, from which he earned his license in 1944. He worked briefly as a school inspector and then became a journalist for Ruz al-Yusuf, Akhir sa'a, and Sabah al-khayr, of which he became editor-in-chief in 1959. He published a novel, al-Rajul al-ladhi faqad zillahu, translated as The Man Who Lost His Shadow, for which the Egyptian government

awarded him an arts and sciences medal in 1962 and the state "Encouragement Prize." He took charge of the Middle East News Agency in 1965–1966, and was editor-in-chief of al-Jumhuriyya from 1966 to 1968. He traveled to Czechoslovakia, the USSR, the Sudan, and East Germany in the late 1960s. Although briefly barred from writing and publishing after the 1971 Corrective Revolution, he resumed writing novels and served as editor of Ruz al-Yusuf from 1973 to 1977. After that he published other novels, including al-Jabal [The Mountain] and Zaynab wa al-'arsh [Zaynab and the Throne], as well as film scenarios and short stories. A member of the Supreme Council for Culture, he received the Saddam Husayn Literary Prize in 1989 and another Egyptian state prize in 1995 for his literary achievement. In the early 1990s Fathi offended the Nasirite Party, some of whose members called for a ban on his writings. He died of cancer in Cairo.

Bibliographic Sources
'Abd al-Qadir, Faruq, in Ruz al-Yusuf, no. 3620 (27 Oct. 1997): 72–75.
al-Ahram Archives, file 4617.
Akhir sa'a, 2 Aug., 13 Sept. 1995.
'Aqid, "I'tirafat mutaakhkhira li-Fathi Ghanim."
EAL, I, 248.
Elon, "Ideology and Structure."
Ghanim, in al-Hayat, 3 Aug. 1990.
Najib, A'lam Misr, 361–362.
Segev, Fundamentalism, 78–79.
Shalabi, Muhammad, Ma'a ruwwad al-fikr.
WWAW, 1997–1998, 255.

al-Ghazali, Shaykh Muhammad
(22 September 1917–9 March 1996)
Islamist writer. Born in Giza, he received his diploma as an 'alim (Muslim scholar) from al-Azhar's Faculty of Religion in 1941, earned another diploma in missionary work in 1943, and yet another in education in 1945. Active in the Society of Muslim Brothers, he began his career as a preacher and a mosque inspector for the awqaf ministry, of which he eventually became undersecretary. His effort to unseat HUDAYBI in 1953 led to his dismissal from the Brothers. Ghazali later taught in several colleges at al-Azhar, at Umm al-Qura and 'Abd al-'Aziz Universities in Saudi Arabia, the College of Shari'ah in Qatar, and Amir 'Abd al-Qadir University in

Algeria. A strong advocate of *shura* (political consultation), he called for strict, Quran-based standards for accepting hadiths ascribed to the Prophet. He received the King Faysal Prize, as well as an Egyptian achievement award and the First Class Medal of the Republic in 1989, and prizes from Saudi Arabia and Pakistan. He wrote a response, *Min huna na'lam* (translated as *Our Beginning in Wisdom*), to KHALID MUHAMMAD KHALID's reformist tract, *Min huna nabda* (translated as *From Here We Start*). He also wrote *al-Islam al-muftara 'alayhi bayn al-shuyu'iyyin wa al-rasmaliyyin* [Islam as Misrepresented by the Communists and Capitalists] and *Taamullat fi al-din wa al-hayat* [Meditations on Religion and Life], along with more than twenty-five other religious books. In 1987 he became a member of Egypt's Supreme Council on Islamic Affairs and in 1990 arranged the release of 149 Egyptian prisoners in Iran. Ghazali's aim was to promote an enlightened, more profound approach to Islam in order to protect Muslim countries from the encroachment of alien values. He died in Saudi Arabia and is buried in Medina.

Bibliographic Sources
al-Ahram Archives, file 5126.
Hasana, *Fiqh al-da'wa*, chap. 7.
Ghazali, Muhammad, *al-Sunna al-nabawiyya*.
'Imara, *al-Shaykh Muhammad al-Ghazali*.
Kishk, *al-Shaykh Muhammad al-Ghazali*.
Nisf al-dunya, 1–22 Feb. 1998, series on Ghazali's early poetry.
OEMIW, II, 63–64, article by Nazih N. Ayubi.
Qaradawi, *al-Shaykh al-Ghazali*.
al-Sha'b, 2 Apr.–25 June 1997, articles by Ghazali, Ni'mat Ahmad Fuad, and Muhammad al-'Imara.
Shalabi, Muhammad, *al-Shaykh al-Ghazali*.

al-Ghazali [al-Jabali], Zaynab
(2 January 1917–)
Leading female Islamist. Born in Cairo, she lost both her father and her male guardian before she was ten. They had encouraged her to aspire to a legal career, studying law in Paris and *fiqh* (Islamic jurisprudence) in Cairo, but her eldest brother (who became her guardian) did not want her to become educated, although the second-eldest brother seems to have offered some support. In 1937 she joined both the Society of Muslim Brothers and the Egyptian Feminist Union, but

soon turned against the latter and proceeded to form the Muslim Women's Association, independent of the Muslim Brothers (although in 1948 she swore personal allegiance to HASAN AL-BANNA). She gave lectures to women at the Ibn Tulun Mosque, ran an orphanage, aided needy families, and mediated family quarrels. Like the Muslim Brothers, the Women's Association demanded that the Quran become Egypt's constitution. For her role in secretly regrouping the Muslim Brothers in the early 1960s, she was jailed from 1965 to 1971. NASIR's men forced her to remove her Islamic dress, tried to rape her, and threatened to give her 500 lashes; only King Faysal's intervention saved her from execution. She organized the Muslim Sisters under SADAT. Invited to run in the 1984 parliamentary elections, she refused to cooperate with the New Wafd. Although she had frequently spoken to groups or attended conferences outside Egypt, the Egyptian government barred her from foreign travel in 1987, setting off some controversy and legal proceedings. She is quoted as saying, "A woman should never say no to her husband unless he is acting against the rules of Islam."

Bibliographic Sources
al-Ahram Archives, file 15051.
al-Ahrar, 10, 24 Jan. 1983.
al-Anba, 4, 7 Feb. 1997.
Cooke, "Zaynab al-Ghazali: Saint or Subversive?"
Ghazali, Zaynab, *Ayyam min hayati*.
Hoffman, "An Islamic Activist: Zaynab al-Ghazali."
Hoffman-Ladd, "Polemics."
Jawadi, *Mudhakkirat al-mara*, 71–86.
OEMIW, II, 64–66, article by Valerie J. Hoffman-Ladd.
Sullivan, Earl L., *Women in Egyptian Public Life*, 115–117.
al-Watan al-'arabi, no. 538:12 (5 June 1987): 28–33.
Zuhur, *Revealing Reveiling*.

Ghurbal, Muhammad Shafiq
(4 January 1894–19 October 1961)
Pioneer historian of modern Egypt. Ghurbal was born in Alexandria, graduated from the Higher Teachers College in 1915, and studied at the University of London, where his M.A. thesis was supervised by Arnold Toynbee and later published as *The Beginnings of the Egyptian*

Question and the Rise of Mehemet Ali. He taught modern history in secondary schools, at the Teachers College, and then at Cairo University, eventually becoming dean of its Faculty of Arts. He was a technical adviser to the Education Ministry and deputy minister of social affairs. He wrote *Tarikh al-mufawadat al-misriyya al-britaniyya, 1882–1936* [History of the Anglo-Egyptian Negotiations], of which only the first volume was published, and a biography of MUHAMMAD 'ALI. He became a member of the Arabic Language Academy in 1957. He also directed the Arab League's Institute for Higher Arab Studies until his death in Cairo.

Bibliographic Sources
'Abd al-Hayy, *'Asir hayati,* 152–159.
Abu Hadid, Muhammad Farid, and Arnold Toynbee, "Muhammad Shafiq Ghurbal," in *MMLA* 15 (1962): 153–162.
al-Ahram, 20 Oct. 1961, 7.
'Allam, *Majma'iyyun,* 286–288.
Anis, Muhammad, in *al-Majalla,* no. 58 (Nov. 1961): 13.
Crabbs, "Politics, History, and Culture," 403.
Fahmi, Mansur, "al-Ustadh Muhammad Shafiq Ghurbal."
Jami'i, *al-Jami'a al-misriyya.*
Jindi, Anwar, *al-Muhafaza wa al-tajdid,* 541–543.
MTM 18 (1971), special issue.
Mustafa, Ahmad 'Abd al-Rahim, "Shafiq Ghurbal muarrikhan."
Najib, *A'lam Misr,* 416.
Qadi, Shukri, *Miat shakhsiyya,* 232–234.
Times (London) (23 Oct. 1961): 15b; (27 Oct. 1961): 17e.
Yusuf, Niqula, *A'lam min al-Iskandariyya,* 295–299.
Zirikli, *al-A'lam,* VI, 159.

Gorst, Sir [John] Eldon

(25 June 1861–12 July 1911)
Foreign Office official and colonial administrator who served as British agent and consul general in Egypt from 1907 to 1911. Born in New Zealand but reared in London, Gorst attended Eton and Trinity College, Cambridge. In 1885 he became both a barrister and a member of the diplomatic corps, going to Egypt the following year as controller of direct taxes, becoming undersecretary for finance (1892), adviser to the Interior Ministry (1894), and financial adviser (1898). In 1904 he returned to London, where as

undersecretary of state he, in effect, represented CROMER in the Foreign Office.

With a new Liberal Party government in power, Gorst was sent to replace Cromer with instructions to give Egyptians greater responsibility to manage their internal affairs. As British agent, Gorst, with his *politique d'entente,* quickly improved relations with Khedive 'ABBAS II, brought more Egyptians into responsible government positions, and weakened the National Party. However, his efforts to rein in the burgeoning corps of Anglo-Egyptian officials offended many old Egypt hands. The appointment of BUTRUS GHALI as prime minister, popularly ascribed to Gorst, angered the Nationalists and many other Muslims, leading to press attacks and eventually to Butrus Ghali's assassination. The revival of the Press Law alienated Europeans as well as Egyptians and proved unenforceable. Gorst's attempt to extend the Suez Canal Company's concession in 1909–1910 to raise additional funds for development in Egypt and the Sudan was disliked by all Egyptians; when he put the issue to the General Assembly, vehement opposition from the Nationalist press led to its rejection. This rejection, combined with the murder of Butrus Ghali, caused Gorst to abandon his lenient policy in favor of a harsher one, using the Exceptional Laws and various penal measures to stifle the Nationalists. He had almost restored British control when he became stricken with cancer and went back to England to die. An unprepossessing but egotistical man, disliked by the older British colonial administrators in Egypt and distrusted by Egyptians as sphinxlike, Gorst was never accorded the respect that his intelligence and strong will warranted, although he received the grand cordons of the Osmanieh and Mejidieh orders and was a Knight Commander of Sts. Michael and George. His "autobiographical notes" and diaries are at St. Antony's College, Oxford.

Bibliographic Sources
Alexander, *Truth About Egypt,* 102–105.
Boyle, *Servant of the Empire,* 107–127.
Coles, *Recollections and Reflections.*
Cromer, *Modern Egypt,* II, 286, 488.
DNB (1901–1911), 133–134.
Foreign Office List, 1912, 423.
Mellini, *Sir Eldon Gorst.*
Mohamed, *In the Land of the Pharaohs.*

Rothstein, *Egypt's Ruin.*
Shafiq, *Mudhakkirati*, II, i.
Tignor, *Modernization,* 291–300.
Times (London) (13 July 1911): 5c; (15 July 1911): 5a.
Vansittart, *Mist Procession,* 56.

Wills and Barrett, *Anglo-African Who's Who*, 62.
Who Was Who (1890–1916), addenda, xxviii.
Wright, *Twentieth Century Impressions of Egypt,* 113–114.
Yusuf, Mustafa al-Nahhas Jabr, *Siyasat al-ihtilal.*
Zakhura, *Mirat al-'asr*, II, 89–90.

H

Hafiz, 'Abd al-Halim
(21 June 1929–30 March 1977)
Popular singer, composer, and actor, sometimes called *al-Andalib al-Ahmar* (the Black Nightingale). 'Abd al-Halim was born in the village of al-Halawat, near Hihya (Sharqiyya). His father was a merchant who so admired his parliamentary representative, 'Abd al-Halim al-Shamsi ('ALI AL-SHAMSI's brother), that he named the baby after him. 'Abd al-Halim attended the local *kuttab,* then the Zaqaziq Boys' Elementary School (where he led the school band), and graduated from the Institute of Arab Music in 1948. Having heard MUHAMMAD 'ABD AL-WAHHAB play the oboe, he chose to study with him. His first job was teaching music at the Tanta Girls' Elementary School; he then taught in Zaqaziq. In 1949 he worked for a radio musical troupe as an oboist and two years later began his broadcast career as a singer. He first won renown by singing in the half-year celebration of the July 1952 Revolution. He starred in his first film in 1955 and went on to make more films than 'Abd al-Wahhab and UMM KULTHUM combined. In 1959 he began teaching voice at the Cinema Institute. His repertory exceeded 300 songs, written by most of modern Egypt's poets. In 1962 he and Muhammad 'Abd al-Wahhab formed a recording company, "Sawt al-fann." He made a singing tour of Amman, Beirut, Kuwait, Baghdad, Paris, and London in 1967. His last film, *Abi fawq al-shajara* [My Father Is Up the Tree], ran in 1969 for thirty-six weeks, a record that has never been surpassed. 'Abd al-Halim received awards from Egypt and Jordan. Dogged by ill health, he was hospitalized several times and died young. He was a handsome but con-firmed bachelor (reportedly he wished to marry costar Su'ad Husni), and his home has become like a shrine since his death. His brother, Isma'il Sha'bana, was also a singer, but less well known.

Bibliographic Sources
al-Ahram Archives, file 546.
Akhir sa'a, 1 Apr. 1985.
Amin, Mustafa, *Shakhsiyyat,* II, 348–364.
Butrus, *A'lam al-musiqa,* 267–268.
Darwish, Mustafa, *Dream Makers,* 32.
al-Majalla, no. 268 (27 Mar. 1985).
Najib, *A'lam Misr,* 291.
Qadi, Shukri, in *al-Jumhuriyya,* 1 Apr. 1986.
Ramzi, *Nujum al-sinima,* 145–158.
Zaki, 'Abd al-Hamid Tawfiq, *al-Mu'asirun,* 84–86.

al-Hakim, Tawfiq
(8 October 1898–26 July 1987)
Playwright, novelist, and essayist. Tawfiq was born in Ramleh, Alexandria, to an Egyptian landowning father and an aristocratic Turkish mother. His family moved often because of his father's work as a district magistrate. Tawfiq was first exposed to drama by seeing an Arabic adaptation of *Romeo and Juliet,* possibly performed by SALAMA AL-HIJAZI's troupe, in Disuq. He attended many dramatic productions in Cairo, began studying classical Greek and French drama, and was already writing plays while still a pupil at the Muhammad 'Ali Secondary School. Obeying his father's wishes, he attended the government Law School, graduating third from the bottom of his class in 1924. His parents, hoping to distract him from writing for the stage, sent him to Paris for more legal studies, but he failed to earn his doctorate and returned to Egypt in 1928. Hakim then worked for the *Niyaba* of the Alexandria Mixed Courts and in 1929 was promoted to deputy public prosecutor. His legal experiences were encapsulated in a novel, *Yawmiyyat naib fi al-aryaf* [Diaries of a Prosecutor in the Country], published in 1937; a later English translation was entitled *The Maze of Justice.* During this period he also wrote *Ahl al-kahf* [The Sleepers in the Cave], *Rasasa fi al-qalb* [A Bullet in the Heart], and *Shahrazad* [Sheherazade]. His plays scandalized his *Niyaba* colleagues, and he was obliged to resign.

In 1933 Hakim published a novel, *'Awdat al-ruh* [Return of the Spirit], an allegory of

Egypt's modern renaissance that stirred up many Egyptians, including NASIR. Hakim took charge of the Education Ministry's research department in 1934 and of the Social Affairs Ministry's information service in 1939, but retired from the government in 1943. In 1951 TAHA HUSAYN named him director of Dar al-Kutub, a post he would have soon lost without Nasir's timely intervention. Hakim was elected to membership in the Arabic Language Academy in 1954, Nasir appointed him to the Supreme Council for the Arts in 1956, and he later represented Egypt at UNESCO in Paris, where he was exposed to the theater of the absurd. He served on the board of *al-Ahram* from 1961 and in that year received his first state prize for literature. A government theater that opened in 1963 was named for him. Among his plays produced in the Nasir era are *al-Sultan al-hair* [The Perplexed Sultan], a historical drama about the Mamluks with contemporary implications, and *Ya tali' al-shajara* [The Tree Climber], influenced by the theater of the absurd. He was appointed in 1965 to the Supreme Council for the Arts, Letters, and Social Sciences.

Although he had written regularly for *al-Ahram* throughout the Nasir era, Hakim denounced Nasir's policies in 1972 in a controversial book, *'Awdat al-wa'y*, translated as *The Return of Consciousness* (1985). He was one of the first Egyptian writers to call for a peace treaty with Israel, perhaps owing to his disillusionment with Nasir but more probably to his love of Egypt and lack of respect for Arabs. He recanted later, when the peace treaty did not yield the benefits he had hoped for. The Egyptian Academy of Fine Arts awarded Hakim an honorary doctorate in 1975. He was named honorary president of *al-Ahram*'s administrative board in 1981 and also became a member of the Supreme Council for the Press. In 1983 he published a biting attack on Egypt's religious leaders called *Ahadith ma'a Allah* [Conversations with God], arousing debates throughout the Arab world. A controversial writer, he was respected by Arabs generally even when they disagreed with him.

Bibliographic Sources

'Abd al-'Aziz, *al-Milaff al-shakhsi li-Tawfiq al-Hakim.*
Abdel Wahab, "The Sultan's Dilemma."

Adham, Isma'il, and Ibrahim Naji, *Tawfiq al-Hakim.*
al-Ahram Archives, file 122.
'Allam, *Majma'iyyun*, 93–94.
Allen, "Egyptian Drama After the Revolution."
———, *Modern Arabic Literature*, 111–124.
Amin, Mustafa, *Shakhsiyyat*, II, 40–74.
'Awad, Louis, *Aqni'at al-nasiriyya al-sab'a.*
'Awad, Ramses, *Tawfiq al-Hakim al-ladhi la ta'rifuhu.*
Badawi, M.M., *Modern Arabic Drama*, 8–87.
Barbour, "'*Audatu r-ruh*—an Egyptian Novel."
Brockelmann, *GAL*, S III, 242–250.
Brugman, *Introduction*, 276–288.
Buyers, *Annual Obituary, 1987*, 355–357.
Colby, *World Authors 1980–1985*, 384–389.
Eban, "Modern Literary Movement in Egypt."
EAL, I, 263–265.
Fontaine, *Mortrésurrection.*
Fuad, Ni'mat Ahmad, *Qimam adabiyya*, 255–280.
Gershoni, "An Intellectual Source for the Revolution."
Hafiz, Ahmad, *Ayyam min shabihim*, 47–58.
Hakim, Tawfiq, *Sijn al-'umr.*
Hopwood, *Egypt: Politics and Society*, 136–160.
Hutchins, "The Theology of Tawfiq al-Hakim."
'Id, Raja, *Dirasa fi adab Tawfiq al-Hakim.*
Jindi, Anwar, *al-Muhafaza wa al-tajdid*, 685–690.
Khafaji, *Suwar min al-adab al-hadith*, IV, 55–63.
Kilpatrick, Hilary, "Egyptian Novel," in *CHAL*, 229–232.
———, *Modern Egyptian Novel*, 41–51.
Landau, *Studies in the Arab Theater*, 138–147 et passim.
Long, *Tawfiq al-Hakim.*
Mallakh, *al-Hakim bakhilan.*
Mandur, *Masrah Tawfiq al-Hakim.*
Le Monde, 28 July 1987.
Muntasir, "Tawfiq al-Hakim."
Murad, *Tawfiq al-Hakim wa al-thawra al-misriyya.*
Mustafa, Ahmad 'Abd al-Rahim, *Tawfiq al-Hakim.*
Muti'i, *Mawsu'a*, 113–120.
Naqqash, Raja, *Maq'ad saghir amam al-sitar*, 7–25.
Qal'aji, *Ma'a Tawfiq al-Hakim.*
Ra'i, 'Ali, "Arabic Drama Since the Thirties," in *CHAL*, 368–384.
———, *Tawfiq al-Hakim.*
Ramadi, *Min a'lam al-adab*, 121–142.
Rooke, *In My Childhood*, 242–248 et passim.
Sakkut, *Egyptian Novel*, 85–97.
Schoonover, "Tawfiq al-Hakim and al-'Aqqad."
Shukri, Ghali, *Thawrat al-mu'tazil.*
Starkey, *From the Ivory Tower.*
———, "Tawfiq al-Hakim."
al-Tali'a 10:12 (Dec. 1974): 5–20, Hakim and Lutfi al-Khuli letters.
Tarabishi, Georges, *Lu'bat al-hulw wa al-waqi'."*
Tutungi, *Tawfiq al-Hakim and the West.*
Zahlawi, *Udaba mu'asirun*, 161–163.

Yusuf, Niqula, *A'lam min al-Iskandariyya*, 305–311.

Halim, Prince. *See* 'ABD AL-HALIM, MUHAMMAD

Halim, 'Abbas
(9 October 1897–6 July? 1978)
Nabil (Prince) of the MUHAMMAD 'ALI dynasty who became a labor leader. Born in Alexandria and educated in Germany, he served as an aide-de-camp to Kaiser Wilhelm II, became a fighter pilot for Germany in World War I, and later joined the Ottoman air corps. After the war, he traveled for several years before he was readmitted to Egypt. A patron of athletics (including sports for the poor), Halim headed the Royal Automobile Club and the Royal Flying Club. Having quarreled with King FUAD, his cousin, he backed the Wafd in 1930 against ISMA'IL SIDQI's efforts to change Egypt's constitution. In that December he was elected president of the pro-Wafdist National Federation of Trade Unions in Egypt. He made sure that the federation's leaders were actual workers and that its goals furthered their class interests regarding wages, working conditions, housing, education, and unemployment compensation. His leading associates, though, were skilled, semiautonomous workers and small proprietors, not industrial laborers. His attempt to establish a workers' party in 1931 alarmed his Wafdist allies, but he and NAHHAS agreed that the National Federation would leave politics to the Wafd. Eclipsed for several years because of Sidqi's repressive policies, the National Federation resumed its efforts to organize workers in 1934, after Sidqi had been replaced by 'ABD AL-FATTAH YAHYA. The police cordoned off 'Abbas Halim's Cairo palace, setting off demonstrations in which one worker was killed and others injured. Another demonstration ensued at the slain worker's funeral. 'Abbas Halim was arrested but released after his well-publicized hunger strike. As the National Federation grew, the Wafd tried to draw it away from Halim, who was forming ties with Misr al-Fatat. The labor movement became split between the Wafd and the prince. When the Wafd regained power in 1936, Halim left labor politics, and the National Federation died out.

He tried again in 1937 to lead a labor group, the Committee to Organize the Workers' Movement, but it allowed him only nominal leadership. He reappeared in 1939 as "supreme president" of the Cairo Tramway Workers' Union, which hoped to exploit Halim's ties with King FARUQ and enmity to the Wafd. He negotiated with the tramway company on behalf of the transport workers, gaining some benefits for them in July 1940. He combined the transport workers' organizations into the Joint Transport Federation, and when this new group struck in September 1941, he negotiated on its behalf for higher wages, but failed to fulfill his promises to the workers. This failure, along with the Wafd's return to power in 1942, undermined Halim; Britain interned him and a few friends for two years. Once he could resume his activities, the workers shunned him for his ties with Faruq, who was no longer popular. As Marxist ideas of working-class solidarity spread, his influence waned in the late 1940s. After the 1952 Revolution, he received a fifteen-year sentence, which was later annulled. His property was sequestered but restored to him in 1975 by the Council of State. His post-1952 press interviews reveal shocking (possibly apocryphal) details about others in the Egyptian royal family.

Bibliographic Sources
al-Ahram Archives, file 1437.
Beinin and Lockman, *Workers on the Nile*, 195–217 et passim.
Burke's Royal Families, II, 29.
al-Musawwar, 7 Nov.–26 Dec. 1958, memoirs.
Sabah al-khayr, 12 Feb. 1959, interview.

Hamama, Fatin
(27 May 1931–)
Film actress, often called the First Lady of the Egyptian Screen. She was born in Cairo's 'Abdin quarter, the daughter of a teacher named Ahmad al-Hamama, who brought her to the office of MUHAMMAD 'ABD AL-WAHHAB (or, according to other accounts, her mother entered her in a children's beauty contest). Muhammad Karim saw her photograph in *al-Musawwar* and chose her for a child's part in his 1940 film, *Yawm Sa'id* [Happy Day]. She attended the Amira Fawqiyya Secondary School, but after her family moved to Doqqi, she studied at the Institute for Theater and Cinema, where her teachers in-

cluded ZAKI TULAYMAT and ZAKI MUBARAK, between acting stints, which included *Rasasa fi al-
qalb* [A Bullet in the Heart] in 1943, *Awwal al-
Shahr* [First Day of the Month] in 1945, and
Dunya [World] in 1946. Because of her innocent
good looks, Hamama was often typecast in B-
grade movies depicting her as a constant victim
of oppression, but as a role model for middle-
class Egyptian girls, she became immensely
popular. After a brief marriage to director 'Izz
al-Din Zulfiqar, she met OMAR SHARIF while
playing with him in *Sira' fi al-Mina* [Feud in the
Port] and married him. They were divorced ten
years later. She left Egypt in 1965 under pressure from NASIR's *Mukhabarat,* lived for six
years in Europe, and worked with YUSUF SHAHIN
on a Moroccan film. At UMM KULTHUM's urging,
she returned to Cairo in February 1970 and resumed her star role during the 1970s and 1980s.
She was given a special award for her fifty-year
career as a film star in December 1991. She has
not acted in a film since 1993, when she starred
in the critically acclaimed but money-losing *Ard
al-ahlam* [The Land of Dreams] but has reportedly filmed her memoirs for television, using
Richard Burton's London flat. She served as a
judge for the 1993 "Miss Africa" contest and the
Montpellier Film Festival. She declined a lucra-
tive offer from Islamists to don the *hijab* (veil)
and end her career. As an actress and in real life,
she has a strongly empathic personality.

Bibliographic Sources
al-Ahram Archives, file 506.
al-Ahram Weekly, 4 Apr. 1991.
al-'Alam al-yawm, 20 Nov. 1992.
al-Anba, 11 Dec. 1995.
Darwish, Mustafa, *Dream Makers,* 30.
al-Hayat, 10 Feb. 1998.
al-Idha'a, 6 Apr. 1991.
al-Ittihad, 18 Aug. 1991.
al-Musawwar, 12 Apr. 1991.
Najib, *A'lam Misr,* 357.
Nisf al-dunya, 15 Dec. 1996.
Ramzi, *Nujam al-sinima,* 191–206.
Sabah al-khayr, 3 June 1993.
WWAW, 1997–1998, 283.

al-Hamuli, 'Abduh

(1836, 1840, or 1845–12 May 1901)
Pioneer musician, singer, and composer. Born in
Tanta, the son of a coffee bean dealer, 'Abduh

and his elder brother quarreled with their parents, ran away from home, and took refuge with
a musician, whose occupation would not have
been respected by most Egyptians of that era.
'Abduh became enamored of singing, and his
new protector took him to Cairo to sing in a cof-
feehouse near what are now the Ezbekiyya Gardens, also marrying his protégé to his daughter
(the first of 'Abduh's five wives). 'Abduh had a
beautiful voice and developed a new and innovative style. He sojourned in Istanbul and adapted
Turkish motifs into Arabic vocal music. He was
the first to merge two song meters and did much
to raise the quality of singing and the status of
singers. Among his songs were *Sharibt al-sabr
min ba'd tasafi* [I Drank Patience After Reach-
ing a Compromise], *al-Rabb yaltif bi-'abdih*
[The Lord Is Kind to His Servant], *Matti' hay-
atak bil-ahbab* [God Makes Your Life Enjoyable
with Loved Ones], and *'Ahd al-ikhwa nahfuzuh
bi al-ruh* [We Keep the Covenant of Brotherhood in Spirit]. He is remembered for founding a
school of Egyptian singers that included many
who would achieve fame in the early twentieth
century. He died of tuberculosis in Helwan.

Bibliographic Sources
Abu Hadid, *'Isamiyun,* 99–110, article by Mahmud
    al-Hifni.
Amin, Ahmad, in *al-Hilal* 56:8 (Aug. 1947):
    20–24.
Bishri, 'Abd al-'Aziz, *al-Mukhtar,* II, 31–40.
Butrus, *A'lam al-musiqa,* 54–60.
al-Hilal 9:8 (June 1901): 505–512.
Jindi, Anwar, *al-Sharq fi fajr al-yaqza,* 223–227.
Jundi, *A'lam al-adab,* II, 566–567.
Mutran, "al-Musiqa al-sharqiyya wa 'Abduh al-
    Hamuli."
Rafi'i, 'Abd al-Rahman, *'Asr Isma'il,* I, 288–289.
Ramadi, *Adab wa tarab,* 169–184.
Rizq, Qustandi, *al-Musiqa al-sharqiyya.*
Zaki, 'Abd al-Hamid Tawfiq, *A'lam al-musiqa,*
    19–24.
Zaydan, Jurji, *Mashahir al-sharq,* 2nd ed., II, 341.
——, *Tarikh adab al-lugha,* IV, 228–229.
Zirikli, *al-A'lam,* IV, 171–172.

Hamza, 'Abd al-Qadir

(1880–6 June 1941)
Journalist and historian. Born in Shubra Khit
(Buhayra), he attended the Ras al-Tin Secondary
School in Alexandria, received his *license* from

the Khedivial Law School, and began his legal practice in 1902. He soon changed to journalism, worked with LUTFI AL-SAYYID in editing *al-Jarida* in 1907, and edited *al-Ahali* in Alexandria from 1910 to 1923, when he became editor of *al-Balagh*. He proved himself a brave defender of the Egyptian cause, knew both MUSTAFA KAMIL and SA'D ZAGHLUL, and was appointed to the Senate. He was elected to membership in the Arabic Language Academy in 1940. He translated several English books on Egypt's modern history into Arabic. He died in Cairo.

Bibliographic Sources
al-Ahram, 7 June 1941, 5.
al-Akhbar, 18 July 1963, article on Hamza and Salama Musa.
'Allam, *Majma'iyyun*, 178–179.
Daghir, *Masadir*, II, i, 322–323.
Fahmi, Zaki, *Safwat al-'asr*, 647–649.
Hamza, *Adab al-maqala*, VIII.
———, "Sahibat jalalat al-sihafa."
Jindi, Anwar, *al-Muhafaza wa al-tajdid*, 643–651.
———, *al-Sihafa al-siyasiyya*, 276–283.
Mahmud, Hafiz, "al-'Amaliqa al-sitta," 106–116.
Mazini, Ibrahim 'Abd al-Qadir, in *al-Ahram*, 14 May 1944.
Qadi, Shukri, *Khamsun shakhsiyya*, 221–225.
al-Risala, 16, 23 June 1941; 4 August 1941.
Rizq, Fathi, *Khamsa wa sab'una najman*, 188–192.
Tanahi, Tahir, "Hal al-sihafi adib?"
Zirikli, *al-A'lam*, IV, 44–45.

Hanna, Murqus
(4 September 1872–18 June 1934)
Coptic lawyer, politician, and orator. Son of Father Yuhanna, Murqus was born in Mansura and studied law in Cairo, Montpellier, and Paris, where he also earned a degree in political economy. Upon returning to Egypt in 1891, he was named deputy public prosecutor in Damanhur but resigned after having written a book on Egyptian administrative law. He practiced law in Asyut, Cairo, and Alexandria. He joined the National Party in the time of MUSTAFA KAMIL and became one of the charter members of the Wafd after World War I. The British military authorities arrested him in 1922 because of his participation in revolutionary activities. Murqus was sentenced to death in July but released after about a year. He was elected leader of the Lawyers Syndicate several times. He served as minister of

public works, finance, and foreign affairs in several cabinets of differing political persuasions. He was a strong supporter of the National University and of education for girls. His daughter married politician MAKRAM 'UBAYD.

Bibliographic Sources
Carter, *Copts*, 164.
Fahmi, Zaki, *Safwat al-'asr*, 211–220.
Habib, *Abu Jilda*, 116–120.
Labib, "The Copts in Egyptian Society," 313–314.
Meinardus, *Christian Egypt: Faith and Life*, 29–30.
Mujahid, *al-A'lam al-sharqiyya*, I, 123–124.
QTQ, 213–214.
Rafi'i, 'Abd al-Rahman, *Fi a'qab al-thawra*, I, 141, 263, 270.
Reid, "National Bar Association," 620–621.
Taqwim "al-Hilal" (1935): 37.
Thabit, Karim, in *al-Hilal* 42:9 (July 1934): 1107–1108.
Times (London) (19 June 1934): 13g.
Walili, *Mafakhir al-ajyal*, 173–179.
Wright, *Twentieth Century Impressions of Egypt*, 108.
Zirikli, *al-A'lam*, VII, 204.

Haqqi, Yahya
(7 January 1905–9 December 1992)
Novelist, short-story writer, and critic. Born in Cairo's Sayyida Zaynab district, Haqqi earned his *license* from the government Law School in 1925 and held several legal posts. He entered Egypt's diplomatic corps in 1929, serving until 1952, and traveled widely in the Middle East and Europe. He was appointed director of the Arts Bureau in 1955 and three years later became arts adviser to Dar al-Kutub. He also edited *al-Majalla*, starting in 1962. His best-known novel, *Qandil ibn Hashim* [Ibn Hashim's Lamp], was published in 1944 (as a novella amid a collection of short stories) and later translated into many foreign languages. His other works include *Khalliha ila Allah* [Leave It to God] and *al-Bustanji* [The Gardener]. His autobiographical writings include *Kunasat al-dukkan* [Sweepings of the Store] on his early life and *Durus wa dhikrayat* [Lessons and Memories] on his first post in Jidda in 1929–1930. He won the King Faysal Prize for Literature in 1990.

Bibliographic Sources
Abdel Mooti, *Yahya Haqqi*.
al-Ahram Archives, file 449.

Allen, *Modern Arabic Literature*, 124–129.
al-'Arabi, no. 449 (Apr. 1996).
'Atiyya, Na'im, *Yahya Haqqi*.
Badawi, M.M., *Modern Arabic Literature*, 83–97.
Cooke, *Anatomy of an Egyptian Intellectual*.
EAL, I, 271–272.
Fuad, Ni'mat Ahmad, *Qimam adabiyya*, 327–388.
Hafez, Sabry, "Modern Arabic Short Story," in *CHAL*, 303–305.
Haqqi, Nuha, ed., *Rasail Yahya Haqqi ila ibnatihi*.
Haqqi, Yahya, *Khalliha ila Allah*.
———, *Qandil Umm Hashim ma'a sira dhatiyya*.
———, *The Saint's Lamp and Other Stories*.
———, *Un égyptien à Paris*.
———, *Yahya Haqqi*.
Husayn, Mustafa Ibrahim, *Yahya Haqqi*.
Ma'ati, *Wasiyyat sahib al-qandil*.
Naji, Najib, *al-Nuzu' ila al-'alimiyya*.
Radwan, Fathi, *Afkar al-kibar*, 95–119.
Sharuni, Yusuf, *Sab'un sham'a fi hayat Yahya Haqqi*.
'Uthman, 'Abd al-Fattah, *al-Uslub al-qisasi 'inda Yahya Haqqi*.
WWAW, 1993–1994, 269.

Harb, [Muhammad] Tal'at

(25 November 1867–21 August 1941)
Financier, founder of Bank Misr, and entrepreneur, often called the Father of Egypt's Economic Independence. Born in Cairo to a family that claimed tribal Arab origins, he graduated from the Khedivial Law School, worked for the State Domains Administration from 1888 to 1905, and became a financial manager for a few large landowners and the director of several companies. An ardent patriot and devout Muslim, he wrote books glorifying Islamic civilization, defending the veiling of women, and opposing the proposed extension of the Suez Canal Company concession. While arguing against that project, he called for the establishment of a purely Egyptian bank, a portent of his later efforts. Visiting Germany shortly before World War I, he was impressed by its banking system.

In April 1920 Harb and his associates established Bank Misr, which became a holding company for many other business enterprises spawned by his intelligence and efforts. He was remarkably open to new ideas; he created Misrair, now Egypt's national airline, and in 1937 he was making his business trips to Syria, Iraq, and the Hijaz by plane. Another of his innovations was Misr Studios, Egypt's first large cinema company, inaugurated in 1934. He pioneered in strengthening economic ties between Egypt and other Arab countries, making him an influential figure among early Arab nationalists. Nevertheless, Bank Misr suffered a liquidity crisis in 1939 and needed assistance from the Egyptian government to survive. Harb resigned from the presidency of Bank Misr and personally chose his successor, but some feel that he was the victim of a political conspiracy by AHMAD MAHIR and HUSAYN SIRRI. He died in Cairo.

Bibliographic Sources
Abaza, Fikri, in *al-Hilal* 45:4 (Feb. 1937): 367–372.
'Abduh, Ibrahim, *Tal'at Harb*.
'Abduh, Ibrahim, and 'Abd al-'Azim, *Tidhkar Muhammad Tal'at Harb*.
Abu Hadid, *'Isamiyyun*, 25–34.
Amin, Ahmad, *Fayd al-khatir*, III, 81–86.
Bishri, 'Abd al-'Aziz, *Fi al-mirat*, 95–100.
Cole, "Feminism, Class, and Islam," 387–407.
Daghir, *Masadir*, II, ii, 312–314.
Davis, *Challenging Colonialism*.
Deeb, "Bank Misr."
Falaki, *Batl al-istiqlal al-iqtisadi*.
Hasan, Ilhami, *Muhammad Tal'at Harb*.
Jawdat, "Tal'at Harb."
Jindi, Anwar, *A'lam wa ashab aqlam*, 203–211.
Kahhala, *Mu'jam*, V, 105–106.
Kamil, Rashid, *Tal'at Harb*.
al-Katib, no. 143 (Jan. 1973): 33–34.
Mahmud, Hafiz, *Asrar al-madi*.
MMIA 5:6 (June–July 1925): 329–331.
al-Muqtataf 72:1 (Jan. 1928): 85–89, interview with Tal'at Harb.
——— 87:6 (June 1935): 70–80.
——— 94:5 (May 1939): 538–541, interview with Tal'at Harb.
Muhammad Tal'at Harb.
Musa, Salama [S], "Sa'a ma'a Tal'at Harb Bey."
Muti'i, *Haula al-rijal min Misr*, I, 95–108.
———, *Mawsu'a*, 452–460.
Najib, *A'lam Misr*, 280–281.
Qadi, Shukri, *Khamsun shakhsiyya*, 48–52.
Rafi'i, 'Abd al-Rahman, in *al-Hilal* 57:1 (Jan. 1949): 38–39.
Radwan, Fathi, *Tal'at Harb*.
Rifa'i, Husayn 'Ali, *Bank Misr fi khamsat 'ashr 'aman*.
Rifa'i, Muhammad 'Ali, *Rijal wa mawaqif*: II, 157–243.
Sadoul, *Cinema*, 81–83.
Tignor, "Bank Misr and Foreign Capitalism."
———, "The Egyptian Revolution of 1919."
'Umar, Mahmud Fathi, *Abtal al-hurriyya*, 72–82.
Zirikli, *al-A'lam*, VI, 175–176.

Hasan, Dr. Salim

(15 April 1886–29 September 1961)
Egyptologist. Born in Mit Naji (in Mit Ghamr
district, Daqahliyya), Hasan was educated at
the Higher Teachers College, graduating in
1912 from AHMAD KAMAL's short-lived Egyptology Department. Unable to get a job at the
Egyptian Museum, he taught history and languages at the Nasiriyya (Cairo), Tanta, Asyut,
and Khedivial Secondary Schools until he was
hired as an assistant curator at the museum in
1921. He was sent on a government mission to
the Sorbonne from 1923 to 1927 and later
earned his Ph.D. in 1935 from Vienna. He was
invited to join the Cairo University faculty as
an assistant professor in 1928 and became the
first Egyptian professor of Egyptology in 1931
and later the assistant director of the Egyptian
Antiquities Administration. Hasan conducted
many excavations in Giza, studying the Sphinx
and its relationship to the second Giza Pyramid.
He led the movement to save the Nubian antiquities when the construction of the Aswan High
Dam was being planned and was deputized by
NASIR to visit the major museums of the world
containing Egyptian antiquities in 1959 so that
he could complete his research. His writings include *Hymnes religieux du Moyen Empire*
(1928), *Excavations at Giza*, 10 parts (1929–
1960), and *Tarikh Misr al-qadima*, 16 volumes
(1940–1962). In 1960 he sued the Ministry of
Culture and National Guidance for defamation
after he had conducted a complete inventory of
the museum, during which he determined that
FARUQ had stolen many antiquities. His Egyptian nationality and abrasive personality
combined to delay his advancement in Egypto-
logical circles longer than he—or his compatri-
ots—would have liked. He died in Cairo. He
was admitted posthumously to the International
Academy of Sciences—the first Arab scholar to
achieve that.

Bibliographic Sources
al-Ahram, 5 Nov. 1960, 30 Sept. 1961, 7 Oct. 1994.
al-Ahram Archives, file 984.
Dawson, *Egyptology,* 133–134.
Jindi, Anwar, *A'lam wa ashab aqlam*, 179–184.
al-Masa, 2 Nov. 1959, 3 Oct. 1961.
Mukhtar, "Salim Hasan."
New York Times (1 Oct. 1961): 86.
Reid, "Indigenous Egyptology," 240–241, 243.

————, "Nationalizing the Pharaonic Past," 141–
144.
Zirikli, *al-A'lam*, III, 117.

Hasanayn, Muhammad Ahmad

(31 October 1889–19 February 1946)
Arab explorer, sportsman, and close associate of
the Egyptian royal family. The son of Shaykh
Muhammad Hasanayn and the grandson of an
Egyptian admiral, Muhammad Ahmad was born
in Bulaq and educated in Cairo and at Oxford,
returning to Egypt in 1914, serving during World
War I as the Arabic secretary to General Sir John
Maxwell. He excelled in sports, especially fencing. An avid adventurer, he was sent by King
FUAD to explore Egypt's Western Desert from
the Mediterranean to Darfur, discovered several
hitherto unknown oases, and published a report
of his finds, *Fi Sahra Libya*, translated into English as *The Lost Oases* (1925), which later influenced the writing of *The English Patient*. The
Egyptian government called on him to negotiate
with Italy over its border with Libya in 1924, after which Fuad appointed him as a royal adviser.
Hasanayn's first wife was the daughter of Sayf
Allah Yusri and Princess Chivékiar, who had
previously been married to Fuad. He served
Fuad for fifteen years, at times chairing the
Royal Council, at others holding diplomatic
posts in Washington and London. Many believe
that after the king's death, Hasanayn secretly
married or had an affair with Queen Nazli,
Fuad's widow and the mother of FARUQ, over
whom Hasanayn exercised great influence during his early reign. Hasanayn's death in an automobile accident deprived the king of a capable
(if pro-British) mentor at a critical time in
Egypt's history.

Bibliographic Sources
al-Ahram, 31 May 1940; 20 Feb. 1946.
Fahmi, Zaki, *Safwat al-'asr*, 267.
Geographical Journal 107 (Jan. 1946): 77–78.
Hamamsi, *Hiwar wara al-aswar.*
Kahhala, *Mu'jam*, II, 93–94.
Mahallawi, *al-Malika Nazli*, 143–169.
McLeave, *Last Pharaoh*, 50–52.
al-Misri, 20 Feb. 1946.
Mujahid, *al-A'lam al-sharqiyya*, II, 853–854.
Musa, Salama [S], "Sa'a ma'a Ahmad Hasanayn
    Bey."
Muti'i, *Haula al-rijal min Misr*, III, 25–37.
————, *Mawsu'a*, 30–36.

Tabi'i, *Min asrar as-sasa.*
Times (London) (20 Feb. 1946): 4e-f, 7d; (21 Feb. 1946): 7e.
Warburg, "Lampson's Ultimatum to Faruq."
Yusuf, Hasan, *al-Qasr wa dawruhu fi al-siyasa.*
Zayyat, Ahmad Hasan, in *al-Risala* 8: 390 (23 Dec. 1940): 1843–1846.
Zirikli, *al-A'lam*, I, 252.

Hatim, Dr. Muhammad 'Abd al-Qadir

(3 September 1918–)
Information specialist, officer, and cabinet minister. Born in Alexandria, Hatim graduated from the Military Academy in 1939 and from the Staff College in 1952. He earned a B.A. in political economy at the London School of Economics (1947) and an M.A. in political science (1954) and a Ph.D. in information (1960) from Cairo University's Law Faculty. One of the Free Officers who staged the 1952 Revolution, he served in 1953 as NASIR's assistant for press relations and then became a general adviser. Elected to the National Assembly in 1957, Hatim became deputy minister for presidential affairs in 1959, minister of information, national guidance, and culture from 1962 to 1966, and became deputy prime minister in 1964. He left the government from 1966 to 1971 because he refused to work with the "Marxists" in the Arab Socialist Union during that time. He rejoined when SADAT ousted his rivals in 1971, again serving as deputy prime minister and information minister until 1974. He chaired the board of *al-Ahram* in 1974–1975 and also served as an adviser to Sadat and MUBARAK until 1996. He was the general overseer of the specialized national councils from 1974 until his retirement. He headed the Egyptian Political Science Society in 1952 and received an honorary doctorate from the University of Aix-en-Provence in 1986. He is the author of *Information and the Arab Cause* (1974), as well as books in English on life in ancient Egypt and about Islamic ethics. An amateur artist, Hatim has exhibited some of his paintings. He did much to develop the art of public information for the Arabs and is considered the father of television broadcasting in Egypt.

Bibliographic Sources
al-Ahram Archives, file 37.
Akhir sa'a, 24 July 1985.

Egypt, Ministry of Information, *al-Mawsu'a al-qawmiyya,* II, 1006.
Hatim, "Hadhihi qissatuna ma' al-shuyu'iyyin."
———, in *Mayu,* 26 July 1982.
———, in *al-Nasr* (July 1983): 24–25.
Mallakh, Kamal, in *al-Ahram al-iqtisadi,* 6 Jan. 1986.
Najib, *A'lam Misr,* 424–425.
Ruz al-Yusuf, 22 July 1985.
Shimoni, *BDME,* 100–101.
WWAW, 1997–1998, 302.

Haykal, Muhammad Hasanayn

(1923–)
Political journalist, writer, and editor. Originally from a Cairo middle-class family, he graduated from a public secondary school and attended classes at Cairo University and the American University in Cairo but did not graduate. Haykal began his journalistic career as an unpaid reporter for the *Egyptian Gazette* and *Ruz al-Yusuf,* covering the Battle of al-'Alamayn and Egypt's parliamentary debates. He then became a reporter for *Akhir Sa'a,* winning the King FARUQ prize for investigative journalism for his reports on the 1947 cholera epidemic. He covered the Palestine struggle from 1946 to 1949 for *Akhbar al-Yawm,* interviewing David Ben-Gurion and King 'Abdallah, and meeting Major JAMAL 'ABD AL-NASIR for the first time. Traveling widely, he also covered the Greek Civil War, the Iranian Musaddiq crisis, and the 1952 U.S. presidential campaign (supported at the time by a State Department Leader Grant). Haykal claimed an intimate involvement with the Free Officers, especially Nasir, at the time of the 1952 Revolution; whether or not this claim is true, Haykal certainly was closer to Nasir throughout his period in power than any other journalist. He edited *Akhir Sa'a* in the early 1950s and then *al-Akhbar,* of which he became editor-in-chief in 1956, but became estranged from the AMIN brothers. After numerous attempts by *al-Ahram* to lure him, he finally agreed to be its editor in 1957. He built up this paper into the most prestigious and influential one in Egypt and arguably the whole Arab world. Haykal also became adviser, confidant, and spokesman for Nasir and is widely credited with ghostwriting Nasir's *Falsafat al-thawra* [The Philosophy of the Revolution]. A firm believer in press freedom and scientific management, he made the physical facilities of *al-Ahram*

among the most modern anywhere in the world, and the newspaper spawned various influential periodicals, ranging from the Marxist *al-Tali'a* to the conservative *al-Ahram al-iqtisadi*. Haykal's weekly column, *Bi al-saraha* [Speaking Frankly], was read throughout the Arab world as an indicator of Nasir's thinking. Haykal served briefly in 1970 as Nasir's minister of information and national guidance.

A loyal Nasirist, he broke with SADAT because of the latter's growing ties with the United States and his inclination to make peace with Israel. In 1974 Haykal was dismissed as editor and chairman of *al-Ahram* and barred from publishing articles in the Egyptian press, although he continued to write in Arabic newspapers in Lebanon, as well as to publish books and articles written in English and directed at American readers. Among his publications of that era were *Nasser: The Cairo Documents* (1973) and *The Sphinx and the Commissar* (1978). He was interrogated by the Egyptian police and the state prosecutor in 1977–1978, forbidden to travel abroad, and imprisoned during Sadat's purge in September 1981. Under MUBARAK he has not regained his former influence on policy decisions or his editorial power, but is respected as an intellectual, writer, and journalist. Haykal wrote a scathing attack on Sadat, *Autumn of Fury* (1983); a memoir of the 1956 Suez War, *Twisting the Lion's Tail* (1986); and an exposé of contacts between various Arab leaders and Israel, *Secret Channels* (1996). He has been suggested as a possible mediator between Egypt and other Arab countries, such as Libya. His memoirs of the June War were published in 1990 as *1967: al-Infijar* [1967: The Explosion]. His memories of events in which he was an observer or participant are valuable but sometimes self-serving.

Bibliographic Sources
Egypt, Ministry of Information, *al-Mawsu'a al-qawmiyya*, II, 915.
Fuda, *Nujum Shari' al-Sihafa*, 19–25.
Najib, *A'lam Misr*, 406.
Nasir, *Press, Politics, and Power.*
Rizq, Fathi, *Khamsa wa sab'una najman*, 440–449.
Sheehan, "Most Powerful Journalist in the World," xi–xxxv.
———, "The Second Most Important Man in Egypt."
Stewart, "The Rise and Fall of Muhammad Haykal."
WWAW, 1997–1998, 278.

Haykal, Dr. Muhammad Husayn

(20 August 1888–8 December 1956)

Writer, politician, and lawyer. Muhammad Husayn was born in Kafr Ghannam, near Simbalawin (Daqahliyya), to a landowning family, educated at his village *kuttab*, Jamaliyya Elementary and Khedivial Secondary Schools in Cairo, the Khedivial Law School (1909), and the University of Paris (1912), where he wrote his doctoral dissertation in political economy on the Egyptian public debt. Homesick while he was living in Egypt, he also wrote a bucolic short novel called *Zaynab*, published anonymously in 1914 (since then it has been republished under his name many times, and an English translation came out in 1989). Upon returning to Egypt in 1913 he practiced law in Mansura, wrote for *al-Jarida*, published a magazine called *al-Sufur* during World War I, and taught at the Law School from 1917 to 1922. When the 1919 Revolution broke out, he backed the Wafd and SA'D ZAGHLUL but broke with them over the 'Adli-Curzon negotiations in 1921. At this time he, 'ADLI YAKAN, and some other educated Egyptians formed the Constitutional Liberal Party. In 1922 Haykal became editor of its newspaper, *al-Siyasa*, for which he later founded an influential weekly edition, *al-Siyasa al-usbu'iyya*. He kept up his literary production with a two-volume study of Jean-Jacques Rousseau, *Fi awqat al-faragh* [In Moments of Leisure], *Tarajim misriyya wa gharbiyya* [Egyptian and Western Biographies], and *Waladi*, a moving eulogy of a son who died in childhood. In 1934, at a time when the Constitutional Liberals were vying for popular favor with the Wafd, the Palace, and the rising Muslim groups, he published *Hayat Muhammad* [The Life of Muhammad], an attempt to apply modern scholarship to the biography of the Prophet and to reconcile the principles of personal freedom, which he had long espoused, with Islamic teachings. Increasingly pious, he made the *hajj* in 1936 and published *Fi manzal al-wahy* [In the Dwelling Place of Conscience], relating his experience as a pilgrim. Haykal went on to write biographies of many of the Prophet's companions in later years. He served as education minister in three cabinets during the late 1930s and 1940s, as president of the Constitutional Liberal Party from 1943 to 1952, and as speaker of the Senate from 1945 to 1950. Some of his educational reforms were to set up regional boards to promote decentralization, to integrate the parallel elementary and the primary school systems, to create a school for training women teachers of Arabic language and civilization, to permit women employees and teachers to marry, and to found industrial schools that combined academic and practical training. His prerevolutionary land-reform proposals were voted down, but he is credited with having sponsored the creation of the Faculties of Law and Letters at the University of Alexandria. He signed the Arab League Charter in 1945, headed Egypt's delegation to the United Nations in 1946, and chaired the Inter Parliamentary Union meeting in 1947. He published an additional novel, *Hakadha khuliqat* [Thus Was She Created], shortly before his death as well as his memoirs, *Mudhakkirat fi al-siyasa al-misriyya* [Memories of Egyptian Politics], of which two volumes appeared during his lifetime and one posthumously. He was elected to the Arabic Language Academy in 1940. An ambitious man with many talents, Haykal felt torn between secularism and Islam, freedom and authority, and his party's democratic principles and his belief that Egypt should be governed by its most educated citizens.

Bibliographic Sources

al-Ahram, 9 Dec. 1956.

al-Ahram Archives, file 222.

'Allam, *Majma'iyyun*, 269–270.

Allen, *Arabic Novel*, 31–35.

———, "The Beginnings of the Arabic Novel," in *CHAL*, 190–192.

———, *Modern Arabic Literature*, 140–146.

'Aqqad, 'Abbas Mahmud, in *Akhbar al-yawm*, 22 Dec. 1956.

Barakat, [Muhammad] Bahi al-Din, *Safahat min al-tarikh*, 185–189.

Brockelmann, *GAL*, S III, 202–211.

Brugman, *Introduction*, 234–243, 357–361.

Dayf, *al-Adab al-'arabi*, 270–276.

EAL, I, 278–279.

EI2, VII, 441–442, article by C. Vial.

Elad, *Village Novel.*

Gershoni, "Imagining the East."

Gibb, *Studies*, 291–296.

Haqqi, Yahya, *Fajr al-qissa al-misriyya.*

Haykal, Muhammad Husayn, *al-Adab wa al-hayat*, 5–26.

———, *Mudhakkirat fi al-siyasa al-misriyya.*

———, *Mudhakkirat al-shabab.*

Hijazi, Ahmad 'Abd al-Mu'ti, *Haykal wa haula.*

Hijazi, Anwar, *'Amaliqa*, 282–287.

Jindi, Anwar, *Adwa*, 88–89, 106–109, 120–123.

———, *al-Muhafaza wa al-tajdid*, 316–333.

———, *al-Sihafa al-siyasiyya*, 258–266.

Johansen, *Muhammad Husayn Haikal.*

Jundi, *A'lam al-adab*, II, 471–472.

Kahhala, *Mu'jam*, IX, 262–263.

Khadduri, *Arab Contemporaries*, 193–210.

Khafaji, *Suwar min al-adab*, 64–71.

Khemiri and Kampffmeyer, *Leaders*, 15, 20–22, 37.

Kilpatrick, Hilary, "Egyptian Novel," in *CHAL*, 223–226.

———, *Modern Egyptian Novel*, 20–26.

Kull shay wa al-dunya, no. 427 (10 Jan. 1934): 4–5.

Mahmud, Hafiz, "al-'Amaliqa al-sitta."

Makhzanji, *Nazra tahliliyya,*

Muhammad, Muhammad Sayyid, *Haykal wa "al-Siyasa al-Usbu'iyya."*

Muti'i, *Mawsu'a*, 504–512.

Najjar, *al-Duktur Haykal.*

New York Times (10 Dec. 1956): 31.

Pérès, "al-Manfaluti wa Haykal."

Radwan, Fathi, *'Asr wa rijal*, 465–598.

Ra'i, *Dirasat fi al-riwaya*, 23–53.

Ramadi, *Min a'lam al-adab*, 50–56.

Rizq, Fathi, *Khamsa wa sab'una najman*, 144–151.

Safran, *Egypt in Search*, 131–134, 169–175.

Sakkut, *Egyptian Novel,* 11–21.

Sayyid, Ahmad Lutfi, *al-Duktur Muhammad Husayn Haykal.*

Semah, *Four Egyptian Literary Critics*, 69–105.

Shamis, "Shakhsiyyat fi hayat Shawqi" (Sept. 1978).

Sharaf, 'Abd al-'Aziz, *Fann al-maqal al-suhufi.*

———, *Muhammad Husayn Haykal fi dhikrahi.*

———, *Muhammad Husayn Haykal wa al-fikr al-qawmi al-misri.*

Shiliq, *Hizb al-ahrar al-dusturiyyin.*

Smith, Charles D., "The 'Crisis of Orientation.'"

———, "*Hakadha khuliqat.*"

———, *Islam and the Search for Social Order.*

———, "Love, Passion, and Class."

Tawfiq, 'Awad, and Hasan Sabri, *Wuzara al-ta'lim*, 95–99.

Taymur, Mahmud, *al-Shakhsiyyat al-'ishrun*, 58–69.

al-Thaqafa 9:1 (Jan. 1982), special issue.

'Usfur and Nabil Faraj, *Muhammad Husayn Haykal.*

Wadi, *al-Duktur Muhammad Husayn Haykal.*

Wessels, *Modern Arabic Biography of Muhammad*, 35–48.

Yaghi, *Fi al-juhud al-riwaiyya.*

Zahlawi, *Udaba mu'asirun*, 114–122.

Zalat, Ahmad, *al-Duktur Muhammad Husayn Haykal.*

Zirikli, *al-A'lam*, VI, 107.

Hijazi, Shaykh Salama

(4 February 1852–4 October 1917)
Pioneer singer, actor, and stage director. Born in Alexandria's Ras al-Tin quarter to a sailor father and a bedouin mother, he was trained as a Quran reciter. He spent his mornings at the local *kuttab* and worked afternoons as a barber's apprentice. He later worked as a muezzin and a Quran reader, visiting many people's homes. Exposed to many of the great Arab singers of his time, he also witnessed performances by European theatrical troupes as a youth and came to know some Syrian actors. His contacts with great artists would serve him well. From 1885 to 1889 he worked with the theatrical troupe of al-Qardahi and Haddad, successfully playing the lead role in his musical play, *Mayy wa Horus* [Mayy and Horus]. In 1905 he organized his own troupe, in which he was a frequent actor and singer, at a theater that he founded in Cairo near the Ezbekiyya Gardens called *Dar al-Tamthil al-Arabi* (House of Arabic Acting), popularizing musical theater in Cairo. His troupe toured Syria and North Africa and helped to win respect for music and theater among Arabic-speaking Muslims. Among its members were JURJ ABYAD, NAJIB AL-RIHANI, and ZAKI TULAYMAT. He composed songs like *Fuadi, ya jamil, yahwak* [My Heart, O Beautiful One, Loves You]. Hijazi adapted *Hamlet*, *The Misers*, and *Crime and Punishment* for the Arabic stage. His dramatic and musical achievements are especially remarkable, given his lack of formal training. He died in Mansura.

Bibliographic Sources
'Ashur, Nu'man, *Butulat misriyya*, 179–199.
Bishri, 'Abd al-'Aziz, *al-Mukhtar*, II, 86–90.
Butrus, *A'lam al-musiqa*, 147–159.
Danielson, *Voice of Egypt*, 43–45.
Fadil, *Salama Hijazi*.
Fishawi, 'Abd al-Fattah, in *Sawt al-sharq* (Oct. 1953).
Hifni, Mahmud Ahmad, *al-Shaykh Salama Hijazi*.
al-Hilal 26:2 (Nov. 1917): 186–189.
Jundi, *A'lam al-adab*, II, 568–569.
Tulaymat, Zaki, in *al-Hilal* 63:1 (Jan. 1955): 180–187.
Yusuf, Niqula, *A'lam min al-Iskandariyya*, 424–430.
Zaki, 'Abd al-Hamid Tawfiq, *A'lam al-musiqa*, 125–131.
Zirikli, *al-A'lam*, III, 106–107.

al-Hilali, Ahmad Najib

(1 October 1891–11 December 1958)
Lawyer, teacher, cabinet minister, and twice premier. Born in Asyut to a wealthy family, Hilali was educated at the Tawfiqiyya School and was hoping to study medicine, but his father advised him to study at the Khedivial Law School, from which he graduated in 1912. He opened a law office and worked in the *Niyaba*, especially the royal cases section, where he became a chancellor in 1931. In 1923 he was appointed a professor in the government Law School. The next year he became secretary-general in the Ministry of Public Instruction and then served as royal adviser for education. He was MUHAMMAD TAWFIQ NASIM's education minister from November 1934 to January 1936 and later served on the committee that revised Egypt's commercial, civil, and corporate codes. He joined the Wafd Party in 1938 and held the education portfolio in MUSTAFA AL-NAHHAS's 1937–1938 and 1942–1944 cabinets, publishing *A Report on Educational Reform in Egypt* (1943), a big step toward free universal public education. His ministry established Egypt's first day-care center in 1942 and reduced the school-entering age from seven to five. It extended the school day for compulsory primary education and the length of the agricultural secondary school curriculum from three years to five, also adding a year to the girls' schools. The University of Alexandria (then called Faruq University) was opened while he was minister. Later estranged from the Wafdist leaders, Hilali attacked them for corruption and broke with the party in 1951. He headed independent cabinets for four months in 1952 after the Cairo fire and again on the day before the 1952 Revolution. His basic policy, while in power, was to clamp down on demonstrations and press freedom and to curb any Wafdist excesses. After the Revolution, he advised FARUQ to abdicate and resigned his own post. Imprisoned briefly by the Revolutionary Command Council in September 1952, Hilali was set free and resumed his legal practice. Although the RCC reportedly sought his advice on how to negotiate with the British, it publicly condemned him and barred him from politics. Devastated by his wife's death in 1958, he died in Ma'adi less than a month later, before his rights were restored and his reputation could be rehabilitated. He wrote books on contracts and the sale of

property. He was a mild-mannered, capable statesman.

Bibliographic Sources
al-Ahram, 12 Dec. 1958.
————, 17 Aug. 1951, interview of Hilali.
————, 23 Apr. 1952, interview with Dorothy Thompson.
al-Ahram Archives, file 218.
Current Biography (1952): 263–264.
Muti'i, *Mawsu'a*, 82–88.
New York Times (12 Dec. 1958): 14.
Qadi, Shukri, *Khamsun shakhsiyya*, 67–70.
Tawfiq, 'Awad, and Hasan Sabri, *Wuzara al-ta'lim*, 85–89.
Times (London) (13 Dec. 1958): 8; (15 Dec. 1958): 14.
al-Wafd, 27 Oct. 1988.
Zirikli, *al-A'lam*, I, 263.

al-Hilbawi, Ibrahim

(1858–20 December 1940)

Lawyer and politician. Born in Kafr al-Zayyat (Buhayra province) to a family of Maghribi origin, he attended al-Azhar but did not complete his studies there. He coedited *al-Waqai' al-Misriyya* with SA'D ZAGHLUL (but at a lower salary) in 1880; in later life, they were political rivals. Like Sa'd, Hilbawi backed 'URABI's movement and later was arrested but released, due to lack of evidence against him. He began working as a lawyer in 1893. He became an adviser to the personal *awqaf* and treasury of Khedive 'ABBAS. In 1906 he was the prosecuting attorney in the Dinshaway trial, for which many Egyptians never forgave him. He later tried to make amends by defending many of the Nationalists without charge. Best known as a trial attorney, Hilbawi was elected the first head of the Egyptian Lawyers' Syndicate in 1912. Initially a member of the Wafd's Central Committee, he became one of the founders of the Constitutional Liberal Party when it was formed in 1922. His memoirs have recently been published.

Bibliographic Sources
al-Ahram (21 Dec. 1940): 2; (23 Dec. 1940): 6.
'Aqqad, 'Abbas Mahmud, *Rijal 'araftuhum*, 181–190.
Bishri, 'Abd al-'Aziz, *Fi al-mirat*, 37–42.
Hilbawi, "Ahamm hadith fi majra hayati."
————, *Mudhakkirat Ibrahim Hilbawi*.
Jindi, 'Abd al-Halim, *Jaraim wa ightiyalat*.
Mujahid, *al-A'lam al-sharqiyya*, II, 427–429.

Najib, *A'lam Misr*, 82.
Reid, *Lawyers and Politics*, 41, 49, et passim.
al-Shabab 1:2 (2 Mar. 1936): 5, 9; 1:3 (9 Mar. 1936).

al-Hudaybi, Hasan

(December 1891–11 November 1973)

Successor to HASAN AL-BANNA as supreme guide of the Muslim Brothers. Hudaybi was born in a village near Shibin al-Qanatir to worker parents and began his education at its *kuttab*. Although his father wanted to send him to al-Azhar, Hasan chose a legal career, attended the Khedivial Secondary School, graduated from the government Law School in 1915, and served his apprenticeship in MUHAMMAD HAFIZ RAMADAN's office. He practiced law in Cairo and Suhaj, became a judge in 1924, and joined the Brothers in 1943. Following the assassination of Supreme Guide al-Banna, Hudaybi was named his successor in 1951, partly because he was not associated with terrorism or the secret branch within the society, and he accordingly resigned from the bench. He cultivated FARUQ as an ally against the Wafd. Arrested on Black Saturday, he was promptly released for lack of evidence that he or the society planned the burning of Cairo. He backed AHMAD NAJIB AL-HILALI's abortive reform efforts and then the Free Officers.

Although he welcomed the 1952 Revolution, when he rejected the officers' offer to admit three leading Brothers to the new cabinet, Hudaybi's relations with NASIR cooled. The creation of the Liberation Rally also antagonized Hudaybi, who feared that it would eclipse the society. His demand to end martial law and lift censorship angered Nasir, as did his secret meetings with the British Oriental secretary during the Suez Canal negotiations. Former Banna supporters within the society objected to Hudaybi's tendency to bypass its governing council. The Egyptian government dissolved the society in January 1954 and arrested many of its leaders, including Hudaybi, who went to jail for two months. After massive demonstrations supporting the nominal president, NAJIB, Nasir agreed in March 1954 to release Hudaybi, end martial law, lift censorship, and allow freedom of expression to all viewpoints; in fact Nasir was laying a trap to expose his opponents, who staged mass demonstrations. But Hudaybi backed Nasir's government, which soon suppressed all political movements except the Brothers. Because the government went on arresting officers associated with the society, especially its secret branch, Hudaybi wrote to Nasir, accusing the RCC of breaking promises. Ignoring Nasir's invitation to meet, he set out on a tour of eastern Arab countries. When Britain and Egypt announced their 1954 Agreement, Hudaybi publicly attacked it in a Beirut newspaper. Upon returning to Egypt, he went into hiding but sent Nasir another letter, proposing an open debate on their differences. The government instead increased its campaign against the society. Its secret branch survived— but outside Hudaybi's control—and plotted to kill Nasir. When the attempt failed, the plotters were arrested, as were thousands of Brothers, including Hudaybi. He was tried and given a death sentence, which was later commuted to penal servitude because of his age. He was released in 1961 but tried again (for taking money from abroad and for trying to revive the secret branch) and was imprisoned from 1965 to 1971. His *Sab'at asila fi al-'aqida wa al-radd 'alayha: takhatti al-su'ubat wa al-'aqabat* [Seven Questions and Answers About Doctrine: Surmounting Difficulties and Obstacles] was published five years after his death. Cautious and conservative, he could not moderate the society's emotionalism and violence.

Bibliographic Sources
al-Ahram Archives, file 15025.
Mitchell, *Muslim Brothers*, 86–87.
Najib, *A'lam Misr*, 182–183.
al-Nur, 10 June 1997.
al-Wafd, 17 Jan. 1985, 19 July 1993, 12 Dec. 1994.

Husayn, Ahmad
(8 March 1911–26 September 1982)
Leader of Misr al-Fatat. Born in the Jamaliyya section of Cairo, he graduated from the Khedivial Secondary School and from the Cairo University Law Faculty in 1933, then worked as a lawyer and journalist, writing for *al-Siyasa*. He and Fathi Radwan founded Misr al-Fatat (Young Egypt) in August 1933 in the belief that the existing political parties had forsaken their patriotic ideals. They also inaugurated the "Piastre Plan," inviting all Egyptians to invest one piastre (then worth U.S. five cents) in locally owned and managed manufacturing firms. He became a

strong and charismatic leader, especially of Egyptian Muslim youth, and was thought to enjoy King FARUQ's support against the Wafd Party. He was an implacable foe of the Muslim Brothers, whom he called *al-Ikhwan al-mujrimin* (the Criminal Brothers). Accused of insulting the monarchy, he was arrested several times and was imprisoned in January 1952 on suspicion of having incited the burning of Cairo, but was released on the day after the Revolution. His disciples included NASIR and SADAT, who later put many of his ideas into practice, but he held no post in their governments. Instead Husayn went into exile for a few years, then returned to Egypt, and devoted his time to writing books, including a 1,500-page dictionary of Egypt's history. He became totally paralyzed in 1969 and died in relative obscurity. His memoirs have appeared in *al-Sha'b* in June–September 1981, July–December 1994, and August 1997, continuing to the present. He is generally viewed as an ultranationalist with no fixed principles.

Bibliographic Sources
al-Ahram Archives, file 920.
Gershoni and Jankowski, *Redefining the Egyptian Nation*, 98–108.
Husayn, 'Adil, in *al-Sha'b*, 15 Mar. 1988.
Husayn, Ahmad, *Imani*.
———, *Mawsu'at tarikh Misr*.
Jankowski, *Egypt's Young Rebels*, passim.
Muti'i, *Mawsu'a*, 37–43.
———, in *al-Akhbar*, 29 Oct. 1979.
Najib, *A'lam Misr*, 89–90.
New York Times (27 Sept. 1982): D9.
Qadi, Shukri, *Khamsun shakhsiyya*, 111–114.
Sa'id, Rif'at, *Ahmad Husayn*.
al-Sha'b, 27 Sept. 1982.
al-Tali'a 1:3 (Mar. 1965): 155–162.
Vatikiotis, *Nasser and His Generation*, 67–84.

Husayn, Dr. Ahmad
(1902–29 November 1984)
Pioneer rural sociologist and Egyptian ambassador to Washington. Ahmad Husayn was born in Helwan and pursued his higher education in Germany, receiving his doctorate in agricultural economics from the University of Berlin. He began his official life as an Egyptian government inspector in 1928 and organized the first comprehensive rural health centers. He served as minister of social affairs in the 1950 Wafdist cabinet, even though he was not a party mem-

ber, but later refused to hold the same portfolio under AHMAD NAJIB AL-HILALI. He inaugurated *Maslahat al-Fallah* (Peasants' Welfare Society) in 1952 and played a major role in setting up Egypt's rural social centers. NASIR appointed him Egypt's ambassador to the United States in 1953, a post that he accepted on the condition that he have direct contact with the president. His efforts to bring the two countries together were stymied by U.S. reluctance to commit large sums for economic aid to Egypt and by Egypt's growing suspicion of Washington's interference. It was he whom Dulles rebuffed by withdrawing the U.S. offer to finance the Aswan High Dam project in July 1956. His sudden dismissal by Nasir in May 1958 humiliated him, and he returned to private life. Later, he wrote a number of reports for the United Nations about rural development and received official decorations from the Egyptian and the French governments.

Bibliographic Sources
al-Ahram Archives, file 586.
al-Akhbar, 30 Nov. 1984.
Alterman, "American Aid to Egypt in the 1950s."
Najib, *A'lam Misr*, 90.

Husayn, 'Aziza Shukri
(30 May 1919–)
Social welfare expert and leading advocate of family planning. Born in Zifta to an Egyptian father (a surgeon) and a Turkish mother, she attended the Mère de Dieu College for Girls in Cairo and graduated in 1942 from the American University in Cairo with a degree in social sciences. She became active in the feminist movement and in volunteer efforts to develop rural Egypt. In 1947 she married Dr. AHMAD HUSAYN, who shared many of her interests. In 1952 she initiated a project to teach handicrafts to women of a Gharbiyya village called Sandyun. She later worked for the Arab League to promote general rural development. She lectured at the University of Chicago and other American universities on the Egyptian women's movement, especially while her husband was ambassador, and became involved in women's issues at the United Nations as early as 1954. In 1962 she became the first woman to represent Egypt at the UN and served on its Status of Women Commission for

fifteen years. A member of the Supreme Council for Population and Family Planning in Cairo, Husayn founded the local Family Planning Association in 1967. In 1977 she became president of the International Union for Family Planning and concurrently turned down an offer to join the cabinet as minister of social affairs. She publicly condemned female genital mutilation in 1979. She mobilized more than two hundred Egyptian nongovernmental organizations to host the International Conference on Population and Development, held in Cairo in 1994. She has received decorations from the Egyptian government, the Food and Agricultural Organization, and the Maharishi Foundation and honorary degrees from the University of Maine and the American University in Cairo.

Bibliographic Sources
al-Ahram Archives, file 5432.
al-Ahram Weekly, 8 July 1993.
al-Anba, 25 Aug.–6 Sept. 1996.
Network of Egyptian Professional Women, *Egyptian Women in Social Development*, 135–138.
Sabah al-khayr, 6 Mar. 1996.
WWAW, 1997–1998, 314–315.

Husayn, Kamal al-Din
(June 1920–19 June 1999)
Free Officer, cabinet minister, and premier. Born in Kafr al-Manaqir, Banha, Husayn graduated from the Military Academy in 1939, and then from the Staff College. He taught there before the 1952 Revolution. One of the Free Officers, he served on the Revolutionary Command Council. After supervising the National Guard, he became minister of social affairs in January 1954 and education minister in June 1956. He headed the Liberation Army in Port Sa'id during the Suez War. He tried to resign his ministerial position in December 1957 over a university withdrawal policy that he felt was too permissive, but NASIR would not let him. Numerous educational reforms were instituted at all levels during his ministry. He was named head of the Supreme Council for the Arts, Letters, and Social Sciences in 1958 and of the National Union's Egyptian branch in 1959. He became minister of local administration in 1961 and, after Syria's withdrawal from the UAR, also vice president for social services and minister of local administration and housing. After serving in

May 1962 as secretary-general for the National Congress of Popular Forces and then as a member of the ASU executive, he left politics in 1963, mainly because the nationalization of property was affecting his family's interests. He and other retired Free Officers offered Nasir their services just before the June 1967 War. Under house arrest for opposing Nasir's policies during the late 1960s, Husayn was released by SADAT in 1970. He was elected to the People's Assembly but was later expelled after he publicly accused Sadat of "punishing the Egyptian people." He died of liver cancer.

Bibliographic Sources
al-Ahram Archives, file 9.
al-'Arabi, 7 July 1997.
Hamrush, *Thawrat Yulyu*, IV, 145, 238, 342–347.
Najib, A'lam Misr, 379.
New York Times, 22 June 1999.
al-Sharq al-awsat, 23–24 Feb. 1982.
al-Siyasa, 8 Jan. 1982.
Tawfiq, 'Awad, and Hasan Sabri, *Wuzara al-ta'lim,* 142–160.

Husayn, Dr. Taha
(14 November 1889–28 October 1973)
Writer, educational administrator, and minister, often called the Dean of Arabic Letters and *Qahir al-Zalam* (Conqueror of Darkness). Born in 'Izbat al-Kilu, near Maghagha (Minya) and blind from age two, he attended a *kuttab* and had memorized the Quran by the time he was nine. Entering al-Azhar in 1902, he came under the influence of MUHAMMAD 'ABDUH and his circle of modernists. He began writing for *al-Jarida* and became a protégé of LUTFI AL-SAYYID, who later aided his academic career; he also wrote for *al-Liwa*, where JAWISH urged him to reject the ulama's conservatism and to seek education abroad. When al-Azhar denied Taha an *'al-imiyya* (an Islamic scholar's degree), he began attending lectures at the Egyptian University and in 1914 was the first student to earn a Ph.D. there. He went to France in 1915 and earned a *doctorat d'état* at the Sorbonne in 1919 for his thesis, *La philosophie sociale d'Ibn Khaldoun*. He also earned the *diplôme supérieur* in ancient history, Greek, and Latin at the Sorbonne. He married his reader, Suzanne, whom he had met while visiting Montpellier.

After returning to Egypt in 1919 Taha became a lecturer in classics and ancient history at the Egyptian University and in 1925, upon its reorganization as Cairo University, was given the chair of Arabic literature. The next year he published a book, *Fi al-shi'r al-jahili* [On Pre-Islamic Poetry], questioning the authenticity of pre-Islamic Arabic poetry and of some of the Quran's narrative chapters, arousing protests at al-Azhar and in Parliament. He withdrew his book, replacing it in 1927 with a revised version, *Fi al-adab al-jahili* [On Pre-Islamic Literature]. Dean of the Arts Faculty at Cairo University (1929–1932), he was dismissed for political reasons by ISMA'IL SIDQI's education minister. Having previously backed the Constitutional Liberals, he then joined the Wafd and became an editor of its newspaper, *Kawkab al-Sharq*, until the Wafd's return to power, when he again became dean (1936–1938).

In 1938 Husayn published his well-known *Mustaqbil al-thaqafa fi Misr*, later translated into English as *The Future of Education in Egypt*, arguing that Egypt was more a Mediterranean country than an Arab or Islamic one and that it should adopt the West's thought patterns in order to share in its civilization. He served as a technical adviser to the Wafdist education minister in 1942 and as rector of Cairo University. Admitted to the Arabic Language Academy in 1940, he became its president in 1963. Husayn was editor of *al-Katib al-misri* in 1946–1948. He was named president of Faruq (Alexandria) University in 1944 and education minister from 1950 to 1952. His ministry implemented a parliamentary mandate making education free and compulsory from age six to twelve, leading to dramatic enrollment increases, especially at the kindergarten and elementary levels. He received the first state prize for literature in 1952. He abstained from politics after the 1952 Revolution, except for a short stint as editor of *al-Jumhuriyya*, but continued to publish books and articles that were widely read throughout the Arab world, including memoirs, three volumes of which have been translated as *An Egyptian Childhood* (1932, reprinted 1990), *The Stream of Days* (1943, revised 1948), and *A Passage to France* (1976). A strong westernizer, Taha Husayn wielded influence more through his personality than through the ideas he espoused, many of which are now under counterattack by

Islamists in Egypt and elsewhere. Villa Ramtan, his home near the Pyramids, has been turned into a museum.

Bibliographic Sources

Abaza, Tharwat, "'Amid al-adab wa jiluhu."
———, *Shu'a' min Taha Husayn.*
'Abd al-Fattah, Muhammad, *Ashhar mashahir,* 66–80.
'Abd al-Ghani, Mustafa, *Taha Husayn wa al-siyasa.*
'Abd al-Hayy, *'Asir hayati,* 83–89.
'Abd al-Sabbur, *Madha yabqa minhum,* 3–32.
Abu al-Hasan, *Taha Husayn wa dimuqratiyat al-ta'lim.*
Ahmad, Muhammad Khalaf Allah, *Taha Husayn wa Mahmud Taymur.*
al-Ahram Archives, file 120.
al-Ahram Weekly, 5 Dec. 1991.
'Allam, *Majma'iyyun,* 129–134.
Allen, *Modern Arabic Literature,* 146–153.
'Alusi, *Taha Husayn bayn ansarihi wa khusumihi.*
'Awad, Louis, *al-Hurriyya wa naqd al-hurriyya,* 5–44.
'Awad, Yusuf, *al-Ru'ya al-hadariyya.*
Badawi, 'Abd al-Rahman, *Ila Taha Husayn.*
———, *Taha Husayn.*
Badawi, M.M., *Modern Arabic Literature,* 172–190.
Berque, "L'Islam vu par Taha Husayn."
"Bibliography of Taha Husayn."
Brockelmann, *GAL,* S III, 284–302.
Brugman, *Introduction,* 273–277.
Buqtur, "Sadiqi Taha Husayn."
Busool, "Development of Taha Husayn's Islamic Thought."
Cachia, *Taha Husayn.*
Current Biography (1953): 290–292; (1973): 455.
Dayf, *al-Adab al-'arabi,* 277–287.
EAL, I, 296–297.
Eban, "The Modern Literary Movement in Egypt."
Egypt, Niyabat Misr, *Muhakamat Taha Husayn.*
Francis, *Aspects de la littérature arabe,* 11–101.
———, *Taha Hussein romancier.*
Fuad, Ni'mat Ahmad, *Qimam adabiyya,* 109–174.
Ghamrawi, *al-Naqd al-tahlili.*
Gibb, *Studies,* 276–279.
Hafiz, Ahmad, *Ayyam min shababihim,* 15–23.
Hanna, Suhail ibn-Salim, "L'autobiographie," 59–72.
al-Hayat, 1 Nov. 1973.
al-Hilal 74:2 (Feb. 1966), special issue.
Hourani, *Arabic Thought,* 324–340.
Husayn, Suzan Taha, *Ma'ak.*
Husayn, Taha, *al-Ayyam.*
———, "Zawjati."
Ibrahim, Ibrahim I., "Taha Husayn."
Jad, *Form and Technique,* 108–110, 123–124.
Jayyusi, *Trends,* I, 146–152.

Jeffery, "Three Cairo Modernists."
Jindi, Anwar, *al-Sihafa al-siyasiyya,* 401–411.
———, *Taha Husayn.*
Karim, Samih, *Madha yabqa min Taha Husayn.*
———, *Taha Husayn fi ma'arikihi al-adabiyya wa al-fikriyya.*
Kayyali, *Ma'a Taha Husayn.*
Khemiri and Kampffmeyer, *Leaders,* 34–37.
Khoury, R.G., "Taha Husayn (1889–1973) et la France."
Kilani, Sayyid, *Taha Husayn.*
Kilpatrick, *Modern Egyptian Novel,* 35–41.
Louca, "Taha Hussein and the West."
Mahran, *Taha Husayn.*
Majallat Jam'iyyat al-Shubban al-Muslimin (Apr. 1932), special issue.
Mallakh, *Qahir al-zalam.*
Malti-Douglas, *Blindness and Autobiography.*
Maqalih, *'Amaliqa.*
Mubarak, Zaki, "'Aduwi Taha Husayn."
Mughith, *Taha Husayn.*
Muhammad, Ahmad al-Sawi, in *al-Hilal* 36 (1928): 1181–1183.
Muhammad, Muhammad 'Awad, in *al-Hilal* 47:2 (Dec. 1938): 128–133.
Musa, Salama [S], "Sa'a ma'a al-Duktur Taha Husayn."
———, in *al-Hilal* 32 (1924): 516–520.
al-Musawwar (20 Oct. 1989): 14–16.
Muti'i, *Haula al-rijal min al-Azhar,* 131–150.
———, *Mawsu'a,* 220–227.
Nallino, "Notizie biobibliografiche."
Nasr, Muhammad, *Safahat min hayatihim,* 115–125.
Nassar, Husayn, *Dirasat hawl Taha Husayn.*
Nawfal, Yusuf Hasan, "Taha Husayn sha'iran."
New York Times (29 Oct. 1973): 38.
OEMIW, II, 148–149, article by Fedwa Malti-Douglas.
Qalamawi, *Dhikra Taha Husayn.*
Qultah, *Taha Husayn.*
Radwan, Fathi, *Afkar al-kibar,* 7–72.
Ramadi, Muhammad Jamal al-Din, in *al-Hilal* 59:10 (Oct. 1951): 45–49.
———, *Min a'lam al-adab,* 3–14.
Rejwan, "Taha Hussein, 1889–1973."
Rooke, *In My Childhood,* 85–89 et passim.
Sa'b, *Shakhsiyyat 'araftuha,* 37–44.
Safran, *Egypt in Search,* 129–131, 153–157, 166–169, 175–179.
Sakkut, *Egyptian Novel,* 31–36, 85–97.
Sakkut and Jones, *A'lam al-adab al-mu'asir fi Misr.*
Schoonover, "Taha Husayn."
Semah, *Four Egyptian Literary Critics,* 109–150.
Shalash, *Taha Husayn.*
Sharaf, 'Abd al-'Aziz, *Taha Husayn.*
Shukri, Ghali, *Madha yabqa min Taha Husayn.*
al-Siyasa, 10–14 June 1991.
Taha, M., "Taha Husayn."

Tahar, *Taha Hussein.*
Taqi al-Din, *Taha Husayn.*
Tawfiq, 'Awad, and Hasan Sabri, *Wuzara al-ta'lim*, 115–124.
Taymur, Mahmud, *al-Shakhsiyyat al-'ishrun*, 14–22.
al-Thaqafa (Nov. 1974), special issue.
Times (London) (29 Oct. 1973): 17f.
Tomiche, "Taha Hussein."
'Umar, Najah, *Taha Husayn*
'Usfur, *al-Maraya al-mutajawira.*
'Uthman, Ahmad, "Fi dhikra al-rabi'a."
Zahlawi, *Udaba mu'asirun*, 122–129.
Zayyat, Muhammad Hasan, *Ma ba'da "al-Ayyam."*
el-Zayyat, "Taha Hussein and the Arab World."
Zirikli, *al-A'lam*, III, 231–232.
Zuhayri, "Mudhakkirat 'an Taha Husayn."

Husayn Kamil

(21 November 1853–9 October 1917)
Sultan of Egypt from 1914 until his death. Born and educated in Cairo, he was the son of ISMA'IL and hence a younger brother of Khedive TAWFIQ. He completed his studies in Paris. As Isma'il's public works director, he ordered the construction of the railroad from central Cairo to Helwan and opened the first state school for girls at al-Suyufiyya. When Isma'il was exiled in 1879, Husayn Kamil accompanied him for three years, then returned to Egypt and supervised the farming of his own lands, also serving on the boards of several Egyptian and foreign companies. He organized the first agricultural fair and inaugurated a flower show in the Ezbekiyya Gardens in 1896. One of the leaders of the Islamic Benevolent Society, he was sympathetic to Egypt's peasants and hostile to the National Party. He chaired the Legislative Council in 1909–1910, resigning after the General Assembly rejected the Suez Canal Company concession extension. On 19 December 1914, when 'ABBAS HILMI II was deposed and Egypt was severed from the Ottoman Empire, the British named Husayn Kamil the first "sultan" of Egypt. Two attempts were made on his life during his reign, but he died in Cairo from natural causes. The British protectorate and wartime conditions kept him from using his managerial abilities.

Bibliographic Sources
Antaki, *al-Nujum*, 16–18.
Asaf, *Dalil*, 167–170.
Burke's Royal Families, II, 35–36.
Durri [al-Hakim], *al-Nukhba al-durriyya*, 32–35.
EI2, III, 624–625, article by P.J. Vatikiotis.
Fahmi, Zaki, *Safwat al-'asr*, 17–23.
Fuad, Faraj Sulayman, *al-Kanz al-thamin*, 9–25.
al-Hilal 23:4 (Jan. 1915): 268–272.
———— 26:2 (Nov. 1917): 148–150.
Kilani, Muhammad Sayyid, *al-Sultan Husayn Kamil.*
Mujahid, *al-A'lam al-sharqiyya*, I, 23–24.
New York Times (10 Oct. 1917): 4.
Qadi, Shukri, *Khamsun shakhsiyya*, 27–30.
Tanahi, Tahir, *'Ala firash al-mawt*, 46–49.
Tawfiq, 'Awad, and Hasan Sabri, *Wuzara al-ta'lim*, 34–35.
Times (London) (10 Oct. 1917): 5, 7.
Zakhura, *Mirat al-'asr*, I, 42–45; II, 9–16.
Zirikli, *al-A'lam*, II, 252.

I

Ibrahim

(1789–20 November 1848)

General, governor of Syria, and acting viceroy of Egypt. The presumed eldest son of MUHAM-MAD 'ALI, Ibrahim was born near Qavalla (Macedonia) and first came to Egypt in 1805 with his brother Tusun. Ibrahim was sent by Muhammad 'Ali on the campaign to the Hijaz and Najd in 1813 and took command of the Sudan expedition in 1821 and the Egyptian forces opposing the Greek struggle for independence in 1824. In 1831 he led the Syrian campaign, taking Acre, Damascus, Homs, and Aleppo. The Ottomans sent an expeditionary force against him, but Ibrahim defeated it at Alexandretta and invaded Anatolia. When his forces crossed the Taurus Mountains and threatened to take Istanbul, the European powers threatened to intervene to protect the sultan, so Ibrahim signed the Convention of Kütahya, giving Egypt suzerainty over Syria. Ibrahim became governor of the new province, situated his capital at Antioch, and introduced many of his father's reforms. Another Ottoman effort to dislodge him from Syria failed in 1838. Abdulmejid, after he became sultan in 1839, made an alliance with the British to expel Ibrahim's forces from Syria. Ibrahim was defeated and obliged to return to Egypt in 1840, but Muhammad 'Ali was permitted under the Convention of London to pass control of Egypt down to his heirs. He did so in 1848, naming Ibrahim governor with the Ottoman government's concurrence. Ibrahim went to Istanbul to receive his decree of investiture, became ill, and died shortly after his return to Cairo. He is popularly thought to have espoused Arab nationalist ideals during his governorship of Syria, thus stressing its ties with Egypt. His ties with Muhammad 'Ali were clouded by the latter's suspicion that he was not truly Ibrahim's father. Nevertheless, Ibrahim was an able commander and governor.

Bibliographic Sources
Abu 'Izz al-Din, *Ibrahim Basha fi Suriya*.
'Aqqad, 'Abbas Mahmud, in *al-Hilal* 56:11 (Nov. 1948): 8–20.
Asaf, *Dalil*, I, 147–150.
Burke's Royal Families, II, 30–32.
CHE 1 (1948), special issue.
Crabites, *Ibrahim of Egypt*.
Durri [al-Hakim], *al-Nukhba al-durriyya,* 16–17.
EI2, III, 999–1000, article by Paul Kahle and P.M. Holt.
EMME, II, 843–844, article by Ali E.H. Dessouki.
Fahmi, Zaki, *Safwat al-'asr*, 39–40.
al-Hilal 8:17–18 (15 June 1900): 513–519.
——— 56:11 (Nov. 1948), special issue.
al-Kitab 6 (Nov. 1948), special issue.
Mardam, *A'lam al-qarn al-thalith 'ashr*, 120–121.
Nubar, *Mémoires*, 17–56.
Rafi'i, 'Abd al-Rahman, in *al-Hilal* 55:3 (Mar. 1947): 8–13.
———, *'Asr Muhammad 'Ali*, 153–162, 245–361.
Rustum, *Disturbances in Palestine, 1834*.
———, *Hurub Ibrahim Pasha*.
———, *Egyptian Expedition to Syria 1831–1841*.
Sayyid-Marsot, *Egypt in the Reign*, 81–85 et passim.
Tugay, *Three Centuries*, 91–97.
Walili, *Mafakhir al-ajyal*, 22.
Zakhura, *Mirat al-'asr*, I, 25–28.
Zaki, 'Abd al-Rahman, *A'lam al-jaysh*, I, 17–33.
———, in *al-Hilal* 46:4 (Feb. 1938): 411–412; and 56:11 (Nov. 1948): 85–89.
———, *Ibrahim Pasha*.
Zaydan, Jurji, *Mashahir al-sharq*, 1st ed., I, 29–30.
Zirikli, *al-A'lam*, I, 70.

Ibrahim, Dr. 'Ali

(1880–28 January 1947)

Surgeon, cabinet minister, artist, and musician. Ibrahim's family originated in Fuwwa, but he was born in Alexandria. He was educated at the Medical School in Cairo, where his mentors were Drs. 'UTHMAN GHALIB and Muhammad al-Durri, a leading surgeon; Ibrahim earned his doctorate in 1901. He backed the 1919 Revolution and the "Piastre Project" for manufacturing tarbushes and spinning wool in Egypt. Head of the Egyptian Medical Society, he became the first Egyptian dean of the Faculty of Medicine at

Cairo University in 1929, later becoming its rector from 1941 to 1946. He also served as minister of health. Ibrahim was given the Mejidi medal by the Ottoman government in 1905 and was knighted by King George VI in 1939. He published numerous medical books and articles in Egypt's medical journal. His hobbies included music and photography. He also collected ceramics and carpets and wrote research articles about them. Maintaining close ties with writers and poets, including AHMAD SHAWQI, Ibrahim became in 1944 the first physician to enter the Arabic Language Academy. He died in Cairo.

Bibliographic Sources
Abu Hadid, *'Isamiyyun*, 58–59, entry by Dr. Sa'id 'Abduh.
al-Ahram (29 Jan. 1947): 6.
'Allam, *Majma'iyyun*, 197–198.
Bishri, 'Abd al-'Aziz, *Fi al-mirat*, 55–62.
Egyptian Medical Society, "Takrim 'Ali Pasha Ibrahim."
Jindi, Anwar, *A'lam wa ashab aqlam*, 285–291.
al-Kitab 3:5 (Mar. 1947): 673–674, obituary.
al-Katib al-Misri 5:18 (Mar. 1947): 337–339.
Madkur, Ibrahim, in *al-Hilal* 81:3 (March 1973): 22–31.
Najib, *A'lam Misr*, 335–336.
Shamis, *'Uzama*, 153–161.
Yusuf, Niqula, *A'lam min al-Iskandariyya*, 256–261.
Zirikli, *al-A'lam*, IV, 252–253.

Ibrahim, [Muhammad] Hafiz

(4 February 1871–12 July 1932)
Egyptian nationalist poet, often called *Sha'ir al-Nil* (Poet of the Nile). Hafiz was born on a river houseboat near Dayrut; when he was four, his father died. His mother brought him to Cairo, where he received his elementary education. He attended secondary school in Tanta, where his mother's brother lived. While still a boy, he wrote poetry, influenced by classical poets and by BARUDI. Hafiz began practicing law, without formal training, with some lawyers in Tanta and Cairo, and then entered the Military Academy, graduating in 1891 with a commission in the artillery. He served under KITCHENER in the Sudan campaign, spending time in Suwakin and Khartum, where he formed a secret nationalist society with some fellow officers. Apprehended by the British, he was court-martialed and transferred to the reserves. Hafiz then sought MUHAMMAD

'ABDUH's protection and took a police post at a monthly salary of £E 4 until he was pensioned off. He became an editor of *al-Ahram*, winning fame for his poetry and prose, inspired by MUSTAFA KAMIL. He was appointed head of the literary section of Dar al-Kutub in 1911, remaining there until shortly before his death, which occurred in Cairo.

The poetry of Hafiz, neoclassical in style, expressed popular feelings and humor in terms that ordinary people could understand. He often recited his poetry publicly to large groups of listeners and freely contributed his verses to the Egyptian press. Often his verse addressed social problems or political events, thus affirming his support for Egyptian national aspirations. Especially famous are his attacks on the British for the Dinshaway Incident and for quelling the women's demonstration during the 1919 Revolution. In addition to his two-volume *diwan* (not published until after his death, at the expense of the Education Ministry), he translated Victor Hugo's *Les Misérables* and a book on political economy from French into Arabic. Hafiz was closer to the people than his famous rival SHAWQI, but the two were reconciled before they died and are now equally revered throughout the Arab world.

Bibliographic Sources
Abu Hadid, *'Isamiyun*, 89–98.
Abu Shadi, "Muhammad Hafiz Ibrahim."
'Ali, Muhammad Kurd, "Hayat Hafiz Ibrahim."
Amin, Ahmad, introduction to Dar al-Kutub ed. of *Diwan Hafiz Ibrahim*.
Apollo (July 1933), special issue.
'Aqqad, 'Abbas Mahmud, *Shu'ara Misr*, 8–20.
Arberry, A.J., "Hafiz Ibrahim and Shawqi."
Badawi, M.M., *Critical Introduction*.
Bishri, 'Abd al-'Aziz, *Fi al-mirat*, 113–122.
Brockelmann, *GAL*, S III, 57–71.
Brugman, *Introduction*, 45–51.
Dahhan, *Sha'ir al-sha'b*.
Dayf, *al-Adab al-'arabi* (1957), 82–85; (1961), 100–109.
EAL, I, 386.
Egypt, Supreme Council for the Preservation of Arts and Letters, *Dhikra Hafiz Ibrahim*.
EI2, III, 59, article by Umberto Rizzitano.
EMME, II, 841–842, article by Kenneth S. Mayers.
Fahmi, Zaki, *Safwat al-'asr*, 643–646.
Ghannam, *Hafiz Ibrahim*.
Hamuda, 'Abd al-Wahhab, *al-Tajdid fi al-adab*, 103–119.
Hasan, Muhammad 'Abd al-Ghani, *A'lam min al-sharq wa al-gharb*, 108–112.

Haykal, Muhammad Husayn, *al-Adab wa al-hayat.*
al-Hilal 40:10 (Aug. 1932): 1390–1391.
——— 76:11 (Nov. 1968), special issue on Hafiz, Shawqi, and Mutran.
Hindawi, *Hafiz Ibrahim sha'ir al-Nil.*
Hittah, Muhammad Kamil, introduction to *Layali satih,* by Muhammad Hafiz Ibrahim.
Husayn, Taha, *Hafiz wa Shawqi.*
Ibrahim, 'Abd al-Fattah, *Shu'arauna al-dubbat,* 53–95.
Ibrahim, Muhammad Hafiz, *Diwan Hafiz Ibrahim.*
———, *Layali satih.*
Jawdat, *Balabil* (1960), 139–155; (1972), 166–177.
Jayyar, *Ma'rakat al-Mazini wa Hafiz.*
Jayyusi, *Trends,* I, 51–54.
Jindi, 'Abd al-Hamid Sanad, *Hafiz Ibrahim.*
Jum'a, Muhammad Kamil, *Hafiz Ibrahim.*
Jundi, *A'lam al-adab,* II, 463–464.
Kahhala, *Mu'jam,* IX, 168–171.
Khafaji, *Qissat al-adab,* V, 218–251.
Khouri, *Poetry,* 77–88.
al-Kitab 4 (Oct. 1947), special issue on Shawqi and Hafiz.
Kurd 'Ali, *Mu'asirun,* 162–209.
Mahfuz, Ahmad, *Hayat Hafiz Ibrahim.*
Maqalih, *'Amaliqa.*
Masiha, *Hafiz Ibrahim.*
Mazini, Ibrahim 'Abd al-Qadir, *Shi'r Hafiz Ibrahim.*
Mikhail, Sa'd, *Adab al-'asr,* 232–241.
Misri, 'Abd al-Sami', *Sha'ira al-'uruba.*
Mubarak, Zaki, *Hafiz Ibrahim.*
Mujahid, *al-A'lam al-sharqiyya,* II, 774–778.
al-Muqattam, 8 Mar. 1937, article by Ibrahim Disuqi Abaza.
Musa, Salama, "Hafiz Ibrahim Bey."
———, "Sa'a ma'a Hafiz Ibrahim Bey."
Qadi, Shukri, *Khamsun shakhsiyya,* 179–182.
Qumayha, *Sawt al-Islam fi shi'r Hafiz Ibrahim.*
Radwan, Fathi, *'Asr wa rijal,* 120–160.
Rafi'i, 'Abd al-Rahman, *Shu'ara al-wataniyya* (1954), 95–157; (1966), 211–232.
Rafi'i, Mustafa Sadiq, in *al-Muqtataf* 81:10 (Oct. 1932): 266–276.
Ramadi, *Min a'lam al-adab,* 215–230.
Sabri, Muhammad, *Shu'ara al-'asr,* I, 100–141.
Saharti, Mustafa 'Abd al-Latif, *Adab al-tabi'a,* 89–91.
Sandubi, *al-Shu'ara al-thalatha.*
Sayrafi, Hasan Kamil, *Hafiz wa Shawqi.*
Sharara, 'Abd al-Latif, *Hafiz.*
Shawi, Yahya 'Abd al-Amir, *Hafiz Ibrahim.*
Tahir, *Muhadarat 'an Hafiz Ibrahim.*
Tanahi, Tahir, *'Ala firash al-mawt,* 133–138.
——— in *al-Hilal* 41:1 (Nov. 1932): 25–32.
———, *Suwar wa zilal.*
'Ubayd, Ahmad, *Dhikra al-sha'irayn.*
———, *Mashahir shu'ara,* I, 181–216.
Zalat, 'Abd al-Salam Mahmud, *al-Janib al-insani.*
Zirikli, *al-A'lam,* VI, 76.

Ibrahim, Yahya

(1861–22 March 1936)

Judge, cabinet minister, and last premier before the 1923 Constitution. Born in Bahbashin, a village near Beni Suef, Ibrahim was educated at the main Coptic college in Cairo and the Khedivial Law School, where he later taught. He translated a French book on administration in 1885. He became a judge in the Alexandria National Court in 1888 and later in Zaqaziq and Beni Suef, and in 1907 he became president of the National Court of Appeals. His cabinet posts included education (1919–1920 and 1922–1923), premier and interior (1923–1924), and finance (1925–1926). As education minister he sought to reduce illiteracy by establishing twenty-two night schools for workers. While he was prime minister the 1923 Constitution and the Election Law were promulgated and SA'D ZAGHLUL was allowed to return from exile. Ibrahim was the first president of the Ittihad Party in 1925. Although well intentioned, he could not withstand pressure from either King FUAD or the British Residency to execute the policies that they wanted.

Bibliographic Sources

Fahmi, Zaki, *Safwat al-'asr,* 173–179.
Mujahid, *al-A'lam al-sharqiyya,* I, 173.
Rafi'i, 'Abd al-Rahman, *Fi a'qab al-thawra,* I, 99–138.
Tajir, *Harakat al-tarjama,* 133.
Tawfiq, 'Awad, and Hasan Sabri, *Wuzara al-ta'lim,* 60.
Times (London) (23 Mar. 1936): 11c.
Wright, *Twentieth Century Impressions of Egypt,* 102.
Zakhura, *Mirat al-'asr,* II, 332.
Zirikli, *al-A'lam,* VIII, 135.

Ibrahim Bey Muhammad

(–1816?)

Mamluk leader of Egypt, successor of MUHAMMAD ABU AL-DHAHAB, and rival to MURAD BEY MUHAMMAD as Egypt's ruler from 1775 to 1798. A rapacious and tyrannical ruler, Ibrahim Bey fled to Syria when Napoleon invaded Egypt. He returned after the French occupation and opposed the Ottoman governor, KHUSRAW, but he played no further role in Egypt's history. He and his followers encamped near present-day Dongola, thus evading MUHAMMAD 'ALI's massacre of the Mamluks in 1811. News of his death reached Cairo in March 1816.

Bibliographic Sources
Browne, Haji Abdallah, *Bonaparte in Egypt*, 54, 93.
Dehérain, *L'Égypte turque*, 144–153.
*EI*2, III, 992, article by P.M. Holt.
Jabarti, *'Ajaib al-athar*, IV, 263–264.
Volney, *Voyage en Égypte*, "État politique," chap. vi.

Idris, Dr. Yusuf

(19 May 1927–1 August 1991)
Physician, fiction writer, and playwright. Born in al-Birum (Sharqiyya province), Idris earned his first medical degree at Cairo University in 1951, later gaining credentials in psychiatry and public health. Before the 1952 Revolution he was jailed four times for his political activities and may well have conspired to murder the chief of Cairo police, Salim Zaki, in 1948. He worked briefly as a physician in Qasr al-'Ayni and health inspector for the Ministry of National Guidance and for the Islamic Congress, but drifted into writing on social problems for the press. His first collection of short stories, *Arkhas al-layali* [The Cheapest Nights], published in 1954, gained widespread public attention. His first play, *The Farhat Republic,* was produced in 1957. He married a Mexican Communist in 1957 but divorced her the following year; he later married a Frenchwoman. In 1958–1959 he served as medical adviser to the Islamic Congress secretary, ANWAR AL-SADAT, who wanted to distribute medical aid to the emerging African states. Idris began to bring Western experimental techniques into his work during the 1960s. Although eager to visit the West, he made several visits to the USSR and Eastern Europe, where his writings were widely distributed. Regrettably, he also became addicted to hard drugs, including heroin and cocaine, and in 1962 he suffered a heart attack while appearing on Egyptian State Television.

In 1966 Idris was awarded the Medal of the Republic after he had refused a prize from *al-Hiwar*, apparently because of revelations that its financial backer, the Council for Cultural Freedom, was being supported by the Central Intelligence Agency. He hoped to create an indigenous Arab drama derived from the shadow and puppet plays that have been a staple of Islamic culture for centuries, as in *al-Farafir* [The Small Birds] produced in 1966 and *al-Mukhattatun* [The Striped Ones] in 1969. The latter play criticized the NASIR regime's restrictions on intellectual freedom. He was unanimously elected in 1970 to head the Society of Drama Writers and the next year as vice president of the Journalists' Syndicate. Idris was admitted to the administrative board of the Society of Writers and Composers in 1972. In 1973 he began writing for *al-Ahram*. He underwent a heart operation in London in 1976. In the following year he was invited to lecture in Abu Dhabi, and in 1982 he attended a conference of short-story writers in India.

Idris in his later years wrote psychological plays inspired by the theater of the absurd. He tried to develop an Arabic style that could express the most subtle and tender nuances of the mind and spirit. He never felt adequately appreciated at home or abroad. In 1984 he sued the Culture Ministry, the prime minister, and *al-Ahram* for an unfavorable review of his work. Disappointed at being turned down in favor of NAJIB MAHFUZ for the Nobel Prize, he accepted the Saddam Husayn Prize for Arabic Literature in 1988, but he never recovered from his chagrin. He died in London. A village library in Baynum (near Faqus, Sharqiyya) is named after him.

Bibliographic Sources
Abdel Wahab, *Modern Egyptian Drama*, 351–493, "The Farfoors."
al-Ahram, 3 Oct. 1997.
al-Ahram Archives, file 998.
Akhir sa'a, 31 May 1995.
Allen, "The Artistry of Yusuf Idris."
———, *Critical Perspectives*.
———, *Modern Arabic Literature*, 153–160.
Badawi, M.M., *Modern Arabic Drama*, 153–164.
Cohen-Mor, *Yusuf Idris*.
EAL, i, 387–388.
Egypt, Ministry of Information, *al-Mawsu'a al-qawmiyya*, II, 1310–1311.
Hafez, "Modern Arabic Short Story," in *CHAL*, 308–310.
International Who's Who of the Arab World, 249.
Kilpatrick, *Modern Egyptian Novel*, 113–126.
Kuppershoeck, *Short Stories of Yusuf Idris*.
Mikhail, Mona, *Mahfouz and Idris*, 27–28.
al-Musawwar, 31 May 1996.
New York Times (3 Aug. 1991): A26.
Nisf al-dunya (2 Nov. 1997): 89–92.

Sirhan, *Yusuf Idris.*
Somekh, "The Function of Sound."
———, "Language and Theme."
Vatikiotis, *Middle East*, 15–18, 206–209.

'Illaysh, Shaykh Muhammad
(1802–22 October 1882)

Mufti and opponent of AL-AFGHANI. Born in Cairo to a family originally from Tripolitania, 'Illaysh studied at al-Azhar and later taught there. He became the chief Maliki mufti in 1854. He strongly opposed Khedive TAWFIQ during the 'URABI Revolution and was arrested, dragged from his home when he was totally paralyzed, and thrown into a prison hospital, where he died. His publications include a two-volume collection of his verdicts, books about jurisprudence, oratory, religious duties, morphology, and grammar. He was reputedly hardworking, quarrelsome, and puritanical.

Bibliographic Sources

Amin, Ahmad, *Muhammad Abduh*, 17–19.
Blunt, *Gordon at Khartoum*, 8.
Brockelmann, *GAL*, S II, 738–739.
Cheikho, *al-Adab al-'arabiyya*, II, 94.
Fikri, 'Ali, *Subul al-najah*, II, 79–81.
Kahhala, *Mu'jam*, IX, 12.
Makhawif, *Shajarat al-nur al-zakiyya*, 385.
Mubarak, 'Ali, *Khitat*, IV, 41–44; VIII, 74.
Schölch, *Egypt for the Egyptians!* 348.
Zakhura, *Mirat al-'asr*, I, 196–197.
Zaydan, Jurji, *Tarikh adab al-lugha*, IV, 305.
Zirikli, *al-A'lam*, VI, 19–20.

Ishaq, Adib
(21 February 1856–12 June 1885)

Newspaper editor, playwright, and poet. Born in Damascus and educated at mission schools, Ishaq moved with his family to Beirut, where he worked in the Customs office and involved himself in literary and dramatic pursuits, translating French plays into Arabic. He came to Alexandria in 1876 and collaborated with Salim al-Naqqash in producing Arabic plays. Moving to Cairo, he became a protégé of Khedive ISMA'IL and of RIYAD. A pioneer of Arabic journalism, he founded *Misr* and *al-Tijara*. He later shifted his political allegiance to SHARIF and published

Misr al-Qahira in Paris, assailing Riyad's policies. Ishaq, who returned to Egypt when Sharif regained power in 1881, also supported BARUDI in 1882, serving as a secretary to the National Assembly. He soon broke with the 'Urabists, however, and went back to Syria. He returned briefly to Egypt after the British had suppressed their movement but was again deported. Kedourie reports his death as having occurred in 1884; all other sources give 1885. Although Adib's politics were protean, his guiding principle was to preserve the Ottoman Empire more than to promote Arab nationalism, as some Arabs believe. His writings include *Nuzhat al-ahdaq fi masari' al-'ushshaq* [Balm for the Pupils (of the Eyes) in the Destruction of the Passionate Lovers], *Tarajim Misr fi hadha al-'asr* [Famous Men of Egypt in This Era], translations of several French plays, and a collection of his poems and press articles, published posthumously under the title of *al-Durar* (Pearls).

Bibliographic Sources

'Abbud, Marun, "Adib Ishaq."
———, *Ruwwad al-nahda*, 235–248.
Abdel Malek, *Idéologie*, 440–443.
'Abduh, Ibrahim, *A'lam al-sihafa*, 116–124.
Barbour, "Arabic Theatre in Egypt."
Cheikho, *al-Adab al-'arabiyya*, II, 133–135.
Daghir, *Masadir*, II, i, 111–114.
Dawn, *From Ottomanism to Arabism.*
EAL, I, 397–398.
EI2, IV, 111–112, entry by Umberto Rizzitano.
Fikri, 'Ali, *Subul al-najah*, II, 214–216.
Hamza, *Adab al-maqala*, II, 9–61.
al-Hilal 2:23 (1 Aug. 1894): 705–707.
Hourani, *Arabic Thought*, 195–196.
Ishaq, *'al-Durar*, 5–22.
Jundi, *A'lam al-adab*, II, 348–350.
Kedourie, "The Death of Adib Ishaq."
Kudsi-Zadeh, "Afghani and Freemasonry in Egypt."
Landau, *Parliaments and Parties*, 31–22, 101–102.
Louca, *Voyageurs*, 127–132.
Muruwwa, "Adib Ishaq," 59–62.
Najm, "al-Silat al-thaqafiyya bayna Misr wa Lubnan."
Nasr, Nasim, "Adib Ishaq."
Ninet, *Arabi Pacha*, 37–38, 43.
Nusseibeh, *Ideas of Arab Nationalism*, 142–145.
Rafi'i, 'Abd al-Rahman, *'Asr Isma'il*, I, 260.
Rizq, *Khamsa wa sab'una najman*, 75–85.
Schölch, *Egypt for the Egyptians!* 333–334.
Sharabi, *Arab Intellectuals and the West.*
Tarrazi, *Tarikh al-sihafa*, II, 105–109.

Zaydan, Jurji, *Mashahir al-sharq,* 1st ed., II, 75–80.

——, *Tarikh adab al-lugha,* IV, 249–250.

Zirikli, *al-A'lam,* I, 285.

al-Islambuli, Khalid
(November 1957–15 April 1982)

SADAT's convicted assassin. Khalid was born in Mallawi (near Minya). His father was a legal adviser to the nationalized sugar refinery in Naj' Hammadi and his mother was of Turkish extraction. Khalid attended al-'Uruba Secondary School; he graduated in 1978 from the Military Academy and was commissioned in the artillery corps. He belonged to one of the *Jama'at* and opposed Sadat's peace treaty with Israel. His immediate motive was to avenge the arrest of his brother, Muhammad, leader of the student *jama'a* at Asyut University, in the roundup of Sadat's opponents in September 1981. He was also inspired by *al-Farida al-ghaiba* [The Hidden Imperative] by 'Abd al-Salam Faraj, ideologue for *al-Jihad al-Jadid,* which called for replacing Sadat's regime by an Islamic state. Khalid had charge of an armored transport vehicle in the 6 October military parade. He managed to replace the soldiers assigned to ride with him by three accomplices and to conceal the grenades and ammunition gathered by his allies in his duffel bag, which was not searched. When his vehicle reached the reviewing stand, it stopped, the conspirators pretended to salute Sadat and then opened fire. As Sadat collapsed, Khalid shouted, "I have killed the Pharaoh!" Although several of the conspirators were killed by Sadat's security forces, Khalid and some of his wounded confederates were eventually brought to trial. He was one of five (out of the twenty-four) defendants who were executed.

Bibliographic Sources
al-Ahram, 23 Mar. 1982.
al-Ahram Archives, file 28459.
al-Anba, 20 Dec. 1984.
'Arusi, *Ashhar qadaya al-ightiyalat,* 623–647.
al-Dustur, 3 Jan. 1996 and 21 Dec. 1997, prison memoirs.
Hamuda, 'Adil, *Ightiyal al-rais.*
Heikal, *Autumn of Fury.*
Sayyid-Ahmad, *'al-Islambuli.*
al-Sha'b, 27 Aug. 1985.
Wilson, Colin, *Encyclopedia of Modern Murder,* 111–112.

Isma'il
(12 January 1830–6 March 1895)

Modernizing viceroy, later khedive, of Egypt from 1863 to 1879. Born in Cairo and educated at the princes' school founded by his grandfather at Qasr al-Ayni and at France's military academy in St-Cyr, Isma'il then went to Istanbul to serve on the sultan's council. On returning to Cairo, he chaired the corresponding council there. After he succeeded his uncle, SA'ID, in 1863, he tried to modernize Egypt by ordering the construction of factories, irrigation works, and public buildings. His reign saw the start of many cultural institutions, including the Cairo Opera House, Dar al-Kutub, the Geographical Society, the Egyptian Museum, and various primary, secondary, and higher schools, such as Dar al-'Ulum. The Suez Canal was completed while he was viceroy. Isma'il established Egypt's system of provincial and local administration and convoked its first representative assembly. Other developments included the organization of the National, Mixed, and Shari'a Courts, the creation of a postal service, and the extension of rail and telegraph lines throughout Egypt. He sent explorers to the African interior and armies to conquer most of the Sudan.

Isma'il tried to make Egypt more independent of the Ottoman Empire, obtaining the title of "khedive," the authority to pass down his khedivate to his eldest son, and the right to contract loans without obtaining the sultan's prior permission. His industrial, military, and construction projects proved expensive, and he also sponsored many other extravagant schemes having no long-term value to Egypt, such as his many palaces and the expensive luxuries that he purchased for his wives and mistresses. Initially he financed his reforms by revenues from the expanded output of Egyptian cotton, demand for which soared during the American Civil War, but when textile manufacturers were able to buy cotton from other sources, Isma'il resorted to higher taxes and loans obtained from European bankers on ever less favorable terms. Increasingly hard-pressed to repay them, he resorted to unorthodox fiscal measures such as the 1871 *Muqabala* (by which landowners who paid six times the annual land tax were given a perpetual 50 percent tax reduction), selling the Egyptian government's shares in the Suez Canal Company, and finally accepting European financial control through the Caisse de la Dette Publique. In 1878, beset by a low Nile, poor harvests, and rising military outlays, he surrendered much of his authority to a "European cabinet," headed by NUBAR, with English and French ministers. In March 1879 a riot by officers who had been put on half pay led to the resignation of the European cabinet and its replacement by one headed by SHARIF. The European bondholders and their governments suspected that Isma'il had engineered the uprising to regain his absolute rule. In June their envoys in Istanbul called on Sultan Abdulhamid to replace Isma'il with his son, TAWFIQ. Isma'il left Egypt and lived out his years in Naples. Although Isma'il was visionary, he was willful; he was ambitious for Egypt's development and his own aggrandizement. His achievements, however, were eclipsed by his fiscal mismanagement, which later led to Egypt's subjection to Britain.

Bibliographic Sources

'Abd al-Karim, Ahmad 'Izzat, *Tarikh al-ta'lim fi Misr*, II, 397–775.
Asaf, *Dalil*, 158–166.
Ayyubi, *'Ahd al-Khidiwi Isma'il*.
Bell, *Khedives and Pashas*, 3–23.
Blunt, *Gordon at Khartoum*, 277–281 et passim.
———, *Secret History*.
Burke's Royal Families, II, 34.
Crabites, *Ismail*.
Cromer, *Modern Egypt*, I, 11–146.
de Leon, *Egypt Under Ismail Pasha*.
———, *Khedive's Egypt*, 153–175.
Dicey, *Story of the Khedivate*, 47–226.
Douin, Georges, *Histoire du règne du Khédive Ismail*.
*EI*2, IV, 192–193, article by P.J. Vatikiotis.
Fahmi, Zaki, *Safwat al-'asr*, 44–45.
Farman, *Egypt and Its Betrayal*.
Fuad, Faraj Sulayman, *al-Kanz al-thamin*, 52–58.
Gran, "Writing of Egyptian History."
Guindi and Tagher, *Ismail d'après des documents officiels*.
Haykal, Muhammad Husayn, in *al-Siyasa al-usbu'iyya* (21 May 1927): 10–12.
Hesseltine and Wolf, *Blue and the Grey on the Nile*.
al-Hilal 3:14 (15 Mar. 1895): 521–533, 553–556.
Hunter, *Egypt Under the Khedives*, 70–79.
Jerrold, *Egypt Under Ismail-Pacha*.
Kafafi, *al-Khidiwi Isma'il*.
Landes, *Bankers and Pashas*, 128–134.
Loring, *Confederate Soldier*, 72–182.
Lott, *Nights in the Harem*, II, 282–350.
Malortie, *Egypt*.
Marlowe, *Making of the Suez*, 174–200.
———, *Spoiling the Egyptians*, 104–252.
Marsot, "The Porte and Ismail Pasha's Quest."
McCoan, *Egypt*, 85–92 et passim.
Milner, *England in Egypt*, 215–222 et passim.
Mujahid, *al-A'lam al-sharqiyya*, I, 19–20.
Mustafa, Ahmad 'Abd al-Rahim, *'Alaqat Misr bi-Turkiya*.
Rafi'i, 'Abd al-Rahman, *'Asr Isma'il*.
Ramadan, 'Abd al-'Azim, "Jaysh Isma'il."
Russell, W.H., "Why Did We Depose Ismail?"
[Sabri] Sabry, M., *Genèse de l'esprit national*.
———, *Episode de la question d'Afrique*.
Sacré and Outrebon, *L'Egypte et Ismail Pacha*.
Sammarco, *Règne du khédive Ismail*.
———, *Les règnes de 'Abbas, de Sa'id, et d'Isma'il*.
[Shukri] Shukry, Muhammad Fuad, *Khedive Ismail and Slavery*.
Stewart, *Middle East: Temple of Janus*, 1–58.
Tajir, *Harakat al-tarjama*, 80–98.
Tanahi, Tahir, *'Ala firash al-mawt*, 30–36.
Tignor, "New Directions in Egyptian Modernization."
Tugay, *Three Centuries*, 128–145.
Tusun, *al-Ba'that al-'ilmiyya*, 314–317.
Zakhura, *Mirat al-'asr*, I, 35–37.
Zaki, 'Abd al-Rahman, *A'lam al-jaysh*, I, 66–67.
Zananiri, *Le Khédive Ismail et l'Égypte*.
Zaydan, Jurji, *Mashahir al-sharq*, 1st ed., I, 34–45.
Zincke, *Egypt of the Pharaohs and the Khedive*.
Zirikli, *al-A'lam*, I, 308.

J

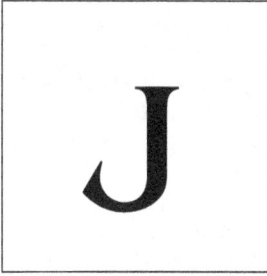

al-Jabarti, 'Abd al-Rahman
(1754–22 June 1822 or 1825)

Historian, biographer, and chronicler of events in Egypt in the late eighteenth and early nineteenth centuries. Born in Cairo to a wealthy and highly educated family that had originated in Ethiopia, Jabarti was educated at al-Azhar, where he studied with MURTADA AL-ZABIDI. He assisted that renowned scholar in collecting biographies on behalf of the Syrian scholar, al-Muradi. When Zabidi died in 1791, Jabarti abandoned the project but later resumed writing it as a combined annal and biographical dictionary of scholars, mystics, mamluks, and merchants. As a clerk in NAPOLEON's council during the French occupation, he came to know some of the scholars who came with the expedition. During MUHAMMAD 'ALI's rise to power, Jabarti became the chief Hanafi mufti but soon differed with that ambitious viceroy. When one of his sons was killed, Jabarti became blind from crying and died soon after, some sources say of natural causes, others that he was hanged. His chronicle of events from A.H. 1100 to 1236 (1685–1821), *Ajaib al-athar fi al-tarajim wa al-akhbar* [Amazing Records from Biographies and History], was banned by Muhammad 'Ali and published as a whole only in 1879. It has been translated into English by a committee of scholars. An older French translation, less reliable, also exists. LANE claimed that Jabarti also wrote a cleaned-up version of the *Thousand and One Nights*. As a scholarly chronicler of events, Jabarti provides a concise basis for historians to test their hypotheses about early modern Egypt.

Bibliographic Sources

'Abd al-Karim, Ahmad 'Izzat, *'Abd al-Rahman al-Jabarti*.
Anis, "Haqaiq 'an 'Abd al-Rahman al-Jabarti."
———, *Madrasat al-tarikh al-misri*.
'Ashur, Nu'man, *Butulat misriyya*, 27–44.
———, *Suwar min al-butula*, 17–28.
Ayalon, David, "The Historian al-Jabarti."
———, "The Historian al-Jabarti and His Background."
———, "Studies in al-Jabarti."
Bosworth, "al-Jabarti and the Frankish Archaeologists."
Brockelmann, *GAL*, S II, 730.
Brugman, *Introduction*, 7–8.
Cheikho, *al-Adab al-'arabiyya*, I, 21.
Crabbs, *Writing of History*, 43–66.
Cuoq, "al-Jabarti."
EAL, I, 403–404.
*EI*1, I, 1027; *EI*2, II, 355–357, article by David Ayalon.
Fuad, 'Atif Ahmad, "'Abd al-Rahman al-Jabarti."
Gran, *Islamic Roots*, 71–74.
al-Hilal 82:6 (June 1974): 6–45.
Holt, P.M., "al-Jabarti's Introduction."
Jabarti, *'Ajaib al-athar*, I, 203.
———, *Napoleon in Egypt*.
Jindi, Anwar, *A'lam wa ashab aqlam*, 219–225.
Kahhala, *Mu'jam*, V, 133–134.
Philipp, "The French and the French Revolution."
———, *al-Jabarti's History of Egypt*.
Qadi, Shukri, *Khamsun shakhsiyya*, 131–134.
Sharqawi, *Dirasat fi tarikh al-Jabarti*.
———, *Misr fi al-qarn al-thamin 'ashr*.
Shaybub, Khalil, *'Abd al-Rahman al-Jabarti*.
Shayyal, *al-Tarikh wa al-muarrikhun*, 10–27.
Wiet, *Fihris ajaib al-athar*.
Zaydan, Jurji, *Tarikh adab al-lugha*, IV, 283–284.
Zirikli, *al-A'lam*, III, 304.

Jahin, Salah
(25 December 1930–21 April 1986)

Cartoonist, poet, playwright, and actor. Born in Cairo and originally named Muhammad Salah al-Din Hilmi, Jahin was the son of a National Court judge and the grandson of the Nationalist journalist Ahmad Hilmi. Jahin received his schooling in Asyut and Tanta and his *license* from the Law Faculty of Cairo University. He began writing for *Ruz al-Yusuf* in 1955 and contributed cartoons to *Sabah al-khayr* from the time it was founded. After he joined the staff of *al-Ahram* in March 1962, his cartoons became highly influential. He wrote poems in colloquial Arabic, as well as an operetta, several stage and television plays (in some of which he also acted), and patriotic songs. Among his earliest were *Ihna al-sha'b* [We Are the People] and *Wallahi zaman, ya silahi* [By God, It's Time, O My Weapon], which served as Egypt's national anthem under NASIR and SADAT. Jahin first visited the USSR in 1957 and wrote an adulatory account of his impressions of Moscow. The government put him in charge of a committee to write children's books in 1962. He received a state prize in arts and letters in 1965. After serving as editor of *Sabah al-khayr* in 1966, he resumed drawing cartoons for *al-Ahram* in 1967. His energy flagged after Egypt's defeat in the June 1967 War. Owing to his leftist views, he faded from prominence under Sadat, but his poetry and art remained popular among many Egyptians.

Bibliographic Sources
al-Ahram Archives, file 3500.
al-Ahram al-riyadi, 27 Apr. 1994.
Anani, "Salah Jahin sha'iran."
Armbrust, *Mass Culture*, 60–62 et passim.
'Ayyad, Rauf, in *Sabah al-khayr,* no. 1582 (1 May 1986): 44–45.
Booth, Marilyn, "Poetry in the Vernacular," in *CHAL*, 463–482.
EAL, I, 407–408.
Egyptian Gazette (22 Apr. 1986): 2.
Kushayk, "Salah Jahin, 1930–1986."
Qadi, Shukri, *Khamsun shakhsiyya,* 169–172.
Qattan, *Ayyam ma'a Salah Jahin.*
Ra'i, 'Ali, in *al-Ahram,* 17 Apr. 1996.
Rizq, *Khamsa wa sab'una najman,* 559–565.
Sabah al-Khayr, 23 Dec. 1993, memorial issue.
Sayf, *Salah Jahin wa 'alamuhu al-shi'ri.*
al-Shabab, no. 221 (Dec. 1995).
Shadhili, "Man huwa Salah Jahin?"
Ziyada, Ahmad, *Salah Jahin.*

Jalal, Muhammad 'Uthman

(1829–16 January 1898)

Short-story writer, playwright, and translator. The son of a court clerk, Jalal was born in the village of Wana al-Qas (Beni Suef). He was educated at the School of Languages in Cairo and went on to work as a clerk and translator in several of the Egyptian ministries. His patron, CLOT Bey, had him appointed to the Medical Council in 1857. He later worked in the War and Interior Ministries, and several of the military manuals that he wrote were published. Together with IBRAHIM AL-MUWAYLIHI, he founded in 1869

Nuzhat al-afkar, one of the first Arabic periodicals in Egypt. Jalal is known especially for his translation and adaptation of Molière's plays. He later served as a judge in the Mixed Court of Alexandria and the National Court of Appeal in Cairo, where he died.

Bibliographic Sources
'Abduh, Ibrahim, *A'lam al-sihafa*, 103–104.
'Aqqad, 'Abbas Mahmud, *Shu'ara Misr*, 111–118.
Ballas, "Italat 'ala manhaj Muhammad 'Uthman Jalal."
Brockelmann, *GAL*, II, 627–628; S II, 725.
Cheikho, *al-Adab al-arabiyya*, II, 100–102.
Durri [al-Hakim], *al-Nukhba al-durriyya*, 30–31.
*EI*1, III, 686; *EI*2, VII, 437–438, article by M. Sobernheim and P.C. Sadgrove.
Hasan, Muhammad 'Abd al-Ghani, and 'Abd al-'Aziz Disuqi, *Rawdat al-madaris*, 348–352.
al-Hilal 30:6 (Mar. 1922): 555–559, on translating Molière.
Kamal al-Din, "Muhammad 'Uthman Jalal."
Khozai, *Development of Early Arabic Drama,* 169–223.
Mujahid, *al-A'lam al-sharqiyya*, II, 515–517.
Najm, *Muhammad 'Uthman Jalal.*
Shamis, *'Uzama*, 92–100.
Tajir, *Harakat al-tarjama*, 103–104.
Taymur, Muhammad, *Hayatuna al-tamthiliyya*, 133.
Wasfi, Huda, "Molière et le théâtre égyptien," 259–270.
———, "al-Shaykh Matluf."
Zaydan, Jurji, *Tarikh adab al-lugha*, IV, 221.
Zirikli, *al-A'lam*, VI, 262–263.

al-Jamasi, Muhammad 'Abd al-Ghani

(9 September 1921–)

Army officer, strategist, and cabinet minister. Born in al-Batanun (Minufiyya), Jamasi graduated from Madrasat al-Masa'i al-Mashkura in Shibin al-Kum in 1936 and from the Military Academy in 1939. Although commissioned in cavalry, he was temporarily assigned to border duty. While serving in the Western Desert during World War II, he learned much about tank warfare in desert conditions. He made trips to the United States in 1948 and 1949 for further study of this specialty. He did advanced study in Egypt's Staff College in 1950–1951 and thereafter served on the general staff. He headed a tank division during the Suez War and took charge of modernizing all armor units in 1957. In 1960–1961 he studied at the Frunze Military

Academy in the USSR; after his return, he took charge of the Armor School, a post he held from 1961 to 1966. After studying at the NASIR Supreme Military Academy in 1965–1966, he took charge of land armored forces in 1966 and the Second Army in 1967. At the time of the June War he headed the army operational branch. He then rose through the ranks from chief of staff for the Eastern military zone, to deputy director of the Reconnaissance and Intelligence Department (1968–1970), to commander of the Egyptian operational group on the Syrian front (1970–1971), chief of the Armed Forces Training Department (1971–1972), head of military operations and deputy chief of staff of the Egyptian armed forces (1972–1973), finally becoming chief of staff (1973–1974). It is said that he drafted the plans for Operation Badr in a small notebook. He took the lead role in field operations during the October War and then headed Egypt's delegation at the Kilometer 101 talks. From 1974 to 1978 he was minister of war and war production and commander-in-chief of the armed forces, also becoming a deputy premier in 1975. In addition, he was assistant military secretary to the Arab League and represented Egypt in the Arab Organization for Military Industrialization. In 1978 Jamasi became SADAT's main military adviser and negotiator with the Israelis. After Camp David, Jamasi left public life. He received medals from the Saudi and Egyptian governments and from the Egyptian-Syrian-Jordanian Joint Command.

Bibliographic Sources
al-Ahram Archives, file 5.
Egypt, Ministry of Information, *al-Mawsu'a al-qawmiyya,* II, 1003.
Jamasi, *Mudhakkirat al-Jamasi.*
Shimoni, *BDME,* 87.
Weizman, *Battle for Peace.*
WWAW, 1993–1994, 237–238.

al-Janzuri, Dr. Kamal

(12 January 1933–)
Economic planner, cabinet minister, and premier. Janzuri was born in Minuf. He graduated from Cairo University in 1952 and took part in the revolutionary regime's earliest planning efforts. He then earned a doctorate in economics from Michigan State University. He taught for a while at the Institute for National Planning, then

served in 1972 as an adviser to the Saudi government on economic development. He became Egypt's assistant minister for regional planning in November 1974. He was governor of New Valley in 1976 and of Beni Suef in 1977, shortly before taking charge of the Planning Institute. He was appointed minister of planning in 1982, to which was added the portfolio for international cooperation from July 1984 to October 1987. He remained planning minister and was named premier in January 1996, a post he held until October 1999. As prime minister, Janzuri implemented many administrative and economic reforms to promote industrial development, foreign investment, and tourism.

Bibliographic Sources
al-Ahram Archives, file 35175.
al-'Alam al-yawm, 5 Jan. 1998.
al-Musawwar, 5 Jan. 1996.
Najib, *A'lam Misr,* 378.
WWAW, 1997–1998, 249.

al-Jarim, 'Ali

(25 December 1881–8 February 1949)
Neoclassical poet and literary scholar. Born in Rosetta, he began his education in a *kuttab* and went on briefly to al-Azhar but transferred to Dar al-'Ulum, graduating in 1908. After studying briefly in England, Jarim taught in a commercial school and was appointed to Dar al-'Ulum's education faculty in 1913. He became an Arabic language inspector in the Education Ministry in 1917 and deputy principal of Dar al-'Ulum in 1940, retiring two years later. He wrote a number of historical novels, of which his best-known work, *Khatimat al-tawaf* [Conclusion of the Circuit], deals with the flight of the poet al-Mutanabbi from Kafur's Egypt in the early tenth century, continuing until his murder by robbers in al-Wasit. Jarim represented Egypt at several scientific and cultural conferences and also was a member of the Arabic Language Academy from its founding in 1932. He aspired (in vain) to succeed to SHAWQI's position as "prince of Arab poets." He died in Cairo.

Bibliographic Sources
'Abd al-Jawad, Muhammad, *Taqwim Dar al-'Ulum,* 162.
'Allam, *Majma'iyyun,* 199–201.

Amin, Ahmad, in *al-Thaqafa* 11:529 (14 Feb. 1949): 6–7.
Brockelmann, *GAL*, S III, 172–174.
Brugman, *Introduction*, 313–314.
Daghir, *Masadir*, II, i, 247–249.
EAL, I, 411–412.
Harb, Muhammad al-Ghazali, *'Ali al-Jarim.*
Jarim, 'Ali, *Salasil al-dhahab.*
Jarim, Badr al-Din, in *al-Hilal* 60:2 (Nov. 1952): 46–49.
Jundi, *A'lam al-adab*, II, 472–473.
Kahhala, *Mu'jam*, VII, 108–109.
Khafaji, *Qisas min al-tarikh*, 238–243.
Khalafallah, "L'évolution."
Khatir, *'Ali al-Jarim.*
Qadi, Shukri, *Miat shakhsiyya*, 184–186.
Sakkut, *Egyptian Novel*, 63–66.
Shayib, Ahmad, *al-Jarim al-sha'ir.*
Sulayman, 'Abd al-Jawad, in *al-Risala* 18:867 (13 Feb. 1950): 181–182; 7:870 (6 Mar. 1950): 271–273; (13 Mar. 1950): 319–322.
Tanahi, Tahir, in *al-Hilal* 57:3 (Mar. 1949): 40–41.
Zirikli, *al-A'lam*, IV, 294.

Jawhari, Shaykh Tantawi
(1862–12 January 1940)
Teacher, writer, and Islamic modernist. Born in Kafr 'Awad Allah Hijazi, near Zaqaziq, Jawhari studied in his village *kuttab*, al-Azhar, and at Dar al-'Ulum, from which he graduated in 1893. He taught at various primary and secondary schools, except for a brief interval at Dar al-'Ulum (1908–1914) and at the Egyptian University, until he retired in 1922. He wrote a series of articles in the National Party organ, *al-Liwa*, which he later republished in book form as *Nahdat al-umma wa hayatuha* [The Awakening and Life of the Nation]. His main work was a twenty-six-volume Quran commentary, *al-Jawahir fi tafsir al-Quran al-karim* (1923–1935). Jawhari's strong belief in spiritualism alienated him from most Azharites, his works were banned for a time in the Dutch East Indies, and his Quran commentary could not be circulated in Saudi Arabia.

Bibliographic Sources
'Abd al-Jawad, Muhammad, *Taqwim Dar al-'Ulum*, 192.
Adams, *Islam and Modernism*, 200 n, 234–237.
al-Ahram (18 Sept. 1927): 1, 6; (13 Jan. 1940): 8.
al-Balagh, 12 Jan. 1940.
Baljon, *Modern Koran Interpretation.*
Brockelmann, *GAL*, S III, 195, 327–329.
Carra de Vaux, *Penseurs*, V, 275–284.
Daghir, *Masadir*, II, i, 282–284.
De Jong, "The Works of Tantawi Jawhari."
EI2, supp., 262–263, article by Frederick de Jong.
Gibb, *Studies*, 291, 316 n.
Goldziher, *Richtungen*, 352.
Hartmann, "Ein modernägyptischer Theolog und Naturfreund."
Jadu, *al-Shaykh Tantawi Jawhari.*
Janbulati, *Fi dhikra Tantawi Jawhari.*
Jawhari, Tantawi, author's introduction to *Kitab al-Arwah.*
Jindi, Anwar, *al-Muhafaza wa al-tajdid*, 609–612.
Jomier, "Le Cheikh Tantawi Jawhari."
Kahhala, *Mu'jam*, X, 42.
Mujahid, *al-A'lam al-sharqiyya*, I, 318–319.
Tanikhi, Mahmud, in *Sahifat Dar al-'Ulum* 6:3 (Jan. 1940): 4–8.
Zakhura, *Mirat al-'asr*, II, 225–228.
Zirikli, *al-A'lam*, III, 230–231.

Jawish, Shaykh 'Abd al-'Aziz
(21 June 1872–25 January 1929)
Pan-Islamic journalist, orator, and educator, sometimes called Shaykh Shawish. He was born in Alexandria to a Tunisian father and a Turkish mother and studied at al-Azhar, Dar al-'Ulum, and London's Borough Road Teacher's Training College. Jawish taught Arabic briefly at Cambridge. Upon returning to Egypt, he worked as an Arabic language inspector for the Education Ministry but resigned in 1908 to become editor of the National Party daily, *al-Liwa*. The newspaper was then gaining popularity, and at its height it reached a circulation of 18,000 and employed a staff of 162 editors, reporters, and workers. Jawish soon became notorious for his attacks on the British occupation and also on the Coptic editors of a rival newspaper, *al-Watan*, leading many Egyptians and foreigners to think that he hated the Copts generally. He was tried four times for his anti-British articles, served two prison sentences, and eventually went into exile. Settling in Istanbul, he became editor of *al-Hilal* and *al-Hidaya*, the Arabic-language publications of the Committee of Union and Progress, and during World War I of *Die islamische Welt* and *al-'Alam al-islami*, published in Berlin by the German Foreign Office. After the war he worked for Mustafa Kemal (Atatürk) but broke with him when he abolished the sultanate. In late 1923 Jawish returned secretly to Cairo, where he resumed work in the Education Ministry. Jawish was elected vice president of Jam'iyyat al-Shubban al-Mus-

limin (Muslim Youth Association) shortly before his death in Cairo. He wrote books on educational methods and on Islam. Although he was admired by young Egyptians as a revolutionary speaker and writer, his bombastic style alienated more conservative—and almost all Christian—supporters of the National Party.

Bibliographic Sources
Abbas Hilmi papers, Durham University, Box 70.
'Abd al-Jawad, Muhammad, *Taqwim Dar al-'Ulum*, 290.
'Abduh, Ibrahim, *Tatawwur al-sihafa al-misriyya*, 183–186.
'Abduh, Muhammad Amin, "Dhikra Dinshaway."
———, "Hadithat al-Kamilin."
Ahmad, Anwar, "Muhakamat al-Shaykh Jawish."
al-Ahram (26 Jan. 1929): 5; (27 Jan. 1928): 5.
al-'Alam, 4 Mar. 1910.
Alexander, *Truth About Egypt*, 141–142, 163–166.
'Aqqad, 'Abbas Mahmud, *Rijal 'araftuhum*, 176–180.
Bowman, *Middle-East Window*, 76–77.
Cleveland, "Islam as Political Ideology."
Cunningham, *Today in Egypt*, 245–249.
Daghir, *Masadir*, II, i, 250–252.
Goldschmidt, "Egyptian Nationalist Party," 323–330.
———, "National Party," 25–26.
Hijazi, Anwar, *'Amaliqa*, 246–249.
al-Hilal 37:4 (Mar. 1929): 520.
Jawish, Nasir, introduction to *al-Islam din al-fitra*.
Jindi, Anwar, *'Abd al-'Aziz Jawish*.
———, *A'lam lam yunsifhum jiluhum*, 10–12.
———, *A'lam wa ashab aqlam*, 242–252.
———, *al-Sihafa al-siyasiyya*, 184–186.
Khafaji, *Qisas min al-tarikh*, 41–80.
———, *Qissat al-adab*, V, 62–70.
Khatib, Muhibb al-Din, "Mudhakkirat. . ."
Mazini, Ibrahim 'Abd al-Qadir, in *al-Siyasa al-usbu'iyya*, no. 152 (2 Feb. 1929): 10.
Mujahid, *al-A'lam al-sharqiyya*, III, 1043–1045.
Murqus, *Sihafat al-Hizb al-Watani*.
Muti'i, *Haula al-rijal min al-Azhar*, 151–167.
———, *Mawsu'a*, 268–274.
Qadi, Shukri, *Miat shakhsiyya*, 163.
Qunaybir, *'Abd al-'Aziz Jawish*.
Radwan, Fathi, *Dawr al-'Amaim*, 109–129.
———, *Mashhurun*, 25–54.
Rifa'i, Muhammad 'Ali, *Rijal wa mawaqif*, I, 235–314.
Rizq, *Khamsa wa sab'una najman*, 106–114.
Saghir, *al-Hizb al-watani*.
Shaykha, *'Abd al-'Aziz Jawish*.
———, *Aqlam thaira*, 101–120.
Shayyal, *A'lam al-Iskandariyya*, 257–270.
al-Siyasa (27 Jan. 1929): 5.
Tanahi, Tahir, in *al-Hilal* 62:2 (Feb. 1954): 64–67.
Thabit, Karim, "Kayfa habat al-Shaykh Jawish."
Times (London) (4, 8, 13 July 1910); (26 Jan. 1929): 11f.
Walili, *Mafakhir al-ajyal*, 93–99.
Wright, *Twentieth Century Impressions of Egypt*, 217–218.
Yusuf, Niqula, *A'lam min al-Iskandariyya*, 249–255.
Zirikli, *al-A'lam*, IV, 17.

al-Jazzar, 'Abd al-Hadi
(23 March 1925–7 March 1965)

Populist painter whose name is usually written Elgazzar. Originally from al-Qabbari, Alexandria, his family moved to the Delta village of Burma and then to Cairo's Sayyida Zaynab district, where Jazzar was exposed to many popular traditions and observances as he was growing up. He attended the Hilmiyya Secondary School, where he had as a teacher Husayn Yusuf Amin, who would later form the Group for Contemporary Art in 1946. Amin encouraged Jazzar's tendency to integrate his fantasies and senses as well as his visual observations into his paintings, which convey a feeling for Egyptian popular life in a semiabstract mode. Al-Jazzar began formal study at the Faculty of Fine Arts in 1944. He was jailed in 1949 for his painting "Hunger," which the government viewed as pro-Communist. He traveled on a student mission to Italy in 1958–1961, studying for an M.A. at the Institute for Restoration and Art Technology in Rome. He took part in many national and foreign exhibits, including those in Venice and São Paolo. He received a silver medal at the Brussels World's Fair in 1958, an Egyptian state prize in 1962, and a gold medal for his surrealistic painting on the Aswan High Dam, displayed in Cairo in 1964. Many of his works are displayed at the Museum of Modern Art in Cairo, and he also painted the murals for Cairo's Tribunal Complex in 1958. Often called surrealist, his artistic work is more in the tradition of revolutionary populism.

Bibliographic Sources
al-Ahram, 30 Apr. 1995.
al-Ahram Archives, file 14974.
al-Ahram al-dawli, 3 Nov. 1987.
al-Ahram Weekly, 20 Apr. 1995.
al-Anba, 27 Apr. 1993.
Karnouk, *Modern Egyptian Art*, 49–57.
al-Musawwar, 1 Mar. 1985.

Sharuni, Salih, '*Abd al-Hadi al-Jazzar.*
WWAW, 1997–1998, 251.

Jomard, Edmé-François

(17 November 1777–23 September 1862)
French engineer and Egyptologist. Born in Versailles, Edmé-François was the fourteenth child
of a silk merchant. He was educated in the College Mazarin (Institut de France), the École des
Ponts et Chaussées, and the École Polytechnique. A member of NAPOLEON's Commission
on Egypt, he led in the writing and editing of the
Description de l'Égypte. He was named *conser-
vateur* of the Bibliothèque Nationale in 1828. As
first director of Egypt's educational mission, he
also helped to train students sent by MUHAMMAD
'ALI to France. In 1859, as the last surviving
member of Bonaparte's Institut d'Égypte, he
founded a new society, the Institut Égyptien, to
conduct research on Egypt. He died in Paris.

Bibliographic Sources
Boselli, "Edmé-François Jomard."
Charles-Roux, François, *Edmé-François Jomard.*
Cortambert, *La vie et les oeuvres de M. Jomard.*
Dawson, *Egyptology*, 152.
DBF, XIII, 760–762, article by T. de Morembert.
De la Roquette, "La vie et les travaux de M. Jo-
    mard."
Du Bus, "E.-F. Jomard."
Godart de Soponay, "Notice nécrologique."
Guigniant, *Funérailles de M. Jomard.*
Houth, "Jomard l'Égyptien."
Louca, *Voyageurs*, 33–36.
Nouvelle biographie générale, 811–814.
Schnepp, introduction to *Mémoires ou travaux
    présentés*, v–xv.
Silvera, "Edmé-François Jomard."
Tusun, *al-Ba'that al-'ilmiyya*, 7–9.

Jum'a, Sha'rawi

(1920–28 November 1988)
Arab Socialist Union leader and cabinet minister, widely regarded as NASIR's most influential
companion after June 1967. Jum'a was born in
Cairo, graduated from the Military Academy in
1942, and earned a master's degree in military
sciences in 1951. He then worked as an instructor at the Military Academy and in 1958 at the
General Staff Headquarters. Working for the
Mukhabarat from 1957 to 1961, he then became
governor of Suez. He was minister of state for
presidential affairs, director of the Institute for
Socialist Studies, and head of the ASU's security
department in 1964. He was interior minister
from 1966 to 1971. He served as secretary-general of the central committee of the ASU in
1969, then as deputy premier for services in
1970. As a leading member of the faction favorable to 'ALI SABRI, Jum'a tried to resign on 13
May 1971; he was one of the leaders purged by
SADAT in his Corrective Revolution two days
later. Tried for conspiracy and sentenced to execution, soon reduced to life imprisonment, he
was released in January 1977 for health reasons
and played no further role in politics, although
he was often interviewed by the press.

Bibliographic Sources
al-Ahali, 24 Sept. 1987.
al-Ahram al-iqtisadi, 13 Apr. 1987.
al-Ahram Archives, file 246.
Majallat Misr, 22 Sept. 1986.
'Ukasha, Tharwat, in *al-Musawwar*, 24 June 1988.
al-Wafd, 23 May 1994.
al-Watan al-'arabi, 1986.
WWAW, 1997–1998, 252.

al-Jumayyil, Antun

(1887?–12 January 1948)
Journalist and writer. He was born in Beirut to
Maronite parents and was educated at St.
Joseph, graduating in 1901. Jumayyil taught
Arabic there for a while and in 1908 began editing the college's newspaper, *al-Bashir.* Moving
to Cairo in 1920, he collaborated with Amin
Taqi al-Din in publishing the magazine *al-
Zuhur* and worked for the Finance Ministry as a
translator, until he was named editor-in-chief of
al-Ahram in 1933, a position he held until his
death. He served in the Egyptian Senate. Jumayyil belonged to the Arabic Language Academy in Cairo from 1942 on, the Arab Scientific
Society in Damascus, and other learned societies. His writings include biographies of
KHALIL MUTRAN, AHMAD SHAWQI, and WALI AL-
DIN YAKAN, and books about the Mediterranean
and on household management.

Bibliographic Sources
'Abd al-Qadir, "Mudhakkirat."
al-Ahram, 14 Jan. 1948.
'Allam, *Majma'iyyun*, 84–85.
Amin, Ahmad, in *al-Thaqafa* 10, no. 473 (20 Jan.
    1948): 4.

Daghir, *Masadir*, II, i, 276–278.

Hasan, Muhammad ʿAbd al-Ghani, *Aʿlam min al-sharq wa al-gharb*, 153–162.

———, *Tarajim ʿarabiyya*, 225–238.

Jindi, Anwar, *al-Muhafaza wa al-tajdid*, 203–207.

———, *al-Sihafa al-siyasiyya*, 99–103.

Jumayyil, Antun, "Ahamm hadith fi majra hayati."

Jundi, *Aʿlam al-adab*, II, 395–396.

Khafaji, *Suwar min al-adab*, 76–83.

Mazini, Ibrahim ʿAbd al-Qadir, in *al-Ahram*, 23 Feb. 1948.

al-Risala 16, no. 759 (19 Jan. 1948): 98–99.

Rizq, Fathi, *Khamsa wa sabʿuna najman*, 315–318.

Tanahi, Tahir, "Hal al-sihafi adib?"

———, "al-Hubb al-ruhi."

Tarrazi, *Tarikh al-sihafa*, II, 17–18.

Taymur, Mahmud, "Antun al-Jumayyil."

———, *al-Shakhsiyyat al-ʿishrun*, 70–77.

UNESCO, *Aʿlam al-Lubnaniyyin*, 205.

Zahlawi, *Udaba muʿasirun*, 99–113.

Zakhura, *Mirat al-ʿasr*, III, 36–37.

Zirikli, *al-Aʿlam*, II, 27.

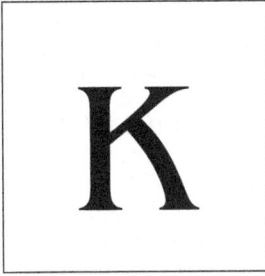

K

————, *A'lam wa ashab aqlam*, 47–53.
Kahhala, *Mu'jam*, II, 53–54.
Kurd 'Ali, *Mu'asirun*, 101–103.
————, *al-Qadim wa al-hadith*, 343–346.
MMIA 3:9 (Sept. 1923): 295–307, articles by
    Muhammad Kurd Ali and 'Isa Iskander Ma'luf.
Mujahid, *al-A'lam al-sharqiyya*, II, 851–852.
Mukhtar, "Ahmad Kamal al-athari al-awwal fi
    Misr."
al-Muqtataf 63:5 (Nov. 1923): 273–277.
Reid, "Indigenous Egyptology," 236–237.
————, "Nationalizing the Pharaonic Past," 131–
    133.
Shayyal, *al-Tarikh wa al-muarrikhun*, 144–151.
Tajir, *Harakat al-tarjama*, 144–151.
Wilson, John, *Signs and Wonders upon Pharaoh*.
Zirikli, *al-A'lam*, I, 199.

Kamal, Ahmad

(29 June 1851–4 August 1923)
Pioneer Egyptian archaeologist and Egyptologist. The son of Hasan ibn Ahmad al-Misri, from
an old Cairo family, Ahmad attended the Mubtadayan and Tajhiziyya Schools, then studied with
Heinrich Brugsch at the first school of Egyptology in Cairo. He became a secretary-interpreter
in the Antiquities Service and later assistant curator of the Egyptian Museum, for which he
translated guidebooks into Arabic in 1892–1893
and 1903. He helped to classify the museum's
holdings and supervised their transfer from Bulaq to Giza and then to the present site in central
Cairo. He also conducted minor excavations
throughout Egypt. His writings included *Stèles
ptolémaiques et romaines* (1904–1905) and *Ta-
bles d'offrandes*. His research also stressed the
connection between ancient Egyptian and the
Semitic languages, notably Arabic, on which he
published articles in *al-Manar* and *al-Muqtataf*.
His ambitious twenty-two-volume Egyptian-
Arabic dictionary was never published. He directed a short-lived school of Egyptology from
1910 to 1912. Because Egyptology was dominated during his lifetime by Europeans, he never
received the honors that he might otherwise have
earned.

Bibliographic Sources
Abou-Ghazi, "Ahmad Kamal, 1849–1923."
A'lam "al-Muqtataf," I, 315–318.
Brockelmann, *GAL*, S II, 735.
Cheikho, in *al-Mashriq* 24:11 (Nov. 1926): 866.
Dawson, *Egyptology*, 3.
Fahmi, Zaki, *Safwat al-'asr*, 331–336.
Habib, "Tarikh kashf 'an al-athar."
Jindi, Anwar, *A'lam lam yunsifhum jiluhum*, 19–22.

Kamil, Mustafa

(14 August 1874–10 February 1908)
Nationalist leader, orator, and editor. The son of
an army officer from an ethnic Egyptian family,
Mustafa was born in Cairo and educated in government schools, the French Law School in
Cairo, and the University of Toulouse, where he
received his law degree in 1894. Among his earliest supporters were François Deloncle, a
French imperialist deputy who hoped to use him
against Britain, and the well-known editor of *La
nouvelle revue*, Juliette Adam. An ardent opponent of the British occupation, Mustafa drew
close to Khedive 'ABBAS HILMI II and Sultan
Abdulhamid II, both of whom supported him
materially as well as morally in his campaigns to
persuade European countries and peoples to demand the evacuation of Egypt promised by successive British governments. Together with
MUHAMMAD FARID, AHMAD LUTFI AL-SAYYID,
and other Egyptians, he formed a secret group
called the Society for the Revival of the Nation,
initially under the aegis of the khedive. The society soon became known as the National Party,
for which Mustafa founded a daily Arabic newspaper, *al-Liwa*, in 1900 and a boys' school that
bore his own name. As the prospect of French
support waned after the Fashoda Incident, he
gradually distanced himself from 'Abbas, publicly breaking with him in 1904. Mustafa continued to seek the support of the Ottoman Empire
and to promote pan-Islam, but he also hailed
Japan's rising power in his book, *al-Shams al-
mushriqa* [The Rising Sun]. He backed Ottoman
claims to part of the Sinai Peninsula during the

1906 Taba Incident (in which the British forced the Ottomans to withdraw their troops from Taba and their claim to part of the Sinai Peninsula) and condemned British atrocities in Egypt following that same year's Dinshaway Incident.

In October 1906 Mustafa became reconciled with the khedive, who offered him financial assistance to found *The Egyptian Standard* and *L'Étendard égyptien* as Nationalist dailies to influence European opinion. In December 1907 he formally set up the National Party, which elected him as its first president. Stricken with tuberculosis (although some thought that he was poisoned), he took to his bed and died in Cairo. His funeral occasioned a massive demonstration of popular grief. Mustafa Kamil is remembered as a fervent patriot, demanding the British evacuation of Egypt and constitutional government, and as an occasional supporter of the Ottoman Empire and pan-Islam. A museum bearing his name, near the Cairo Citadel, memorializes his contribution to the Egyptian nationalist movement and contains his tomb, which serves also for Muhammad Farid and 'ABD AL-RAHMAN AL-RAFI'I. His statue adorns a square that bears his name in central Cairo, and many Egyptian towns and villages have streets named after him.

Bibliographic Sources

Abbas Hilmi papers, Durham University, Box 4/1–55.

'Abd al-Latif, Muhammad Fahmi, "Mustafa Kamil wa Pierre Loti."

'Abduh, Ibrahim, *A'lam al-sihafa*, 138–144.

Adam, Juliette, *L'Angleterre en Égypte*, 144–197.

Agliette, "Mustafa Kamil, 1874–1908."

Alexander, *Truth About Egypt*, 28–41, 139–140.

Anis, *Safahat matwiya*.

'Aqqad, 'Abbas Mahmud, *Rijal 'araftuhum*, 39–51.

'Ashur, Nu'man, *Butulat misriyya*, 153–162.

———, *Suwar min al-butula*, 71–80.

Baron, "Nationalist Iconography."

Bindari, *Za'im al-nahda Mustafa Kamil*.

Blunt, *My Diaries*.

Brockelmann, *GAL*, S III, 332–333.

Carra de Vaux, *Penseurs*, V, 285–296.

CE, VI, 1747–1748, article by Yunan Labib Rizq.

Crabbs, *Writing of History*, 146–166.

Daghir, *Masadir*, II, i, 649–652.

Dunya, 'Abd al-'Aziz Hafiz, *Rasail tarikhiyya*.

*EI*1, II, 824–825; *EI*2, VII, 715–716, articles by Max Meyerhoff.

Fikri, 'Ali, *Subul al-najah*, III, 257–264.

Gharaba, *Shakhsiyyat*, 205–211.

Goldschmidt, "Egyptian Nationalist Party," 310–322.

———, "National Party," 11–15.

Haddad, George, "Mustafa Kamil."

Hamza, *Adab al-maqala*, V.

Haykal, Muhammad Husayn, *Tarajim misriyya*, 139–162.

Hijazi, Anwar, *'Amaliqa*, 224–237.

al-Hilal 16:6 (1 Mar. 1908): 321–333.

——— 56:2 (Feb. 1948), special issue.

Ibrahim, Shihata 'Isa, *'Uzama al-wataniyya*, 173–208.

'Imara, *al-Jami'a al-islamiyya*.

'Imari, Ahmad Suwaylim, *Mustafa Kamil*.

'Isa, Mamduh, "Mustafa Kamil fi al-madrasa."

Jamal, *Awraq Mustafa Kamil*.

Jami'i, "Mustafa Kamil wa tasis al-Hizb al-Watani."

Jam'iyya al-Misriyya li al-dirasat al-Tarikhiyya, *Mustafa Kamil*.

Jawda, *Nawabigh al-shabab*, 76–92.

Kahhala, *Mu'jam*, XII, 269–270.

Kamil, 'Ali Fahmi, *Mustafa Kamil Basha*.

Kamil, Mustafa, *Lettres égyptiennes françaises*.

Kurd 'Ali, *al-Qadim wa al-hadith*, 340–342.

Landau, *Parliaments and Parties*, 107–126.

Louca, *Voyageurs*, 244–245.

Maqdisi, Anis, in *al-Hilal* 63:1 (Jan. 1955): 109–110.

Marzuq, *al-Khataba al-siyasiyya fi Misr*, 89–109.

Mujahid, *al-A'lam al-sharqiyya*, I, 169–171.

Murqus, *Maqalat Mustafa Kamil*.

———, *Sihafat al-Hizb al-Watani*.

Mustafa Kamil muqiz al-wataniyya.

Muti'i, *Haula al-rijal min Misr*, III, 321–333.

———, *Mawsu'a*, 618–624.

Najjar, *Mustafa Kamil raid al-wataniyya*.

OEMIW, II, 398, article by Amira El Azhary Sonbol.

Qadi, Shukri, *Khamsun shakhsiyya*, 35–38.

Qutb, "Ayna anta, ya Mustafa Kamil."

Radwan, Fathi, *Mustafa Kamil*.

Rafi'i, 'Abd al-Rahman, "Mustafa Kamil."

———, in *al-Hilal* 49:3 (Apr. 1941): 497–504.

———, in *al-Hilal* 66:2 (Feb. 1958): 13–17.

———, *Mustafa Kamil*.

Ramadan, 'Abd al-'Azim, *Mustafa Kamil*.

Rashad, *Mustafa Kamil*.

Rathmann, "Mustafa Kamil."

Rida, Muhyi al-Din, *Abtal al-wataniyya*, 9–24.

Sayyid, Afaf Lutfi, *Egypt and Cromer*, 155–184.

Shafiq, *Mudhakkirati*, II, i, ii.

Steppat, *Nationalismus und Islam bei Mustafa Kamil*.

Tanahi, Tahir, *'Ala firash al-mawt*, 65–77.

———, in *al-Hilal* 66:2 (Feb. 1958): 18–25.

Tawfiq, Najib, *Mustafa Kamil*.

'Umar, Mahmud Fathi, *Abtal al-hurriyya*, 46–56.

Walili, *Mafakhir al-ajyal*, 78–86.

Zaydan, Jurji, *Mashahir al-sharq*, 1st ed., I, 288–301.

———, *Tarikh adab al-lugha,* IV, 316–317.

Zayyan, *Mustafa Kamil.*

Zirikli, *al-A'lam*, VII, 238–239.

Kamil, Yusuf

(26 May 1891–11 December 1971)
Painter. Born in Cairo, he began his education at the Bab al-Sha'riyya Elementary School, went on to the Khedivial School for Arts and Crafts, and then Yusuf Kamal's School of Fine Arts. Yusuf was sent on an educational mission to Rome, where he graduated from the Academy of Fine Arts in 1924 and from Mussolini's new art school two years later, specializing in illustration. After his return to Egypt he taught in several preparatory and secondary schools before joining the Academy of Fine Arts, later becoming head of its painting department. In 1948 he became director of Cairo's Museum of Modern Art and two years later was dean of the Academy. He exhibited his work in Italy, Lebanon, the USSR, and India. He painted NASIR's portrait in 1958. Given a state prize in 1960, he was appointed to the Supreme Council for the Arts, Letters, and Social Sciences in 1965. Two of his canvases are on display at the Modern Art Museum in Cairo: a portrait of a lady, and a picture of a group of young girls at play. A prize has been given in his memory by the Academy of Fine Arts since 1965, and a Cairo street bears his name.

Bibliographic Sources
al-Ahram, 28 Dec. 1982, 7 Nov. 1997.
al-Ahram Archives, file 1639.
Iskandar, *Khamsun sana min al-fann,* 24–25.
al-Jil, 28 Jan. 1963.
al-Jumhuriyya, 7 July 1961.
Karnouk, *Modern Egyptian Art,* 5.
Mallakh, Kamal, in *al-Ahram,* 12 Dec. 1971, 2 May 1980, 14 Aug. 1981.
al-Masa, 11 July 1961.
al-Musawwar, 4 June 1993.
Ruz al-Yusuf, 1 July 1961.

Karim, Dr. Sayyid

(16 February 1911–)
Architect, writer, and editor, sometimes called the Flying Engineer. Born in Mit Bira, near Benha, Sayyid was the son of a civil engineer who worked for the Egyptian government and also a distant descendent of Sayyid MUHAMMAD KARIM's brother. He entered Cairo University's Engineering Faculty, but his artistic skills were noted by MUSTAFA FAHMI, who had him transferred to Architecture. In 1938 he became the first Egyptian to earn a doctorate in architectural engineering, receiving his degree from the University of Zurich. He opened Egypt's first architectural consulting firm and in 1939 founded *al-'Imara*, its first magazine for architecture and the arts, which he edited until the government sequestered it in 1962. He also taught architectural engineering at Cairo University. Sayyid drafted the designs for the renovation of Cairo in 1952 and the plans for Madinat Nasr, Hurghada, al-'Arish, Amman, and tourist villages in Algeria and Morocco. He also prepared the plan for protecting Egyptian monuments from the threat of flooding due to the Aswan High Dam. He designed Cairo's Shams Building, the Kuwait Museum complex, the Arab pavilions at the Brussels World Fair, the Journalists' Syndicate building, the offices of *Akhbar al-Yawm* and of *Ruz al-Yusuf*, Asyut University Hospital, the United Arab Airlines office in Paris, and many palaces in the Gulf Region. His concerns also extended to protecting the shoreline of the countries bordering on the Mediterranean by designing a Gibraltar barrage that was never built. He won an international prize from the Pioneers of Architecture in 1958 and was made an honorary member of the International Planners Organization in 1963. He opposed neo-Islamic architecture, saying that the early Arabs, if they had been able to produce steel and reinforced concrete, would not have used arches and domes. As for HASAN FATHI's "architecture for the poor," he argued that it was better to empower poor people to afford more modern buildings. Recently he has published books purporting to prove, from reading hieroglyphic texts, that Egypt's civilization began six millennia before most scholars believe it started.

Bibliographic Sources
al-Ahram Archives, file 1346.
al-Ahram Weekly, 3 Dec. 1992.
al-Idha'a, 2 Jan. 1960.
al-Jil, 8 May 1961.
al-Jumhuriyya, 30 June 1961.
Karim, Sayyid, "al-Tabi' al-qawmi wa al-'imara fi Misr."

Sakr, *Early Twentieth Century Islamic Architecture*, 16.
al-Siyasa, 21 Sept. 1990.
Volait, *La Revue Imara (1939–1962)*.
al-Wafd, 5 Nov. 1992; 4 May 1995.

Karim, Sayyid Muhammad
(?–5 September 1798)
Alexandria's director of customs during NAPOLEON's invasion of Egypt. His name is sometimes rendered Kurayyim. Born in Alexandria, Sayyid was originally a weigher of goods and was promoted until he took complete charge of the accounts and the Customs office. Because of his resistance to Napoleon's occupation of Alexandria, he was interned by KLÉBER on 20 July 1798, imprisoned in an Abu Qir harbor tower, and then transferred to Cairo, to be judged by Napoleon, who demanded payment of a large fine within twelve hours. When the sum was not forthcoming, he was tortured, humiliated, and executed by a firing squad. Karim's severed head was raised on a post with a sign: "This is the fate of anyone who opposes the French." His relatives rescued the head and buried it with his body. Egyptians view him as an early nationalist hero.

Bibliographic Sources
'Awad, Ahmad Hafiz, *Fath Misr al-hadith*.
Baqli, *Abtal al-muqawama*, 11–25.
Basyuni, "Insaf batal shadid."
Browne, Haji Abdallah, *Bonaparte in Egypt*, 40–42.
Dunya, 'Abd al-'Aziz Hafiz, *al-Shahid Muhammad Karim*.
Gharaba, *Shakhsiyyat*, 47–52.
Ibrahim, Shihata 'Isa, *'Uzama al-wataniyya*, 7–18.
Jabarti, *'Ajaib al-athar*, III, 62–63.
Qadi, Shukri, *Miat shakhsiyya*, 261–263.
Rafi'i, 'Abd al-Rahman, *Tarikh al-haraka al-qawmiyya*, I, 165–188.
Shayyal, *A'lam al-Iskandariyya*, 231–236.
'Umar, Mahmud Fathi, *Abtal al-hurriyya*, 1–7.
Zirikli, *al-A'lam*, VII, 14.

Khalid, Shaykh Khalid Muhammad
(15 June 1920–29 February 1996)
Islamic teacher, reformer, and writer, sometimes called Freedom's Knight. Born in Hihya (Sharqiyya), Khalid received his *'alimiyya* in 1947 from al-Azhar's Faculty of Shari'a, followed by a teaching certificate. He was briefly a Sufi in his youth; by 1951 he belonged to the Society of Muslim Brothers. During the NASIR years he worked as a teacher and in the cultural bureau of the Education Ministry. A member of the Supreme Council for the Arts and Sciences, he published some thirty books, including *Min huna nabda* (translated into English as *From Here We Start*), *Muwatinun, la ra'aya* [Citizens, not Subjects] and *Rijal hawl al-rasul* [Men Around the Prophet], upholding a reformist interpretation of Islam. Later in life, he tended to promote Islamic authenticity in his writings, as in *al-Dawla fi al-Islam* [The State in Islam], which called for a government based on Muslim principles.

Bibliographic Sources
Abdel-Malek, *Arab Political Thought*, 116–119.
al-Ahram Archives, file 3790.
al-Akhbar, 8 Mar. 1996.
Ba'thi, *Shakhsiyyat islamiyya wa mu'asira*, 131–163.
al-Musawwar, 15 Mar. 1996.
OEMIW, II, 412–413, article by William E. Shepard.
Ruz al-Yusuf, 4 Mar. 1996.
al-Shabab, no. 225 (Apr. 1996).
Tafahum, "A Cairo Debate on Islam."
al-Wafd, 3 Mar. 1996.

Khalil, Dr. Mustafa
(18 November 1920–)
Engineer, cabinet minister, and premier. Mustafa was born in Kafr Tusfa, near Benha (Qalyubiyya). He graduated from Cairo University's Faculty of Engineering in 1941, then worked as an inspector for the Egyptian railways. He was sent on an educational mission to the United States, where he worked for the Chicago and Milwaukee Rail Line and earned his M.A. and Ph.D. in engineering from the University of Illinois, after which he taught at Ain Shams University. He was NASIR's minister of communications and housing from 1956 to 1965 and of industry and energy from 1965 to 1966, also serving as deputy prime minister in 1964. He left the Egyptian government in 1966 but came back to head the Supervisory Council for State Broadcasting and Television in 1970. He was elected head of the Engineers' Syndicate in 1975. He became the last secretary-general of the ASU in 1976 and presided over its division into three

manabir (pulpits, or platforms), which evolved into separate political parties in 1978. He accompanied SADAT to Jerusalem in 1977 and took part in the negotiations with Israel, which he has visited many times since. Appointed prime minister in October 1978, he also served as foreign minister from May 1979–1980. When Sadat assumed the premiership in 1980, Khalil became deputy chairman of the National Democratic Party. Although less influential under MUBARAK than under Sadat, he retains his party post, is a respected member of the president's inner circle, and maintains relations with Israeli leaders. He serves on the Board of Trustees of the American University in Cairo and chairs the board of the Arab International Bank. He is the author of a book on the American oil crisis. He continues to give interviews on the peace process and in 1998 called for a unified Jerusalem to be shared between Israelis and Palestinians, modeled on Vatican City.

Bibliographic Sources
al-Ahram Archives, file 19.
Egypt, Ministry of Information, *al-Mawsu'a al-qawmiyya*, II, 1193–1194.
Najib, *A'lam Misr*, 469.
Shimoni, *BDME*, 138–139.
Weizmann, *Battle for Peace*, 59–61 et passim.
WWAW, 1997–1998, 379.

Khayrat, Abu Bakr

(10 April 1910–25 October 1963)
Musician, engineer, and first dean of the Conservatoire. Born in Cairo, he was trained in Cairo University's Faculty of Engineering, graduating at the head of his class in 1930, after which he worked briefly for the Public Works Ministry and then was sent on an educational mission to Paris, where he studied at the École des Beaux Arts. Upon receiving his diploma in 1935, he also won a prize for his final project, an accomplishment unmatched by any other Egyptian. Meanwhile, he also received musical training, starting at age five with instruction on the violin, then in composition and piano. Even while a practicing architect in Cairo, he tried his hand at musical composition, writing the "Symphony of Isis" and a number of other compositions for orchestra, chorus, or piano. He became dean of the National Institute of Music, or "Conservatoire," in 1959 and received a state prize in the follow-

ing year. He helped to design the new Opera Building, the Ballet Center, the Conservatoire, SAYYID DARWISH Hall, the Higher Institute for Dramatic Studies, and various hospitals and other large buildings. A music prize bearing his name has been awarded annually since 1993, and a Cairo street has been renamed after him.

Bibliographic Sources
al-Ahali, 9 May 1995.
al-Ahram Archives, file 254.
al-Ahram al-dawli, 28 Oct. 1988.
'Ala al-Din, 21 Mar. 1996.
Khuli, Samiha, in *al-Musawwar*, 26 Nov. 1982.
al-Umma, 25 Feb. 1991.

al-Khuli, Shaykh Amin

(1 May 1895–9 March 1966)
Islamic reformer and exponent of enlightened fundamentalism. Born in Minufiyya to an agricultural family with ties to the ulama, Amin was educated in his local *kuttab* and in government schools in Cairo, where he lived with his maternal grandfather. Although he took part in the 1919 Revolution, he never joined a political party. He graduated from the Shari'a Judges School in 1920 and soon afterward was appointed to teach there. He was sent to staff the Egyptian consulates in Rome (1923) and Berlin (1926), taking advantage of his residency in Europe to learn about foreign cultures. Upon returning to Cairo in 1927, he resumed teaching at the Shari'a Judges School until it was abolished in 1928. He then became an Arabic instructor at Cairo University and rose to be vice dean of its Arts Faculty, a post he held until he resigned in 1953 due to political differences with the government. He became an adviser to Dar al-Kutub and director of the cultural office in the Education Ministry, retiring in 1955. He briefly edited *al-Qada al-shar'i* and published *al-Adab*. He wrote plays, short stories, and books on philosophy, rhetoric, religion, psychology, and history. Among his works are *Manahij al-tajdid fi al-lugha wa al-nahw wa al-tafsir* [Methods of Renewal in Language, Grammar, and Quranic Interpretation] and *al-Mujaddidun fi al-Islam* [Renewers in Islam]. He also gave a series of Egyptian state radio broadcasts about Quran interpretation. Devoted more to teaching than to writing, he founded a school of thinkers who called themselves *al-Umana*, based on his name.

Elected to the Arabic Language Academy in 1961, Khuli was viewed as a successor to MUHAMMAD 'ABDUH. He married 'AISHA 'ABD AL-RAHMAN, who continued his work after his death.

Bibliographic Sources
al-Ahram, 21 Feb. 1997.
al-Ahram Archives, file 1214.
al-Ahram al-dawli, 14 Apr. 1996.
al-Ahram Hebdo, 26 July 1995.
'Awad, Louis, in al-Ahram, 11 Mar. 1966.
Fuad, Ni'mat Ahmad, in al-Ahram, 12 Mar. 1986; 7 Dec. 1997.
Jansen, Interpretation of the Koran, 64–68.
Jindi, Anwar, al-Muhafaza wa al-tajdid, 718–722.
al-Majalla, no. 589 (22–28 May 1991).
Nadwat Amin al-Khuli, al-Asala wa al-tajdid.
al-Riyad, 10 Jan. 1988.
Sabah al-Khayr, 30 May 1996.
Sa'fan, Amin al-Khuli.
Shukri, Ghali, in al-Ahram, 9 Dec. 1992.
Uktubir, 12 Apr. 1996.

Khurshid, Ahmad

Ottoman official. Appointed mayor of Alexandria after the French evacuated Egypt in 1801, he was named Egypt's governor in 1804 at MUHAMMAD 'ALI's behest. Allied with Britain's diplomatic representative, Khurshid tried to get Muhammad 'Ali and his Albanians removed from Egypt, bringing in the *Delhi* (madmen) troops from Syria. Muhammad 'Ali managed to win the *Delhi*s to his side and, backed by a demonstration of ulama and guild leaders in Cairo, had himself named governor of Egypt in May 1805. Khurshid, abandoned by his troops, was besieged in the Cairo Citadel, which he left only after he saw the Ottoman decree investing Muhammad 'Ali as Egypt's governor.

Bibliographic Sources
Ghorbal, Beginnings, 224, 227–228.

Khusraw Pasha

Ottoman official and first governor of Egypt after the French were expelled. Originally a Georgian slave untrained in either war or administration, he commanded a weak Ottoman force that could withstand neither the Mamluks nor MUHAMMAD 'ALI's Albanian troops. After Khusraw tried to send back the latter with false promises to pay them, they deposed him in 1803, starting a protracted power struggle.

Bibliographic Sources
Ghorbal, Beginnings, 207, 211.
Rafi'i, 'Abd al-Rahman, Tarikh al-haraka al-qawmiyya, II, 290–313.

Killearn. *See* LAMPSON, MILES.

Kitchener, Sir [Horatio] Herbert, First Earl

(24 June 1850–5 June 1916)
British officer, colonial administrator, and agent and consul general in Cairo from 1911 to 1914. Born to an Anglo-Irish landowning family, Kitchener studied in Switzerland and at the military academy in Woolwich. Commissioned into the Royal Engineers in 1871, he conducted land surveys in Palestine, Cyprus, and the Sinai. He joined the Egyptian army in 1883 and took part in the unsuccessful Gordon rescue mission. He served in Zanzibar and the eastern Sudan before becoming adjutant general to the Egyptian army in 1888. Soon after his accession, Khedive 'ABBAS chose Kitchener, with Britain's concurrence, as commander-in-chief of the Egyptian army, but their friendship soured in 1894, when Kitchener thought that 'Abbas had insulted the British officers in that army and demanded a public apology. In 1896–1898 he organized and led the campaign to regain the Sudan from the Mahdi's successors and repulsed France's effort to occupy the Nile headwaters at Fashoda.

Kitchener played a major role in Britain's victory over the Boers in South Africa in 1899–1902, then became commander of the Indian army. After GORST's death, Kitchener was sent to Egypt by the Liberal cabinet to pacify the country and improve its economic condition. Serving as Britain's chief diplomatic representative and de facto colonial administrator, he subdued the Nationalists, improved the irrigation system, persuaded the Egyptian government to pass the Five *Feddan* Law, established the Agriculture Ministry, and revised the Organic Law. He pressured National Party leaders to leave Egypt and banned most of their papers. Twice he narrowly escaped assassination. He kept Egypt out of the Ottoman Empire's Libyan and Balkan

Wars. Prior to the outbreak of World War I his relations with 'Abbas deteriorated to the point that Kitchener was thinking of deposing him. At that time, Kitchener was importuned by Prime Minister Asquith to enter the British cabinet as his war minister. Although popular and often perceptive, Kitchener did not like being a wartime mobilizer in London as much as he did governing Egypt, to which he always hoped to return someday.

Bibliographic Sources
'Aqiqi, *al-Mustashriqun*, II, 493–494.
Arthur, *Life of Lord Kitchener.*
Cassar, *Kitchener.*
EMME, II, 1034, article by Peter Mellini.
Magnus, *Kitchener.*
Moseley, *With Kitchener in Cairo.*
Royle, *Kitchener Enigma.*
Warner, *Kitchener.*

Kléber, Jean-Baptiste

(9 March 1753–14 June 1800)
General in NAPOLEON's army and his successor as commander of the French forces in Egypt. The son of a Strasbourg mason, Jean-Baptiste hoped to become an architect; he studied at the Munich military academy, joined the Bavarian army in 1777, and then served in the Austrian army, but returned to Alsace in 1785 as a building inspector. He joined the local national guard in 1789 and took part in the successful siege of Mainz in 1793. For distinguished service against the Vendée rebels, he was promoted to the rank of general and aided in the French occupation of the Rhineland. Napoleon invited him to command a division in his Army of Egypt, where Kléber frequently saw action against the Ottomans, notably in the Battle of Mount Tabor during the abortive siege of Acre. When Napoleon returned to France in 1799, he left Kléber in command of all his forces. Early in 1800 Kléber signed the abortive Convention of al-'Arish. Soon after it was annulled, he levied a heavy tax on the Muslim population, leading to a series of revolts, which he suppressed with the aid of Greek and Coptic Christians. He appointed mainly Coptic tax collectors, but subjected them to French supervision, and made needed repairs to St. Catherine's Monastery in the Sinai. He later attempted to effect a reconciliation with Egypt's Muslims. He successfully secured Cairo from an Ottoman attack by his victory at Heliopolis. Shortly afterward, Kléber was stabbed to death by a Syrian at his Cairo headquarters. He was a soldier's soldier, lacking in charisma and poise before groups, but intelligent and capable.

Bibliographic Sources
CE, V, 1416–1417, article by Harald Motzki.
Chandler, David G., *Dictionary of the Napoleonic Wars*, 225–226.
Chuquet, *Quatre généraux de la Révolution.*
Connelly, *Napoleonic France*, 276, article by Milton Finley.
DBF, XVIII (Paris, 1993), 1191–1192.
Doriant, "Le bicentennaire de la naissance de Kléber."
Ernouf, *Le général Kléber.*
Font-Réaulx, *Le général Kléber.*
Garçot, *Kléber, 1753–1800.*
Goncourt and Goncourt, *Portraits intimes.*
Herold, *Bonaparte in Egypt.*
LaJonquière, *L'expédition en Égypte.*
Laurens, *L'expédition d'Égypte.*
———, *Kléber en Égypte.*
Miot, *Memories.*
Morpain, *Kléber: documents inédits.*
Pajol, *Kléber.*
Palmer, *Encyclopedia of Napoleon's Europe*, 167.
Pesloüan, *Kléber, 1753–1800.*
Puryear, *Kleber and Menou.*
Tulard, Fayard, and Fierro, *Histoire et dictionnaire*, 913.

L

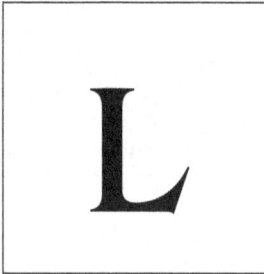

Lampson, Sir Miles Wedderburn, First Baron Killearn

(24 August 1880–18 September 1964)
British diplomat. Originally from Killearn (Stirlingshire) and educated at Eton, he entered the Foreign Office, serving in Japan and China and then briefly in Siberia after World War I. Lampson attended the Washington Naval Conference, headed the Foreign Office's Central European Department, and was Britain's minister in Peking from 1926 to 1933. He was appointed high commissioner for Egypt and the Sudan in December 1933. His early diplomatic achievement was the signing of the 1936 Anglo-Egyptian Treaty, after which his title changed to ambassador. His firm stance ensured that Egypt would remain a base for Britain's Eighth Army and Mediterranean Fleet during World War II, although Egypt remained a nonbelligerent for most of the war. Suspecting King FARUQ and his advisers of favoring the Axis Powers, Lampson forced the king on 4 February 1942 to accept a Wafdist cabinet to uphold the 1936 treaty. Although Lampson's behavior has often been assailed, especially by Egyptians, others argue that the British Empire could not have survived World War II if it had not stood firm in Egypt before its victory at al-Alamayn. Lampson was elevated to the peerage as Baron Killearn in 1943. As Egyptian agitation grew for the British evacuation after the war, the Labour government removed him from Cairo, naming him high commissioner for Southeast Asia. Some of his Egyptian diaries were published in 1972, translated into Arabic, and printed in *al-Ahram;* the full text is in the Middle East Centre, St. Antony's College, Oxford. A tough negotiator, Lampson disdained rising nationalism in Egypt, where a subtler diplomacy would have averted ill feeling toward Britain.

Bibliographic Sources
'Abd al-Ra'uf, *Dubabat hawl al-qasr.*
Abu al-Majd, *Sanawat ma qabla al-Thawra.*
Anis, *4 Fibrayir 1942.*
DNB (1961–1970), 627–628.
EMME, III, 1069, article by Jean-Marc Oppenheim.
Evans, *Killearn Diaries.*
Grafftey-Smith, *Bright Levant*, 133–138, 232–235.
Lampson, *Politics and Diplomacy in Egypt.*
New York Times (19 Sept. 1964): 27.
Salim, Jamal, *Qiraa jadida.*
Smith, Charles D., "4 February 1942."
Times (London) (19 Sept. 1964): 10e; (22 Sept. 1964): 15a.
Warburg, "Lampson's Ultimatum to Faruq."
Who Was Who (1961–1970), 630.

Lane, Edward William

(17 September 1801–10 August 1876)
British Arabic scholar, born in Hereford, the son of a clergyman and of the niece of artist Thomas Gainsborough. Although trained as an engraver, Lane became fascinated by Egypt and went there in 1825 to explore the country and write and illustrate a book about its monuments and people. The resulting work, "Description of Egypt," was never published, although parts later appeared in Sophia Lane Poole's (Lane's sister's) *Englishwoman in Egypt* (1844–1846) and in his *Cairo Fifty Years Ago* (prepared by his grandnephew, Stanley Lane-Poole, and published in 1896). After a second trip to Egypt, during which he settled in Cairo for three years, Lane wrote a pioneer ethnographic study of Egyptian society entitled *An Account of the Manners and Customs of the Modern Egyptians* (1836). He later wrote an annotated translation of the *Thousand and One Nights* (1838–1841) and *Selections from the Kur-an* (1843). With support from the Duke of Northumberland, Lane went to Egypt for a third time to gather material for his *Arabic-English Lexicon* (1863–1893). Returning to England in 1849, Lane devoted the rest of his life to the *Lexicon*. At the time of his death, he had nearly completed the sixth volume. Stanley Lane-Poole supervised the publication of that and the remaining two volumes. Egyptians and foreigners still acknowledge the importance of his work.

Bibliographic Sources
Ahmed, Leila, *Edward W. Lane.*
'Aqiqi, *al-Mustashriqun,* I, 493–494.
Arberry, Arthur J., *Oriental Essays,* 87–121.
Dawson, *Egyptology,* 162.
DNB, XI, 521–525, article by Stanley Lane-Poole.
Lane-Poole, *Life of Edward William Lane.*
Poole, *The Englishwoman in Egypt.*
Tajir, *Harakat al-tarjama,* 44–45.
Thompson, "Edward William Lane as an Artist."
———, "Edward William Lane as Egyptologist."
———, "Edward William Lane in Egypt."
———, "Edward William Lane's 'Description of
   Egypt.'"
———, "'I Felt Like an Eastern Bridegroom.'"
———, "'Of the Osmanlees, or Turks.'"
———, "Reassessment of Edward William Lane."

al-Laythi, Shaykh 'Ali

(1821–25 January 1896)
Poet and friend of the khedivial family. Born in Bulaq, 'Ali lost his father at an early age, so his mother took him to live near the Mosque of Imam Layth, hence his surname. He studied at al-Azhar, then went to al-Jabal al-Akhdar in Tripolitania, where he became a Sufi disciple of al-Sanusi and lived for three years, tending camels and sheep, helping to build a *zawiya* (Sufi hostel), and studying hadiths and related subjects. He returned to Cairo about 1846 and became famous for his intimate knowledge of the khedivial court and its politics, although he was exiled by SA'ID to Aswan for teaching astrology and divination and was briefly rusticated after backing the 'URABI movement. Tall and dark-skinned, he had a serene, often jolly, disposition, yet could be extremely serious about politics. He accompanied several princes of the khedivial family to Vienna and wrote an interesting account of his observations there, as well as a *diwan* of poetry that he did not want to have published (it never was). He was close to MAHMUD SAMI AL-BARUDI and MUHAMMAD 'ABDUH. He died in Cairo.

Bibliographic Sources
'Allam and 'Abd al-Hamid Hasan, *Nathr Hifni
   Nasif.*
'Aqqad, 'Abbas Mahmud, *Shu'ara Misr,* 99–110.
Ayyubi, *'Ahd al-Khidiwi Isma'il,* I, 250–253.
Brockelmann, *GAL,* S III, 83.
Brugman, *Introduction,* 7–8.
Cheikho, *al-Adab al-'arabiyya,* II, 98–99.
Daghir, *Masadir,* III, ii, 1120–1121.

EAL, II, 463–464.
Hasan, Muhammad 'Abd al-Ghani, and 'Abd al-
   'Aziz Disuqi, *"Rawdat al-Madaris,"* 395–399.
al-Hilal 4:11 (1 Feb. 1896): 439.
Jundi, *A'lam al-adab,* II, 429–430.
Kahhala, *Mu'jam,* VII, 66–67.
Khafaji, *Qissat al-adab,* III, 99–101.
Malaika, Sadiq, *Dhawn al-fuqaha fi al-tarikh,* 154–
   157.
Mujahid, *al-A'lam al-sharqiyya,* II, 751–754.
Rafi'i, 'Abd al-Rahman, *'Asr Isma'il,* I, 261.
Taymur, Ahmad, *A'lam al-fikr al-islami,* 52–57.
———, in *al-Hilal* 41:8 (June 1933): 1033–1038.
———, in *al-Risala,* no. 57 (6 Aug. 1934): 1304–
   1305.
———, *Tarajim,* 140–143.
Zaydan, Jurji, *Tarikh adab al-lugha,* IV, 219–220.
Zirikli, *al-A'lam,* IV, 275–276.

Lesseps, Ferdinand de

(19 November 1805–7 December 1894)
French diplomat, entrepreneur, and creator of the Suez Canal. Born in Versailles, the son of a French consul of Basque origin who had earlier served in Egypt and a Spaniard who would become the great aunt of the future Empress Eugénie, Ferdinand was reared in Pisa and Paris and educated (at state expense) in the Lycée Napoleon (Collège Henri IV). After briefly studying law, he took a job in the army commissariat and then became an apprentice consul, working for his uncle, a consul in Lisbon, and later with his father in Tunis. Soon after his father's death in 1832, Ferdinand was appointed vice-consul in Alexandria, where he got to know most of the leading European and Muslim inhabitants, learned Arabic, and explored the countryside on horseback. During this time he met Prince SA'ID, then an adolescent under strict orders from his father, MUHAMMAD 'ALI, to lose weight. Lesseps befriended the boy, fed him macaroni, taught him French, and took him riding; years later the friendship would serve Lesseps well. In 1838 he was transferred to Holland and then to various consulates in Spain. During the 1840s he became attracted to Saint-Simon's ideas, among which was building a canal across the Isthmus of Suez. Betrayed by the government of Louis Napoleon's Second Republic while he was consul in Rome, Lesseps resigned in disgrace from the foreign service and retired to his wife's family farm for five years.

The death of 'ABBAS I and succession of Lesseps's friend to the governorship of Egypt brought him back to Alexandria. On renewing his friendship with Sa'id, he wrote him a memorandum on the advantages of a maritime canal joining the Mediterranean to the Red Sea. Easily convinced of the merits of the project, Sa'id announced the Suez Canal as his own decision to an assemblage of foreign consuls. It took just five days for Lesseps to draft a formal agreement, by which Sa'id granted the Suez Canal Company a ninety-nine-year concession to build and operate the projected waterway. Permission from the Ottoman sultan, which Sa'id set as a prerequisite, proved hard to get, and although merchants in London (as elsewhere) saw the advantages of the canal project to world shipping, the British government opposed the Suez Canal. The French emperor, Napoleon III, allied with Britain in the Crimean War, also resisted the project at first but eventually was won over by his wife, Empress Eugénie. For a while even Sa'id turned against the project and refused to meet with Lesseps. Only after the work had begun did those governments support the project. Although Lesseps persuaded many capitalists to invest in his company, the capital requirements of building the canal exceeded his estimates, and Sa'id had to commit large sums from his own pocket, shares that were assumed by the Egyptian government when Sa'id died and was succeeded by his nephew ISMA'IL.

As construction began, British and other hostile observers noted the reliance on Egyptian corvée labor and persuaded the Ottoman government to pressure Egypt to pay the workers, further raising construction costs. Fortunately for Lesseps, the excavating machine had just proved feasible. Napoleon III arbitrated the forced labor issue between the Canal Company and the Egyptian government, arranging a settlement by which Egypt paid 84 million francs (U.S.$17 million) as compensation for the loss of corvée labor, just as Lesseps was finding the new machinery cheaper than his lost conscripts. British efforts to persuade the Ottomans to block this settlement failed after the grand vezir was suddenly relieved of a personal debt to a Paris bank. Construction went on despite Anglo-French diplomatic rivalry and a cholera epidemic in Egypt. Once the French National Assembly passed an act authorizing the Suez Canal Company to issue preferred shares, Lesseps assured everyone that the Suez Canal would be opened by 1869. The khedive planned a celebration that included visits by many European heads of state, much new building in Cairo, and several months of ceremonies.

The canal began operation, with Lesseps heading the company that he had founded. His hope that all the governments of the world would buy shares, making his enterprise truly international, was not realized, but the Egyptian government's brush with bankruptcy in 1875 enabled Britain to buy its shares at a bargain rate, with Lesseps's blessing. But his own power declined, especially after TAWFIQ replaced Isma'il in 1879. His inability to deter British troops from invading Egypt via the canal in 1882 to quell 'URABI's revolution underscored his waning influence. The efforts of Lesseps to recapture some of his former glory by organizing the construction of a Panama canal led to financial scandals in Paris, a trial, and further disgrace. A man of boundless energy, charm, and vision, he was eulogized in the *Times* at his death: "He alone did more to restore to France the glory diminished by her disasters than all the miserable politicians taken together who pursued him with their hate." However, his hope that the Suez Canal would benefit Egypt was never realized, and most Egyptians now view him as the archetypal exploiter of their country.

Bibliographic Sources
Beatty, *Ferdinand de Lesseps.*
Blunt, *Gordon at Khartoum,* 122–129.
Bonin, *Suez: du Canal à la finance.*
Bonnet, *Ferdinand de Lesseps.*
Bouvier, *Les deux scandales de Panama.*
Chaloner, "De Lesseps and the Suez Canal."
Charles-Roux, J., *L'Isthme et le Canal du Suez.*
Courau, *Ferdinand de Lesseps.*
Crowther, *Six Great Engineers,* 11–39.
Eckstein, *Ferdinand von Lesseps.*
Elbée, *Un conquistador de génie.*
Farnie, *East and West of Suez.*
Hoskins, Halford L., *British Routes to India,* 303–319, 343–372, 495–568.
Kinross, *Between Two Seas.*
Lesseps, *History of the Suez Canal.*
———, *Le percement de l'Isthme de Suez.*
Marlowe, *Making of the Suez.*
Merruau, *L'Égypte contemporaine.*
Schonfield, *Ferdinand de Lesseps.*
———, *Suez Canal in Peace and War,* 21–41.
Taboulet, "De Lesseps et l'Égypte avant le canal."

Times (London) (8 Dec. 1894): 6a; (15 Dec. 1894): 5e; (17 Dec. 1894): 5e.

Wilson, Arnold T., *Suez Canal.*

Wright, *Twentieth Century Impressions of Egypt,* 143–153.

Linant de Bellefonds, Louis Maurice Adolphe

(23 November 1799–19 July 1883)

French engineer, geographer, and explorer. He was born in Lorient and planned to pursue his father's career as a seaman. After passing his examination in 1814 Louis went to Canada and the United States to survey the coasts, then accompanied the Comte de Forbin on a tour of several Middle Eastern countries. On arriving in Egypt in 1818 he worked for a time as a draftsman and entered the service of MUHAMMAD 'ALI, taking part in expeditions in Egypt, Arabia, and the Sudan. He explored the White Nile and the Sudan under the auspices of the Association for Promoting the Discovery of the Interior Parts of Africa. He made many drawings of ancient monuments, some of which are no longer extant, helped to design some of Muhammad 'Ali's irrigation projects, and proved the feasibility of building the Suez Canal, as befit a disciple of Saint-Simon. Linant's papers and drawings are reportedly in the possession of R. Bankes, Kingston Lacy, Wimborne, Dorset.

Bibliographic Sources

Anderson, *Communications with India, China, etc.*
Charles-Roux, J., *L'Isthme et le Canal du Suez.*
Dawson, *Egyptology,* 179–180.
Habib, *Hawamish,* 88–91.
Hanotaux, *Histoire,* VI, 238.
Kinross, *Between Two Seas,* 36–37, 62–63.
Laborde, *Voyage de l'Arabie Pétrée.*
Linant, *Journal d'un voyage à Merue.*
Mazuel, *L'oeuvre géographique.*
Times (London) (6 Aug. 1883): 6c.
Zayn al-Din, Isma'il Muhammad, *al-Ajanib,* 140–147.

Lloyd, Sir George Ambrose, Baron Lloyd

(19 September 1879–5 February 1941)

British high commissioner from 1925 to 1929. He was educated at Eton and at Trinity College, Cambridge, but did not complete his degree, because of the death of his parents. After a few years in his father's steel tubing business, Lloyd embarked on a career of public service. He became an honorary attaché in Istanbul and then headed a commission to inquire into future British trade with the Ottoman Empire and the Persian Gulf. Elected to the House of Commons as a Conservative in 1910, he traveled during recesses to Europe and the Near East. He held various staff positions during World War I, serving briefly at Gallipoli in 1915 and Basra in 1916. He was later attached to the Arab Bureau, where he came to know many of the Arab leaders. He then served for five years as governor of Bombay, improving housing and irrigation, but also curbing nationalist agitation. He again won a seat in the 1924 parliamentary elections, but in the following year he replaced ALLENBY as high commissioner for Egypt and the Sudan. Lloyd tried to establish firm control over Egyptian affairs, but the Foreign Office criticized his policies and undermined his position by negotiating a treaty with 'ABD AL-KHALIQ THARWAT in 1927. When a Labour government took power in 1929, the new foreign secretary obliged him to resign. Lloyd then served on the boards of several companies, strongly upheld imperial causes, and took charge of the British Council in 1937. His views on rearmament, collective security, and Indian policy agreed with those of Winston Churchill, hence Lloyd's return to official life in 1940, when he became colonial secretary and then leader of the House of Lords. Although sustained by idealism and resolution, his devotion to British imperialism, amply expressed in his two-volume *Egypt Since Cromer* (1933–1934), made him unsympathetic to Egyptian national aspirations.

Bibliographic Sources

Adam, Colin Forbes, *Life of Lord Lloyd,* 61–76, 193–225.
Charmley, *Lord Lloyd and the Decline.*
Current Biography (Jan. 1941): 520–522.
DNB (1941–1950), 512–514.
Foreign Office List, 1930, 314.
Grafftey-Smith, *Bright Levant,* 100–112.
Near East 28 (8 Oct. 1925): 434–435.
New York Times (6 Feb. 1941): 21.
Parkinson, "The Rt. Hon. Lord Lloyd of Dolobran."
Times (London) (6 Feb. 1941): 7d–e; (7 Feb. 1941): 7e; (8 Feb. 1941): 6f; (12 Feb. 1941): 7d.
Who Was Who (1941–1950), 691.

Loraine, Sir Percy

(5 November 1880–23 May 1961)
British high commissioner from 1929 to 1933.
Percy was educated at Eton and New College,
Oxford, and fought in the Boer War. He entered
the foreign service in 1904 and served in Istanbul
and Tehran, then in Rome, Peking, Paris, and
Madrid. He attended the Paris Peace Conference
and later served as minister in Tehran and then in
Athens. He succeeded Lloyd as high commissioner for Egypt and the Sudan, but his policy of
letting King FUAD control the government led the
Foreign Office to remove him in 1933. Loraine
was sent to Ankara, where he developed close
ties with Kemal Atatürk and strengthened Anglo-
Turkish relations. In 1939–1940 he served as
Britain's last ambassador to Italy before the outbreak of World War II. Churchill made no use of
his Middle East knowledge during World War II,
and he retired from public life. He was made a
knight commander of the Order of Sts. Michael
and George in 1925.

Bibliographic Sources
Foreign Office List, 1962, 450.
Geographical Journal 127 (Sept. 1961): 387.
Grafftey-Smith, *Bright Levant,* 119–127.
Illustrated London News 238 (3 June 1961): 941.
New York Times (24 May 1961): 41.
Times (London) (24 May 1961): 18a; (26 May
    1961): 17e; (30 May 1961): 15b; (13 June
    1961): 14e.
Waterfield, *Professional Diplomat.*
Who Was Who (1961–1970), 690–691.

Lutfi, 'Umar

(1867–14 November 1911)
Legal expert and father of the Egyptian coopera-
tive movement. 'Umar was born in Alexandria;
his father was Sayyid Yusuf 'Ashur, who had
represented Morocco at MUHAMMAD 'ALI's

court. 'Umar went to the Islamic Benevolent Society's school in Alexandria, École des Frères in
Cairo, and graduated from the School of Administration in 1886. After graduation, he served in
the government's department of legal cases,
SA'D ZAGHLUL's law office, and the *Niyaba.*
Later he became an instructor at the Khedivial
Law School, teaching criminal law and investigation, and served as its deputy director for sixteen years. He set up the *Nadi al-Madaris al-
'Ulya* (Higher Schools Club) in Cairo, serving as
its first president, and later founded many agricultural syndicates and other organizations. Lutfi
represented Egypt at the International Congress
of Orientalists in Geneva in 1894. He published
books in Arabic and French on various aspects
of the law and lectured at the Egyptian University. A supporter of the National Party (of which
his brother, Ahmad, was vice president), he died
in Cairo.

Bibliographic Sources
African Times and Orient Review 2:17–18
    (Nov.–Dec. 1913): 223–225.
al-Hilal 20:6 (1 Mar. 1912): 323–333.
Jindi, Anwar, *A'lam lam yunsifhum jiluhum,* 13–15.
———, *A'lam wa ashab aqlam,* 310–316.
Kahhala, *Mu'jam,* VII, 305.
Majallat al-Majallat al-'arabiyya 3 (Apr.–June
    1903): 216–232.
Mujahid, *al-A'lam al-sharqiyya,* II, 487–488.
al-Muqtataf 73:2 (Oct. 1928): 201–205.
Muti'i, *Haula al-rijal min Misr,* I, 143–156.
———, *Mawsu'a,* 382–390.
Rafi'i, 'Abd al-Rahman, *Muhammad Farid,* 290–
    302.
Shayyal, *al-Tarikh wa al-muarrikhun,* 180.
Walili, *Mafakhir al-ajyal,* 100–101.
Wright, *Twentieth Century Impressions of Egypt,*
    105–106.
Zaydan, Jurji, *Tarikh adab al-lugha,* IV, 304.
Zirikli, *al-A'lam,* V, 59.

M

frivolous singing and dancing. Her comeback failed. She did act later in the movie *al-Ghandura* [The Dandy], but did not regain her popularity. She spent the rest of her life in obscurity and genteel poverty.

Bibliographic Sources
al-Ahram, 13 Mar. 1965.
Butrus, *A'lam al-musiqa,* 233–235.
Najib, *A'lam Misr,* 480–481.
Zaki, 'Abd al-Hamid Tawfiq, *A'lam al-musiqa al-misriyya,* 147–151.

Mahdiyya, Munira
(1884–12 March 1965)

Actress and singer. Originally from a poor peasant family, Munira began her career as a dancer in Zaqaziq's coffeehouses, then in Cairo's Ezbekiyya district, where she was discovered by a vaudeville manager, 'Aziz 'Id, and presented as an entertainer between two acts. Gifted with a powerful voice, attractive figure, and sparkling blue eyes, she soon became popular in her own right and began singing the songs of Shaykh SALAMA AL-HIJAZI, moving over to his troupe around 1915. When the troupe broke up after the shaykh's death, she became the first woman to form her own troupe. She was especially known for her renditions of Bizet's *Carmen*, and under JURJ ABYAD's influence she tried to adapt the music to a more Arab style, which rendered her even more popular with her Cairene audience. She also tried to adapt Massanet's *Thais*, which, despite its pharaonic theme, did not gain the same acceptance. She was more successful, though, in adapting the Italian opera, *Edna*, because of its easier music, and acquired the nickname *Sultanat al-turb* (Sultana of Song). Toward the end of 1926 her troupe adapted the story of Antony and Cleopatra, aided by composer MUHAMMAD 'ABD AL-WAHHAB and poet AHMAD SHAWQI, but her voice was not equal to the music; nevertheless, in 1926 she won the prize offered by the Public Works Ministry to the best singer. She took part in inaugurating Egyptian state broadcasting in 1934 and sang before Kemal Atatürk. After a brief retirement, Munira rented BADI'A MASABNI's hall in 1938 and began her performance with readings from the Quran, which startled the audience, accustomed to more

Mahfuz, Najib
(10 December 1911–)

Novelist and film writer, winner of the 1988 Nobel prize for literature. The son of a minor government official who was a strict Muslim and an ardent nationalist, Najib was the youngest of seven children. The family lived in the Jamaliyya quarter but moved to 'Abbasiyya when he was thirteen. He attended a local *kuttab,* graduated in 1925 from the Husayniyya Elementary School, and got his secondary education at Fuad I High School. To improve his weak English, he translated James Baikie's *Ancient Egypt* into Arabic; SALAMA MUSA arranged to have it published as *Misr al-qadima* in 1932. A protégé of MUSTAFA 'ABD AL-RAZIQ, Mahfuz graduated from Cairo University's Faculty of Arts in 1934 with a degree in philosophy and spent two additional years working for an M.A. (which he did not complete). He worked as a secretary in the university (1936–1939), parliamentary secretary at the *awqaf* ministry (1939–1953), technical director for artistic censorship at the Culture Ministry (1953–1960), administrative head of the cinema organization (1960–1970), and adviser to the Culture Ministry and weekly writer for *al-Ahram.* He belongs to the National Council for Culture, the Supreme Council for Letters, the Writer's Union, and the Short Story Club.

Mahfuz began writing as an elementary school pupil, published his first story in 1932, his first collection of stories in 1938, and his first novel in 1939, aided by Salama Musa, then the editor of *al-Majalla al-jadida.* After writing three historical novels on pharaonic themes as disguised attacks on Egyptian politicians ruling under British tutelage, Mahfuz published a number of novels about life in Cairo, notably *al-Qahira*

115

al-jadida [New Cairo], *Khan al-Khalili*, and *Zuqaq al-midaqq* (published in English translation as *Midaq Alley* in 1966). For a while after the 1952 Revolution he had a literary dry spell, partly due to his dislike of military dictatorship and possibly to a psychological crisis, although he did write some film scripts. He then wrote his famous Cairo trilogy: *Bayn al-Qasrayn* (translated as *Palace Walk*), *Qasr al-Shawq* (translated as *Palace of Desire*), and *al-Sukkariyya* (translated as *Sugar Street*), portraying three generations of a Cairo family and the evolution of Egyptian politics, society, and culture during the twentieth century. In 1959 *al-Ahram* published in serial form his controversial novel, *Awlad haratina* (translated as *Children of Gebelawi*), which treats Judaism, Christianity, and Islam in allegorical terms offensive to strict Muslims; it has never been printed as a book in Egypt and has caused many Islamists to condemn him. His novel *Miramar*, written just before the June War, assailed the NASIR government's pretensions and shortcomings. A later work, *al-Maraya* (translated as *Mirrors*), presents fifty-five autobiographical sketches representing multiple viewpoints. His *al-Hubb taht al-matar* [Love in the Rain] shows the 1967 War's impact on Egypt's younger generation. Following the October War, Mahfuz was one of the first Egyptian writers to call for peace with Israel, and his books were officially boycotted—but still read—by Arabs outside Egypt. His Nobel Prize, the first to be awarded to an Arab writer, recognized his ability to express the hopes and fears of the Egyptian people and to shape classical Arabic into a vehicle of popular speech. Because he spoke out in defense of Salman Rushdie and supported the secularists on other issues, he was stabbed (almost fatally) in 1994 by a young Muslim extremist. He has made few public appearances since that time. He received Egyptian state prizes in 1962, 1968, and 1988 and the prestigious French Arts and Letters Award in 1995. His works have been translated into English, French, German, Italian, Russian, and Serbo-Croatian.

Bibliographic Sources

'Abd al-Hayy, *'Asir hayati*, 126–314.
Abu al-Majd, "Rajul al-shari' yaqul."
al-Ahram Archives, file 1196.
'Alim, *Taamulat fi 'alam Najib Mahfuz.*
Allen, *Modern Arabic Literature*, 192–204.
———, "Some Recent Works of Najib Mahfuz."
Badawi, M.M., *Modern Arabic Literature*, 19–22, 167–171, 221–230.
Beard and Haydar, *Naguib Mahfouz.*
Brugman, *Introduction*, 293–305.
Dawwara, Fuad, *Najib Mahfuz.*
EAL, II, 490–492.
Egypt, Ministry of Information, *al-Mawsu'a al-qawmiyya*, II, 1261–1262.
Enany, *Naguib Mahfouz.*
Faraj, Nabil, *Najib Mahfuz.*
Ghitani, *Najib Mahfuz yatadhakkir.*
Gordon, Haim, *Naguib Mahfouz's Egypt.*
Hafiz, Ahmad, *Ayyam min shababihim*, 59–68.
Hilal, "al-Nubugh al-fardi."
Jomier, "La vie d'une famille du Caire."
al-Katib, no. 22 (Jan. 1963), special issue.
al-Khuli, "Taslim wa tasallum."
Kilpatrick, "Egyptian Novel," in *CHAL*, 238–246, 253–259.
———, *Modern Egyptian Novel*, 71–113.
Le Gassick, "An Analysis of *al-Hubb tahta al-matar.*"
Mahfuz, Najib, *Atahaddath ilaykum.*
Mahmud, Fatima al-Zahra Muhammad, *al-Ramziyya fi adab Najib Mahfuz.*
Mahrez, *Egyptian Writers*, 17–38, 78–95.
Mikhail, Mona, *Mahfouz and Idris*, 8–24.
Milson, "Najib Mahfuz and Jamal 'Abd al-Nasir."
———, *Najib Mahfuz.*
———, "Reality, Allegory, and Myth."
Moosa, *Early Novels of Naguib Mahfouz.*
Muti'i, *Mawsu'a*, 632–637.
Nasr, Muhammad, *Safahat min hayatihim*, 240–250.
Peled, *Literary Works of Najib Mahfuz.*
Ramadi, *Min a'lam al-adab*, 176–182.
Sakkut, *Egyptian Novel*, 72–76, 114–142.
———, "Najib Mahfuz's Short Stories."
———, "Udaba Misr fi al-qarn al-'ishrin."
Shukri, Ghali, "Hawl al-minbar al-dawli li-jaizat al-Nubil."
———, *al-Muntami.*
———, *Min al-Jammaliyya ila Nubil.*
Somekh, *Study of Najib Mahfuz's Novels.*
Stock, "Naguib Mahfouz Turns 85."
Times Literary Supplement, 23 Sept. 1981.
Wessels, "Nagib Mahfuz and Secular Man."
WWAW, 1997–1998, 418–419.

Mahir, Dr. Ahmad

(30 May 1888–24 February 1945)

Lawyer, cabinet minister, premier, and party leader. Born to a prominent landowning family known for its nationalism (his father was Muhammad Mahir and his uncle, 'ABD AL-RAHMAN FAHMI), Ahmad earned his *license* from the Khedivial Law School and a doctorate from the

University of Montpellier. He later taught at the Khedivial Law School and the Higher School of Commerce. He joined the Wafd during the 1919 Revolution and was elected as a Wafdist to Parliament in 1924, briefly serving under SA'D ZAGHLUL as education minister. In that capacity he abolished the bedouin school and set up an industrial night school for workers. Accused of belonging to a terrorist group involved in assassinating Sir Lee Stack, he left the government. He became estranged from the Wafd after Sa'd's death, although he served as speaker of the Wafdist Parliament in 1936. His efforts to effect a reconciliation between young King FARUQ and the Wafd led to his expulsion from the party. He and NUQRASHI proceeded to set up the Sa'dist Party, which claimed to represent the principles of the Wafd's late founder, but their new movement soon sided with the king against the Wafd. Following the 1938 election, which the Wafd boycotted, the Sa'dists formed a coalition government with the Constitutional Liberals, and Mahir became finance minister. In 1940 he was again elected speaker of Parliament. In October 1944 after Faruq dismissed the Wafdist cabinet, led by MUSTAFA AL-NAHHAS, which had been forced on him by the British, Ahmad Mahir became head of a coalition government. He was assassinated in February 1945 by a young nationalist (probably a member of Misr al-Fatat) just after he had won parliamentary endorsement for the Egyptian government's declaration of war against the Axis Powers, so that it might take part in the San Francisco Conference to set up the United Nations. An honest and patriotic statesman strongly attached to Sa'd Zaghlul, he was not politically close to his brother 'ALI.

Bibliographic Sources
Abu Ruwa', *al-Shahid Ahmad Mahir.*
Amin, Mustafa, *Shakhsiyyat,* I, 34–47.
Barakat, Muhammad Bahi al-Din, *Safahat min al-tarikh,* 181–184.
Hijazi, Anwar, *'Amaliqa,* 271.
Mujahid, *al-A'lam al-sharqiyya,* I, 142–143.
Muti'i, *Haula al-rijal min Misr,* II, 53–66.
———, *Mawsu'a,* 75–81.
Sawadi, *Aqtab Misr bayn al-thawratayn.*
Tawfiq, 'Awad, and Hasan Sabri, *Wuzara al-ta'lim,* 67.
Times (London) (26 Feb. 1945): 4g, 6f.
'Umar, Mahmud Fathi, *Abtal al-hurriyya,* 83–93.
Zirikli, *al-A'lam,* I, 201.

Mahir, 'Ali

(29 November 1882–24 August 1960)
International law expert, cabinet minister, and four-time premier. 'Ali was from a landowning family famous for its opposition to the British; his father was Muhammad Mahir and his uncle, 'ABD AL-RAHMAN FAHMI. Born in Cairo, he attended the Khedivial Secondary School and graduated from the Khedivial Law School in 1905. He worked for a time in the *Niyaba* in Cairo. Although he joined the Wafd in 1919, he drifted into the court party surrounding Sultan (later King) FUAD, whose power he helped to strengthen. 'Ali Mahir became dean of the Law School in 1923, chaired the assembly that drafted the 1923 Constitution, and was elected to Parliament as an independent in 1924, resigning his academic position. When the Wafd Party was out of power, he held many cabinet portfolios, including education (1925–1926), finance (1928–1929), and justice (1930–1932). His major concern as education minister was to expand the number and improve the organization of the elementary schools, so as to implement the constitutional provision for free compulsory education. He served as prime minister in early 1936 while Egypt was resuming parliamentary government and as *chef du cabinet* for both King Fuad (in 1935) and his son, FARUQ (in 1936–1937), fighting against the Wafdists in Parliament. He formed a royalist government in August 1939, serving as both foreign and interior minister. Although he acquiesced in the expulsion of German and Austrian nationals from Egypt and the increase of the British garrison after the outbreak of World War II, he became increasingly anti-British once Italy entered the war and an Axis victory seemed likely. When he named nationalists to cabinet positions, the British suspected him of secret contacts with Nazi Germany and Fascist Italy. Threatened with deposition by Britain's ambassador, Sir MILES LAMPSON, Faruq reluctantly called for 'Ali's resignation in favor of HASAN SABRI in June 1940. In opposition, 'Ali became Faruq's chief confidant, and the British actually considered abducting him and smuggling him out of Egypt for the duration of the war. When they suspected that Faruq was about to reappoint him to head a neutralist ministry, amid large-scale popular demonstrations in Cairo, they forced the king to appoint a Wafdist cabinet, and 'Ali was kept under

house arrest for the rest of the war. In January 1952, after the Cairo fire led to NAHHAS's fall from power, he headed another royalist government. When the Free Officers ousted Faruq in July of that year, they asked 'Ali (or he persuaded them) to form a civilian government, but he soon resigned because he opposed their land reform law and other revolutionary ideas. In January 1953 he was asked to chair a projected constitutional committee, but the Free Officers did not seek its advice. He proposed a summit meeting of political leaders in late March 1954, then played no further role in Egypt's politics. 'Ali died in Geneva. His efforts to use the Palace, al-Azhar, Young Egypt, and the army to weaken the Wafd's popularity never won him the power he craved, but his efforts helped to undermine the 1923 Constitution as a basis for Egypt's government.

Bibliographic Sources

Abu al-Majd, "Misr ma qabla al-thawra."
al-Ahram, 18 Aug. 1939; 23 July 1953; 25 Aug. 1960; 8 Mar. 1973.
al-Ahram Archives, file 217.
al-Ahrar, 29 Mar. 1982.
al-Akhbar, 22 Mar. 1976.
'Azmi, *al-Ayyam al-mia*.
Berque, *Egypt*, 460–465.
Jab Allah, *'Ali Mahir*.
Lashin, *Adwa 'ala mawqif wizarat 'Ali Mahir*.
Mustafa, Kamal, *'Ali Mahir Basha*.
Muti'i, *Mawsu'a*, 368–375.
New York Times (25 Aug. 1960): 29.
Qadi, Shukri, *Khamsun shakhsiyya*, 57–60.
Radwan, 'Abd al-Rahman Mustafa, *'Ali Mahir*.
Sayyid, 'Isam Diya al-Din, *Hadith 17 yunyu 1940*.
Tawfiq, 'Awad, and Hasan Sabri, *Wuzara al-ta'lim*, 69–71.
Tripp, "Ali Mahir."
Zirikli, *al-A'lam*, IV, 321–322.

Mahmud, Muhammad

(1877–1 February 1941)

Politician, cabinet minister, and premier. Born in Sahil Salim (near Asyut) to a wealthy Upper Egyptian family (he inherited 1,600 *feddan*s from his father, MAHMUD SULAYMAN, and increased his landholdings during his lifetime), Muhammad was educated in Asyut, Cairo, and at Balliol College, Oxford. He held various administrative positions, becoming governor of Fayyum, the Suez Canal district, and Buhayra. He joined the Wafd during the 1919 Revolution and was interned with SA'D ZAGHLUL in Malta. He soon broke with Sa'd, however, and became one of the founders of the Constitutional Liberal Party in 1922, serving initially as its vice president and becoming its president in 1929. He entered the cabinet in 1926, became finance minister in 1927, and premier in 1928–1929. During his term of office, he reached a tentative agreement with the Foreign Office, but Britain insisted on having the approval of the Wafd Party, which demanded restoring parliamentary democracy under the 1923 Constitution, so Mahmud resigned in 1929. He was a member of the coalition of politicians that negotiated the 1936 Anglo-Egyptian Treaty. After King FARUQ dismissed the Wafdist government in 1937, Mahmud formed a caretaker coalition cabinet. His Constitutional Liberal Party regained power in the 1938 parliamentary elections boycotted by the Wafd, and he became prime minister in 1938–1939. He published a volume of his speeches under the title *al-Yad al-qawiyya* [The Strong Hand], and a memorandum on the 1929 Anglo-Egyptian negotiations. He was intelligent and patriotic, but nervous and intolerant of opposition. In 1927 a British observer remarked: "He is at times held back by the fact that he does not consider any Egyptian but himself clever enough to run the country without the English, and so wants to keep them here till he has maneuvered himself to the head of affairs."

Bibliographic Sources

'Abd al-Raziq, Mustafa, in *al-Hilal* 49:3 (Apr. 1941): 353–355.
Abu al-Majd, *Muhammad Mahmud*.
———, *Sanawat ma qabla al-thawra*.
Amin, Mustafa, *Shakhsiyyat*, I, 18–33.
Barakat, Muhammad Bahi al-Din, *Safahat min al-tarikh*, 178–180.
Deeb, *Party Politics*, 113 n, et passim.
Fuad, Faraj Sulayman, *al-Kanz al-thamin*, 280.
Hammud, *al-Mu'tadilun fi al-siyasa al-misriyya*.
Mujahid, *al-A'lam al-sharqiyya*, I, 165–166.
al-Musawwar, no. 852 (7 Feb. 1941): 12.
Muti'i, *Haula al-rijal min Misr*, III, 294–305.
———, *Mawsu'a*, 533–540.
Rafi'i, 'Abd al-Rahman, *Fi a'qab al-thawra*, II, 85–95.
Rizq, Yunan Labib, *Tarikh al-wizarat al-misriyya*, 322–323.
al-Siyasa al-usbu'iyya, 16 Feb. 1941.
Times (London) (3 Feb. 1941): 7d; (24 Feb. 1941): 7c.
Zirikli, *al-A'lam*, VII, 90–91.

Mahmud, Mustafa

(1921–)

Physician, journalist, writer, and Islamic activist. Originally from Minufiyya, Mahmud received his bachelor's degree in medicine from Cairo University in 1952 and worked as a physician until 1966. He then devoted his time to writing for *Ruz al-Yusuf, Sabah al-khayr, Akhir sa'a,* and *al-Ahram.* Evolving from secularism, materialism, and Marxism, his ideas moved toward Islam, as he explained in his autobiography, *Rihlati min al-shakk ila al-iman* [My Journey from Doubt to Faith]. He founded the Islamic Center, Mahmud Hospital, the Medical Center, and the Treatment Unit, all located in Cairo's Muhandisin quarter and supported by donations by Gulf Arab friends. He has a popular television program called *Science and Faith.* His plays include *al-Zilzal* [The Earthquake] and *al-Shaytan yaskun baytana* [The Devil Lives in Our House]. In 1997 his one-act play *A Visit to Paradise and Hell* was banned by the State Censorship Board after it had been approved by the rector of al-Azhar. Mahmud has also published novels and collections of short stories. He received a state prize in 1970 and a public opinion award in 1990.

Bibliographic Sources
al-Ahram Archives, file 3334.
Ayubi, *Political Islam,* 197–198.
Conermann, *Mustafa Mahmud.*
Najib, *A'lam Misr,* 475.
Nisf al-dunya, 16, 23, 30 Nov. 1997.
OEMIW, III, 23–24, article by Denis J. Sullivan.
Sullivan, Denis J., *Private Voluntary Organizations.*

Majdi, Salih

(1826–7 November 1881)

Writer, translator, and civil servant. His father's family came originally from Mecca, and Salih was born in the Giza village of Abu Rajwan. He was educated in Helwan and the School of Languages in Cairo. He received military training and served as a translator in the Military School during TAHTAWI's administration. Under ISMA'IL he established the translation bureau for the education council. He later shifted to the judiciary and translated many technical books from French into Arabic. The khedive charged him with translating the *Code Napoléon.* He became a judge in the Cairo National Court shortly be-

fore his death. 'ALI MUBARAK reported that Majdi published more than sixty-five books and treatises. He was the father of Muhammad Salih Majdi, the poet.

Bibliographic Sources
Asaf, *Dalil,* 307–310.
Cheikho, *al-Adab al-'arabiyya,* II, 18–20.
Fikri, 'Ali, *Subul al-najah,* III, 192–194.
Fuad, Faraj Sulayman, *al-Kanz al-thamin,* 212.
Hasan, Muhammad 'Abd al-Ghani, and 'Abd al-'Aziz Disuqi, *Rawdat al-madaris,* 342–345.
al-Hilal 7:14 (15 Apr. 1899): 417–418.
Majdi, Muhammad Salih, introduction to *Diwan al-Sayyid Salih Majdi Bey.*
Mubarak, 'Ali, *Khitat,* VIII, 22–25.
al-Muqtataf 57 (1920): 465–468.
Shayyal, *al-Tarikh wa al-muarrikhun,* 91–99.
Tajir, *Harakat al-tarjama,* 99–100.
Zaydan, Jurji, *Mashahir al-sharq,* 1st ed., II, 126–128.
———, *Tarikh adab al-lugha,* IV, 194.
Zirikli, *al-A'lam,* VI, 165.

Makram, Sayyid 'Umar

(1755–15 April 1822)

Popular leader and *naqib al-ashraf* during the French occupation. Born in Asyut and educated at al-Azhar, 'Umar led a crowd of Cairo residents against NAPOLEON's invasion. When their resistance failed, he escaped to al-'Arish and then Jaffa, but after Napoleon captured these cities, 'Umar Makram returned to Cairo. When the Ottoman army invaded Egypt from Syria in 1800 and threatened to oust the French, he led another popular uprising, which lasted thirty-seven days, until the French victory in the Battle of Heliopolis. He escaped again and did not return until the British and Ottoman armies had expelled the French from Egypt. Upon returning to Cairo and resuming his duties as *naqib,* he backed MUHAMMAD 'ALI's rise to power, but when he demanded a voice in Egypt's affairs, he was expelled to Damietta and four years later to Tanta. He petitioned the pasha for permission to make the *hajj* to Mecca and, upon his return, resumed living in Cairo. Soon afterward, a small rebellion broke out. Suspecting 'Umar's involvement, Muhammad 'Ali expelled him again to Tanta, where he died. Egyptians remember him as an early hero of their independence struggle. A central Cairo mosque bears his name.

Bibliographic Sources
Abu Hadid, *al-Sayyid 'Umar Makram.*
——, *Sirat al-Sayyid 'Umar Makram.*
'Ashur, Nu'man, *Butulat misriyya*, 9–26.
Baqli, *Abtal al-muqawama*, 123–124.
Gharaba, *Shakhsiyyat*, 87–92.
Hijazi, Anwar, *'Amaliqa*, 65–76.
Himada, "'Umar Makram, 1755–1822."
Ibrahim, Shihata 'Isa, *'Uzama al-wataniyya*, 19–52.
Jabarti, *'Ajaib al-athar*, IV.
Radwan, Fathi, *Dawr al-'amaim*, 21–24.
Rafi'i, 'Abd al-Rahman, *'Asr Muhammad 'Ali*, 60–64, 84–104.
——, *Tarikh al-haraka al-qawmiyya*, II, 263–266.
Sayyid-Marsot, *Egypt in the Reign*, 44–55.
Shinnawi, 'Abd al-'Aziz Muhammad, *'Umar Makram.*
'Umar, Mahmud Fathi, *Abtal al-hurriyya*, 8–9.
Zirikli, *al-A'lam*, V, 67–68.

Malet, Sir Edward

(10 October 1837–29 June 1908)
British diplomat and agent and consul general in Egypt from 1879 to 1883. Malet came from a family of diplomats and, after three years at Eton, entered the foreign service at the age of seventeen. He served as attaché to his father in Frankfurt, then in Brussels. He saw service in Argentina, Brazil, the United States, France, China, Athens, and Rome. He served as minister plenipotentiary in Istanbul during 1878, the year of the San Stefano and Berlin Treaties, forming close ties with Abdulhamid. In October 1879 Malet was sent to Egypt, soon after Khedive TAWFIQ had succeeded his father, and pressed for financial and administrative reforms. Sympathetic at first to 'URABI's demand for constitutional government, Malet insisted that Egypt must repay its public debts and sought Ottoman military intervention under European supervision; otherwise, he believed that joint Anglo-French action would be needed. When riots broke out in Alexandria in May 1882, he refused asylum on a British warship and stayed in the city to try to restore confidence among the Europeans. He suddenly became gravely ill and left to regain his health; he returned in time to accompany General WOLSELEY on his entry into Cairo in September 1882. He opposed executing 'Urabi and his associates. Malet then collaborated with Lord Dufferin in making plans for the reorganization of Egypt's government, but his health remained poor. He was replaced later in 1883 by Sir Evelyn Baring, later Lord CROMER; Malet became Britain's ambassador to Belgium and then Germany. His incomplete memoirs, edited by Lord Sanderson after his death, were published as *Egypt, 1879–1883*. There is also a section on his Egyptian experiences in his general memoirs, *Shifting Scenes*. Ambitious and capable of influencing Tawfiq, he lacked the necessary self-assurance and familiarity with Egypt to uphold Britain's interests effectively.

Bibliographic Sources
Blunt, *Gordon at Khartoum*, 38–43.
Cromer, *Modern Egypt*, I, 181–182, 205–206, 288–289, 345.
DNB (1901–1911), II, 555–557.
Foreign Office List, 1909, 403.
Malet, *Egypt, 1879–1883.*
——, *Shifting Scenes*, 50–81.
Times (London) (30 June 1908): 13d.
Who Was Who (1897–1915), 469.

al-Mallakh, Kamal

(26 October 1918–29 October 1987)
Archaeologist, writer, artist, film critic, and journalist. Kamal was born in Asyut, graduated in 1943 from the Architecture Department of the Faculty of Fine Arts at Cairo University and earned an M.A. in the language and architecture of ancient Egypt five years later. He worked as a structural engineer and as an instructor at the Faculty of Fine Arts, the Cinema Institute, and the American University in Cairo. He then became a technical drawer and critic for *al-Ahram*, starting in 1950, and briefly wrote for *al-Akhbar* and its sister periodicals in 1952. He discovered the Solar Boat of Cheops and directed the excavations around the Pyramids and the Sphinx. He was among the signers of the artists' manifesto "For a Revolutionary Independent Art," which set the tone for Egypt's modern artists. Mallakh received prizes from Italy, Lebanon, Ethiopia, France, and Egypt for his discoveries, and was given honorary membership in the National Geographic Society. He wrote at least seventeen books on art, history, and travel, including a guide to Cairo, Giza, Saqqara, and Memphis. He made numerous radio broadcasts, films, and lectures on Egyptian antiquities. He founded the Society of Film Writers and Critics and served as its president from 1985 until his death. He was a member of the

Supreme Council for the Arts, Letters, and Social Sciences and also the Supreme Council for Antiquuities. Starting in 1958, Mallakh wrote a daily column on the back page of *al-Ahram,* concentrating on entertainment and culture; he served as the newspaper's deputy editor-in-chief from 1975 until his sudden death in Cairo of a heart attack. Two of his paintings were hung in the Modern Art Museum, an exhibition of his photographs was held in 1989, and a club printed a book of poems in his memory.

Bibliographic Sources
al-Ahram, 30 Oct. 1987.
al-Ahram Archives, file 353.
Farah, Fayiz, in *Watani,* 9 Nov. 1997.
Mallakh, "Hikayati ma'a al-markab."
Mansur, Anis, "Wa lakinnana dahikna akthar."
WWAW, 1997–1998, 428.

Mandur, Dr. Muhammad

(5 July 1907–19 May 1965)
Literary critic, lawyer, professor, and journalist. Born in the Delta village of Kafr Mandur (Sharqiyya), Muhammad Mandur attended the primary school in Minya al-Qamh and secondary school in Tanta. He entered Cairo University in 1925, studying law and literature, the latter with TAHA HUSAYN, who encouraged him to become a critic and instilled in him a strong belief in Western culture; he earned his *license* in letters in 1929 and in law the following year. He won a scholarship for advanced study at the Sorbonne, where he spent nine years, gaining a reading knowledge of ancient Greek, French, and English. Obliged by the outbreak of World War II to return to Egypt without having completed his doctorate, he was appointed, with the help of AHMAD AMIN, as a lecturer at Cairo University's Journalism School. He also began writing for *al-Thaqafa.* He was appointed to the literary faculty at the newly founded University of Alexandria in 1942 and completed his doctorate the next year under the supervision of Ahmad Amin. In 1944 he became an editor for several literary magazines and shortly thereafter editor-in-chief of *al-Wafd al-Misri;* when SIDQI closed it down in 1946 on charges of being Communist, he became editor of *Sawt al-Umma,* another Wafdist daily. Mandur opened a law office in 1948 and was elected to Parliament as a left-wing Wafdist in late 1949. He also taught at the Drama Insti-

tute from the time it was founded, becoming head of its Department of Dramatic Literature in 1959. When *Sawt al-Umma* was closed after the 1952 Revolution, he wrote for other magazines, including *al-Majalla.* His 1956 trip to Romania and the USSR influenced some of his later writings, and he won the State Encouragement Prize for Literature in 1962.

Mandur's published books include *Min al-adab wa al-naqd* [About Literature and Criticism], *al-Fann al-tamthili wa al-masrah* [The Acting Art and the Stage], *Masrahiyyat Shawqi* [SHAWQI's Plays], *al-Naqd al-manhaji 'ind al-'Arab* [Systematic Criticism Among the Arabs], *Qadaya jadida fi adabina al-hadith* [New Causes in Our Modern Literature], *Ajhizat al-thaqafa* [Cultural Institutions], *al-Masrah al-nathri* [Prose Drama], and *Fi al-adab wa madhahibih* [Concerning Literature and Its Schools]. He also published translations from French and ancient Greek. His literary criticism evolved from one of "art for art's sake" into one of social engagement, reflecting changing political and intellectual trends in Egypt, as well as his own social origins.

Bibliographic Sources
'Abd al-Hayy, *'Asir hayati,* 177–185.
'Abd al-Sabur, *Rihla 'ala al-waraq,* 45–52.
Abdel-Malek, *Arab Political Thought,* 114–116.
al-Ahram (20 May 1965): 1.
'Ashri, *Thaqafatuna bayna al-asala wa al-mu'asara,* 18–19, 71–86.
'Atiya, Ahmad Muhammad, and Mahdi al-'Abidi in *al-Adab* 13 (Oct. 1965).
'Awad, Louis, *Dirasat fi adabina al-hadith,* 93–96.
———, *al-Thawra wa al-adab,* 8–35.
'Aziz, *Udaba 'ala tariq al-nidal al-siyasi,* 105–142.
Barrada, *Muhammad Mandur.*
Brugman, *Introduction,* 402–409.
Daghir, *Masadir,* III, ii, 1285–1289.
Dawwara, Fuad, *Muhammad Mandur.*
———, "Shaykh al-nuqqad yatahaddath."
EAL, II, 505–506.
al-Hilal 73:7 (July 1965): 4–7.
Jayyusi, *Trends,* II, 522–529.
Jindi, Anwar, *al-Muhafaza wa al-tajdid,* 773–776.
Khafaji, *Suwar min al-adab,* 6–17.
Mahasini, Wadad Sakakini, in *al-Ma'rifa,* no. 43 (Sept. 1965): 43–48.
Muti'i, *Haula al-rijal min Misr,* I, 209–221.
———, *Mawsu'a,* 549–556.
Naqqash, Raja, in *al-Hilal* 76:6 (June 1968): 4–17.
———, *Udaba mu'asirun,* 90–134.
Omrani, "Les tournants de la critique arabe."

Qandil, *Shaykh al-nuqqad Muhammad Mandur.*
Riyad, Henry, *Muhammad Mandur.*
Rizq, Fathi, *Khamsa wa sab'una najman,* 193–203.
Semah, *Four Egyptian Literary Critics,* 153–209.
———, "Muhammad Mandur and the 'New Poetry.'"
Shukri, Ghali, *Muhammad Mandur.*
———. *Thawrat al-fikr,* 241–313.
Tahir, Ali Jawad, in *al-Adib* 24:7 (July 1965): 52–53.
al-Tali'a (May 1966): 130–152.
Zaki, Ahmad Kamal, *al-Naqd al-adabi,* 132–141.
Zirikli, *al-A'lam,* VII, 111.

al-Manfaluti, Mustafa Lutfi
(30 December 1876–12 July 1924)
Writer and poet. Born in the Upper Egyptian village of Manfalut to a father descended from al-Husayn and famed for his piety and knowledge of the Shari'a and a mother of the Turkish Shurbaji family, Mustafa was reared in Cairo. His formal schooling was limited to al-Azhar, where he became a poet and also a disciple of MUHAMMAD 'ABDUH. Tried and jailed in 1897 for a poem deemed insulting to Khedive 'ABBAS, Mustafa was released after a year. He then broke with 'Abduh, wrote a laudatory poem to the khedive, and began writing weekly articles for *al-Muayyad.* He also won a prize offered by FARAH ANTUN's *al-Jami'a* for a poem about the Nile. In 1909 he became an Arabic editor in the Education Ministry under SA'D ZAGHLUL, whom he followed into the Justice Ministry in 1910. He became secretary to the Legislative Assembly in 1913 and later the Chamber of Deputies, serving until his death. Some of his articles were reissued in *al-Nazarat,* which became his most popular body of writings because he upheld traditional Muslim values. He argued with MAHMUD 'AZMI, who wanted to introduce the beret, in defending traditional male headgear. His poems tended to be short, highly emotional, and deeply committed to Islam. His popular novels, largely derivative from Western romances fashionable among Egyptians in his day, have not withstood the test of time, but his Arabic literary style was widely admired and enabled him to bring the novel as a literary form to the attention of many Egyptians who might otherwise not have been attracted to it.

Bibliographic Sources
'Abbud, Marun, *Judud wa qudama,* 221–226.
'Abd al-Fattah, Muhammad, *Ashhar mashahir,* II, 178–224.
'Abd al-Hadi, Ahmad, *al-Manfaluti.*
Abu al-Anwar, *Mustafa Lutfi al-Manfaluti.*
'Aqqad, 'Abbas Mahmud, *Muraja'at fi al-adab,* 170–184.
———, *Rijal 'araftuhum,* 62–74.
'Ashur, Nu'man, *Butulat misriyya,* 225–242.
Barbour, "al-Manfaluti—an Egyptian Essayist."
Becka, *DOL,* III, 117.
Bencheneb, Sa'd al-Din, "Deux sources d'al-Manfaluti."
Brockelmann, *GAL,* S III, 195–202.
Brugman, *Introduction,* 83–88.
Butti, *Sihr al-shi'r,* 230–239.
Daghir, *Masadir,* II, i, 730–733.
Dayf, *al-Adab al-'arabi,* 227–233.
Disuqi, 'Umar, *al-Manfaluti.*
*EI*2, VI, 414–415, article by Ch. Vial.
Farrukh, *Arba'a udaba mu'asirun.*
Fuad, Faraj Sulayman, *al-Kanz al-thamin,* 268–270.
Gibb, *Studies,* 258–268.
Hall, *Egypt in Silhouette,* 213–229.
al-Hilal 33:1 (Oct. 1924): 36–40.
Jayyusi, *Trends,* I, 140–144.
Jindi, Anwar, *al-Muhafaza wa al-tajdid,* 188–195.
Jundi, *A'lam al-adab,* II, 469–470.
Kahhala, *Mu'jam,* XII, 272–274.
Khafaji, *Qissat al-adab,* V, 3–16.
Manfaluti, *al-Nazarat,* 9–31; see also introduction.
Mazini, Ibrahim 'Abd al-Qadir, *Diwan,* II, 1–32.
Mikhail, Sa'd, *Adab al-'asr,* 256–262.
Mujahid, *al-A'lam al-sharqiyya,* II, 815–819.
Musa, Salama, "Mustafa Lutfi al-Manfaluti."
Pérès, "Le roman arabe."
Qadi, Shukri, *Miat shakhsiyya,* 292–294.
Qalamawi, Suhayr, in *al-Hilal* 70:9 (Sept. 1962): 7–11.
Radwan, Fathi, *Dawr al-'amaim,* 133–142.
Ramadi, *Min a'lam al-adab,* 73–79.
Sabri, Muhammad, *Shu'ara al-'asr,* I, 220–224.
Saharti, Ahmad 'Abd al-Hamid, *al-Manfaluti.*
Shalabi, Muhammad, *Mustafa Lutfi al-Manfaluti.*
Shalash, *Unknown Works.*
Tanahi, Tahir, *'Ala firash al-mawt,* 115–124.
———, in *al-Hilal* 38:2 (Dec. 1929): 201–206.
———, "al-Manfaluti al-sha'ir."
———, "Mashahir al-'alam fi tufulatihim."
———, "al-Sayyid Mustafa Lutfi al-Manfaluti."
'Ubayd, Ahmad, *Kalimat al-Manfaluti.*
———, *Mashahir shu'ara,* I, 320–341.
Walili, *Mafakhir al-ajyal,* 138–141.
Zaki al-Din, *al-Kuttab al-thalatha,* 65–126.
———, *al-Manfaluti.*
Zayyat, Ahmad Hasan, in *al-Risala,* no. 210 (12 July 1937): 1121–1122; (9 Aug. 1937): 2702.
Zirikli, *al-A'lam,* VII, 239–240.

Mansur, Anis

(18 August 1924–)

Journalist and popular writer. Born in Mansura, Anis earned a *license* in philosophy from Cairo University in 1947, receiving his M.A. the next year under the supervision of 'Abd al-Rahman Badawi. He taught philosophy at Ain Shams University while contributing articles to *al-Asas*. In 1950 he began working for *Ruz al-Yusuf* and later moved to *al-Ahram*, translating short stories and poems from German into Arabic. He also wrote stories of his own and translated Rommel's memoirs into Arabic. In 1953 he joined the staff of *Akhbar al-Yawm* and served as editor of *al-Jil, Hiya*, and finally *Akhir Sa'a*. In 1974 he became editor of *Uktubir*, founded by SADAT, and two years later took over the administration of Dar al-Ma'arif Publishing House. In 1980 he became editor-in-chief of *Mayu*, the National Democratic Party's magazine. He began writing his daily column, *"Mawaqif,"* in *al-Ahram* and became a member of the Consultative Assembly. As of 1997 he had reportedly written 177 books, among them *Hawla al-'alam fi 200 yawm* [Around the World in 200 Days] and *Fi salun al-'Aqqad* [In al-'Aqqad's Salon]. His stage plays include *Hilmak ya Shaykh 'Allam* [Your Dream, Shaykh Allam] and *al-Ahya al-mujawira* [The Neighboring Quarters]. He has translated plays by Dürrenmatt and Arthur Miller, among others, and some 200 short stories as well. He has also written serial dramas for television, one of which, *al-Ladhi yuhibb Fatima* [The One Who Loves Fatima], caused some press controversy in 1996; sometimes he has acted in his own plays. He received state prizes in 1963 and 1981, a book award in 1995, and at least four citations from the Television and Broadcasting Writers Association.

Bibliographic Sources
al-Ahram Archives, file 1495.
al-Ahram al-riyadi, 3–24 Aug. 1994.
Akhir sa'a, 31 Oct. 1995.
Dozier, "An Angry Old Man."
Elon, *Flight into Egypt*, 21–22, 152–155.
Fuda, *Nujum Shari' al-Sihafa*, 89–94.
Gharib, *Anis Mansur.*
Nasr, Muhammad, *Safahat min hayatihim*, 40–47.
Rizq, Fathi, *Khamsa wa sab'una najman*, 461–467.
Shalabi, Muhammad, *Ma 'a ruwwad al-fikr.*
al-Siyasi al-misri, 10, 17 July 1994.
WWAW, 1997–1998, 431.

al-Maraghi, Shaykh [Muhammad] Mustafa

(5 March 1881–21 August 1945)

Islamic scholar, reformer, and rector of al-Azhar. Born in Maragha (near Jirja, Suhaj province), Mustafa was educated at al-Azhar and became a disciple of MUHAMMAD 'ABDUH. He entered the Shari'a Court judiciary and served from 1908 to 1919 as the chief judge in the Sudan. In 1919 he became the head inspector within the Justice Ministry. He headed the Cairo Shari'a Court in 1920–1921 and became a member of the Supreme Shari'a Court in 1921, serving as its president from 1923 to 1928. He played a pivotal role in the 1926 Cairo Caliphate Congress, in which the delegates discussed restoring the caliphal office that had just been abolished by Mustafa Kemal [Atatürk]. Maraghi was rector of al-Azhar in 1928–1929 and from 1935 until his death, the interstice being caused by King FUAD's personal antipathy toward him. His reforms included the introduction of modern sciences and foreign languages into al-Azhar's curriculum. An opponent of *taqlid* ([blindly] following ancient Muslim customs), he called for the renewed exercise of *ijtihad* and for reconciliation among the various *madhhab*s (legal rites) and sects of Islam. He exercised much influence over young King FARUQ and supported the king's campaign for the Islamic caliphate (after having opposed similar claims advanced by Faruq's father). Invited to join the Arabic Language Academy in 1940, Maraghi resigned two years later because of the pressure of his other duties. He encouraged MUHAMMAD HUSAYN HAYKAL to write his biography of Muhammad. Maraghi wrote several books about Quranic interpretation and one that advocated translating the Quran into foreign languages. He died in Cairo and was buried in Alexandria. He was unique in enjoying the confidence of almost all Egyptian politicians of his day, except for King Fuad.

Bibliographic Sources
'Abd al-Hamid, Muhammad Muhyi al-Din, "Muhammad Mustafa al-Maraghi."
Adams, *Islam and Modernism*, 208–209.
al-Ahram (22 Aug. 1945): 3; (20 Feb. 1970); (2 Oct. 1997).
al-Ahram Archives, file 7110.
al-Ahram al-masai, 17–19 Jan. 1998.
Akhir sa'a, 6, 13 Sept. 1995.

'Allam, *Majma'iyyun*, 322.
al-Balagh, 24 Aug. 1945.
Bayyumi, Muhammad Rajab, *al-Azhar.*
Baz, *Thair taht al-imama.*
Fuad, Ni'mat Ahmad, in *al-Ahram*, 5 Nov. 1997.
al-Hilal 41:1 (Nov. 1932): 45–47, interview.
Jindi, Anwar, *al-Imam al-Maraghi.*
Kahhala, *Mu'jam*, XII, 34–35.
Kedourie, "Egypt and the Caliphate."
Kramer, Walter, "Shaykh Maraghi's Mission to the Hijaz."
Kurd 'Ali, "al-'Allama al-Maraghi Shaykh al-Azhar."
———, *al-Mu'asirun*, 383–388.
al-Manar 29:4 (17 July 1928): 315–316.
Mujahid, *al-A'lam al-sharqiyya*, I, 400–401.
Musa, Salama [S], "Shaykh Jami' al-Azhar."
al-Musawwar, 19 May 1995; 15 June 1995; 7, 14, 21 July 1995.
Muti'i, *Mawsu'a*, 526–532.
New York Times (23 Aug. 1945): 23.
OEMIW, III, 44–45, article by Amira El Azhary Sonbol.
Qadi, Shukri, *Khamsun shakhsiyya*, 115–118.
Ruz al-Yusuf, 4 Sept. 1995; 2, 9 Oct. 1995.
Sa'idi, *al-Mujaddidun*, 545–549.
Sayyid-Marsot, *Egypt's Liberal Experiment*, 190.
Sudani, *al-Asrar al-siyasiyya*, 294–302.
Tanahi, Tahir, "Shaykh Jami' al-Azhar."
Tantawi, Muhammad Sayyid, in *al-Ahram*, 28 May 1996.
al-Thaqafa, no. 348 (28 Aug. 1945): 949–950, obituary.
Times (London) (27 Aug. 1945): 7f.
Uhiba, *Manhaj al-Maraghi fi al-tafsir.*
Wajdi, "Wafat al-ustadh al-imam."
Wingate Papers, Durham University Box 469/10, "Remarks on Failure of British Officials to Understand Egyptians."
———, Box 466/9/8, draft biography, no author indicated.
Zawahiri, *al-Siyasa wa al-Azhar*, 55–70.
Zirikli, *al-A'lam*, VII, 103.

Mar'i, Sayyid

(26 August 1913–22 October 1993)
Politician, landowner, and economist. Originally from Sharqiyya province, Sayyid Mar'i studied agricultural engineering at Cairo University, graduating in 1937. Fascinated with agrarian reform, planning, and development, he was first elected to Parliament in 1944 as a Sa'dist. He helped to form the Agricultural Syndicate and was appointed president of the Agricultural Loan Bank in 1955. After the 1952 Revolution he played a major role in formulating NASIR's land redistribution program, becoming minister of state for agrarian reform in 1956. During the union with Syria, Mar'i was minister of agriculture and land reform. He was also on the executive committee of the National Union in 1956–1961 and of the Arab Socialist Union from 1962, serving also as its secretary-general in 1971–1973. Agriculture and land reform minister from June 1967, he was also deputy prime minister from November 1970 until December 1971. Mar'i was one of SADAT's most trusted advisers, and his son was married to Sadat's daughter. Although nominated to head the UN Food and Agriculture Organization, Mar'i was not elected. He chaired the People's Assembly from 1975 to 1978 and then assisted and advised Sadat until the latter's assassination. He retired from public life in 1984. Mar'i was a large landowner dedicated to agrarian reform and a politician highly adept at adjusting to the changing tides of government power.

Bibliographic Sources
al-Ahram, 23, 25, 27, 29 Oct. 1993.
Mar'i, *Awraq siyasiyya.*
Najib, *A'lam Misr*, 250.
Shimoni, *BDME*, 155–156.
Springborg, *Family, Power, and Politics.*
WWAW, 1993–1994, 423.

Mariette, François Auguste Ferdinand

(11 February 1821–19 January 1881)
French founder of Egypt's Antiquities Service, excavator of many archaeological sites, and organizer of the Egyptian Museum. Mariette was born in Boulogne-sur-Mer and was educated at the Collège de Boulogne. Unable to complete his education, he went to England to work as a teacher and model designer, then returned to France to earn his *baccalauréat-ès-lettres* at Douai. Supporting himself as a French teacher, he became interested in ancient Egyptian hieroglyphics, which he taught himself. In 1849 he took a position at the Louvre Museum, where he transcribed all its inscriptions. Sent to Egypt to acquire Coptic manuscripts in 1850, Mariette began excavating the Memphis Serapeum, where he won fame for his discoveries, many of which he smuggled out of Egypt. In 1855 he became assistant curator of the Louvre's Egyptian Department. Later, he resumed his work in

Egypt and, as an employee of the Egyptian government, campaigned vigorously for the preservation of Egyptian monuments, which were rapidly being carried away or destroyed. He began many excavations in the Nile Valley, eventually covering thirty-five sites with more than 2,780 workers, maintaining high standards of archaeological workmanship. He established the Egyptian Museum in Bulaq and guarded it with zeal bordering on possessiveness. He also helped compose the libretto for *Aida*. Mariette's prodigious publications did not encompass all his discoveries; many of his notes were destroyed when his Cairo house was flooded in 1878. His last act was to help form the School of Oriental Studies, now the French Archaeological Institute; its founding committee arrived just before he died. His remains were interred in a sarcophagus now set in front of the Egyptian Museum.

Bibliographic Sources
'Aqiqi, *al-Mustashriqun*, I, 331.
Bierbrier, "Auguste Mariette."
Carré, Jean-Marie, *Voyageurs*, II, 223–234.
Dawson, *Egyptology*, 194–196.
Deseille, *Auguste Mariette*.
———, *Les debuts de Mariette-Pacha*.
Drioton, "Le musée de Boulac."
Egypt, *Rapports sur la marche du Service des Antiquités*, 147–159.
Fikri, 'Ali, *Subul al-najah*, III, 163–172.
Garnot, *Mélanges Mariette*.
al-Hilal 5:16 (15 Apr. 1897): 601–608.
——— 11:4 (15 Nov. 1902): 114–118.
Mariette, *Mariette Pacha*.
Maspéro, *Bibliothèque Égyptologique*.
Revue des deux mondes 43 (15 Feb. 1881): 768–792, article by Eugene Melchior de Vogue.
Wallon, *F.A.F. Mariette*.
Zaydan, Jurji, *Mashahir al-sharq*, 1st ed., II, 117–125.

al-Marsafi, Shaykh Husayn
(1815–27 January 1890)
Scholar, teacher, and writer. Born in Marsafa, near Banha, the son of an Azharite scholar, Husayn became blind at the age of three but completed a course of study at al-Azhar and became a teacher there himself, mainly of Arabic language. In 1872 'ALI MUBARAK named him professor of Arabic Linguistics at Dar al-'Ulum, where he taught until 1888, writing *al-Wasila al-adabiyya ila al-'ulum al-'arabiyya* [The Literary

Means to the Arabic Sciences], published in two parts, and "Dalil al-mustarshid fi fann al-insha" [The Student's Guide to the Art of Composition], which remains in manuscript. The first to formulate the concept of an Arabic literary renaissance (*nahda*), he promoted Western methods for teaching language and literature. In October 1881 he published the essay "Risalat al-kalim al-thaman," which defined eight terms that were entering popular discourse during the 'URABI era: *umma* (nation), *watan* (homeland), *hukuma* (government), *'adl* (justice), *zulm* (oppression), *siyasa* (politics), *hurriyya* (freedom), and *tarbiya* (education). He taught at the School for the Blind and learned how to read and write braille. A liberal who remained faithful to Islamic precepts, Marsafi was more moderate than 'Urabi's disciples.

Bibliographic Sources
'Abd al-Jawad, Muhammad, *al-Marsafi*.
'Abd al-Latif, Muhammad Fahmi, in *Majallat al-Azhar* 28 (1956–1957): 977–980.
Abdel-Malek, *Idéologie*, 329, 416–417.
Ahmed, J.M., *Intellectual Origins*, 21–23.
Brugman, *Introduction*, 324–327.
Carré, Jean-Marie, *Voyageurs*, II, 223–234.
Cheikho, *al-Adab al-'arabiyya*, II, 94–95.
Delanoue, *Moralistes*, II, 357–379, 650–651.
EI2, VI, 602, article by G. Delanoue.
Hasan, Muhammad 'Abd al-Ghani, *A'lam min al-sharq wa al-gharb*, 67–81.
———, in *al-Hilal* 81:4 (Apr. 1973): 48–57.
———, "Husayn al-Marsafi."
———, *Tarajim 'arabiyya*, 135–150.
Hasan, Muhammad 'Abd al-Ghani, and 'Abd al-'Aziz Disuqi, *Rawdat al-madaris*, 352–355.
Kahhala, *Mu'jam*, III, 310.
Mandur, *al-Naqd*, 7–24.
Mujahid, *al-A'lam al-sharqiyya*, II, 704–705.
Rafi'i, 'Abd al-Rahman, *'Asr Isma'il*, I, 253–254, 269.
Shamis, 'Abd al-Mun'im, in *al-Katib* (Oct. 1977): 44–51.
Zaydan, Jurji, *Tarikh adab al-lugha*, IV, 239.
Zirikli, *al-A'lam*, II, 232.

al-Masabni, Badi'a
(1892–23 July 1974)
Singer, dancer, actress, and theater owner. Badi'a was originally from Syria; her father owned a soap factory near Damascus, but after it burned down, he vanished. Her mother took young Badi'a with her to South America but, hating life

in exile, returned after eight months to stay with various relatives, often moving between Beirut and Damascus. After learning to sew to earn her living, Badi'a quarreled with her mother and fled to Cairo to seek her fortune. Interested in acting, she managed to play some bit parts in JURJ ABYAD's theatrical troupe, then moved on to Ahmad al-Shami's troupe, in which she emerged as a star singer and dancer, playing for exclusively female audiences. After a brief and unhappy marriage to a young lawyer, Badi'a went back to dancing in the night clubs of Beirut, Damascus, and Aleppo. An Ottoman officer befriended her during World War I and saved her from destitution. NAJIB AL-RIHANI discovered her during a postwar visit to Syria with his troupe; she followed him back to Cairo and was invited to join his troupe, after which she starred in many of Rihani's productions in Egypt and Syria. They married in 1923 and spent their honeymoon with the troupe, touring South America. Quarreling after they returned to Cairo, she left both him and his troupe and proceeded to set up her own theater, for which she hired many star actors. Her theater's popularity enabled her to launch such new stars as Asmahan and her brother, FARID AL-ATRASH. She took on the role of mistress of ceremonies and pioneered in hosting foreign traveling troupes. She made her first film in 1935. Badi'a made her fortune during World War II, both because she entertained the Allied troops and because she received secret subventions from the Allies for her parodies of Hitler. Her main theater was located on what is now Shari' al-Jumhuriyya, near Opera Square, where her mocking treatment of the nationalist demonstrators on Black Saturday may have incited them to burn Shepheard's Hotel. She also owned a summer theater on the site of the present Dokki Sheraton. Evading the Egyptian tax collectors, she managed to smuggle her savings, about £E 500,000, to Lebanon in 1953 and bought a farm in Shatura, raising chickens and cattle. She died in obscurity.

Bibliographic Sources
al-Ahram, 15 July 1959.
al-Ahram Archives, file 2967.
Akhir sa'a, 22 Nov. 1950.
Danielson, "Artists and Entrepreneurs," 297.
al-Kawakib, 26 Apr. 1966.
Mahallawi, Hanafi, Layali al-Qahira.
Mallakh, Kamal, in al-Ahram, 27 July 1974.

Masabni, *Mudhakkirat Badi'a Masabni.*
al-Masrah, no. 48 (22 Nov. 1926): 16.
al-Usbu' al-'arabi, 26 Feb. 1968.
al-Wafd, 22 Feb. 1994.

Maspéro, Sir Gaston Camille Charles
(23 June 1846–30 June 1916)
French Egyptologist. The son of Italian immigrant parents, Maspéro was born and educated in Paris, attending the Lycée Louis-le-Grand and the École Normale. He later became professor of Egyptology at the École des Hautes Études and then at the Collège de France in 1874. He went to Cairo in 1880 as director of an expedition that evolved into the Institut Français d'Archéologie Orientale. In 1881 he succeeded MARIETTE as director of the Egyptian Museum and of the Antiquities Service. Although he went back to France in 1886, he returned to Egypt in 1899 to resume direction of the Antiquities Service, which he did much to develop in the next fifteen years. A list of his publications contains at least 1,200 items, among which are the *Cairo Catalogue*, *Histoire ancienne des peuples d'Orient*, and *Egypt: Ancient Sites and Modern Scenes*. He was knighted by the British government and received an honorary doctorate from Oxford University.

Bibliographic Sources
'Aqiqi, al-Mustashriqun, I, 332–333.
CE, V, 1561, article by Aziz S. Atiya.
Cordier, Bibliographie de Gaston Maspéro.
Dawson, Egyptology, 197–198.
Khumayyis, Sayyid, in al-Hilal 77:5 (June 1969): 71–75.
Wright, Twentieth Century Impressions of Egypt, 135.

al-Mazini, Ibrahim 'Abd al-Qadir
(19 August 1889–10 August 1949)
Humorous writer, journalist, editor, literary critic, and modernist poet. Al-Mazini was born in Cairo, but the exact date of his birth is disputed (some say 1890). His family traced its origins to the Minufiyya village of Kum Mazin. His lawyer father divorced his mother; his older brother squandered much of her money; and Ibrahim grew up in poverty. He went to the Nasiriyya Elementary School. Upon graduating

from the Khedivial School in 1905, he started to study medicine but fainted upon entering the operating room; he then turned to law, but finally attended the Higher Teachers College, from which he graduated in 1909. He taught at various secondary schools for the next decade, but found that his real métier was journalism. He was especially gifted at translating articles from the English press into Arabic. Influenced by his association with 'ABD AL-RAHMAN SHUKRI, al-Mazini wrote Arabic poetry for a while, publishing the two-volume *al-Diwan* with 'AQQAD in 1921, then shifted to prose after reading widely in English, Russian, and Arabic literature. He initially attached himself to AMIN AL-RAFI'I and served as an editor for *al-Akhbar* from 1919 to 1926. He then edited the weekly version of *al-Siyasa* from 1926 to 1930 and its daily version for the next two years. As editor of *al-Ittihad* from 1932 to 1934, he was once tried for having attacked the late SA'D ZAGHLUL. He edited *al-Balagh* for the last fifteen years of his life, developing close ties to 'ABD AL-QADIR HAMZA. He wrote for other newspapers and for weekly and monthly magazines; he briefly published his own review, *al-Usbu'*, of which only four issues appeared.

Mazini helped to found the journalists' syndicate in 1941 and was elected its first vice president. Because he wrote for such a variety of newspapers, his own political stance seemed protean, but he always opposed the Wafd. He was one of the first Egyptians to back the Palestinians against Zionism, writing articles in favor of Arab nationalism. Among his published books, *Ibrahim al-Katib* (1931), which some critics treat as autobiographical (despite his denial), was translated by Majdi Wahba into English as *Ibrahim the Writer* (1976). His poetry was deeply subjective, at times derived from classical Arabic or English models, but often moving and humorous. Elected to the Arabic Language Academy in 1947, he belonged also to its Damascus counterpart.

Bibliographic Sources
'Abbud, Marun, *Judud wa qudama*, 216–220.
'Abd al-Latif, Nasr al-Din, in *al-Hilal* 81:9 (Sept. 1973): 118–126.
'Abd al-Sabur, "al-Mazini sha'iran."
Abu Salmi, in *al-Risala*, no. 140 (9 Mar. 1936): 371–372.
al-Adib 8:9 (Sept. 1949): 63–64, obituary.

al-Ahram Archives, file 822.
'Allam, *Majma'iyyun*, 8–9.
Allen, *Modern Arabic Literature*, 214–219.
Badawi, M.M., "al-Mazini the Novelist."
Brockelmann, *GAL*, S III, 157–164, 280.
Brugman, *Introduction*, 138–147.
Counillon, "À propos d'une nouvelle d'al-Mazini."
Daghir, *Masadir*, II, i, 682–687.
Dayf, *al-Adab al-'arabi*, 261–269.
EAL, II, 521–522.
EI2, VI, 955–958, article by Ch. Vial.
Fuad, Ni'mat Ahmad, *'Abd al-Qadir al-Mazin.*
———, *Adab al-Mazini.*
———, *Qimam adabiyya*, 415–438.
———, in *al-Thaqafa* 14:712 (18 Aug. 1952): 20–21; 716 (15 Sept. 1952): 14–17.
Gershoni, "Emergence of Pan-Nationalism," 82–85.
Gibb, *Studies,* 281–284, 301–302.
Hawwal, *al-Sukhriyya fi adab al-Mazini.*
Hutchins, *al-Mazini's Egypt.*
Jad, *Form and Technique*, 45–50, 88–89, 115–127.
Jayyar, *Ma'rakat al-Mazini wa Hafiz.*
Jayyusi, *Trends*, I, 152–153.
Jindi, Anwar, *al-Muhafaza wa al-tajdid*, 466–480.
———, *al-Sihafa al-siyasiyya*, 387–400.
Jundi, *A'lam al-adab*, II, 473–474.
Jones and Sakkut, *Ibrahim 'Abd al-Qadir al-Mazini.*
Kahhala, *Mu'jam,* I, 99–100.
Kan'an, Hasan, in *al-Risala* 18:905 (7 Nov. 1950): 1245–1246.
Khafaji, *Suwar min al-adab*, IV, 72–75.
Khemiri and Kampfmeyer, *Leaders*, 27–29.
Khidr, 'Abbas, in *al-Risala* 17:842 (22 Aug. 1949): 1249–1250, 1266–1268; 848 (3 Oct. 1949): 1432.
Kilpatrick, "Egyptian Novel," *CHAL*, 228–229.
———, *Modern Egyptian Novel*, 26–30.
al-Kitab 4:8 (Oct. 1949): 322–323, obituary.
Kurayyim, Samih, in *al-Ahram*, 11 Aug.–8 Sept. 1989.
Mandur, *Muhadarat 'an Ibrahim al-Mazini.*
———, *al-Shi'r fi Misr ba'd Shawqi.*
Mazini, Ahmad, in *al-Hilal* 57:9 (Sept. 1949): 88–89.
Mazini, Ibrahim 'Abd al-Qadir, "Ahamm hadith fi majra hayati."
———, "Asatidhati."
———, *Qissat hayah.*
———, "Ummi."
Mubarak, Zaki, in *al-Risala* 11 (1943): 626, Mazini vs. Taha Husayn.
Nasif, Mustafa, *Dirasa fi adab al-Mazini.*
Radwan, Fathi, *'Asr wa rijal*, 161–199.
Ramadi, *Min a'lam al-adab*, 143–149.
al-Risala 17:851 (24 Oct. 1949): 1509–1511; 852 (31 Oct. 1949): 1535–1537, 1554–1555.
Rizq, Fathi, *Khamsa wa sab'una najman*, 163–169.
Rooke, *In My Childhood*, 60–61 et passim.

Saharti, *Adab al-tabiʿa*, 106–107.
Sakkut, *Egyptian Novel*, 22–27.
Saussey, "Ibrahim al-Mazini."
Shalash, ʿAli, in *al-Sharq al-awsat*, 24 Aug. 1991.
Shukri, ʿAbd al-Rahman, in *al-Muqtataf* 50:1 (Jan. 1917): 87–89.
Tanahi, Tahir, in *al-Hilal* 57:10 (Oct. 1949): 33–45.
Taymur, Mahmud, *al-Shakhsiyyat al-ʿishrun*, 43–49.
al-Thaqafa, no. 555 (15 Aug. 1949): 6; no. 602 (10 July 1950): 24–28; no. 603 (17 July 1950): 12–16; no. 604 (24 July 1950): 17–20.
ʿUbayd, Ahmad, *Mashahir shuʿara*, I, 12–44.
Wahhabi, *Marajiʿ tarajim*, I, 22–25.
Zayyat, Ahmad Hasan, in *al-Risala*, no. 845 (12 Sept. 1949): 1333.
Zirikli, *al-Aʿlam*, I, 72.

Mazlum, Ahmad

(1858–9 May 1928)
Cabinet minister and parliamentary leader. Ahmad Mazlum was born in Cairo, the child of a Turkish landowning family; he was educated in Egypt and in England, where he studied economics. Master of ceremonies under Khedive ISMAʿIL, he later served as a judge and public prosecutor in the National Courts, then as a Mixed Courts judge, and finally as chancellor of the National Court of Appeals. He served as governor of the Suez Canal. During the premiership of MUSTAFA FAHMI, he was minister of justice and later of finance. He was elected to the Legislative Assembly in 1913 and was named its president. Mazlum was *awqaf* minister in the cabinet of MUHAMMAD SAʿID, to whom he was related by marriage. Elected to represent Alexandria in the Chamber of Deputies, he was elected president of the body; later he was appointed to the Senate. He received the MUHAMMAD ʿALI medal and sixteen other decorations during his lifetime. His portrait, painted by MAHMUD SAʿID, is displayed in Cairo's Modern Art Museum.

Bibliographic Sources
Antaki, *al-Nujum*, 30–31.
Bishri, ʿAbd al-ʿAziz, *Fi al-mirat*, 89–94.
al-Hilal 36:7 (May 1928): 902.
Mujahid, *al-Aʿlam al-sharqiyya*, I, 67–68.
Najib, *Aʿlam Misr*, 116–117.
Times (London) (10 May 1928): 15b.
Walili, *Mafakhir al-ajyal*, 187.
Zakhura, *Mirat al-ʿasr*, II, 78.

McMahon, Sir [Arthur] Henry

(28 November 1862–26 December 1949)
British officer, colonial administrator, and high commissioner for Egypt and the Sudan. Born in Simla (India) to a military family, McMahon attended Haileybury and the Royal Military College at Sandhurst, where he was the top 1882 graduate. He served on the Punjab Frontier Force, then in the Indian Political Department from 1890 to 1914, rising to the post of foreign secretary in the government of India in 1911. He was responsible for demarcating the boundaries between Baluchistan and Persia and between India and China. At the start of World War I, when KITCHENER took charge of the War Office and Britain proclaimed a protectorate over Egypt and the Sudan, McMahon was named the first high commissioner. He maintained order in a troubled time, as two attempts were made to kill Sultan HUSAYN KAMIL, the reservists rioted, and Egypt was overcrowded with troops from all parts of the British Empire. He is best known for the Husayn-McMahon Correspondence, his exchange of letters with Sharif Husayn of Mecca, in which he is thought to have guaranteed that the sharif's family, the Hashimites, would rule Palestine, Syria, and Iraq once they had overthrown Ottoman rule there in World War I (he later denied that Palestine had been included in those lands). He was recalled suddenly at the end of 1916 and later served as president of the Bank of Persia. An avid sportsman and a lively conversationalist, McMahon knew little about Egypt and its needs.

Bibliographic Sources
DNB (1941–1950), 563–564.
Grafftey-Smith, *Bright Levant*, 20–23.
al-Hilal 23:4 (Jan. 1915): 3–11.
Jewish Agency for Palestine, *Documents*.
Kedourie, *In the Anglo-Arab Labyrinth*, 34–38.
Storrs, *Orientations*, 222–225.
Times (London) (6 Apr. 1939): 7b.
——— (30 Dec. 1949): 7d.
Who Was Who (1941–1950), 741.
Zakhura, *Mirat al-ʿasr*, II, 85–87.

Menasce, Baron Jacques Lévi de

(January 1850–1916)
Jewish communal leader. His family had settled in Egypt for a long time, and his mother was of the equally established Qattawi family. Jacques

studied in Egyptian schools, completing his education in France and Britain. He then worked in branches of his family firm in London, Liverpool, and Istanbul before returning to Egypt in 1874. A cotton and sugar merchant, he expanded his landholdings. He headed the Egyptian Land Company, the Free Publications Company, and the Delta Company. He was a board member of the National Bank, the Khedivial Bourse, the Life Insurance Company, the Tram Company, the Alexandria and Ramleh Railway Company, and the Salt and Soda Company. He helped to raise money to build Victoria College. He received a First-Class Franz-Josef Medal from the Austrian government (which had ennobled his father), the Third-Class Mejidi and Second-Class Osmanli Medals from the Ottoman government, and the Chevalier Medal from France.

Bibliographic Sources
Antaki, *al-Nujum*, 104–105.
Dawson, *Who Was Who in Egyptology*, 1st ed., 106.
Encyclopedia Judaica, XI, 1315.
Landau, *Jews in Nineteenth Century Egypt*, 146–147.
Mizrahi, *L'Égypte et ses juifs*, 69.
Wilbour, *Travels in Egypt*.
Wright, *Twentieth Century Impressions of Egypt*, 448.
Zakhura, *Mirat al-'asr*, I, 515–517; II, 142–144.

Menou, Jacques "Abdallah"

(7 September 1750–13 August 1810)
Successor to NAPOLEON and KLÉBER as commander of France's Army of Egypt. The son of an officer, Jacques had served the Comte de Provence and the Legion of Flanders. Chosen by the nobility to represent them in the 1789 Estates-General, he later returned to military life, commanding a regiment in the Army of the Rhine. In 1798 he joined the Army of Egypt, received seven wounds when the French stormed Alexandria, and became governor of Rosetta and then of Alexandria. After the Battle of Abu-Kir he commanded the siege of the castle. He acquired notoriety by marrying a Muslim Egyptian woman and converting to Islam. Upon succeeding Kléber in 1800, Menou projected a complete reform of Egypt's government and the collection of its taxes, but popular uprisings and the British blockade undermined his scheme. In 1801 he was defeated by the Ottomans and the British.

Upon returning to France, he held several political and military posts in Napoleon's empire. He was widely ridiculed for his stout figure and unmartial bearing, conversion to Islam, and belief in a permanent French occupation.

Bibliographic Sources
Bahgat, "Acte de mariage."
CE, V, 1591–1592, article by Harald Motzki.
Chandler, David G., *Dictionary of the Napoleonic Wars*, 279.
Connelly, *Napoleonic France*, 334–335, article by Milton Finley.
Dehérain, *L'Égypte turque*, 497–527.
Herold, *Bonaparte in Egypt*, 363–388.
Ivray, *La vie aventureuse du Général Menou*.
Khoury, René, "Le mariage musulman."
LaJonquière, *L'expédition en Égypte*.
Laurens, *L'expédition d'Égypte*.
Mackesy, *British Victory in Egypt*.
Miot, *Memories*.
Palmer, *Encyclopedia of Napoleon's Europe*, 190.
Puryear, *Kleber and Menou*.
Rigault, *Le Général Abdallah Menou*.
Shukri, Muhammad Fuad, *'Abd Allah Jak Minu*.
Tulard, Fayard, and Fierro, *Histoire et dictionnaire*, 980–981.

Milner, Sir Alfred, Viscount

(23 March 1854–13 May 1925)
Financial adviser and British statesman. The son of a physician, he was educated at King's College (London) and Balliol and New Colleges (Oxford). Milner worked as a teacher, lawyer, and journalist before going into politics, serving as private secretary to his friend G.J. Goschen, when the latter was chancellor of the Exchequer. Milner entered Egyptian service in 1889, serving as undersecretary of state for finance from 1890 to 1892. The publication of his *England in Egypt* (1892, with many subsequent revisions) convinced many English-speaking people that the British were successfully rehabilitating Egypt and hence should postpone their promised withdrawal from the country. His reputation as a colonial administrator was established, however, in South Africa, where he was governor of Cape Colony during the Anglo-Boer War. He later served in Lloyd George's war cabinet and undertook various missions abroad. Thus he was called upon, as colonial secretary, to head the commission of inquiry that went to Egypt in November 1919, after the revolution inspired by SA'D ZAGHLUL and the Wafd. Although the com-

missioners were boycotted by nearly all politically articulate Egyptians because the terms of their mission called for maintaining the British protectorate imposed in 1914, Milner grasped the depth of public feeling on this issue. His report, therefore, called for a reduced British role as protector, but this idea was rejected by the British cabinet. He also engaged in talks, ultimately futile, with Sa'd on terms for an independent Egypt allied with Britain. Although Milner was a perspicacious analyst of English and Egyptian interests, his ideas for reconciling them came to be appreciated only after his death. He is better remembered for his services in South Africa than in Egypt.

Bibliographic Sources

Crankshaw, *Study of Viscount Milner.*
Deighton, "The Impact of Egypt on Britain," 247–249.
DNB (1922–1930), 588–602.
Gollin, *Proconsul in Politics.*
Halperin, *Lord Milner.*
Headlam, *The Milner Papers.*
Marlowe, *Milner: Apostle of Empire.*
McIntyre, *Boycott of the Milner Mission,* 35.
Nimock, *Milner's Young Men.*
O'Brien, *Milner.*
Wills and Barrett, *Anglo-African Who's Who,* 116–117.
Wrench, *Alfred, Lord Milner.*

al-Misri, 'Aziz 'Ali

(1879–15 June 1965)

Arab nationalist officer and politician, sometimes called Abu al-Thairin. Of mixed Arab and Circassian background, 'Aziz was born in Cairo, graduated from the Tawfiqiyya Secondary School in 1896, studied at Istanbul's Military Academy and General Staff College, and was commissioned in the Ottoman army in 1904. Soon thereafter he became a member of the Committee of Union and Progress, but after it restored the Ottoman Constitution, he moved toward Arab nationalism, founding a secret society called *Qahtaniyya* (named for Qahtan, legendary ancestor of the southern Arabs) in 1909 and an Arab officers' group called *'Ahd* (Covenant) in 1913, all while he was a commissioned Ottoman officer. Arrested, tried for treason, and sentenced to death early in 1914, 'Aziz was freed by the Ottoman government and allowed to go to Egypt after protests erupted in the Arab lands and the

British ambassador interceded for him. When the Arab revolt began in 1916, 'Aziz served briefly as Sharif Husayn's chief of staff; he later joined the Egyptian army.

In the interwar years 'Aziz joined a few fringe groups dedicated to reorienting Egypt toward Arab nationalism and then some pro-Nazi organizations. He was appointed to head the Cairo Police School by MUHAMMAD MAHMUD in 1928. Named by King FUAD to tutor Prince FARUQ when he was cramming for admission to Woolwich in 1935, he soon resigned after a quarrel with AHMAD HASANAYN, and he spent the next eighteen months in Germany. In January 1938 Mahmud named him inspector general of the Egyptian army, and in the following year, Premier 'ALI MAHIR named him chief of staff, but he was disliked by the officer corps. The British accused him of undermining Egypt's cooperation in World War II, as mandated by the 1936 Anglo-Egyptian Treaty, and insisted on his dismissal in February 1940. He deserted the Egyptian army and tried to reach the Axis forces in the Western Desert, but was caught in 1941 and put on trial. Because of legal technicalities, he was released by the NAHHAS government in 1942. In 1951 he tried to lead the Egyptian volunteer fighters against the British in the Suez Canal Zone. 'Aziz was greatly respected by the Free Officers, with whom he helped conspire for the 1952 Revolution. They named him Egypt's ambassador to Moscow in 1953 and wanted to make him president in place of MUHAMMAD NAJIB, but he retired in 1954. He was fiercely nationalistic, but his enthusiasm often went beyond his political judgment. He died in Cairo.

Bibliographic Sources

Abu al-Majd, *'Aziz 'Ali al-Misri wa suhbatuh.*
———, in *al-Musawwar,* 7 Feb. 1980; 2–30 Jan. 1981.
'Abd al-Hamid, Muhammad, in *al-Anba,* 11 Apr.–9 Sept. 1989.
al-Ahram, 16 June 1965.
———, 4 Oct. 1951; 21 July 1959, memoirs.
al-Ahram Archives, file 2371.
al-Ahram al-Iqtisadi (15 Sept. 1967): 52–57.
al-Akhbar, 16 June 1965; 19 June 1972; 23 Aug. 1976.
Hijazi, Anwar, *'Amaliqa,* 250–256.
al-Hilal 22:8 (May 1914): 626–627.
Khadduri, *Arab Contemporaries,* 7–18.
———, "Aziz Ali al-Misri and the Arab Nationalist Movement."

Mumin and Manhal, *Min talai' yaqzat al-umma*.
al-Musawwar, 14 Jan. 1965; 25 June 1965.
Muti'i, *Haula al-rijal min Misr*, I, 193–206.
————, *Mawsu'a*, 340–349.
Radwan, Fathi, series in *al-Watan*, 19 Apr.–17 May
  1984.
Sadat, Anwar, articles in *Mayu*, 8 June, 22 June, 12
  July 1981.
Subayh, *Batal la nansahu.*
Zirikli, *al-A'lam*, IV, 231.

Mubarak, 'Ali

(1823–15 November 1893)

Official, cabinet minister, and writer. Born in Birimbal (Daqahliyya province) to a family of ulama, 'Ali decided at an early age to enter government service. Educated in his village *kuttab*, then at Abu Za'bal, the Cairo and Paris Polytechnics, and the artillery school at Metz, he served a year in the French army before returning to Egypt in 1849. He came to 'ABBAS I's attention by developing an economical method of facilitating the passage of boats through the Delta Barrages and was promoted from teaching artillery to managing all the government primary and preparatory schools and the Polytechnic. Dismissed from government service by SA'ID, he served in the Crimean War, then held various low-paying positions and was repeatedly dismissed from government service. ISMA'IL's accession enabled 'Ali to advance through various government posts, becoming director of education and public works and then of communications and railways (1868), *awqaf* and again communications (1869), education again (1870, 1872), and public works again (1871–1872). His national education program, based on resolutions passed by the Assembly of Delegates and called the "Rajab [1284] Decree," became the basis of Egypt's government school system. He also focused on creating thousands of state-supported *kuttab*s, appointing inspectors, training teachers, and publishing *Rawdat al-madaris* [The Garden of Schools], Egypt's first education journal. He served on the privy council (1873–1874), became head of the office of engineering and adviser of the Public Works Department (1875), and rejoined the cabinet as director of education (1878). He would later serve in three cabinets under TAWFIQ. Often he was dismissed from government posts because he lacked protection, even within the village elite,

and depended wholly on his ruler's patronage. Strongly patriotic, he urged Egyptians to view government work as an opportunity to serve the people, not merely to enrich themselves. He did benefit materially from his posts, but less than other officials. He was proud of his ethnic Egyptian background, cared about his students and peasants, and advanced the careers of several notable Egyptians. He wrote a patriotic story inspired by the traditional *maqamat* (a genre of Arabic literature, written in rhymed prose), *'Alam al-Din*, and a detailed description of nineteenth-century Egypt still used by historians, *al-Khitat al-Tawfiqiyya al-jadida* [New Guide to the Districts Ruled by Tawfiq]. He died in Cairo.

Bibliographic Sources
'Abd al-Karim, Ahmad 'Izzat, *Tarikh al-ta'lim fi
  Misr*, I, 22–27, 110–114; II, 50–52, 100–112,
  116–125, 135–138, 583–586.
'Abd al-Karim, Muhammad, *'Ali Mubarak*.
Abu Hadid, *'Isamiyyun*, 35–44.
al-Ahram (16 Nov. 1894): 2.
A'lam "al-Muqtataf," 145–156.
Amin, Ahmad, *Zu'ama al-islah*, 184–201.
Asaf, *Dalil*, 214–218.
Ayyubi, *'Ahd al-Khidiwi Isma'il*, II, 192–196.
Baer, "Ali Mubarak's *Khitat*."
Bahrawi, *'Ali Basha Mubarak*.
Bell, *Khedives and Pashas*, 192–196.
Brockelmann, *GAL*, II, 633–634; S II, 733.
Brugman, *Introduction*, 65–68.
Crabbs, *Writing of History*, 109–119.
Delanoue, *Moralistes*, 488–564.
Durri, *Tarjamat hayat 'Ali Mubarak*.
Dykstra, "Ancient Egypt in the Writings of 'Ali
  Mubarak."
EAL, II, 535–536.
*EI*1, I, 297–298.
*EI*2, I, 396, article by K. Vollers.
Fikri, 'Ali, *Subul al-najah*, III, 117–122.
Fliedner, *'Ali Mubarak und seine Hitat*.
Gharaba, *Shakhsiyyat*, 27–33.
Goldziher, "'Ali Pascha Mubarak."
Heyworth-Dunne, J., *Introduction*, 142, 243.
Hijazi, Anwar, *'Amaliqa*, 90–95.
al-Hilal 2:6 (15 Nov. 1893): 187–188; 7 (1 Dec.
  1893): 219–220; 8 (15 Dec. 1893): 250–251; 10
  (15 Jan. 1894): 289–295; 19 (1 Jun. 1894): 576.
Hunter, *Egypt Under the Khedives*, 123–138.
'Imara, Muhammad, *'Ali Mubarak*.
Jam'iyya al-Khayriyya al-Islamiyya, *Sirat al-
  marhum 'Ali Mubarak Basha*.
Kahhala, *Mu'jam*, VII, 173–174.
Kenny, Lorne, "'Ali Mubarak."
Khafaji, *Qissat al-adab*, III, 49–50.

Khalaf Allah, *'Ali Mubarak.*
Lashin, *al-Fikr al-siyasi 'inda 'Ali Mubarak.*
Louca, *Voyageurs,* 75–100.
Mubarak, 'Ali, *Khitat,* IX, 37–61.
Mujahid, *al-A'lam al-sharqiyya,* I, 100–102.
al-Muqtataf 18:3 (Dec. 1893): 145–154; 4 (Jan. 1894): 239–245.
Najjar, *'Ali Mubarak abu al-ta'lim.*
Qadi, Wadad, "East and West in Mubarak's *'Alam al-Din.*"
Rafi'i, 'Abd al-Rahman, *'Asr Isma'il,* I, 208–241.
Reimer, "Contradiction and Consciousness."
Schölch, *Egypt for the Egyptians!* 322–323.
Shaked, "Biographies of 'Ulama in Mubarak's *Khitat.*
Shamis, *'Uzama,* 70–77.
Sharqawi, *'Ali Mubarak.*
Shayyal, *al-Tarikh wa al-muarrikhun,* 99–112.
Shinnawi, Mahmud, and al-'Ashd, *Ali Mubarak.*
Tawfiq, 'Awad, and Hasan Sabri, *Wuzara al-ta'lim,* 31–33.
Tusun, *al-Ba'that al-'ilmiyya,* 237–244.
Walili, *Mafakhir al-ajyal,* 42.
Zakhura, *Mirat al-'asr,* I, 39–42.
Zaki, 'Abd al-Rahman, *A'lam al-jaysh,* I, 103–106.
Zaydan, Jurji, *Mashahir al-sharq,* 1st ed., II, 32–38.
Zayid, Sa'id, *'Ali Mubarak wa a'maluhu.*
Zirikli, *al-A'lam,* IV, 322.

Mubarak, [Muhammad] Husni

(4 May 1928–)

Officer, pilot, vice president, and Egypt's president since 1981. Husni Mubarak was born in Kafr al-Musayliha (Minufiyya); his father was an inspector for the Justice Ministry and wanted his son to enter the Higher Teachers College in Cairo. After completing Kafr al-Musayliha Elementary and Shibin al-Kom Secondary School (where he played hockey and excelled in Arabic and history), Husni chose to enter the Military Academy in 1947, graduating eighteen months later, after which he graduated from the Air Force Academy in 1950. After a brief stint as a fighter pilot, he taught at that academy from 1952 to 1959 and spent the following academic year at the Soviet General Staff Academy, learning to fly the Ilyushin jet fighter. In 1964–1965 he did advanced studies at the Frunze Military Academy. He was commandant of the Air Force Academy in 1967–1969, chief of staff of the air force in 1969–1972, and then became deputy war minister and commander-in-chief of the air force, where he spearheaded Egypt's preparations for the October War. Because of the air force's stellar performance in the war, he received Egypt's three highest military medals and was promoted to the rank of air marshal in 1974. The following year Mubarak was appointed vice president by SADAT, whom he served loyally for the rest of Sadat's life. He became president after the assassination, was nominated within a week by the National Democratic Party (whose executive board he had chaired since 1979), and was confirmed by a referendum without opposition. His policies have included keeping close ties with the United States, on whose economic aid Egypt was becoming dependent; strengthening state control over the economy to promote efficiency, raise general living standards, and curb government corruption; reestablishing diplomatic and economic ties with the Arab states without breaking Egypt's relations with Israel; and curbing the resurgent Islamists. He narrowly escaped assassination in Addis Ababa in 1995; his assailants are thought to be Egyptian and Sudanese Islamists. He has striven recently to improve Egypt's economy and to promote the peace process between Israel and the Palestinians. Less flamboyant than his predecessors, Mubarak inspires neither loyalty nor aversion among Egyptians.

Bibliographic Sources
al-Ahram Archives, file 3.
Ansari, "Mubarak's Egypt."
Baker, *Sadat and After.*
Bianchi, "Egypt: Drift at Home, Passivity Abroad."
Cantori, "Egyptian Policy Under Mubarak."
Cooper, *Transformation of Egypt.*
Current Biography 43 (Apr. 1982): 29–32.
Dessouki, "The Primacy of Politics."
Egypt, Ministry of Information, *al-Mawsu'a al-qawmiyya,* I, 11–14.
Encyclopedia of World Biography, Supplement (New York, 1987), article by Donald M. Reid.
Merriam, "Egypt After Sadat."
Miller, "Mubarak's Venture in Democracy."
Newhouse, "Letter from Cairo."
———, "Diplomatic Round."
Ramadan, 'Abd al-'Azim, *al-Sira' al-ijtima'i.*
Reich, *Political Leaders,* 367–372, article by Louis J. Cantori.
Solecki, *Hosni Mubarak.*
Sonbol, Amira, "Egypt."
Springborg, *Mubarak's Egypt.*

Mubarak, Dr. Zaki 'Abd al-Salam

(5 August 1892–22 January 1952)
Writer, poet, and teacher, often called *al-Dakatira* for having earned three doctorates. Zaki was born to a peasant family in the Minufiyya village of Sanatris; his father had Sufi associations that affected Zaki as a boy. He was educated at his local *kuttab,* at al-Azhar, where he received his *'alimiyya* in 1915, and at the Egyptian University. Already an avid reader and writer of poetry, he was arrested during the 1919 Revolution for inciting the crowds through his patriotic poems and refused to sign a loyalty oath to secure his release from a nine-month prison term. He received his first doctorate in literature in 1924 from the Egyptian University for a thesis on morals according to al-Ghazali. The publication of his thesis raised a storm at al-Azhar because of his criticism of the celebrated theologian's mysticism. After teaching briefly at Cairo University and writing for *al-Balagh,* he went to Paris in 1927, studied literature there, and earned his second doctorate in 1931 from the Sorbonne for a thesis on technical prose in the fourth Hijri century. After his return to Egypt, he took charge of Arabic language instruction at the American University in Cairo and the Lycée Française. He earned his third doctorate at Cairo University in 1937 for a dissertation about Sufism. He was sent to Baghdad to teach at Iraq's Higher Teachers College but returned after nine months. For seven years he served as editor of *al-Risala.* He was appointed an inspector in the education ministry and professor of Arabic literature for the Institute of Art and Drama, also working for Dar al-Kutub. Mubarak wrote approximately thirty books and became well known for his literary feuds with TAHA HUSAYN and 'AQQAD. His memoirs and recollections were recorded in *al-Hadith dhu shujun* and *Dhikrayat Baris.* He was well on his way to earning a fourth doctorate, with a thesis on al-Ghazali, from Alexandria University, when he was severely injured in a traffic accident. He survived only a few hours and died in Cairo. He received a decoration from Iraq in 1947. Having earlier donated his home to serve as the first elementary school in Sanatris, he is now honored by a cultural palace in that village bearing his name. His literary gifts enabled him to bridge French and Arabic culture.

Bibliographic Sources
al-Ahram Archives, file 2021.
al-Ahram al-dawli, 15 Oct. 1990; 5 June 1994.
al-Akhbar, 2 Jan. 1981; 8 Feb. 1992.
al-Balagh, 20 July 1948; 2 Aug. 1948; 21 Feb. 1950.
Brockelmann, *GAL,* S III, 302–305.
Buyumi, Muhammad Rajab, in *al-Risala* 20 (1952): 190, 446, 452.
———, in *al-Thaqafa,* Jan. 1982.
"Cinquante ans de littérature égyptienne," *Revue du Caire,* special issue, 1953.
Daghir, *Masadir,* II, i, 688–692.
Darwish, al-'Arabi Hasan, *Zaki Mubarak sha'iran.*
Hijazi, Anwar, *'Amaliqa,* 296–302.
Hilali, *Zaki Mubarak fi al-'Iraq.*
al-Idha'a, 27 Jan. 1990; 12 Aug. 1991.
Jindi, Anwar, *Zaki Mubarak.*
Jumayyil, Zuhayr, and Mubarak, *al-Fikr al-tarbawi 'inda Zaki Mubarak.*
Jundi, *A'lam al-adab,* II, 475–476.
Kahhala, *Mu'jam,* X, 8–9.
al-Kawakib (12 Oct. 1965): 14–15.
Khalaf, *Zaki Mubarak.*
al-Misri, 24 Jan. 1952.
Mubarak, Karima Zaki, *Zaki Mubarak.*
Mubarak, Zaki, *Zaki Mubarak naqidan.*
Muti'i, *Haula al-rijal min al-Azhar,* 97–112.
———, *Mawsu'a,* 164–170.
Nawwar, Ibrahim, articles in *al-Jumhuriyya,* 28 Jan., 2 May 1966.
Radwan, Fathi, *Afkar al-kibar,* 73–94.
Radwan, Muhammad Mahmud, *Safahat majhula min hayat Zaki Mubarak.*
Ramadi, *Min a'lam al-adab,* 103–110.
Taymur, Mahmud, in *al-Hilal* 74:5 (May 1966): 4–10.
———, *Ittijahat al-adab al-'arabi,* 158–171.
Uktubir, no. 1120 (12 Apr. 1998): 64–65.
Zirikli, *al-A'lam,* III, 47–48.

Mufattish. See SIDDIQ, ISMA'IL.

Muftah, Raghib

(21 December 1898–)
Historian of Coptic music. Born in Cairo, Raghib Muftah studied agriculture in Germany and returned to Egypt, where he met an English musicologist interested in the ancient Coptic liturgy. Working with a blind cantor, Mikhail Jirjis al-Batanuni, Muftah and the Englishman wrote down the notes and recorded the chants on paper tape, which was the only recording medium available to them in the 1930s. Believ-

ing that this music reflected the traditions of pharaonic Egypt, which had long ago influenced the development of Western music, they lectured on this topic at Oxford, Cambridge, and other universities in 1931. Working alone, Muftah went on to transcribe around sixteen volumes of the various liturgies used by the Copts. Eventually, he was able to set up a music section (under his own direction) within the Institute of Higher Coptic Studies in 1954 and to obtain more modern audiotaping equipment, as well as the collaboration of other musicologists. The American University in Cairo Press agreed to publish the music, with some timely intervention by the Coptic patriarch, Pope Shinuda, and the Library of Congress has preserved all of Muftah's recordings and transcriptions. Since 1994 he has restored most of St. Cyril's liturgy, which had been thought to be lost due to the deaths of the last cantors who knew this music.

Bibliographic Sources
CE, VI, 1717–1747.
Moftah, "Coptic Music" (1958).
———, "Coptic Music" (1968).
Najib, *A'lam Misr*, 211.
Stock, "Preserving Pharaoh's Psalms for Christ."

Muhammad 'Ali

(1769–2 August 1849)
Ottoman officer, reforming viceroy from 1805 to 1848, and founder of the dynasty that ruled Egypt until 1952. Born in Qavalla (Macedonia), Muhammad 'Ali was the son of a tobacco merchant who was also a soldier. His military (and possibly naval) experience was gleaned from fighting bandits and pirates in his province. He became an officer in the Ottoman army despite his lack of formal education; he did not learn to read until he was forty-five. He came to Egypt in 1801 as second-in-command of a 300-man Albanian regiment in the Ottoman army, allied with the British, to drive out the French invaders. He persuaded the Mamluks to aid the Ottomans and his Albanians against the French. He then maneuvered the ulama and Mamluk factions into ousting the Ottoman-appointed governors, KHUSRAW and then KHURSHID, so that he could himself be named to their post in 1805. He went on contending with the remaining Mamluks, until he had them massacred in 1811.

Acting as a loyal vassal of the Ottoman sultan, Muhammad 'Ali sent troops to suppress the Wahhabi rebellion in Arabia, thus conquering the Hijaz for Egypt. Constructing a Nile River fleet, he also sent forces to conquer the eastern Sudan in 1821, hoping to staff his armies with Blacks, but most could not survive Egypt's climate. He replaced them with Egyptian peasants, who had not been conscripted since antiquity. He ordered dams, dikes, canals, and catch basins built to improve Nile irrigation, and many cash crops were introduced, including long-staple Egyptian cotton. By putting all agricultural land under a state monopoly, he controlled the output and price of cash crops, thus raising the funds needed to pay for his other reforms.

Muhammad 'Ali was the first non-Western ruler who tried to industrialize his country on a Western model. He sent student missions to European universities, military academies, and technical institutes; he also imported Western instructors to staff the academies and schools that he founded in Egypt to train officers, engineers, physicians, and administrators. He set up factories to spin and weave textiles and to manufacture munitions, staffing them with Egyptian peasant conscripts. He created an arsenal in Alexandria for naval ship construction, enabling Egypt to take part in the Morean campaign against the Greek war for independence, but most of the Egyptian fleet was sunk at Navarino and the Ottomans eventually lost that war. When the Ottomans reneged on their promise to award Crete to Muhammad 'Ali, his son IBRAHIM invaded Syria in 1831 and governed that region for eight years. When the Ottomans tried to retake Syria, Ibrahim defeated them, the reigning sultan died, and the Ottoman fleet deserted Istanbul for Alexandria. Britain and Austria intervened against the victors, finally ousting Ibrahim from Syria but promising that Muhammad 'Ali could pass down his governorship of Egypt to his heirs. Once Egypt accepted the 1840 London Convention, it had to abide by the 1838 Anglo-Ottoman trade agreement, causing most of the state-run factories to close because they could not compete against British manufactures. He also had to limit his army to 18,000 soldiers.

The viceroy then lost interest in his westernizing reforms. He let his factories and schools decay and gave away many state-controlled lands to family members or to favored officers and officials of his government. Treated with silver nitrate for a bowel complaint, the cure affected his mental powers. In 1848 he agreed to relinquish his governorship to Ibrahim, who died soon afterward, leaving the post to 'ABBAS HILMI I. Muhammad 'Ali was one of the ablest men ever to govern Egypt and did much to increase the country's power and wealth, but he showed no concern for his subjects' welfare and established a system of personal rule that, in the hands of less capable descendants, would prove ruinous to his dynasty and injurious to Egypt. He died at Ras al-Tin Palace.

Bibliographic Sources

'Abbas, *al-Nizam al-ijtima'i fi Misr.*

'Abd al-Karim, Ahmad 'Izzat, *Tarikh al-ta'lim fi 'asr Muhammad 'Ali.*

Abdel-Malek, *Idéologie*, 23–38.

Asaf, *Dalil*, 133–146.

Baer, *History of Landownership in Modern Egypt*, 1–70.

————, *Studies in the Social History of Modern Egypt.*

Barakat, A., *Tatawwur al-milkiyya al-zira'iyya.*

Burke's Royal Families, II, 27–28.

Cameron, *Egypt in the Nineteenth Century*, 38–43, 58–215.

Carra de Vaux, *Penseurs*, V, 224–235.

Carré, Jean-Marie, *Voyageurs*, II, 279–299.

Cattaoui, *Mohamed-Aly et l'Europe.*

————, *La règne de Mohamed Aly.*

Charles-Roux, François, *Thiers et Méhémet-Ali.*

Clot-Bey, *Mohammed-Ali, vice-roi d'Égypte.*

Cuno, "Origins of Private Ownership of Land in Egypt."

Dehérain, *Le Soudan égyptien.*

Dodwell, *Founder of Modern Egypt.*

Douin, *Mohamed Aly, pacha du Caire.*

————, *Mohamed Aly et l'expédition d'Alger.*

Driault, *La formation de l'empire de Mohamed Aly.*

————, *Mohamed Aly et Napoléon.*

Durri [al-Hakim], *al-Nukhba al-durriyya*, 10–16.

*EI*1, III, 681–684.

EI2, VII, 423–431, article by E.R. Toledano.

Fahmi, Zaki, *Safwat al-'asr*, 24–39.

Fahmy, *All the Pasha's Men.*

Fakhiri, *Awwal athar li-Muhammad 'Ali.*

Faraj, al-Sayyid, *Hurub Muhammad 'Ali.*

Fikri, 'Ali, *Subul al-najah*, III, 316–319.

Fuad, Faraj Sulayman, *al-Kanz al-thamin*, 26–36.

Ghorbal, *Beginnings*, 207–232, 279–284.

————, "Dr Bowring and Mohammed Ali."

Gran, *Islamic Roots*, 31–33, 111–121.

Hamont, *L'Égypte sous Méhémet-Ali.*

Herrmann, *Mehemet Aly: Pascha von Ägypten.*

al-Hilal 1:8 (1 Apr. 1893): 337–352; 9 (1 May 1893): 390–401.

———— 10:17 (1 June 1902): 517–541.

———— 13:8 (1 May 1905): 442–449.

———— 57:11 (Nov. 1949): 7–12, letters to his sons; 40–41, pictures.

Hoskins, Halford L., "Mohamed Ali and Modern Egypt."

Hourani, "Ottoman Reform and the Politics of Notables."

Hunter, *Egypt Under the Khedives*, 14–32.

Jami'i, *Tarikh Misr al-iqtisadi.*

Jawhari, Mahmud, "Kayfa kana Muhammad 'Ali." *al-Kitab* 8 (Nov. 1949), special issue.

Kuhnke, *Lives at Risk*, 3–4, 17–23, 98–99.

Lawson, *Social Origins of Egyptian Expansionism.*

Mengin, *Histoire de l'Égypte.*

"Mohamed Ali jugé par lui-même," *CHE* 2 (1949): 18–60.

Mouelhy, "Mohammad Ali et l'éducation."

————, "Le wali Mohammed Ali et son divan."

al-Muqtataf 30:7 (July 1905): 521–532; 8 (Aug. 1905): 637–646; 9 (Sept. 1905): 717–725; 10 (Oct. 1905): 796–808; 11 (Nov. 1905): 901–909; 12 (Dec. 1905): 992–1000.

———— 31:1 (Jan. 1906): 105–107.

Nubar, *Mémoires de Nubar Pacha*, 3–56.

Owen, *Cotton and the Egyptian Economy.*

Politis, *Le conflit turco-égyptien de 1838–1841.*

Qadi, Shukri, *Khamsun shakhsiyya*, 19–22.

Rafi'i, 'Abd al-Rahman, *'Asr Muhammad 'Ali.*

Rajabi, *Tarikh al-wazir Muhammad 'Ali Basha.*

Rif'at, Muhammad, in *al-Hilal* 45:6 (Apr. 1937): 617–621, 689–691.

Rivlin, *Agricultural Policy.*

Rustum, "Syria Under Mehemet Ali."

Sabry, *L'Empire égyptien.*

Sa'idi, *al-Mujaddidun*, 476–482.

Sammarco, "I documenti diplomatici."

Sayyid-Marsot, *Egypt in the Reign.*

Shayyal, Jamal al-Din, in *al-Hilal* 54:2 (Feb. 1946): 237–240.

Shukri, Muhammad Fuad, *Bina dawlat Misr Muhammad 'Ali.*

————, *al-Hamla al-firansiyya.*

Sulayman, Muhammad, *Rasail sair,* 196–208.

Tagher, "Bibliographie analytique et critique."

————, "Mohamed Aly et les anglais."

————, "Mohamed Aly étudiait l'histoire."

Tignor, "Muhammad Ali: Modernizer of Egypt."

Toledano, "Mehmet Ali Pasa or Muhammad 'Ali Basha?"

Tucker, *Women in Nineteenth Century Egypt.*

Tugay, *Three Centuries*, 72–90.

Tusun, *Safha min tarikh Misr.*

'Umar, Mahmud Fathi, *Abtal al-hurriyya*, 17–23.

Walili, *Mafakhir al-ajyal*, 7–22.

Weygand, *Histoire militaire de Mohamed Aly.*

Wiet, "Les déplacements de Mohammed Ali."

————, *Mohamed Ali et les beaux-arts.*

Zakhura, *Mirat al-'asr*, I, 17–24.

Zaki, 'Abd al-Rahman, *A'lam al-jaysh*, 1–15.

————, *Muhammad 'Ali wa 'asruhu.*
————, *al-Tarikh al-harbi.*
Zaydan, Jurji, *Mashahir al-sharq,* 1st ed., I, 1–28.
Zirikli, *al-A'lam,* VI, 298–299.

Muhammad 'Ali, al-Amir
(9 November 1875–18 March 1955)
Twice heir to the Egyptian throne, horse breeder, painter, art collector, and writer. The second son of Khedive TAWFIQ and younger brother of 'AB-BAS HILMI II, Amir was born in Cairo and was educated there and in Switzerland. He had an excellent knowledge of French, English, and Turkish, and he traveled to many parts of the world, about which he wrote various books. During FUAD's reign, he supported the Wafd but later turned against NAHHAS. He served on FARUQ's regency council in 1936–1937 and was heir apparent until the king's son was born in 1952. He owned Manyal Palace, now a museum, on the island of Roda. A handsome, cosmopolitan bachelor, he wrote Arabic and French memoirs, some of which appears in Tugay's *Three Centuries.* After the 1952 Revolution, he moved to Lausanne, where he died.

Bibliographic Sources
al-Ahram, 2 Feb. 1970.
al-Ahram Archives, file 28155.
Antaki, *al-Nujum,* 15–16.
Durri [al-Hakim], *al-Nukhba al-durriyya,* 46–49.
Fahmi, Zaki, *Safwat al-'asr,* 95–98.
Kahhala, *Mu'jam,* XI, 46.
Musa, Salama [S], "Hadith ma'a al-Amir Muhammad 'Ali."
New York Times (19 Mar. 1955): 15.
Thabit, Karim, in *al-Hilal* 37:1 (Nov. 1928): 10–14.
Tugay, *Three Centuries,* 170–171.
Zakhura, *Mirat al-'asr,* I, 48–50.
Zirikli, *al-A'lam,* VI, 307.

Muharram Bey
(?–21 December 1847)
Military and naval commander and governor of Alexandria under MUHAMMAD 'ALI, whose daughter, Tevhide, he married. Originally from Qavalla, Muharram was appointed to command the Egyptian fleet in 1826. After most of his ships were sunk at Navarino the following year, he resigned and resumed his post as governor of Alexandria, where he was immensely popular. A neighborhood is named after him.

Bibliographic Sources
Fahmy, *All the Pasha's Men,* 176.
Rafi'i, 'Abd al-Rahman, *'Asr Muhammad 'Ali,* 451.
Walili, *Mafakhir al-ajyal,* 32.
Zaki, 'Abd al-Rahman, *A'lam al-jaysh,* 59–61.
————, "Taqrir Amir al-Bahr Muharram Bey."

Muhyi al-Din, Dr. [Ahmad] Fuad
(16 February 1926–5 June 1984)
Physician, professor, cabinet minister, and premier. Born in Kafr al-Shukr (Qalyubiyya) to a landowning family, Fuad received his first degree in medicine in 1949 and his doctorate in radiology from Cairo University in 1958. He also studied political economy in the Cairo Law Faculty in 1951–1953 and 1957–1958. He had been one of the members of the National Committee of Workers and Students that confronted the British occupation in 1946. He was a teaching assistant at Qasr al-'Ayni in 1949 and became a general instructor there in 1958. Elected to serve in five sessions of the National (later Popular) Assembly, he became ASU secretary-general in Qalyubiyya (1965) and was appointed governor of Sharqiyya (1968), Alexandria (1971), and Giza (1973), whereupon he entered the cabinet, first as minister of state for local administration (1973), minister of youth (1974), of health in the same year, and of Popular Assembly affairs (1976). He became deputy prime minister in 1980, then first deputy to SADAT when the latter took charge of the cabinet in 1981. In addition to being secretary-general of the Arab Socialist Party of Egypt in 1977, he played a leading role in the National Democratic Party. Muhyi al-Din became prime minister in 1982 and served until he died in his office two years later of a heart attack, probably due to a hard reelection campaign, during which the opposition press had predicted that he would lose the premiership and become speaker of the Assembly instead. He was a political technician loyal to Sadat and MUBARAK.

Bibliographic Sources
al-Ahram, 6 June 1984.
al-Ahram Archives, file 422.
Ghanim, Fathi, in *Ruz al-Yusuf,* 11 June 1984.

al-Jumhuriyya, 6 June 1984.
Muhyi al-Din, "'Ashar sanawat ma'a al-Sadat."
Najib, *A'lam Misr*, 367.
New York Times (7 June 1984): D22.
Shimoni, *BDME*, 166–167.
WWAW, 1997–1998, 471.

Muhyi al-Din, Khalid

(17 August 1922–)

Officer, politician, and journalist. Khalid Muhyi al-Din was born in Kafr al-Shukr (Daqahliyya) to a landowning family. He graduated in 1940 from the Military Academy, served as a cavalry officer, and in 1951 earned a B.A. in commerce from Cairo University. Although associated with Hadeto, he probably never joined that Communist group, but he did have early ties to the Democratic Movement for National Liberation. A member of the Free Officers and the Revolutionary Command Council, he called for the restoration of constitutional government and hence was assumed to have backed NAJIB against NASIR, leading to his resignation and brief exile. Leading the left wing of the officers' group, Khalid founded and edited *al-Masa* (a leftist daily) in 1956, served on the central committee of the National Union, became a member of the National Assembly in 1957, chaired the Egyptian Peace Council, and hence became a member of the World Peace Movement's presidential council in 1958. He was one of four men appointed by Nasir to set up the first conference of the Afro-Asian Peoples' Solidarity Organization in 1957–1958. He briefly chaired the board of *al-Akhbar* in 1964 and the Press Council in 1965. He became a member of the eight-man executive committee of the ASU in 1964, chaired the Aswan High Dam Committee, and was awarded the Lenin Peace Prize in 1970.

Because of his politics, he was jailed for two months after the May 1971 Corrective Revolution. His power waned under SADAT. Within the ASU he took the leadership of the leftist platform that evolved into the National Progressive Union Party and was one of its three delegates elected to the People's Assembly in 1976. He was suspected of inciting the 1977 Food Riots. In 1978 he founded and edited his party's organ, *al-Ahali*, and in the next year he was charged with antistate activities but was never tried. As a former RCC member, he was spared when Sadat jailed other dissidents in 1981. He has continued

to make many public appearances in Egypt and abroad. Now a member of the leftist "loyal opposition" to MUBARAK, he published *Li-hadha nu'aridu Mubarak* [For This We Oppose Mubarak] in 1987 and a memoir called *Wa al-an atakallam* [And Now I Will Speak]. The latter has been translated as *Memories of a Revolution, Egypt 1952*. Khalid won a parliamentary seat in 1990, after three previous defeats, and has emerged as an elder statesman.

Bibliographic Sources

al-Ahram, 5 Dec. 1992.
al-Ahram Archives, file 418.
Gordon, Joel, *Nasser's Blessed Movement*, 129–131.
Hammad, "Kayfa takhallas Majlis al-Thawra."
Egypt, Ministry of Information, *al-Mawsu'a al-qawmiyy*a, I, 341.
Najib, *A'lam Misr*, 199.
Shimoni, *BDME*, 167.
WWAW, 1997–1998, 471.

Muhyi al-Din, Zakariyya

(7 May 1918–)

Officer, politician, and vice president from 1961 to 1968. A native of Qalyubiyya, Zakariyya (who was KHALID's first cousin and a distant relative of FUAD MUHYI AL-DIN) studied at 'Abbasiyya Elementary School, Fuad I Secondary School, and the Military Academy, graduating with NASIR and SADAT in 1938. He got to know Nasir, however, at Manqabad in 1939 and later served in the Sudan. After graduating from the General Staff College in 1948, Zakariyya went off at once to serve in Palestine, including the siege at Faluja. He then became an instructor at the Military Academy and later at the Staff College. Joining the Free Officers on the eve of the 1952 Revolution, he became a member of the RCC. Taking charge of military intelligence, he served as interior minister from 1953 to 1962; his responsibilities also covered state security and organizing the secret service (*Mukhabarat*). He became vice president one month before the United Arab Republic broke up. He was also premier and interior minister from October 1965 to September 1966, when he resigned because of his support for an IMF recommendation to devalue Egypt's currency and perhaps also because of differences over the Yemen Civil War. He became vice president, however, served on the

ASU Executive Committee, superintended the MUHAMMAD 'ALI dynasty's sequestered properties, and organized the popular resistance forces in May 1967. When Nasir resigned at the end of the June War, he designated Zakariyya as his successor, but the latter declined to serve after massive protest demonstrations. He continued to serve as vice president and also as deputy prime minister until he left the cabinet in March 1968. He has held no government post since that time, although he was considered as a possible successor to Nasir in 1970. He publicly opposed Sadat's peace initiative with Israel. Zakariyya is thought to have opposed the extension of Arab socialism and closer ties with the USSR, but he could not persuade Nasir to adopt his policies. He has received eighteen decorations from Arab and foreign governments.

Bibliographic Sources
al-Ahram Archives, file 7.
Egypt, Ministry of Information, *al-Mawsu'a al-qawmiyya,* I, 372–373.
Najib, *A'lam Misr,* 224–225.
Shimoni, *BDME,* 167–168.
al-Tali'a (Nov. 1965): 6–26.
Waterbury, *Egypt of Nasser and Sadat,* 96–97.
WWAW, 1997–1998, 471.

Mukhtar, Mahmud

(10 May 1891–27 March 1934)
Sculptor. Born in a village near al-Mahalla al-Kubra, Mahmud attended his village *kuttab,* then studied in Prince Yusuf Kamal's School of Fine Arts in Cairo, graduating in 1911, and was sent to complete his studies at the École Supérieure des Beaux Arts in Paris. During his stay there, he was attracted to the heroic interpretations by the sculptor Antoine Bourdelle and to the Art Deco movement. In addition, he was strongly influenced by his teacher Guillaume Laplagne and by his early exposure to Egyptian Arab folk epics. Although he enjoyed the bohemian life of a Paris artist, he remained firmly patriotic. Upon returning to Cairo, he sculpted the statue called *Nahdat Misr* (The Awakening of Egypt), a model of which had been displayed in an art exhibit in France in 1920. In May 1928 the statue was placed in front of Cairo's main railway station; it was later moved to the mall leading to the University of Cairo. He began a statue of SA'D ZAGHLUL but died of tuberculosis before he

could finish it. He also did portrait busts of Sa'd, 'ADLI YAKAN, Dr. 'ALI IBRAHIM, and several Europeans. Mukhtar's best work combines pharaonic formalism with a romantic celebration of Egypt's folklore and environment. His sculptures, well known and loved by the Egyptian people, are mostly housed in the Mukhtar Museum (actually a park) in Zamalek.

Bibliographic Sources
Abou-Ghazi and Boctor, *Moukhtar ou le reveil de l'Égypte.*
Abu Ghazi, *al-Maththal Mukhtar.*
———— in *al-Hilal* 73:3 (Mar. 1965): 146–162.
————, *Mukhtar.*
Abu al-Majd, *Amin al-Rafi'i,* 161–167.
al-Ahram (28 Mar. 1934): 10.
Bishri, 'Abd al-'Aziz, *Fi al-mirat,* 183–190.
al-Hilal 42:7 (May 1934): 801–808, illustrated obituary.
Iskandar, *Khamsun sana min al-fann,* 15–22.
Jindi, Anwar, *A'lam wa ashab aqlam,* 422–434.
Karnouk, *Modern Egyptian Art,* 11–18.
al-Musawwar, no. 495 (6 Apr. 1934): 2.
Ostle, "Modern Egyptian Renaissance Man."
Shal, *Mahmud Mukhtar.*
Zirikli, *al-A'lam,* VII, 187.

Murad Bey Muhammad

(?–22 April 1801)
Mamluk leader, successor to MUHAMMAD BEY ABU AL-DHAHAB, and rival to IBRAHIM BEY MUHAMMAD as Egypt's leader from 1775 to 1798. He commanded the Mamluk cavalry that was defeated by NAPOLEON's army in the Battle of Imbaba. As Napoleon occupied Cairo and tried to make peace with him, he fled to Upper Egypt. Murad Bey spurned his offer of the governorship of Jirja province and tried to offer money to the French forces to leave Egypt. He repeatedly evaded French attempts to capture him and later offered to ally himself with the British, whom he would have allowed to occupy Alexandria, Damietta, and Rosetta. The Mamluks would also have paid the Ottomans an annual tribute and a war indemnity. He died of the plague before he could conclude this agreement and is remembered as a cruel and extortionate ruler.

Bibliographic Sources
Browne, Haji Abdallah, *Bonaparte in Egypt,* 54–56, 92–93.
Crecelius, "*Waqfiyah* of Muhammad Bey Abu al-Dhahab," 102.

Dehérain, *L'Égypte turc*, 140–153, 510–514.
Herold, *Bonaparte in Egypt*, 230–262.
Jabarti, *'Ajaib al-athar*, III, 230–232.
Volney, *Voyage en Égypte,* "État Politique," chap.
vi.

Musa, Nabawiyya
(1886–30 April 1951)
Schoolteacher, administrator, and pioneer feminist. Nabawiyya was born in Zaqaziq; her father,
an army officer, died before she was born, and
her mother reared her in Cairo. She was educated in the girls' section of 'Abbas Primary
School and the Saniyya School Teachers Training Program, graduating in 1906. She began
teaching at the girls' section of the 'Abbas Primary School and petitioned for the right to take
the state baccalaureate examination, then limited
to boys. When she was allowed to take the test at
home in 1907, she scored in the top third of that
class, but no other girl pupil was allowed to sit
for the examination until after 1922. Although
barred from enrolling in the new Egyptian University, she was invited to teach in the women's
extramural section of the university in 1909, and
her lectures were published in *al-Ahram* in 1912.
In 1909 she also became principal of the Girls'
School in Fayyum, the first of many administrative assignments. In 1910 she became principal
of the Women Teachers Training School in
Mansura and in 1915 of the Wardian Women
Teachers Training School in Alexandria. Nine
years later the Egyptian government made her
the chief inspector of state schools for girls.
Fired in 1926 by the Education Ministry for insubordination (or for exposing acts of sexual ha-
rassment and misconduct), she then concentrated on running two private girls' schools that
she had founded, a primary school in Alexandria
and a secondary school in Cairo. She focused on
expanding opportunities for women, writing
pseudonymous articles for Cairo newspapers,
publishing *al-Mara wa al-'amal* [Women and
Work] in 1920 and other books on women's education, and founding in 1937 a weekly magazine
for girls called *al-Fatat*. Her public career ended
in 1942 when she was jailed for protesting
against the government's submission to the
British, but she was cleared in court and later secured her government pension rights. Upon her
death in Alexandria, she bequeathed to the state
the schools she had founded. In a period of rapid
westernization, she upheld high standards of
conduct for Egyptians, both men and women.

Bibliographic Sources
'Abd al-Halim, *Nisa*, 18–24.
al-Ahram, 29 Apr. 1954; 14 May 1956.
al-Ahram Archives, file 2075.
Akhir lahza, 1 June 1956.
Badran, "Feminism and Nationalism in Autobiog-
  raphy.
———, *Feminists*, 38–44, 53–60, 65–69, 91–92.
———, "Feminist Politics," in Spagnolo, *Prob-
  lems,* 27–48.
———, "Feminist Vision."
Badran and Cooke, *Opening the Gates*, 257–269.
EAL, II, 554.
Kahhala, *A'lam al-nisa,* 4th ed., V, 163.
Kazim, "al-Raida Nabawiya Musa.
Mikhail, Mona, *Images of Arab Women.*
al-Muqtataf 38:4 (Apr. 1911): 330–336.
Musa, Nabawiyya, "Dhikrayati."
OEMIW, III, 179–180, article by Margot Badran.
Qadi, Shukri, *Khamsun shakhsiyya*, 119–122.
Salim, Latifa Muhammad, "Changing Position of
  the Egyptian Woman."
Zirikli, *al-A'lam*, VIII, 7–8.

Musa, Salama
(4 January 1887–4 August 1958)
Journalist, writer, and socialist. Salama Musa was
born in Kafr al-Afi, near Zaqaziq (Sharqiyya), to
a Coptic family; his father died soon after. Salama
attended a Muslim *kuttab*, a Coptic school, and
then a government primary school. He studied at
the Khedivial Secondary School from 1903 to
1907, but his intellectual formation owed more to
the influence of FARAH ANTUN, a secularist writer,
and to AHMAD LUTFI AL-SAYYID than to school.
Drawing on a monthly pension that he had inherited from his father, he traveled in 1907 to Istanbul and then to Europe, spending a year in France
to learn more about the French language and culture, for which he had a lifelong predilection. After three months back in Cairo, writing for *al-
Liwa*, Musa went to London for four years,
initially studying law, and came under the influence of the Fabian Society. Returning to Egypt in
1913, he tried to found a socialist magazine, *al-
Mustaqbal* [The Future], but the government ordered him to suspend publication. He spent most
of World War I teaching in a village near Zaqaziq
and observing peasant living conditions. After his
mother died in 1916, he taught at the Tawfiqiyya

School in Cairo. He tried to form a socialist party in 1920. He taught briefly, got married, and then became an editor for *al-Hilal* and *Kull shay* in 1923–1929, initially writing under the pen name "S." In 1927 he published attacks on the Lebanese press in Egypt. In 1929 he founded *al-Majalla al-jadida*, which lasted for twelve years despite a suspension for his attacks on ISMA'IL SIDQI's cabinet. In 1935 he formed *Jam'iyyat al-Misri li al-Misri* (The Society of the Egyptian for the Egyptian) to introduce Gandhi's idea of national self-sufficiency into Egypt.

An avowed secularist, he introduced the writings of Darwin, Nietzsche, and Freud to Egyptian readers and scandalized his readers by calling for writing Arabic in the Roman alphabet. Musa wanted Egypt to embrace European thought and civilization, espoused the theory of evolution by natural selection, and advocated an egalitarian socialism somewhat influenced by Marxism, although he was never an avowed Communist. After *al-Majalla al-jadida* was suspended in 1942, he worked for a year as an editor for the Social Affairs Ministry, then resumed editing leftist journals outside the government. He was jailed in 1946 on trumped-up charges of sabotage, but really for attacking the monarchy. In 1949 he established the Egyptian Peace Society. After the 1952 Revolution he was named supervisor of the science section in *Akhbar al-Yawm*, a post that he held until he died. He wrote himself or translated about forty-five published books, but his radical views limited his influence on Egyptians. NAJIB MAHFUZ, however, called Salama Musa his "spiritual father." Musa, for his part, acknowledged his own debt to Farah Antun, Lutfi al-Sayyid, and YA'QUB SARRUF.

Bibliographic Sources
'Abd al-Latif, Kamal, *Salama Musa.*
Abu Jaber, "Salamah Musa."
al-Adib 17:8 (Aug. 1958): 52–53; 18:9 (Sept. 1959): 61.
al-'Ahd al-jadid, 13 Aug. 1958.
al-Ahram, 8 Aug. 1958; 26 Apr. 1963; 26 Jan. 1965; 20 Sept. 1995.
al-Ahram Archives, file 659.
al-Ahram Hebdo, 9 Aug. 1995, interview with Najib Mahfuz.
al-Akhbar, 9 Sept. 1981; 18 July 1963; 20 May 1965.
'Awad, Louis, *Literature of Ideas in Egypt.*
Ayalon, Ami, *Press,* 237–240.
Brockelmann, *GAL,* S III, 213–215.
CE, VII, 208–209, article by Ali el-Din Hilal Disuqi (Dessouki).
Coury, "Who 'Invented' Egyptian Arab Nationalism?—II," 472–473.
Dessouki, "Musa on Religion and Secularism," 23–24.
EAL, II, 554–555.
Egger, *Salamah Musa.*
Fuda, *Nujum Shari' al-Sihafa,* 134–139.
Gibb, *Studies,* 284–285.
Haim, "Salama Musa."
Hanna, Sami, and Gardner, "Salama Musa, 1887–1958.
Hanna, Suhail ibn-Salim, "L'autobiographie."
Ibrahim, Ibrahim A., "Salama Musa."
Jindi, Anwar, *al-Muhafaza wa al-tajdid,* 364–378.
al-Jumhuriyya, 5 Aug. 1960; 9 Sept. 1968.
Khemiri and Kampffmeyer, *Leaders,* I, 31–33.
Khuri, Jacqueline, in *al-Ahram* (8 Aug. 1958): 8.
Mallakh, Kamal, in *al-Ahram* (6 Aug. 1958): 6.
Musa, Salama, *Tarbiyat Salama Musa.*
Muti'i, *Mawsu'a,* 178–184.
Perlmann, "The Education of Salama Musa."
QTQ, 116–117.
Radwan, Fathi, *'Asr wa rijal,* 249–296.
Ramadi, *Min a'lam al-adab,* 57–63.
Rizq, Fathi, *Khamsa wa sab'una najman,* 134–143.
Sa'id, Rif'at, "al-Fikr al-ishtiraki al-misri."
Sharqawi, *Salama Musa.*
Shukri, Ghali, *Salama Musa.*
Zahlawi, *Udaba mu'asirun,* 81–91.
Zirikli, *al-A'lam,* III, 107–108.

Musharrafa, Dr. 'Ali Mustafa

(11 July 1898–16 January 1950)

Leading scientist and expert in atomic physics. 'Ali was born in Damietta, son of a small landowner who committed suicide during the cotton crisis, shortly before 'Ali took his elementary school certificate examination. He excelled in his studies at all levels, receiving a baccalaureate degree in mathematics and physics from the Higher Teachers College in 1917. The government sent him in that year on an educational mission to Nottingham College, where he earned another bachelor's degree, and to London, where he completed a doctorate in mathematics and science in 1923. He then taught in Cairo University's Faculty of Science, becoming its dean in 1936. He was one of the founders of the Egyptian Academy of Science in 1944. He became vice president of Cairo University in the following year and was a visiting professor at Princeton University in 1947. He was the first foreigner ever to be elected to the Royal College in England. Albert Einstein respected greatly Musharrafa's command of nuclear physics, and he was invited to work in the Manhattan Project, but he refused. Musharrafa wrote five books, collaborated in writing four others, fifty-three scholarly articles, and thirty-five scientific studies in various foreign languages. He also played the piano and the violin, translated foreign songs into Arabic, enjoyed tennis, cycling, and gardening, and urged exploration of the Arabian Desert for uranium. After his sudden death, King FARUQ shocked Egypt's intellectuals by sending no representative to his funeral. A mathematics prize is named for him.

Bibliographic Sources
al-Ahram, 18 Aug. 1972; 16 Jan 1979; 18 Jan. 1985; 24 Mar. 1995; 4 Mar. 1996; 15 Jan. 1998.
al-Ahram Archives, file 1622.
Jawadi, Muhammad Muhammad, *Musharrafa*.
Muti'i, *Mawsu'a*, 376–381.
Qadi, Shukri, *Miat shakhsiyya*, 187.
Uktubir, no. 977 (12 July 1995): 65–67.

Mustafa, Shukri

(1942–19 March 1978)
Militant Islamist leader. Born in Asyut, Mustafa enrolled in the Faculty of Agriculture at Asyut University and was arrested in 1965 for distributing leaflets for the Society of Muslim Brothers on campus. He was imprisoned, first in Tura and later the Abu Za'bal concentration camp, until released by SADAT in 1971. Influenced by SAYYID QUTB's writings, Mustafa returned to Asyut to complete his education and to develop his Society of Muslims, often called *Takfir wa al-Hijra* (Identifying Unbelief and Fleeing Evil), which advocated reforming Egypt's corrupt society before fomenting revolution against the state. Members of his society withdrew from their families and developed communal living arrangements in caves or cramped city apartments. His tendency to use violence to punish defectors from his society brought him into conflict with the Egyptian police, who arrested many of the Muslim Society's leaders but failed to capture Mustafa. In July 1977 his group captured a former minister of *awqaf* and religious affairs to secure the release of its imprisoned members; when the government did not respond, it killed its ministerial hostage. After a prolonged and ferocious manhunt that resulted in scores of casualties and hundreds of arrests, Shukri and four other leaders of the Muslim Society were tried, sentenced to death, and hanged. The society collapsed, but its members joined other groups, such as al-Jihad, the organization that later killed Sadat.

Bibliographic Sources
Ansari, "The Islamic Militants."
Ayubi, *Political Islam*, 78, 143.
Esposito, *Islam and Politics*, 217–218.
Ibrahim, Saad Eddin, "Egypt's Militant Islamic Groups."
Kepel, *Muslim Extremism*, 70–105 et passim.
OEMIW, III, 211–212, article by Denis J. Sullivan.
Segev, *Fundamentalism*, 44–50.
Voll, "Fundamentalism in the Sunni Arab World."

Mutran, Khalil

(1 July 1872–1 June 1949)
Journalist and poet, often called *Sha'ir al-Qutrayn* (the Poet of the Two Countries). Mutran was born in Ba'lbek to a Palestinian father; his family claimed pure Arab descent. Mutran attended the Greek Catholic school in Beirut, where one of his teachers was Nasif al-Yaziji, and learned good Arabic and French. He left Lebanon for France in 1890, supposedly because of his Arab nationalist views. Although he planned to immigrate to Chile in 1892, he settled instead in Egypt, where he found his first job at *al-Ahram*. He established his own bimonthly magazine, *al-Majalla al-misriyya*, in 1900, publishing some of his own writings and also poems by MAHMUD SAMI AL-BARUDI. In 1903–1904 he put out a daily newspaper, *al-Jawaib al-misriyya*, which backed MUSTAFA KAMIL's nationalist movement. He collaborated with HAFIZ IBRAHIM in translating a French book on political economy. He translated plays by Shakespeare, Corneille, Racine, Victor Hugo, and Paul Bourget into Arabic. Owing to business reverses, he later took a post as secretary to the Agricultural Syndicate and helped to found Bank Misr. In 1935 he also became director of the National Theater. Throughout his career he published poetry, for which he became widely popular throughout the Arab world. After making a long journey through Syria and Palestine in 1924, he called himself Poet of the Arab Countries. His poetic allusions, though, were more evocative of a love for Lebanon, or of Egypt's pharaonic past, than of Arab nationalism as such. His poems, published in four *diwan*s during his lifetime,

show both classical Arab and French influences; there is great versatility and variety in their style and content. After SHAWQI died, he chaired *Apollo* until his own death.

Bibliographic Sources

'Abd al-Fattah, Muhammad, *Ashhar mashahir*, I, 139–159.

'Abd al-Hamid, M., in *al-Adib* 37:1 (Jan. 1978): 3–6.

Abu Shadi, *Shu'ara al-'arab*.

Adham, Isma'il Ahmad, *Khalil Mutran*.

———, in *al-Muqtataf* 94:4 (Apr. 1939): 405–418; 95:3 (Aug. 1939): 312–327; 95:4 (Sept. 1939): 467–478; 95:5 (Oct. 1939): 538–550.

al-Ahram Archives, file 1340.

Allen, *Modern Arabic Literature*, 228–234.

'Aqqad, 'Abbas Mahmud, "Khalil Mutran."

'Ata, *Khalil Mutran*.

'Atri, *Khalil Mutran*.

Badawi, M.M., *Critical Introduction*, 68–84.

Brockelmann, *GAL*, S III, 86–96.

Brugman, *Introduction*, 56–62.

Daghir, *Masadir*, II, i, 703–709.

Dayf, *al-Adab al-'arabi*, 121–217.

Disuqi, 'Abd al-'Aziz, *Jama'at Apollo*.

EAL, II, 562–563.

EI2, IV, 966–968, article by A.G. Karam.

Fahmi, Zaki, *Safwat al-'asr*, 640–643.

Ghadban, "Khalil Mutran."

Husayn, Muhammad Muhammad, *al-Ittijahat al-wataniyya*, II, 96, 122, 260–261.

Ibn al-Sharif, *Khalil Mutran*.

Jahim, *Khalil Mutran al-sha'ir*.

Jamal al-Din, *Khalil Mutran*.

Jawdat, *Balabil* (1960), 109–117; (1972), 106–111.

Jayyusi, *Trends*, I, 54–64.

Jundi, *A'lam al-adab*, II, 376–378.

Juraydini, Sami, in *al-Hilal* 55:4 (Apr. 1947): 83–84.

Kahhala, *Mu'jam*, IV, 122–124.

Khouri, *Poetry*, 140–172.

Kurani, As'ad, in *al-Hilal* 47:4 (Feb. 1939): 430–432.

Kurd 'Ali, *Mu'asirun*, 213–223.

Mandur, *Khalil Mutran*.

Mansur, Sa'id Husayn, *al-Tajdid fi shi'r Khalil Mutran*.

Mikhail, Sa'd, *Adab al-'asr*, 147–152.

Moreh, *Modern Arabic Poetry*, 59–65.

Musa, Salama, in *al-Hilal* 39:9 (June 1924): 967–970.

———, in *al-Hilal* 32:9 (July 1928): 1034–1038.

Mutran, "Ahamm hadith fi majra hayati."

Nasr Allah, *Khalil Mutran*.

Nu'ayma, *al-Ghurbal*.

Ostle, R.C., "Khalil Mutran."

Rafi'i, 'Abd al-Rahman, *Shu'ara al-wataniyya*, 158–188.

Ramadi, *Khalil Mutran*.

———, *Min a'lam al-adab*, 237–242.

———, *Sha'ir al-sharq al-'arabi*.

Saadé, *Halil Mutran*.

Sabri, Muhammad, *Khalil Mutran*.

Sa'd, Saib, *Khalil Mutran*.

Saharti, *Adab al-tabi'a*, 96–97.

———, *Khalil Mutran*.

Sandubi, *al-Shu'ara al-thalatha*.

Sayrafi, Hasan Kamil, "Shawqi wa Hafiz wa Mutran."

Sharaf, 'Abd al-'Aziz, *Mukhtarat al-zuhm*.

Sharara, A., *Khalil Mutran*.

Tanahi, Tahir, *Hayat Mutran*.

Tulaymat, *al-Kitab al-dhahabi li-mahrajan Khalil Mutran*.

UAR, *Mahrajan Khalil Mutran*.

'Ubayd, Ahmad, *Dhikra al-sha'irayn*.

'Uwayda, Kamil Muhammad Muhammad, *Khalil Mutran*.

Wakil, Mukhtar, *Khalil Mutran wa madrasatuhu*.

———, *Ruwwad al-shi'r al-hadith*, 14–29.

Zakhura, *al-Suriyyun fi Misr*, II, 3, 227–260.

Zirikli, *al-A'lam*, II, 320.

al-Muwaylihi, Ibrahim
(1846–29 January 1906)

Writer, journalist, and publisher. From a family of silk merchants originally from Muwaylih, a Red Sea Arabian port city, Ibrahim was born in Cairo and began his political career as Khedive ISMA'IL's appointee on the Council of Merchants and the Court of First Instance. He left Egypt with Isma'il when the latter was obliged to abdicate in 1879, serving as a tutor to his children. He helped AFGHANI and 'ABDUH publish *al-'Urwa al-wuthqa* in 1884–1885. For the next decade he lived in Istanbul, where he served on the Education Council and engaged in various forms of political intrigue, later described in a series of anonymous articles, entitled "Ma hunalik" [What's Up], published in *al-Muqattam* soon after his return to Cairo in 1895. He published a weekly political and literary magazine, *Misbah al-sharq*, from 1898 to 1903, contributing a series of articles patterned after his brother's famous *Hadith 'Isa ibn Hisham*, called *Mirat al-'alam aw hadith Musa ibn 'Isam* [Mirror of the World, or the Story of Musa Son of Isam]. As he became ever more involved with khedivial politics, *Misbah al-sharq* languished and died. Although al-Muwaylihi was a brilliant stylist in the traditional mode, his political intrigues came to overshadow his literary efforts.

Bibliographic Sources
'Abd al-Latif, Muhammad Fahmi, *Falasifa*, 27–40.
———, in *al-Thaqafa* 14:711 (11 Aug. 1952): 15–16.
'Abduh, Ibrahim, *A'lam al-sihafa*, 103–106.
Allen, *Study of "Hadith 'Isa ibn Hisham."*
———, "Nazli Circle," 79–84.
Berque, *Egypt*, 116–117.
Blunt, *Gordon at Khartoum*, 354–359, 401–409, 458–459.
Brockelmann, *GAL*, S III, 194.
Cheikho, "al-Adab al-'arabiyya."
Daghir, *Masadir*, III, ii, 1305–1307.
EAL, II, 566.
EI2, VII, 813, article by Roger Allen.
Hamza, *Adab al-maqala*, III.
al-Hilal 14:7 (Apr. 1906): 383–387, obituary.
Jindi, Anwar, *al-Muhafaza wa al-tajdid*, 89–93.
Jundi, *A'lam al-adab*, II, 438–439.
Kahhala, *Mu'jam*, I, 43.
Keddie, *Sayyid Jamal al-Din "al-Afghani,"* 235–268.
Khafaji, *Qissat al-adab*, V, 16–20.
Mouelhy, "Ibrahim el-Mouelhy Pacha," *CHE* 2 (1949): 313–328.
———, in *al-Risala* 6:249 (11 Apr. 1938): 617–620; 250 (18 Apr. 1938): 658–662.
Mujahid, *al-A'lam al-sharqiyya*, II, 650–651.
al-Muqtataf 31:3 (Mar. 1906): 264–265, obituary.
Rafi'i, 'Abd al-Rahman, *'Asr Isma'il*, I, 255–256.
Rizq, Fathi, *Khamsa wa sab'una najman*, 86–88.
Schölch, *Egypt for the Egyptians!* 327.
Tarrazi, *Tarikh al-sihafa*, II, 275–278.
Widmer, Gottfried, "Ibrahim al-Muwailihi."
Zaydan, Jurji, *Mashahir al-sharq*, II, 113–118.
Zirikli, *al-A'lam*, I, 45.

al-Muwaylihi, Muhammad Ibrahim

(30 March 1868–28 February 1930)
Journalist and writer. The son of IBRAHIM AL-MUWAYLIHI, Muhmmad Ibrahim was born in Cairo and educated at al-Azhar and at the Princes' School set up for Khedive ISMA'IL's sons, learning Turkish, French, and English. He followed Isma'il and his own father to Naples in 1879 and later to the Ottoman court in 1885. Returning to Egypt in 1895, he edited *Mirat al-Sharq* and *al-Muqattam* and held administrative posts in Qalyubiyya and Gharbiyya. He founded *Misbah al-Sharq* with his father in 1898, publishing chapters of *'Isa ibn Hisham* as *maqamat* in its pages. After his father's death, he quit journalism and waited three years until he was appointed by Khedive 'ABBAS to manage the *awqaf*, which he did up to 1915. Dismissed from his post and under house arrest, he devoted himself to writing. Paralyzed in his last years, al-Muwaylihi died in his Helwan home.

Bibliographic Sources
'Abd al-Latif, Muhammad Fahmi, *Falasifa*, 41–52.
'Abd al-Muttalib, 'Abd Allah, *Muwaylihi al-saghir*.
al-Ahram, 2 Mar. 1930.
'Allam, "Safahat min al-adab al-'arabi."
Allen, "Beginnings of the Egyptian Novel," in *CHAL*, 184–186.
———, "*Hadith 'Isa ibn Hisham* by Muhammad al-Muwaylihi."
———, "*Hadith 'Isa ibn Hisham*: The Excluded Passages."
———, *Period of Time.*
———, "Poetry and Poetic Criticism."
———, "Some New al-Muwailihi Materials."
———, *A Study of "Hadith 'Isa ibn Hisham."*
'Aqqad, 'Abbas Mahmud, *Rijal 'araftuhum*, 76–88.
Bencheneb, "Edmond About et al-Muwaylihi."
———, "Études de litterature arabe moderne."
Berque, *Egypt*, 212–214.
Bishri, 'Abd al-'Aziz, *al-Mukhtar*, I, 218–235, 296–308.
———, in *al-Risala* 2:72 (19 Nov. 1934): 1886–1888; 73 (26 Nov. 1934); 74 (3 Dec. 1934): 1966–1968.
Blunt, *My Diaries.*
Brockelmann, *GAL*, S III, 194–195.
Cheikho, "al-Adab al-'arabiyya," *al-Mashriq* 23:5 (May 1925): 377–379.
Daghir, *Masadir*, II, i, 734–735.
Dayf, *al-Adab al-'arabi*, 234–241.
Dhuhni, *Misr bayn al-ihtilal wa al-thawra*, 8–64.
EAL, II, 566–567.
EI2, VII, 814–815, article by Roger Allen.
Gibb, *Studies*, 289–290.
Hawwari, *Naqd al-mujtama'.*
Kahhala, *Mu'jam*, VIII, 204–205.
Khafaji, *Qissat al-adab*, V, 21–32.
Louca, *Voyageurs*, 225–237.
Mouelhi, "Mohammad el Mouelhi Bey."
Mubarak, Zaki, in *al-Risala* 10:485 (19 Oct. 1942): 995–997; 486 (26 Oct. 1942): 1016–1019; 487 (2 Nov. 1942): 1035–1038; 488 (9 Nov. 1942): 1049–1050.
Mujahid, *al-A'lam al-sharqiyya*, II, 764–766.
Pérès, "Les éditions successives de *Hadit Isa Ibn Hisam.*"
———, "*Hadith Isa ibn Hisham* de Mohamed al-Muwailihi."
Ramadi, *Adab wa tarab*, 108–116.
Ramitch, *Usrat al-Muwaylihi.*
Schölch, *Egypt for the Egyptians!* 327.
Zirikli, *al-A'lam*, V, 305–306.

N

Nabarawi, Saiza

(24 May 1897–24 February 1985)

Pioneer feminist. Daughter of an employee at the Minshawi palace, Qurashiyya (Gharbiyya), Saiza Nabarawi was originally named Zaynab Muhammad Murad. Owing to the divorce of her parents, both of whom remarried, she was reared by a childless cousin of her mother, 'Adila Nabarawi, who changed the child's name to Saiza (often written Céza) Nabarawi. She lived mainly in Paris, the home of her stepmother's mother, from age five to fifteen, attending the Institut St Germain-des-Prés and later the Lycée de France. Obliged by her stepmother's suicide to return to Egypt, she soon ran afoul of her father, who chastised her for wearing a European hat and ordered her to don the veil. For several years she attended Alexandria's Notre Dame de Sion School, graduating in 1913, but was barred by her father from studying at the French Law School. A friend of her late stepmother befriended the girl and exerted a liberalizing influence, opposing her authoritarian father, who died in 1922. Soon afterward Saiza helped to form the Egyptian Feminist Union, moved into HUDA SHA'RAWI's house, removed her face veil in a defiant public gesture, and became editor of the EFU's first journal, L'Égyptienne. When barred from observing the 1925 inaugural meeting of the Egyptian Parliament, which by then was open to women journalists only if they were foreign, she protested to the interior minister in vain, but she was allowed to attend the monthly banquets of Egyptian and foreign journalists.

Nabarawi had a political program: she campaigned for a law to set a minimum marriage age of eighteen for boys and sixteen for girls to ensure sufficient education for both, helped to lead the campaign to boycott the 1931 elections under the royalist constitution, and wrote an article in 1934 calling for women's suffrage and the right to run for public office. She married an artist named Mustafa Najib in 1937 and named their only daughter after Huda, but the couple was divorced in 1941. In 1951 she helped to found the Women's Political Resistance Committee against the British forces in the Suez Canal, as well as a Youth Committee within the EFU. Although she had been EFU vice president from 1923 to 1953, political differences with its mainstream caused her to resign. Later she was made a life member of the EFU's successor, the Huda Sha'rawi Society.

She was also active in international politics. She attended feminist conferences in Rome, Naples, Paris, Paris, Istanbul, Amsterdam, and Beirut during the 1920s and 1930s. Nabarawi and Huda campaigned even in France for women's suffrage, not yet achieved, in 1933. At the Women's International Association Conference in Copenhagen in 1939, she spearheaded a move to uphold the rights of Palestinian women in response to a drive to support Jewish women who were being oppressed by the Nazis. With Huda, she helped to set up the Arab Feminist Union in 1944 and to lead the first protests against the use of atomic weapons in 1946. She served briefly as a consultant at the World Peace Society headquarters in Geneva in 1958, took part in World Peace Conferences held in Stockholm in 1961 and Moscow in 1962, and was elected vice president of the Women's International Democratic Federation in 1964. She was awarded the Lenin Prize in 1970 by the Soviet ambassador in Cairo. In later years she assailed Islamists who pressured women to resume veiling. Nabarawi publicly opposed any form of oppression, whether inspired by gender or by imperialism.

Bibliographic Sources

'Abd al-Halim, *Nisa*, 49–55.
al-Ahram Archives, file 1003.
Akhir sa'a, 6 Feb. 1985.
Badran, Margot, in *al-Ahram Weekly*, 13 Feb. 1997.
———, *Feminists*, 98–99 et passim.
Badran and Cooke, *Opening the Gates*, 279–281.
EAL, II, 568.
Hawwa, 27 May 1995.
Jundi, *A'lam al-adab*, II, 533.

Najib, *A'lam Misr*, 252.
Ruz al-Yusuf, 4 Mar. 1985.
Sabah al-khayr, 31 Jan. 1985; 27 Feb. 1986.

Nada, Hamid
(19 November 1924–27 May 1990)
Painter and art teacher, sometimes called Shaykh al-Fannanin. Hamid was born and reared in Cairo's Khalifa quarter: he began painting in 1946 and was trained at the Academy of Fine Arts, graduating in 1951 and later teaching at the school. He later received a grant for higher studies in Luxor in 1957, then earned a diploma in painting from the San Fernando Academy in Madrid in 1961. A founder of the Alexandria School of Fine Arts in 1957, he taught there for a while. He became head of the Art Department of the Cairo Academy of Fine Arts in 1977. Nada displayed his paintings in many Egyptian and foreign exhibitions, starting in 1946, and was given awards by the Alexandria *biennale* in 1957 and 1959, the Egyptian government in 1974, Kuwait in 1975, and Iraq in 1988. He often incorporated folktales and legends into his art and sometimes depicted historical events, such as MUSTAFA KAMIL's funeral procession. Largely representational at first, his style grew more abstract as he matured, and he came to be regarded as Egypt's leading surrealist. His influence on younger painters, many of whom he taught, was considerable. Many of his paintings are now displayed in the Museum of Modern Art in Cairo.

Bibliographic Sources
al-Ahram, 1 June 1991; 25 Aug. 1995.
al-Ahram Archives, file 13365.
al-Ahram al-dawli, 2 Jan. 1986.
al-Hayat, 1 Aug. 1991.
Karnouk, *Contemporary Egyptian Art*, 101.
———, *Modern Egyptian Art*, 57–72.
al-Musawwar, 1 June 1990.
Najib, *A'lam Misr*, 172.

al-Nadim, al-Sayyid 'Abd Allah
(10 December 1845–10 October 1896)
Nationalist editor, poet, and speaker, sometimes called *Khatib al-Thawra* (the Orator of the 'URABI Revolution). He was born in the Manshiyya quarter of Alexandria to a poor family descended from Hasan, the Prophet's grandson. 'Abd Allah's father, a baker of peasant origin

who had been conscripted into MUHAMMAD 'ALI's army, enrolled him at the local *kuttab* and then the mosque school of Shaykh Ibrahim, where he had an excellent mentor who taught him oratory and composition, encouraged him to read great literature, and took him to literary clubs in Alexandria. He even began to compose poetry, to the distress of his father, who told him to choose between adhering to his studies and forgoing all financial support. Choosing the latter, 'Abd Allah spent six months in Upper Egypt, then went to Cairo, where he managed to get training as a telegraph operator and found a job in 1863 at Khedive ISMA'IL's mother's palace in Cairo. Later, after he came under the influence of JAMAL AL-DIN AL-AFGHANI, he lost his position, the result of a dispute with the palace's chief Black eunuch. He later worked as a Quranic tutor and farmer in Badawa (Daqahliyya) for an *'umda*, with whom he soon quarreled, as a shopkeeper in Mansura, and as a literary companion to the inspector general for Lower Egypt, where he gained a reputation for improvising clever verses.

Influenced by al-Afghani and by Egypt's troubled condition in 1877–1878, Nadim drifted into journalism, writing articles for the newspapers *al-Mahrusa* and *al-Asr al-jadid*, and for *Misr* and *al-Tijara*, published by ADIB ISHAQ. In 1881 he began publishing his own weekly paper, *al-Tankit wa al-tabkit*, followed shortly by *al-Taif*, in which he first declared his nationalist views. He soon became a leading proponent of 'Urabi and his movement, writing some of the most ardent articles in support of Egyptian nationalism and delivering revolutionary speeches while the 'Urabists held power. After the British occupied Egypt, Nadim went into hiding for nine years, an exile he described later in *Kan wa yakun* [It Was and Is]. Once discovered and arrested, he was expelled from Egypt. He lived in Jaffa for a year until he was invited back by 'ABBAS HILMI II. He published *al-Ustadh*, a Cairo weekly opposed to the British occupation, in 1892–1893, thus becoming one of the few human links between the 'Urabist movement and MUSTAFA KAMIL, then a law student editing his own journal, *al-Madrasa*. Nadim called for an anti-imperialist alliance of Eastern peoples, drastic improvements in Egyptian education, and freedom based on individual rights and duties. Accused by the British of stirring up fanaticism, Nadim was exiled again from Egypt in 1893. He went to Istanbul, where the Ottoman government employed him in its Education Department and then as an inspector of publications, and he died there. Nadim was an inspiring, often humorous, speaker and writer who did much to popularize nationalism in Egypt. Some of his writings were collected by his brother and published as *Sulafat al-Nadim*.

Bibliographic Sources
'Abd al-Fattah, Muhammad, *Ashhar mashahir*, II, 146–176.
'Abd Allah Nadim.
Abdel-Malek, *Idéologie*, 449–483.
'Abduh, Ibrahim, *A'lam al-sihafa*, 125–129.
Amin, Ahmad, *Fayd al-Khatir*, VI, 144–178.
———, *Zu'ama al-islah*, 202–248.
'Aqqad, 'Abbas Mahmud, *Shu'ara Misr*, 87–97.
'Ashur, Nu'man, *Butulat misriyya*, 89–101.
———, *Suwar min al-butula wa al-abtal*, 43–52.
'Atiyyat Allah, *'Abdallah Nadim*.
Baha al-Din, *Ayyam laha tarikh*, 3–34.
Becka, *DOL*, III, 130–131.
Brockelmann, *GAL*, S III, 154, 331.
Buhuth Nadwat al-Ihtifal.
Cheikho, *al-Adab al-'arabiyya*, II, 99–100.
Delanoue, "'Abd Allah Nadim (1845–1896)."
EAL, II, 572.
EI2, VII, 852, article by P.C. Sadgrove.
Fayid, *'Abdallah al-Nadim*.
Fikri, 'Ali, *Subul al-najah*, III, 187–191.
Gharaba, *Shakhsiyyat*, 5–10.
Habib, *Hawamish*, 41–43.
Hadidi, *'Abdallah Nadim khatib al-wataniyya*.
Hafiz, S., *Genesis of Arabic Narrative Discourse*, 1, 13–23.
Hamza, *Adab al-maqala*, II, 114–215.
Hijazi, Anwar, *'Amaliqa*, 133–140.
al-Hilal 5:11 (1 Feb. 1897): 401–408.
Ibrahim, Shihata 'Isa, *'Uzama al-wataniyya*, 109–138.
Jami'i, *'Abdallah Nadim*.
———, *Majallat "al-Ustadh."*
———, *"al-Masamir."*
Jindi, Anwar, *A'lam wa ashab aqlam*, 253–261.
———, *al-Muhafaza wa al-tajdid*, 84–89.
Jundi, *A'lam al-adab*, II, 436–438.
Kahhala, *Mu'jam*, VI, 151–153.
Khalaf Allah, *'Abdallah al-Nadim*.
Mujahid, *al-A'lam al-sharqiyya*, III, 1045–1050.
Nadim, *Sulafat al-Nadim*, I, 3–23.
Qadi, Shukri, *Khamsun shakhsiyya*, 103–106.
Rafi'i, 'Abd al-Rahman, *Shu'ara al-wataniyya* (1954), 13–17.
———, *al-Thawra al-'urabiyya*, 572–579.
Ramadi, *Adab wa tarab*, 122–126.
———, *Sihafat al-fukaha*, 13–18.
Riyad, Hasan Mazlum, in *al-Thaqafa*, no. 409 (29 Oct. 1946): 1252–1254; 416 (17 Dec. 1946): 1431–1432.
Rizq, Fathi, *Khamsa wa sab'una najman*, 60–74.
Sadgrove, *Egyptian Theatre*, 145–149, 152–155, 161, 163.
Sa'id, Naffusa Zakariyya, *'Abdallah Nadim*.
Saqr and Fawzi Sa'id Ibrahim, *'Abdallah Nadim*.
Sawi, Ahmad Husayn, in *al-Hilal* 74:3 (Mar. 1966): 76–85; 10 (Oct. 1966): 75–89.
Schölch, *Egypt for the Egyptians!* 348–349.
Sharqawi, *Masabih*, 127–152.
Shaykha, *Aqlam thaira*, 45–69.
Shayyal, "'Abd Allah Nadim, 1845–1896."
———, *A'lam al-Iskandariyya*, 237–256.
Tarabay, "Des causes du progrès."
Tawfiq, Najib, *'Abdallah al-Nadim*.
———, *al-Thair al-azim 'Abdallah Nadim*.
Taymur, Ahmad, *A'lam al-fikr al-islami*, 120–142.
———, in *al-Hilal* 41:9 (July 1933): 1160–1168.
———, *Tarajim*, 3–30.
Walili, *Mafakhir al-ajyal*, 71–74.
Zaydan, Jurji, *Mashahir al-sharq*, 1st ed., II, 105–112.
Zirikli, *al-A'lam*, IV, 137–138.

al-Nahhas, Mustafa

(15 June 1879–23 August 1965)

Judge, cabinet minister, five-time premier, and Wafd Party leader. Born to a petit bourgeois family in Samanud (Gharbiyya), where his father was a lumber merchant, Mustafa began his education at a French-language school founded by two Copts. Moving to Cairo, he graduated from Nasiriyya Elementary School in 1891 and the Khedivial Secondary School in 1896. After receiving his *license* from the Khedivial Law School in 1900, he worked in Muhammad Farid's law office before opening his own practice in Mansura. In 1904 Nahhas was named a judge in the Tanta National Court by 'Abd al-Khaliq Tharwat. He was dismissed from the bench in 1919 when he joined the Wafd to represent the National Party, which he had quietly backed. Exiled with Sa'd Zaghlul to the Seychelles from 1921 to 1923, Nahhas was chosen upon his repatriation to represent Samanud in the first Chamber of Deputies elected under the 1923 Constitution. He became communications minister in 1924. Reelected to the 1926 Chamber as a deputy from Abu Sir Banna (Gharbiyya) and barred by the British from a cabinet post, he was elected one of the Chamber's two vice presidents and, in the following year, its president.

After Zaghlul died in 1927, Nahhas defeated his nephew in the contest to lead the Wafd Party. He would become prime minister on five different occasions: 1928, 1930, 1936–1937, 1942–1944, and 1950–1952. In most of these cabinets he was also the interior minister, but in 1942–1944 he was foreign minister. He headed the Egyptian delegation to the talks with Britain that produced the 1936 Anglo-Egyptian Treaty. The popularly elected Nahhas government of 1936–1937 also negotiated at Montreux to end the Capitulations and the Mixed Courts. His government also persuaded the Suez Canal Company to admit two Egyptians to its governing board, set up Egypt's military schools for aviators and mechanics, and expanded the Military Academy by opening it to secondary school graduates who could pass a competitive examination, thus admitting many of the future Free Officers. However, Nahhas was almost assassinated in November 1937. When his hastily formed youth group, the "Blue Shirts," broke into the Sa'dist Party clubhouse to intimidate its members and staged a noisy demonstration in front of 'Abdin Palace, King FARUQ seized this chance to oust the Wafdist cabinet. The king installed a caretaker coalition government of the rival parties and called an election, held in 1938, which was boycotted by the Wafd.

World War II drove Nahhas into an alliance with his erstwhile foes, the British, who made Faruq appoint Nahhas as the head of an all-Wafdist cabinet. Soon after this incident, which tarnished his nationalist credentials for many Egyptians, Nahhas was further discredited by the defection of the Wafdist secretary-general, MAKRAM 'UBAYD, who denounced Nahhas's policies and exposed his corruption in the *Black Book*. Nahhas's wartime cabinet tried to resolve some social issues by raising the farm workers' minimum daily wage, abolishing fees for the state elementary schools, lowering the taxes on small landowners, and legalizing labor unions. His major accomplishment was to initiate the Arab League by convoking the Arab leaders' conference that wrote the Alexandria Protocol, thus committing Egypt to Arab nationalism. On the day after the protocol was signed, though, Faruq finally asked Nahhas to resign.

By the time Nahhas resumed the leadership of Egypt's politics, the country's ties to the Arab world had been tightened by its involvement in the Palestine War. Its defeat had discredited both the king and the constitutional system generally, but the old order made its final bid for popularity by calling a general election for January 1950. The Wafd won most of the parliamentary seats (but less than half of the total votes cast), and Nahhas managed to form a Wafdist government that lasted for almost two years. It passed new laws to benefit poor people, notably one that distributed a million acres to landless peasants; but his main aim was to persuade Britain to renounce its 1936 treaty, leave its Suez Canal base, and hand the Sudan over to Egypt. He failed. After nineteen months of fruitless talks, Nahhas unilaterally abrogated the treaty that he had signed on Egypt's behalf in 1936 and also the 1899 Sudan Convention. The British troops did not leave, but 100,000 Egyptians stopped working for them in the Canal Zone, the remaining British civil servants and teachers in Egypt were summarily dismissed, and extremists began harassing British forces. A shooting incident on 25 January 1952 led to the death of more than fifty Egyptian auxiliary policemen in Ismailia, causing protest demonstrations the next day and the burning of much of downtown Cairo. Faruq gave Nahhas emergency powers to quell the riots but dismissed him the next day for failing to maintain order.

Six months after the fires of Black Saturday had illumined the breakdown of Egypt's political institutions, the Free Officers seized control of the government. Nahhas, vacationing in Europe, hastened back, expecting to be invited to head a new cabinet. NAJIB and NASIR met with him at length before deciding that the powers that he sought for the Wafd were more than they cared to give. In September 1952 the officers ordered all parties to purge themselves of their leaders. Nahhas defied the order, but the officers managed to split the Wafd. Four months later they abolished all political parties and seized their assets. The officers arrested Nahhas and his wife, assuming that she had taken control of the party. Both were tried. He was censured for condoning corruption, she was fined for rigging the Alexandria cotton market, and both were deprived of their political and civil rights until 1960 and confined to their Cairo villa, where they lived in relative obscurity. Nahhas's death in 1965 occasioned a larger funeral than Nasir's government had wanted. The regime refused to bury Nahhas next to Sa'd Zaghlul and banned popular demonstrations in his memory.

Personally honest but easily swayed by less scrupulous colleagues, sometimes jealous of people richer or better connected than himself, principled to the point of obstinacy, Nahhas remained popular because of his solicitude for poor people and his unflinching patriotism.

Bibliographic Sources
Abaza, Fikri, in *al-Hilal* 45:3 (Jan. 1937): 248–251.
Ahmad, Muhammad 'Ali, *Mustafa al-Nahhas Basha.*
al-Ahram (24 Aug. 1965): 1.
al-Ahram Archives, file 219.
Berque, *Egypt*, 520–533 et passim.
Colombe, *L'évolution de l'Égypte,* 102–115.
Current Biography (July 1951): 451–453; (1965): 302.
Deeb, *Party Politics*, 43, 142–149, et passim.
EI2, VII, 904–905, article by Derek Hopwood.
Hadidy, "Mustafa al-Nahhas and Political Leadership."
Hafiz, 'Abbas, *Mustafa al-Nahhas.*
Muti'i, *Haula al-rijal min Misr,* I, 12–27.
———, *Mawsu'a*, 593–602.
New York Times (24 Aug. 1965): 31.
Qurra 'ah, *Nimr al-siyasa al-misriyya.*
Ramadan, 'Abd al-'Azim, *al-Sira' bayn al-Wafd wa al-'arsh.*
Reich, *Political Leaders*, 373–379, article by Arthur Goldschmidt.
Rizq, Yunan Labib, in *al-Wafd*, 21 Aug. 1986.
Sa'd al-Din, *Za'im Misr al-khalid Mustafa al-Nahhas.*
Sa'id, Rif'at, *Mustafa al-Nahhas.*
Shahid, Salih, *Dhikrayati fi 'ahdayn.*
Terry, *The Wafd.*
al-Wafd, 23, 30 Aug. 1984; 13 Sept. 1984; 5 Sept. 1985.
al-Watan, 27–29 Nov. 1983.
Yusuf, Fatima, *Dhikrayat*, 117–229.
Zirikli, *al-A'lam*, VII, 246.

Naji, Dr. Ibrahim

(31 December 1898–24 March 1953)
Physician, poet, and writer. Born in Shubra, Ibrahim was the son of Ahmad Naji, secretary-general of the telegraph service, who had taught himself English, French, and Italian, possessed a large library, and often read aloud to his family from Arabic and European works. Ibrahim began writing poetry as a child and attended the Bab al-Sha'riyya Elementary School and the Tawfiqiyya Secondary School. He enrolled at the Qasr al-'Ayni Medical School in 1916 and received his degree in 1922. After briefly practicing medicine in Cairo, he took a job with the Egyptian State Railways, moving to Suhaj, Minya, and finally Mansura. There he met some of the poets who would later constitute the Apollo Group and also published his earliest translations and his first poem in *al-Siyasa al-usbu'iyya*. Returning to Cairo in 1931, he married the daughter of the city's governor. Somewhat later he took charge of the *awqaf* ministry's Medical Department. When the Apollo Group was formed, Naji became its vice president and was closely tied with AHMAD ZAKI ABU SHADI. Naji published his first poetry collection in 1934 and headed the Writers Syndicate in 1945. Not interested in politics but well connected to the men in power, he led a bohemian life, having many mistresses and spending time in cabarets. After the July 1952 Revolution he was dismissed from his position. Having never saved any money for his retirement, he was reduced to penury and was abandoned by his family and friends by the time he died. A collection of his poems was published posthumously by a government-appointed committee. Some of his translations of Shakespeare's sonnets remain unpublished. He is perhaps best known for writing *al-Atlal* [The Ruins], put to music by AHMAD RAMI and sung by UMM KULTHUM.

Bibliographic Sources
al-Ahram, 8 Nov. 1995, 30 Dec. 1996.
al-Ahram Archives, file 2018.
al-Ahram Weekly, 18, 25 Mar. 1993, translation of *al-Atlal.*
al-Akhbar, 21 Feb. 1985; 27 Mar. 1985.
Allen, *Modern Arabic Literature*, 234–237.
Baqari, *Ibrahim Naji min shi'rihi.*
Brockelmann, *GAL*, S III, 137–139.
Brugman, *Introduction*, 167–173.
Daghir, *Masadir*, II, i, 736–738.
Dayf, *al-Adab al-'arabi*, 154–160.
EAL, II, 576.
EI2, VII, 868–869, article by P.C. Sadgrove.
Filastin, *Ibrahim Naji.*
Fiqi, 'Ali Muhammad, *Ibrahim Naji.*
Fuad, Ni'mat Ahmad, *Naji, al-Shabbi, al-Akhtal al-Saghir*, 22–120.
———, *Naji al-sha'ir.*
———, "al-Tabib al-sha'ir."
Jawdat, *Balabil* (1960), 7–24; (1972), 5–20.
———, *Naji.*
Jayyusi, *Trends,* II, 394–397.
Jindi, Anwar, in *al-Hilal* 81:3 (Mar. 1973): 78–85.
Jundi, *A'lam al-adab*, II, 479–480.
Kahhala, *Mu'jam*, I, 120.

Kayyali, *Diwan Ibrahim Naji,* 783–855.
Khafaji, 'Abd al-Mun'im, in *al-Adib* 12:6 (1953): 76.
———, in *al-Hilal* 89:4 (Apr. 1980): 90–95.
———, *Madhahib al-adab,* 112–134 et passim.
Khalil, *Mu'jam al-udaba al-atibba,* 10–13.
Khashaba, "Shi'r Naji."
Mu'tasim Billah, *Naji.*
Ramadi, *Min a'lam al-adab,* 251–258.
Rami, Ahmad, in *al-Hilal* 61:5 (May 1953): 72–74.
Saharti, Mustafa 'Abd al-Latif, *al-Shi'r al-mu'asir,* 203–206.
Sayrafi, Hasan Kamil, in *Apollo* 3:1 (Sept. 1934): 17.
Sharqawi, Mahmud, in *al-Hilal* 75:9 (Sept. 1967): 60–85.
Tanahi, Tahir, in *al-Hilal* 60:7 (July 1952): 26–29.
Tawfiq, Hasan, in *al-Hilal* 81:5 (May 1973): 138–139.
Taymur, Mahmud, *al-Shakhsiyyat al-'ishrun,* 133–135.
Wadi, *Shi'r Naji al-mawqif wa al-'adat.*
Wakil, Mukhtar, "Ibrahim Naji."
Zahlawi, *Udaba mu'asirun,* 15–24.
Watani, 14 Feb. 1993; 19 June 1997.
Zirikli, *al-A'lam,* I, 76.

Naji, Muhammad

(17 January 1888–5 April 1956)

Painter. Of Turkish and Egyptian extraction (his father was an army officer), Muhammad was born in Muharram Bey, Alexandria, and received his *license en droit* from the University of Lyons in 1910, then spent four years at the Academy of Fine Arts in Florence. During World War I he studied ancient monuments in Alexandria and Luxor (especially Qurna). He went to Paris in 1919, studied with Claude Monet, and spent some time painting in a French village, developing a *pointilliste* style. He returned to Egypt and took part in some of the 1919 Revolution's demonstrations, an experience that drew him back into his Egyptian heritage. His work won a gold medal at the 1922 Paris Salon. He entered the Egyptian foreign service in 1925, serving in Brazil and then in France, but resigned in 1930. He lived in Ethiopia from 1931 to 1933 and then in Greece and Cyprus. In 1934 he opened a studio in Alexandria, where he painted a series of murals on the history of medicine for the Alexandria Hospital. Influenced by the Mexican muralists who stressed art's social mission, his best-known work, "The Renaissance of Egypt," which combines pharaonic with modern motifs,

graces the wall of the Egyptian Senate. Naji also painted portraits of Juliette Adam (MUSTAFA KAMIL's patron), Haile Selassie, and Archbishop Makarios. After World War II he attended a UNESCO artists and writers conference in London and spent some time painting in Spain. In 1947–1950 he headed the Egyptian Academy for Fine Arts in Rome and also served as cultural counselor in the Egyptian Embassy. In 1951 he founded the *Atelier* Society in Cairo. He died in his studio, located near the Pyramids, and his home has now been converted into a museum devoted to his paintings. A few that show Egyptians in rural scenes are exhibited in Cairo's Modern Art Museum. His sister, 'Iffat Naji, also a painter, has written about him and carried on some of the work he began.

Bibliographic Sources
al-Ahram, 31 Oct. 1997.
al-Ahram Archives, file 3168.
Finbert, "Mohammed Naghi."
al-Hayat al-siyahiyya (Aug. 1994): 42–45.
Karnouk, *Modern Egyptian Art,* 25–27.
Mohammed Naghi Retrospective Exhibition.
Muhammad Naji al-fannan al-tathiri al-misri.
al-Musawwar (6 May 1983); (23 May 1989): 38–40.
Naji, 'Iffat, et al., *Muhammad Naji.*
Said, *Contemporary Art in Egypt,* x, 116–120.

Najib, Muhammad

(20 February 1901–28 August 1984)

Officer, politician, and titular leader of the 1952 Revolution. Born in Khartum, he was educated at Gordon College and the Military Academy, which commissioned him as an artillery officer in 1918. He earned a law degree in 1927 and also took advanced courses in economics and political science. He gradually rose through the ranks, becoming a brigade commander (*miralay*) in the Palestine War. He commanded the Frontier Force in 1950 and became director general of the Infantry Corps in 1951. As he was admired by other officers for his integrity and resistance to corruption, the Free Officers wanted him elected president of the Officers' Club early in 1952, but King FARUQ rigged the vote against him, sparking a political crisis. Needing a mature figurehead, the Free Officers made him nominal leader of their revolution against Faruq (although Najib insisted in his memoirs that he had actually been given control earlier). He became premier, war and naval minister, commander-in-chief of the army, and governor-general of Egypt from 1952 to 1953. He was its president from 1953 to 1954, but he had diminishing power, as NASIR used his control over the army and organized labor to counter Najib's support from the Wafd, Muslim Brothers, Communists, and many liberal Egyptians. After the failed attempt by a Muslim Brother to assassinate Nasir, Najib was placed under house arrest for seventeen years, his supporters were purged, and his role in the 1952 Revolution ignored. Released by SADAT in 1971, he attacked Nasir in subsequent articles and interviews and hailed his benefactor, but he was never given another government post. His publications include *Kalimati li al-tarikh* [My Word to History] in 1975 and *Kuntu ra'isan: mudhakkirat Muhammad Najib* [I Was President: The Memoirs of Muhammad Najib] in 1984. Outwardly modest, he was more a father figure than a revolutionary leader. A square in Asyut and streets in Alexandria, Khartum, and Heliopolis bear his name.

Bibliographic Sources
al-Ahram Archives, file 216.
al-Ahrar, 17 Sept., 8 Oct., 23 Oct. 1984.
al-Akhbar, 29 Aug. 1984.
Akhir Sa'a, 25 Jan. 1984; 5 Sept. 1984.
Gordon, Joel, *Nasser's Blessed Movement,* 59, 109–126.
Hammad, "Kayfa qarara Majlis al-Thawra."
———, "Kayfa wajaha Muhammad Najib."
Hamrush, Ahmad, "Dhikrayati 'an Muhammad Najib."
'Isa, Salah, in *al-Sha'b,* 25 Oct. 1991.
Khuli, Lutfi, in *al-Anba,* 5 Sept. 1984.
al-Musawwar, no. 2986 (1 Jan. 1982): 38–41.
Muti'i, *Mawsu'a,* 540–548.
Neguib, *Egypt's Destiny.*
New York Times (29 Aug. 1984): D22.
Qadi, Shukri, *Miat shakhsiyya,* 271–273.
Riyad, Muhammad, "Muhammad Najib al-muftara 'alayh."
Ruz al-Yusuf, 2 Sept. 1984.
Samakuri, *Asrar hukm al-qusur,* 59–72.
al-Wafd, 13, 20, 27 Sept. 1984; 4, 11 Oct. 1984.

Napoleon Bonaparte

(15 August 1769–5 May 1821)
Conqueror of Egypt and emperor of the French. Napoleone Buonaparte (his original name) was born in Corsica, the son of an aristocratic lawyer.

He was sent in 1778 to learn French at a preparatory school in Autun and then to boarding school in Brienne, followed by the Paris Military Academy. After spending several years fighting the French for Corsican independence, he quarreled with his patron and returned to France, where he established his reputation by besieging Toulon and taking it from British control, then campaigned in northern Italy. Napoleon went on to command the Army of Italy, capturing most of the peninsula. The Directory wanted him to conquer England, but he realized that the Royal Navy would stop his troops from crossing the English Channel. He chose instead to strike at Britain's Levant trade and possibly its hold on India by occupying Egypt. He easily defeated the Mamluks at Alexandria and in the Battle of Imbaba, but the British landed at Abu-Kir and destroyed most of his ships. Napoleon launched a counterassault into Palestine in 1799, but failed to capture Acre. The Anglo-Ottoman alliance and the bubonic plague forced him to retreat. He decided to return to France, where he soon took control. His major achievement in Egypt was his introduction of a large corps of scientists and artists who recorded and illustrated the condition of the country, later published as *Description de l'Égypte.* His claim to be a Muslim and his support for the ulama against the Mamluks earned him no local backing. Instead, popular resistance was fierce and could be quelled only by force. His conquest of Egypt and his reforms profoundly disrupted Egyptian politics and society, accelerating changes that would lead to the rise of MUHAMMAD 'ALI and his westernization program. Egypt also gave Napoleon his first opportunity to govern a country.

Bibliographic Sources
'Awad, Ahmad Hafiz, *Fath Misr al-hadith.*
Beaucour, Laissus, and Orgogozo, *Discovery of Egypt.*
Benoist-Mechin, *Bonaparte en Egypte.*
Bernoyer, *Avec Bonaparte en Egypte.*
———, *Bonaparte de Toulon au Caire.*
Boustany, *Journals of Bonaparte in Egypt.*
Browne, Haji Abdallah, *Bonaparte in Egypt,* 65–220.
Chandler, David G., *Campaigns of Napoleon,* 205–249.
Charles-Roux, François, *Bonaparte: Governor of Egypt.*
Connelly, *Napoleonic France,* 166–167, 353–357.

De Moulinaere, *Bibliographie raisonée des té-moignages*.

Ghorbal, *Beginnings*, 9–103.

Gillespie, "Napoleon's Egyptian Campaign."

Herold, *Bonaparte in Egypt*.

Horward, *Napoleonic Military History: Bibliography*, 115–146.

LaJonquière, *L'expédition en Égypte*.

Laurens, *L'expédition d'Égypte*.

Miot, *Memories*.

Palmer, *Encyclopedia of Napoleon's Europe*, 114, 200–202.

Rafi'i, 'Abd al-Rahman, *Tarikh al-haraka al-qawmiyya*.

Raymond, *Égyptiens et français au Caire*.

Schom, *Napoleon Bonaparte*, 106–188.

Shukri, Muhammad Fuad, *al-Hamla al-firansiyya*.

Tulard, Fayard, and Fierro, *Histoire et dictionnaire*, 245–250.

Nasif, Malak Hifni

(25 December 1886–17 October 1918)

Poet, writer, and feminist orator, often called *Bahithat al-Badiya* (Searcher in the Desert). Born in Cairo's Jamaliyya quarter, the daughter of MUHAMMAD HIFNI NASIF, she was educated at home, a French school, 'Abbas Primary School when it opened a girls' section in 1895, and the Saniyya School, becoming the first Egyptian woman to graduate from a modern state elementary school in 1900 and one of two to earn a primary teacher's certificate in 1903. She then taught at the girls' section of 'Abbas Primary School. Although she had refused to marry 'ABD AL-'AZIZ FAHMI, after the intervention of her father's friend Shaykh 'ABD AL-KARIM SALMAN, she agreed in 1907 to marry 'Abd al-Sattar al-Basil, a bedouin tribal leader, who failed to inform her, until after their wedding, that he already had a wife and a daughter whom he expected Malak to tutor. She persevered in the marriage, not wishing to subject her family to scandal, but soon became a pioneer feminist. She wrote for Egyptian, Turkish, French, German, and English newspapers on women's rights, girls' education, the evils of polygyny, and the reasons why Egyptian men should not marry foreigners. Her articles for *al-Jarida* were collected into a book, *al-Nisaiyat*, of which only the first part was printed in 1910. She also wrote poetry in Arabic. She was the only woman to present a list of demands (she was not allowed to speak) at the 1911 Egyptian Congress. Because of the Italian invasion of Tripoli in 1911, Malak organized a school in Cairo to train women as nurses. In 1914 she helped found the Literary Society for the Advancement of Egyptian Women. When her brother, Majd al-Din, was arrested during World War I for his nationalist activities and condemned to death, she paid £E 200 to save him from execution. She was writing a book on women's rights when she died suddenly of the Spanish influenza. She strongly influenced HUDA SHA'RAWI, Egypt's future feminist leader, who eulogized her in a series of articles.

Bibliographic Sources

'Abd al-Halim, *Nisa*, 41–48.

'Abd al-Malik, *Dhikra Bahithat al-Badiy*.

Adams, *Islam and Modernism*, 235–239.

'Aqqad, 'Abbas Mahmud, *Shu'ara Misr*, 20–39.

Badran, "Feminist Vision."

———, *Feminists*, 54–55.

Badran and Cooke, *Opening the Gates*, 134–138, 227–238.

Booth, "Biography and Feminist Rhetoric."

Brockelmann, *GAL*, S III, 256–258.

Cole, "Feminism, Class, and Islam," 387–407.

Daghir, *Masadir*, II, i, 739–741.

Disuqi, 'Umar, *Dirasat adabiyya*, 180–197.

Early, "Cairo Viewed from the Fayyum Oasis."

EI2, VI, 219–220, article by Thomas Philipp.

Fahmi, Qallini, *Muhadarat 'an Mayy*, 53–94.

al-Hilal 27:2 (Nov. 1918): 153–155.

——— 66:11 (Nov. 1958): 16–22.

Husayn, Qadriyya, *Shahirat al-nisa*.

Ibrahim, Emily Faris, in *al-Wurud* (Beirut) 1:3 (1953): 10–13.

Jabari, *Malak Hifni Nasif*.

Jindi, Anwar, *Adwa*, 196–200.

———, *al-Muhafaza wa al-tajdid*, 93–102.

Jundi, *A'lam al-adab*, II, 531–532.

Kahhala, *A'lam al-nisa*, II, 1464–1490.

———, *Mu'jam*, XIII, 5–6.

Mahmud, Muhammad, *al-Shi'r al-nisai*.

al-Manar 21:2 (2 Mar. 1919): 105–109; 21:3 (28 June 1919): 163–168.

Mubarak, Zaki, in *al-Hilal* 44:2 (Dec. 1935): 144–145.

Muhammad, Fathiyya, *Balaghat al-nisa*, I, 4–60.

al-Muqtataf 53:4 (Oct. 1918): 486–488; 5 (Nov.): 497–500; 54:3 (Mar. 1919): 217–221; 4 (Apr.): 338–346; 5 (May): 425–432; 6 (June): 529–535; 55:1 (July 1919): 26–33; 6 (Dec.): 497–506; 56:1 (Jan. 1920): 51–60; 2 (Feb.): 153–163; 3 (Mar.): 201–209.

——— 68:1 (Jan. 1926): 71–76, memorial speeches.

Nasif, Majd al-Din, *Athar Bahithat al-Badiya Malak Hifni Nasif*.

———, *Tahrir al-mara fi al-Islam*, 41–68.

OEMIW, III, 229–230, article by Margot Badran.
Philipp, "Feminism and Nationalist Politics in Egypt."
Qadi, Shukri, Miat shakhsiyya, 298–300.
Qallini, Sha'irat 'arabiyyat, 37–57.
Tanahi, Tahir, 'Ala firash al-mawt, 91–94.
Zeidan, Arab Women Novelists, 21–23.
Zirikli, al-A'lam, VII, 287–288.
Ziyada, Mayy, Bahithat al-Badiya.

Nasif, Muhammad Hifni

(16 September 1856–25 February 1919)
Arabic philologist, judge, and poet. Muhammad was born in Birkat al-Hajj (Qalyubiyya) and educated at al-Azhar, where he was closely associated with MUHAMMAD 'ABDUH. He then advanced through various posts in the educational and then the judicial system, finally becoming the first Arabic language inspector in the Education Ministry. He made many speeches during the 'URABI Revolution, delivering some of them in the streets and mosques, and wrote for the press under the pen name Idris Muhammadayn. He traveled to various Near Eastern and European countries to make propaganda for the nationalist cause. In 1908, after having worked for twenty years in the Niyaba and the judiciary of the National Courts, he became the first president of the Egyptian University and one of its earliest teachers. He helped to found the first Arabic Language Academy. Collaborating with HAFIZ IBRAHIM and others, he wrote a collection of humorous poems. He also wrote a two-volume history of Arabic literature and other books about the Arabic language. The final year of his life was saddened by his wife's illness and the death of his thirty-three-year-old daughter, Malak. His son collected and published his poems posthumously.

Bibliographic Sources

'Abd al-Jawad, Muhammad, Taqwim Dar al-'Ulum, 241.
al-Adib 19:2 (Feb. 1960): 5–6.
'Allam and 'Abd al-Hamid Hasan, Nathr Hifni Nasif.
'Aqqad, 'Abbas Mahmud, Shu'ara Misr, 21–29.
Brockelmann, GAL S II, 728.
EAL, II, 580.
Fikri, 'Ali, Subul al-najah, II, 197–203.
Gharaba, Shakhsiyyat, 139–144.
Ghunaym, Mahmud, Hifni Nasif.
Heyworth-Dunne, James, "Society and Politics."

Habib, Tawfiq, in al-Hilal 27:7 (Apr. 1919): 594–600.
Hijazi, Anwar, 'Amaliqa, 145–148.
Husayn, Taha, in al-Hilal 65:6 (June 1957): 9–13.
Ibrahim, Ahmad Muhibb al-Din, in al-Ahram, 18 Mar. 1947.
Jindi, Anwar, A'lam wa ashab aqlam, 139–146.
Jundi, A'lam al-adab, II, 449.
Kahhala, Mu'jam, IX, 265.
Mikhail, Sa'd, Adab al-'asr, 133–136.
Mujahid, al-A'lam al-sharqiyya, II, 503–505.
Mutran, Khalil, in al-Siyasa al-usbu'iyya, no. 90 (26 Nov. 1927): 12–13.
Nadi Dar al-'Ulum, al-Majmu'a al-thaniyya, 125–133.
Nasif, 'Isam al-Din Hifni, in al-Muqtataf 81:6 (Dec. 1932): 597–601.
Nasif, Majd al-Din, Shi'r Hifni Nasif.
Ramadi, Min a'lam al-adab, 97–102.
———, Sihafat al-fukaha, 65–66.
Sabri, Muhammad, Shu'ara al-'asr, I, 152–158.
Tanahi, Tahir, 'Ala firash al-mawt, 95–99.
Zirikli, al-A'lam, II, 265.

Nasim, Muhammad Tawfiq

(1875–7 March 1938)
Politician, minister, and premier. Of Anatolian Turkish origin, Nasim was born in Cairo and educated at the Jesuit school, graduating from the Khedivial Law School at the top of his class in 1894. He served in the Niyaba until he was appointed as minister of awqaf, then finance, and he twice held the post of premier at King FUAD's behest. He also served as the king's chef du cabinet and speaker of the Senate. He was frequently the rival of his law school classmate, ISMA'IL SIDQI, in courting both the king and the British. Of a calm temperament, Nasim loved literature. His marriage to an Austrian in his last years set off press attacks, based on the public fear that his wife would take his vast wealth out of the country. He divorced the young woman and died in Cairo shortly thereafter.

Bibliographic Sources

Amin, Mustafa, Shakhsiyyat, I, 48–61.
Badrawi, Malak, Isma'il Sidqi, 116–119.
Mujahid, al-A'lam al-sharqiyya, I, 106–107.
New York Times (8 Mar. 1938): 19.
Rafi'i, 'Abd al-Rahman, Fi a'qab al-thawra, I, 89–97; II, 194–195.
Thabit, Karim, in Kull shay wa al-'alam, no. 122 (12 Mar. 1928): 5.
———, "Tawfiq Nasim Basha."
Zirikli, al-A'lam, VI, 66–67.

al-Nasir, Jamal 'Abd
(15 January 1918–28 September 1970)
Army officer, leader of the 1952 Revolution, premier, and president of Egypt from 1956 to 1970, usually called "Nasser." Born in Alexandria, the son of a postal clerk from Beni Murr (Asyut), Nasir studied at al-Nahhasin Elementary and al-Nahda Secondary Schools in Cairo, the Cairo University Law Faculty, and the Military Academy. Commissioned in 1938, he then served in the Western Desert, Manqabad, and the Sudan. From 1941 he taught at the Military Academy, also receiving advanced Staff College training in 1947–1948. In the Palestine War he led a battalion that was besieged for six months at Faluja, winning respect from both Israelis and Egyptians for its tenacity. Promoted to colonel in 1951, he earned a diploma from the Staff College, where he became a lecturer. Much of his energy went into organizing the Free Officers group that conspired to oust King FARUQ and the other governing powers that it believed had led Egypt to defeat in Palestine and fostered corruption and backwardness.

The group executed a successful coup on the night of 22–23 July 1952 and took power, forming a twelve-member Revolutionary Command Council (RCC) headed by Gen. MUHAMMAD NAJIB. Once the officers decided not to relinquish control to civilian politicians, Nasir began a power struggle with Najib, who wanted to restore Egypt's multiparty parliamentary government. Nasir, who favored a one-party regime led by the army, prevailed, and in January 1953 the RCC abolished all political parties except the Muslim Brothers and set up a single organization to replace the parties, the Liberation Rally. Nasir also became deputy RCC secretary-general and in May 1953 deputy premier and interior minister. He had many old regime politicians put on trial and imprisoned. The power struggle with Najib came to a head in February and March 1954, when Nasir tried to use his position to oust his rival, who enjoyed the conspicuous support of the Muslim Brothers, backers of the outlawed political parties, Communists, and other liberal Egyptians. Although Najib seemed to triumph at first, Nasir rallied his officers and some labor leaders and finally maneuvered him out of power. After the Brothers tried to assassinate Nasir in October, he banned their society, executed or jailed its leaders, ousted Najib, and put him under house arrest.

Under Nasir's early leadership, the revolutionary officers made major domestic changes: land reform, expansion of educational and health services, and elimination of much government corruption. In foreign policy, they relinquished Egypt's claims on the Sudan and signed the 1954 Anglo-Egyptian agreement, providing for the evacuation of Britain's forces from the Suez Canal. Nasir even put out clandestine peace feelers to Israel, but they were nullified by a secret Israeli attempt to sabotage U.S.-Egyptian relations known as the Lavon Affair. His evenhanded execution of both Muslim Brothers implicated in the attempt on his life and Egyptian Jews in the Lavon Affair was meant to placate domestic opinion, but it antagonized Israel. In February 1955 Israel raided the Egyptian-administered Gaza Strip, inflicting many casualties and revealing the Egyptian army's weakness. Nasir tried to buy more arms from the West, but his refusal to join the British-sponsored Baghdad Pact caused London and Washington to block any sales. Influenced by Indian Premier Nehru, Nasir attended the Bandung Conference, where he was persuaded to buy arms from Communist regimes. Consequently, Egypt concluded the Czech Arms Deal in September 1955. Anxious to prevent Egypt from falling to communism, the United States and Britain, along with the World Bank, offered aid to help finance construction of the Aswan High Dam, one of the regime's desiderata. In July 1956, after Egypt had accepted their terms, however, U.S. Secretary of State John Foster Dulles retracted the offer. In retaliation, Nasir nationalized the Suez Canal Company, a daring move that won widespread support in Egypt and the Arab world. The West's failure to restore international control of the canal, either by diplomacy or by the Suez War, enhanced his prestige. When Egypt adopted its 1956 Constitution, he was elected president for a six-year term.

As Nasir's leadership became entrenched, he began promoting state-sponsored economic development, including the nationalization of public utilities and basic industries, a policy that he called Arab socialism. He took up a leading role in inter-Arab politics, generally backing Syria and Saudi Arabia against the Hashemite kingdoms of Jordan and Iraq. His Arab nationalism, appealing to the people against their rulers, became a *leitmotif* of Egyptian foreign policy, as did his policy of positive neutrality, by which Egypt avoided forming Cold War alliances while seeking military and economic aid from both sides. Nasir opposed both the Baghdad Pact and the Eisenhower Doctrine and appealed to workers and students (and Palestinian refugees) to undercut pro-Western regimes. In 1958, at Syria's behest, Nasir agreed to an organic union of Egypt and Syria, to be called the United Arab Republic (UAR), which they hoped other Arab countries would later join. Egypt hosted a nongovernmental Afro-Asian Peoples' Solidarity Conference in 1957, brought together the nonaligned African states as the Casablanca Bloc, and attended a neutralist summit in Belgrade in 1961.

Iraq's refusal, after its July 1958 revolution, to join the UAR was a setback, and several other Arab countries that supported Nasir's neutralism also stood aloof. In 1961, after he nationalized most private companies, Syria seceded from the UAR. Although chagrined, Nasir cultivated new allies, especially Algeria, and sent troops to back Yemen's 1962 military coup, precipitating a costly civil war. At home he convoked the National Congress of Popular Forces, drew up the National Charter, and established the Arab Socialist Union (ASU) as the new single political party. The appointment of 'ALI SABRI as prime minister of a cabinet that included a worker and a woman for the first time, signaled Nasir's leftward drift. Although he continued to influence other Arab governments and rejoiced when Ba'thist officers overthrew hostile regimes in Iraq and Syria early in 1963, leading to new Arab unity talks, his regime acquiesced in the continued existence of separate states. Responding to the draining of the Arabs' fresh water supply by Israel's irrigation projects in the Jordan River valley, Egypt convened two Arab summit meetings in 1964, proclaiming plans to divert the Jordan's sources and creating the Palestine Liberation Organization. His ostensible aim was to back Arabs opposing Israel; the consequence was to delay any war with the Jewish state.

In 1966, however, a radical Ba'thist group took power in Syria and began provoking Israel by backing Palestinian *fidaiyin* raids. Egypt's Joint Defense Agreement with Syria failed to restrain the latter, which lost six fighter planes in a dogfight with Israel in April 1967. Advised by Soviet sources that Israel was massing troops to invade Syria, Nasir hastily built up Egypt's forces in the Sinai Peninsula. He demanded the withdrawal of the UN Emergency Force and then blockaded the Tiran Straits against Israeli shipping in the Gulf of Aqaba. Egypt's press, radio, and television competed with the mass media of other Arab states in making anti-Israel threats. Israeli jet fighters attacked Egypt and other Arab powers, starting the June War. Within six days Israel had tripled the land area under its control, including the Gaza Strip and the Sinai, and Nasir had to accept a UN cease-fire. Addressing the nation on television, he took responsibility for the defeat (but accused the United States of aiding Israel) and resigned as president. Mass demonstrations, seemingly spontaneous but probably orchestrated, persuaded him to withdraw his resignation.

Nasir's postwar policies were more subdued. At the Khartum Summit, the Arab leaders rejected any negotiations with Israel, but Nasir made peace with King Faysal and withdrew his troops from Yemen in return for Saudi financial support. He later accepted UN Security Council Resolution 242, but waged a costly War of Attrition against Israel, only to end it abruptly by agreeing to the Rogers Peace Plan in July 1970. It seemed that he was moving toward peace with Israel at the time of his sudden death in September 1970, just after he had mediated a Jordanian-Palestinian civil war.

His successor, ANWAR AL-SADAT, changed many domestic and foreign policies, enabling some Egyptians to attack the oppressive character of Nasir's regime and the failure of his socialist policies. Nevertheless, his personal integrity, commitment to Arab unity, concern for the welfare of poor people, and ability to stand up to the West are honored by many Egyptians. When Sadat's policies worked, Nasir's reputation suffered, but to the degree that Sadat, too, failed, Nasir's memory is still revered by many Arabs.

Bibliographic Sources
Abdel-Fadil, *Political Economy of Nasserism.*
al-Ahram Archives, file 1.
Baghdadi, *Mudhakkirat,* 3 vols.
Baker, *Egypt's Uncertain Revolution.*
Balta and Rulleau, *Nasser.*
Beattie, *Nasser Years.*
Dekmejian, *Egypt Under Nasir.*
*EI*2, Supp., 5–9, article by Derek Hopwood.

EMME, III, 1313–1315, article by Raymond W. Baker.

Gordon, Joel, *Nasser's Blessed Movement*.

Farid, 'Abdel Magid, *Nasser.*

Fawzi, Mahmud, *Thuwwar Yulyu yatahaddathun.*

Hamrush, *Thawrat Yulyu.*

Haykal, Muhammad Hasanayn, *'Abd al-Nasir.*

———, *Cairo Documents.*

Hopwood, *Egypt: Politics and Society*, 34–104.

Jankowski, "Arab Nationalism in 'Nasserism.'"

Karrum, *'Abd al-Nasir al-muftara 'alayh.*

Kerr, *Arab Cold War.*

Lacouture, *Nasser.*

Matar, *Bi-saraha 'an 'Abd al-Nasir.*

Muti'i, *Mawsu'a*, 121–127.

Nasr, Marlene, *Jamal 'Abd al-Nasir.*

Nasser, *Philosophy of the Revolution.*

Neguib, *Egypt's Destiny,* 29–30, 120, 190–192.

Nutting, *Nasser.*

OEMIW, III, 231, article by Derek Hopwood.

Radwan, Fathi, *72 shahran ma'a 'Abd al-Nasir.*

Ramadan, 'Abd al-'Azim, *'Abd al-Nasir.*

Reich, *Political Leaders*, 379–388, article by Ellis Goldberg.

Rejwan, *Nasserist Ideology.*

Sadat, Anwar, *Revolt on the Nile.*

Samakuri, *Asrar hukm al-qusur*, 77–119.

Stephens, *Nasser.*

Stewart, *Middle East: Temple of Janus*, 326–354, 364–370.

St. John, *The Boss.*

Vatikiotis, *Egypt Since the Revolution.*

———, *Nasser and His Generation.*

Vaucher, *Gamal Abdel Nasser et son équipe.*

Waterbury, *Egypt of Nasser and Sadat.*

Wheelock, *Nasser's New Egypt.*

Woodward, *Nasser.*

al-Nawawi, Shaykh Hasuna
(1839–17 May 1925)

Islamic legal expert, chief Hanafi mufti, and reforming rector of al-Azhar. Hasuna was born in Nawa, a village in the Mallawi district of Asyut province, memorized the Quran in his local *kuttab*, and was educated at al-Azhar. He became an instructor in Islamic jurisprudence at Dar al-'Ulum and then at the Khedivial School of Law and held various judiciary positions. His colleagues petitioned Khedive 'ABBAS to appoint him as the leader of al-Azhar. He became the chief mufti of Egypt in 1898 and rector of al-Azhar twice (1896–1899 and 1907–1909). He was elected to the board of the Shar'i Courts but resigned in 1899 because of his opposition to a British plan to appoint two judges from the National Court of Appeals to the Shar'i Court system. He wrote a treatise on teaching Islamic jurisprudence and religion. He died in Cairo. He was the father of 'Abd al-Khaliq Hasuna, second secretary-general of the Arab League.

Bibliographic Sources

al-Ahram (18 May 1925): 5.

Fikri, 'Ali, *Subul al-najah*, II, 67.

Hasan, Muhammad 'Abd al-Ghani, and 'Abd al-'Aziz Disuqi, *"Rawdat al-Madaris,"* 369–371.

al-Manar 10:1 (14 Mar. 1907): 48–51.

Mubarak, 'Ali, *Khitat*, XVII, 14–15.

Mujahid, *al-A'lam al-sharqiyya*, I, 301–302.

Taymur, Ahmad, *A'lam al-fikr al-islami*, 114–119.

Zakhura, *Mirat al-'asr*, I, 190–192.

Zayyati, *Kanz al-jawhar*, 153–156.

Zirikli, *al-A'lam*, II, 229.

Nazli [Zaynab Fadil]
(1853–27 December 1913)

Princess of the khedivial family, hostess of a literary salon, and close friend of many leading Egyptians and Europeans. Daughter of Mustafa Fadil, who was deprived of his right to succeed to the khedivate when his half-brother ISMA'IL changed the succession system, Nazli married an Ottoman foreign minister, Khalil Sharif, and later al-Sayyid Khalil Bu Hajib of Tunisia. Although not openly a Nationalist, she was sympathetic to 'URABI as a possible supporter of Prince HALIM, to MUSTAFA KAMIL, and definitely to SA'D ZAGHLUL, whom she probably introduced to Safiyya, his future wife. Many political and literary leaders, European as well as Egyptian, frequented her salon.

Bibliographic Sources

Allen, "Nazli Circle," 79–84.

Fahmi, Qallini, *Mudhakkirat*, I, 135–136.

Farid, Muhammad, *Memoirs and Diaries*, 126–128.

Jindi, Anwar, *Adwa*, 265–266.

Jundi, *A'lam al-adab*, II, 532.

al-Muqtataf 44:1 (Jan. 1914): 99–100.

Storrs, *Orientations*, 102–107.

Times (London) (29 Dec. 1913): 5–6.

Zeidan, *Arab Women Novelists*, 50–51.

Nimr, Dr. Faris
(6 January 1856–17 December 1951)

Editor of *al-Muqtataf* and one of the pioneers of Arabic journalism. Faris was born to a Greek Orthodox family in Wadi al-Matim (in what is now Lebanon); his father was killed in the 1860 troubles, when Faris was four. His mother took him to Beirut and in 1863 to Jerusalem, where he studied at the British School for five years. He then worked in commerce before becoming one of the first students at the Syrian Protestant College (American University of Beirut). Upon graduating in 1874, he became a tutor in astronomy and mathematics at the college, running its observatory and founding the Syrian Scientific Society in 1882. Six years earlier, he and a classmate, YA'QUB SARRUF, began publishing in Beirut a literary and scientific monthly called *al-Muqtataf*. Following a quarrel with the college authorities over the young men's belief in Darwin's theory of evolution by natural selection, they moved, with their journal, to Cairo in 1884. In 1889 they founded a daily newspaper, *al-Muqattam,* of which Nimr took primary charge. His editorials favored individualism, laissez-faire economics, and the British occupation. Although *al-Muqattam* at first antagonized Egypt's Nationalists, it and *al-Muqtataf* promoted the dissemination of liberalism among educated Egyptians. An excellent orator, Nimr kept his mental and physical powers until his death at an advanced age in Ma'adi. He was one of the founding members of the Arabic Language Academy.

Bibliographic Sources
Abu 'Arja, "*al-Muqattam,*" 26–29.
'Allam, *Majma'iyyun*, 226–227.
Antonius, *Arab Awakening*, 79–89.
Asaf, *Dalil*, 335–336.
*EI*2, VIII, 48–49, article by Y.M. Choueiri.
EMME, III, 1343–1344, article by Guilain P. Denoeux.
Hourani, Albert, in *JRCAS* 39 (1952): 167–169.
Jindi, Anwar, *al-Sihafa al-siyasiyya*, 140–143.
al-Kitab 11 (Jan. 1952): 61, obituary.
al-Muqattam, 17 Dec. 1951.
Tarrazi, *Tarikh al-sihafa*, II, 138–142.
Times (London) (18 Dec. 1951): 4f.
Zakhura, *Mirat al-'asr*, I, 529–356; II, 289–292.
Zeine, *Emergence of Arab Nationalism*, 51–54.
Zirikli, *al-A'lam*, V, 127–128.

Nubar Nubarian

(4 January 1825–13 January 1899)
Armenian official, legal reformer, cabinet minister, and three-time premier. Born in Smyrna (Izmir) and educated in France and Switzerland,

Nubar was brought to Egypt by an uncle, Baghus Yusufiyan, who was MUHAMMAD 'ALI's main interpreter. Nubar worked at his uncle's side for some time and, after his death in 1844, was sent to Paris in that year's educational mission for training at the Egyptian military school there, remaining in France until 1849, although others report that he remained in Egypt and worked for Baghus's successor, Khusraw Bey. Nubar soon became translator and unofficial adviser to IBRAHIM. He married Fulik, the daughter of Kevork Iramian, a member of a rich Istanbul Armenian family whose Ottoman connections would later help him to serve his patrons, notably Khedive ISMA'IL. 'ABBAS HILMI I used Nubar as his chief negotiator with the British to build Egypt's first railway. Having lived in Europe as a boy, Nubar spoke eleven foreign languages, had read widely in Western literature, and knew how to charm Europeans. Although he asked permission to leave government service in 1853, he acceded to Abbas's request to be his chargé d'affaires in Vienna. Recalled by SA'ID when he closed Egypt's agencies abroad, Nubar organized the growing transit traffic between Cairo and Suez, was named secretary to the cabinet, and in 1858 became director of the Communications and Railways Department. He was dismissed the next year, ostensibly because of the delayed delivery of two guns ordered by the viceroy but really because of Nubar's dependence on the British consul general, one of several occasions when Nubar sought British backing.

Isma'il sent Nubar to Istanbul and to Paris to represent his views on the Suez Canal concession. In 1864 he assumed almost total control over public works and railways, becoming in European eyes the mastermind of Egypt's administration, but Isma'il's suspicion that Nubar was abusing his powers led in 1866 to his transfer to foreign affairs. Meanwhile, his rapid accumulation of land and money was making him one of the richest men in Egypt. Nubar helped obtain loans for Isma'il, negotiated with the Ottoman government for the decrees that increased Egypt's autonomy, and worked between 1867 and 1875 to set up the Mixed Courts. He then served for three years as director of the Commerce Department. When Isma'il agreed in August 1878 to turn his powers over to a cabinet modeled after those of Europe, he named Nubar as his premier. This "European cabinet," which included an Englishman as finance minister and a French public works minister, was dismissed by Isma'il in March 1879, following an officers' mutiny. Nubar returned to power in 1884, when Egypt was being pressed to evacuate the Sudan, and served until 1888, a period when Britain's occupation was becoming entrenched. He served as premier a third time in 1894–1895. Adaptable, clever, and suave, he is remembered by Egyptians for enriching himself from his foreign connections at their expense. He died in Paris. His memoirs were published in 1983 in French and in an Arabic translation, *Nubar fi Misr,* in 1991.

Bibliographic Sources
Archarouni, *Nubar Pacha.*
Bell, *Khedives and Pashas*, 145–160.
Bertrand, *Nubar Pacha.*
Blunt, *Gordon at Khartoum*, 170–178, 190–199.
*EI*2, VIII, 93, article by F.R. Hunter.
Ghali, Mirrit Boutros, introduction to *Mémoires de Nubar Pacha.*
al-Hilal 7:9 (1 Feb. 1899): 257–261.
Holynski, *Nubar Pacha devant l' histoire.*
Hunter, *Egypt Under the Khedives*, 165–176.
———, "Self-Image and Historical Truth."
Makhluf, N., *Nubar Basha.*
Mujahid, *al-A'lam al-sharqiyya*, I, 130–131.
al-Muqtataf 22:2 (Feb. 1899): 101–108.
Sayyid, Afaf Lutfi, *Egypt and Cromer*, 69–75.
Schölch, *Egypt for the Egyptians!* 320.
Tagher, "Portrait psychologique de Nubar Pacha."
——— [J.T.], "Nubar Pacha et la reforme judi-caire."
Times (London) (16 Jan. 1899): 10–11.
Tusun, *al-Ba'that al-'ilmiyya*, 330–333.
Walili, *Mafakhir al-ajyal*, 59–61.
Zakhura, *Mirat al-'asr*, I, 77–79.
Zaydan, Jurji, *Mashahir al-sharq*, 1st ed., I, 222–225.

al-Nuqrashi, Mahmud Fahmi
(26 April 1888–27 December 1948)
Educator, politician, and minister. Born in Alexandria to 'Ali and Hanifa al-Nuqrashi, Mahmud graduated from Ras al-Tin Secondary School in 1906 and received his higher education at the Higher Teachers College and the University of Nottingham (England). Upon returning to Egypt in 1909, he taught school, then rose in the administration until he became director of public instruction in Asyut. A Wafdist, he became the deputy governor of Cairo and then deputy interior minister under SA'D ZAGHLUL. Implicated in Stack's murder, Nuqrashi was imprisoned briefly but then cleared. He held ministerial posts in the Wafdist cabinets of 1930 and 1936 but broke with NAHHAS in 1937. Together with AHMAD MAHIR, he formed the Sa'dist Party, which joined several Palace-led coalition governments, in which he served twice as education minister. His reforms included setting up Departments of Oriental Languages and Journalism in Cairo University's Arts Faculty, founding night schools for graduates of the technical and commercial secondary schools, eliminating English from the first year of the elementary schools, and standardizing kindergarten curricula. After Ahmad Mahir was assassinated in 1945, Nuqrashi became Sa'dist Party leader and headed cabinets in 1945–1946 and 1947–1948. He led the 1947 Egyptian delegation to the UN Security Council to demand that Britain withdraw from the Sudan and allow it to unite with Egypt, but did not gain its support. When fighting broke out between Jews and Arabs in Palestine, Nuqrashi hoped to avoid committing Egyptian troops, but King FARUQ ignored his advice and entered the war in May 1948. As defeats in Palestine stirred up discontent within Egypt, Nuqrashi tried to ban the Muslim Brothers and was assassinated by a student member. Known for his integrity and patriotism, he was neither as charismatic as his rival Nahhas nor as flamboyant as his royal patron.

Bibliographic Sources
Abaza, Tharwat, in *al-Ahram*, 27 June 1992.
'Abd Allah, Sa'id 'Abd al-Raziq Yusuf, *Mahmud Fahmi al-Nuqrashi.*
al-Ahram Archives, file 221.
al-Ahrar, 12 Dec. 1993.
Amin, Mustafa, *Shakhsiyyat*, I, 124–142.
'Arusi, *Ashhar qadaya al-ightiyalat*, 401–620.
Luqa, *Rayhanat al-shuhada Mahmud Fahmi al-Nuqrashi.*
Qadi, Shukri, *Khamsun shakhsiyya*, 61–65.
Rafi'i, 'Abd al-Rahman, *Fi a'qab al-thawra*, III, 271–277.
Tawfiq, 'Awad, and Hasan Sabri, *Wuzara al-ta'lim*, 99–101.
Times (London) (29 Dec. 1948): 4d, 5c, 7d.
'Umar, Mahmud Fathi, *Abtal al-hurriyya*, 94–119.
al-Wafd, 14 Dec. 1991; 1 Nov. 1993.
Zirikli, *al-A'lam*, VII, 180–181.

Q

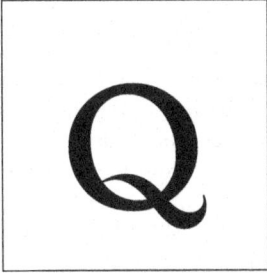

Qadri, Muhammad
(1821–21 November 1888)

Judge and writer. Born in Mallawi to an Anatolian Turkish father and an Egyptian mother, Muhammad was educated in his village *kuttab* and at the School of Languages, where he excelled in the study of foreign languages. Upon his graduation, he became an assistant translator at the school, meanwhile studying the Shari'a and European law codes, until Khedive ISMA'IL chose him to tutor the crown prince. He then worked for the Palace and for the Alexandria Commercial Court, headed the foreign affairs department's translation bureau, and translated the criminal sections of the Napoleonic Code into Arabic for the Mixed Courts and in preparation for the National Courts. He later became a chancellor in the Mixed Courts, justice minister, and education minister. He died in Cairo. His published writings include a work on the Turkish, Arabic, and French languages; a botany textbook; a book on adjudicating *awqaf* issues; and works on criminal law.

Bibliographic Sources

Fikri, 'Ali, *Subul al-najah*, III, 189–192.
Haykal, Muhammad Husayn, *Tarajim misriyya*, 101–109.
Iskarus, Tawfiq, in *al-Muqtataf* 48:3 (Mar. 1916): 253–263.
Khanki, Aziz, in *al-Muhamah* 7:7 (Feb. 1927): 646–650.
Mujahid, *al-A'lam al-sharqiyya*, I, 114–115.
Shamis, *'Uzama*, 78–84.
Tajir, *Harakat al-tarjama*, 104.
Walili, *Mafakhir al-ajyal*, 39–40.
Zirikli, *al-A'lam*, VII, 10.

al-Qalamawi, Dr. Suhayr
(20 July 1911–4 May 1997)

Literary scholar, writer, translator, and professor. Born in Cairo, Qalamawi was educated at the American School for Girls, then was one of the first women to enter Cairo University (after being rejected by the Science Faculty, Suhayr was admitted by TAHA HUSAYN to the Arts Faculty) in 1929, earning her *license* in 1933, the highest in her class. She was the first woman to earn an M.A. (1937) and a Ph.D. (1941), both in Arabic literature. Appointed as an instructor, she rose to be professor of Arabic and, in 1958, department head. Later she became a member of the Popular Assembly and vice president of Dar al-Ma'arif Publishing House. She chaired the first Conference on Popular Arts in 1961 and one sponsored by the Egyptian Organization for Writing and Translation in 1966. Qalamawi represented Egypt at the Conference on the Family, held in Kuwait, in 1972 and two years later at a Beirut conference on personal law. She became chief editor of *al-Funun* in 1971 and was elected to membership in the Supreme Council for the Press in 1975 and of Arts and Letters in 1976 and was a member of the Popular Assembly in 1979–1984. She was the first person to propose holding the Cairo Book Fair, an annual event since 1969. She also participated in preparing a simplified encyclopedia, oversaw the translation of ten Shakespeare plays into Arabic as part of an Arab League project, and oversaw critical editions of more than twenty books in the "Thousand Book Series." She took part in many working conferences on literature, literary criticism, women, and education in Egypt and abroad. Her publications included *Ahadith jiddati* [Tales of My Grandmother] and *al-Naqd al-adabi* [Literary Criticism]. JIHAN SADAT was one of her students. Although Qalamawi tended not to address feminist issues, she opened many doors to other women during her lifetime.

Bibliographic Sources

al-Ahram Archives, file 1398.
al-Ahram Weekly, 8 May 1997.
al-Anba, 16 Mar. 1986.
EAL, II, 628–629.
Hafiz, Ahmad, *Ayyam min shababihim*, 105–108.
al-Hayat, 12 May 1997.
Jundi, *A'lam al-adab*, II, 541.
Qalamawi, *My Grandmother's Cactus*.

Sa'd al-Din, Mursi, in *al-Ahram*, 10 May 1997.
Sa'dawi, Nawal, in *al-Ahram*, 7 May 1997.
Sharuni, Yusuf, *al-Layla al-thaniya ba'da al-alf.*
Uktubir, 18 May 1997.
WWAW, 1997–1998, 526.

Qattawi, Yusuf Aslan
(15 May 1845 or 1861–16 May 1942)
Entrepreneur, engineer, member of Parliament, cabinet minister, and leader of Egypt's Jewish community. Yusuf's family traced its residence in Egypt back to the eighth century; his father served in the governments of 'ABBAS, SA'ID, and ISMA'IL. Trained at the École des Ponts et Chaussées in Paris, Yusuf began his career as an engineer in the Public Works Ministry. He became a member and then the elected president of the Egyptian Chamber of Commerce and served on the boards of Bank Misr (which he helped to found) and other companies. He was elected in 1913 to the Legislative Assembly and in 1923 to the Chamber of Deputies, chairing its budget committee. He was minister of economy and communications in the ZIWAR cabinet of 1924–1925. He became a member of the short-lived Ittihad Party and was an appointed member and speaker of the Senate from 1927 to 1931. His wife was a lady-in-waiting to Queen Nazli, and Yusuf was reputedly close to King FUAD. He was president of Cairo's Sephardic Jewish Council from 1924 to 1942 and was succeeded in that post upon his death by a son, René. Loyal to Egypt, he was strongly opposed to Zionism.

Bibliographic Sources
Antaki, *al-Nujum*, 106–107.
Beinin, *Dispersion of Egyptian Jewry*, 45–46.
EMME, I, 450, article by Michael Laskier.
Encyclopedia Judaica, V, 255.
Fargeon, *Les juifs en Égypte*, passim.
Grünwald, "On Cairo's Lombard Street."
Krämer, *Jews in Modern Egypt*, 94–103.
———, "Rise and Decline of the Jewish Community of Cairo."
Laskier, *Jews of Egypt, 1920–1970*, 36 et passim.
Makariyus, *Tarikh al-Israiliyyin.*
Mizrahi, *L'Égypte et ses juifs*, 67–68.
———, "Jews in Economic Development," 87–88.
Mujahid, *al-A'lam al-sharqiyya*, I, 130–131.
Nassar, Siham, *al-Yahud al-misriyyin*, 20–21.
Raafat, "The House of Yacoub Cattaui."
al-Shams (18 May 1942): 1, 4, obituary.
Zakhura, *Mirat al-'asr*, II, 146.

al-Qaysuni, Dr. 'Abd al-Mun'im
(9 June 1916–21 October 1987)
Egyptian economist. Born in Heliopolis, 'Abd al-Mun'im was taught by the Frères in Bab al-Luq and Khoronfish, then earned his bachelor's degree in commerce from Cairo University (1937) and his doctorate from the London School of Economics (1942). He worked for Barclay's Bank in England (1942–1943), taught economics at Cairo University (1944–1946), directed the Middle East Department of the International Monetary Fund in Washington (1946–1950), and then served with the National Bank of Egypt (1950–1954). He was finance minister in 1954–1966 and again in 1968, also serving for part of that time as deputy prime minister and in 1958 as head of the Supreme Council for Tourism. He was influential in Egyptianizing the economy after the Suez War and in formulating NASIR's economic policies. He was elected to chair the Conference on Commerce and Development in Geneva in 1964. He chaired the Arab International Bank in 1971–1976 and again in 1978. Because Qaysuni again served the Egyptian government as minister for economic and financial affairs in 1976–1978, he was blamed for the 1977 Food Riots. He was also planning minister in 1977–1978 and later served under MUBARAK as adviser to the Finance Ministry. A patriotic technocrat, his economic views were conservative for the Arab socialist era, but better suited to SADAT's policy of *infitah*. He received decorations from Egypt, Lebanon, and West Germany.

Bibliographic Sources
'Abd al-Hayy, *'Asir hayati*, 20–28.
al-Ahram, 22 Oct. 1987.
al-Ahram Archives, file 16.
International Who's Who of the Arab World, 275–276.
Najib, *A'lam Misr*, 324.
New York Times (22 Oct. 1987): B8.
Uktubir, 28 Apr. 1985–12 Jan. 1986; *al-Akhbar*, 16 Feb. 1986–20 Feb. 1987, Qaysuni memoirs.

Qutb, Sayyid
(9 October 1906–29 August 1966)
Muslim thinker and writer. Born in Musha (near Asyut), the son of a respected farmer (said to be of Indian origin) who belonged to the National Party, Sayyid was educated at his village *kuttab*, a

Cairo secondary school, and Dar al-'Ulum, where he became interested in English literature. After graduating in 1933, he worked for *al-Ahram* and wrote literary articles for *al-Risala* and *al-Thaqafa*, taught Arabic, and served as an education inspector in Qina. He was sent to study educational administration in the United States from 1948 to 1950, during which time he grew disenchanted with the West as he observed the apparent moral corruption of American society and its anti-Arab bias caused by the Palestine War.

Upon returning, Qutb criticized Egypt's British-influenced educational programs and called for a more Islamic curriculum, becoming a Muslim Brother around 1951. He developed close ties to some of the Free Officers, notably KAMAL AL-DIN HUSAYN, who wanted to make him education minister, and served as the first secretary-general of the Liberation Rally. He resigned from the government in 1953, taking charge of the Muslim Brothers' propaganda and editing their newspaper. Imprisoned with the other Brothers after their failed attempt to assassinate NASIR, he began writing books that were smuggled out of Egypt and published abroad, notably *al-'Adala al-ijtima'iyya fi al-Islam* (translated into English as *Social Justice in Islam*), *Fi zilal al-Quran* (translated as *In the Shade of the Quran*), and *Ma'alim fi al-tariq* [Landmarks on the Way]. Disillusioned with Nasir's government, he argued that each person is an arena in the battle between godly and satanic forces. He called for a small community of good people to expel evil and establish righteousness in the world. Drawing on Quranic passages, he taught that Jews and Christians will always implacably oppose Islam and that Muslims must combat Zionism, "crusaderism," and communism to protect their community and its values. Qutb's thirty-volume interpretation of the Quran has become a standard reference work in mosques and homes throughout the Muslim world. Released in 1964, he was jailed again in 1965 and subjected to press vilification before being hanged for treason in August 1966. Since his death his ideas have inspired many individuals and groups, such as *al-Takfir wa al-Hijra, al-Jihad al-Jadid*, and other Islamist *jama'at* in Egypt, as well as politicized Muslims in many other countries.

Bibliographic Sources

Abu-Rabi', *Intellectual Origins of Islamic Resurgence*, 92–219.
al-Ahram Archives, file 9629.
Akhavi, "Sayyid Qutb."
al-Anba, 17–24 June 1994; 15–17 Feb. 1997.
'Arusi, *Muhakamat Sayyid Qutb*.
Balihi, *Sayyid Qutb*.
Binder, *Islamic Liberalism*, 170–205.
Cahiers de l'Orient Contemporain 58: 324; 59: 50; 60: 39–40; 61: 44–45; 62: 40–41.
Carré, Olivier, "Note sur la politique."
Choueiri, *Islamic Fundamentalism*, 93–160.
Diyab, Muhammad Hafiz, *Sayyid Qutb*.
EAL, II, 642.
EI2, IX, 118–119, article by J.J.G. Jansen.
Fadl Allah, *Ma'a Sayyid Qutb*.
Faiz, *Tariq al-da'wa fi zilal al-Quran*.
Haddad, Yvonne Yazbeck, "Quranic Justification."
———, "Ideologue of Islamic Revival."
Haim, "Sayyid Qutb."
Hamuda, 'Adil, *Sayyid Qutb*.
al-Hayat, 13 Oct. 1996.
Kepel, *Muslim Extremism*, 27–34, 37–69.
Khalidi, *Sayyid Qutb min al-milad ila al-istishhad*.
———, *Sayyid Qutb: al-shahid al-hayy*.
Moussalli, *Radical Islamic Fundamentalism*.
Musallam, "Prelude to Islamic Commitment."
———, "Sayyid Qutb and Social Justice, 1945–1948."
OEMIW, III, 400–404, article by Shahrough Akhavi.
al-Qabas, 11 May 1989.
Qutb, Muhammad Ali, *Sayyid Qutb*.
Qutb, Sayyid, *Tifl min al-qarya*.
Rooke, *In My Childhood*, 172–175 et passim.
Rouleau, Eric, articles in *Le Monde*, 23, 30–31 Aug. 1966; 1 Sept. 1966.
Roussillon, *Sayyid Qutb*.
Sagiv, *Fundamentalism*, 36–42.
Saharti, Mustafa 'Abd al-Latif, *Adab al-tabi'a*, 112–113.
al-Sha'b, 11, 18, 25 Nov. 1986.
Shepard, *Sayyid Qutb and Islamic Activism*.
Sivan, *Radical Islam*.
Voll, "Fundamentalism in the Sunni Arab World," 368–372.
Zirikli, *al-A'lam*, III, 147–148.

R

al-Rafiʿi, ʿAbd al-Rahman

(8 February 1889–3 December 1966)
Lawyer, journalist, member of Parliament, cabinet minister, and pioneer historian of Egypt's nationalist movement. ʿAbd al-Rahman was born in Cairo's Khalifa quarter to a father originally from Tripoli (now in Lebanon) and a mother whose family had once been connected with the Palace. He was educated in Zaqaziq and then the Gharbiyya (Cairo) Elementary School, the Ras al-Tin (Alexandria) Secondary School, and the Khedivial Law School, from which he graduated in 1908, after which he worked as a writer and editor for *al-Liwa*. MUSTAFA KAMIL reportedly wanted to send him to Paris to study journalism after he finished his legal studies, but Mustafa's untimely death thwarted the project. ʿAbd al-Rahman practiced law for a time in Mansura, then in Zaqaziq, and then in Cairo. He wrote articles regularly for the newspapers of the National Party, sometimes with his brother, AMIN AL-RAFIʿI, a leading journalist, and served on the party's administrative board from 1911. He published his first book, *Huquq al-shaʿb* [The People's Rights] in 1912. He was arrested and his papers seized at the outbreak of World War I.

Although Rafiʿi spearheaded the early organization of the 1919 Revolution, he did not join the Wafd. Elected from Mansura as a Nationalist to many sessions of the Chamber of Deputies and in 1939 to the Senate, he led a coalition of Nationalists who objected to HAFIZ RAMADAN's joining the cabinet, arguing that party members should not take part in any government as long as the British occupied Egypt. Nevertheless, he later served as minister of supply in HUSAYN SIRRI's 1949 caretaker government. The NASIR

regime appointed him to head the Lawyers' Syndicate in 1954. He received a state prize in 1961 and was appointed in 1965 to membership in the Higher Council for the Arts, Letters, and Sciences. He was a prolific chronicler of Egypt's political history, with books on the French occupation, MUHAMMAD ʿALI, ISMAʿIL, the ʿURABI Revolution, Mustafa Kamil, MUHAMMAD FARID, the 1919 Revolution, its aftermath, and the 1952 Revolution, of which he approved. A towering figure in Egypt's historiography, he is buried beside Mustafa Kamil and Muhammad Farid.

Bibliographic Sources
Abaza, Fikri, in *al-Musawwar*, 9 Dec. 1966.
ʿAbd al-Hayy, *ʿAsir hayati*, 143–151.
al-Ahram, 4 Dec. 1966.
al-Ahram Archives, file 911.
ʿAlwan, *ʿAbd al-Rahman al-Rafiʿi*.
Bakr, Ihsan, in *al-Ahram*, 9 Feb. 1964.
Crabbs, "Egyptian Intellectuals and the Revolution."
———. "Politics, History, and Culture."
Jindi, Anwar, *Adwa*, 126–127.
al-Jumhuriyya, 12 Feb. 1986.
Jundi, *Aʿlam al-adab*, II, 422.
Kurayyim, Samih, in *al-Ahram*, weekly articles 24 Nov.–15 Dec. 1989.
Mustafa, "ʿAbd al-Rahman al-Rafiʿi."
Mutiʿi, *Haula al-rijal min Misr*, III, 119–133.
———, *Mawsuʿa*, 228–235.
Najjar, "ʿAbd al-Rahman al-Rafiʿi."
Qadi, Shukri, *Khamsun shakhsiyya,* 135–139.
Radwan, Fathi, *Mashhurun*, 77–96.
Rafiʿi, ʿAbd al-Rahman, *Mudhakkirati*, 78–82.
Tawfiq, Najib, *Ashhar al-usrat*, 154–162.
al-Wafd, 1 Apr. 1997, on historians' conference about al-Rafiʿi.
Zirikli, *al-Aʿlam*, III, 311.

al-Rafiʿi, Amin

(17 December 1886–29 December 1927)
Nationalist journalist. Amin al-Rafiʿi was born to a family of Syrian origin in Zaqaziq; he was educated there and in Alexandria, then graduated from the Khedivial Law School in Cairo. He joined the National Party under MUSTAFA KAMIL and wrote his first articles for its newspapers, *al-Liwa*, *al-ʿAlam*, and *al-Shaʿb*. After being interned for ten months during World War I, he was suddenly released at the instance of Sultan HUSAYN KAMIL and Prime Minister RUSHDI and offered the government's assistance, as a means of pressuring the British in the event that, once

163

the war ended, they failed to end the protectorate as they had promised in 1914. He subsequently bought control of *al-Akhbar* and became one of the Wafd's strongest backers in the beginning, until he broke with SAʻD ZAGHLUL over its policies. He had been elected to the first session of Parliament as a Nationalist; when the members were locked out of their building, it was Amin who proposed that they meet instead at the Continental Hotel in downtown Cairo. He was the author of a book about British negotiations on the Egyptian question and a set of travel memoirs, as well as numerous articles. The Wafdist leader NAHHAS visited Amin shortly before his death in Cairo.

Bibliographic Sources

Abu al-Majd, *Amin al-Rafiʻi, munadil misri.*
———, *Amin al-Rafiʻi, raid sihafat al-ray fi Misr.*
———, *Amin al-Rafiʻi: shahid al-wataniyya al-misriyya.*
ʻAnbar, *Amin al-Rafiʻi.*
Daghir, *Masadir*, II, i, 371–372.
Hamza, *Adab al-maqala*, VII.
Jindi, Anwar, *Aʻlam wa ashab aqlam*, 69–77.
———, *al-Sihafa al-siyasiyya*, 229–240.
Jundi, *Aʻlam al-adab*, II, 421–422.
Kahhala, *Muʻjam*, III, 9.
Mahmud, Hafiz, "al-ʻAmaliqa al-sitta," 106–108.
al-Manar 28:10 (22 Jan. 1928): 793–795.
Mujahid, *al-Aʻlam al-sharqiyya*, III, 990–991.
Nawfal, ʻAbdallah Habib, *Tarajim ʻulama Tarablus*, 249.
Qadi, Shukri, *Khamsun shaykhsiyya*, 217–220.
Rafiʻi, ʻAbd al-Rahman, *Fi aʻqab al-thawra*, II, 23–30.
Rizq, Fathi, *Khamsa wa sabʻuna najman*, 126–133.
Shamis, *ʻUzama*, 145–152.
Tawfiq, Najib, *Ashhar al-usrat*, 163–178.
Walili, *Mafakhir al-ajyal*, 92–93.
Zirikli, *al-Aʻlam*, II, 17.

al-Rafiʻi, Mustafa Sadiq

(January 1880–10 May 1937)

Popular neoclassical writer. Mustafa was born in Bahtim (Qalyubiyya), the son of a Shariʻa Court judge who had come originally from Tripoli (now in Lebanon), and got his elementary education there. Rendered deaf by a childhood illness, he could not attend al-Azhar and took a job as a Shariʻa Court clerk in Talkha and later in Tanta. He attended the literary salon of MAYY ZIYADA, with whom he was briefly in love, and in other ways played an active role in Egypt's literary life.

He became King FUAD's court poet in 1926. He led the opposition to the perceived threat to Egypt's Arabic-Islamic heritage, notably WILLCOCKS's effort to adapt Egyptian Colloquial Arabic to written form. He was renowned for his piety and the variety of his fields of knowledge. His best-known work, *Iʻjaz al-Quran* [The Quran's Inimitabilty], greatly impressed SAʻD ZAGHLUL. A proud and often abrasive writer, he feuded with TAHA HUSAYN and ʻAQQAD for both personal and literary reasons. He eventually broke with the Palace and, when his money began to run out, became a columnist for *al-Risala* in 1934. His literary conservatism and romantic prose won him a lasting popular following.

Bibliographic Sources

ʻAbd al-Hamid, Ismaʻil, *al-Udaba al-khams*, 2–32.
Abu Rayya, *Min rasail al-Rafiʻi.*
———, in *al-Risala*, no. 985 (19 May 1952): 556–559.
ʻAjlan, *al-Islam fi adab al-Rafiʻi.*
ʻAryan, *Hayat al-Rafiʻi.*
———, in *al-Risala*, no. 227 (8 Nov. 1937): 1816–1818.
ʻAzzam, ʻAbd al-Wahhab, *al-Awabid.*
Badri, *al-Imam Mustafa Sadiq al-Rafiʻi.*
Bayyumi, Muhammad Rajab, *Mustafa Sadiq al-Rafiʻi.*
Brockelmann, *GAL*, S III, 71–76.
Brugman, *Introduction*, 88–93.
Daghir, *Masadir*, II, i, 375–381.
Dayf, *al-Adab alʻarabi*, 242–250.
EAL, II, 644.
Eliraz, "Egyptian Intellectuals," 103, 107, 111, 118.
Fuad, Niʻmat Ahmad, *Dirasa fi adab al-Rafiʻi.*
Ghamrawi, Muhammad Ahmad, in *al-Risala*, no. 256 (30 May 1938): 887–888, 902–907.
Hafiz, ʻAbd al-Salam Hashim, *al-Rafiʻi wa Mayy.*
Hajj, *Mustafa Sadiq al-Rafiʻi.*
Haykal, Muhammad Husayn, *Fi awqat al-faragh*, 202–220.
al-Hilal 45:8 (June 1937): 870–873, obituary.
——— 89:5 (May 1980): 43–46 and other articles.
Husayn, Taha, *Hadith al-arbaʻa*, III, 11, 24–40.
Ibn Masʻud, *Nathr Mustafa Sadiq al-Rafiʻi.*
ʻImari, Muhammad ʻAbd al-Qadir, *Muhakamat al-zaman aw Taha Husayn.*
ʻIryan, *Hayat al-Rafiʻi.*
ʻIsa, Ahmad Muhammad, in *al-Muqtataf* 91:7 (Dec. 1937): 529–540.
Jindi, Anwar, *al-Muhafaza wa al-tajdid*, 455–463.
Jundi, *Aʻlam al-adab*, II, 414–420.
Kahhala, *Muʻjam*, XII, 256–258.
Khafaji, *Qissat al-adab*, V, 71–88.
Mahmud, ʻAli ʻAbd al-Hamid, *Mustafa Sadiq al-Rafiʻi.*

Makhluf, Hasanayn Hasan, *Mustafa Sadiq al-Rafi'i.*
Mazhar, Isma'il, in *al-Muqtataf* 91:1 (June 1937): 20–24.
Mikhail, Sa'd, *Adab al-'asr*, 263–271.
Mujahid, *al-A'lam al-sharqiyya*, II, 811–815.
Musa, Salama, in *al-Hilal* 32:3 (Jan. 1924): 400–404.
Nashat, *Mustafa Sadiq al-Rafi'i.*
Nawfal, 'Abdallah Habib, *Tarajim 'ulama Tarablus*, 211.
Qutb, Sayyid, in *al-Risala*, no. 257 (6 June 1938): 933–938.
Rafi'i, Mustafa Sadiq, "al-Kutub allati afadatni."
Ramadi, *Min a'lam al-adab*, 111–117.
Sabri, Muhammad, *Shu'ara al-'asr*, I, 213–220.
Shak'a, *Mustafa Sadiq al-Rafi'i.*
Sutuhi, *Mustafa Sadiq al-Rafi'i.*
Tawfiq, Najib, *Ashhar al-usrat*, 179–195.
Wakil, al-'Awadi, *Qadiyyat al-saffud.*
Zirikli, *al-A'lam*, VII, 235.

Ramadan, Muhammad Hafiz
(1879–7 February 1955)
Lawyer, member of Parliament, and cabinet minister. Muhammad was born in Cairo. The son of a businessman, he graduated from the Khedivial Law School in 1904 and had a thriving legal practice. He joined the National Party and served on its administrative board. He founded and edited *al-Liwa al-misri* in 1921 and became National Party president in 1923. He was elected to almost every session of Parliament and served in several anti-Wafd coalition governments, but his party leadership was challenged in 1940 by younger Nationalists who objected to his participation in governing Egypt while British troops continued to occupy the country. He was elected head of the Egyptian Lawyers' Syndicate in 1926. He published memoirs entitled *Abu al-Hawl qala li* [The Sphinx Told Me] and *Ahadith wa mudhakkirat fi al-qadiyya al-misriyya* [Speeches and Memoirs on the Egyptian Cause]. After the 1952 Revolution he left public office and died in Cairo.

Bibliographic Sources
Abu al-Majd, *Sanawat ma qabla al-thawra.*
al-Ahram (8 Feb. 1955): 11.
al-Ahram Archives, file 40884.
Bishri, 'Abd al-'Aziz, *Fi al-mirat*, 101–106.
Kahhala, *Mu'jam*, IX, 171.
Mazini, Ahmad Fathi, *Qudat*, 144.
Muti'i, *Haula al-rijal min Misr*, II, 175–186.
———, *Mawsu'a*, 439–445.

Ramadan, Muhammad Hafiz, *Safha siyasiyya*, 5–9.
Rizq, Yunan Labib, *al-Ahzab al-siyasiyya.*
Who's Who in Egypt and the Near East, 380.
Zirikli, *al-A'lam*, VI, 77.

Rami, Ahmad
(9 August 1892–4 June 1981)
Poet and songwriter, sometimes called *Sha'ir al-Sha'b* (the People's Poet). Ahmad was born in Cairo's Nasiriyya district to a family of Circassian origin; his father was then a medical student at Qasr al-'Ayni but later became a Palace doctor. Ahmad spent part of his childhood on the island of Thassos, which belonged to Khedive 'ABBAS II, coming back to Cairo at age eight to live with his grandfather. He attended the Muhammadiyya Elementary and Khedivial Secondary Schools in Cairo and wanted to go to law school, but unable to pay the fees, he graduated from the Higher Teachers College in 1914. Unable at first to find a job at a government school, he taught in a private one in Sayyida Zaynab and then at al-Qurabiyya and al-Munira. Rami published his first *qasida* (ode) in *al-Riwaya al-jadida* in 1910 and his first *diwan* in 1918. Owing to his literary interests, he became a librarian for the Teachers College in 1920 and later worked for Dar al-Kutub and in 1938 for the League of Nations Library in Geneva. He was sent to Paris on an educational mission and received a *license en lettres* in Persian from the École des Langues Orientales in 1924, after which he wrote an Arabic translation of the *Ruba'iyyat* of 'Umar Khayyam. He published his second and third collections of poetry in 1925. He also wrote the words to more than 500 songs and is famous for having written around 200 of the lyrics sung by UMM KULTHUM, to whom he was greatly devoted. He contributed articles to *al-Hilal* between 1936 and 1954 and wrote plays for both the stage and the screen. He was named vice president of the Dar al-Kutub Board in 1948 and literary adviser to the Egyptian State Broadcasting in November 1954. He received the State Prize for Literature in 1965 and an honorary doctorate from the Academy of the Arts in 1976.

Bibliographic Sources
Abaza, Tharwat, in *al-Ahram*, 23 Nov. 1981.
'Abd al-Hayy, *'Asir hayati*, 160–168.
al-Ahram Archives, file 522.
al-Akhbar, 5 June 1981.

Amin, Mustafa, *Shakhsiyyat*, II, 276–291.
al-Anba, 4 Nov. 1997.
Brockelmann, *GAL*, S III, 129–130.
Brugman, *Introduction*, 147–150.
Fuad, Ni'mat Ahmad, *Ahmad Rami*.
Hall, *Egypt in Silhouette*, 208–212, 260–268.
Jawdat, *Balabil* (1960), 39–53; (1972), 30–38.
———, in *al-Hilal* 61:4 (Apr. 1953): 58–65.
Mahmud, Hafiz, in *al-Jumhuriyya*, 8 June 1981.
Mallakh, Kamal, in *al-Ahram*, 5 June 1981.
al-Musawwar (5 Aug. 1965): 46–48.
Qadi, Shukri, *Khamsun shakhsiyya*, 199–203.
Rami, *Mudhakkirat Ahmad Rami*.
Shawrib, *Ahmad Rami*.
Shusha, *Ahmad Rami*.
Tabarak, *Rami wa Umm Kulthum*.
'Ubayd, Ahmad, *Mashahir shu'ara*, 45–62.
Umm Kulthum, "Ahmad Rami."
'Uwayda, Kamil Muhammad Muhammad, *Ahmad Rami*.

Rida, Sayyid Muhammad Rashid

(18 October 1865–22 August 1935)
Writer, editor, and Muslim reformer. Born near Tripoli to Syrian parents, educated in *kuttab*s and Ottoman government schools, Rida became the chief disciple of the leading Islamic scholar of al-Azhar, MUHAMMAD 'ABDUH, continuing and developing his reformist teachings. They founded an influential Arabic monthly, *al-Manar*, which disseminated their ideas throughout the Muslim world. He also wrote a commentary on the Quran and a three-volume biography of 'Abduh. From 1912 to 1914 he directed a school for the training of Muslim preachers. His ideas were influenced by Wahhabi puritanism, calling for a return to the pristine Islam of Muhammad and his associates, hence its name, *Salafiyya* (way of the righteous ancestors). He was also a founder of the Ottoman Decentralization Party, which advocated loyalty to the sultanate within a looser state that would extend greater freedom to the Arabs, whom he saw as the core of the Islamic community. During World War I Rida aided the Arab nationalists in Cairo who worked for future independence. He chaired the first Syrian Arab Congress in 1920 and served on a Syro-Palestinian delegation in Geneva, opposing Zionism in Palestine and French colonialism in Syria. Hoping to revive the caliphate, he took part in Islamic congresses in Mecca in 1926 and Jerusalem in 1931. Independent of specific political parties and movements, Rida wielded much moral influence in his later years but proved a marginal figure in the history of Arab nationalism and veered increasingly outside the Islamic mainstream. After his death in Cairo, his movement and magazine vanished.

Bibliographic Sources
Abu Rayya, Mahmud, in *al-Risala* 8 (Aug. 1940): 1355; 11:530 (30 Aug. 1943): 700; 12:584 (11 Sept. 1944): 747–749.
Adams, *Islam and Modernism*, 177–204.
'Adawi, *Rashid Rida*.
Antonius, *Arab Awakening*, 109, 159–160.
'Aqqad, 'Abbas Mahmud, *Rijal 'araftuhum*, 169–174.
Arslan, *Rashid Rida*.
Badawi, Zaki, *Reformers of Egypt*, 97–139.
Bitar, Muhammad Bahjat, "al-Musab al-'amm."
Brockelmann, *GAL*, S III, 321–323.
Busool, "Rashid Rida's Struggle."
———, "Shaykh Muhammad Rashid Rida's Relations."
Daghir, *Masadir*, II, i, 396–401.
Durnayqa, *al-Sayyid Rashid Rida*.
EAL, II, 662.
EI2, VIII, 446–448, article by Werner Ende.
Gibb, *Modern Trends*, 34, 131.
Haddad, Mahmoud, "Arab Religious Nationalism."
Hourani, *Arabic Thought*, 222–244.
———, "Rashid Rida and the Sufi Orders."
Ibish, *Muhammad Rashid Rida*.
Jindi, Anwar, *A'lam wa ashab aqlam*, 153–160.
———, *al-Muhafaza wa al-tajdid*, 110–116.
———, *Tarikh al-sihafa al-islamiyya*, I, passim; II, 319–321.
Jomier, *La commentaire coranique du "Manar."*
———, "Les raisons d'adhésion du Sayyid Rashid Rida au nationalisme arabe."
Jundi, *A'lam al-adab*, II, 357–360.
Kahhala, *Mu'jam*, IX, 310–312.
Kan'an and al-Shawish, *Mukhtasar tafsir "al-Manar."*
Kerr, *Islamic Reform*.
Kramer, Martin, *Islam Assembled*.
Kurd 'Ali, *Mu'asirun*, 334–337.
Laoust, *Le caliphat dans la doctrine de Rashid Rida*.
———, "Le réformisme orthodoxe des 'salafiyya.'"
al-Manar 11:9 (25 Oct. 1908): 706–716; 11:11 (22 Jan. 1909): 936–953; 21:7 (24 Apr. 1920): 377–382; 8 (17 June 1920): 428–433; 9 (14 Aug. 1920): 498–504; 22:10 (31 Oct. 1921): 795–797; 28:3 (2 May 1927): 240.
Marrakushi, *Tafkir Muhammad Rashid Rida*.
Mubarak, Zaki, "Ruh al-Shaykh Rashid Rida."
Muqbil, *Ruwwad al-islah*.
OEMIW, III, 410–412, article by Emad Eldin Shahin.
Reid, *Farah Antun*, 23 et passim.

al-Risala 3:112 (26 Aug. 1935): 1397; 114 (9 Sept. 1935): 1452–1455.
Safran, *Egypt in Search*, 75–84.
Sa'idi, *al-Mujaddidun*, 539–544.
Samarrai, *Rashid Rida al-mufassir.*
Shahin, "Muhammad Rashid Rida's Perspectives."
Shakir, "Ustadhuna al-imam."
Sharabasi, *Rashid Rida.*
Shawabika, *Muhammad Rashid Rida.*
Tauber, "Rashid Rida as Pan-Arabist."
Wajdi, Muhammad Farid, in *al-Manar* 35:5 (Sept. 1933): 400; 7 (30 Nov. 1935): 520–535.
Wielandt, *Offenbarung.*
Wingate Papers, Durham University, Boxes 101/17/2, 3–10, 134/3, 135.
Zirikli, *al-A'lam*, VI, 126.

Rifqi, 'Uthman
(1839–30 January 1886)
Army officer. Born to a Circassian tribe in the Caucasus mountains, Rifqi launched his military career in Egypt as a twelve-year-old cadet; he began teaching at the Alexandria Infantry School at fifteen. He became a colonel in 1861 and a general in 1876. He served as governor of the Red Sea Coast, commander of the Eleventh Infantry Brigade in the Crete and Ethiopia campaigns, and deputy minister of defense in 1879. War minister from 1879 to 1881, his alleged favoritism to Turks and Circassians over native Egyptians in the army officer corps sparked a mutiny led by AHMAD 'URABI in February 1881, and he was dismissed by RIYAD and exiled to Istanbul. He later commanded Egypt's forces in the eastern Sudan under General Gordon.

Bibliographic Sources
Kahhala, *Mu'jam*, VI, 253–254.
Mujahid, *al-A'lam al-sharqiyya*, I, 97–98.
Rafi'i, 'Abd al-Rahman, *al-Thawra al-'Urabiyya*, 90–95.
Rashid Rustum memoirs, cited in Zaki, 'Abd al-Rahman, *A'lam al-jaysh*, 156.
Schölch, *Egypt for the Egyptians!* 332.
Zaki, 'Abd al-Rahman, *A'lam al-jaysh*, 155–156.

al-Rihani, Najib
(1892–8 June 1949)
Comic actor and playwright, sometimes called *al-Filusuf al-dahik* (the Laughing Philosopher). His mother originated from Mount Lebanon; his father, a horse trader who later opened a small factory in Cairo, came from Iraq. Najib was born in the Bab al-Sha'riyya quarter of Cairo. He was educated by the Frères and briefly worked as a bank clerk. Stagestruck from an early age, he joined Ahmad al-Shami's troupe, then briefly that of JURJ ABYAD (who swore he would never learn how to act), and then that of Aziz 'Id in 1915. He eventually settled on one stage in 1916 and became famous as a comedian under the name of "Kishkish Bey." He traveled to Syria, Tunisia, Algeria, France, and the United States, presenting various plays. Najib wrote fifty plays, earning comparison with Molière. He also starred in a silent movie and six talking films, the most famous of which was his last, *Ghazwat al-Banat* [The Flirtation of Girls], costarring Layla Murad. He was married twice, first to a Frenchwoman, then to BADI'A MASABNI. His closest friend was the popular poet, Badi' Khayri, after whom he named his son. After his death in Alexandria, his friends published his memoirs, *Mudhakkirat Najib al-Rihani: za'im al-masrah al-fukahi* [Memoirs of Najib al-Rihani: The Leader of the Comic Stage].

Bibliographic Sources
Abu Sayf, *Najib al-Rihani.*
al-Ahram Archives, file 483.
Amin, Mustafa, *Shakhsiyyat*, II, 186–205.
al-Anba, 21 Jan.–18 Feb. 1989.
Darwish, Mustafa, *Dream Makers*, 20.
al-Kawakib, 10 June 1958, 19 June 1959, 21 June 1961.
al-Kitab 8 (Sept. 1949): 304–305.
al-Misri, 12, 13 June 1949.
al-Qabas, 24 Oct. 1984; 5, 18 Nov. 1984.
Ramzi, *Nujum al-sinima*, 321–334.
Taymur, Mahmud, *al-Shakhsiyyat al-'ishrun*, 78–95.
al-Watan, 18 Mar. 1998.
Zirikli, *al-A'lam*, VIII, 10–11.

Riyad, Mahmud
(8 January 1917–25 February 1992)
Officer, diplomat, and Arab League secretary-general. Born in Qalyubiyya, Riyad graduated from the Military Academy in 1939 and later from the Staff College. He represented Egypt on the Egyptian-Israeli Mixed Armistice Commission from 1949 to 1952 and then served from 1954 to 1955 as director of the Arab Affairs Department within the Egyptian Foreign Ministry. He was ambassador to Syria from 1955 until the creation of the United Arab Republic in Febru-

ary 1958, whereupon he became a presidential adviser on foreign affairs. In 1961 he was named deputy head of Egypt's permanent mission to the United Nations and became its head in the following year. He was foreign minister from 1964 to 1972, also holding the rank of deputy premier from 1970. SADAT removed him from his cabinet in January 1972 and gave him the essentially honorific title of special adviser to the president. In 1974 he became secretary-general of the Arab League, holding that post until April 1979, when Egypt's membership in that organization was suspended because of its separate treaty with Israel. Riyad, who strongly opposed Sadat's policy toward Israel, resigned at that time. Thereafter, he played no role in politics. He was more a diplomat-technician than the shaper of Egypt's foreign policies.

Bibliographic Sources
Current Biography 53 (Mar. 1992): 61.
Egypt, Ministry of Information, *al-Mawsu'a al-qawmiyya*, II, 1130.
Karkouti, "Egypt and the Arabs: Interview."
Najib, *A'lam Misr*, 453.
New York Times (26 Feb. 1992): 32.
Riad, *Mudhakkirat Mahmud Riyad*.
———, *Struggle for Peace in the Middle East*.
Shimoni, *BDME*, 193.
WWAW, 1988–1989, 542.

Riyad, Mustafa

(1834–18 June 1911)
Officer, official, cabinet minister, and three-time premier, usually called Riaz Pasha. He spoke Turkish as his first language but was widely believed to have come from a Smyrna Jewish family that had converted to Islam. Mustafa's father was director of the Egyptian mint under MUHAMMAD 'ALI, and Mustafa was educated in government schools and graduated from the Mafruza [Select] Military Academy. He began his career as a clerk in the Finance Ministry and then joined the Egyptian army officer corps as a clerk and then as a musician. Around 1850 Riyad became an aide-de-camp to ABBAS I, who in 1851 promoted him in rank; he then became governor of Giza province from 1853 to 1856. SA'ID made him administrative chief of Fayyum and then governor of Qina. ISMA'IL promoted him again upon his accession, named him keeper of the seal, admitted him to the Council of Jus-

tice, and, in 1864, made him director of his private estates. A personal clash with Isma'il led to Riyad's sudden dismissal from all his posts in 1868.

Riyad was soon recalled as Isma'il's chief treasurer, perhaps because the khedive needed an honest official who knew both Arabic and Turkish. In 1872 he was named adviser to Prince TAWFIQ. In 1873–1874 he was director of education, building on the foundations laid by 'ALI MUBARAK. He was responsible for bringing JA-MAL AL-DIN AL-AFGHANI to Egypt. He endowed the revenue from some 1,800 acres of Delta farmland to support the newly created Dar al-Kutub. After serving briefly in 1874 as adviser to the director of interior, he held the portfolios for foreign affairs (1874–1875), agriculture (1875, 1877–1878), justice (1875–1876 and 1877), education again (1876–1877), and commerce (1877–1878). His education policy stressed improvement over expansion of the school system and required foreign and private schools to conform to Egyptian regulations. Riyad headed the 1878 commission of inquiry empowered to look into Egypt's financial condition, collaborating with the European creditors against Isma'il. He was minister of both interior and justice in Prince Tawfiq's short-lived cabinet of March 1879, but did not serve in the "Egyptian" (i.e., pro-Isma'il) cabinet of SHARIF. He went to Europe until he was recalled by Tawfiq to serve as his interior minister after the latter's accession later that year. A month later the new khedive asked Riyad to head a cabinet, in which he also held portfolios for interior and finance. He worked mainly on reorganizing Egyptian government finances, which were nearing bankruptcy. Together with the European commissioners, he balanced Egypt's books, using the 1880 Law of Liquidation. He ignored the Assembly of Delegates, neutralized most of his opponents, including NUBAR and Sharif, and co-opted Afghani's remaining partisans by appointing his disciple MUHAMMAD 'ABDUH editor of *al-Waqai' al-misriyya*. He underestimated the Egyptian army officers, however, ignoring their petition for the dismissal of 'UTHMAN RIFQI as war minister. The officers finally mutinied, and in February 1881 he had to accede to their demands. Riyad tried to improve officers' conditions, but they made further demands on the government in August. Finally they massed at 'Abdin Palace in September, demanding that Tawfiq convoke the Assembly of Delegates, enlarge his army, and dismiss Riyad. Tawfiq complied, and Riyad stayed in Europe as long as 'URABI was in power.

During the early years of the British occupation, his opposition was welcomed by many nationalists, and he backed the creation of *al-Muayyad* in 1889 as a Muslim-owned daily newspaper to compete against the Syrian-owned *al-Muqattam* and *al-Ahram*. Riyad served as premier from 1888 to 1891 and again in 1893–1894; he is credited with reducing taxes, abolishing the corvée, extending rail lines, and setting up the reformed National Courts. He resigned after having failed to back 'ABBAS HILMI II against KITCHENER and played no further role in the government. In 1911 he chaired the Egyptian Congress that was convened to oppose the demands of the Coptic Congress, held earlier that year in Asyut. Capable but often tactless, Riyad backed the introduction of European science and technology. In contrast, he fiercely resisted Britain's growing power over Egyptian finance, justice, and government, while favoring closer ties with the Ottoman Empire.

Bibliographic Sources
Abbate Pacha, *Séance solemnelle.*
Aghion and Poilay, "Excursion dans les grands domains."
Antaki, *al-Nujum*, 36–38.
Asaf, *Dalil*, 211–214.
Ayyubi, *'Ahd al-Khidiwi Isma'il*, II, 197–210.
Bell, *Khedives and Pashas*, 121–141.
Cromer, *Modern Egypt*, II, 342–345.
Fikri, 'Ali, *Subul al-najah*, III, 250–254.
al-Hilal 19:10 (1 July 1911): 570–576, obituary.
Hunter, *Egypt Under the Khedives*, 158–169.
Kahhala, *Mu'jam*, XII, 252–253.
al-Manar 14:6 (27 June 1911): 474–477; 7 (26 July 1911): 555–559.
Milner, *England in Egypt*, 13th ed., 126–127.
Mujahid, *al-A'lam al-sharqiyya*, I, 123–124.
Rafi'i, 'Abd al-Rahman, *al-Thawra al-'urabiyya*, 45–48.
Shumayyil, "Isma'il wa Riyad."
Tawfiq, 'Awad, and Hasan Sabri, *Wuzara al-ta'lim*, 35–36.
Walili, *Mafakhir al-ajyal*, 53–54.
Wright, *Twentieth Century Impressions of Egypt*, 60, 380.
Zakhura, *Mirat al-'asr*, I, 74–76.
Zaki, Ahmad, in *al-Hilal* 20:5 (Feb. 1912): 275–288.
———, *Un mot sur Riaz Pacha.*
———, in *al-Muqtataf* 39:2 (Aug. 1911): 105–112; 3 (Sept.): 209–216; 4 (Oct.): 321–332.
Zirikli, *al-A'lam*, VII, 233.

al-Rubi, 'Ali
(?–September 1891)

'Urabist army officer. Born in Fayyum and educated in his village *kuttab* and at al-Azhar, al-Rubi was commissioned into the Egyptian army, rising to the rank of colonel during his service in Ethiopia. He then held civilian posts within the War and Interior Ministries, served as president of the Mansura court, and then returned to the army. According to some sources, he was the founder of the first "National Party" in 1876 and one of its extremist leaders. In 1882 he served as *wakil* (deputy) for the Sudan and field commander of the Egyptian army in Maryut and hence in the Battle of Tel al-Kabir. After the British occupied Cairo, he was tried and sentenced to twenty years' exile in Musawwa', but was later moved to Suakin, where he died.

Bibliographic Sources
Jami'i, *'Abdallah Nadim*, 85.
Mujahid, *al-A'lam al-sharqiyya*, I, 156–157.
Rafi'i, 'Abd al-Rahman, *al-Thawra al-'urabiyya*, 587–589.
Schölch, *Egypt for the Egyptians!* 331.
Taha, Samir Muhammad, *Ahmad 'Urabi.*
Zaki, 'Abd al-Rahman, *A'lam al-jaysh*, 156–157.

Rushdi, Husayn
(1863–14 March 1928)

Lawyer, cabinet minister, and four-time premier. Born in Cairo to a Turkish family named Topuzzadeh, he studied law in Geneva, Cairo, and Paris. Rushdi was appointed by the government to be attorney for the Finance Ministry, later became an education inspector, and then a judge. He was also active in the Islamic Benevolent Society. His first wife, Eugénie Le Brun (d. 1908), was a French writer and feminist pioneer. He later married a sister-in-law of Sharif Husayn of the Hijaz. He became justice minister in the BUTRUS GHALI cabinet from 1908 to 1910, then served as foreign minister until SA'D ZAGHLUL's resignation in 1912, whereupon he resumed the justice portfolio.

After MUHAMMAD SA'ID resigned in April 1914, 'ABBAS HILMI II named Rushdi the new premier (and interior minister). He served as regent while the khedive was in Istanbul, hence was acting head of state when World War I began and when the Ottoman Empire, Egypt's nominal suzerain, declared war on Britain. When the protectorate was declared on 19 December 1914, Rushdi agreed to stay on as premier, but on the understanding that the protectorate would end after the war. Following the Armistice, he encouraged Sa'd and others to speak to High Commissioner WINGATE about sending a delegation to the Foreign Office to discuss Egypt's future. When the British refused to see any delegation, Rushdi resigned as premier, although he did stay on as education minister until November 1919. Serving later as deputy premier, he accompanied 'ADLI YAKAN to negotiate with the Foreign Office in 1921. He was later appointed to the Senate by King FUAD and chaired that body until his death. He played a thankless role in Egyptian politics with courage and integrity.

Bibliographic Sources
al-Ahram, 18 Mar. 1927, interview.
Bishri, 'Abd al-'Aziz, al-Mukhtar, I, 194–203.
———, in al-Muqtataf 72:5 (May 1928): 497–503.
Fahmi, Zaki, Safwat al-'asr, 167–172.
Fuad, Faraj Sulayman, al-Kanz al-thamin, 84.
Hijazi, Anwar, 'Amaliqa, 166–173.
Kull shay wa al-dunya, no. 33 (28 June 1926): 9.
———, no. 117 (6 Feb. 1928): 5, 17.
Luthi, Introduction, 286.
Mujahid, al-A'lam al-sharqiyya, I, 82–83.
al-Musawwar, no. 180 (23 Mar. 1928): 5.
Rafi'i, 'Abd al-Rahman, Thawrat sanat 1919, 3rd ed., I, 68–70.
Shaarawi, Harem Years, 81–82.
Shafiq, Mudhakkirati, II, i, 17.
Sudani, al-Asrar al-siyasiyya, 286–288.
Thabit, Karim, in al-Hilal 36:9 (June 1928): 929–931.
Times (London) (15 Mar. 1928): 14d, 19a; (20 Mar. 1928): 16d.
Walili, Mafakhir al-ajyal, 152–154.
Wright, Twentieth Century Impressions of Egypt, 92.
Zakhura, Mirat al-'asr, II, 65–71.
Zirikli, al-A'lam, II, 237.

Russell, Sir Thomas Wentworth
(22 November 1879–10 April 1954)

Chief of Cairo police. Russell was born at Wollaton Rectory, near Nottingham; his father was a country parson from the well-known Russell family. His mother having died when he was seven, Thomas got his education from a succession of English governesses, Cheam School, Haileybury, and Trinity College, Cambridge, where he read classics. Influenced by a cousin, Percy Machell, he was persuaded to seek a career in Egypt instead of India. He learned French, took a year of Arabic with E.G. Browne, and went to Egypt in 1902. He began work with the coast guard, near Alexandria, and later became a police subinspector in Buhayra province. He went on to various provincial police posts as a subinspector and beginning in 1905 as an inspector, eventually serving in all of the fourteen provinces Egypt had at the time, as well as in the nearby desert areas, hence dealing with both *fallahin* and bedouin. In 1911, just after becoming engaged to marry, he became assistant commandant of the Alexandria police force. Two years later he was named commandant of the Cairo police, a post he accepted with reluctance but was to occupy until 1946. Known as Russell Pasha, he was respected by Egyptians even when they demonstrated angrily against British policies. He also led the struggle to interdict the importation of hashish and other illegal drugs into Egypt. When asked in 1922 to head the Palestine police, he turned down the offer. His wife, Dorothea, wrote a guide to Cairo's mosques. Their daughter married author Christopher Sykes.

Bibliographic Sources
Illustrated London News (24 Apr. 1954): 663.
Jarvis, Desert and Delta, 84–86.
New York Times (11 Apr. 1954): 86.
Russell, Sir Thomas, Egyptian Service.
Seth, Russell Pasha.
Times (London) (12 Apr. 1954): 11c; (14 Apr. 1954): 10b; (24 June 1954): 8f.
Who Was Who (1951–1960), 957.

S

and may have turned Sadat against him. He gave many press interviews in retirement, portraying himself as a patriotic Egyptian and neither pro-American (as he probably was in 1952) nor pro-Soviet. He died in Cairo.

Bibliographic Sources
Abdel-Malek, *Arab Political Thought*, 208–211.
al-Ahram, 4 Aug. 1991.
al-Ahram Archives, file 23.
al-Ahram al-iqtisadi, 3 Jan. 1983, interview.
al-'Arabi, 22 July–11 Aug. 1997.
New York Times (4 Aug. 1991): 46.
al-Ray al-'amm, 10–12 Oct. 1971.
Sabri, 'Ali Baligh, *'Ali Sabri yatadhakkir.*
Shimoni, *BDME*, 197–198.
'Uruq, *Qiraa fi awraq 'Ali Sabri.*
WWAW, 1990–1991, 486.

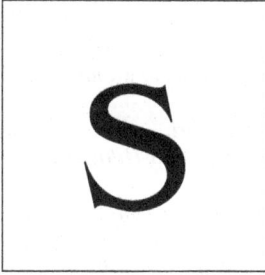

Sabri, 'Ali Baligh

(30 August 1920–3 August 1991)
Air force officer, cabinet minister, and premier. Born in Sharqiyya province to a family of Turkish aristocratic origin, Sabri graduated from the Military Academy in 1939 and completed flight training in 1940. Although not one of the original Free Officers, Sabri was close to them and served as their liaison with the U.S. embassy before the 1952 Revolution. He served as political director of the president's office (1953–1956) and as minister for presidential affairs from 1956 through the UAR era (1958–1961), also serving on the National Union central executive in 1958. NASIR named Sabri prime minister and a member of the presidential council in 1962. From 1965 to 1967 he was vice president of Egypt and from 1965 to 1969 was also secretary-general of the ASU, which he tried to pattern after the Soviet Communist Party, although his influence waned after Egypt's June 1967 defeat.

Upon Nasir's death in 1970, the USSR hoped that Sabri would succeed him, and SADAT initially named him as one of his two vice presidents. However, as one of the Nasirist politicians whom Sadat accused of plotting against his regime, Sabri was ousted from all his posts in the May 1971 Corrective Revolution. He was tried for treason and condemned to death, but his sentence was commuted to life imprisonment and he was pardoned and released by Sadat in May 1981. Sabri's reputation for favoring the USSR and communism aided his rise to power in the early 1960s, but Egyptians were aware of his ties to several major landowning families. The conservative Arab regimes, on which Egypt came to depend after the June War, disliked him

Sabri, Hasan

(1875–14 November 1940)
Politician, cabinet minister, and premier. Trained at the Higher Teachers College and the Khedivial Law School, Hasan Sabri then was appointed headmaster of the Muhammad 'Ali School in Cairo. He later taught mathematics, history, and geography at al-Azhar. He was elected to represent Shirbin (Gharbiyya) in the Chamber of Deputies in 1926 and in the Senate in 1931, later becoming the vice president of this body. In 1933 'ABD AL-FATTAH YAHYA named him finance minister. In 1934 he became Egypt's last minister to London before its legation was raised to embassy status. Returning to Egypt, he became 'ALI MAHIR's commerce and communications minister and later served in that post and then as war minister under MUHAMMAD MAHMUD. Upon taking charge of the cabinet in 1940, Sabri took the office of foreign minister and later added the interior portfolio. His sudden death while reading the annual speech from the throne before Parliament was never explained. A nonpartisan technocrat, he was committed to carrying out the 1936 Anglo-Egyptian Treaty.

Bibliographic Sources
Abbas Hilmi Papers, Durham University, Box 221/1–22.
al-Ahram (15 Nov. 1940): 1.
Amin, Mustafa, *Shakhsiyyat*, I, 110–122.
Najib, *A'lam Misr*, 177.
New York Times (15 Nov. 1940): 5.
Times (London) (15 Nov. 1940): 5c, 9f.

Sabri, Isma'il
(16 February 1854–21 March 1923)
Poet and civil servant. Born in Cairo, Isma'il began his education at the Mubtadayan School and completed his legal studies in Aix-en-Provence in 1878. He proceeded to hold a number of Egyptian judicial and government posts: he was governor of Alexandria and undersecretary of justice. He began writing poetry for *Rawdat al-madaris* when he was sixteen and gradually evolved from a traditional toward a neoromantic style. After his retirement in 1907, he continued to write poetry, kept in touch with contemporary authors, frequented MAYY ZIYADA's literary salon, and came to be called *Shaykh al-Shu'ara* (the Senior Poet). He was cautiously sympathetic to nationalism.

Bibliographic Sources
'Abd al-Ghani, 'Abd al-Hamid, in *al-Risala* 9 (1933): 24–26.
Abu al-Ma'ali, *Shaykh al-shu'ara Isma'il Sabri Basha.*
al-Ahram (21 Mar. 1923): 5.
'Aqqad, 'Abbas Mahmud, *Shu'ara Misr*, 31–39.
Becka, *DOL*, III, 163.
Bishri, 'Abd al-'Aziz, *al-Mukhtar*, I, 84–85, 141–144, 187–188.
Brockelmann, *GAL*, S III, 18–21.
Brugman, *Introduction*, 33–35.
Daghir, *Masadir*, II, i, 534–536.
Dayf, *al-Adab al-arabi*, 92–99.
EAL, II, 673.
EI2, IV, 194–195, article by U. Rizzitano.
Fikri, 'Ali, *Subul al-najah*, II, 203–207.
Gharaba, *Shakhsiyyat*, 219–213.
Hamuda, 'Abd al-Wahhab, *al-Tajdid fi al-adab*, 103–118.
Hasan, Muhammad 'Abd al-Ghani, and 'Abd al-'Aziz Disuqi, "*Rawdat al-madaris*," 274–277.
Haykal, Muhammad Husayn, *Tarajim misriyya*, 168–180.
Hijazi, Anwar, *'Amaliqa*, 141–144.
Husayn, Taha, in *al-Hilal* 47:4 (Feb. 1939): 404–406.
———, in *al-Hilal* 57:9 (Sept. 1949): 39–41.
Jayyusi, *Trends*, I, 39–42.
Jundi, *A'lam al-adab*, II, 446–447.
Kahhala, *Mu'jam*, II, 282–283.
Kurd 'Ali, *Mu'asirun*, 111–311.
Mandur, *Muhadarat 'an Isma'il Sabri.*
Mikhail, Sa'd, *Adab al-'asr*, 73–77.
Mujahid, *al-A'lam al-sharqiyya*, II, 678–680.
Qadi, Shukri, *Miat shakhsiyya*, 49–51.
Rafi'i, 'Abd al-Rahman, *Shu'ara al-wataniyya* (1954), 30–40.
Rafi'i, Mustafa Sadiq, in *al-Muqtataf* 62:5 (May 1923): 451–460.
Ramadi, *Min a'lam al-adab*, 191–198.
Sabri, Muhammad, *Adab wa tarikh*, 109–179, 288–292.
———, *Isma'il Sabri.*
Shinnawi, Kamil, in *al-Hilal* 70:11 (Nov. 1962): 3–7.
Tanahi, Tahir, *'Ala firash al-mawt*, 109–114.
Tawfiq, Najib, *Isma'il Sabri.*
'Ubayd, Ahmad, *Mashahir shu'ara*, 158–167.
Zayn, *Diwan Sabri*, 27–43.
Zirikli, *al-A'lam*, I, 315.

Sabri, Dr. Muhammad
(1890?-18 January 1978)
Historian and literary critic, usually surnamed al-Surbuni. Son of an itinerant farm inspector originally from Bilbays, Muhammad Sabri was born in al-Marj (Qalyubiyya province). After learning to read and write in his village *kuttab*, he was educated at the Nahhasin Elementary School in Cairo. His predilection for memorizing poetry consoled him after the premature death of his mother and enabled him to publish his first book, *Shu'ara al-'asr* [Poets of Our Era] (1910), but delayed the completion of his studies at the Khedivial School. He passed the secondary examination in 1913 and went to Paris in that same year, drawn by the poetry of Lamartine and Victor Hugo. Despite the outbreak of World War I, he completed his *license* at the Sorbonne in 1919, one year after TAHA HUSAYN, worked in Paris as a secretary to the Wafd, probably thanks to his prior acquaintance with SA'D ZAGHLUL's private secretary, and wrote a two-volume account of the 1919 Revolution and a pamphlet in French about the Egyptian question. It was Sa'd who first encouraged Sabri to write history instead of poetry, and Sabri remained loyal to the Wafd's leader for the rest of his life. In 1924 he presented his doctoral dissertation on the origins of Egyptian nationalism.

Returning to Egypt to teach at the Higher Teachers College, Sabri wrote *Tarikh Misr al-hadith min Muhammad 'Ali ila al-yawm* [Modern History of Egypt from Muhammad 'Ali Until Today] (1926). He then taught at Dar al-'Ulum. In 1930 he published his study in French on the Egyptian empire under MUHAMMAD 'ALI, followed three years later by a similar study on Egypt under ISMA'IL and the intervention of the British and the French. He was named director of the Egyptian study mission in Geneva in 1937 and married a Frenchwoman, who divorced him in 1951. At NUQRASHI's behest, he wrote a history in French on the Egyptian Sudan, later expanded and published in Arabic in 1948 as *al-Imbiraturiyya al-sudaniyya fi al-qarn al-tasi' 'ashr* [The Sudanese Empire in the Nineteenth Century]. Although the 1952 Revolution led to his dismissal, in 1956 the Egyptian government commissioned him to write a history of the Suez Canal after its nationalization, leading to *Asrar qadiyyat al-tadwil wa ittifaqiyyat 1888* [Secrets of the Internationalization Cause and the 1888 Agreement], published in 1957, followed the next year by *Fadihat al-Suways* [The Suez Scandal]. In his later years he wrote books about AHMAD SHAWQI and on history, literature, and society, both largely unnoticed, and died in poverty and obscurity.

Bibliographic Sources
al-Ahram, 11 Feb. 1978.
al-Ahram Archives, file 2781.
al-Ahram al-dawli, 21 Aug. 1994.
al-Masa, 18 Nov. 1962.
Muti'i, *Mawsu'a*, 206–213.
Radwan, Fathi, *Afkar al-kibar.*
Tamawi, *Sabri al-Surbuni.*

al-Sadat, [Muhammad] Anwar

(25 December 1918–6 October 1981)
Officer, writer, politician, and president from 1970 to 1981. Born in Mit Abu al-Kum, near Tala (Minufiyya), to an Egyptian father, who was an army clerk, and a Sudanese mother, Anwar was reared in Cairo and educated at al-Jami'a Elementary and Raqi al-Ma'arif Secondary School. He was in the first class admitted on a competitive basis to the Military Academy, graduating in 1938 and commissioned as an infantry officer. He backed Misr al-Fatat and the Muslim Brothers in his youth and secretly contacted German agents early in World War II. Expelled from the army, he was jailed in 1942 but escaped in 1944. He was arrested again in 1946 on suspicion of conspiring to assassinate AMIN 'UTHMAN. Imprisoned during the two-year trial, he was acquitted and released in April 1948. After working as a journalist, he managed to regain his military commission in January 1950. He joined the Free Officers and took part in plan-

ning the 1952 Revolution. Close to NASIR, he joined the Revolutionary Command Council (RCC), serving as its liaison with the Muslim Brothers and other right-wing groups. He was a member of the revolutionary court in 1953 and a minister of state from 1954 to 1956, edited the government newspaper, *al-Jumhuriyya*, from 1953 to 1956, and served as secretary-general for the Islamic Conference in 1954 and the National Assembly in 1957. Sadat wrote books about Nasir and the revolution (published in 1958 and 1961 respectively), chaired the UAR National Assembly in 1960–1961, and was president of the Afro-Asian Peoples' Solidarity Organization in 1962. He was secretary of the 1962 National Council of Popular Forces, which approved the National Charter, and he became a member of the Presidential Council in that year. Nasir named him vice president in 1969 to halt the rise of 'ALI SABRI's leftists within his ruling circle but allegedly planned to replace him. Upon Nasir's death, Sadat was elected by a plebiscite to succeed him as Egypt's president and ASU chairman. Egypt's leaders hoped in choosing him to avert a power struggle between the right, led by ZAKARIYYA MUHYI AL-DIN, and the leftists, although the latter group expected Sadat to fall from power, enabling them to take control.

Sadat proved to have his own policies and powerful backers. In May 1971 he quashed a leftist conspiracy by purging Sabri and his allies. While signing the Soviet-Egyptian Treaty in May 1971 and visiting Moscow in October 1971 and May 1972, he actually drew nearer to the conservative Arab states, notably Saudi Arabia. He set up the abortive Federation of Arab Republics but resisted organic union with Libya. He hoped to gain U.S. support in 1972 by ousting 20,000 Soviet experts, mainly military ones, although some historians argue that Moscow approved this measure and that key advisers remained to help Sadat's army before and during the October War. Early in his presidency, he sought peace talks with Israel, but demanded its prior commitment to withdraw from the Sinai Peninsula and settle the Palestine refugee problem. When Israel rejected these terms in 1971, Sadat warned that he would take military action. He and Syria's Hafiz al-Asad planned a joint attack on the Israel-occupied Sinai and Golan Heights for 6 October 1973. Caught by surprise, the Israelis were driven back as the Egyptian army crossed the Suez Canal. Israel soon counterattacked and repulsed Egypt's and Syria's forces, but the October War was widely viewed in the Arab world as restoring Egypt's honor and enhancing Sadat's reputation at Nasir's posthumous expense.

Sadat used his hard-won prestige to extricate Egypt from the war against Israel and to regain control of the Sinai. Henry Kissinger's "shuttle diplomacy" helped Egypt recover the western peninsula, including its oil wells and the Gidi and Mitla passes, in two interim agreements reached in 1974 and 1975. The peace negotiations stalled, however, on the issue of Palestinian participation. Sadat broke the deadlock in November 1977 by his dramatic flight to Jerusalem. Addressing the Israeli Knesset, he offered peaceful coexistence between the Arabs and Israel, provided that Israel agreed first to withdraw from all the lands it had occupied in June 1967 and negotiated a solution to the Palestinian Arab problem. He tried to negotiate directly with Israeli Premier Menachem Begin, but talks soon faltered. U.S. President Jimmy Carter invited both leaders to an open-ended summit at his summer retreat, where the three men and their advisers hammered out a set of agreements known as the Camp David Accords, for which Sadat and Begin were awarded the 1978 Nobel Peace Prize. Further negotiations led to the 1979 Egyptian-Israeli Peace Treaty. The other Arab states condemned these accords and tried with inducements and threats to persuade Sadat not to sign the treaty. When he rejected their appeals, they broke diplomatic ties, cut off financial support, and expelled Egypt from the Arab League. Sadat preferred greater political and economic dependence on the United States to submitting to the other Arab states' demands, but the talks that Egypt and Israel had agreed to hold for Palestinian autonomy stalled and eventually ended.

Sadat's foreign policies, partly a reaction against Nasir's Arab and Soviet orientation, also reflected Egypt's deteriorating economy. His solution was to renounce Arab socialism by gradually restoring capitalism, a policy that he called *infitah,* and luring foreigners to invest in local manufacturing industries. From 1974 to 1978 the oil-rich Arab states invested heavily, but American and European involvement fell short of Sadat's expectations. The reopening of the Suez Canal, revival of tourism, and rising remit-

tances from Egyptians working abroad (mainly in other Arab countries) helped Egypt's economy. Regrettably, investors preferred Egyptian real estate, consumer goods, and luxury hotels to new factories. The state-owned industries developed under Nasir languished, as did state-provided services in health, education, welfare, and transport. Income inequalities widened. The 1977 Food Riots expressed the dissatisfaction felt by many Egyptians, and Sadat used his Israeli peace initiative to distract the public. When his policies came under attack, he censored the press, passed the Law of Shame, and in September 1981 rounded up many of his suspected opponents and sent them to prison without trial.

Sadat gradually gave up his simple lifestyle, moved into palaces, befriended rich and powerful Egyptians and foreigners, and let some of his friends and relatives use their connections for personal gain. Members of the Islamist opposition, whom he had at first used to fight communism and Nasirism and then tried to curb, attacked his abuse of power. His peace with Israel, economic and social issues, his opulent lifestyle, and his perceived opposition to Islam were all factors leading to his assassination while reviewing a parade on the anniversary of the October War. Many foreign leaders, including three former U.S. presidents and Menachem Begin, flew to Cairo to attend his funeral, but most Egyptians were barred from the procession, and few mourned his death. A superb actor and a shrewd diplomat, often highly patriotic, he lost his popular touch and tied Egypt's position too closely to U.S. policies. Two of his books, *Revolt on the Nile* (1957) and *In Search of Identity: An Autobiography* (1978), serve as partial memoirs; some of his diaries have been published as *The Public Diaries of Anwar al-Sadat.*

Bibliographic Sources
'Abd al-Hayy, *'Asir hayati,* 9–19.
al-Ahram Archives, file 2.
Ajami, "The Sorrows of Egypt."
Alterman, *Sadat and His Legacy.*
'Arusi, *Ashhar qadaya al-ightiyalat,* 621–647.
Baker, *Egypt's Uncertain Revolution.*
———, *Sadat and After.*
Cooper, *Transformation of Egypt.*
EI2, VIII, 716–718, article by Derek Hopwood.
EMME, III, 1570–1572, article by Fred Lawson.
Finklestone, *Anwar Sadat.*
Heikal, *Autumn of Fury.*
Hinnebusch, *Egyptian Politics Under Sadat.*

Hirst and Beeson, *Sadat.*
Hopwood, *Egypt: Politics and Society*, 105–121.
al-Musawwar, no. 2985 (25 Dec. 1981): 24–33.
Muti'i, *Mawsu'a*, 106–112.
New York Times (7 Oct. 1981): 10.
Reich, *Political Leaders*, 453–460, article by Marius Deeb.
Samakuri, *Asrar hukm al-qusur*, 125–138.
WWAW, 1981–1982, 1218.

al-Sadat, Jihan

(1933–)

Feminist, political activist, and the second wife of ANWAR AL-SADAT. Jihan was born in Roda Island to an Egyptian Muslim father and a British mother, was educated in a Christian missionary school, and earned her B.A. in Arabic in 1973 from Cairo University. She later earned an M.A. from Cairo, writing her thesis on Shelley's poetry and its influence on Egyptian culture. During Sadat's presidency, she headed the organization *al-Wafa wa al-amal*, set up to aid soldiers wounded in the October War, formed a private charitable organization to teach women marketable skills, and emerged as a leading women's rights advocate. She represented Egypt at the 1975 International Women's Year Conference, held in Mexico City. Her role also was evident in the 1979 divorce legislation called "Jihan's Law," which required the husband to register his divorce and to inform his wife of it and which gave the wife a claim to larger alimony and child-support payments, also lengthening the period when she could retain custody of her children. Although polygyny (which is rare in Egypt) was not outlawed, the first wife's consent was made a prerequisite for a man's taking a second wife. Many Muslims opposed these changes as contrary to the Shari'a, and parts of the 1979 legislation were voided in 1985 by the Constitutional Court.

Jihan was often criticized by conservatives for playing too prominent a role in Egypt's public life during her husband's presidency, and after his assassination she spent much of her time with her daughter in the United States, where she lectured at several American universities and caused some press controversy over her compensation and her claim to speak for the women of Egypt. She returned to live in Egypt in 1993 and earned her doctorate in English literature from Cairo University.

Bibliographic Sources
Abu al-Su'ud, Su'ad, *Qissati ma'a Jihan al-Sadat.*
al-Ahram, 8 Sept. 1974, interview.
al-Ahram Archives, file 2.
al-Anba, 29 Dec. 1985; 11 Jan. 1986.
Fawzi, Mahmud, *Jihan al-Sadat.*
Imam, 'Abd Allah, *Jihan.*
International Herald Tribune, 14 June 1986.
International Who's Who of the Arab World, 436.
Jawadi, *Mudhakkkirat al-mara*, 17–32.
Kamal, *Nisa Anwar al-Sadat.*
Mahallawi, *Sayyidatan min Misr.*
Roosevelt, "The Fascinating Women of Egypt."
Sa'da, Ibrahim, in *al-Akhbar*, 23 May 1987.
Sadat, Jihan, *A Woman of Egypt.*
Sullivan, Earl L., *Women in Egyptian Public Life*, 89–92.
al-Watan al-'arabi, 19 Oct. 1984; 1, 8, 15 Nov. 1984; 6 Dec. 1984.

al-Sa'dawi, Nawal [al-Sayyid]

(27 October 1930–)

Physician, author, and feminist. Born to a family of modest means in the Qalyubiyya village of Kafr Tahla (other sources say she was born in Cairo one year later), Nawal attended a British mission school in Minufiyya and the Helwan Secondary School, earned her bachelor's degree in medicine (specializing in surgery and chest diseases) at al-Qasr al-'Ayni in 1954 and her master's degree in public health at Columbia University Medical School in 1966. She began her medical practice in 1955. Two years later she published in *Ruz al-Yusuf* a memoir, based on her early life and training, part of which appears in her *Memoirs of a Woman Doctor.* She taught for some years in the medical faculty and became editor of *al-Sihha* [Health] magazine and the director of information in the Ministry of Health, but she was dismissed in 1972 for publishing *al-Mara wa al-jins* [Women and Sex], one of a series of books that she wrote on topics viewed as taboo by most Egyptians. She later became a consultant for the UN and published in 1980 an exposé of women's conditions in the Arab world, *The Hidden Face of Eve,* that drew attention to the practice of female genital mutilation. Arrested by SADAT for alleged "crimes against the state" in 1981, Sa'dawi later described her experiences in *Memoirs from the Women's Prison,* published in English in 1988. She has also written many novels about Egyptian women. In 1982 she founded the Arab

Women's Solidarity Organization, which opposed the Egyptian government's revisions in the personal status laws in 1984–1985 and the U.S.-led intervention against Iraq in 1991. The organizataion was banned in 1991 by Egypt's minister of social affairs, and all challenges to the government's action have been unavailing. Sa'dawi has participated in numerous conferences in Egypt and abroad, taught at Washington (St. Louis) and Duke Universities in the United States, and been praised for her courage by Egyptian and foreign feminists. Some, however, criticize her addressing so many political issues at once. After a period of self-imposed exile, she returned to Egypt in 1996, gave interviews attacking the Islamists, and joined YUSUF SHAHIN's peace mission to Baghdad in 1997. She has received honorary degrees from York University (Canada) and the University of Illinois.

Bibliographic Sources
al-Ahali, 28 Jan. 1998.
al-Ahram Archives, file 6216.
al-Ahram Weekly, 10 Aug. 1995.
Badran and Cooke, *Opening the Gates*, 203–219, 392–404.
EAL, II, 673–674.
Egypt, Ministry of Information, *al-Mawsu'a al-qawmiyya*, II, 1274.
Graham-Brown, "Feminism in Egypt."
Jawadi, *Mudhakkirat al-mara*, 121–126.
Khater, "Egypt's Feminism."
Lerner, "Nawal el-Saadawi."
Malti-Douglas, *Men, Women, and Gods.*
———, *Women's Body, Women's Word.*
al-Musawwar, 16 June–6 Oct. 1995, memoirs.
Sa'dawi, *Awraqi . . . hayati.*
———, *Nawal El Saadawi Reader.*
Tarabishi, Georges, *Untha didda al-unutha.*
Times Literary Supplement, 22 Dec. 1989.
WWAW, 1997–1998, 553.
Zeidan, *Arab Women Novelists*, 124–139.

[Muhammad] Sa'id

(17 March 1822–17 January 1863)

Egypt's viceroy from 1854 to 1863. The fourth surviving son of MUHAMMAD 'ALI, he was taught by Palace tutors. Sa'id was a bright pupil but painfully shy, perhaps because he was overweight; his father required him to make daily calls on the various European consuls and address them in French. Thus he overcame his shyness, became fluent in French, and was befriended by the young French consul, FERDINAND DE LESSEPS,

with fateful consequences for Egypt's later history. Sa'id became an ensign in the Egyptian navy at age thirteen, and Muhammad 'Ali promptly made him its commander, a position he retained through the reign of 'ABBAS I, despite the bad relations between them. Upon succeeding 'Abbas as viceroy, Sa'id quickly improved ties with France and with some of the Turks and Egyptians whom 'Abbas had exiled. He also shifted his interest to the army and sought to increase Egypt's independence from the Ottoman Empire. Most Western historical accounts praise Sa'id's reign for granting the concession to build the Suez Canal, befriending the Europeans, promulgating the 1855 Land Law, phasing out remnants of Muhammad 'Ali's monopolies, admitting peasants to the officer corps of the Egyptian army, and upgrading Egypt's irrigation, transport, and communications systems. But Sa'id's reign led to massive European immigration, foreign indebtedness, and political interference by Western consuls. The deindustrialization of Egypt, popularly ascribed to 'Abbas but really owing to Muhammad 'Ali's changing policies after 1841, continued under Sa'id. He also granted more power in the administration and the army to the rural notables and their sons, but the ethnic Egyptians' first taste of power occurred only after his death. He outlawed the slave trade in Egypt and formally freed the slaves living there, but slavery lasted for several decades after his reign. Sa'id was a weak ruler and his reign was an era of quiescence in Egypt's modernization, yet also a portent of the changes to come under Khedive ISMA'IL and the British occupation. He died in Alexandria. His name was given to its rival port city created by the Suez Canal, Port Sa'id.

Bibliographic Sources
Asaf, *Dalil*, 155–156.
Ayyubi, *'Ahd al-Khidiwi Isma'il*, I, 2–7.
Durri [al-Hakim], *al-Nukhba al-durriyya*, 24–27.
EI2, VIII, 859–860, article by C.E. Bosworth.
Fahmi, Zaki, *Safwat al-'asr*, 43–44.
Farnie, *East and West of Suez*, 33–34.
Fuad, Faraj Sulayman, *al-Kanz al-thamin*, 49–51.
Loring, *Confederate Soldier*, 47.
Mardam, *A'yan al-qarn al-thalith 'ashr*, 123–124.
Marlowe, *Making of the Suez*, 72–175.
Merruau, *L'Égypte contemporaine.*
Nubar, *Mémoires de Nubar Pacha*, 127–208.
Rafi'i, 'Abd al-Rahman, *Asr Isma'il*, 2nd ed., 23–66.
Sayyid-Marsot, *Egypt in the Reign*, 90–92.

Toledano, *State and Society,* 43–49.
Tugay, *Three Centuries,* 100–102.
Zakhura, *Mirat al-'asr,* I, 32–33.
Zaki, 'Abd al-Rahman, *A'lam al-jaysh,* 32–33.
Zaydan, Jurji, *Mashahir al-sharq,* 1st ed., I, 32–33.
Zirikli, *al-A'lam,* VI, 140–141.

Sa'id, Dr. 'Abd al-Hamid

(1882–1 July 1940)

Nationalist and Muslim activist. The son of
Ibrahim Sa'id, who owned 700 *feddans* in Gharbiyya, he was educated in Paris, earning a doctorate of laws. He volunteered to fight in the Ottoman army during the Balkan Wars and then in
World War I, when he served in Syria and the
Hijaz. At war's end he was in Istanbul, where he
facilitated the escape of Muhammad Farid,
'Abd al-'Aziz Jawish, and the other Nationalists, and then spent time in Switzerland and Italy.
Returning later to Egypt, despite his misgivings
about the 1923 Constitution, Sa'id ran for and
was elected to represent Kafr al-Shaykh in every
session of the Chamber of Deputies. He argued
strongly for religious education in the state
schools and opposed all traces of foreign cultural
influence. He later presided over the Muslim
Youth Association (*Jam'iyyat al-Shubban al-
Muslimin*). He strongly opposed the 1936 Anglo-Egyptian Treaty. He died in Cairo.

Bibliographic Sources
Abbas Hilmi papers, Durham University, file 120.
al-Ahram (2 July 1940): 6.
Bishri, 'Abd al-'Aziz, *Fi al-mirat,* 77–82.
Deeb, *Party Politics,* 218 n.
Heyworth-Dunne, Jamal al-Din, *Religious and Po-
litical Trends,* 11–12.
Jindi, Anwar, *A'lam wa ashab aqlam,* 212–218.
Kull shay wa al-dunya, no. 426 (3 Jan. 1934): 21;
429 (24 Jan. 1934): 14–15.
al-Musawwar, no. 821 (5 July 1940): 17
OM 20 (1940): 436.

Sa'id, Ahmad

(1927–17 Aug. 1994)

Influential radio broadcaster during Nasir's
presidency. Born in Cairo, he graduated from the
Faculty of Law in 1949 and began working in
broadcasting in 1950. He took charge of "Voice
of the Arabs" in 1953 and made it into a major
political influence on Arab listeners in the 1950s
and 1960s, especially his own program, *Akadhib*

tukshifuha haqaiq [Lies Revealed by Truths],
and his radio commentaries. He also wrote occasional articles for *Akhir sa'a, Ruz al-Yusuf,* and
al-Hilal. Sa'id played a major role in developing
Egypt's television broadcasting, introducing the
use of satellite transmission and the microwave.
He quit broadcasting in 1971 to practice law, but
later became press counselor for Egypt's embassy in Ottawa in March 1982.

Bibliographic Sources
al-Ahram Archives, file 6430.
al-Idha'a wa tilivizyun, 20 July 1996.
Najib, *A'lam Misr,* 96.
al-Siyasa, 30 Nov. 1994; 1 Dec. 1994.

al-Sa'id, Amina

(1914–13 August 1997)

Novelist, journalist, and editor. Born in Shanisa
(Asyut province), her father was a Nationalist
physician who was jailed in Cairo during the
1919 Revolution. Her family soon moved to
Cairo, where she attended the Shubra Secondary
School for Girls. There she met Huda Sha'rawi,
who invited her to speak at the Egyptian Feminist Union, whose youth group, al-Shaqiqat (Sisters) she joined. She became one of Huda's disciples and served as her Arabic secretary. Amina
sought admission to the Commerce Faculty at
Cairo University, but was rejected due to her
sex; however, she was admitted to its Faculty of
Arts in 1931. She soon shocked Muslim conservatives by taking up tennis. In 1935 she was one
of the first women to receive a degree in English. Even before graduation, she began writing
for *Kawkab al-sharq* and wrote for *Akhir sa'a*
and *al-Musawwar* in the late 1930s. In 1945 she
became editor of the ephemeral *al-Mara al-jadida,* published by the Arab Feminist Union, in
which she remained active through the Nasir
years, when it could function only under state
control. Remaining in Dar al-Hilal Publishing
House, she founded *Hawwa,* a women's mass-
circulation magazine, in 1955. She served on the
board of the Egyptian Press Syndicate in 1956
and became its vice president in 1959. She was
the first woman to serve on the editorial board of
Dar al-Hilal and later became the president of its
administrative council, a post that she held from
1975 until her retirement in 1981. In 1960 Amina led a women's demonstration against Bayt

al-ta'a (House of Obedience), a coercive institution not abolished by the government until 1967. Her publications include two novels and a collection of her articles from *Hawwa*. She also translated Kipling's *Jungle Book* and Alcott's *Little Women* into Arabic. Blessed with a dynamic personality and articulate in her defense of women's rights and responsibilities, she often represented Egypt and "Arab women" at international conferences. She opposed any attempt to permit female genital mutilation or to oblige women to resume wearing the veil. Upon her death in Cairo, she willed her library to the Huda Sha'rawi Society. She received Egyptian government decorations in 1963, 1975, and 1982.

Bibliographic Sources
al-Ahram, 3 Sept. 1995; 14, 16 Aug. 1997; 17 Aug. 1997.
al-Ahram Archives, file 308.
al-Ahram Weekly, 20 June 1991.
Akhir sa'a (23 Aug. 1995): 40–43.
Amin, Mustafa, *Shakhsiyyat*, I, 272–286.
Badran, *Feminists*, 101, 143, 149, 249–250.
Badran and Cooke, *Opening the Gates*, 357–365.
EAL, II, 676–677.
Fawzi, M. *Adab al-azafir al-tawila.*
Fuda, *Nujum Shari' al-Sihafa*, 193–198.
Hanna, Milad, "Amina al-Sa'id."
al-Hawwa, Apr.–May 1993, interviews by Ni'mat Riyad.
al-Musawwar, 17 Aug. 1997, special issue.
Raghib, *A'lam al-tanwir*, 83–96.
Sa'd al-Din, Mursi, in *al-Ahram Weekly*, 17 Aug. 1997.
Sa'id, Amina, "Min yawmiyyat taliba."
WWAW, 1997–1998, 564.

Sa'id, Mahmud
(8 April 1897–8 April 1964)
Artist and lawyer. Originally from Alexandria's Anfushi district, he attended Victoria College, spent six months in a Jesuit school, passed his elementary and preparatory state examinations independently in 1911 and 1912, and attended the Hilmiyya and 'Abbasiyya Schools before passing the general secondary examination in 1915. He was trained as a lawyer at the government Law School in Cairo and in France. He also took painting lessons with an Italian artist in Alexandria and studied fine arts at l'Académie Julien in Paris. He began working in the *Niyaba* of the Mixed Courts in 1922, heading the public prosecutor's office in Mansura, Alexandria, and

Cairo, later becoming a judge, and eventually being appointed chancellor of the Alexandria Court of Appeals, before he resigned in 1947 to devote full time to his artistic muse. Sa'id's brightly colored oil paintings depicting peasant life are especially well known. The Museum of Modern Art in Cairo features his work, including many of his portraits, on its main floor. Appointed to the Supreme Council for the Arts in 1956, he resigned two years later. He displayed his work at the Venice Biennale several times, also in the Louvre in 1949, and he was the first Egyptian artist to win the state prize in art in 1959. He was also the maternal uncle of Queen Farida, painted her portrait, and encouraged her own artistic talents, which blossomed only later.

Bibliographic Sources
'Abd al-Karim, Lotus, *al-Malika Farida*, 133–136.
al-Ahram, 9 May 1997.
al-Ahram Archives, file 933.
Akhir sa'a, 29 Nov. 1995.
Iskandar, *Khamsun sana min al-fann*, 84.
Karnouk, *Contemporary Egyptian Art*, ix, 106–111.
———, *Modern Egyptian Art*, 18–25.
al-Musawwar, 4 Dec. 1992.
Nisf al-dunya, 3 July 1994.

Sa'id, Muhammad
(18 January 1863–20 July 1928)
Politician, cabinet minister, and twice premier. Born in Alexandria to a family of Turkish origin, he was educated at the Khedivial Law School. He married a niece of AHMAD MAZLUM. Sa'id rose up through the *Niyaba* of the Mixed Courts and the judiciary, becoming interior minister under BUTRUS GHALI from 1908 to 1910, then succeeding him as premier upon his assassination. Although widely assumed to be a Nationalist, he opposed the National Party while in power. He resigned in 1914 and held no government post during World War I, but during the 1919 Revolution he chaired the cabinet again and also held the interior portfolio. Elected to the first and second sessions of the Chamber of Deputies, he served as education and justice minister in SA'D ZAGHLUL's cabinets and briefly held the agriculture portfolio after his resignation. As education minister he drafted the rules for foreign educational missions, set up night schools for adult technical education, and admitted girls to boys' kindergartens when there were unfilled spaces.

He was the first to form a committee to study implementing the constitutional provision that education was to be free and compulsory for all Egyptians. He was widely viewed in his lifetime as a political manipulator without fixed principles. Muhammad Sa'id was the maternal grandfather of Queen Farida and the father of MAH-MUD SA'ID, who painted his portrait.

Bibliographic Sources
Alexander, *Truth About Egypt*, 312.
Fahmi, Zaki, *Safwat al-'asr*, 179–183.
Fuad, Faraj Sulayman, *al-Kanz al-thamin*, 81.
al-Hilal 27:8 (June 1919): 851.
Marshall, *Egyptian Enigma*, 57–61.
Mujahid, *al-A'lam al-sharqiyya*, I, 108–109.
al-Musawwar, no. 198 (27 July 1928): 32.
Tawfiq, 'Awad, and Hasan Sabri, *Wuzara al-ta'lim*, 65–66.
Times (London) (21 July 1928): 12c, 14b.
Walili, *Mafakhir al-ajyal*, 155–157.
Wright, *Twentieth Century Impressions of Egypt*, 92.
Zakhura, *Mirat al-'asr*, II, 65–67.
Zirikli, *al-A'lam*, VI, 143.

Salim, Mamduh Muhammad

(1918–25 February 1988)
Police general, administrator, and premier. Born in Alexandria, he graduated from the Police Academy in 1940. From 1960 to 1970 he managed NASIR's security during his trips abroad. He served as commander of the Alexandria police from 1964 to 1967, then as governor of Asyut from 1967 to 1970, of Gharbiyya from August to November 1970, and of Alexandria in 1970–1971. Salim took charge of arresting the "Centers of Power" (the Nasirites) during the May 1971 Corrective Revolution, after which he joined SA-DAT's cabinet, serving as interior minister in 1971–1975, deputy premier in 1972–1975, then prime minister from 1975 to 1978 (also interior minister in 1977). He was the leader of the Arab Socialist Union during those years and took charge of its centrist *minbar* (section [pulpit]) in 1976. He also led the suppression of the January 1977 Food Riots, which occasioned the worst bloodletting in Egypt's history since 1919. Named special assistant to the president in October 1978, after the foreign minister had resigned in protest against Sadat's signing the Camp David Accords, he went on serving in this capacity under MUBARAK. He was also a member of the Higher Council for Nuclear Energy. He modernized Egypt's security forces, revoked exit visa requirements for Egyptians, and pressed for democratic reforms within Sadat's government. Salim received awards from the Lebanese and Egyptian governments in the 1970s and made trips to various Communist and Third World countries during the 1980s. He died in a London hospital. He served Sadat and Mubarak more as a strongman than an ideologue.

Bibliographic Sources
al-Ahram, 26 Feb. 1988.
al-Ahram Archives, file 200.
al-Ahrar, 12–13, 15–16 Aug. 1995.
al-Jumhuriyya, 29 Feb., 2 Mar. 1988.
Mansur, Anis, in *al-Ahram*, 28 Feb. 1988.
Najib, *A'lam Misr*, 479.
New York Times (26 Feb. 1988): D17.
New York Times Biographical Service 19 (Feb. 1988): 236.
Shimoni, *BDME*, 204–205.
WWAW, 1997–1998, 576.

Salim, Salah

(25 September 1920–18 February 1962)
One of the Free Officers, cabinet minister, and journalist. Born in Sinikat (Sudan) and reared in the Hilmiyya Jadida section of Cairo, he was educated at the Ibrahimiyya School and graduated from the Military Academy in 1938 and from the General Staff College in 1948. Salah was one of the officers who plotted the 1952 coup and later became an RCC member. He served as minister of national guidance and minister of state for Sudan affairs in 1953. Strongly committed to the unity of the Nile Valley, Salim campaigned in the Sudan to win popular support for union with Egypt and earned his nickname, the Dancing Major, from being photographed dancing in his underwear with a group of naked Sudanese, but accusations that he was bribing Sudanese politicians later caused the country's first president to block his appointment as Egypt's ambassador to Khartum. He also was noted for his quick tongue, which sometimes put him in trouble with the press or with his fellow Free Officers. A famous instance occurred in a Beirut press conference in which he said that Egypt gave precedence to having British forces evacuate the Suez Canal over the liberation of Palestine. After a quarrel with NASIR, he left the cabinet and

served from 1956 to 1959 as editor of *al-Sha'b*, later becoming administrative head of Tahrir Publishing and Printing and in 1960 president of the Press Syndicate. He took charge of the executive committee for the National Union in Cairo in November 1959. Despite his youth and robust constitution, he suffered from kidney trouble aggravated by a heart condition. After seeking medical treatment in Moscow and Boston and returning to Cairo, he was the first of the Free Officers to die. The modern circumferential highway around eastern Cairo bears his name.

Bibliographic Sources
al-Ahram Archives, file 278.
al-Akhbar, 19 Feb. 1962.
al-Dustur, 23 July 1997.
International Herald Tribune, 19 Feb. 1962.
Mandur, Muhammad, in *al-Jumhuriyya*, 21 Feb. 1962.
Muhyi al-Din, *Memories of a Revolution*.
Muti'i, *Mawsu'a*, 213–220.
Najib, *A'lam Misr*, 268.
New York Times, 19 Feb. 1962.
Radwan, Fathi, in *al-Watan*, 12 July 1964.
al-Rajul, no. 40 (Aug. 1995): 80–81.

Salman, Shaykh 'Abd al-Karim

(23 June 1849–17 May 1918)
Muslim reformer, writer, and Shari'a judge. Born in Jambaway, near Itay al-Barud (Buhayra), he attended his village *kuttab* and studied at al-Azhar, where he knew AFGHANI and 'ABDUH; after 'URABI's defeat he succeeded 'Abduh as main editor of *al-Waqai' al-Misriyya* at a time when it contained literature and scholarly research. He was an inspector in the Shar'i judicial system and became a member of the Supreme Shari'a Court in 1897. Serving with Muhammad 'Abduh on the governing council of al-Azhar, he kept voluminous minutes on its activities. He was a strong advocate of reform.

Bibliographic Sources
Adams, *Islam and Modernism*, 207–208.
Asaf, *Dalil*, 324–327.
Fuad, Faraj Sulayman, *al-Kanz al-thamin*, 167.
Jundi, *A'lam al-adab*, II, 442.
Kahhala, *Mu'jam*, V, 315.
al-Manar 20:10 (6 Oct. 1918): 437–440.
Mujahid, *al-A'lam al-sharqiyya*, I, 338–339.
Rida, Muhammad Rashid, *Tarikh al-Ustadh al-Imam*, I, 278, 1017–1019.
Zirikli, *al-A'lam*, IV, 51–52.

Salt, Henry

(14 June 1780–30 October 1827)
British diplomat and collector of antiquities. A native of Lichfield, he was trained as a portrait painter and worked as a secretary-draftsman to George Annesley, ninth Viscount Valentia, whom he accompanied on his travels between 1802 and 1806. Valentia sent Salt into the interior of Ethiopia, where Salt met the Emperor Egwala Seyon, who gave him a letter to King George III, who in turn sent Salt back to Ethiopia at the head of an official embassy in 1809, Britain's first to that country. While in Ethiopia, Salt wrote an extensive topographical and archaeological survey, published in 1814. With help from Lord Valentia and other influential politicians, Salt was appointed British consul general in Cairo in 1815. Arriving there in March 1816, he soon gained influence in MUHAMMAD 'ALI's court, due to NAPOLEON's defeat as well as to the fact that other European consuls remained in Alexandria. Authorized by a trustee of the British Museum to bring back "antiquities and curiosities," Salt built several collections of Egyptian antiquities on his own account and for the museum. His first collection was sold to Soane's Museum, his second to the king of France, and his third at auction after his death, which occurred in Egypt. Much of his diplomatic work was directed against the French influence in Egypt.

Bibliographic Sources
Bosworth, "Henry Salt."
Dawson, *Egyptology*, 258.
DNB, XVII, 701–702.
Halls, *Life and Correspondence of Henry Salt*.
McNaught, *Henry Salt*.

al-Sanhuri, Dr. 'Abd al-Razzaq

(11 August 1895–20 June 1971)
Legal expert, judge, cabinet minister, and designer of civil codes for Egypt and other Arab countries. Born in Alexandria, Sanhuri began his official life in 1912 by working in its Customs House. He graduated from the government Law School in 1917, worked as an assistant public prosecutor, and briefly taught at the Shari'a Judges School in 1920. He was sent on an educational mission to France, earning his first doctorate in political economy and law under the supervision of Édouard Lambert, former Law

School director, in 1921. Sanhuri earned a second doctorate later for his study of the caliphate. He joined the *Niyaba* upon his return and was appointed deputy public prosecutor in 1926. He also became a professor of civil law at Cairo University and began writing books about contracts, civil procedure, and international law. He represented Egypt at the Paris Congress of Comparative Law held in 1932. Appointed dean of the Law Faculty in 1936, he soon lost the post because of his political and personal hostility to NAHHAS, but he spent a year in Iraq as dean of its law school, also drafting Iran's civil code. He was one of the founders of the Sa'dist Party in 1937. He helped to phase out the Mixed Courts (in which he was, for three years, a judge) and drafted revisions to Egypt's civil code during intervals when the Wafd Party was out of power. He was justice minister (1944) and education minister (1945–1946 and 1946–1949). His educational reforms spanned every level and every branch of public instruction, including the publication of new translations of books to promote pupils' knowledge of their literary heritage. He led the Egyptian delegation at the London Conference on Palestine in 1946, at the UN General Assembly in 1947, and at the Security Council in 1947. In 1946 he was elected to membership in the Arabic Language Academy and in 1949 to the presidency of the Council of State, an advisory judicial body, where he directed the revision of Egypt's civil code. Because Sanhuri wanted to restore constitutional government in 1954, NASIR made him retire after demonstrators forced their way into the Council of State and attacked him. He then left Egypt and helped draft the civil codes of Syria, Jordan, and Libya, as well as Kuwait's commercial code. Egypt awarded him its prize for social sciences in 1970, shortly before his death.

Bibliographic Sources

'Abd al-Birr, M., "al-Sanhuri."
al-Ahram (21 June 1971): 1, 9; (31 Mar. 1997).
al-Ahram Archives, file 764.
'Allam, *Majma'iyyun*, 158–160.
'Amudi, Muhammad Sa'id, in *al-'Ukaz* (Jidda, 23 Jumada II 1390).
Arabi, "al-Sanhuri's Reconstruction."
'Azmeh, *Islamic Law.*
Bellefonds, "'Abd al-Razzak al-Sanhuri."
Castro, "'Abd al-Razzak Ahmad al-Sanhuri."
EI2, IX, 18–19, article by Enid Hill.
Hill, *'Abd al-Razzaq al-Sanhuri and Islamic Law.*
———, "al-Sanhuri and Islamic Law."
Khadduri, *Political Trends*, 240–244.
Khattab, Diya Shit, *'Abd al-Razzaq Ahmad al-Sanhuri.*
Mursi, A., "Ustadh al-asatidha."
Muti'i, *Mawsu'a*, 254–260.
OEMIW, I, 7–8, article by Emad Eldin Shahin.
Qadi, Shukri, *Khamsun shakhsiyya*, 75–79.
Qulali, "Kalimat al-Duktur Muhammad Mustafa al-Qulali."
Reid, *Lawyers and Politics*, 153–155.
Sanhuri, N., and T. al-Shawi, *'Abd al-Razzaq al-Sanhuri.*
Tawfiq, 'Awad, and Hasan Sabri, *Wuzara al-ta'lim*, 101–108.
Ziadeh, *Lawyers*, 118–118, 137–147.
Zirikli, *al-A'lam*, III, 350.

Sannu', Ya'qub

(9 February 1839–30 September 1912)
Humorous writer, journalist, playwright, and pioneer Egyptian nationalist, called *Abu al-Naddara al-Zarqa* (the Wearer of Blue Spectacles). Born in Cairo to a Jewish family of Italian origin, he was taught the rudiments of Islam as well as of Judaism and in 1852 was sent to Leghorn to study at the expense of a generous nephew of MUHAMMAD 'ALI. Sannu' spent three years studying political economy, international law, natural science, and the fine arts, also gaining exposure to the theater and to nascent Italian nationalism. He returned to the court of SA'ID, whom he admired, to serve as a tutor, then began teaching in the Cairo Polytechnic in 1862. His classroom duties were preempted by his extracurricular meetings with students who would later become supporters of 'URABI. Because Khedive ISMA'IL's reform program included opening an opera house and a comic theater in Cairo, Egyptians, among them Sannu', came to know European drama. He began writing and producing comic plays, using Cairo colloquial Arabic, for Egyptian audiences, and became the first director to put women actors on the Egyptian stage. After meeting JAMAL AL-DIN AL-AFGHANI in 1871, he also began composing political satires. His first plays were performed in a small theater in Cairo's old city, but he soon moved to one near the Ezbekiyya Gardens and eventually to Qasr al-Nil Palace, where he performed before the khedive, who called him Egypt's Molière. As his Arabic plays and his adaptation of French plays became better

known, his satires grew bolder, and the British convinced Isma'il that the influence of Sannu' was subversive. The khedive forbade him to write or produce further plays. He formed two secret literary societies, both noteworthy for including members from all the major religions, but they were closed in 1875; he would later claim that they were precursors of the first National Party. Sannu' made peace with Isma'il in 1876 and was named court poet, but they soon quarreled again. As he became involved in the Freemasonic movement, he lampooned ever more stridently the court and its hangers-on.

Encouraged by Afghani and 'ABDUH, he published a comic newspaper, partly in colloquial Arabic, called *Abu Naddara Zarqa*, in which he satirized both the khedive and the sultan, but hailed Prince 'ABD AL-HALIM as Egypt's potential savior. His was the first Egyptian newspaper to print cartoons. Threats against the editor and even his printer did not deter him, so Isma'il banished him from Egypt in 1878. Sannu' fled to Paris, where he met other Near Eastern émigrés and went on putting out newspapers attacking Isma'il and his successors, gleaning support from various sources, including Prince Halim. The British also banned his papers in Egypt.

A pioneer of both drama and journalism in Egypt, Sannu' now stands out for having been at the same time a Jew and an Egyptian nationalist, but in his own time he was hailed for his witty social comedies and his satires against native and foreign rulers.

Bibliographic Sources
Abdel-Malek, *Idéologie*, 320–324.
'Abduh, Ibrahim, *Abu Nazzara*.
———, *A'lam al-sihafa*, 50–67.
Ali, Mohamed, *Souvenirs de jeunesse*, 84.
Amer, *Lughat al-masrah al-'arabi*, 76–107.
Baignières, *L'Égypte satirique*.
Blunt, *Gordon at Khartoum*, 45–47.
———, *My Diaries*, 71, 376.
Brockelmann, *GAL*, S III, 265–266.
Daghir, *Masadir*, II, i, 549–552.
EAL, II, 688.
*EI*2, I, 141–142, article by Jacob M. Landau.
Encyclopedia Judaica, XIV, 850.
Gendzier, *Practical Visions of Ya'qub Sanu'*.
Ghunaym, 'Abd al-Hamid, *Sannu', raid al-masrah al-misri*.
al-Hilal 77:6 (June 1969): 116–123, text of a rediscovered play.

Jerrold, *Belgium of the East*, 38–40.
———, *Egypt Under Ismail-Pacha*.
Jewish Encyclopedia (1905), XI, 50–51.
Kahhala, *Mu'jam*, XIII, 248.
Khozai, *Development of Early Arabic Drama*, 123–168.
Landau, "Abu Naddara."
Louca, "Le harem du khédive."
———, "Masrah Ya'qub Sannu'."
———, *Voyageurs*, 153–197.
Malaika, Sadiq, *Dhawu al-fukaha fi al-tarikh*, 247–250.
Moosa, "Ya'qub Sanu' and the Rise of Arab Drama."
Najm, *al-Masrahiyya*, 77–91.
———, *Ya'qub Sannu'*.
Ninet, *Arabi Pacha*, 225–226.
Qadi, Shukri, *Khamsun shakhsiyya*, 249–252.
Ramadi, *Sihafat al-fukaha*, 19–22.
Rizq, Fathi, *Khamsa wa sab'una najman*, 49–59.
Sadgrove, *Egyptian Theatre*, 89–124.
Schölch, *Egypt for the Egyptians!* 334–335.
Tagher, Jeannette, in *CHE* 2 (1949): 192–207.
Tarrazi, *Tarikh al-sihafa*, II, 281–286; III, 8–9.
Zaki, 'Abd al-Hamid Tawfiq, *al-Mu'asirun*, 171–175.
Zirikli, *al-A'lam*, VIII, 198.

Sarruf, Dr. Ya'qub

(18 July 1852–9 July 1927)

Scientist, translator, and founding editor of *al-Muqtataf* and *al-Muqattam*. Born in Hadath, a village near Beirut, Ya'qub came from an obscure family, but his father is said to have come from Damascus. One of the first students to register at the Syrian Protestant College, he received a B.S. in 1870 and began work as a teacher in Tripoli and Sidon. He later became an instructor of natural philosophy and mathematics at the college. He also wrote poetry. While in Beirut, he, Shahin Makariyus, and FARIS NIMR founded *al-Muqtataf*, a scientific monthly that drew heavily at first on foreign newspapers and magazines. Sarruf and Nimr resigned from the college in 1885 because of their belief in Darwin's theory of natural selection and moved to Cairo, where they continued to publish their magazine, broadening its contents to include translated novels and short stories. In 1889 they established *al-Muqattam*, a daily newspaper with an avowedly pro-British slant, as a rival to *al-Ahram*. Sarruf spent most of his life editing and writing scientific articles for *al-Muqtataf*. He published numerous scientific and philosophical works translated from English, a book comparing famous Arabs and Englishmen, and about twenty short stories. He was also the first Arabic writer to explain and advocate socialism.

Bibliographic Sources

'Abbud, Marun, *Ruwwad al-nahda*, 219–220.
'Abduh, Ibrahim, *A'lam al-sihafa*, 91–98.
Abu 'Arja, *"al-Muqattam,"* 29–30 et passim.
Abu Diyya, "al-Afkar al-Masuniyya fi majallat *al-Muqtataf.*"
Alfi, "Dr. Sarruf wa fann al-zira'a."
'Amiri, *Nuzhat al-albab*, 213–214.
'Aqqad, 'Abbas Mahmud, *Rijal 'araftuhum*, 115–127.
Arslan, Shakib, in *al-Muqtataf* 73:1 (July 1928): 8–13; 4 (Oct. 1928): 137–142; 6 (Dec. 1928): 429–439.
Asaf, *Dalil*, 334–335.
Brockelmann, *GAL*, S III, 215–217.
Brugman, *Introduction*, 228–231.
Clayton, *An Arabian Diary*, 347–348.
Daghir, *Masadir*, II, i, 540–548.
EAL, II, 693.
EI2, IX, 66, article by J. Fontaine.
al-Hilal 35:10 (Aug. 1927): 115–118, short obituary.
———— 36:1 (Nov. 1927): 94–96, detailed obituary.
Jindi, Anwar, *al-Muhafaza wa al-tajdid*, 49–54.
Jundi, *A'lam al-adab*, II, 345–346.
Kahhala, *Mu'jam*, XIII, 253–254.
Khabbaz, *Mukhtarat "al-Muqtataf."*
al-Kitab al-dhahabi li-yubil "al-Muqtataf" al-khamsin.
Kurd Ali, in *MMIA* 8:1–2 (Jan.–Feb. 1928): 57–60.
————, *Mu'asirun*, 468–475.
Maqdisi, *al-Funun al-adabiyya*, 239–257.
Mazhar, *Mu'addat al-madaniyya al-haditha*, 192–204.
al-Muqattam, 14 July 1927.
al-Muqtataf 72:4 (Apr. 1928): 361, 417–419, article by Mahmud Jirdaq.
Sarruf, *Ya'qub Sarruf.*
Shafiq, *Mudhakkirati*, I, 284–286.
Tarrazi, *Tarikh al-sihafa*, II, 124–129; IV, 106, 166.
'Umar, 'Abd Allah, in *al-Majalla al-thaqafiyya wa al-tahwirat al-mu'asira* (Kuwait) (1984): 9–68.
UNESCO, *A'lam al-lubnaniyyin*, 139.
Zakhura, *Mirat al-'asr*, I, 465–472.
Zirikli, *al-A'lam*, VIII, 202.
Ziyada, Mayy, *al-Sahaif*, 188–196.

al-Sayyid, Ahmad Lutfi

(15 January 1872–5 March 1963)
Lawyer, writer, editor, cabinet minister, and educational leader, called *Ustadh al-jil* (Professor of the Generation) for his influence on younger Egyptians. Born to an Egyptian landowning family in Barqin, near Simbalawin (Daqahliyya), Lutfi began his education in the local *kuttab*, then attended al-Mansura Elementary and the Khedivial Secondary School, after which he was supposed to attend al-Azhar, but instead entered the Khedivial Law School in 1889. While a student there, he founded Egypt's first law review, *al-Tashri'* [Legislation], together with ISMA'IL SIDQI and 'ABD AL-KHALIQ THARWAT. After graduating in 1894, he worked as a deputy public prosecutor in Beni Suef, Fayyum, and Mit Ghamr, becoming head prosecutor in Minya in 1896. In that year he joined the secret society that became the basis for the National Party and was advised by Khedive 'ABBAS II to live in Switzerland for a year to acquire Swiss nationality so that he could edit a nationalist newspaper, protected by the Capitulations from prosecution under the Press Law. While there, he fell under the influence of MUHAMMAD 'ABDUH and soon distanced himself from the khedive and from MUSTAFA KAMIL's pan-Islamic tendencies. Returning to Egypt, he continued his work in the *Niyaba*, but he resigned in 1905 because of his growing alienation from the British. Opening a law firm with 'ABD AL-'AZIZ FAHMI, he defended the peasants in the Dinshaway trial.

Early in 1907, a group of Egyptian liberals established *al-Jarida* and named Lutfi as its editor, a post he held until 1914. Its shareholders formed the Umma Party as a middle force between the khedive and the Nationalists, with Lutfi as its secretary. Because he strongly upheld individual rights and constitutional liberties, his editorials opposed 'Abbas's autocratic pretensions and rejected ties with the Ottoman Empire and pan-Islam. He focused on promoting sound Egyptian patriotism based on education and a sense of self-worth. Although rejecting the National Party's extremism, he admired Mustafa Kamil personally and cooperated with MUHAMMAD FARID during Britain's *politique d'entente* with Abbas. *Al-Jarida* folded in July 1915, after Britain declared its protectorate, but Lutfi had resigned a few months earlier. He was the director of Dar al-Kutub from 1915 to 1922.

In 1918 Lutfi was one of the first to join the Wafd, but he soon withdrew from politics. In 1923–1932 and 1935–1941 he was the rector of Cairo University and championed academic freedom and the admission of women. He translated Aristotle's *Nichomachean Ethics* and other writings into Arabic. He also held several cabinet posts, served in the Senate from 1942, and chaired the Arabic Language Academy (to which he had been elected in 1940) from 1945 until his death. As education minister in 1928–1929 he reorganized the Law and Medical Faculties of Cairo University, formed a committee to improve Arabic instruction, and took charge of Egypt's ancient monuments and cultural centers. Some of his *al-Jarida* editorials were reprinted as *al-Muntakhabat* [Selected Passages] in 1937 and 1949, *Safahat matwiya min tarikh al-haraka al-istiqlaliyya fi Misr* [Unwritten Pages from the History of Egypt's Independence Movement] in 1946, and *Taammulat fi al-falsafa wa al-adab wa al-siyasa wa al-ijtima'* [Meditations in Philosophy, Literature, Politics, and Society] also in 1946. His memoirs, published in *al-Musawwar* in 1950, were reissued as *Qissat hayati* [The Story of My Life] in 1963. An advocate of reason who preferred a scholarly life to a political career, he did not seek to inspire the masses, but his influence on Egypt's intellectuals was immense.

Bibliographic Sources

Adams, *Islam and Modernism*, 224–225.
Ahmed, J.M., *Intellectual Origins*, 85–112.
al-Ahram Archives, file 1269.
'Allam, *Majma'iyyun*, 60–65.
Amin, Mustafa, *Shakhsiyyat*, II, 5–19.
'Aqqad, 'Abbas Mahmud, *Rijal 'araftuhum*, 223–256.
'Ashur, Nu'man, *Butulat misriyya*, 265–286.
'Awad, Louis, "Ahmad Lutfi al-Sayyid."
Barakat, [Muhammad] Bahi al-Din, "Abu al-Jami'a."
———, *Safahat min al-tarikh*, 104–107.
Bishri, 'Abd al-'Aziz, *Fi al-mirat*, 63–70.
Dayf, *al-Adab al-'arabi*, 251–261.
Delanoue, "Ahmad Lutfi al-Sayyid."
EAL, II, 480.
EI2, V, 838–839, article by Charles Wendell.
Fahmi, Zaki, *Safwat al-'asr*, 384–390.
Fuad, Faraj Sulayman, *al-Kanz al-thamin*, 262–265.
Fuad, Ni'mat Ahmad, *Qimam adabiyya*, 19–64.
Hamza, *Adab al-maqala*, VI.
Haykal, Muhammad Husayn, *Fi awqat al-faragh*, 152–158.
———, *Mudhakkirat fi al-siyasa al-misriyya*, I.
Hijazi, Anwar, *'Amaliqa*, 211–215.
Hourani, *Arabic Thought*, 171–182.
Husayn, Muhammad Muhammad, *al-Ittijahat al-wataniyya*, I, 78–88; II, passim.
Husayn, Taha, *Hadith al-arba'a*, III, 47–57.
Jami'i, *al-Jami'a al-misriyya wa al-mujtama'*.
Jawdat, Salih, in *al-Hilal* 71:6 (June 1963): 44–49.
Jindi, Anwar, *al-Sihafa al-siyasiyya*, 198–200.
al-Jumhuriyya, 6 Apr. 1985; 26 Aug 1985.
Khadduri, *Arab Contemporaries*, 175–192.
Madkur, Ibrahim, "Lutfi al-Sayyid bayn al-muslihin."
Musa, Salama, "al-'Uzama al-khamsa fi Misr al-yawm," 652–653.
Muti'i, *Haula al-rijal min Misr*, III, 39–51.
———, *Mawsu'a*, 68–74.
Najjar, *Ahmad Lutfi al-Sayyid*.
———, *Lutfi al-Sayyid*.
New York Times (6 Mar. 1963): 4.
Radwan, Fathi, *'Asr wa rijal*, 393–464.
Reid, *Cairo University*, 14–17, 74, 123–124.
Rizq, Fathi, *Khamsa wa sab'una najman*, 100–105.
Safran, *Egypt in Search*, 90–97.
Sayyid, Afaf Lutfi, *Egypt and Cromer*, 185–195.
———, "Lutfi al-Sayyid al-insan."
Sayyid, Ahmad Lutfi, *Dhikra Ahmad Lutfi al-Sayyid*.
Sayyid, Jalal, "Lutfi al-Sayyid."
Tanahi, Tahir, in *al-Hilal* 71:4 (Apr. 1963): 19–23.
Tawfiq, 'Awad, and Hasan Sabri, *Wuzara al-ta'lim*, 74–76.
Taymur, Mahmud, "Lutfi al-Sayyid."
———, *al-Shakhsiyyat al-'ishrun*, 9–13.
Times (London) (28 June 1928): 16c.
Wendell, "Ahmad Lutfi al-Sayyid: In Memoriam."
———, *Evolution of the Egyptian National Image*.
Zakhura, *Mirat al-'asr*, II, 412–413.
Zirikli, *al-A'lam*, I, 200.

Scott, Sir John

(1841–1 March 1904)

English lawyer, judge, and legal reformer. The son of a solicitor, he was born in Wigan, educated at Bruce Castle and at Pembroke College, Oxford, and was called to the Bar at the Inner Temple in 1865. He practiced before the British Consular Court in Alexandria (1872–1874) and was then recommended by the British consul general to serve as a judge in the newly formed International (or Mixed) Court of Appeal, serving as its vice poresident until 1882. After an eight-year stint as a judge in the Bombay High Court, CROMER invited him back to Egypt as adviser to the Justice Ministry. Overcoming the resistance of Prime Minister RIYAD and the French, Scott reformed the administration of Egypt's National Court system, earning high praise from MILNER and the nickname Scott the Just from Upper Egyptians. These reforms included reducing the number of judges needed to hear civil and criminal cases and establishing strict standards for new judicial appointments. He was awarded a knighthood in 1894 and, when he left Egyptian service in 1898, the highest ranks in the Osmaniyya and Mejidiyya orders from Khedive 'ABBAS. He later served as deputy judge advocate in the British army during the Boer War. He died in Norwood (England) of heart and liver trouble.

Bibliographic Sources
Egyptian Gazette, 4 Mar. 1904.
Milner, *England in Egypt*, 13th ed., 131–132, 280–283.
Tignor, *Modernization*, 131–138.
Times (London) (3 Mar. 1904): 5c.

Sève, Octave-Joseph-Anthelme, "Sulayman Pasha"

(April 1787–12 March 1860)
French army officer in Egyptian service. Born in Lyons, the son of a factory owner, he excelled in the study of mathematics as an aspiring naval officer, but he had to quit the navy after he killed a senior officer in a duel. Joining NAPOLEON's army, Sève saw action in Italy, in Russia, and in Napoleon's hundred-day attempt to regain power. Sève's career derailed by the Bourbon restoration, he left France in 1816 for Persia. When Sève reached Egypt, MUHAMMAD 'ALI offered him an instructorship in his new army. Sève managed to assert his authority over a corps of young Georgian and Circassian Mamluks, arresting some of their cadets who had tried to shoot him during their target practice. He even taught European military techniques to IBRAHIM, just back from his war against the Wahhabis in Arabia. In a few years he managed to weld a polyglot array of Turks, Circassians, and Arabs, to which were added Egyptian peasants, into a 130,000-man army that could be doubled, in case of need, by bedouin irregulars, auxiliaries, and cadets. Sève married into Muhammad 'Ali's family; converted to Islam, taking the name Sulayman; and was promoted to the rank of colonel. He aided Ibrahim in the Morean campaign against the Greeks and later in Egypt's Syrian campaign against the Ottomans. Although his role was diminished by the London Convention, he remained commander general of the Egyptian army, preparing it for the Crimean

War. He died in Cairo. He and his wife, Fatima, who were renowned for their hospitality, are buried in Old Cairo, near the site of their Nile-side palace, which was torn down when the Corniche was widened. One of his daughters married MUHAMMAD SHARIF, and he was the great-grandfather of King FARUQ.

Bibliographic Sources
Carré, Jean-Marie, *Voyageurs*, I, 208–209.
Fikri, 'Ali, *Subul al-najah*, III, 319–327.
Guemard, "Le tombeau et les armes parlantes."
al-Hilal 6:4 (15 Oct. 1897): 121–125.
Houghton, *Monographs*, 1–17.
Ivray, *Un chef au service de l'Égypte*.
Mardam, *A'yan al-qarn al-thalith 'ashr*, 296–299.
Rafi'i, 'Abd al-Rahman, *'Asr Muhammad 'Ali*, 379–380 et passim.
Vingtrinier, *Soliman-pacha, Colonel Sève*.
Walili, *Mafakhir al-ajyal*, 23.
Weygand, *Histoire militaire de Mohammed Aly*.
Zaki, 'Abd al-Rahman, *A'lam al-jaysh*, 35–44.
Zaydan, Jurji, *Mashahir al-sharq*, 1st ed., I, 165–170.
Zayn al-Din, Isma'il Muhammad, *al-Ajanib*, 57–63.

al-Shadhili, Sa'd al-Din

(1 April 1922–)
Army officer, diplomat, and writer. Born in Cairo, he was educated in the Basyun village *kuttab*, Khedive Isma'il Secondary School, Cairo University, and the Military Academy, where he was commissioned in 1943. He later took advanced paratrooper training at Fort Benning, Georgia, in 1952–1952 and in the USSR in 1958–1959. After five years' service in the Guards Regiment, he was a platoon commander in the Palestine War. He was commander of the Parachute School (1954–1956), a paratroop battalion (1956–1958), and the UAR contingent in the UN Congo force (1960–1961). He served as Egypt's defense attaché in London from 1961 to 1963. He then became brigadier commander of the Egyptian forces in the Yemen Civil War (1965–1966), the Shadhili Group in the June War, the Special Forces (1967–1969), and the Red Sea district (1970–1971). As commander-in-chief of the Egyptian armed forces (1971–1973), he is generally credited with leading the Egyptians' successful crossing of the Suez Canal in the October War. After a quarrel with SADAT, he was removed from all military command and

sent as Egypt's ambassador to Britain in 1974–1975, then to Portugal until 1978. An expatriate critic of Sadat's policies, he founded the Egyptian National Front in 1980 and began publishing *al-Jabha* magazine. Accused of publishing Egyptian military secrets, he was secretly tried in absentia and sentenced to three years' imprisonment. He remained abroad until 1992, when he returned from Algeria; he served half his sentence before MUBARAK released him in September 1993. He has given many press interviews since then, warning against Israel's political and military strategy and criticizing Sadat's conduct of the October War. He received decorations from Egypt, the UN, Korea, Syria, Yemen, West Germany, and the PLO.

Bibliographic Sources
al-Ahali, 19 Jan.–2 Feb. 1994.
al-Ahram Archives, file 4106.
EMME, IV, 1649, article by David Waldner.
Najib, *A'lam Misr*, 235.
Shazly, *Crossing of the Suez*.
WWAW, 1993–1994, 597.

al-Shafi'i, Husayn Mahmud
(8 February 1918–)
Officer and cabinet minister. Originally from Tanta, he graduated from the Military Academy in 1938, was commissioned as a cavalry officer, and took advanced training at the Staff College in 1953. He saw action in the Palestine War and later took charge of the Cavalry Division. One of the Free Officers who staged the 1952 Revolution, he joined the RCC. He became war and marine minister in 1954, then minister for labor and social affairs up to 1958. During the union with Syria, Shafi'i held the same portfolios, attending ILO meetings in Geneva in 1959 and 1960, and also adding that of the Planning Ministry. Shortly before the breakup of the UAR he became a vice president. In 1962 he joined the ASU Executive Board. He headed the Arab Olympic Committee during the 1960s and became head of the Egyptian Equitation Society. He took charge of the Central Accounting Office in 1965. He again became minister of social affairs, plus *awqaf*, in 1967–1968. During that time he chaired the revolutionary court that tried fifty-five officers accused of plotting against NASIR. He resigned his vice presidency in 1968 when he was elected to the ASU Supreme Council, but served again as vice president under SADAT from 1970 to May 1975, when the two men fell out over a power issue. Shafi'i opposed Sadat's peace initiative and denounced the Camp David Accords in October 1978. Since then he has dropped out of public life but has given press interviews and is reportedly writing his memoirs.

Bibliographic Sources
al-Ahram Archives, file 8.
al-Anba, 1–15 July 1986; 4–7 Apr. 1996.
al-Dustur, 18 Dec. 1986; 23 July 1997.
Egypt, Ministry of Information, *al-Mawsu'a al-qawmiyya*, I, 322.
al-Hayat, 25 July 1995.
Imam, Salih, *Husayn al-Shafi'i*.
al-Misri, 25 Aug. 1996; 1 Sept. 1996.
al-Shabab, 1 July 1991; 16 Apr., 14 May 1995.
WWAW, 1997–1998, 597.

Shafiq, Ahmad
(18 May 1860–17 October 1940)
Civil servant and historian. Born in Cairo, he graduated from the Khedivial Law School and the École des Sciences Politiques in Paris. The first vice president of the Egyptian University, he also headed the Khedivial Council under 'ABBAS HILMI II, whom he followed into exile during World War I. He was involved in various Arab political issues after the war and wrote *Hawliyyat Misr al-siyasiyya* [The Political Annals of Egypt], *Mudhakkirati fi nisf qarn* [My Memoirs of Half a Century], and *A'mali ba'd mudhakkirati* [My Activities Since My Memoirs], useful sources for historians, as well as *L'Égypte moderne et ses influences étrangères*.

Bibliographic Sources
Abbas Hilmi Papers, Durham University, Box 166/1–954.
Hamdi, 'Abd al-Hamid, in *al-Siyasa al-usbu'iyya*, no. 61 (7 May 1927): 1–2.
'Inan, Muhammad 'Abdallah, in *al-Siyasa al-usbu'iyya*, no. 143 (1 Dec. 1928): 20.
Jindi, Anwar, *Adwa*, 117–120.
———, *al-Muhafaza wa al-tajdid*, 243–249.
Kahhala, *Mu'jam*, I, 245.
MMIA 8 (1928): 306.
Mujahid, *al-A'lam al-sharqiyya*, II, 845–846.
Qutb, Sayyid, in *al-Ahram*, 19 Oct. 1940.
Rifa'i, 'Abd al-'Aziz, *Ahmad Shafiq*.
Shafiq, *Mudhakkirati*, I, introduction.
Zirikli, *al-A'lam*, I, 135–136.

Shafiq, Dr. Durriyya [Raja'i]

(14 December 1908–20 September 1975)
Feminist, poet, and editor. Born in Tanta to a
mother who came from a rural notable family
and a father who was a government civil engineer, she spent her childhood in Mansura and
Tanta. She was educated in Roman Catholic
schools there and in Alexandria, and (with
timely financial aid from HUDA SHA'RAWI) at the
Sorbonne, where she earned her *license ès lettres*
and went on to become the first Egyptian woman
to earn a doctorate there, writing her dissertation
on Egyptian women and Islam. She also married
her first cousin, Nur al-Din Raja'i, who at that
time was working for his doctorate in law in
Paris. After her return to Egypt in 1945, she tried
unsuccessfully to get a teaching position in
Cairo University's Arts Faculty, where AHMAD
AMIN was dean at the time. Instead, she taught at
the Alexandria College for Girls and the Saniyya
School and then worked for a time as an inspector for the Education Ministry. In 1945 she
founded both a magazine and a political organization called *Bint al-Nil* (Daughter of the Nile)
to promote female education and women's political rights. She also published a children's magazine, *Katkut*, from 1946 to 1948. Backed by
Princess Chévikiar (the first wife of the late
King FUAD and a leader of Egypt's aristocracy),
Durriyya edited the magazine of the New
Woman Society, *La femme nouvelle*. In her campaign for women's suffrage, she led a disruptive
demonstration into the Egyptian Parliament and
also tried to turn *Bint al-Nil* into a political party,
which was promptly closed down when NASIR's
government banned all parties. In 1954 she went
on a hunger strike for women's suffrage and
other political rights, contacting foreign journalists and taking refuge in the Indian Embassy.
Participating in this demonstration was her final
and most dramatic action in favor of women's
enfranchisement, which would be written into
the 1956 Constitution. She also demonstrated
against the Israeli occupation of the Sinai and
Gaza in 1956–1957, but because she directed
this hunger strike as well against Nasir's restrictions on individual freedoms, she lost the support of such feminists as SAIZA NABARAWI and
INJI AFLATUN, and even *Bint al-Nil* expelled her
from its membership list. Nasir put her under
house arrest in 1957. Although SADAT ended her
confinement in 1970, she had lost her will for

freedom and became withdrawn and depressed.
She later fell from her sixth-story balcony, probably a suicide, a tragic ending to a life of militant
and provocative feminism.

Bibliographic Sources
'Abd al-Halim, *Nisa*, 57–64.
al-Ahram Archives, file 5401.
Amin, Mustafa, *Shakhsiyyat*, I, 257–271.
Badran, Margot, in *al-Ahram Weekly*, 3 Oct. 1996.
———, *Feminists*, 153–154.
Badran and Cooke, *Opening the Gates*, 352–356.
Luthi, *Introduction*, 287–288.
Nelson, *Doria Shafik*.
OEMIW, IV, 39–40, article by Eleanor Abdella
    Doumato.
Subki, *al-Haraka al-nisaiyya*, 122–123.
Sullivan, Earl L., *Women in Egyptian Public Life*,
    33.
WWAW, 1997–1998, 597.

Shahin, Yusuf

(25 January 1926–)
Cinema director, producer, and actor. Born in
Alexandria to a Syrian Melchite lawyer and a
Greek Orthodox mother, he attended a Catholic
primary school, Victoria College, the University
of California at Berkeley, and the Pasadena Play-
house, which awarded him a master's degree in
1950. Unique among Egyptian directors in having
made several autobiographical films, his first
movie, *Baba Amin* (1950), expressed his feelings
toward his father in the context of a social commentary then rare in Egyptian cinematography.
His marriage to a Frenchwoman and his own het-
erogeneous background shaped his presentation
of a Jewish-Arab love story in *Iskandariyya leh?*
[Why Alexandria?]. Later productions include
Sira' fi al-wadi [The Blazing Sun] in 1954, *Bab
al-Hadid* [The Railway Station] in 1958, *al-Nasir
Salah al-Din* [The Victor Saladin] in 1963, *al-
Ikhtiyar* [The Choice] in 1970, *al-'Asfur* [The
Swallow] in 1973, and *al-Wida' ya Bunabart*
[Farewell, Bonapart] in 1985. He admired NASIR
and saw himself as a leftist, hence his neorealistic
film based on 'ABD AL-RAHMAN AL-SHARQAWI's
novel, *al-Ard* [The Land] (1968), but he detested
Arab socialism's heavy-handed bureaucracy; because of that bureaucracy he went into voluntary
exile for two years. He received awards from the
Egyptian government in 1964, from Tunisia in
1970, from Berlin in 1978, and from France in
1987. A recent film, *al-Masir* [Destiny], dealing

with the life and writings of Ibn Rushd and viewed as an attack on Muslim extremists, was screened at the 1997 Cannes Film Festival, where he received a life achievement award. Later in 1997 he declined an invitation from the Van Leer Institute to attend the Jerusalem Film Festival. In January 1998 he headed an Arab delegation to Baghdad in support of Iraq's children and in protest against the UN embargo.

Bibliographic Sources
al-Ahram, 1 June 1997.
al-Ahram Archives, file 605.
al-Ahram Hebdo, 23 Oct. 1996, interview with Najib Mahfuz.
Berrah, Levy, and Cluny, *Cinémas arabes,* 175–176 et passim.
Bosseno, "Youssef Chahine l'Alexandrin."
Cahiers du Cinéma (1996), special issue by Thierry Jousse.
Cluny, *Dictionnaire des nouveaux cinémas arabes.*
Darwish, Mustafa, *Dream Makers,* 43.
Derives (Montréal) 43 (1984), special issue.
Katz, *Film Encyclopedia,* 235–236.
Khan, *Introduction to Egyptian Cinema.*
Khayati, *Cinémas arabes.*
Kiernan, "Cultural Hegemony and National Film Language."
Newell-Smith, *Oxford History of the World Cinema,* 663–665, insert article by Roy Armes.
QTQ, 283–284.
al-Riyad, 28 May 1997.
Sadoul, *Dictionary of Film Makers,* 231–232.
Sawi, Muhammad, *Sinima Yusuf Shahin.*
Shiri, *Directory of African Film-Makers,* 44.
Thomas, *Directory of Films and Filmmakers, II,* 133–134, article by Roy Armes.
Thoraval, *Le cinéma égyptien,* 71–78.
Thoraval interview in *Le Progrès égyptien,* 6 Mar. 1972.
Toubiana, "Entretien avec Youssef Chahine."
Wakeman, *World Film Directors, II,* 199–206, article by Miriam Rosen.

Shaltut, Shaykh Mahmud

(23 April 1893–12 December 1963)
Scholar, teacher, and reformist rector of al-Azhar under NASIR. Born in Minyat Bani Mansur near Itay al-Barud (Buhayra), he entered the Alexandria Religious Institute in 1906 and graduated in 1918 from al-Azhar, where he taught for most of his life, initially as a protégé of MARAGHI. He wanted to combine the modern sciences with traditional Islamic studies and called for opening the gate of *ijtihad* (judicial interpretation). Driven

from al-Azhar by his conservative opponents, he worked as a lawyer from 1931 to 1935, then returned to al-Azhar, where he was appointed dean of the Faculty of Shari'a. He represented Egypt at the International Law Congress held in The Hague in 1937, giving a paper on criminal law in the Shari'a. In 1941 he was appointed to the Council of High Ulama, then was admitted to the Arabic Language Academy in 1946. He was an adviser to the 1957 Islamic Congress. He served as rector of al-Azhar from 1958 until his death. A gifted orator, he was the author of twenty-six printed works, including an incomplete *tafsir* (Quranic interpretation), a study of women and the Quran, and a book on Muhammad's preaching style. He spearheaded al-Azhar's modernization, but failed to ensure its independence from the Egyptian government. Honoring a visit he had made in 1960 to Indonesia, its government gave £E 4 million to Itay al-Barud in 1988 to fund elementary, preparatory, and secondary schools connected with al-Azhar. One of his innovations, *Majma' al-Buhuth al-Islamiyya* (the Islamic Research Center), has turned into a body for literary censorship and intimidation of authors deemed heretics.

Bibliographic Sources
'Abd al-'Azim, *Mashyakhat al-Azhar mundhu inshaiha hatta al-an,* II, 181–243.
'Abd al-Raziq, 'Ali, in *MMIA* 19 (1939): 147–153.
al-Ahram, 13, 14 Dec. 1963; 10 Mar. 1992.
al-Ahram Archives, file 118.
al-Ahram al-masai, 30 Dec. 1997–1 Jan. 1998.
'Allam, *Majma'iyyun,* 340–341.
———, in *MMLA* 19: 154–162.
Daghir, *Masadir,* IV, 387–389.
EI2, IX, 260–261, article by Werner Ende.
Ende, "Die Azhar, Saih Saltut und die Schia."
Khafaji, *al-Azhar fi alf 'am,* III, 113.
Lemke, *Mahmud Saltut.*
Majallat al-Azhar 30 (1958–1959), special issue.
OEMIW, IV, 42–43, article by Amira El Azhary Sonbol.
Tantawi, Muhammad Sayyid, in *al-Ahram,* 9 July 1996.
Zayyat, Ahmad Hasan, "al-Shaykh Mahmud al-Shaltut."
Zebiri, *Mahmud Shaltut and Islamic Modernism.*
Zirikli, *al-A'lam,* VII, 173.

al-Shamsi, 'Ali

(1885–11 February 1962)
Member of Parliament and prominent businessman. From a Sharqiyya mercantile and landown-

ing family (his father, Amin al-Shamsi, was a cotton merchant who had earlier backed 'URABI), 'Ali earned his *license en droit* in France and was elected to the Legislative Assembly in 1914, but was exiled during World War I because of his association with the Egyptian Youth Congress and the National Party in Geneva. His pamphlet *Egypt and the Right of Nations* upheld Egypt's demand for independence from Britain but was interpreted as compromising by the National Party leaders. He joined the Wafd while still in Europe and returned to a tumultuous reception in Alexandria in 1922. He became finance minister in 1924 and thus had to write the indemnity check of behalf of the Egyptian government following Sir Lee Stack's assassination, an act that barred Shamsi's return to the Finance Ministry. He was elected to represent al-Qinayat (Sharqiyya province) in the 1926 Parliament. Education minister from 1926 to 1927, he left the Wafd and became close to 'ABD AL-KHALIQ THARWAT. Shamsi's educational reforms included standardizing the stages of public instruction, division of secondary instruction between scientific and literary branches, school administration, technical and administrative inspection, textbook selection, and the organization of Cairo University. Joining the United Front in 1935, he served on the team negotiating the 1936 Anglo-Egyptian Treaty and at the Montreux Conference in 1937. He then represented Egypt at the League of Nations. He made a speech in 1939 at Egypt's Chamber of Deputies, warning that the country was becoming overpopulated, and proposed reform policies that, if adopted, might have forestalled the upheaval that followed. He became the first Egyptian chairman of the National Bank of Egypt in 1940; he also served on the board of the Suez Canal, Cairo Water, and Tura Cement Companies. As the uncle of SAYYID MAR'I, Wahid Rafat, and 'ALI SABRI, all of whom served Egypt after the 1952 Revolution, he bridged the gap between the old regime and the new.

Bibliographic Sources
Bishri, 'Abd al-'Aziz, *Fi al-mirat*, 141–148.
Egyptian Mail, 24 Dec. 1994, article by Samir Raafat.
Farid, Muhammad, *Memoirs and Diaries*.
Mallakh, Kamal, in *al-Ahram*, 12 Feb. 1962.
al-Masa, 14 Feb. 1962.

Mutawalli, "Shakhsiyyat rasmaliyya."
Najib, *A'lam Misr*, 342.
Thabit, Karim, in *al-Hilal* 37:4 (Feb. 1929): 402–405; 41:6 (Apr. 1933): 736–738.
Tawfiq, 'Awad, and Hasan Sabri, *Wuzara al-ta'lim*, 72–74.
Who's Who in Egypt and the Near East, 575–576.

Sharaf, Sami
(1929–)
Intelligence operative and close associate of JAMAL 'ABD AL-NASIR. Sami graduated from the Military Academy in 1949 and was commissioned in the Artillery Corps. He became Nasir's secretary in 1955 and helped to set up the *Mukhabarat*. He was the cousin of General MUHAMMAD FAWZI, whom he urged Nasir to appoint as defense minister. Billed as "the second most powerful man in Egypt" after the June War, he was chosen to represent Cairo on the ASU governing board in 1968. British and U.S. intelligence alleged that he was on the Soviet KGB payroll from 1959 on. He was minister of state for presidential affairs in 1970 under both Nasir and SADAT, who purged him in the Corrective Revolution despite his friendship with the commander of the presidential guard. Convicted of plotting against Sadat, he was given a death sentence, which was commuted to hard labor without parole. However, he was released in May 1981 and was allowed to reenter politics in 1987. He is now secretary-general of the Nasirite Party, and his revelations in the early 1990s about Nasir's policies raised a small tempest in the Cairo press.

Bibliographic Sources
al-Ahram Archives, file 5638.
al-'Arabi, 10 Jan. 1994–8 May 1995.
al-Kifah al-'arabi, 26 Oct. 1991–24 May 1993.
al-Misri, 16–20 Oct. 1996.
Najib, *A'lam Misr*, 232.
Sharaf, Sami, *'Abd al-Nasir.*
Uktubir, no. 425 (16 Dec. 1984).

Sha'rawi, Huda
(22 June 1879–12 December 1947)
Pioneer Egyptian feminist leader. Born in Minya, she was a daughter of MUHAMMAD SULTAN, and she was reared and taught to read the Quran and tutored in Arabic, Persian, Turkish, and Islamic subjects by Muslim women tutors in Cairo. She

wrote poetry in both Arabic and French. Against her will, she was married to her cousin, 'Ali Sha'rawi. Even as a young woman, she showed her independence by entering a department store in Alexandria to buy her own clothes instead of having them brought to her home. She helped to organize *Mubarrat Muhammad Ali,* a women's social service organization, in 1909 and the Union of Educated Egyptian Women in 1914, the year in which she traveled to Europe for the first time. She helped lead the first women's street demonstration during the 1919 Revolution and was elected president of the Wafdist Women's Central Committee. In 1923 Sha'rawi founded and became the first president of the Egyptian Feminist Union, which sent her to an international feminist meeting in Rome. Upon her return, she removed her face veil in public for the first time, a signal event in the history of Egyptian feminism. She led Egyptian women pickets at the opening of Parliament in January 1924 and submitted a list of nationalist and feminist demands, which were ignored by the Wafdist government, whereupon she resigned from the Wafdist Women's Central Committee. She continued to lead the Egyptian Feminist Union until her death, publishing the feminist magazine *l'Égyptienne* (and *al-Misriyya*), and representing Egypt at women's congresses in Graz, Paris, Amsterdam, Berlin, Marseilles, Istanbul, Brussels, Budapest, Copenhagen, Interlaken, and Geneva. She was instrumental in 1944 in convening the first Arab Feminist Conference and in 1945 in forming the Arab Feminist Union, which called for solidarity with the Arabs of Palestine. She also proposed internationalizing the Suez Canal and, shortly before her death, abolishing nuclear weapons. Even if only some of her demands were met during her lifetime, she laid the groundwork for later gains by Egyptian women and remains the symbolic standard-bearer for their liberation movement.

Bibliographic Sources
Adams, *Islam and Modernism*, 231, 236, 239.
al-Ahram, 15 June 1979.
al-Ahram Archives, file 1692.
al-Ahram Hebdo, 13 Dec. 1995.
al-Ahram Weekly, 17 Mar. 1994.
al-Akhbar, 25 May 1979.
Akhir sa'a, no. 1970 (26 July 1972).
Amin, Mustafa, *Shakhsiyyat*, I, 225–245.
Arafa, *Egyptian Feminist Union.*
Badran, "Dual Liberation."
———, *Feminists*, 32–38.
———, "Feminist Politics."
Badran and Cooke, *Opening the Gates*, 41–48, 337–340.
Bishri, 'Abd al-'Aziz, *Fi al-mirat*, 123–132.
Brockelmann, *GAL*, S III, 263–264.
Daghir, *Masadir*, III, i, 637–639.
Dhikra faqidat al-'uruba . . . Huda Hanim Sha'rawi.
Eliraz, "Egyptian Intellectuals," 101–102.
EAL, II, 704–705.
Fernea and Bezirgan, *Middle Eastern Muslim Women Speak,* 193–200.
International Dictionary of Women's Biography, 425.
Kahf, "Huda Sha'rawi's *Mudhakkirati.*"
Kahhala, *Mu'jam*, XIII, 146.
Muhammad, Fathiyya, *Balaghat al-nisa*, I, 61–85.
Musa, Salama, in *al-Hilal* 35:6 (Apr. 1927): 650–654.
OEMIW, IV, 44–46, article by Margot Badran.
Philips, "Feminist Movement in Egypt."
Qadi, Shukri, *Khamsun shakhsiyya,* 123–127.
Qusi, *Lamha tarikhiyya 'an al-nahda al-niswiyya.*
Raghib, *Huda Sha'rawi wa 'asr al-tanwir.*
Sabah al-khayr, 6 Feb. 1986.
Sa'id, Amina, in *al-Hilal* 61:1 (Jan. 1952): 59–64.
——— 89:2 (Feb. 1980): 50–52.
Sha'rawi, *Mudhakkirat.*
Subki, *al-Haraka al-nisaiyya.*
Thabit, Karim, in *al-Hilal* 38:1 (Nov. 1929): 14–17.
Waddy, *Women in Muslim History.*
Woodsmall, *Muslim Women.*
Zirikli, *al-A'lam*, VIII, 78–79.

al-Sha'rawi, Shaykh Muhammad Mutawalli

(15 April 1911–17 June 1998)
Popular Islamist preacher, writer, and cabinet minister. Born in Daqadus, near Mit Ghamr (Daqahliyya), he was educated in Zagaziq and graduated from al-Azhar's Arabic Language Faculty in 1941, receiving an *ijaza* (teaching certificate) in 1943. He taught in its institutes in Tanta, Zaqaziq, and Alexandria, then worked in Saudi Arabia from 1950 to 1963. In his youth he demonstrated in support of restoring MARAGHI to his position as rector of al-Azhar and for a time backed the Muslim Brothers, even writing a manifesto in May 1937 for HASAN AL-BANNA, but later broke with the society over its use of violence. Shaykh al-Sha'rawi became deputy for propaganda and office director for the former

rector of al-Azhar, Shaykh Hasan Mamun, then was delegated to 'Abd al-'Aziz University in Riyadh in 1972. He became minister of *awqaf* and al-Azhar affairs in 1976. One of his *fatwas* opposed cosmetic surgery but favored any operation that would relieve suffering. He received honorary doctorates from the University of Minufiyya in 1985 and from Mansura in 1990. He kept close ties with the Saudi government and resisted attempts to form a Muslim political party in Egypt. His best-known publication was an interpretation of the Quran, but he wrote many other books and advocated Muslim principles without antagonizing the MUBARAK regime. He died at his home near the Pyramids after a long illness.

Bibliographic Sources
al-Ahali, 25 Aug. 1993.
al-Ahram (18 June 1998): 1, 3.
al-Ahram Archives, file 199.
Jansen, "Endorsement by Shaykh al-Sha'rawi."
Najib, *A'lam Misr*, 441.
al-Shaykh al-Imam Muhammad Mutawalli al-Sha'rawi.
al-Shaykh al-Sha'rawi bayn al-Islam wa al-siyasa.
al-Shaykh al-Sha'rawi min al-qarya ila al-qimma.

Sharif, Muhammad

(26 November 1826–19 April 1887)
Army officer, cabinet minister, and three-time premier. Born in Cairo to the Ottoman grand qadi, who usually lived in Istanbul, he later accompanied his father when the latter was sent by the sultan to be a judge in Mecca. MUHAMMAD 'ALI saw him as a boy, took a fancy to him, and offered to rear him as one of his own sons. He was enrolled in the Princes' School and went with them on the 1844 education mission to Paris. Sharif spent two years at St-Cyr military academy and became the captain of a French regiment. He returned to Cairo in 1849 to become a captain under Colonel SÈVE (Sulayman Pasha), whose daughter he married, and may have been a clerk to Prince 'ABD AL-HALIM. He was in Istanbul during 'ABBAS I's last year as viceroy, but returned after the accession of SA'ID, who promoted him to colonel and put him in command of an infantry regiment.

Sharif entered the civil administration as director of the Foreign Affairs Department in 1857. He mixed well with Europeans and was scrupulously honest, but was extremely proud of his Turkish background and contemptuous toward Armenians and Egyptians. He chaired the Council of Justice from 1861 to 1863 and later in 1867. He briefly directed education, then returned to foreign affairs in 1863; took charge of interior in 1866, adding public works for a time; served on four occasions as acting viceroy when ISMA'IL was away from Egypt; and headed the Department of Justice from 1872 to 1875, adding commerce in 1874 and again from 1876. He also drafted the plans for the first representative assembly in 1866. As prime minister in 1879, then in 1881–1882, and in 1882–1884, Sharif acquired an undeserved reputation for favoring constitutional government and 'URABI's movement. Liked by Europeans and Turco-Egyptian notables, he built up vast landholdings in Egypt. He was dominated by Isma'il and TAWFIQ and rarely tried to assert his convictions, except when he resigned in 1884 rather than countenance surrendering Egyptian control over the Sudan. He retired to a life of study and reading.

Bibliographic Sources
Ayyubi, *'Ahd al-Khidiwi Isma'il*, II, 166–172.
Bell, *Khedives and Pashas*, 163–181.
Blunt, *Gordon at Khartoum*, 124–128 et passim.
———, *Secret History*, 192–196, 250, et passim.
Cromer, *Modern Egypt*, II, 334–335.
de Leon, *Khedive's Egypt*, 181–182.
Des Boves, *Son excéllence Chérif Pacha.*
Des Michels, *Souvenirs de carrière.*
EI2, IX, 340, article by C.E. Bosworth.
Fikri, 'Ali, *Subul al-najah*, III, 244–250.
al-Hilal 2:2 (15 Sept. 1893): 33–37.
Hunter, *Egypt Under the Khedives*, 151–158.
Kusel, *Englishman's Recollections of Egypt,* 122–125.
Mujahid, *al-A'lam al-sharqiyya*, I, 109–110.
Muti'i, *Mawsu'a*, 192–198.
Rafi'i, 'Abd al-Rahman, *'Asr Isma'il*, II, 206–223.
Ramadan, Tal'at Isma'il, *Muhammad Sharif Pasha.*
Sayyid, Afaf Lutfi, *Egypt and Cromer*, 7–8 et passim.
Schölch, *Egypt for the Egyptians!* 322.
Times (London) (20 Apr. 1887): 13d; (21 Apr. 1887): 5b.
Tusun, *al-Ba'that al-'ilmiyya*, 246–251.
Walili, *Mafakhir al-ajyal*, 57–59.
Zakhura, *Mirat al-'asr*, I, 125–129.
Zaki, 'Abd al-Rahman, *A'lam al-jaysh*, 110–112.
Zaydan, Jurji, *Mashahir al-sharq*, 1st ed., I, 216–219.

Sharif, Omar

(10 April 1932–)

Cinema actor and expert bridge player. Originally named Michel Chalhub, he was born in Alexandria and educated at Cairo's Victoria College. He worked briefly as a salesman for a lumber export firm and in 1953 was selected by YUSUF SHAHIN to play the male lead opposite FATIN HAMAMA in *al-Sira' fi al-Wadi* [Struggle in the Valley (usually translated as *The Blazing Sun*)]; when he married her two years later, he converted to Islam and adopted his present name, which in Arabic is 'Umar al-Sharif. He starred in twenty-four Egyptian and two French coproduction films during the following five years. Egypt awarded him a prize for his role in *Juha* in 1959. He began his international career with a supporting role in *Lawrence of Arabia* and starred in other British and American movies, including *Behold a Pale Horse*, *Doctor Zhivago*, and *Funny Girl*. After playing the title role in *Che Guevara*, his career in Western cinema faded, although he remained prominent in high society as a champion bridge player. More recently, he has settled in Cairo and resumed acting in Egyptian films, such as *Ayyub* and *al-Aragöz*. He was considered for the directorship of the Cairo Film Festival but was passed over because he has retained dual French and Egyptian nationality.

Bibliographic Sources
al-Ahram Archives, file 499.
al-Ahrar, 12 Jan. 1998.
Current Biography Yearbook (1970), 390–392.
Darwish, Mustafa, *Dream Makers*, 31.
Egypt, Ministry of Information, *al-Mawsu'a al-qawmiyya*, I, 746.
Jabara et al., "Arab Image."
Katz, *Film Encyclopedia*, 1237–1238.
Sawi, *'Umar al-Sharif.*
Sharif, Omar, *The Eternal Male.*
Thomas, *Directory of Films and Filmmakers*, III, 907–909, article by Doug Tomlinson.
WWAW, 1997–1998, 608–609.

al-Sharqawi, Shaykh 'Abd Allah

(1737–19 October 1812)

Islamic legal expert. Born in the Sharqiyya village of al-'Arin, he studied at al-Azhar, taught there, and eventually became its rector in 1794. He founded the *riwaq* (hostel) for Azhari students from Sharqiyya and became the head of NAPOLEON's first appointed Council of Ulama. He was forced to sign a manifesto warning Egyptians against opposing the French. He died in Cairo. He wrote books on history, Shafi'i jurisprudence, hadith, and various other Islamic subjects.

Bibliographic Sources
Baqli, *Abtal al-muqawama*, 93–99.
Brockelmann, *GAL*, II, 631–632; S II, 729.
Dibs, *Tarikh Suriyya*, VIII, 699.
EAL, II, 707.
Fikri, 'Ali, *Subul al-najah*, II, 55–57.
Ghayth, "Shuyukh Jami' al-Azhar."
Gran, *Islamic Roots*, 44–46.
al-Hilal 18:4 (1 Jan. 1910): 198–199.
Jabarti, *Ajaib al-athar*, IV, 159–165.
Jami'at al-Duwal al-'Arabiyya, *al-Fihris al-tamhidi*, 362.
Kahhala, *Mu'jam*, VI, 41–42.
Mubarak, 'Ali, *Khitat*, III, 63.
Rafi'i, 'Abd al-Rahman, *Tarikh al-haraka al-qawmiyya*, I.
Shayyal, *al-Tarikh wa al-muarrikhun*, 27–30.
'Umar, Mahmud Fathi, *Abtal al-hurriyya*, 10–12.
Walili, *Mafakhir al-ajyal*, 27–28.
Zayyati, *Kanz al-jawhar*, 133–135.
Zirikli, *al-A'lam*, IV, 78.

al-Sharqawi, 'Abd al-Rahman

(10 November 1920–10 November 1987)

Leftist novelist, journalist, and playwright. Born in Minufiyya, he earned his law *license* from Cairo University in 1943. He worked in both law and journalism, but initially served as head inspector of investigations within the Education Ministry. He edited the literary sections of *al-Sha'b* and *al-Jumhuriyya* in the 1950s and was administrative chairman of *Ruz al-Yusuf* from 1971 to 1977. He became secretary-general in 1954 of the Supreme Council for the Arts and Culture and in 1978 of the Afro-Asian Peoples' Solidarity Organization, becoming its president in 1985. Sharqawi's first novel, *al-Ard* (translated by Desmond Stewart as *Egyptian Earth*), depicted peasants' privations before the 1952 Revolution, a theme that he developed further in another novel, *al-Fallah* (1970). He wrote a weekly column for *al-Ahram* under NASIR, but broke with SADAT after the latter formed the Supreme Press Council (of which Sharqawi was briefly a member) in 1975. His manifesto, *Muhammad rasul al-hurriyya* [Muhammad, Messenger of Freedom], preached a form of Islamic socialism; it was followed by a series of biographies of early Muslim leaders. The play that he wrote about the Prophet's grandson, al-Husayn, was banned by Egyptian censors. He received state prizes for literature in 1972 and 1974 and belonged to the Press Syndicate, the Writers Union, and the Story Club. His family donated £E 10,000 to establish a literary prize in his memory.

Bibliographic Sources
'Abd al-Ghani, Mustafa, *'Abd al-Rahman al-Shar-qawi.*
———, *al-Sharqawi mutamarridan.*
al-Ahram, 11 Nov. 1987; 8 Sept. 1987.
al-Ahram Archives, file 3885.
al-Akhbar, 13 Nov. 1987.
Allen, *Modern Arabic Literature,* 293–298.
Badawi, M.M., *Modern Arabic Drama,* 217–220.
Becka, *DOL,* III, 171–172.
EAL, II, 707.
EI2, IX, 353, article by Pierre Cachia.
Kilpatrick, "Egyptian Novel," *CHAL,* 249–250.
———, *Modern Egyptian Novel,* 126–140.
Muti'i, *Haula al-rijal min Misr,* III, 125–147.
———, *Mawsu'a,* 236–242.
New York Times (11 Nov. 1987): B8.
New York Times Biographical Service 18 (Nov. 1987): 1175.
Raghib, *A'lam al-tanwir,* 97–112.
Ra'i, "Arabic Drama Since the Thirties," *CHAL,* 360–361.
Ramadan, 'Abd al-'Azim, in *al-Wafd,* 16 Nov. 1987.
Ruz al-Yusuf, 16 Nov., 23 Nov. 1987.
Sa'd, Ahmad Sadiq, *Safahat min al-Yasar al-Misri.*
Sa'id, Rif'at, *al-Sihafa al-yasariyya fi Misr.*
al-Wafd, 3 Dec. 1987.
al-Watan al-'arabi, no. 37 (27 Nov. 1997).
WWAW, 1997–1998, 609.

Shawqi, Ahmad

(16 October 1868–14 October 1932)
Distinguished Arabic poet and playwright, often called *Amir al-Shu'ara* (Prince of Poets). He came from a wealthy family of mixed Turkish, Circassian, Kurdish, and Greek origin and having close connections to the khedivial house. Born in Cairo, he was educated at a *kuttab,* a primary school, the Khedivial Secondary School, then the School of Languages (later the Khedivial Law School) in Cairo from 1885 to 1889, and studied in Montpellier and Paris in 1889–1891 at Khedive TAWFIQ's expense. Shawqi was fascinated by France and impressed by the monuments and the "great commercial and industrial developments" in London, which he visited during his European stay. Upon returning to Egypt, he went to work in the French chancery of 'ABBAS HILMI II and began writing poetry, often glorifying his patron, who came to appreciate his work because of its popularity among educated Egyptians. He read one of his poems at the 1894 International Congress of Orientalists in Geneva. Shawqi wrote poems attacking RIYAD for praising the British occupation in 1904 and CROMER when he left Egypt in 1907. He mourned Sultan 'Abd al-Hamid's deposition in 1909 and would later pen an elegy to the caliphate upon its abolition by Kemal Atatürk. After 'Abbas was deposed in 1914, Shawqi was exiled to Barcelona, where he read classical Arabic poetry and visited the monuments of al-Andalus. After returning to Egypt in 1919, his appeal to Muslim sentiments won him public recognition as the greatest living Arabic poet. He was elected to the Senate in 1923 and was formally named "Prince of the Arab Poets" by his colleagues, including HAFIZ IBRAHIM, at a Cairo ceremony in 1927. His enemies called him the Poet of Arab Princes because of his 'Abdin Palace ties, but his work remains a model for neoclassical Arabic poetry. He also began writing verse dramas. He was named to head the Apollo Group in 1932, more for his fame than for his classical literary style. He is still widely read and admired throughout the Arab world, and his Giza mansion has been converted into a museum.

Bibliographic Sources
Abbas Hilmi Papers, Durham University, Box 274/1–287.
'Abbud, Marun, *al-Ruus,* 320–326.
'Abd al-Fattah, Muhammad, *Ashhar mashahir,* I, 3–32.
'Abd al-'Izz, *Ahmad Shawqi.*
Aboushadi, "Shawqi, Hafiz, and Matran."
al-Ahram (15 Oct. 1932): 1–3; (16 Oct. 1932): 1.
Amin, Mustafa, *Shakhsiyyat,* II, 167–186.
Apollo 1:4 (Dec. 1932); 5 (Jan. 1933), special issues.
'Aqqad, 'Abbas Mahmud, *Shu'ara Misr,* 155–188.
Arberry, Arthur J., "Hafiz Ibrahim and Shawqi."
Arslan, *Shawqi aw sadaqat arba'in sana.*
'Atawi, *Ahmad Shawqi.*
Badawi, M.M., *CHAL,* 47–48, 67–71, 358–360.
———, *Modern Arabic Drama,* 207–215.
Bishri, 'Abd al-'Aziz, *Fi al-mirat,* 169–176.
———, *al-Mukhtar* I, 86–94, 118–127, 145–146, 169–175.
Boudot-Lamotte, *Ahmad Shawqi.*

Brockelmann, *GAL*, S III, 21–48.
Brugman, *Introduction*, 35–45.
Bustani, Butrus, *Udaba al-'arab*, III, 173–250.
Daghir, *Masadir*, II, i, 504–514.
Danielson, *Voice of Egypt*, 112–117.
Dayf, *al-Adab al-'arabi*, 110–121.
———, *Shawqi sha'ir al-'asr al-hadith*.
al-Diwan 1 (1921): 3–45; 2 (1921): 33–84, 'Aqqad and Mazini articles.
EI2, IX, 379–380, article by Antoine Boudot-Lamotte.
Fahmi, Mahir Hasan, *Shawqi*.
Fahmi, Zaki, *Safwat al-'asr*, 336–339.
Farhud, *Malhat al-shi'r Ahmad Shawqi*.
Farrukh, *Ahmad Shawqi*.
———. *Kalima fi Ahmad Shawqi*.
Gabrieli, "Commemorazione di Ahmad Shawqi."
Ghandur, *Muhadarat 'an masrahiyyat Shawqi*.
Guidi, "L'onoranzo al poeta egiziano Shawqi."
Hamuda, 'Abd al-Wahhab, *al-Tajdid fi al-adab*, 19–32.
Hanna, Sami, "Ahmad Shauqi."
Hasan, 'Abbas, *al-Mutanabbi wa Shawqi*.
Hasan, Muhammad 'Abd al-Ghani, *A'lam min al-sharq wa al-gharb*, 95–107.
Hawi, *Ahmad Shawqi*.
Haykal, Muhammad Husayn, *al-Adab wa al-hayat*, 121–180.
Hijazi, Anwar, *'Amaliqa*, 192–197.
al-Hilal 35:8 (June 1927): 898–909, two articles.
——— 41:1 (Nov. 1932): 17–24, obituary.
——— 55:10 (Oct. 1947); 66:10 (Oct. 1958); 76:11 (Nov. 1968).
Hufi, Ahmad Muhammad, *al-Islam fi shi'r Shawqi*.
———, *Wahy al-nasib fi shi'r Shawqi*.
———, *Wataniyyat Shawqi*.
Hunayn, *Shawqi 'ala al-masrah*.
Husayn, Taha, *Hafiz wa Shawqi*.
'Imari, Ahmad Suwaylim, *Adab Shawqi*.
'Inani, 'Ali, *Dhikra Shawqi*.
Jarim, "Sadiqi Ahmad Shawqi."
Jawdat, *Balabil* (1960), 67–87; (1972), 47–71.
Jayyusi, *Trends*, I, 46–51.
Jumayyil, Antun, *Shawqi*.
Jundi, *A'lam al-adab*, II, 457–459.
Kahhala, *Mu'jam*, I, 246–250.
Kayyali, *al-Rahilun*, 43–60.
Khouri, *Poetry*, 55–77.
al-Kitab 4 (Oct. 1947), special issue.
Kurd 'Ali, *Mu'asirun*, 59–94.
Landau, *Studies in the Arab Theater*, 125–138.
Mahfuz, Ahmad, *Hayat Shawqi*.
al-Majalla 12:144 (Dec. 1968), special issue.
Mandur, *A'lam al-shi'r*.
Mikhail, Mona, "Shawqi."
Mikhail, Sa'd, *Adab al-'asr*, 7–22.
Misri, 'Abd al-Sami', *Sha'ira al-'uruba*.
MMIA 13:2 (Feb. 1933): 69–113; 3–4 (Mar.–Apr. 1933): 156–161.
Mubarak, Zaki, *Ahmad Shawqi*.

———, *al-Muwazana bayn al-shu'ara*.
Mujahid, *al-A'lam al-sharqiyya*, II, 658–663.
Musa, Salama, "Ahmad Shawqi Bek."
Nashashibi, *al-'Arabiyya wa sha'iruha al-akbar Ahmad Shawqi*.
———, *al-Batl al-khalid Salah al-Din*.
Nasif, 'Ali al-Najdi, *al-Din wa al-akhlaq fi shi'r Shawqi*.
Nasr, Nasim, *Shawqi wa mirat adabihi*.
Pérès, "Ahmad Sawqi."
Qadi, Shukri, *Khamsun shakhsiyya*, 175–178.
Radwan, Fathi, *'Asr wa rijal*, 87–119.
Rafi'i, 'Abd al-Rahman, *Shu'ara al-wataniyya* (1954), 41–94.
Ramadi, *Min a'lam al-adab*, 199–214.
Rubinacci, "'Magnun Laila' di Ahmad Sawqi."
Sabri, Muhammad, *al-Shawqiyyat al-majhula*.
———, *Shu'ara al-'asr*, I, 48–99.
Saharti, Mustafa 'Abd al-Latif, *Adab al-tabi'a*, 91–93.
———, *al-Shi'r al-mu'asir*, 151–157.
Sandubi, *al-Shu'ara al-thalatha*, 6–252.
Sayrafi, Hasan Kamil, *Hafiz wa Shawqi*.
———, in *al-Muqtataf* 112:2 (Feb. 1948): 124–136; 3 (Mar.): 219–225; 4 (Apr.): 281–290.
Shahid,'Irfan, *al-'Awda ila Shawqi*.
Shamis, "Shakhsiyyat fi hayat Shawqi."
Shawkat, *al-Masrahiyya fi shi'r Shawqi*.
Shawqi, Ahmad, "Ahammu hadith fi majra hayati."
Shawqi, Husayn, *Abi Shawqi*.
Shayib, *Ahmad Shawqi*.
Tanahi, Tahir, *'Ala firash al-mawt*, 151–157.
———, *Suwar wa zilal min hayat Shawqi wa Hafiz*.
Tarabulsi, *Khasais al-uslub fi "al-Shawqiyyat."*
Tattawi, *al-Turath wa al-mu'arada 'inda Shawqi*.
Thabit, Karim, "Ziyara li al-amir al-sha'ir."
UAR, *Mahrajan Ahmad Shawqi*.
'Ubayd, Ahmad, *Dhikra al-sha'irayn*.
———, *Mashahir shu'ara*, 62–99.
'Uthman, Muhammad Fathi, *Sharh al-Burda*.
Wahhabi, *Maraji' tarajim*, I, 276–291.
Yarid, *Ahmad Shawqi*.
Zakhura, *Mirat al-'asr*, III, 113–115.
Zaki, Muhammad Amin, *Mashahir al-Kurd*, I, 84.
Zalat, 'Abd al-Salam Mahmud, *al-Janib al-insani*.
Zirikli, *al-A'lam*, I, 136–137.

Shinuda III, al-Baba

(3 August 1923–)

Coptic patriarch. Awarded a *license* in English language and literature from Cairo University in 1947, he interrupted his studies to volunteer for the Palestine War; he earned a baccalaureate in theology from the Higher Coptic College in 1950. He took holy orders in 1954 and was given his first priestly assignment in 1956. He became the director of Coptic religious education in 1962 and was elected patriarch on 20 October 1971. Recently his patriarchate has been troubled by quarrels with Coptic émigrés who feel that he has not upheld their interests. Visiting the United States in 1997, he denounced congressional efforts to make U.S. aid conditional on fairer treatment of Egypt's Copts, arguing that Copts and Muslims already enjoy equal rights without foreign intervention. Attacking Israel's management of Christian holy places, he announced that he would not visit Jerusalem until it was freed from Jewish control. He also condemned U.S. air strikes against Iraq in 1998.

Bibliographic Sources
al-Ahram, 21 Jan. 1998.
al-Ahram Archives, file 22279.
al-Musawwar, 17 Apr. 1998.
Najib, *A'lam Misr*, 257.
Ruz al-Yusuf, no. 3618 (13 Oct. 1997).
Tincq, "Siege Mentality."
Uktubir, nos. 1084–1088 (3–31 Aug. 1997).
Watani, 8 July 1997.
WWAW, 1997–1998, 187–188.

Shukri, 'Abd al-Rahman

(12 October 1886–15 December 1958)
Romantic poet, teacher, and critic. Born in Alexandria to a family of North African origin that had supported the 'URABI movement, Shukri graduated from secondary school in 1904. After two years at the Khedivial Law School, he was expelled for his pro-Nationalist activities in the 1906 student strike. He enrolled in the Higher Teachers College, graduated in 1909, and was sent on an education mission to Sheffield University in 1909–1912, receiving a B.A. in literature and history and acquiring a great admiration for the English Romantic poets. He published his first *diwan* in 1909 with the encouragement of IBRAHIM AL-MAZINI, his second in 1912, and his third in 1916. Together with 'AQQAD and Mazini, he defended the English Romantics and denounced the influence of French literature. Later Shukri broke with them and forsook poetry for teaching. In 1934 he became principal of a secondary school and later served briefly as an education inspector before retiring in 1938. He wrote many articles after 1936 on education, psychology, and literature. Eight volumes of his poems were published after his death.

Bibliographic Sources
Abu Shadi, *Shu'ara al-'arab*, 42–46.
Adham, 'Ali, in *al-Majalla* (Feb. 1959): 13–27.
al-Ahram (17 Dec. 1958); (20 Dec. 1981): 12; (1 Jan. 1995).
al-Ahram al-dawli, 17 Aug. 1997.
al-Ahram Archives, file 1542.
al-Akhbar, 16 Dec. 1958.
Allen, *Modern Arabic Literature*, 301–305.
'Aqqad, Abbas Mahmud, "'Abd al-Rahman Shukri fi al-mizan."
Badawi, M.M., *Critical Introduction*, 84–105.
———, "Shukri the Poet."
Bayyumi, Muhammad Rajab, in *al-Adib* 28:12 (Dec. 1969): 6.
Brockelmann, *GAL*, S III, 125–128.
Brugman, *Introduction*, 112–121.
Daghir, *Masadir*, III, i, 647–650.
Daud, *'Abd al-Rahman Shukri.*
Dayf, *al-Adab al-'arabi*, I, 128–135.
EAL, II, 715–716.
EI2, IX, 498, article by S. Moreh.
Farhud, *al-Ittijahat al-fanniyya.*
———, *'Abd al-Rahman Shukri.*
Ghurab, *'Abd al-Rahman Shukri.*
Jayyusi, *Trends*, I, 157–163.
Jindi, Anwar, *al-Kuttab al-mu'asirun*, 94–98.
Kahhala, *Mu'jam*, XIII, 395–396.
Khouri, *Poetry*, 173–195.
Moreh, *Modern Arabic Poetry*, 65–79.
Moreh and Milson, *Modern Arabic Literature*, 240–242.
N. Sh. [Na'um Shuqayr], in *al-Muqtataf* 47:11 (Nov. 1915): 507–510.
Najm, Muhammad Yusuf, in *al-Abhath* 3 (1960): 220–247.
Qadi, Shukri, *Khamsun shakhsiyya*, 183–186.
Sakkut, *'Abd al-Rahman Shukri.*
Salama, Yusri Muhammad, *'Abd al-Rahman Shukri.*
Shatti, *'Abd al-Rahman Shukri.*
Shukri, 'Abd al-Rahman, in *al-Muqtataf* 95:1 (June 1939): 33–40; 2 (July 1939): 70; 3 (Aug. 1939): 284–290.
Tamawi, *'Abd al-Rahman Shukri.*
'Ubayd, Ahmad, *Mashahir shu'ara*, 249–267.
Wakil, Mukhtar, *Ruwwad al-shi'r al-hadith*, 30–47.
Yusuf, Niqula, Introduction to *Diwan 'Abd al-Rahman Shukri.*
Zirikli, *al-A'lam*, III, 335–336.

Shumayyil, Dr. Shibli

(1850–1 January 1917)
Pioneer scientist, physician, writer, and social reformer. Born in Kafr Shima (in what is now Lebanon) to a Greek Catholic literary family, he studied medicine at the Syrian Protestant College

(one of his classmates was YA'QUB SARRUF), Paris, and Istanbul. He went to Egypt in 1875 and practiced medicine in Tanta for a while. He returned to the Syrian Protestant College to teach medicine in 1882, but because of his controversial opening lecture championing Darwin's theory of evolution, he was barred from teaching there and from practicing medicine in Syria. After opening his practice in Alexandria, he published a medical journal, *al-Shifa*, from 1887 to 1889. He later moved his clinic to Cairo, where he tried to form a socialist party in 1910 and published, together with SALAMA MUSA, *al-Mustaqbal*, a socialist journal that was banned by the British, in 1914. He published numerous scientific articles in other Arabic journals and led the effort to popularize Darwinian theory in the Arab world. He also translated Hippocrites into Arabic, wrote a commentary on Ibn Sina, published books criticizing Ottoman rule in Syria, and wrote novels, plays, and poems. He died of an asthma attack. Among the earliest proponents of secularism and socialism and an opponent of doctrinaire religion, he was cherished for his jovial personality, moral courage, and kindness to the poor and the weak.

Bibliographic Sources
'Abbud, Marun, *Ruwwad al-nahda*, 253–256.
A'lam "al-Muqtataf," 288–292.
Anawati, "Shibli Shumayyil, Medical Philosopher and Scientist."
Brockelmann, *GAL*, S III, 212–213.
Daghir, *Masadir*, II, i, 497–500.
EI2, IX, 501–502, article by P.C. Sadgrove.
Fakhry, "Shibli Shumayyil."
Fayyad, Niqula, in *al-Muqtataf* 37:7 (July 1910): 676–681.
Haroun, *Sibli Sumayyil*.
al-Hilal 25:5 (Feb. 1917): 422–426, obituary and Khalil Mutran poem; 9 (June): 726–732, memoirs; 26:1 (Oct. 1917): 49–50; 30:8 (May 1922): 815–817; 32:1 (Feb. 1923): 24–28; 33:2 (Feb. 1924): 137–142.
Hourani, *Arabic Thought*, 248–253.
Jindi, Anwar, *A'lam wa ashab aqlam*, 185–193.
Kahhala, *Mu'jam*, IV, 294.
Khalil, *Mu'jam al-udaba al-atibba*, I, 190–195.
Kurd 'Ali, *Mu'asirun*, 241–247.
LeCerf, "Chibli Chemayyel."
Mazhar, "Shibli Shumayyil."
Meier, *"al-Muqtataf" et le débat sur le Darwinisme*.
Mumin and Manhal, *Min talai' yaqzat al-umma*, 93–111.
Qabbani, 'Abd al-Qadir, in *al-Manar* 19:10 (18 Apr. 1917): 625–632.
Ramadi, *Sihafat al-fukaha*, 29–31.
Reid, *Farah Antun*, 75–77, 116–117, et passim.
———, "Syrian Christians and Early Socialism."
Sa'id, Rif'at, *Thalathat Lubnaniyyin*, 14–68.
Sarruf, Ya'qub, in *al-Muqtataf* 50:2 (Feb. 1917): 105–112; 3 (Mar. 1917): 225–231; 4 (Apr. 1917): 266–269.
Shalhut, Yusuf, in *al-Muqtataf* 34:1 (Jan. 1909): 170–174; and 3 (Mar. 1909): 284–288.
Tarrazi, *Tarikh al-sihafa*, III, 74–76.
UNESCO, *A'lam al-Lubnaniyyin*, 147.
Zaydan, Emile, in *al-Hilal* 25:6 (Mar. 1917): 456–460.
Zaydan, Jurji, in *al-Hilal* 25:5 (Feb. 1917): 422–426.
Zirikli, *al-A'lam*, III, 155.

al-Siba'i, Yusuf
(10 June 1917–18 February 1978)

Army officer, minister, journalist, and writer. Born in Cairo's Darb al-Ahmar district, he was the son of Muhammad al-Siba'i, a famous teacher and writer. Yusuf published his first short story in *Majallati* in 1933. He graduated from the Military Academy as a cavalry officer in 1937 and from the Staff College in 1944, also taking specialist training in tank maneuvers in 1942. He taught military history at the Military Academy from 1943 to 1949, when he became chief senior teacher in the military secondary school and its director in the following year. In 1952 he became director of the Military Museum, shortly after having graduated from Cairo University's Journalism Institute. After the revolution, he gave up his military career in favor of a literary one. He helped found *Nadi al-Qissa* (Short Story Club), which published the work of several creative writers. He also served as editor of *al-Risala al-jadida* from 1953 to 1958, secretary-general of the Supreme Council for the Arts and Literature in 1956, and chairman of the Writers' Association and of the Cinema Critics' Association. He chaired the first congress of the Afro-Asian Peoples' Soldiarity Organization in December 1957 and was elected its secretary-general in 1958, chairing its 1962 and 1966 congresses. He was named to the board of *Ruz al-Yusuf* in 1960 and became editor-in-chief of *Akhir Sa'a* in 1966. In 1969 he was named board chairman of Dar al-Hilal and editor-in-chief of *al-Musawwar*. He served as minister of culture in 1973–1976. Appointed board chairman and editor-in-chief of *al-Ahram* in 1976, he was elected head of the Journalists' Syndicate and vice president of the Egyptian Writers Association in 1977. The author of many popular novels, short stories, and screenplays, he was killed by Palestinian *fidaiyin* attacking an Afro-Asian Peoples' Solidarity Conference meeting in Cyprus, turning many Egyptians against the Palestinians at a critical stage in the negotiations with Israel. His writings remain popular, and the attempt by al-Azhar's Islamic Research Center to ban his novel, *Azrael's Deputy*, in 1996 (thirty years after its publication) met loud protest. He received several prizes from Egypt, an award from Italy, and the Lenin Peace Prize.

Bibliographic Sources

Afro-Asian Peoples' Solidarity Organization, *Youssef El-Sibai*.

al-Ahram, 18 Feb. 1994; 21 Jan. 1997; 13 Feb. 1998.

al-Ahram Archives, file 605.

EAL, II, 717–718.

Fuda, *Nujum Shari' al-Sihafa*, 33–39.

Khidr, *Suhufiyyun mu'asirun*, 159–186.

New York Times (19 Feb. 1978): 15.

Ramadi, *Min a'lam al-adab*, 161–175.

Ramsay, *Novels of an Egyptian Romanticist*.

Rizq, Fathi, *Khamsa wa sab'una najman*, 344–350.

Wahid, *Yusuf al-Siba'i*.

Siddiq, Isma'il

(1821–14 November 1876?)

Egyptian official under Khedive ISMA'IL, generally called the *Mufattish* (Inspector General). Siddiq's father was a poor peasant; his mother was Isma'il's wet nurse, and hence the two boys grew up together. He got little schooling, spoke only Arabic, and rarely dealt with Europeans, yet he became one of Egypt's richest and most powerful officials. Starting as a local inspector for the khedivial estates under 'ABBAS HILMI I and SA'ID, he eventually became their inspector general. Upon his accession, Isma'il raised his salary and made him director general of all khedivial properties. Siddiq took on more responsibilities until he became in 1866 inspector general for all Egypt, the position that made him famous. In 1867 he joined the Regency Council that governed Egypt while Isma'il was visiting Paris; the next year he took charge of the Finance Department. He married a freed slave of

IBRAHIM, Isma'il's father, and his son later married an adopted daughter of the khedive. Although untrained in finance, Siddiq had a flexible mind that enabled him to adapt to new situations and to understand his patron's wishes. He became adept at bargaining with Egypt's creditors, devising new stratagems to collect taxes, and supervising provincial officials. He accumulated farm lands, Cairo palaces, and immense sums of money. Isma'il, despite his ties to Siddiq, watched him closely and grew increasingly suspicious about his fortune, gained mostly by graft and extortion. Dismissed from all his positions, Siddiq "vanished" suddenly in November 1876; in fact, he was being pursued by the new *Caisse de la Dette Publique*. Arrested by the khedive's Privy Council, he was tried, found guilty, and secretly murdered—allegedly by MUSTAFA FAHMI—although the government covered up his violent death. In a critical era of Egypt's history, he was an official with unparalleled power, immense wealth, strong patronage, few scruples, and no education.

Bibliographic Sources

Abu Lughod, "Transformation of the Egyptian Elite."

Ayyubi, *'Ahd al-Khidiwi Isma'il*, II, 263–266, 358–409.

de Leon, *Khedive's Egypt*, 183–198.

Farman, *Egypt and Its Betrayal*, 214–255.

Hunter, *Egypt Under the Khedives*, 144–153.

Nubar, *Mémoires de Nubar Pacha*, 471–474.

Rae, *Egypt Today*, 9–13, 16.

Sami, *Taqwim al-Nil*, III, iii, 1449–1455.

Wilson, C.R., *Chapters from My Official Life*.

Sidnawi, Salim

(1856–1908)

Department store entrepreneur. Born in Damascus to a financial agent, Salim got a rudimentary education at home and was apprenticed to a European tailor. He moved to Cairo in 1879, preceded by his younger brother, Sim'an, who had an aptitude for commerce, had worked for an uncle who was a silk merchant, and had built up a retail firm entrusted to him by another Syrian who died without issue. Living frugally in one room, the two bachelor brothers built up their clothing store by their industry, honesty, and knowledge of the European silk trade, moving from Hamzawi to the fashionable Muski district in 1885. Salim specialized in sales and accounts and Sim'an in their store's management. Once the store became Egypt's largest, they opened branches in Alexandria, Lyons, Paris, and Manchester. They also invested in land and buildings. They married in middle age and fathered sons who inherited the firm, which eventually set up branches throughout Egypt. Like Egypt's other department stores, Sidnawi's was nationalized in 1961, but unlike many others, it has managed to survive.

Bibliographic Sources
Fahmi, *Safwat al-'asr*, 720–723.
Harris, Murray, *Egypt Under the Egyptians*, 168.
al-Hilal 16:8 (May 1908): 471.
Mutran, *Salim Bey Sidnawi*.
Zakhura, *Mirat al-'asr*, II, 419–424.

Sidqi, 'Atif

(21 August 1930–)
Lawyer, professor, cabinet minister, and premier. 'Atif was born in Sanhara, near Tukh (Qalyubiyya); his father was a judicial chancellor and vice president of the Court of Cassation. He received his *license* from Cairo University's Faculty of Law in 1951 and a doctorate in finance and economics from the Sorbonne in 1958, after which he was a professor of general finance at Cairo University from 1958 to 1973. His book on Soviet taxation earned him a state prize in 1965. He served as cultural attaché in the Egyptian Embassy in Paris from 1973 to 1980 and was elected in 1974 to membership in UNESCO's board. From 1980 to 1985 he was president of the government's advisory council for economic and financial affairs (becoming a deputy premier in 1982), then briefly served as head of the government's auditing office, and then minister for international cooperation from 1987 to May 1991, when he became prime minister. Muslim extremists made an attempt on his life in November 1993. After he left the cabinet in January 1996 he supervised the national specialized councils. In 1970 and 1974 he received French decorations and in 1995 a state prize, the proceeds of which he donated to Cairo University.

Bibliographic Sources
al-Ahram Archives, file 15443.
al-Ahram al-iqtisadi, 1 Apr. 1993.
al-Anba, 27 Nov. 1993.

Najib, *A'lam Misr*, 286.
Ruz al-Yusuf, 18 Jan. 1993.
WWAW, 1997–1998, 626.

Sidqi, Dr. 'Aziz

(1 July 1920–)
Engineer, cabinet minister, and premier. A native of Cairo, he received his *license* in architecture from Cairo University's Engineering Faculty in 1944, his M.S. from the University of Oregon, and his Ph.D. in regional planning from Harvard University in 1946. He then worked as an instructor in the Faculty of Engineering at Alexandria University and as a technical adviser to the prime minister. In 1953 he became general director of the Liberation Province project. He served as minister of industry from 1956 to 1963, then deputy prime minister for industry and mineral wealth in 1964–1965, later becoming NASIR's adviser for production in 1966–1967, and finally minister of industry, petroleum, and mineral wealth from 1968 to 1971. He was also elected to the National Assembly in 1969. Under SADAT, he became a deputy prime minister in 1971 and prime minister in 1972–1973, giving way to Sadat just before the October War and becoming his special assistant. He represented Egypt at many international conferences on industrial affairs. He received Egyptian state decorations in 1982 and 1983.

Bibliographic Sources
al-Ahram Archives, file 20.
Egypt, Ministry of Information, *al-Mawsu'a al-qawmiyya*, I, 686–687.
Najib, *A'lam Misr*, 331.
WWAW, 1997–1998, 626.

Sidqi, Isma'il

(15 February 1875–9 July 1950)
Lawyer, cabinet minister, and twice premier. he was born in Alexandria, where his father, Ahmad Shukri, was undersecretary of interior and his mother was the daughter of SA'ID's *chef du cabinet*. Sidqi graduated from the Collège des Frères in 1889 and went on to the Khedivial Law School, where he worked with MUSTAFA KAMIL on *al-Madrasa* and with AHMAD LUTFI AL-SAYYID on *al-Tashri'*, Egypt's first law review. He advanced rapidly through the *Niyaba* and the judiciary, became administrative secretary to the

Alexandria municipality by passing a competitive examination, and served as agriculture minister from 1914 to 1917, when he resigned because of a compromising scandal.

A member of the original Wafd in 1918, he was interned in Malta with SA'D ZAGHLUL in March 1919. Sidqi later broke with Sa'd and helped to establish the Constitutional Liberal Party in 1922. He served as interior minister in 1924–1925, worked closely with King FUAD, and founded the Sha'b Party to support his campaign for prime minister under the 1930 Constitution. He headed a strong cabinet in 1930–1933, but Fuad's dismissal of him for being too powerful in his own right weakened Sidqi's influence and undermined the Sha'b Party. He served on the Egyptian delegation that negotiated the 1936 Anglo-Egyptian Treaty. He headed a second cabinet from February to December 1946, concluding the abortive Bevin-Sidqi Agreement, which he believed could have ensured Egypt's control over the Sudan. He returned to the Senate and openly opposed Egypt's entry into the Palestine War. One of the most personable and clever politicians of his era, Sidqi was loyal to the monarchy. Nevertheless, because of his frank criticism of King FARUQ's behavior, he did not receive the state funeral to which he was entitled as a holder of the Grand Cordon of MUHAMMAD 'ALI. Egyptian nationalists never forgave his attempt to supersede the 1923 Constitution to serve King Fuad and the British.

Bibliographic Sources

Amin, Mustafa, *Shakhsiyyat*, I, 62–78.
Badrawi, Malak, *Isma'il Sidqi*.
Deeb, *Party Politics*, 232–264 et passim.
EI2, IV, 198–199, article by Abbas Kelidar.
Mutawalli, "Shakhsiyyat rasmaliyya," 34–35.
Muti'i, *Haula al-rijal min Misr*, I, 78–92.
———, *Mawsu'a*, 89–98.
Qurra'ah, *Namir al-siyasah al-misriyah*.
Radi, *Sidqi wa al-Ikhwan wa Wafd al-Sudan*.
Sidqi, Isma'il, *Mudhakkirati*.
Wright, *Twentieth Century Impressions of Egypt*, 99.
Zirikli, *al-A'lam*, I, 315.

Siraj al-Din, [Muhammad] Fuad

(2 November 1910–)

Landowner, lawyer, and leader of the old and New Wafd Party. Fuad was born in Kafr al-Garayda (Gharbiyya); his father and grandfather were '*umda*s and landowners. His mother came from the Badrawi 'Ashur landowning family, into which Fuad later married. He received his *license* from Cairo University's Law School in 1931, worked in the *Niyaba* until his father died in 1934, and then went home to manage the family estates. He ran successfully in the 1936 parliamentary elections as a Wafdist, aided by MAKRAM 'UBAYD. He soon came to know NAHHAS and became a financial adviser to his young wife. When Nahhas returned to power in February 1942, he appointed Fuad, despite his youth, as agriculture minister. He remained loyal to Nahhas when Makram 'Ubayd broke with the Wafd, and Fuad became interior minister in 1943.

After the Wafd cabinet fell in 1944, Fuad went back to managing his estates and serving on several corporate boards, including the Egyptian Coca-Cola Company. Although he won a Senate seat in 1946, he strove to become his party's secretary-general, a post that he gained in 1948 and used to maneuver the left-wing Wafdists out of influential positions. In 1949 he joined SIRRI's coalition cabinet as communications minister. He campaigned in the general elections that led to the Wafd's return to power in 1950 and assumed the portfolio for interior, later adding those of finance and even, for a while, education. He and other members of his faction used their positions to engage in questionable business deals on the side. The aging Premier Nahhas became suspicious of Fuad, who also faced a rival clique loyal to AHMAD NAJIB AL-HILALI. He tried both to co-opt and to coerce the leftists and resisted attempts to limit maximum landholdings. The high-living Wafdists were also making their peace with King FARUQ, but rumors of manipulating the Alexandria cotton market, buying titles, and European sprees discredited both sides. In January 1952 he ordered a poorly armed police force in Ismailia to resist the British, leading to heavy casualties and the Cairo fire. The Wafd cabinet was dismissed the next day, and he was briefly detained for smuggling arms.

Abroad when the 1952 Revolution occurred, he hastened back, hoping to be appointed by the Free Officers, but he balked at their land reform program. Fuad resigned from the Wafd but was arrested twice and released each time. Tried for rigging the cotton market, granting favors to the king, inadequately planning the abrogation of the Anglo-Egyptian Treaty, and negligence during the burning of Cairo, he received a fifteen-year prison sentence. Quietly released later, he remained under house arrest. Not until 1975 was his family allowed to regain some of its confiscated lands. In 1977 he revived the Wafd Party as a vehicle for regaining power at the expense of SADAT, who promptly banned it. Although jailed on Sadat's orders in 1981, he managed to resume his political activities under MUBARAK. His New Wafd, allied with the Muslim Brothers, finished second to the National Democratic Party in the 1984 parliamentary elections. Fuad remains a prominent, albeit elderly, figure on the Egyptian political stage. He is sometimes called the Last of the Pashas.

Bibliographic Sources
Abou al-Kheir, "Dialogue Finally Begins."
'Awda, *al-Basha wa al-thawra.*
Deeb, "Continuity in Modern Egyptian History," 50–51.
Egypt, Ministry of Information, *al-Mawsu'a al-qawmiyya,* II, 1045–1046.
Ghiryani, *Fuad Siraj al-Din.*
'Isa, Salah, *Muhakamat Fuad Siraj al-Din.*
Kishk, Jalal, in *al-Hawadith,* no. 1074 (10 June 1977): 27–28; 1077 (1 July 1977): 24–26; 1107 (27 Jan. 1978): 31.
Kurum, *Radd 'ala Siraj al-Din.*
Reid, "Fuad Siraj al-Din and the Egyptian Wafd."
———, "Return of the Egyptian Wafd."
Siraj al-Din, *Limadha al-hizb al-jadid.*

Sirri, Husayn

(12 December 1892–15 December 1960)
Engineer, politician, and three-time premier. Born in Cairo, he was the son of ISMA'IL SIRRI, also an engineer and long-serving works minister. Husayn graduated from the Sa'idiyya School in 1910 and earned a diploma in engineering from London in 1915. On returning to Egypt, he worked for the Public Works Ministry's Irrigation Department and became an expert in that field, publishing treatises on the Nile defense works, irrigation, the Qattara Depression, water policy, and state finances. He first became public works minister in 1928. In 1937 he was appointed to the Senate and became undersecretary of state for public works. After the fall of the Wafd government, he became public works minister again, serving in three cabinets until 1939, when he assumed the portfolio for war and marine. He was minister of finance in 1939–1940,

of public works again in 1940, and of communications later in that year. After HASAN SABRI's sudden death, Sirri served as premier and interior minister from November 1940 to 1942 (also as foreign minister for part of that time), but resigned in 1942, in part because both the Wafd and the Palace were against him, before the 4 February incident. He went into business for several years and became a technical expert for the Suez Canal Company in 1948. He was again called on to serve as premier and interior and foreign minister in 1949–1950, until the Wafd Party returned to power. He then served as director of the royal cabinet but resigned after a year, intimating disapproval of some of King FARUQ's policies. He headed a short-lived cabinet, with portfolios for foreign affairs and war and marine, in July 1952, just before the Revolution. He was a nonpartisan engineer and administrator.

Bibliographic Sources
al-Ahram, 12 Jan. 1950.
———, 4 May 1973.
Najib, *A'lam Misr,* 187.

Sirri, Isma'il

(January 1860–22 January 1937)
Engineer, cabinet minister, and landowner. Of Hijazi (or Maghribi) background, he was born in Minya, educated at the Collège des Frères, and sent on an Egyptian government mission to France's École Central Polytechnique des Arts et Métiers, from which he received his *license* in 1883. His main interest was in river irrigation: he supervised the canalization and drainage of Upper Egypt and served on consultant panels for France on the Lower Rhone River and for Italy on the Po River irrigation schemes. In Egypt he began work as assistant engineer at the Delta Barrages, becoming subinspector in Minya in 1888, director of irrigation for Giza and part of Asyut and later in 1892 for Gharbiyya and Minufiyya provinces, and then supervised a large-scale irrigation project in his native Minya. He was public works minister for seventeen years in various Egyptian cabinets. He was also a member of the Egyptian Senate and was elected president of the Egyptian Scientific Society. He published several technical books and translated a European chemistry textbook into Arabic.

Bibliographic Sources
Bishri, 'Abd al-'Aziz, *Fi al-mirat*, 71–76.
Fuad, Faraj Sulayman, *al-Kanz al-thamin*, 87.
Mujahid, *al-A'lam al-sharqiyya*, I, 71–72.
Sihafi al-'Ajuz [Tawfiq Habib], in *al-Ahram*, 22 Jan. 1937; 3 Feb. 1937.
Taqwim "al-Hilal" 10 (1938), 26.
Wright, *Twentieth Century Impressions of Egypt*, 92.
Zaghlul and Sirri, *Hawla mashru'at al-rayy al-kubra.*
Zakhura, *Mirat al-'asr*, I, 289–292; II, 108–111.
Zirikli, *al-A'lam*, I, 314.

Sirri, Jadhibiyya Hasan

(1925–)
Painter, usually known as Gazbia Sirry. Born in Cairo, she graduated from the Higher Institute for Fine Arts in 1948. Her work ranges from large abstractions to modest depictions of popular life. Some of her paintings are exhibited at the Cairo Museum of Modern Art, the Science Museum, the Opera House, and al-Ahram's main building. She became a professor at Helwan University in 1970 and received a state prize in that year for her artistic achievements.

Bibliographic Sources
Iskandar, *Khamsun sana min al-fann*, 99–100.
Karnouk, *Contemporary Egyptian Art*, 23–26.
Najib, *A'lam Misr*, 155.
Saad El Din, *Gazbia Sirry.*
Said, *Contemporary Art in Egypt*, 78–79.
WWAW, 1997–1998, 630.

Stone, Charles Pomeroy

(20 September 1824–24 January 1887)
U.S. Army officer and leader of the first U.S. military mission to Egypt. Born in Greenfield, Massachusetts, Stone graduated in 1845 from the U.S. Military Academy at West Point and saw action in the Mexican War, serving under General Winfield Scott. After the war he took twenty months' leave to study armies in Europe, briefly visiting Egypt in 1850. He surveyed the Northwest Territories for the U.S. Army and then served the Mexican government as chief of the scientific commission for the State of Sonora. He rejoined the Union Army and in 1861 took charge of setting up the defenses for Washington, D.C., but an error of military judgment led to his arrest and detention, effectively ruining his career as a U.S. officer. In 1868 he was brought to Khedive ISMA'IL's attention by the khedive's American adviser, Thaddeus Mott, who knew General Sherman; the latter recommended Stone at the rank of brigadier general. Stone was appointed chief of staff, even though Egypt did not yet have a general staff, but he set up military schools for cavalry, artillery, and other branches of the army, as well as for the sons of officers and sergeants. To keep his American staff busy, he organized expeditions to explore the Red Sea coast, the Upper Nile, and much of what is now the Sudan, seeking sites for sources of fresh water, future forts, railroads, telegraph lines, and agriculture. When the financial stringencies of the Dual Financial Control led to severe cutbacks in the army, most Americans were discharged from Egyptian service, but Stone stayed on to serve TAWFIQ until he dissolved the Egyptian army following the 'URABI Revolution and the British occupation. Stone returned to the United States, where his last duty was to supervise the erection of the Statue of Liberty in New York harbor.

Bibliographic Sources
American National Biography, XX, 845–846.
Brinton, *American Effort in Egypt*, 98–100, 115–116.
Cox, "Egypt's First Military Rebellion."
Crabites, *Americans in the Egyptian Army.*
Hesseltine and Wolf, *Blue and Gray on the Nile.*
Idenogle, "The Khedive's Cartographers."
Lester, "Stone of Egypt."
Loring, *Confederate Soldier*, 350–362.
Suruji, *al-Jaysh al-misri.*
Zayn al-Din, Isma'il Muhammad, *al-Ajanib*, 72–74.

Sulayman, Mahmud

(1841–22 January 1929)
Nationalist leader. From a prominent Upper Egyptian landowning family of Hijazi origin, he was born in Sahil Salim (al-Badari district of Asyut province) and tutored at home and then at his maternal uncle's house in Cairo. He studied at al-Azhar until he returned at age twenty-two to his village to serve as its *'umda*. About 1868 he was named *nazir* (head) of Abu Tij and later promoted to deputy governor of Jirja and then of Asyut. Elected to the National Assembly during Khedive TAWFIQ's reign, he gave the speech

from the throne. A patriot whose opinions were heard and respected, he was named vice president of the Legislative Council in 1895. He became the first president of the Umma Party when it was founded in 1907 and coeditor of *al-Jarida* with AHMAD LUTFI AL-SAYYID. He was vice chairman of the Egyptian Congress chaired by RIYAD Pasha in response to the 1911 Coptic Congress. He supported SA'D ZAGHLUL in 1919 and copresided with him over the Wafd's Central Committee. He was the father of MUHAMMAD MAHMUD, who was interned with Sa'd on Malta. He endowed a mosque in his village and an industrial school in Abu Tij.

Bibliographic Sources
al-Ahram (23 Jan. 1929): 5.
Bishri, 'Abd al-'Aziz, "Yawmiyyat."
Fuad, Faraj Sulayman, *al-Kanz al-thamin*, 277–280.
Haykal, Muhammad Husayn, *Tarajim misriyya*, 181–187.
Hijazi, Anwar, *'Amaliqa*, 100–104.
al-Hilal 37:5 (Mar. 1929): 519, obituary.
Mujahid, *al-A'lam al-sharqiyya*, I, 168–169.
Walili, *Mafakhir al-ajyal*, 159–162.
Wright, *Twentieth Century Impressions of Egypt*, 384.
Zakhura, *Mirat al-'asr*, II, 153–154.

Sulayman Pasha. *See* SÈVE.

Sultan, Muhammad
(1825–August 1884)
Upper Egyptian landowner, local governor, National Assembly deputy, and speaker. Born in Zawiyat al-Amwat (Minya), although Sultan came from a well-established but impoverished family, he managed to become *shaykh al-balad* in his village and then *nazir* of the district of al-Qulusna. Hasan al-Shari'i, a large landowner, enabled him to meet and to entertain SA'ID on a trip to Upper Egypt. By March 1860 Sultan had become governor of Beni Suef, and three years later he was transferred to Asyut, where he helped to subdue a peasant uprising. Under ISMA'IL he became governor of Gharbiyya in 1864, then inspector of the viceroy's estates in December 1865, and seven months later deputy director of the Inspectorate for Upper Egypt. In this post he served directly under ISMA'IL SIDDIQ, the famous *Mufattish*, and amassed numerous estates in Upper Egypt,

mainly in Minya. His control over government posts and lands was so great that he was sometimes called King of Upper Egypt. He chaired the *Majlis Ahkam* in Khartum in 1872 and served as inspector of the khedivial properties in Minya in 1875–1876. Elected to the Chamber of Delegates in 1876, he presided over that body through the 'URABI Revolution, which he initially supported and later renounced. He also chaired the Legislative Council in 1883. He died of cancer in Cairo. He was the father of HUDA SHA'RAWI.

Bibliographic Sources
Fahmi, *Mudhakkirat*, I, 49–63.
al-Hilal 91:8 (June 1933): 1033–1038.
Hunter, *Egypt Under the Khedives*, 138–144.
———, "Muhammad Sultan Pasha.
Mujahid, *al-A'lam al-sharqiyya*, I, 161–162.
Rafi'i, 'Abd al-Rahman, *al-Thawra al-'urabiyya*, 199, 590–594.
Rifa'i, 'Abd al-'Aziz, *Muhammad Sultan amam al-tarikh*.
Sami, *Taqwim al-Nil*, III.
Schölch, *Egypt for the Egyptians!* 337.
Shaarawi, *Harem Years*, 27–32.
Taha, Samir Muhammad, *Muhammad Sultan*.
Taymur, Ahmad, *Tarajim*, 31–39.
al-Wafd, 20 Oct. 1988.
Walili, *Mafakhir al-ajyal*, 186.

Sumayka, Murqus
(1864–2 October 1944)
Archaeologist, art historian, and founder of the Coptic Museum. He was born to a Coptic notable family in Cairo. He began his career in the railway administration and served for many years in the General Assembly, Legislative Council, Legislative Assembly, the Higher Education Council, the Geographical Society, and on the Coptic Council (*Majlis Milli*). He was treasurer and president of the Coptic Girls College. He served from 1906 on the Committee for Arabic Monuments, heading its technical division from 1919 to 1939. Founder of the Coptic Museum in 1910, he wrote the *Short Guide to the Coptic Museum and the Principal Churches of Cairo*, published in 1937, a guide to its collection of Coptic and Arabic manuscripts, and also memoirs that have not been published. He died in Alexandria.

Bibliographic Sources
al-Ahram (3 Oct. 1944): 4; (20 Feb. 1947).
CE, VI, 1700, article by Mirrit Boutros Ghali.

Ghali, Mirrit Boutros, "Marcus Simaika Pacha."
Habib, *Abu Jilda*, 38.
Mujahid, *al-A'lam al-sharqiyya*, II, 952–953.
Najib, *A'lam Misr*, 467.
QTQ, 214–215.
Reid, "Archaeology, Social Reform, and Modern Identity."
Zirikli, *al-A'lam*, VII, 204.

al-Sumbati, Riyad

(30 November 1906–9 September 1981)
Singer, *'ud* player, and composer. Born in Sumbat, near Damietta, and the son of a professional singer from Mansura, he was taught to accompany his father on the *'ud*. He knew UMM KULTHUM as a child (their fathers were acquainted with each other). After getting some training in Mansura, he taught music in schools there for a time. He moved to Cairo in 1927 and first studied and then taught at the Institute of Arab Music beginning in 1933. One of his pupils there was FARID AL-ATRASH. Sumbati sang at the inauguration of Egyptian state broadcasting in 1934. He turned to composition, wrote an operetta, *Arus al-sharq* [The Bride of the East], and coauthored an opera, *Semiramis*. He then devoted his time to writing music for poetic odes and composed many of the long odes and songs that were sung by Umm Kulthum. Sumbati produced one film, *Habib qalbi* [Darling of My Heart], in 1952. There are a few songs that he himself sang, such as *Rabbi subhanik* [My Lord Is Your Prayer] and *'Ala 'udi* [On My Lute]. He reportedly wrote more than 500 songs during his career. He headed the Society of Song Writers and Composers in 1961. Immensely popular, he received a state prize in 1961, an honorary doctorate from the Academy of the Arts, and a prize from UNESCO in 1977.

Bibliographic Sources
al-Ahram Archives, file 3267.
Amin, Mustafa, *Shakhsiyyat*, II, 333–347.
al-Anba, 12–15 Jan 1990; 19 Nov. 1995.
Butrus, *A'lam al-musiqa*, 230–232.
Danielson, *Voice of Egypt*, 114–117.
al-Ittihad al-fanni, 12 Oct. 1992.
al-Kawakib, 11 Sept. 1981.
Mallakh, Kamal, in *al-Ahram*, 10 Sept. 1981.
al-Musawwar, 18 Sept. 1981.
al-Nahar, 9 Sept. 1984.
Sabri, 'Abd al-Qadir, *Amir al-naghm Riyad al-Sumbati*.
al-Siyasa, 30 Nov.–6 Dec. 1991.
Uktubir, no. 1092 (28 Sept. 1997): 58–60.
Zaki, 'Abd al-Hamid Tawfiq, *A'lam al-musiqa*, 93–97.

T

al-Jumhuriyya, 11 Nov. 1959; 20 Nov. 1968.
Jundi, *A'lam al-adab,* II, 481–483.
Kahhala, *Mu'jam,* VII, 238–239.
al-Kitab 9:1 (Jan. 1950): 3–4, obituary
Malaika, Nazik, *Muhadarat fi shi'r 'Ali Mahmud Taha.*
Mandur, Muhammad, in *al-Thaqafa* 11:570 (28 Nov. 1949): 7.
New York Times (18 Nov. 1949): 29.
Qadi, Shukri, *Khamsun shakhsiyya,* 187–190.
Ramadi, *Min a'lam al-adab,* 243–250.
Rifa'i, Muhammad 'Ali, in *al-Sha'b,* 9 Dec. 1958.
Saharti, Mustafa 'Abd al-Latif, *al-Shi'r al-mu'asir,* 99–203, 210–211.
Sayyid-Ahmad, al-Sayyid Taqi al-Din, *'Ali Mahmud Taha.*
Zahlawi, *Udaba mu'asirun,* 152–157.
Zayyat, *Wahy "al-Risala,"* III, 188–192, 323–326.
Zirikli, *al-A'lam,* V, 21.

Taha, 'Ali Mahmud

(1901–17 November 1949)

Romantic poet. Born in Mansura to fairly wealthy parents of partially Arab descent, he graduated from the College of Applied Sciences in 1924 with a diploma in architecture. He later served in a succession of government engineering posts, moving to Cairo around 1930 and rising to the position of deputy director of Dar al-Kutub in 1949. He began publishing his poetry in *al-Sufur* in 1918 and produced translations of a number of French and English poems. Among the reasons for his fame was the poem *al-Jundul* [The Gondola], set to music and sung by MUHAMMAD 'ABD AL-WAHHAB. His best-known *diwan, al-Mallah al-taih* [The Lost Sailor], was published in 1934. He traveled to various European countries both before and after World War II and based some of his poems on his observations, notably *Buhayrat Como* [Lake Como]. An advocate for Arab nationalism, he influenced poets from other Arab countries.

Bibliographic Sources
'Abidin, *Bayn sha'irayn mujaddidayn.*
Allen, *Modern Arabic Literature,* 309–313.
Badawi, M.M., *Critical Introduction,* 137–145.
Becka, *DOL,* III, 179–180.
Brockelmann, *GAL,* S III, 169.
Brugman, *Introduction,* 173–181.
Daghir, *Masadir,* II, i, 565–568.
Dayf, *al-Adab al-'arabi,* 161–168.
———, *Dirasat,* 136–153.
EAL, II, 752.
Faris, Bishr, in *al-Balagh,* 10 May 1940; 17 June 1940.
Halwaji, 'Abd al-Sattar, *'Ali Mahmud Taha.*
Jawdat, "Sahib al-Jundul fi wataniyyatihi."
Jayyusi, *Trends,* II, 397–410.

al-Tahtawi, Shaykh Rifa'a Rafi'

(1801–27 May 1873)

Writer and educational reformer. Originally from Tahta, where he was born to an Upper Egyptian family of impoverished ulama that descended from the Prophet. Tahtawi was educated at al-Azhar and in Paris, where he was sent as the imam for the first student mission in 1826. His observations there were published as *Takhlis al-ibriz fi talkhis Bariz* [Refinement of Pure Gold in the Summary of Paris]. Back in Egypt Tahtawi became a translator for the School of Medicine in 1832 and for the Gunnery School on 1833. In 1835 he was named director of the new School of Languages. In 1841 he became the editor of *al-Waqai' al-misriyya* and the director of MUHAMMAD 'ALI's translation bureau, which translated mainly scientific and practical books from French to Arabic, until it was closed in 1849. Exiled to the Sudan under 'ABBAS I, he became director of an Egyptian primary school in Khartum, where he translated Fenelon's *Télémaque.* Under SA'ID he headed the European section of the Cairo governorate and then became deputy director of the Military Academy. Tahtawi directed the revived translation bureau under ISMA'IL from 1863 to 1873 and worked to expand the Bulaq Press. He wrote several original works, including two volumes of a projected complete history of Egypt, a book on education entitled *al-Murshid al-amin fi tarbiyat al-banat wa al-banin* [The Honest Guide for Training Girls and Boys], and a guide for Egypt's political and social development called *Manahij al-albab al-misriyya fi mabahij al-adab al-ʿasriyya* [Courses for Egyptian Minds in the Joys of Contemporary Manners]. This work advocated benevolent autocracy, bounded by the Shariʿa but modified to meet the needs of the modern world, stressing agricultural development, the education of girls as well as boys, and the development of a national community (*watan*, or "homeland"). Tahtawi's ideas promoted the growth of Egyptian nationalism and the adaptation of European social concepts to Islam. In 1870 he became editor of Egypt's first education journal, *Rawdat al-madaris*. Showered in his last years with titles and gifts, he died in Cairo, a relatively wealthy man.

Bibliographic Sources

Abdel-Malek, *Arab Political Thought*, 27–30.
ʿAbduh, Ibrahim, *Aʿlam al-sihafa*, 28–35.
———, *Tarikh "al-Waqʿi al-Misriyya,"* 34–35.
———, *Tatawwur al-sihafa al-misriyya*, 33–34, 51–52, 56–57.
Abu Hamdan, *Rifaʿa Rafiʿ al-Tahtawi*.
Abu Lughod, *Arab Rediscovery of Europe*, 50–53, 88–96, 115–120, 137–140.
Ahmed, J.M., *Intellectual Origins*, 10–15.
Amin, Ahmad, *Fayd al-khatir*, V, 69–113.
Ampère, *Voyage en Égypte*.
ʿAshur, Nuʿman, *Butulat misriyya*, 45–56.
———, *Suwar min al-butula wa al-abtal*, 29–36.
ʿAwad, Louis, in *al-Ahram*, 16, 23 Feb. 1968; 15 Mar. 1968.
Badawi, Ahmad Ahmad, *Rifaʿa al-Tahtawi*.
Brockelmann, *GAL*, II, 481; S II, 731–732.
Brugman, *Introduction*, 18–25.
Carra da Vaux, *Penseurs*, V, 235–244.
Cheikho, *al-Adab al-ʿarabiyya*, II, 8–11.
Choueiri, *Arab History and the Nation-State*.
Cole, "Rifaʿa al-Tahtawi."
Crabbs, *Writing of History*, 67–86.
Daghir, *Masadir*, II, i, 569–573.
Delanoue, *Moralistes*, II, 384–487.
EAL, II, 753–754.
EI1, III, 1235–1236.
EI2, VIII, 525–526, article by K. Öhrnberg.
EMME, IV, 1725–1727, article by Abdel Aziz EzzelArab.
Fikri, ʿAli, *Subul al-najah*, II, 177–182.
Gran, *Islamic Roots*, 97, 161–163.
Hamid, *Japanese and the Egyptian Enlightenment*.
Hamza, *Adab al-maqala*, I, 103–157.
Hasan, Muhammad ʿAbd al-Ghani, and ʿAbd al-ʿAziz Disuqi, *"Rawdat al-Madaris,"* 324–328.
Heyworth-Dunne, J., "Rifaʿa Badawi Rafiʿ al-Tahtawi."
Hijazi, Anwar, *ʿAmaliqa*, 77–81.
Hijazi, Muhammad Fahmi, *Usul al-fikr al-ʿarabi*.

al-Hilal 3:12 (15 Feb. 1895): 441–446.
Hourani, *Arabic Thought*, 67–83, 144, 294.
Husry, *Origins*.
———, *Three Reformers*, 11–31.
ʿImara, *Rifaʿa al-Tahtawi*.
ʿInani, Muhammad, in *al-Katib* 181 (1 Apr. 1976): 36–49.
Jindi, Anwar, *Aʿlam wa ashab aqlam*, 161–169.
———, *al-Muhafaza wa al-tajdid*, 18–29.
Jomard, "L'École Égyptienne de Paris."
Jundi, *Aʿlam al-adab*, II, 425.
Kahhala, *Muʿjam*, IV, 168–169.
al-Katib, no. 148 (July 1973): 82–92.
Lewis, *Muslim Discovery of Europe*, 133, 219–220, 281–282.
Livingston, "Western Science and Educational Reform."
Louca, in *Connaissance de l'étranger*, ed. Peyre, 286–291.
———, in *al-Majalla* 5:53 (May 1961): 40–50.
———, "Les Parisiens dans le Miroir de Rifaʿa."
———, *Voyageurs*, 55–74.
Majdi, Salih, *Hilyat al-zaman*.
Mardam, *Aʿyan al-qarn al-thalith ʿashr*, 223–227.
Mubarak, ʿAli, *Khitat*, XIII, 53–60.
Mutiʿi, *Haula al-rijal min al-Azhar*, 81–96.
———, *Mawsuʿa*, 157–163.
Naddaf, "Rifaʿah al-Tahtawi and the West."
Najjar, *Rifaʿa al-Tahtawi*.
Nusseibeh, *Ideas of Arab Nationalism*.
Qadi, Shukri, *Khamsun shakhsiyya*, 253–257.
Rachad, "Rifaa Rafée el Tahtaoui."
Radwan, Fathi, *Dawr al-ʿamaim*, 27–45.
Rafiʿi, ʿAbd al-Rahman, *ʿAsr Muhammad ʿAli*, 498–543.
———, *Shuʿara al-wataniyya* (1954), 7–12.
Ramadi, *Adab wa tarab*, 82–101.
Rizq, Fathi, *Khamsa wa sabʿuna najman*, 17–26.
Saʿid, Rifʿat, in *al-Katib* 8 (1968): 100–107.
Sami, *al-Taʿlim fi Misr*.
———, *Taqwim al-Nil*, III, i, 38, 50.
Sandubi, *Aʿyan al-bayan*, 90–98.
Sayyid-Ahmad, Ahmad Ahmad, *Rifaʿa Rafiʿ al-Tahtawi*.
Shamis, *ʿUzama*, 53–60.
Shaybub, Siddiq, *Shakhsiyyat ʿarabiyya*, 7–47.
Shayyal, *Rifaʿa al-Tahtawi*.
———, *al-Tarikh wa al-muarrikhun*, 49–83.
Stowasser, *Ein Muslim entdeckt Europa*.
Tahtawi, *Petit aperçu historique*.
Tajir, *Harakat al-tarjama*, 32, 52–56.
Tarrazi, *Tarikh al-sihafa*, I, 92–96.
Tusun, *al-Baʿthat al-ʿilmiyya*, 46.
UAR, *Mahrajan Rifaʿa Rafiʿ al-Tahtawi*.
Vial, "Precursor du feminisme en Egypte."
Walili, *Mafakhir al-ajyal*, 37–39.
Wielandt, *Das Bild der Europäer*, 24–28.
Yarid [Yared], *Arab Travellers and Western Civilization*.

Yusuf, Mahmud, in *al-Hilal* 81:6 (July 1973): 56–61.

Zaydan, Jurji, *Mashahir al-sharq* (1st ed.), II, 18–23.

———, *Tarikh adab al-lugha*, IV, 296–297.

Zaydan, Yusuf, *Rifa'a Rafi' al-Tahtawi.*

Zirikli, *al-A'lam*, III, 29.

Zolondek, "al-Tahtawi and Political Freedom."

Taqla, Bishara

(22 August 1852–15 June 1901)

Lebanese journalist and cofounder of *al-Ahram.* Born in Kafr Shima to a Greek Catholic family, he was educated in his village school and at the National School in Beirut, where one of his teachers was Butrus al-Bustani, and at the Patriarchal School. In partnership with his brother, SALIM, he founded *al-Ahram* in 1875 in Alexandria, first as a weekly, later as a daily, newspaper. They tried to back Khedive ISMA'IL, RIYAD, SHARIF, and the 'URABI movement, but did not always succeed in warding off harm, as the 'Urabists destroyed their press in Alexandria. The Taqla brothers escaped to Syria at the height of the 'Urabi Revolution, then returned after the British occupation, which they supported at first. Protected by France, they favored its interests and maintained closer ties to the Ottoman Empire than their rival, *al-Muqattam.* After his brother died, Bishara became the sole owner, moved the newspaper to Cairo in 1898, and continued to expand its format and circulation as long as he lived.

Bibliographic Sources

'Abduh, *A'lam al-sihafa*, 107–115.

Barakat, Daud, "Ma 'araftuhu 'an Madam Taqla Basha."

Broadley, *How We Defended Arabi*, 334.

Cheikho, *al-Adab al-'arabiyya*, II, 151.

———, *Tarikh al-adab al-'arabiyya*, 20–21.

EMME, IV, 1741, article by As'ad AbuKhalil.

Hartmann, *Arabic Press of Egypt*, 10–11.

al-Hilal 9:8 (15 June 1901): 521–524.

Mutran, *Bishara Taqla Basha.*

Ninet, *Arabi Pacha*, 82–84.

Schölch, *Egypt for the Egyptians!* 334.

Tagher, "La naissance du *al-Ahram.*"

Tarrazi, *Tarikh al-sihafa*, III, 50–51.

Zakhura, *Mirat al-'asr*, I, 544–549; II, 425.

———, *al-Suriyyun fi Misr*, 153–163.

Zirikli, *al-A'lam*, II, 52.

Zolondek, "*al-Ahram* and Westernization."

Taqla, Salim

(1849–11 August 1892)

Lebanese cofounder of *al-Ahram.* He was born in Kafr Shima (in what is now Lebanon) to a Greek Catholic family known as Bani Bardawil. Educated in his native village and in the National School in Beirut, he taught Arabic for a while at the Patriarchal School there and wrote a textbook for his pupils. He went to Alexandria in 1874 and got a license to start *al-Ahram* as a weekly newspaper. As interested in writing poetry as in putting out a newspaper, he soon sought his brother's aid in publishing *al-Ahram*, whose presses were destroyed during the 'URABI Revolution. After briefly fleeing to Syria, he returned to Egypt and resumed publishing the paper. He became ill and went back to Lebanon, dying in Bayt Mari.

Bibliographic Sources

'Abduh, Ibrahim, *A'lam al-sihafa*, 107–115.

———, *Tarikh jaridat "al-Ahram."*

Abu Hadid, *'Isamiyyun*, 83–88.

al-Ahram, 6 Feb. 1965.

'Amiri, *Nuzhat al-albab*, 212–213.

Broadley, *How We Defended Arabi*, 334.

Cheikho, *al-Adab al-'arabiyya*, II, 149–151.

Daghir, *Masadir*, II, i, 220–221.

EMME, IV, 1742, article by As'ad AbuKhalil.

al-Hilal 1:1 (1 Sept. 1892): 19–20, obituary.

——— 4:3 (1 Oct. 1895): 82–85.

Kahhala, *Mu'jam*, IV, 244–245.

Ma'luf, *Dawani al-qatuf fi sirat Bani Ma'luf*, 401.

Ninet, *Arabi Pacha*, 82–84.

Schölch, *Egypt for the Egyptians!* 335.

Zakhura, *Mirat al-'asr*, I, 544–549.

———, *al-Suriyyun fi Misr*, 178–184.

Zaydan, Jurji, *Mashahir al-sharq*, II, 1st ed., 99–101; 2nd ed., 104–106.

Zirikli, *al-A'lam*, III, 117.

Tawfiq, Muhammad

(30 April 1852–7 January 1892)

Khedive of Egypt from 1879 to 1892. Eldest son of Khedive ISMA'IL by a palace concubine, Tawfiq was born and reared in Cairo, studying in Manyal and then at the Tajhiziyya School. Unlike most members of his dynasty, he never studied outside Egypt. Starting at age nineteen, he held various administrative posts under his father: president of his privy council, director of the interior and of public works, and head of the cabinet in 1879. Pressured by Egypt's European creditors, the Ottoman sultan named Tawfiq to succeed his father in June 1879. The new khedive tried to placate the Europeans, exiling JAMAL AL-DIN AL-AFGHANI and imposing the financial stringencies demanded by Egypt's creditors. These measures alienated many army officers and civil officials, leading to mutinies against War Minister RIFQI in February 1881 and Premier RIYAD in September of that year. Historians disagree on whether Tawfiq himself encouraged the rebels; it is certain, though, that by 1882 'Urabists had taken over the cabinet and were plotting to depose him. Following the Alexandria riots in June 1882, when Britain threatened to bombard the port's fortifications, Tawfiq turned against his Egyptian cabinet, the British invaded, and 'URABI was defeated.

For the rest of his life Tawfiq claimed that he owed his throne to the British intervention, which led to the dismissal of his cabinet, the dissolution of the army, and British control over Egypt. He accordingly heeded the "advice" offered him by Britain's diplomatic representatives in Cairo, Sir EDWARD MALET and Sir Evelyn Baring (Lord CROMER). The Egyptian army, rebuilt by the British, failed to quell the Mahdist revolt in 1884–1885, costing Egypt the Sudan. Among the reforms instituted during Tawfiq's reign were the reorganization of the National Courts, the formation of the Legislative Council and General Assembly under the 1883 Organic Law, various irrigation projects, restoration of mosques and other religious buildings, and reform of the benevolent *awqaf*. He died unexpectedly in Helwan. Although reputedly devoted to the people's welfare and genuinely mourned at the time because he died young, Egyptians now recall him as a weak viceroy who acquiesced in the British occupation of their country and its loss of the Sudan.

Bibliographic Sources
'Aqqad, in *al-Hilal* 60:10 (Oct. 1952): 5–8.
Asaf, *Dalil*, 172–189.
Bell, *Khedives and Pashas*, 27–53.
Blunt, *Gordon at Khartoum*.
Butler, *Court Life*.
Cromer, *Modern Egypt*, II, 327–333.
Dicey, *Story of the Khedivate*, 227–231, 445–456.
Durri [al-Hakim], *al-Nukhba al-durriyya*, 38–45.
Fahmi, Zaki, *Safwat al-'asr*, 56–69.
Farman, *Egypt and Its Betrayal*, 262–273.
Fuad, Faraj Sulayman, *al-Kanz al-thamin*, 59–67.
Loring, *Confederate Soldier*, 183–192.
Miéville, *Under Queen and Khedive*, 142–144, 235–239.
Milner, *England in Egypt* (1920), 133–136.
Mujahid, *al-A'lam al-sharqiyya*, I, 39–40.
al-Muqtataf 16:5 (Feb. 1892): 289–292, obituary.
New York Times (8 Jan. 1892): 8.
Plauchot, *L'Égypte et l'occupation anglaise*, 51–59.
Rafi'i, 'Abd al-Rahman, *al-Thawra al-'urabiyya*.
Sayyid, Afaf Lutfi, *Egypt and Cromer*, 68–69.
Tanahi, Tahir, *'Ala firash al-mawt*, 37–45.
Tugay, *Three Centuries*, 146–151.
Zakhura, *Mirat al-'asr*, I, 38–42.
Zand, *Muhammad Tawfiq*.
Zaydan, Jurji, *Mashahir al-sharq*, I, 1st ed., 46–48; 2nd ed., 48.
Zirikli, *al-A'lam*, VI, 65–66.

al-Tawil, Shaykh Hasan

(1834–3 July 1899)

Maliki legal expert. He was born in Minyat Shahala (Minufiyya) and was educated in Tanta and at al-Azhar. He became a military instructor under SA'ID, a proofreader for the War Ministry's printing office, and inspector for the Education Ministry. However, he was imprisoned on suspicion of practicing witchcraft. After his release he was appointed to teach philosophy at the newly opened Dar al-'Ulum. He openly backed the Mahdi's revolt in the Sudan, antagonizing the British. Faithful to the ideas of Ibn Taymiyya, Tawil opposed innovation in Islam. One of his disciples was AHMAD TAYMUR.

Bibliographic Sources
Daghir, *Masadir*, II, i, 582–583.
Fikri, 'Ali, *Subul al-najah*, II, 83–87.
al-Hilal 7:20 (15 July 1899): 629.
Kahhala, *Mu'jam*, III, 202.
al-Manar 2:17 (7 July 1899): 269–270.
Mujahid, *al-A'lam al-sharqiyya*, II, 295.
Taymur, Ahmad, *A'lam al-fikr al-islami*, 93–101.
———, in *al-Hilal* 41:10 (Aug. 1933): 1353–1357.
———, *Tarajim*, 120–129.
Zirikli, *al-A'lam*, II, 183.

Taymur, Ahmad

(6 November 1871–26 April 1930)

Writer and scholar. Ahmad was born in Cairo to a wealthy family of Kurdish origin; his grandfather was an Ottoman officer who had accompanied MUHAMMAD 'ALI to Egypt in 1801, and his father was the head of his European chancery. Because Ahmad lost both his parents at an early age, he was reared by his literary elder sister,

'AISHA AL-TAYMURIYYA, who made sure that he learned French, Turkish, and Persian as well as Arabic. Tutored at home, he became a dedicated Arabic scholar. He accumulated a large library and hosted a literary salon attended by many men of letters. He also encouraged the literary activities of his sister and of his sons, MUHAMMAD and MAHMUD. He was a member of *al-Majma' al-'Ilmi al-'Arabi* (Arab Scholarly Society). Upon his death, he bequeathed his collection of more than 4,000 books and manuscripts to Dar al-Kutub. Modest and retiring, he wrote some scholarly works that were published in his lifetime and many others that appeared posthumously.

Bibliographic Sources

'Abd al-Latif, Muhammad Fahmi, in *al-Risala*, no. 60 (27 Aug. 1934): 1424–1427.
Bayyumi, Muhammad Rajab, "Ahmad Taymur."
Brockelmann, *GAL*, S III, 217 n.
Daghir, *Masadir*, II, i, 231–235.
EAL, II, 761.
Gottheil, "Ahmad Taimur Pasha."
Hasan, Muhammad 'Abd al-Ghani, introduction to *A'lam al-fikr al-islami*, 1–10.
Hijazi, Anwar, *'Amaliqa*, 206–210.
al-Hilal 24:8 (May 1916): 687, bibliography.
——— 38:8 (June 1930): 903, obituary.
Husayn, Taha, introduction to *Awham shu'ara al-'arab*, by Ahmad Taymur.
Jindi, Anwar, *A'lam wa ashab aqlam*, 17–24.
———, *Qissat Mahmud Taymur*.
Jundi, *A'lam al-adab*, 461–462.
Kahhala, *Mu'jam*, I, 166–167.
Kurd 'Ali, Muhammad, in *MMIA* 11 (1931): 129–147.
———, *Mu'asirun*, 37–47.
———, in *al-Muqtataf* 64 (1924): 502–504.
al-Manar 30:10 (28 May 1930): 784–790.
MMIA 4 (1924): 240; 8 (1928): 363–366, article by 'Isa Iskandar Ma'luf; 20 (1940): 26, 63.
Mujahid, *al-A'lam al-sharqiyya*, II, 838–841.
Rifa'i, Muhammad 'Ali, in *al-Muqtataf* 80:3 (Mar. 1932): 342–345.
Salama, Ibrahim, introduction to *al-Barqiyyat*, by Ahmad Taymur.
Schacht, "Ahmad Pascha Taymur, ein Nachruf."
Schaede, "Ahmad Taymur Pasa."
Taqwim "al-Hilal" (1930), 61.
Tawfiq, Najib, *Ashhar al-usrat*, 48–53.
Taymur, Ahmad, *Dhikra Ahmad Taymur*.
———, *Tarajim*, 157–163.
———, *Tarikh al-usra al-taymuriyya*, 89–92.
Zakhura, *Mirat al-'asr*, II, 329–331.
Zaki, Muhammad Amin, *Mashahir al-Kurd wa Kurdistan*, I.
Zaydan, Jurji, *Tarikh adab al-lugha*, IV, 111–112, his library.
Zirikli, *al-A'lam*, I, 100.
———, in *al-Muqtataf* 77 (1930): 129–132.

Taymur, Mahmud
(16 June 1894–25 August 1973)

Writer of novels, short stories, plays, and critical essays. Born in Darb al-Sa'ada, Cairo, he was a son of AHMAD TAYMUR and the younger brother of MUHAMMAD, who influenced him as a boy, as did the literary pursuits of his father and his aunt, 'AISHA AL-TAYMURIYYA. The children put out a domestic newspaper and built a theater in their home. They were much influenced by AL-MANFALUTI and Khalil Jibran. Mahmud studied at al-Nasiriyya Elementary and Ilhamiyya Secondary School and in Switzerland, where he went for his health. He also spent six months at the Agriculture School but withdrew due to illness. Although he sometimes held government jobs (e.g., a clerkship in the Justice Ministry in 1927), he was independently wealthy and could devote most of his life to literature. Muhammad initiated him to the theater, where their teachers were AL-MUWAYLIHI and HAYKAL. Mahmud's first stage experience was with ZAKI TULAYMAT. He tried to reproduce popular dialogue, hence his initial preference for colloquial Arabic. His earliest stories, published in 1919, were written in the Egyptian dialect, but he later changed to classical Arabic. His first anthology of short stories came out in 1925; others soon followed. He visited France and Switzerland for the first time in 1925, gained exposure to foreign theaters, and came to know Russian literature. In later years he began to write novels, starting with *Nida al-majhul* [Appeal of the Unknown], published in 1939. In addition, he wrote critical essays, travel books, and collective biographies, but critics have stressed his ability to depict Egyptian popular life in his fiction. He was invited to conferences in Beirut, the University of Peshawar, and Damascus. In 1947 he was awarded the first prize for fiction by the Arabic Language Academy, of which he became a member in 1950. He gave guest lectures at al-Azhar and various Egyptian universities and taught part-time at the Cinema Institute. He edited *Majallat al-qissa* in 1962 and became a member of the Supreme Council for the Arts, Letters, and Social Sciences in 1965.

Among his translated work is *Hakamat al-Mahkama* [The Court Ruled], which appears in Mahmoud Manzalawi's *Arabic Writing Today: Drama*. He received the Fuad I Literature Prize in 1950, the Wacyf Ghali Franco-Egyptian Prize and the Cedars of Lebanon Medal in 1951, and state prizes in 1962 and 1963. He was honored by Moscow's School of Oriental Studies in 1962. He died in Lausanne while on vacation. Both the Egyptian government and the Alexandria branch of *Nadi al-Qissa* (the Short Story Club, which he helped found) now award prizes in his name for young writers.

Bibliographic Sources
'Abd al-Ghani, Ahmad Zaki, "Mahmud Taymur."
'Abd al-Hayy, *Asir hayati*, 135–142.
Abdel-Magued, *Modern Arabic Short Story*.
Abu Salim, *Mahmud Taymur*.
Acta Orientalia Belgica/Correspondance d'Orient, no. 10 (1966): 137–154.
al-Ahram, 26 Aug. 1973; 23 Aug. 1996.
al-Ahram Archives, file 986.
'Allam, *Majma'iyyun*, 333–337.
Allen, *Modern Arabic Literature*, 317–323.
Badawi, M.M., *Modern Arabic Drama*, 88–111.
Badr, *Tatawwur al-riwaya al-'arabiyya*.
Becka, *DOL*, III, 183–184.
Brockelmann, *GAL*, S III, 218–226, 255–256.
Brugman, *Introduction*, 254–263.
Chakroun, "Les frères Taymour."
Dayf, *al-Adab al-'arabi*, 299–307.
Drozdik, "La conception linguistique de Mahmud Taymur."
EAL, II, 761–762.
EI2, VI, 75–77, article by C. Vial.
Fawzi, Husayn, in *al-Ahram* (31 Aug. 1973): 5.
Fuad, Ni'mat Ahmad, *Qimam adabiyya*, 389–414.
Gabrieli, "La Napoli di Mahmud Taymur."
———, "L'opera letteraria di Mahmud Taimur."
———, "Uno scritto di Mahmud Taimur."
Hafez, Sabry, "Modern Arabic Short Story," *CHAL*, 282–285, 293–294.
Hafiz, Ahmad, *Ayyam min shababihim*, 39–44.
Hakim, Nazih, *Mahmud Taymur: raid al-qissa al-'arabiyya*.
al-Hayat, 28 Aug. 1973; 6 Sept. 1996.
Ibn al-Sharif, *Adab Mahmud Taymur*.
Ibyari, *'Alam Taymur al-qasasi*.
———, *Fann al-qissa 'inda Mahmud Taymur*.
———, *Mahmud Taymur*.
Jindi, Anwar, *Qissat Mahmud Taymur*.
Landau, *Studies in the Arabic Theatre*, 149–153.
MMIA 2 (1922): 206.
Nasr, Muhammad, *Safahat min hayatihum*, 208–214.
Peled, *al-Aqsusa al-taymuriyya fi marhalatayn*.
Pérès, "Le roman dans la littérature arabe moderne."
Ramadi, *Min a'lam al-adab*, 150–160.
Schoonover, "Mahmud Taymur."
Tawfiq, Najib, *Ashhar al-usrat*, 75–86.
Taymur, Ahmad, *Tarikh al-usra al-taymuriyya*, 103–114.
Tewfiq, *Nouvelles/Mahmoud Teymour*.
Vásquez, *El Cairo de Mahmud Taymur*.
Vial, "L'étude du roman et de la nouvelle en Égypte."
Widmer, "Mahmud Taymur."
Wielandt, *Frühwerk Mahmud Taymurs*.
Zirikli, *al-A'lam*, VII, 165.

Taymur, Muhammad
(1892–24 February 1921)
Writer, poet, and playwright. Born to a wealthy and educated family living in Darb al-Sa'ada in Cairo, he began writing poetry at age ten and started a family newspaper with his brother, MAHMUD. They also wrote and performed plays at home modeled on those of SALAMA HIJAZI. Sent to study medicine in Berlin, he left after three months to study law in Paris and Lyons. Equally uninterested in law and preferring to read French literature, he did not return to France when World War I broke out but studied agriculture for a while in Cairo. He also began to publish poetry in *al-Sufur*, campaigned for the opening of the National Theater, and even acted in a play before becoming a court chamberlain to HUSAYN KAMIL. After the sultan's death, he resigned from his post and promptly returned to the stage. His acting career ended when he got married, but he continued to write plays and short stories. His plays were mainly in Egyptian colloquial Arabic; his short stories contained realistic depictions of popular life but were written in simplified standard Arabic, often dominated by dialogue, and are considered among the pioneering Egyptian works in this genre. He also wrote some essays that were published posthumously. A great admirer of Guy de Maupassant, he passed on his enthusiasm and many of his literary ideas to his younger brother, Mahmud. He died in Cairo.

Bibliographic Sources
al-Ahram (28 Feb. 1921): 3.
'Ashur, Nu'man, *Butulat misriyya*, 201–223.
Badawi, M.M., "Arabic Drama: Early Developments," *CHAL*, 349–353.
Brockelmann, *GAL*, S III, 217–218, 271–273.

Brugman, *Introduction*, 244–246.
Daghir, *Masadir*, II, i, 236–237.
EAL, II, 762–763.
Fuad, Ni'mat Ahmad, *Qimam adabiyya*, 392ff.
Hall, *Egypt in Silhouette*, 238–243.
Hijazi, Anwar, *'Amaliqa*, 316–321.
Jindi, Anwar, *A'lam lam yunsifhum jiluhum*, 29–31.
Kahhala, *Mu'jam*, VIII, 233–234.
Khidr, *Muhammad Taymur.*
Landau, *Studies in the Arab Theatre*, 147–148.
Maghribi, 'Abd al-Qadir, in *MMIA* 3 (1923): 284.
MMIA 8 (1928): 320.
Mujahid, *al-A'lam al-sharqiyya*, II, 773.
Tawfiq, Najib, *Ashhar al-usrat*, 75–86.
Taymur, Ahmad, *Tarikh al-usra al-Taymuriyya*, 95–102.
Taymur, Mahmud, introduction to *Muallifat Muhammad Taymur.*
———, *Marathi al-Marhum Muhammad Taymur.*
———, *Ma tarahu al-u'yun*, 8–13.
———, *al-Shakhsiyyat al-'ishrun*, 153–162.
Tulaymat, introduction to *Hayatuna al-tamthiliyya.*
———, in *al-Risala* 8:349 (11 Mar. 1940): 455–457.
Wahid, *Masrah Muhammad Taymur.*
Zirikli, *al-A'lam*, VI, 22.

al-Taymuriyya, 'Aisha

(November 1840–26 May 1902)

Pioneer woman poet, writer, and feminist. Born in Bab al-Khalq, Cairo, she was the daughter of Isma'il Taymur, a Turkish-born official in MUHAMMAD 'ALI's European chancery, and an upper-class Circassian woman who tried to quash 'Aisha's literary leanings. Tutored at home, she learned the Quran, Arabic and Persian rhetoric, and composition, becoming an avid reader of the books in her father's library, while defying her mother's efforts to teach her sewing and embroidery. Her knowledge of Arabic, Turkish, and Persian enabled her to write poetry in all three languages. Her marriage in 1854 to Muhammad Tawfiq al-Islambuli, a second cousin, obliged her to move to Istanbul and to suspend her literary pursuits, although one of their daughters, Tawhida, who shared her mother's love of poetry, relieved her of some of her housekeeping duties and gladdened her life for a time. After her husband and daughter died, however, she returned around 1875 to her brother AHMAD's palace in Cairo and received instruction in poetic composition from two women tutors. Some of her poems were of the erotic type known as *ghazal*, shocking to some

but probably a reason for their popularity. The publication of her poems was delayed by the death of her daughter and the inflammation of her eyes resulting from weeping for seven years. The first to call for equality between men and women, 'Aisha corresponded with a number of women intellectuals in her later years and inspired the early growth of Egyptian feminism.

Bibliographic Sources
'Abbud, Marun, *Ruwwad al-nahda*, 175–176.
'Abd al-Halim, *Nisa*, 97–106.
'Abd al-Rahman, 'Aisha, introduction to *Hilyat al-tiraz.*
'Amiri, *Nuzhat al-albab*, 186–187.
'Aqqad, 'Abbas Mahmud, *Shu'ara Misr*, 149–154.
Badran, *Feminists*, 14–15.
Badran and Cooke, *Opening the Gates*, 125–133.
Booth, "Biography and Feminist Rhetoric."
Brockelman, *GAL*, S II, 724; S III, 174.
Daghir, *Masadir*, II, i, 238–240.
EAL, II, 763.
Fahmi, Mansur, *Mayy Ziyada wa raidat al-adab.*
Fawwaz, *al-Durr al-manthur*, 303.
Hatem, "Aisha Taymur's Tears."
al-Hilal 10:17 (1 June 1902): 544–546.
'Ibada, "'Aisha al-Taymuriyya."
Jindi, Anwar, *Adwa*, 195–196.
Jundi, *A'lam al-adab*, II, 525–528.
Kahhala, *A'lam al-nisa*, II, 908–925.
———, *Mu'jam*, V, 55–56.
Kilani, Muhammad Sayyid, in *al-Risala* 19:949 (10 Sept. 1951): 1026–1028, 1059–1060.
Mahmud, Muhammad, *al-Shi'r al-nisai*, 11–18.
Maskuni, *Min 'abqariyyat nisa*, 26–124.
Muhammad, Fathiyya, *Balaghat al-nisa*, I, 86–114.
al-Muqtataf 27:7 (July 1902): 605, 692–696.
——— 63:3 (Sept. 1923): 242–248.
Qallini, *Sha'irat 'arabiyyat*, 9–34.
Rafful, *al-Tariq ila al-i'rab.*
Rafi'i, 'Abd al-Rahman, *'Asr Isma'il*, I, 257–258.
Sabri, Muhammad, *Shu'ara al-'asr*, I, 173–178.
Tawfiq, Najib, *Ashhar al-usrat*, 54–62.
Taymur, Ahmad, *Tarikh al-usra al-Taymuriyya*, 85–89.
Taymur, Mahmud, *al-Shakhsiyyat al-'ishrun*, 163–167.
'Aisha 'Abd al-Rahman, introduction to *Hilyat al-tiraz*, 3–31.
Zaki, Muhammad Amin, *Mashahir al-Kurd*, II, 239–244.
Zaydan, Jurji, *Tarikh adab al-lugha*, IV, 224.
Zeidan, *Arab Women Novelists*, 59–63.
Zirikli, *al-A'lam*, III, 240.
Ziyada, Mayy, *'Aisha Taymur.*
———, in *al-Muqtataf* 62:2 (Feb. 1923): 154–159; 3 (Mar.) 251–259; 5 (May): 463–468; 6 (June): 561–570; 64:1 (Jan. 1924): 9–18; 2 (Feb.):

121–128; 3 (Mar.): 281–288; 66:1 (Jan. 1925): 59–66; 2 (Feb.): 158–164; 3 (Mar.): 281–287; 4 (Apr.): 408–414; 68:1 (Jan. 1926): 35–39.

Thabit, Karim

(1902–13 March 1964)

Journalist and King FARUQ's adviser. The son of a *Muqattam* editor of Lebanese origin, Karim was born and educated in Cairo. After he graduated from the American University in 1925, he worked as a translator for several foreign embassies. He was a reporter for *al-Siyasa, al-'Alam,* and then *al-Dunya,* of which he became the editor when it merged with *al-Hilal.* During World War II he worked for *al-Muqattam,* becoming its editor-in-chief in 1946. Meeting Faruq in that year, he soon became his press adviser and public spokesman. A flatterer who wrote what people paid him to write and told people what they wanted to hear, he became the leading figure in the clique surrounding the king. He is popularly thought to have influenced Faruq's decision to enter the 1948 Palestine War as a means of reviving his popularity. Thabit wrote various biographies, including one of SA'D ZAGHLUL, and a history of the MUHAMMAD 'ALI dynasty. Although he resigned from the Palace in October 1951, he was tried for corruption by the Revolutionary Court in 1953, convicted and sentenced to hard labor for life, but was set free because of his health in 1960. His memoirs were serialized in several popular dailies, but he is remembered as a sycophant who helped to corrupt the king.

Bibliographic Sources
al-Ahram (6 Oct. 1951); (14 March 1964): 1; (20 March 1964).
al-Ahram Archives, file 10659.
al-Ahram al-masai, 24 Mar. 1993.
Akhir sa'a (26 Jan. 1949): 39.
Mahmud, Hafiz, in al-Jumhuriyya, 30 Sept. 1968.
McBride, Farouk, 140, 185–187.
McLeave, Last Pharaoh, 113–114.
al-Misri, Oct. 1952, memoirs.
Zakhura, al-Suriyyun fi Misr, 405–406.
Zirikli, al-A'lam, V, 224–225.

Thabit, Dr. Mahjub

(1884–21 May 1945)

Physician, writer, and labor organizer. He was born in Dongola (Sudan), where his father was an engineer. The family moved to Cairo in the year of his birth. Trained as a medical doctor, he made many speeches during the 1919 Revolution and was exiled with SA'D ZAGHLUL. Later he was elected to the Egyptian Parliament, where he advocated the introduction of military training in the schools and supported the organization of labor unions. He also was appointed professor of Legal Medicine at Cairo University and was among its leading doctors. Passionately devoted to the welfare of both the Sudan and Egypt, he was widely respected as a genuine nationalist. He died in Cairo.

Bibliographic Sources
al-Ahram (22 May 1945): 4.
Bishri, 'Abd al-'Aziz, Fi al-mirat, 43–54.
al-Ithnayn, 28 May 1945.
Jindi, Anwar, A'lam wa ashab aqlam, 342–351.
Kahhala, Mu'jam, VIII, 180.
Kurd 'Ali, Mu'asirun, 329–333.
al-Misri, 25 May 1945.
al-Muqattam, 24 May 1945.
Ramadi, Sihafat al-fukaha, 76–78.
Sudani, al-Asrar al-siyasiyya, 18–242.
Zirikli, al-A'lam, V, 283–284.

Thabit, Munira

(1906?–September 1967)

Pioneer woman journalist. She was the daughter of an employee in the Interior Ministry and of an educated Turco-Egyptian woman. When the first Parliament was elected under the 1923 Constitution, she confronted SA'D ZAGHLUL directly with her demands for legal equality between men and women. In 1925 she was the first Egyptian woman to enroll in the French Law School in Cairo, completing her legal training in Paris and becoming the first Egyptian woman to earn a *license en droit* and to argue before the Mixed Courts. Faced with insuperable barriers because of her sex, however, she turned to journalism. She founded the magazine *l'Espoir* in 1925. Aided by veteran journalist 'ABD AL-QADIR HAMZA, she founded *al-Amal* in 1926 as the first Wafdist women's periodical. She and Hamza fell in love and married, but their marriage foundered when he asked her to give up her journalistic career (or, some say, because he already had a wife). Consequently *l'Espoir* folded and *al-Amal* could come out only irregularly. At this point, ANTUN JUMAYYIL invited her to write a regular column for *al-Ahram*, which she kept up until his death in 1948, campaigning for women's suffrage and other rights. She was able to persuade the Education Ministry to stop requiring women teachers to resign once they married. She was also the first to call for a journalists' syndicate and club. She was also an early Arab nationalist, taking part in the Eastern Women's Congress in 1938, writing a "Red Book" in response to Britain's White Paper on Palestine, and representing Egyptian and Palestinian women at the 1939 Copenhagen feminist conference. She wrote a series of articles assailing the 1946 Bevin-SIDQI talks, as well as the 1936 Anglo-Egyptian Treaty. She volunteered for civil defense duty during the Suez War and ran, unsuccessfully, for Parliament in 1957. Poor health marred her later years, and she died in obscurity.

Bibliographic Sources
'Abd al-Halim, *Nisa*, 33–40.
al-Ahram Archives, file 5807.
Amin, Mustafa, "Shakhsiyat la tunsa."
Badran, *Feminists*, 153.
Jundi, *A'lam al-adab*, 533.
Mahmud, Hafiz, in *al-Jumhuriyya*, 16 Sept. 1967, 25 Nov. 1968.
Najib, *A'lam Misr*, 480.
Thabit, Munira, *Mudhikkirat fi 'ishrin 'am*.
al-Watan, 24 Feb. 1998.

Tharwat, 'Abd al-Khaliq
(1873–22 September 1928)
Judge, cabinet minister, and twice premier. Of Turco-Egyptian extraction, he attended the Abdin Elementary School, the Higher Teachers College, and the government Law School, where he was one of the founders of Egypt's first law review. Tharwat worked for the State Domains (*Daira Saniyya*) administration after his graduation, then for the Justice Ministry. He was deputy chairman of Qina's National Court and then became director of administration for the National Courts as a whole. In 1907 he served briefly as chancellor of the National Court of Appeals, then became governor of Asyut province (1907–1908), head of the *Niyaba* (1908–1914), minister of justice (1914–1919), interior (1921, 1922, and 1927–1928), and foreign affairs (1922 and 1926–1927), deputy premier, and prime minister from 1922 to 1923 and from 1927 to 1928, when he retired due to the

onset of diabetes. Elected to the Chamber of Deputies in 1924, he was appointed to the Senate in 1925. He served on the boards of the Islamic Benevolent Society and the Egyptian University until his death and was respected by his colleagues, foreign and Egyptian, for his legal expertise. Although he strove for Egypt's independence, he worked with the Palace and the British. Some Wafdists accused him of corruption and resented his opposition. He died suddenly in Paris.

Bibliographic Sources
Bishri, 'Abd al-'Aziz, *Fi al-mirat*, 31–37.
Crabites, "Abdel Khalek Saroit Pasha."
Fuad, Faraj Sulayman, *al-Kanz al-thamin*, 131.
Grafftey-Smith, *Bright Levant*, 105–106.
Hijazi, Anwar, *'Amaliqa*, 216–223.
Husayn, Taha, "Tharwat wa *al-Shi'r al-jahili*."
Maliji, *'Abd al-Khaliq Tharwat*.
Mujahid, *al-A'lam al-sharqiyya*, I, 94–95.
Musa, Salama, "al-'Uzama al-khamsa fi Misr al-yawm," 651–652.
Rafi'i, 'Abd al-Rahman, *Fi a'qab al-thawra*, I, 63–70, 270.
Sayyid-Marsot, *Egypt's Liberal Experiment*, 62–64, 99–103.
Siba'i, *Abtal Misr*.
Sudani, *al-Asrar al-siyasiyya*, 285–286.
Times (London) (24 Sept. 1928): 21c; (28 Sept. 1928): 19a.
Walili, *Mafakhir al-ajyal*, 157–158.
Zakhura, *Mirat al-'asr*, II, 80.
Zirikli, *al-A'lam*, III, 291.

al-Tilmisani, 'Umar
(4 November 1904–22 May 1986)
Supreme guide of the revived Society of Muslim Brothers and editor of its weekly, *al-Da'wa*. Born in Cairo's Darb al-Ahmar quarter to a family of Algerian descent, 'Umar attended the *kuttab* of Nawa (Qalyubiyya) and the Islamic Benevolent Society Elementary School. He completed secondary school in 1924 and graduated from Cairo University Law School in 1931. Then a Wafdist, he joined the Muslim Brothers two years later. He took a position at the Finance Ministry in 1933, moving to the *Niyaba* in 1936. He refused the offer of a judgeship in order not to compromise his integrity, due to his work as a Brother.

He was one of the Brothers jailed following the abortive attempt on NASIR's life in 1954, serving a fifteen-year term, which was renewed briefly in 1969. After SADAT let the society resume its activities, Tilmisani succeeded HU-DAYBI as supreme guide in 1973. He revived the publication of *al-Da'wa* in 1976; in it he inveighed against secularism and the power of the Jews, even ascribing Atatürk's reforms to his alleged Jewish background, and against "Crusaders," meaning both the Christian West and Egypt's Copts. He blamed the riots in al-Zawiya al-Hamra on a "Crusader conspiracy" against Islam. He was one of the 1,600 political and religious leaders jailed by Sadat in September 1981 but was freed by MUBARAK two months later. He never secured permission to resume issuing *al-Da'wa*, nor could he persuade the government to legalize the society, despite his claim that 75 percent of all Egyptians want to live under Islamic law. He called for the gradual application of the Shari'a to Egypt's laws, but opposed violence and terrorism. He died in a Cairo hospital of kidney and liver failure, and his funeral at the 'Umar Makram Mosque drew 5,000 mourners.

Bibliographic Sources
al-Ahram, 23 May 1986.
al-Ahram Archives, file 37203.
al-Ahrar, 18 Mar. 1985.
Akhir sa'a, 15 Jan. 1986; 28 May 1986.
Hawadith 'arabiyya, 30 May 1986, 25–29.
Jawhari, 'Abd al-Rahim, 'Umar al-Tilmisani mujahidan.
Kepel, Muslim Extremism, 105–106, 124–128.
New York Times (24 May 1986): 28.
al-Siyasiyya, 24 May 1996.
Tilmisani, Dhikrayat la mudhakkirat.

Tulaymat, Zaki
(29 April 1895–22 December 1982)
Playwright, drama teacher, and educational administrator. Born in Cairo, he graduated from the Khedivial Secondary School and studied for three years at the Higher Teachers College but left three months before he would have received his diploma. He worked at the Cairo Zoo from 1921 to 1924. He also acted in several troupes: Hawat, then 'Abd al-Rahim Rushdi, and finally that of JURJ ABYAD. Sent on an educational mission to Paris to study theater at the Comédie Française, he received a diploma in stage production and direction in 1929. From 1937 to 1952 he supervised drama education in the Egyptian schools. He began managing the Na-

tional Theater in 1942 and two years later became dean of the reopened Higher Institute of Drama, serving until 1952. Having received a Tunisian decoration in 1950, four years later he became technical director of the Folkloric Troupe in Tunis and in 1960–1963 and 1966–1968 the director of the Kuwaiti national troupe. He wrote Egypt's first folkloric opera, *Ya layl ya 'ayn* [O Night, O My Eye], in 1957. Among the works that he translated was *The Barber of Seville*. In 1975 he received an Egyptian state merit award and an honorary doctorate from the Academy of Fine Arts. After his death in Ma'adi, his daughter endowed an annual prize in his memory to the top graduate of the Higher Institute of Drama.

Bibliographic Sources
al-Ahram, 23 Dec. 1982.
al-Ahram Archives, file 3066.
al-Akhbar, 25 Dec. 1982.
Akhir sa'a, 23 June 1982.
al-Anba, 31 Mar. 1996.
Brockelmann, GAL, S III, 274.
Fawzi, Mufid, "Akhir hiwar ma'a Zaki Tulaymat."
Nasr, Muhammad, Safahat min hayatihim, 106–114.
Ruz al-Yusuf (27 Dec. 1982): 12–13; (3 Jan. 1983): 48–55; (9 Feb. 1976): 22–26.
Taymur, Mahmud, al-Shakhsiyyat al-'ishrun, 122–132.
Tulaymat, Dhikrayat wa wujuh.
———, "Drama in Egypt."

al-Tunisi, Mahmud Bayram
(4 March 1893–5 January 1961)
Poet. Born in the Anfushi district of Alexandria, where his father was a silk merchant in the Maghribi market, al-Tunisi's original name was Mahmud Muhammad Mustafa Bayram. He was educated at al-Rashad Elementary School. Exiled from Egypt in 1920 for his involvement in the 1919 Revolution and his attacks on the monarchy, he spent some time in Paris, worked in Tunisia from 1932 to 1937, then went to Syria, but later came to Port Sa'id and began writing for *Ruz al-Yusuf* (and other Egyptian papers) in 1939. He was known especially for his *zajal*, often satirizing political figures, which appealed to Egyptians of all classes. He wrote an operetta based on *Madame Butterfly*. He received the State Prize in Arts and Letters in 1961, at the time of his final illness, and UMM

KULTHUM sang for him. He wrote Ramadan poems until six hours before he died in Alexandria. His *Mudhakkirat fi al-manfa* [Memoirs from Exile] was published after his death; he remains a popular hero in Egypt.

Bibliographic Sources
'Abd al-Hayy, *'Asir hayati*, 186–193.
Ahmad, Ahmad Yusuf, *Mahmud Bayram al-Tunisi*.
al-Ahram, 16 Feb. 1965; 12 Aug. 1975.
al-Ahram Archives, file 821.
al-Ahram al-masa'i, 30 Mar. 1996.
Akhar sa'a, 11 Jan 1961; 2 June 1965; 30 June 1965.
'Ashur, Nu'man, in *al-Jumhuriyya*, 11 July 1961.
'Awadayn, "Bayram al-Tunisi."
Banna, Muhammad Kamil, *Bayram al-Tunisi kama 'araftuh*.
———, *Mahmud Bayram al-Tunisi*.
Booth, *Bayram al-Tunisi's Egypt*.
EAL, II, 784–785.
al-Hilal 61:9 (Sept. 1953): 67–68.
——— 93:5 (May 1984), special issue.
——— 104:3 (Mar. 1996).
Jabiri, *Mahmud Bayram al-Tunisi*.
al-Jumhuriyya (6 Jan. 1961): 1; (18 Sept. 1962); (11 Mar. 1965); (3 Mar. 1971); (1 Apr. 1971).
al-Kawakib, 17 Jan. 1961; 6 Apr. 1965; 20 July 1965; 4 Jan. 1966.
Majed, *La presse littéraire en Tunisie*.
al-Masa, 12 Jan. 1962, article by Ahmad Yusuf; 20 Jan. 1965; 17 Jan. 1966.
al-Musawwar, 16 Jan. 1959; 12 Jan. 1961.
Qabbani, *Mahmud Bayram al-Tunisi*.
Ruz al-Yusuf, 27 Feb. 1961.
Sa'd, Kamal, in *Akhar sa'a*, 18 Oct 1961; 25 Oct, 1961; 1 Nov. 1961; 8 Nov. 1961.
Salih, Rushdi, in *Hawwa*, 14 Jan. 1961.
———, in *al-Jumhuriyya*, 21 Mar. 1961; 22 June 1961.
Zirikli, *al-A'lam*, VII, 186.

al-Turk, Niqula Yusuf

(1763–1828)
Scholar, historian, and poet. Born in Dayr al-Qamar (now in Lebanon) to a Greek Catholic family, Niqula (like his father) served the Bashir al-Shihabi family before he accompanied NAPOLEON's expedition to Egypt, about which he wrote a mainly favorable account, *Tamalluk jumhir al-Fransawiyya al-aqtar al-misriyya wa al-bilad al-shamiyya*, which was later translated into French by Desgranges as *Histoire de l'expédition des français en Égypte* and published in 1839. He also wrote an unpublished biography of Ahmad Jazzar

and a history of Mount Lebanon (both listed among the manuscripts in al-Zahiriyya Library in Damascus) and published memoirs and a *diwan* of his poetry. His memoirs were translated into French by Gaston Wiet and published as *Chronique d'Egypte, 1798–1804*. Blind in his old age, he died in Dayr al-Qamar.

Bibliographic Sources
'Abbud, Marun, *Ruwwad al-nahda*, 50–54.
Brockelmann, *GAL*, II, 647; S II, 770.
BIE 6 (1924): 145–146.
Bustani, Fuad Ifram, *Muqaddimat diwan Niqula al-Turk*.
Cheikho, *al-Adab al-'arabiyya*, I, 22–24, 40–44.
Crabbs, *Writing of History*, 59–61.
Daghir, *Masadir*, II, i, 217–219.
Dibs, *Tarikh Suriyya*, VIII, 697.
EAL, II, 786.
Haddad, George M., "Historical Work of Niqula al-Turk."
Hasan, Muhammad 'Abd al-Ghani, *Tarajim 'arabiyya*, 59–76.
Kahhala, *Mu'jam*, XIII, 118.
Makhtutat al-Zahiriyya, 143.
Mardam, *A'yan al-qarn al-thalith 'ashr*, 154–155.
Nasr, Nasim, in *al-Adib* 20:7 (July 1961): 26–27.
Pérès, "L'Institut d'Égypte et l'oeuvre de Bonaparte."
Philipp, "Class, Community, and Arab Historiography."
Shayyal, *al-Tarikh wa al-muarrikhun*, 37–39.
Zaydan, Jurji, *Tarikh adab al-lugha*, IV, 204.
Zirikli, *al-A'lam*, VIII, 47.

Tusun, 'Umar

(8 September 1872–26 January 1944)
Prince, scholar, and philanthropic landowner. Born in Alexandria, he was educated in Switzerland and excelled in sports and hunting during his youth. He knew Arabic, Turkish, French, and English; wrote numerous books and articles on Egypt's history; and backed the nationalist movement materially and morally. When the Italians invaded Tripolitania in 1911, Tusun was among the first to organize help for the Ottoman defenders. Some sources credit him with initiating the Wafd in 1918. He belonged to the Arabic Language Academies of Cairo and Damascus and to the Geographical Society. He served as president of the Alexandria Museum and the Society of Coptic Archaeology. In 1935 he and the Coptic patriarch cochaired the committee to support Ethiopia against the Italian invasion. He

was one of the most popular members of the royal family, partly because of his generosity to many villagers, and partly because of his scholarship and his nationalism. A large funeral followed his death in Alexandria.

Bibliographic Sources
CE, VI, 1841, article by Mirrit Boutros Ghali.
Coles, *Recollections and Reflections*, 43, 160.
Daghir, *Masadir*, II, i, 574–577.
Dhikra al-maghfur lahu al-Amir 'Umar Tusun.
Fahmi, Qallini, *al-Amir 'Umar Tusun.*
Fahmi, Zaki, *Safwat al-'asr*, 72–75.
Ghali, Mirrit Butros, in *Bulletin de la Société d'Archéologie Copte* 10 (1944): v–vi.
Kahhala, *Mu'jam*, VII, 311.
Khanki, 'Aziz, in *al-Akhbar*, 18 Nov. 1954.

Kurd 'Ali, Muhammad, in *al-Balagh*, 26 Jan. 1944.
——, in *MMIA* 7 (1927): 231.
——, *Mu'asirun*, 285–289.
MMIA 17 (1937): 555.
—— 19 (1939): 161–167; 471, autobiography.
Mujahid, *al-A'lam al-sharqiyya*, I, 45–47.
al-Muqtataf 104:3 (Mar. 1944): 223–228.
Rafi'i, 'Abd al-Rahman, *Mudhakkirati,* 78–82.
Tanahi, Tahir, in *al-Hilal* 38:9 (July 1930): 1034–1038.
Thabit, Karim, "Ziyara li al-Amir 'Umar Tusun."
Times (London) (27 Jan. 1944): 7d.
Tugay, *Three Centuries*, 102–103.
Wiet, Gaston, in *BIE* 26 (1944): 1–19.
Zakhura, *Mirat al-'asr*, I, 51–52; II, 60–61.
Zayyat, Ahmad Hasan, in *al-Risala* 12:552 (31 Jan. 1944): 101–102.
Zirikli, *al-A'lam*, V, 48.

U

'Ubayd, William Makram
(25 October 1889–5 June 1961)
Coptic politician, longtime secretary-general of the Wafd Party, and finance minister, sometimes called the Golden Knight of National Unity. Born in Qina to a family originally from Asyut, his father, a contractor, extended the railway from Naj' Hammadi to Luxor, enabling him to buy land from the royal estates, of which Makram would inherit some 150 *feddans*. He attended the American College in Asyut, Tawfiqiyya Secondary School in Cairo, and New College, Oxford, where he read law, graduating in 1908. He then spent two years studying Egyptology in France and entered the University of Lyons, hoping to work for a doctorate in laws. He returned to Egypt and worked for the Justice Ministry from 1913 to 1918 but resigned due to political differences with WILLIAM BRUNYATE, the British adviser. He married the daughter of MURQUS HANNA, an early National Party supporter. After World War I, Makram joined the Wafd, was imprisoned several times, and became the political "son" of SA'D ZAGHLUL, a lifelong association. Soon after Sa'd died in 1927, Makram became the Wafd's secretary-general. He represented Qina in every Parliament in which the Wafd won a majority in free elections and served as communications minister briefly in 1928 and as finance minister in the Wafdist cabinets of 1930, 1936–1937, and 1942. Ever more aghast at the Wafd's corruption and possibly encouraged by King FARUQ, he left the government in 1942 and then published the *Black Book*, attacking the party's leader, MUSTAFA AL-NAHHAS. Makram founded a rival party called the Wafdist Bloc and later served in several coalition governments from which the Wafd was excluded. Politically inactive after the 1952 Revolution, he died of a liver ailment at his home in Manshiat al-Bakri. Some of his speeches and writings were collected posthumously and published in 1990 as *Kalimat wa mawaqif* [Words and Positions]. He also had written a pamphlet in English denouncing the MILNER mission.

Bibliographic Sources
Abaza, Fikri, in *al-Hilal* 45:8 (June 1937): 850–853.
Abu al-Majd, "Qissat al-khilaf."
al-Ahram, 6 June 1961.
al-Ahram Archives, file 400.
Bishri, Tariq, *al-Muslimun wa al-Aqbat.*
Bowie, "The Copts, the Wafd, and Religious Issues," 114–118.
Carter, *Copts.*
CE, V, 1515–1516, article by Mustafa al-Fiqi.
Coury, "Arab Nationalism of Makram 'Ubayd."
Deeb, *Party Politics*, 109 n, et passim.
al-Duha (Mar. 1984): 14–17.
Fiqi, Mustafa, "Makram Ebeid," 22–24.
———, *Makram 'Ubayd.*
Mahna, *Makram 'Ubayd.*
Mayu, 19 Apr.–3 May 1989.
al-Musawwar (8 Nov. 1940): 14; (16 June 1961); (23 June 1989).
Muti'i, *Mawsu'a*, 625–631.
New York Times (7 June 1961): 38.
QTQ, 219–220.
Reid, "National Bar Association," 630–631.
Ramadan, 'Abd al-'Azim, in *al-Jumhuriyya*, 22 Feb. 1977.
Rizq, Yunan Labib, *al-Wafd wa "al-Kitab al-Aswad."*
Shukri, Ghali, in *al-Ahram*, 27 Feb. 1991.
Tadrus, *al-Aqbat*, III, 39–454; IV, 129–134.
Terry, *The Wafd*, 253–258.
Times (London) (7 June 1961): 15a.
'Ubayd, Muna Makram, *Makram 'Ubayd, 1889–1989.*
'Ubayd, William Makram, *Makramiyyat.*
———, "al-Siyasa 'allamatni."
Watani, 11 June 1961; 25 June 1961.

'Ukasha, Dr. Tharwat
(18 February 1921–)
Army officer, culture minister, and writer on art history and music. Born in Cairo, he entered the Military Academy soon after it was open to

young men of modest means and graduated in 1939, also completing advanced study at the Staff College in 1948. In 1951 he earned a doctorate in literature from the Sorbonne and in 1960 a diploma in journalism from Cairo University's Arts Faculty. He fought in the Palestine War and helped plan the 1952 Revolution. He was military attaché in Egypt's Embassies at Bern, Paris, and Madrid between 1953 and 1956 and ambassador to Italy in 1957–1958 before being appointed minister of culture and national guidance. His ministerial achievements included reorganizing the Conservatoire and other higher institutes for the arts, ordering the construction of SAYYID DARWISH Hall and the preservation of that national composer's work, opening a palace of culture in each of Egypt's governorates, and organizing the campaign to save the ancient monuments of Philae and Abu Simbel. He also served several terms on the Supreme Council for Arts and Letters. He left the Culture Ministry for four years to serve as administrative director of the National Bank of Egypt, also becoming a member of the National Assembly in 1964–1966. He took the post of deputy premier in 1966, resumed his culture portfolio in 1967, and was assistant to the president for cultural affairs in 1970–1972. A visiting professor at the Collège de France in 1973, he was elected to corresponding membership in the Royal Academy in 1975 and to membership on the cultural advisory board for the Institut du Monde Arabe in 1990. He has written numerous books on the history of music and especially of art, ranging from ancient Egypt to the Baroque period. His prizes include an armed forces award in 1950, UNESCO silver and gold medals, the French Legion d'Honneur in 1968, the French medal for arts and letters, and an Egyptian achievement award in 1987.

Bibliographic Sources
al-Ahram Archives, file 978.
al-Akhbar, 12 Dec. 1964.
'Awad, Louis, in *al-Ahram*, 25 Feb. 1972.
Najib, *A'lam Misr*, 151.
Sabah, *Mawsu'at Tharwat 'Ukasha.*
Sabah al-khayr, 10 July 1997.
Sa'd al-Din, Mursi, in *al-Ahram*, 27 Dec. 1997.
'Ukasha, *Mudhakkirati.*

'Ulaysh. See 'ILLAYSH.

Umm Kulthum
(4 May 1904?–3 February 1975)

The most famous and popular female vocalist in the Arab world, often called *Kawkab al-Sharq* (Star of the East). Named Fatima Ibrahim al-Baltaji at her birth in Tammay, a Daqahliyya village near Simbalawin, she was the daughter of a local shaykh who called villagers to prayer, led Friday worship, and recited the Quran at *mawlid*s (birthdays of revered Muslims) and other religious occasions. He soon recognized her exceptional musical gifts and brought her with him (dressed as a boy) to sing at *mawlid*s and concerts. She began singing in Cairo in 1920. Eventually her talents came to the attention of the best-known musicians of the day, and she broadened her repertoire and began singing in Cairo cabarets. Because entertainers were still not respected by many Egyptians, her father continued to chaperone her, but she increasingly became her own business manager, and by the late 1920s she was earning large royalties for her recorded songs, both religious and popular. She learned to sing secular as well as religious poems, some of which were written especially for her by well-known writers. She sang regularly on the first Thursday of each month at a small theater near the Ezbekiyya Gardens and later at Cinema Radio. She was invited to sing at the weddings of many notables, at the behest of King FARUQ, later under the patronage of NASIR's government, and at JIHAN SADAT's invitation. She received awards and decorations from Egypt and most of the other Arab countries. Umm Kulthum's funeral drew a large popular turnout, close to the record numbers that had followed Nasir's procession. Her singing did much to raise the status and fame of female entertainers in the Arab world; her songs remain popular.

Bibliographic Sources
'Abd al-'Al, *Umm Kulthum.*
'Abd al-Hakim, *Nisa*, 115–123.
Amin, Mustafa, *Shakhsiyyat*, I, 190–207 et passim.
'Awad, Mahmud, *Umm Kulthum.*
Butrus, *A'lam al-musiqa*, 242–247.
Danielson, *Voice of Egypt.*
EAL, II, 795.
Fuad, Ni'mat Ahmad, *Umm Kulthum.*
Hafiz, Ahmad, *Ayyam min shababihim*, 171–178.
Hammond, "Still Crazy After All These Years."
Kenny, Dallas, "The Magic of Om Kalthoum."
Khatib, Adnan, *Umm Kulthum.*
Mahallawi, *Sayyidatan min Misr.*

Mustafa, Zaki, *Umm Kulthum: ma'bad al-hubb.*
New York Times, 4 Feb. 1975; 6 Feb. 1975.
Rahma, *Kawkab al-sharq Umm Kulthum.*
Ramadi, *Adab wa tarab,* 220–224.
Rami, "Umm Kulthum."
Saiah, *Oum Kalsoum, l' étoile de l' Orient.*
Shusha, *Umm Kulthum.*
Umm Kulthum qitharat al-'arab.
Zaki, 'Abd al-Hamid Tawfiq, *A'lam al-musiqa,* 57–64.
Zarruq, *Muwahhidat al-'arab al-Sayyida Umm Kulthum.*
Zirikli, *al-A'lam,* V, 129–130.

'Urabi, Ahmad

(1 April 1841–21 September 1911)
Nationalist leader and army officer. Born in Qaryat Rizqa (Sharqiyya) to a village shaykh of Iraqi Arab origin who died when Ahmad was very young, he studied for two years at al-Azhar and then entered the Military Academy at SA'ID's behest in 1854–1855, soon earning his commission. He rose rapidly through the ranks under Sa'id, but his career was stalled under ISMA'IL, who favored army officers of Turkish or Circassian origin. After Isma'il's deposition in 1879, 'Urabi may have joined the emerging National Party, but his first known act was to represent a group of discontented ethnic Egyptian officers who were protesting in February 1881 against War Minister RIFQI's favoritism to their Turco-Circassian colleagues. Khedive TAWFIQ and Premier RIYAD planned to arrest 'Urabi's group for insubordination, but other Egyptian officers seized control of the ministry, setting them free. The khedive then replaced Rifqi with MAHMUD SAMI AL-BARUDI as war minister. On 9 September, fearing a counterplot, the Nationalist officers surrounded 'Abdin Palace, confronted Tawfiq, and made him set up a constitutional government headed by SHARIF and enlarge the Egyptian army. Britain and France (especially the latter), concerned about the safety of the Suez Canal and their investments and citizens in Egypt, became increasingly hostile to the 'Urabist movement, stating their views in the Joint Note of January 1882. The Nationalists countered by replacing Sharif with Barudi as premier in February, making 'Urabi the new war minister. Still fearing a khedivial counterplot, the Nationalists took steps to weaken the Turks and

Circassians within the officer corps, also stirring up popular feeling against the European powers, and in some cases threatened the Europeans living in Egypt as well. Riots broke out in Alexandria in June 1882, and many European residents fled for safety, sometimes to the British and French warships that were gathering near its harbor. The Europeans threatened military intervention to back the khedive and to protect their nationals, demanding that the Egyptians remove their harbor fortifications. When 'Urabi refused, British ships bombarded them. In Alexandria fires broke out, caused either by the bombardment (as the Egyptians claimed) or by Egyptian officials (according to the British).

British troops—unaided by France, which had pulled out owing to a ministerial crisis in Paris—landed at Alexandria and later at Ismailia to restore order. 'Urabi and the Egyptian army continued to resist the British invaders, even after the khedive had turned against 'Urabi and declared him a rebel, but they were defeated at Tel el-Kebir on 13 September. Once the British entered Cairo the next day, 'Urabi surrendered and was tried for treason against the khedive. Although ultimately spared execution, he and his followers were exiled to Ceylon. 'ABBAS II let him return to Egypt in 1901, but he did not join the later National Party of MUSTAFA KAMIL, died in obscurity, and was scorned by most educated Egyptians up to the 1952 Revolution. After that, he was rehabilitated by NASIR and his Free Officers, whose occupational and class backgrounds paralleled 'Urabi's own. Now he is viewed as a patriot who resisted the British, the khedive, and the large landowners to promote constitutional government and the people's welfare. His memoirs have been published in several editions, the most detailed being the two-volume *Kashf al-sitar 'an sirr al-asrar* [Lifting the Veil on the Greatest Secrets] in 1925.

Bibliographic Sources
Abdel-Malek, *Arab Political Thought,* 122–125.
'Abduh, Muhammad, "Mudhakkirat 'an al-thawra al-'urabiyya."
Abu al-Su'ud, Fakhri, *al-Thawra al-'urabiyya.*
Ahmad 'Urabi.
'Ashur, Nu'man, *Butulat misriyya,* 71–88.
———, *Suwar min al-butula wa al-abtal,* 37–42.
Blunt, *Gordon at Khartoum,* 1–17.
———, *Secret History,* 99–108.

Broadley, *How We Defended Arabi.*
Chaillé-Long, *Three Prophets.*
Cole, *Colonialism and Revolution.*
Cox, "Arabi and Stone."
Cromer, *Modern Egypt*, I, 176–278.
Egyptian Gazette, 23 Sept. 1911.
Fahmi, Mahmud, *Mudhakkirat Mahmud Basha Fahmi.*
Farman, *Egypt and Its Betrayal*, 301–333.
Fiqi, Ahmad 'Abd al-Majid, *Qissat Ahmad 'Urabi.*
Gharaba, *Shakhsiyyat*, 23–26.
Gregory, *Ahmad Arabi and His Household.*
Greiss, "La crise de 1882 et le mouvement Orabi."
Hafiz, Hasan, *al-Thawra al-'urabiyya fi al-mizan.*
Hijazi, Anwar, *'Amaliqa*, 118–126.
al-Hilal 5:2 (15 Sept. 1896): 42–48, biography.
——— 5:3 (1 Oct. 1896): 82–90.
——— 5:4 (15 Oct. 1896): 122–134, memoirs.
——— 9:17 (1 June 1901): 482–492.
——— 10:2 (15 Oct. 1901): 33–55, reprint 1 Dec. 1967.
——— 19:7 (1 Oct. 1911): 27–41, obituary.
——— 77:10 (Oct. 1969): 68–73, 'Urabi and the Suez Canal.
Ibrahim, Shihata 'Isa, *'Uzama al-wataniyya*, 65–108.
'Isa, Salah, *al-Thawra al-'urabiyya.*
Jambalati and 'al-Tunisi, *Ahmad 'Urabi.*
Jami'i, *al-Thawra al-'Urabiyya fi daw al-wathaiq al-misriyya.*
Khafif, *Ahmad 'Urabi.*
LeGassick, *Defense Statement of Ahmad Urabi.*
Loring, *Confederate Soldier*, 192–207.
Manaf, *al-Thawra al-'urabiyya.*
Mayer, *Changing Past.*
Mujahid, *al-A'lam al-sharqiyya*, I, 140–142.
al-Muqtataf 39:5 (Nov. 1911): 417–424, obituary.
Murshidi, *al-Thawra al-'urabiyya.*
Musa, 'Ayda al-'Azab, *Tis'in sana.*
Mustafa, Ahmad 'Abd al-Rahim, *al-Thawra al-'urabiyya.*
Najjar, *Ahmad 'Urabi Basha.*
Naqqash, Salim Khalil, *Misr li al-misriyyin*, IV, 82–83 et passim.
New York Times (22 Sept. 1911): 11.
Ninet, *Arabi Pacha.*
Qadi, Shukri, *Khamsun shakhsiyya*, 31–34.
Rafi'i, 'Abd al-Rahman, *al-Thawra al-'urabiyya*, 87–94, 556–562.
Ramli, *Thawrat 'Urabi.*
Rathmann, *Neue Aspekte des Arabi-Aufstandes.*
Sabri, M., *Génese de l' esprit national.*
———, *Mémoire d' Arabi Pacha à ses avocats.*
Sa'id, Rif'at, *al-Asas al-ijtima'i*, 127–140.
Salah, *Muhakamat Ahmad 'Urabi.*
Salim, Latifa Muhammad, *al-Quwwa al-ijtima'iyya fi al-thawra al-'urabiyya.*
———, *'Urabi wa ruffaquhu fi Jannat Adam.*

Schofield, "An Autograph Manuscript of 'Urabi Pasha."
Schölch, *Egypt for the Egyptians!* 341–342.
Sharubim, *al-Kafi*, IV, 227–234.
Stewart, *Middle East: Temple of Janus*, 60–106.
Taha, Samir Muhammad, *Ahmad 'Urabi.*
Tanahi, Tahir, *'Ala firash al-mawt*, 72–75.
Tignor, "The Arabi Rebellion."
Times (London) (22 Sept. 1911): 3c, 4e.
'Urabi, *Ahmad 'Urabi.*
Walili, *Mafakhir al-ajyal*, 44–53.
Zakhura, *Mirat al-'asr*, I, 99–124.
Zaki, 'Abd al-Rahman, *A'lam al-jaysh*, 128–132.
Zaydan, Jurji, *Mashahir al-sharq* (1st ed.), I, 229–252.
Zirikli, *al-A'lam*, I, 168–169.

'Uthman, Amin

(1900–5 January 1946)

Lawyer and cabinet minister. Born in Alexandria, he was educated at Victoria College, graduating in 1918, and read law at Brasenose College, Oxford. He was called to the Bar at the Inner Temple in London and later received his *license* and doctorate in law from Paris. 'Uthman taught briefly at Victoria after his return to Egypt, then worked in the government's legal department. Later he became a financial inspector, director of imports for the Alexandria municipality, director of the direct tax department, deputy finance minister, and head of the accounts council. He was secretary-general of Egypt's delegation at the 1936 treaty negotiations. In 1942 he became finance minister in NAHHAS's cabinet. He instituted a national bond drive and the government employees' pension system, but angered many nationalists by saying that Britain and Egypt were conjoined in a "Catholic marriage." After the ministry fell, he went into business. He was a member of the Senate and besides serving on the boards of many companies and banks, he founded a commercial firm called Tradco. Although he belonged to the Wafd Party, in 1945 he founded a "nonpolitical" movement called *Rabitat al-Nahda* (Renaissance League) for Victoria College alumni, although its purport was to strengthen Anglo-Egyptian ties. He was knighted by King George VI into the Order of the British Empire, had an English wife, and raised over £E100,000 for a memorial at al-Alamayn. His assassination in Cairo, probably by Muslim Brothers, signaled Egypt's growing anger against Britain.

Bibliographic Sources
al-Ahram Archives, file 5800.
'Atiyah, An Arab Tells His Story, 54–55, 58, 64, 121–122.
Jami'i, "Ightiyal Amin 'Uthman wa dalalatuhu al-siyasiyya."
Mujahid, al-A'lam al-sharqiyya, I, 73–74.
al-Musawwar, no. 1109 (11 Jan. 1946): 2, 6.
New York Times (6 Jan. 1946): 15.
Ruz al-Yusuf, 9 May 1977.
Times (London) (7 Jan. 1946): 4e and 7e; (8 Jan. 1946): 3e.

'Uthman, 'Uthman Ahmad
(6 April 1917–1 May 1999)
Engineer, contractor, cabinet minister, and deputy premier. 'Uthman was born in Ismailia; his father was an itinerant merchant who carried grain between the Canal region and Gaza. Pleading poverty, the young 'Uthman won a scholarship to Cairo University's Engineering Faculty, graduating in 1940. He founded the Civil Engineering Company, headquartered at Ismailia, in 1941. A longtime backer of the Muslim Brothers, he resented the discrimination that Egyptians suffered in that city at the hands of Europeans. In 1950 he moved the main center of operations of his firm, renamed the Arab Contractors, to Saudi Arabia; there his business flourished with the growth of the oil industry, soon moving into other Arab countries as well. 'Uthman did not neglect Egypt; his firm spearheaded the reconstruction of Port Sa'id following the Suez War and won a $48 million contract for part of the building of the Aswan High Dam. His enthusiasm for working with the Soviets palled, however, when they denied him access to one of their bases after he had won a contract to build shelters for their fighter planes. 'Uthman and his relatives held most of the shares in the Engineering Company for Industries and Contracts, the Nasr Company for Pencils and Graphite Products, and other firms. From 1949 to 1973 he was president of Arab Contractors (NASIR nationalized the Egyptian branch in 1961) and of its Saudi, Kuwaiti, and Libyan affiliates. He also helped to set up the Suez Canal Bank and Ismailia Misr Company for Agricultural Development.

His position improved under SADAT's infitah policy, which 'Uthman supported. He became minister for reconstruction in 1973, adding the portfolio for housing from 1974 to 1976. His son married Sadat's daughter. He represented Ismailia in the People's Assembly (1976–1999), served as deputy premier, and chaired the Engineers' Syndicate, the National Democratic Party, the Committee for Popular Development, and the Ismailia Football Club. He received an honorary LL.D. from Ricker College and decorations from the Egyptian and Soviet governments. His construction projects included the Aswan High Dam, the deepening of the Suez Canal, the Cairo International Airport, the Dhahran Airport, the Kuwait Municipality Centre, the Benghazi sewer system, the Kirkuk Feeder Canal, dams and tunnels on Jordan's Yarmuk River, and a first-class hotel in Khartum. Under Sadat he accumulated power and wealth in ways that many people questioned, as he was at the same time a minister who could issue tenders for contracts and a contractor who could bid on them. By the 1980s the assets of Arab Contractors exceeded $1.5 billion, and 60,000 Egyptian families depended on the company for their livelihood. His memoirs, Safahat min tajribati [Pages from My Experience], raised a controversy for its attacks on Nasir's policies, and a series of articles refuting the book were published by al-Watan. He was less invulnerable under MUBARAK, and some of his misdeeds were publicized in a book by the Engineers' Syndicate. One of his sons sued him. He suffered a heart attack and died in Cairo.

Bibliographic Sources
al-Ahram Archives, file 406.
al-Anba, 21 Dec. 1989, interview.
Arbose, "Osman Ahmad Osman."
Baker, Sadat and After, 15–45.
Egypt, Ministry of Information, al-Mawsu'a al-qawmiyya, I, 673–674.
Heikal, Autumn of Fury, 186–192.
Khamis, 'Abd al-'Aziz, in Ruz al-Yusuf, 9 May–2 June 1977.
Ruz al-Yusuf, 21 June 1992.
al-Sha'b, 26 Aug.–28 Oct. 1986.
'Uthman, 'Uthman Ahmad, Safahat min tajribati.
WWAW, 1997–1998, 517.

W

Hoskins, Halford L. *British Routes to India*, 99–101, 118–120, 227–231, 243 n.
Kinross, *Between Two Seas*, 19–33.
Lieutenant Waghorn, R.N.
Sankey, *"Care of Mr. Waghorn."*
Sidebottom, *The Overland Mail.*
Wright, *Twentieth Century Impressions of Egypt*, 142–143.

Wahba, Yusuf

(1852–7 February 1934)

Legal expert, judge, cabinet minister, and premier. Born in Cairo, he was educated at CYRIL IV's Coptic college, where he became fluent in French and English. He began his career in the Finance Ministry and later moved to the Justice Ministry, where he helped to translate the *Code Napoléon* into Arabic and to develop the National Courts. He also helped to revive the Coptic Council (*Majlis Milli*) against the wishes of Patriarch CYRIL V and to found the Tawfiq Benevolent Society. He later became a chancellor in the Mixed Court of Appeals in Alexandria. When MUHAMMAD SA'ID and his successor resigned from the premiership, Wahba became the Coptic member of the cabinet with the portfolio for foreign affairs. He became finance minister in the first HUSAYN RUSHDI ministry in 1914 and continued to serve in the cabinet during the war and the 1919 Revolution. He agreed to head the government in November 1919 despite massive demonstrations by leading Copts, backed by many Muslims, and narrowly escaped assassination. He later served in the Senate, where he generously arranged for his erstwhile assailant to find employment as a clerk. He coauthored, with Shafiq Mansur [Yakan], *Sharh al-qanun al-madani* [Civil Law Explained] and, with 'Abd al-'Aziz Kuhayl, *Sharh qanun al-tijara al-misri* [Commercial Law Explained].

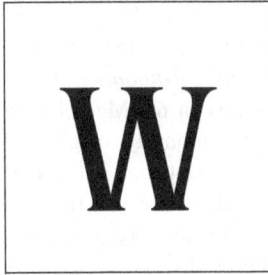

Waghorn, Thomas Fletcher

(20 June 1800–7 January 1850)

British promoter of the overland route to India. Born in Chatham, England, he entered the Royal Navy at the age of twelve. Dismissed after the Napoleonic Wars, he became a merchantman, served in the Bengal Marine, and later in the East India Company's fleet, and thus came to believe that Britain could cut the time and cost of transport between Europe and India by using the Egyptian overland route. In 1829–1830 Waghorn made a test voyage to carry messages from London to Bombay and to return with a reply within three months. Surmounting great hardships, he managed to cover 2,700 miles between London and Suez in forty and a half days. After living for some years among the Egyptian bedouin, he was able to develop a regular caravan route, secure from nomadic raids, with eight halting points between Cairo and Suez. By 1840 he provided a service of English carriages, vans, and horses to convey travelers. He wrote several pamphlets, including *Egypt As It Is* (1837), to promote his enterprise. This was a step toward building the first railroad linking Alexandria to Cairo and ultimately the Suez Canal. DE LESSEPS acknowledged his debt to Waghorn by having the latter's bust erected in Port Tawfiq. Ironically, Waghorn, like many Britons, opposed building the canal. Pensioned off by the East India Company, he died in poverty and obscurity.

Bibliographic Sources
Addison, "Thomas Waghorn and the Overland Route."
Cable, *A Hundred Year History of the P and O*, 53–64.

Bibliographic Sources
al-Ahram (9 Feb. 1934): 9–11.
Asaf, *Dalil*, 303–304.
Fuad, Faraj Sulayman, *al-Kanz al-thamin*, 91.
Kahhala, *Mu'jam*, XIII, 341.
Mujahid, *al-A'lam al-sharqiyya*, I, 134–135.
QMQ, 287.
Taqwim "al-Hilal" (1935), 37.
Times (London) (9 Feb. 1934): 15d.
Zakhura, *Mirat al-'asr*, I, 329–331; II, 93–94.
Zirikli, *al-A'lam*, VIII, 256.

Wahbi, Yusuf

(14 July 1898–17 October 1982)

Stage and screen actor, sometimes known as the Dean of the Arabic Theater. Born in Fayyum, he was the son of a landowner and irrigation inspector for Upper Egypt. Although his father wanted him to become an agricultural engineer, Yusuf began his acting career at the age of seven. He attended the School of Agriculture, the Acting Institute, the Dante Alighieri Institute, and the Armandis Cinema Institute in Milan, graduating in 1922. He also studied under 'Aziz 'Id and formed the Ramses Acting Troupe in March 1923. The troupe would put on 284 plays, most of which he produced. In 1930 he began to act in films, and he made his first radio broadcast in 1936. He became the general director of the National Troupe, now known as the National Theatre, and technical director of the Nahhas and Ramses Film Companies. He received awards from the Italian government, the Vatican, Morocco, Lebanon, and Jordan, as well as the Egyptian Fine Arts Prize in 1958 and an honorary doctorate from the Academy of Fine Arts in 1975. He produced 330 plays, 58 films, 111 radio programs, and 15 television series. The stage at the Academy of Fine Arts is named after him, as is a Fayyum street.

Bibliographic Sources

al-Ahram, 8 Feb. 1998, article by Alfred Faraj.
———, 18 Oct. 1982, obituary and article by Kamal al-Mallakh.
al-Ahram Archives, file 113.
al-Ahram al-masai, 10 Nov. 1996.
Amin, Mustafa, *Shakhsiyyat*, I, 335–352; II, 206–224.
Armbrust, *Mass Culture*, 200–204.
Darwish, Mustafa, *Dream Makers*, 23.
Hafiz, Ahmad, *Ayyam min shababihim*, 191–195.
al-Kawakib, no. 1630 (26 Oct. 1982), special issue.
Nisf al-dunya, 19 July 1992.
Qasim, *Mawsu'at mumaththili al-sinima al-misri*, 443.
Ramzi, *Nujum al-sinima*, 363–381.
Uktubir, no. 266 (29 Nov. 1981).
Yusuf, Fatima, *Dhikrayat*, 56–62 et passim.

Wajdi, Muhammad Farid

(1878–5 February 1954)

Journalist, Islamic scholar, and Quran commentator. Born and reared in Alexandria, he spent part of his youth in Damietta, where his father was deputy governor. Having accompanied his father to Suez, Farid wrote his first book there in 1899, *al-Falsafa al-haqqa fi badi' al-akwan* [True Philosophy in the Marvel of Events]. He also founded a monthly magazine called *al-Hayat*, which he published initially in Suez from 1899 to 1900, then in Cairo from 1906, meanwhile working for the *awqaf* ministry. He wrote a book on philosophy in Arabic and one on Islam and civilization in French (which he later translated into Arabic), and also a collection of *maqamat* that he published initially in his magazine and later as *al-Wajdiyyat*. Then he started a press and briefly published a daily newspaper, *al-Dustur*. He wrote books on Quranic commentary, the rights of women in Islam (responding to QASIM AMIN), the Arabic language, the errors of materialistic philosophy, and a critique of TAHA HUSAYN's *Fi al-Shi'r al-jahili*. Wajdi's major work was his ten-volume *Dairat ma'arif al-qarn al-'ishrin* [Twentieth Century Encyclopedia]. From 1943 to 1952 he published al-Azhar's monthly journal. He seldom attended parties or accepted invitations but graciously received visitors in his home.

Bibliographic Sources

'Abd al-Fattah, Muhammad, *Ashhar mashahir*, II, 114–128.
Adams, *Islam and Modernism*, 243–245.
al-Ahram Archives, file 28157.
Aqqad, *Rijal 'araftuhum*, 157–168.
Brockelmann, *GAL*, S III, 324–325.
Brugman, *Introduction*, 76–77.
*EI*2, VII, 439, article by J.J.G. Jansen.
Haykal, Muhammad Husayn, *Fi awqat al-faragh*, 164–181.
Hasan, Muhammad 'Abd al-Ghani, in *al-Ahram* (17 Feb. 1954): 5, 10.
Hajiri, *Muhammad Farid Wajdi*.
al-Idha'a wa al-tilvizyun, 5, 12 Mar. 1994.
Jansen, *Interpretation of the Koran*, 46–47.
Jindi, Anwar, *A'lam wa ashab aqlam*, 315–325.
———, *Muhammad Farid Wajdi*.
Kahhala, *Mu'jam*, XI, 126–127.
al-Manar 10:5 (Jumada I 1325): 456–480.
al-Muqtataf 55:1 (Jan. 1919): 76–78.
Smith, Wilfrid Cantwell, *Islam in Modern History*, 122–155.
Tanahi, Tahir, in *al-Hilal* 62:3 (Mar. 1954): 46–49.
Wajdi, *al-Wajdiyyat*.
———, "Ahamm hadith fi majra hayati."
Zirikli, *al-A'lam*, VI, 329.

Willcocks, Sir William

(1852–28 July 1932)

Engineer, missionary, and Arabic scholar. Born in India to an engineer who worked for the East India Company, he lost his mother in the 1857 Indian Mutiny and was reared by his father and a series of governesses. He graduated from the Thomason Engineering College in Roorkee, India, and began his career in that country's irrigation department. He was brought to Egypt by Sir Colin Scott-Moncrieff (for whom he had worked in India) in 1883 and soon became inspector of irrigation for the central Delta provinces, where he undertook a series of experiments that led to the abolition of the corvée. In 1889 he published a two-volume study, *Egyptian Irrigation,* which he revised several times during his career. As director of reservoirs during the 1890s he conducted the surveys and calculations that led to the construction of the first Aswan Dam and the Asyut Barrage, greatly increasing the productivity of the Nile Valley and starting the introduction of perennial irrigation in Upper Egypt. He left the service of the Egyptian government in 1897 and managed the Cairo Water Company for two years, extending its area of service and the effectiveness of its filtration system. He then managed the lands of *al-Daira al-Saniyya* until 1905, except for a three-month visit to South Africa in 1901 to advise Lord MILNER on irrigation possibilities in the Transvaal. Next he traveled to the Sudan to study the development potential of the Upper Nile. Willcocks worked for the Ottoman government from 1908 to 1911, improving irrigation in the Tigris and Euphrates Valleys. He visited Canada in 1913 and the United States in 1914 and advised the Romanian government on an irrigation scheme early in World War I. His postwar criticisms of an Upper Nile irrigation project, popularly believed to have inspired Egyptian unrest during the 1919 Revolution, led to a sedition and criminal libel trial in the Supreme Consular Court in Egypt and to his conviction early in 1921. Spared incarceration because of his age, he was urged to leave Egypt and required to cease libeling the projects. He later advised Bengal's government on its irrigation needs. Willcocks was notorious for his belief that more Egyptians could be converted to Christianity if the Bible were translated into their colloquial dialect, a view that raised the level of controversy between champions of classical Arabic and those who believed that Egyptian colloquial Arabic could be a written language.

Bibliographic Sources

Grafftey-Smith, *Bright Levant,* 79–80.
al-Hilal 35:10 (Aug. 1927): 1162–1166, interview.
Taqwim "al-Hilal" (1933), 37.
Times (London) (29 July 1932): 14b; (2 Aug. 1932): 12c; (6 Aug. 1932): 12d.
Who Was Who (1929–1940), 1458.
Willcocks, "In Egypt During the Forty Years."
———, *Sixty Years in the East.*

Wingate, Sir [Francis] Reginald, First Baronet

(25 June 1861–28 January 1953)

British army general and high commissioner of Egypt. Born in Port Glasgow (Scotland), he was educated at the Royal Military Academy, Woolwich, and was commissioned in 1880 as a second lieutenant in the Royal Artillery. Although posted to India, he was sent to Aden, where he learned Arabic, and he joined the Egyptian army in 1883, becoming an aide-de-camp to its commander-in-chief, Sir Evelyn Wood. Wingate took part in the relief expedition for General Gordon, but saw no other active service. He was named assistant military secretary, then assistant adjutant general, and in 1889 director of military intelligence, with special responsibility for the Sudan, about which he wrote *Mahdiism and the Egyptian Sudan* (1891). He also translated the accounts by Father Ohrwalder and R.C. Slatin of their experiences as prisoners of the Mahdi. He accompanied KITCHENER during the 1896–1898 Sudan campaign and succeeded him as commander-in-chief of the Egyptian army, serving from 1899 to 1916; he was concurrently governor-general of the Sudan. Wingate restored order and established British rule in that country, notably expanding cotton production in the Jazira Irrigation Project begun in 1913. He brought Darfur under Anglo-Egyptian control in 1916.

In January 1917 Wingate succeeded Sir HENRY MCMAHON as Egypt's high commissioner. This office proved challenging because of the large influx of British Empire troops during World War I, the shortage of foodstuffs and animals, and rising popular opposition to British rule in Egypt. The fact that he was chosen over Ronald Graham, who was well liked by the British officials in Cairo, put Wingate at a disadvantage, partly offset by his excellent rapport with Egypt's sultan, most high officials, and the Egyptian people. He had to to maintain cooperation between civilian and military officials in Egypt, to carry out the policies of (and provide information to) the Foreign Office, and to direct Britain's role in the Arab revolt. Although relatively ignorant of the internal politics of Britain's Foreign Office (where he faced opposition from Robert Cecil as well as Graham), Wingate was well aware of rising discontent among Egyptians in 1918. His warnings to the British government were ignored, and in November 1918 he received a formal visit at the Residency from SA'D ZAGHLUL and two of the latter's friends, who asked to send a delegation to negotiate with the Foreign Office for an end to the protectorate that Britain had proclaimed in 1914. However, Foreign Secretary Curzon rejected Sa'd's demands and even Wingate's advice that the British government should negotiate with the Egyptian ministers. When the 1919 Revolution broke out, demonstrating that Wingate had better grasped Egypt's situation than the Foreign Office, the British cabinet replaced him with General ALLENBY. Wingate never again held a responsible government position, although he served on the boards of various local organizations and of Gordon College in Khartum. His services to the British Empire as a military commander and civil administrator were never adequately recognized. His papers are in Durham University's Sudan Archive.

Bibliographic Sources
Antaki, *al-Nujum*, 32–33.
Daly, *The Sirdar: Sir Reginald Wingate.*
DNB (1951–1960), 1066–1067.
EMME, IV, 1894, article by Janice J. Terry.
Grafftey-Smith, *Bright Levant*, 58–66.
al-Hilal 25:3 (Dec. 1916): 250–252.
Illustrated London News, 7 Feb. 1953.
New York Times (29 Jan. 1953): 27.
Warburg, *Sudan Under Wingate.*
Who Was Who (1951–1960), 1183–1184.
Wills and Barrett, *Anglo-African Who's Who*, 165–166.
Wingate, *Wingate of the Sudan.*
Wingate Papers, Durham University, Boxes 219, 225–227, 232–233, 245/5–6, 269/8.
Zakhura, *Mirat al-'asr*, II, 114–118.

Wisa, Esther Fahmi
(19 February 1895-August 1990)
Feminist leader, political activist, and social worker. She was born in Asyut; her father, Akhnukh Fanus, was a large landowner and member of the Legislative Assembly. She was brought up by English governesses and educated at the American mission school in Asyut. She was married in 1912 to Fahmi Wisa (1885–1952), her father's first cousin once removed, who was an active Mason and for many years a senator. Influenced by MAKRAM 'UBAYD, Esther became active in the 1919 Revolution and was elected secretary of the New Woman Society formed in April of that year. In January 1920 she called the St. Mark's Cathedral meeting that led to her election as vice president of the Wafdist Women's Central Committee, of which HUDA SHA'RAWI was chosen as the first president. Fluent in English and not easily cowed by powerful personages, she corresponded often with Lord ALLENBY while he was high commissioner, supporting SA'D ZAGHLUL or the nationalist cause. After her young son 'Adli was killed in an automobile accident in Asyut, she lost all desire to live there and moved to Alexandria, where she was active in the Egyptian YWCA from the 1920s until 1983, as well as the Red Crescent's social committee. She set up the Work for Egypt Society, a women's benevolent organization that taught nursing and homemaking skills, and frequently organized balls and fundraising events between 1924 and 1962, when her group was taken over by the Social Affairs Ministry. Soon after the 1952 Revolution, she called on NAJIB to protest against some aspects of the proposed land reform law, which was accordingly modified, and also wrote to NASIR to warn him against letting Egypt become a Communist state. In 1954 and 1956 she went at her own expense to the United States to speak for Egypt and the Palestinian cause, and while there she wrote *The Virgin Heart*. On the fiftieth anniversary of the 1919 Revolution, she was one of four surviving leaders to receive decorations from Nasir. She never let herself be hampered by religion or gender; hoping to promote interfaith understanding, she read all the scriptures.

Bibliographic Sources
al-Ahram Archives, file 4474.
Najib, *A'lam Misr*, 121.

QTQ, 21–22.
Shamis, 'Abd al-Mun'im, in *al-Idha'a wa al-tilvizyun*, 5 Jan 1991.
Wissa, *Assiout*.

al-Tawfiq 2 (May 1959).
Watani, 10 June 1993.
Winslow, "The Child Weavers of Egypt."

Wisa-Wasif, Ramses
(8 November 1911–13 July 1974)
Architect, teacher, and patron of village artists. Ramses was born in Cairo; his father, Wisa Wasif, was one of the few Copts to back the Egyptian National Party and later to chair the Chamber of Deputies. Ramses graduated from the Lycée Française in 1928 and traveled to Paris the following year to study architecture at the École des Beaux Arts, obtaining his *diplome* in 1935 and returning to Cairo in 1936. In 1938 he joined the staff of the Higher School of Fine Arts at Cairo University; he headed the Department of Architecture and Art History in 1965–1969. He designed a Coptic school in Old Cairo and a portion of the Lycée Française, the Coptic cathedrals in Zamalek and Heliopolis, the Dominican Convent in Abbasiyya, and the MAHMUD MUKHTAR Museum in Giza. He also worked with HASAN FATHI in designing New Qurna. Influenced by his London-trained father-in-law, Habib Jurji, he became interested in folk art. As a patron of Egyptian peasant artists, especially children, Wisa-Wasif encouraged them to use their imaginations to weave tapestries representing scenes from village life. His studio in Harraniyya, near the Giza Pyramids, was and continues to be a center of artistic creativity. He received an Egyptian state prize in 1961 and was posthumously awarded the Agha Khan prize for his design of that studio complex. He died in Cairo of a heart attack. His peasant artists' work has been displayed in many foreign cities, as well as in many Cairo hotels and museums.

Bibliographic Sources
al-Ahram Archives, file 17220.
CE, VII, 2051, article by Cérès Wissa Wassef.
Fayza, "Family Life in Modern Egypt," 172–181.
Forman and Wissa Wassef, *Fleurs du Desert.*
———, *Tapestries from Egypt.*
al-Jumhuriyya, 15 July 1974.
Karnouk, *Contemporary Egyptian Art*, 62–63.
Mallakh, Kamal, in *al-Ahram*, 14 July 1974.
Morineau, "Artisinat égyptien."
QTQ, 102–103.

Wolseley, Sir Garnet
(4 June 1833–26 March 1913)
British army officer, imperial administrator, and leader of the 1882 force that occupied Egypt. Born in Dublin to a small landowning family, Garnet was only seven when his father died. He was tutored at home and then attended a local day school. He applied at age fourteen to the Duke of Wellington for a commission-without-purchase, rarely granted at that time. Perhaps in response to his mother's emotional plea and his father's military record, he eventually was commissioned as an ensign in 1852, serving in India, the Crimean War, the Indian Mutiny, China, Canada, the Confederate States (during the American Civil War), the Ashanti Wars, Natal, Cyprus, the Zulu Wars, and the War Office in the years prior to 1882. That year Wolseley was dispatched by the British government to take charge of its forces in Egypt after the bombardment of Alexandria in July. He led the successful invasion of the Suez Canal and Ismailia that enabled his troops to defeat 'URABI's army at Tel el-Kebir. He was promoted to general, appointed a baronet, and voted a £30,000 grant by Parliament, but soon returned to Egypt to organize the 1884 Gordon rescue mission. It failed, perhaps due to Wolseley's debatable decision to advance up the Nile rather than overland from the Red Sea, but the Mahdists would probably have taken Khartum in any event. Wolseley resumed the task of reorganizing Britain's army, preparing for its role in World War I, which he did not live to see.

Bibliographic Sources
DNB (1912–1921), 586–591.
Featherstone, *Wolseley's Conquest of Egypt.*
al-Hilal 8:8 (15 Jan. 1900): 228–229.
Lehmann, *Life of Field-Marshall Lord Wolseley.*
Maurice, *Military History.*
Morris, *Pax Britannica*, 236–237 et passim.
Pictorial Records of the English in Egypt, 303–332.
Times (London) (26 March 1913): 7f, 8e.
Who Was Who (1897–1916), 776.
Wingate Papers, Durham University, Boxes 104, 245/8, 250, 439/599.

Y

Fahmi, Zaki, *Safwat al-'asr*, 161–166.
Haykal, Muhammad Husayn, in *al-Hilal* 42:2 (Dec. 1933): 132–135.
Mujahid, *al-A'lam al-sharqiyya*, I, 155–156.
Muti'i, *Haula al-rijal min Misr*, III, 189–202.
———, *Mawsu'a*, 317–323.
Rafi'i, 'Abd al-Rahman, *Fi a'qab al-thawra*, I, 263–270.
Salim, Muhammad Khalil, *Azmat al-Wafd al-kubra*.
Sayyid-Marsot, *Egypt's Liberal Experiment*, 52–58.
Taqwim "al-Hilal" (1934), 38.
Tawfiq, 'Awad, and Hasan Sabri, *Wuzara al-ta'lim*, 56–58.
Times (London) (23 Oct. 1933): 19c.
Walili, *Mafakhir al-ajyal*, 169–172.
Wright, *Twentieth Century Impressions of Egypt*, 384.
Zakhura, *Mirat al-'asr*, I, 275–277; II, 91–92.
Zirikli, *al-A'lam*, IV, 218.

Yakan, 'Adli

(18 January 1864–22 November 1933)

Politician, cabinet minister, and three-time premier. The great-grandson of MUHAMMAD 'ALI's sister, 'Adli descended from one of Egypt's main landowning families, from which he inherited about 1,000 *feddan*s. He became NUBAR's private secretary in 1885, then deputy governor of Minufiyya in 1891. He went on to serve as deputy governor of Minya and of the Suez Canal, then governor of Fayyum, Minya, Sharqiyya, Daqahliyya, Gharbiyya, and Cairo. He was director general of the *awqaf* department from 1906 to 1909. Elected to the Legislative Assembly in 1913, he also served as foreign minister in the 1914 RUSHDI cabinet until the declaration of the protectorate, then held the portfolio for public instruction (1917–1919) and for interior (1919). As education minister 'Adli made Arabic the main language of both elementary and secondary instruction, set up the first state kindergartens and primary schools, and took the first steps toward creating a government university. He became prime minister for the first time in 1921 and took part in the negotiations with Lord Curzon about Egypt's status that were eventually stymied by the Wafd. He was a founder of the Constitutional Liberal Party in 1922 and interior and prime minister in 1926–1927 and 1929–1930. His policies served the interests of Egypt's landowners, especially those of King FUAD; he could not compete with SA'D ZAGHLUL for popular support. He died in Paris.

Bibliographic Sources
Bili, *'Adli Basha*.
Deeb, *Party Politics*, 114 n, et passim.

Yakan, [Muhammad] Wali al-Din

(2 March 1873–6 March 1921)

Turco-Egyptian poet, writer, and partisan of the Young Turks. The grandson of a nephew of MUHAMMAD 'ALI, he was born in wealthy circumstances in Istanbul. His mother belonged to the Circassian nobility. Yakan was orphaned when he was six, and his paternal uncle, 'Ali Haydar, Egypt's finance minister, adopted him and paid for his education, part of which he received at the Princes' School, learning Turkish, Arabic, and English as well as the natural sciences. He later learned French and Greek. He worked briefly in 1893 for Khedive 'ABBAS and then made two trips to Istanbul, where he became director general of Customs and then a member of the Supreme Council for Public Instruction. He published a newspaper called *al-I'timad* in which he criticized the sultan's government, and he was interned by 'Abd al-Hamid in Sivas (1902–1908).

Set free after the Young Turk Revolution, he stopped briefly in Istanbul. He then returned to Egypt and published in 1909 an exposé of the Hamidian regime, *al-Ma'lum wa al-majhul* [The Known and Unknown], and other works of prose and poetry, which tended to be pro-British, although he described himself as a liberal Ottoman who had become a literary Arab. Prior to World War I he was a clerk in the Justice Ministry and from 1914 to 1919 he served as Arabic secretary to Sultan HUSAYN KAMIL. Then, suffering from asthma, he retired to Helwan, where he died. Some of his essays and translations from French have never been published. Intelligent and high-strung, he fearlessly spoke out for liberty and social reform.

Bibliographic Sources
Brockelmann, *GAL,* S III, 49–56.
Brugman, *Introduction,* 54–56.
Bustani, Ahmad Ifrad, *Wali al-Din Yakan.*
Daghir, *Masadir,* II, i, 765–767.
Darwish, Darwish Muhammad, "Wali al-Din Yakan."
Jumayyil, Antun, "Wali al-Din Yakan."
Jundi, *A'lam al-adab,* II, 464–466.
Kahhala, *Mu'jam,* XIII, 166–168.
Kayyali, *Wali al-Din Yakan.*
Mandur, *Muhadarat 'an Wali al-Din Yakan.*
Mansi, *Wali al-Din katiban wa sha'iran.*
Mas'ud, *Wali al-Din Yakan.*
Mikhail, Sa'd, *Adab al-'asr,* 283–290.
Mujahid, *al-A'lam al-sharqiyya,* II, 804–807.
al-Muqtataf 58:4 (Apr. 1921): 375–378.
Ramadi, *Min a'lam al-adab,* 89–96.
Sabri, Muhammad, *Shu'ara al-'asr,* I, 232–240.
Wahid, *Wali al-Din Yakan.*
Zaki al-Din, *al-Kuttab al-thalatha,* 68–106.
Zirikli, *al-A'lam,* VIII, 118.

Yunus, Mahmud

(3 April 1912–18 April 1976)
Engineer, army officer, and first director of the Suez Canal Authority. Born in the Sayyida Zaynab section of Cairo, he was trained at the Khedivial School (two of his classmates were AHMAD HUSAYN and Fathi Radwan), Cairo University's Engineering Faculty, and the Staff College. He began his career in the mechanical and electrical department of the Public Works Ministry and became an army engineer in 1937. Immediately after the 1952 Revolution, he supervised the inventory of FARUQ's palaces. He became director of the general headquarters of the army's Technical Affairs Office in 1952, chairman and managing director of the General Petroleum Authority in 1954, and counselor to the Ministry of Commerce, Industry, and Mineral Wealth. After NASIR nationalized the Suez Canal Company in 1956, Yunus became its first managing director. His efficient operation of the canal, despite the company-inspired walkout by most of the foreign pilots, belied predictions by some Western experts that Egypt would never be able to manage the waterway. Yunus chaired the Suez Canal Authority in 1957–1965, then served from 1965 to 1967 as deputy prime minister for transport and communications and in 1967–1968 for petroleum and transport. He also headed the Engineers' Syndicate in 1954–1965 and was elected in 1964 to the National Assembly. In March 1968 he left the government and became a consultant to the Italian State Oil Company and then a private consulting engineer in Beirut and Cairo. He died in Ma'adi.

Bibliographic Sources
'Abd al-Hayy, *'Asir hayati,* 29–40.
al-Ahram, 19 Apr. 1976.
al-Ahram Archives, file 424.
al-Jumhuriyya, 28 Aug. 1985.
Najib, *A'lam Misr,* 463–464.
WWAW, 1974–1975, 1713.
Yunis, *Idarat Qanat al-Suways qabl al-tamim wa ba'dah.*

Yusuf, Shaykh 'Ali

(1863–25 October 1913)
Pioneer journalist and founder of *al-Muayyad.* Born in Balsafura, an Upper Egyptian village near Jirja, 'Ali lost his father before he was one year old; his mother took him to Bani 'Adi, where she, too, died. He was educated at the local *kuttab,* in Asyut, and at al-Azhar. Bored by his studies, he took to reading literature, biographies, and history. He began his career as a poet, then coedited a weekly literary magazine, *al-Adab,* for three years. Backed financially and politically by Prime Minister RIYAD, he began in December 1889 to put out *al-Muayyad,* the first Muslim paper to challenge and later surpass in popularity the dominant Syrian dailies, *al-Ahram* and *al-Muqattam.* This success was due not only to timely financial backing but also to the energy and skill of 'Ali and his staff in gathering and publishing important news from the various ministries of the Egyptian government. He also benefited from the legal advice and financial backing of SA'D ZAGHLUL. When 'ABBAS II succeeded to the khedivate, *al-Muayyad* became the Palace organ, often publishing articles by MUSTAFA KAMIL and other Muslim Egyptians hostile to the British occupation. 'Ali later broke with the National Party, as the khedive became reconciled with the British. Because of his lowly background, his marriage in 1904 to the

daughter of Shaykh al-Sadat, against the shaykh's wishes, was opposed by conservative Muslims, but the khedive and the law courts backed him. He became estranged from the nationalist movement; as 'Abbas drew closer to GORST, 'Ali espoused collaboration with the British occupation and created a Palace-based political party. In his last years he distanced himself from the newspaper that he had created, which attained a daily circulation of 20,000. He became a member of the General Assembly, assumed a leadership role in his father-in-law's Sufi order, and presided over the Red Crescent Society, whose creation he had initially proposed in *al-Muayyad* in 1911 when the Italians invaded Tripoli. Although he grew rich from his newspaper, in part because he articulated so well the feelings of his fellow Muslims, he lost much of his money in real estate speculation. He died in Cairo, a disappointed man. The party that he had founded died with him, and even his influential paper did not survive very long after him.

Bibliographic Sources
'Abbas Hilmi II, in *al-Misri*, 13, 15 May 1951.
'Abduh, Ibrahim, *A'lam al-sihafa*, 130–137.
'Aqqad, 'Abbas Mahmud, *Rijal 'araftuhum*, 12–38.
Ayalon, Ami, *Press*, 233–237.
Baha al-Din, *Ayyam laha tarikh*, 47–61.
Daghir, *Masadir*, II, i, 68–70.
Disuqi, 'Umar, "al-Shaykh 'Ali Yusuf."
Farid, Muhammad, *Memoirs and Diaries*, 19, 60 n, 112–114.
Hamza, *Adab al-maqala*, IV.
Hartmann, *Arabic Press of Egypt*, 11–14.
al-Hilal 22:2 (Nov. 1913): 148–151.
Jindi, Anwar, *al-Sihafa al-siyasiyya*, 166–167.
Kahhala, *Mu'jam*, VII, 10–11.
Khafaji, *Qissat al-adab*, IV, 171–174.
Kelidar, "Shaykh Ali Yusuf."
Mujahid, *al-A'lam al-sharqiyya*, III, 1052–1055.
al-Muayyad (26 Oct. 1913): 4.
al-Muqtataf 43:5 (Nov. 1913): 519.
Qadi, Shukri, *Khamsun shakhsiyya*, 213–216.
Radwan, Fathi, *Dawr al-'amaim*, 81–106.
Ramadi, *Adab wa tarab*, 117–121.
Rizq, Fathi, *Khamsa wa sab'una najman*, 89–94.
Salih, Sulayman, *al-Shaykh 'Ali Yusuf*.
Shalabi, 'Ali 'Atiya, *Dhikrayat*.
Tarrazi, *Tarikh al-sihafa*, III, 30–31, 37–40.
Walili, *Mafakhir al-ajyal*, 101–102.
Wood, *Egypt Under the British*, 139–174.
Yusuf, 'Ali, in *al-Muayyad*, 2 Oct. 1906.
Zakhura, *Mirat al-'asr*, I, 537–543.
Zirikli, *al-A'lam*, IV, 262.

al-Yusuf, Fatima
(15 January 1898–9 April 1958)
Stage actress and journalist, usually known as Rose *(Ruz)* al-Yusuf and sometimes depicted as the East's Sarah Bernhardt. Fatima was born in Tripoli (now in Lebanon) and, with her family, came as a girl first to Alexandria and then to Cairo. Fascinated by the stage, she learned how to act from Iskandar Farah, 'Aziz 'Id, and eventually JURJ ABYAD, under whose direction she costarred with YUSUF WAHBI. She shifted to journalism, however, and put out the first issue of her magazine, *Ruz al-Yusuf*, in October 1925, intending to focus it on the theater, but it soon branched out to other current issues. It was independent but tended to be viewed as pro-Wafdist. Because of its political columns and cartoons, it was frequently suspended or suppressed. She tried briefly to publish it as a daily newspaper in 1935, but financial problems hobbled the daily during its two years of existence. She later issued magazines called *al-Raqib*, *al-Sarkha*, *Sawt al-haqq*, *Misr al-hurra*, and *al-Sharq al-adna*. She married three times, twice to actors, and finally to QASIM AMIN's grandson, himself an editor. Her only child was IHSAN 'ABD AL-QUDDUS, the writer, whom she reared and who later became editor of *Ruz al-Yusuf*. Fatima has been memorialized by a plaque in the new Opera House.

Bibliographic Sources
'Abduh, Ibrahim, *Ruz al-Yusuf*.
al-Ahram Archives, file 174.
al-Ahram al-dawli, 12 Dec. 1991.
al-Ahram al-masai, 13 Feb. 1993.
Amin, Mustafa, *Shakhsiyyat*, I, 246–256.
EAL, II, 815.
Fuda, *Nujum Shari' al-Sihafa*, 40–46.
Rizq, Fathi, *Khamsa wa sab'una najman*, 217–227.
Yusuf, Fatima, *Dhikrayat*.

Z

al-Zabidi, Muhammad Murtada
(1732–April 1791)

Expert on Arabic philology and Islamic hadith. He was born in India to parents probably from Wasit (Mesopotamia). His family settled in Zabid (in Yemen) and later relocated to the Hijaz. Having moved to Egypt, Zabidi became known for his virtue and learning, corresponding with rulers from many Muslim lands, and achieving great popularity, to the point that some Maghribis declared that a *hajj* could not be complete without a visit to Zabidi. He died of the plague in Cairo. He is best known for his ten-volume Arabic dictionary, *Taj al-'arus fi sharh al-qamus* [The Bridegroom's Crown in the Dictionary's Explanation]. He also wrote a ten-volume commentary on al-Ghazali's *Ihya 'ulum al-din* [Revival of the Sciences of Religion].

Bibliographic Sources
Brockelmann, *GAL*, II, 371; S II, 398–399, 620, 696.
EAL, II, 817.
*EI*1, III, 691, article by Carl Brockelmann.
Gran, *Islamic Roots*, 54–55 et passim.
Haywood, *Arabic Lexicography*, 89–90.
al-Hilal 11:16 (15 May 1903): 475–481, bibliography.
Ibn Sawda [al-Murri], *Dalil muarrikhi al-Maghrib*, I, 39.
Jabarti, *'Ajaib al-athar*, II, 196–210; VII, 297–298; X, 228.
Kahhala, *Mu'jam*, XI, 282–283.
MMIA 2 (1922): 56, 106.
Mubarak, 'Ali, *Khitat*, III, 94–96.
Zaydan, Jurji, *Tarikh adab al-lugha*, III, 288–289.
Zirikli, *al-A'lam*, VII, 70.

Zaghlul, Ahmad Fathi
(20 February 1863–27 March 1914)

Writer, translator, and judge. He was born in Ibyana, where his father was the *'umda*. His older brother was SA'D ZAGHLUL. Originally called Fath Allah Sabri, Ahmad changed his name while in school. He studied briefly at the School of Languages and earned his *license en droit* in Paris in 1887. He began his career in the legal section of the Interior Ministry, serving for a time as head of the *Niyaba* in Asyut and Alexandria. He presided over the National Court in Cairo for eleven years. At the time he died, he was deputy justice minister. He translated a number of books, notably several by Gustave Le Bon and Edmond Desmoulins's *À quoi tient la supériorité des Anglo-Saxons?* which led many Egyptians to esteem English, as opposed to French, education. Some of his articles were reprinted as *al-Athar al-fathiyya: maqalat fi al-adab wa al-ijtima'* [Fathi's Reflections on Literature and Society].

Bibliographic Sources
'Abd al-Fattah, Muhammad, *Ashhar mashahir*, II, 114–144.
'Abd al-Latif, Muhammad Fahmi, in *al-Risala* 16:773 (26 Apr. 1948): 480–482.
African Times and Orient Review, N.S. 1:3 (7 Apr. 1914): 67.
Ahmed, J.M., *Intellectual Origins*, 44–46, 89.
Brockelmann, *GAL*, S III, 325–326.
Egypt, National Courts, *al-Kitab al-dhahabi li al-mahakim al-ahliyya*, I, 182.
Farid, Muhammad, *Memoirs and Diaries*, 103–104.
Fikri, 'Ali, *Subul al-najah*, III, 198–204.
al-Hilal 22:8 (May 1914): 628–632.
'Isa, Mamduh, in *al-Thaqafa* 11:536 (4 Apr. 1949): 23–24.
Jawdat, Salah, in *al-Muqtataf* 44:6 (June 1914): 578–588.
Jindi, Anwar, *al-Muhafaza wa al-tajdid*, 116–122.
Jundi, *A'lam al-adab*, II, 455–456.
Kahhala, *Mu'jam*, II, 44–45.
Kurd 'Ali, *Mu'asirun*, 95–100.
al-Manar 17:6 (24 May 1924): 472–478.
MMIA 27 (1947): 481–485.
Mujahid, *al-A'lam al-sharqiyya*, II, 443–444.
Muti'i, *Haula al-rijal min Misr*, I, 48–62.
———, *Mawsu'a*, 59–67.
Sayyid, Ahmad Lutfi, *Taammulat*.
Shiliq, *Ahmad Fathi Zaghlul*.
Tajir, *Harakat al-tarjama*, 127–128.

Wright, *Twentieth Century Impressions of Egypt*, 93.
Zakhura, *Mirat al-'asr*, II, 351–352.
Zirikli, *al-A'lam*, I, 194.

Zaghlul, Sa'd

(July 1859?–24 August 1927)

Lawyer, minister, leader of the Wafd, and premier. Born to a prosperous peasant family in Ibyana (Gharbiyya), he was educated in his village *kuttab* and spent four years at al-Azhar, where he became a disciple of AFGHANI and 'ABDUH. In 1881 he briefly edited *al-Waqai' al-misriyya*. He took part in the 'URABI Revolution, following which he was arrested for membership in a secret society but was cleared. He worked as a lawyer and served for a time as a judge in the National Courts before a wealthy patron financed his legal studies in Cairo and Paris. His marriage to SAFIYYA [ZAGHLUL], daughter of Prime Minister MUSTAFA FAHMI, advanced his career greatly. In response to the nationalist upsurge following the 1906 Dinshaway Incident, Sa'd was named education minister. He clashed openly with his British adviser but won popular support for insisting on making Arabic the medium of instruction in government elementary schools. His house served as the meeting place for the founders of the Egyptian University and for a time as its administrative headquarters. His other reforms included setting up agricultural and technical schools, extending the length of secondary education from three years to four and of teachers' training from one year to two (later raised to three), and founding a girls' secondary school at Kubri al-Qubba, Cairo. He was also the first minister to visit the schools himself. He served as justice minister in 1910–1912. In 1913 he was elected to the new Legislative Assembly, where, as the elected vice president, he became leader of the opposition. When the assembly was prorogued during World War I, he withdrew from politics. Considered for a cabinet post in 1917, he was rejected as too anti-British.

After the Armistice, Sa'd and two of his colleagues asked the British high commissioner if they could go to London to discuss Egypt's postwar status, but the Foreign Office refused to see them. Sa'd then proposed to lead an Egyptian delegation, or *wafd*, to the Paris Peace Conference and circulated petitions throughout the country to gain popular support, but the British blocked that idea too. The Egyptian ministers resigned, and riots broke out in Cairo and the provinces in March 1919. Sa'd and three of his friends were arrested by the British and interned in Malta, but the disturbances grew worse. A new high commissioner, General ALLENBY, suppressed the riots but let the *wafd* leaders go to Paris, where they stayed for a year without gaining a hearing at the conference. Sa'd talked with MILNER in 1920, but the two men failed to reach an agreement on Egypt's future status. His return to Egypt revived popular unrest, and he was exiled to Aden, the Seychelles, and Gibraltar. He did not return until the 1923 Constitution had been written. He then converted his delegation into the Wafd Party, which, in the parliamentary elections held late in that year, won a large majority.

In January 1924 FUAD invited Sa'd to form a Wafdist government. His cabinet hoped to reach an agreement on Egypt's status with Britain's new Labour Party government. He barely escaped an attempt on his life in June of that year. His Wafdist government fell after the assassination in Cairo of the commander of the Egyptian army, Sir Lee Stack, in November. Commissioner Allenby handed Sa'd an ultimatum couched in terms the latter viewed as extreme and humiliating. He resigned in protest, and the king named a caretaker government from which the Wafd was excluded. In new elections, held in 1925, the Wafd won a partial victory and Sa'd was elected speaker of the Chamber of Deputies, but the king ordered Parliament closed. In the 1926 elections Zaghlul led the Wafd to another victory but declined to form a government and was reelected speaker. His death in 1927 was mourned throughout Egypt. Hailed as the Father of Egypt's Political Independence, he was popular and patriotic, but often vain and stubborn. He did more to rouse the masses than to expel the British. His memoirs are being published by the Center for the Study and Documentation of Egypt's Contemporary History. By 1998 eight volumes, covering up to May 1918, had appeared. His Cairo house, *Bayt al-Umma*, is a national museum; he is buried in a special mausoleum nearby.

Bibliographic Sources
'Abd al-Nur, *Mudhakkirat Fakhri*.
Abu 'Alam, Sabri, in *al-Muqtataf* 71:3 (Nov. 1927): 241–259; 4 (Dec.): 377–384.

Abu al-Fath, *Ma'a al-Wafd al-Misri*.

————, *al-Masala al-misriyya wa al-Wafd*.

Ahmed, J.M., *Intellectual Origins*, 52–55, 113–117.

Amin, Mustafa, "Kitab majhul bi-qalam Sa'd Zaghlul."

————, *al-Kitab al-mamnu'*.

————, *Shakhsiyyat*, I, 7–17 et passim.

Anis, *Dirasat fi wathaiq thawrat 1919*.

————, "Thawrat 1919 wa Hizb al-'Ummal."

'Aqqad, 'Abbas Mahmud, in *al-Hilal* 36:1 (Nov. 1927): 10–33.

————, "Sa'd Zaghlul ba'da 20 sana."

————, *Sa'd Zaghlul: sira wa tahiyya*.

Asaf, *Dalil*, 244–245.

'Awad, Mahmud, *Sa'd Zaghlul*.

Baha al-Din, *Ayyam laha tarikh*, 77–120.

Barakat, Dawud, in *al-Ahram* (24 Aug. 1927): 1–2; articles in next 40 issues.

Barakat, Muhammad Bahi al-Din, *Safahat min al-tarikh*, 160–174.

Berque, *Egypt*, 279–282.

Bishri, 'Abd al-'Aziz, *Fi al-mirat*, 1, 23–30.

Bishri, Tariq, *Sa'd Zaghlul*.

Blunt, *Gordon at Khartoum*, 71, 74–75, 628.

Brockelmann, *GAL*, S III, 334–335.

Carra de Vaux, *Penseurs*, V, 296–306.

CE, VII, 2074–2075, article by Yunan Labib Rizq.

Daghir, *Masadir*, II, i, 416–421.

Deeb, *Party Politics*, 39–60, 109 n, et passim.

EI2, VIII, 698–701, article by R. Schulze.

Fahmi, Zaki, *Safwat al-'asr*, 132–156.

Fikri, 'Ali, *Subul al-najah*, III, 271–280.

Harris, Murray, *Egypt Under the Egyptians*, 208–224.

Hijazi, Anwar, *'Amaliqa*, 149–162.

al-Hilal 29:8 (May 1921): 732–742, articles and poems about Sa'd.

Hourani, *Arabic Thought*, 209–221.

Ibrahim, Shihata 'Isa, *'Uzama al-wataniyya*, 245–307.

Jabr, Mustafa al-Nahhas, *Mudhakkirat Sa'd Zaghlul*.

Jaziri, *Sa'd Zaghlul*.

Kahhala, *Mu'jam*, IV, 209–210.

Kedourie, *Chatham House Version*, 82–159.

Lashin, *Sa'd Zaghlul wa dawruhu fi al-siyasa al-misriyya*.

————, *Sa'd Zaghlul: wa dawruhu fi al-siyasa al-misriyya hatta sanat 1914*.

al-Manar 28:8 (27 Oct. 1927): 584–592; 9 (24 Nov. 1927): 709–714.

Muhammad, Muhsin, *Sa'd Zaghlul*.

Mujahid, *al-A'lam al-sharqiyya*, I, 145–148.

Muti'i, *Haula al-rijal min al-Azhar*, 113–131.

————, *Mawsu'a*, 171–177.

Nahhas, Yusuf, *Dhikrayat*.

Najjar, *Sa'd Zaghlul*.

Pernot, *Sur la route de l'Inde*, 16–20.

Qadi, Shukri, *Khamsun shakhsiyya*, 45–48.

Qal'aji, *Sa'd Zaghlul*.

Rafi'i, 'Abd al-Rahman, *Fi a'qab al-thawra*.

————, *Thawrat sanat 1919*.

Rida, Muhyi al-Din, *Abtal al-wataniyya*, 41–78.

Rifa'i, Muhammad 'Ali, *Rijal wa mawaqif*, II, 129–155.

Sa'id, Rif'at, *Sa'd Zaghlul*.

Salim, Muhammad Khalil, *Azmat al-Wafd al-kubra*.

————, *Sira' Sa'd fi Urubba*.

————, *Thawrat 1919*.

Sayyid-Marsot, *Egypt's Liberal Experiment*, 44–105.

Schulze, *Die Rebellion der ägyptischen Fallahin 1919*.

Shanuda, *Sa'd Zaghlul nazir al-ma'arif*.

Stewart, *Middle East: Temple of Janus*, 259–271.

Subki, *Sa'd Zaghlul*.

Tanahi, Tahir, *'Ala firash al-mawt*, 125–132.

Tawfiq, 'Awad, and Hasan Sabri, *Wuzara al-ta'lim*, 51–53.

Tawfiq, Najib, *al-Za'im al-khalid Sa'd Zaghlul Basha*.

Thabit, Karim, *Sa'd fi hayatihi al-khassa*.

Times (London) (24 Aug. 1927): 10f, 12b.

Tweedy, "Sa'd Pasha Zaghlul."

————, "Sa'd Zaghlul Pasha."

'Umar, *Abtal al-hurriyya*, 63–71.

Walili, *Mafakhir al-ajyal*, 123–135.

Wingate Papers, Durham University, Boxes 107/3 and 170/3.

Zakhura, *Mirat al-'asr*, II, 100–101.

Zayid, Mahmud, "Nashat Hizb al-Wafd, 1918–1924."

Zayyat, Ahmad Hasan, in *al-Risala* 3:111 (19 Aug. 1935); 112 (26 Aug. 1935): 1361–1362.

————, *Sa'd Zaghlul min aqdiyatihi*.

Zirikli, *al-A'lam*, III, 83.

Zaghlul, Safiyya
(1876–12 January 1946)

Umm al-Misriyyin, the wife of SA'D ZAGHLUL. The youngest daughter of the five-time premier, MUSTAFA FAHMI, she was born in Cairo. Her 1896 marriage to Sa'd may have been facilitated by Princess NAZLI, for Safiyya's father would probably have preferred to marry her into an aristocratic Turkish family like his own. In 1919, when Sa'd was arrested and interned on the island of Malta, she purchased a boat ticket to join him. However, when a group of women demonstrators from Tanta came to her door, chanting "'Aisha was the mother of the believers; Safiyya is the mother of the Egyptians," she realized that she would have to stay in Egypt to help lead the 1919 Revolution. When the Wafd leaders tried to remove Sa'd's papers from their home, she insisted on being treated as if she were a male Wafdist capable of guarding them. She chaired meetings of the Wafd's Central Committee during her husband's exile, led a women's protest demonstration, and issued manifestoes demanding Egypt's independence. Some of Sa'd's followers thought of making her the head of the Wafd Party after his death in 1927, and it is highly probable that she influenced their choice of MUSTAFA AL-NAHHAS over Fath Allah Barakat, a cousin whom she disliked. For the rest of her life, she played a symbolic role within the nationalist movement.

Bibliographic Sources
Abd al-Hakim, *Nisa*, 65–72.
Amin, Mustafa, *Shakhsiyyat*, I, 179–189.
Badran, *Feminists*, 80–81.
Najib, *A'lam Misr*, 265.
Vidal, *Safiyya Zaghlul.*

Zaki, Ahmad

(26 May 1867–5 July 1934)
Arabic philologist, sometimes called the Dean of Arabism, and longtime secretary of the Egyptian cabinet. Born in Alexandria to a Kurdish mother and a Moroccan father, Ahmad attended Cairo's Qurabiyya and Tajhiziyya Schools, followed by the School of Administration. While a student there, he won a competition to become a translator for Ismailia's provincial government at a monthly salary of £E 13; in 1888, thanks to his command of French, he moved to the press bureau of the Interior Ministry. He also became an editor and translator for *al-Waqai' al-Misriyya*, a translation teacher for the Khedivial School, and an Arabic teacher for the French Archaeological Institute in Cairo, all in 1888. In the following year he won a competition for the post of translator for the cabinet, for which he became adjunct secretary in 1897 and secretary-general in 1911, serving until he retired in 1921. During World War I he also recodified Egypt's administrative procedures in keeping with its status as a British protectorate. Because of his wide range of interests and numerous publications, he became a fellow of the Institut d'Égypte, the Royal Geographical Society, and the Royal Asiatic Society in London. He served on the administrative boards of both al-Azhar and the Egyptian University, also holding the chair for Islamic civilization in the latter. He took the lead in setting the Arabic-language equivalents of European loanwords, such as *sayyara* for "automobile," and also alerted the press to the Arabic origins of many Spanish and Portuguese place-names that had been inaccurately transcribed into Arabic. He participated in many conferences of the International Congress of Orientalists and was respected by Europeans for his erudition. He was a staunch nationalist, Egyptian from his youth, later pan-Arab and even pan-Oriental, becoming one of the founders and first secretary-general of *al-Rabita al-Sharqiyya* (the Oriental League). His Giza home, *Bayt al-'Uruba*, became the meeting place for visitors from other Arab countries, even at times a site for reconciliations between quarreling Arab princes, and a repository of Arab antique furniture, jewelry, books, and manuscripts. He also erected a mosque near his home. A prodigious writer of articles and short books, he did not live long enough to complete what would have been the crowning achievement of his scholarship, an Arabic dictionary modeled on the French *Larousse*. He gave his books and manuscripts to Dar al-Kutub.

Bibliographic Sources
'Ata Allah, "Ahmad Zaki."
Brockelmann, *GAL*, S III, 231–233.
Daghir, *Masadir*, II, i, 422–426.
Farès, "Nécrologie: Ahmad Zaki Pacha."
Fuad, Faraj Sulayman, *al-Kanz al-thamin*, 92–106.
al-Hilal 42:10 (Aug. 1934): 1172–1174.
'Isa, Ahmad, in *al-Ahram*, 16 Nov. 1934.
———, in *BIE* 17 (1935): vii–xix.
Jindi, Anwar, *Ahmad Zaki.*
———, *A'lam wa ashab aqlam*, 31–38.
Jundi, *A'lam al-adab*, II, 456–457.
Kahhala, *Mu'jam*, I, 225–226.
Kayyali, *al-Rahilun*, 29–41.
Kurd 'Ali, *Mu'asirun*, 48–58.
Louca, *Voyageurs*, 209–227.
Ma'luf, "Ahmad Zaki Basha."
Mujahid, *al-A'lam al-sharqiyya*, II, 841–844.
al-Muqtataf 85:2 (Oct. 1934): 153–156.
Pérès, *L'Espagne vue par les voyageurs musulmans*, 72–87.
Musa, Salama [S], "Hadith ma'a Ahmad Zaki Basha."
Shamis, 'Abd al-Mun'im, in *al-Katib* (Sept. 1977): 8–19.
Tajir, *Harakat al-tarjama*, 125–126.
Tanahi, Tahir, *'Ala firash al-mawt*, 163–169.
Wright, *Twentieth Century Impressions of Egypt*, 93–94.
Zakhura, *Mirat al-'asr*, II, 151–152.

Zaki, Ahmad, *al-Safr ila al-mutamar.*
Zayyat, Ahmad Hasan, in *al-Risala* (16 July 1934).
Zirikli, *al-A'lam*, I, 126–127.

al-Zawahiri, Shaykh Muhammad al-Ahmadi

(1878–13 May 1944)

Shafi'i judicial expert and rector of al-Azhar. Born in the Sharqiyya village of Kafr al-Zawahiri to a family that traced its lineage to al-Qahtan, he received his *'alimi* (teaching) certificate from al-Azhar, where he studied with MUHAMMAD 'ABDUH and others. He took over from his father the leadership of the Ahmadi Mosque in Tanta, then moved to Asyut to be shaykh of its institute for a while. When the Islamic conference was held in Cairo in 1926 following the abolition of the caliphate in Turkey, he boldly called for its adjournment without a resolution because many Islamic countries were not represented. He then headed the Egyptian delegation to the 1926 Islamic Congress in Mecca. As he strengthened his ties with King FUAD, he replaced MARAGHI as rector of al-Azhar in 1929, describing his experiences in *al-Siyasa wa al-Azhar* [Politics and al-Azhar]. He served until 1935, when he resigned due to ill health. While he was rector, the magazine *Nur al-Islam* was launched and al-Azhar adopted some of the organization of a modern university. An orator, Zawahiri had leanings toward the Shadhili Sufi order. His other books include one on how to organize instruction and a memoir, published posthumously by his son.

Bibliographic Sources

'Abd al-Jawad, Muhammad, *Hayat mujawir fi al-Jami' al-Ahmadi.*
al-Ahram (14 May 1944): 6.
Amin, 'Uthman, in *al-Ahram*, 13 May 1949.
Kahhala, *Mu'jam*, IX, 30–31.
al-Manar 31:5 (20 Dec. 1930): 375–388.
al-Misri, 14 May 1944.
Mujahid, *al-A'lam al-sharqiyya*, I, 359–360.
al-Muqattam, 15 May 1944.
Zawahiri, *al-Siyasa wa al-Azhar.*
Zirikli, *al-A'lam*, VI, 26.

Zaydan, Jurji

(14 December 1861–21 August 1914)

Novelist, Arabic philologist, historian, founder and editor of *al-Hilal*. Born to a poor Greek Orthodox family in Beirut, he was largely self-educated until he entered the Syrian Protestant College (now the American University of Beirut) in 1881. Expelled after one year for taking part in a student strike in support of a lecturer who had espoused Darwin's theory of natural selection, he passed a pharmaceutical examination in Beirut. In October 1883 Zaydan moved to Cairo, intending to complete his medical education at Qasr al-'Ayni. Instead, he decided to become a journalist and began writing articles for *al-Zaman*. He also accompanied the Gordon rescue expedition to the Sudan as an interpreter. He returned to Beirut in 1885 to resume his studies, this time in Hebrew and Syriac, and also wrote his first book, dealing with Arabic philology. After visiting England in 1886, he returned to Beirut and began writing for *al-Muqtataf*. In 1888 he left the magazine and taught briefly at a Greek Orthodox school. In 1892 he founded the monthly (and at times fortnightly) magazine, *al-Hilal*, which he published, built up, and distributed for the rest of his life. He wrote numerous historical novels, compendia of information about Islamic and Egyptian history and literature and popular science. Invited to lecture on early Islam at the newly established Egyptian University, he had to resign because its directors feared an adverse Muslim reaction to having a Christian teaching Islamic history, but he accepted his dismissal in a dignified manner. His autobiography, *Mudhakkirat Jurji Zaydan*, the first of its type in Arabic, was not fully published until 1968. His writings on the early history of the Arabs, if now quite dated, helped to inspire the rise of Arab nationalism in the early twentieth century. His death in Cairo was unexpected.

Bibliographic Sources

'Abbud, Marun, *Ruwwad al-nahda*, 171–172.
'Abbud, Nazir, *Jurji Zaydan.*
Abu Hadid, *'Isamiyyun*, 45–58.
Abu Khalil, *Jurji Zaydan fi al-mizan.*
Alkhayat, *Gurgi Zaydan.*
Allen, "Beginnings of the Arabic Novel," *CHAL*, 187–188.
'Ashmawi, *Waqfa ma'a Jurji Zaydan.*
'Aqqad, 'Abbas Mahmud, *Rijal 'araftuhum*, 191–198.
Brockelmann, *GAL*, II, 483; S III, 186–190.
Brugman, *Introduction*, 218–224.
Crabbs, *Writing of History*, 191–195.
Daghir, *Masadir*, II, i, 442–448.
Desormeaux, "L'oeuvre de George Zaidan."

*EI*1, IV, 1262–1263, article by Ignaz Kratschkovsky.

Fahmi, Zaki, *Safwat al-'asr*, 653–662.

Harb, Joseph, *Jurji Zaydan*.

Hartmann, *Arabic Press of Egypt*, 35–36.

Hasan, Muhammad 'Abd al-Ghani, *Jurji Zaydan*.

———, *Jurji Zaydan*.

———, *al-Kitab al-dhahabi*, by various writers.

——— 22:10 (July 1914): 761–768; 23:1 (Oct. 1914): 2–16; 2 (Nov.): 91–95; 3 (Dec.): 179–184; 4 (Jan. 1915): 309–310.

——— 47:10 (Aug. 1939): 963–982.

——— 62:4 (Apr. 1954): 56–62, extracts from his memoirs.

Jindi, Anwar, *Jurji Zaydan*.

———, *al-Muhafaza wa al-tajdid*, 70–77.

Jundi, *A'lam al-adab*, II, 356–357.

Kahhala, *Mu'jam*, III, 125–126.

Kratschkovsky, "Le roman historique."

Kurd 'Ali, *Mu'asirun*, 143–146.

———, "Sadiqi Jurji Zaydan."

Mujahid, *al-A'lam al-sharqiyya*, III, 1000–1002.

Pérès, "Le roman historique dans la littérature arabe."

Philipp, *Gurgi Zaydan*.

———, "Language, History, and Arab National Consciousness."

Reid, *Cairo University*, 22–24.

———, *Farah Antun*, 110–114.

Rizq, Fathi, *Khamsa wa sab'una najman*, 95–99.

Shaybub, Siddiq, *Shakhsiyyat 'arabiyya*, 107–125.

Shayyal, *al-Tarikh wa al-muarrikhun*, 185–187, 246–247.

Tamawi, *Jurji Zaydan*.

Tanahi, Tahir, *'Ala firash al-mawt*, 87–90.

Tarrazi, *Tarikh al-sihafa*, I, 21; III, 87–90.

UNESCO, *A'lam al-Lubnaniyyin*, 191–198.

Ware, "Women's Emancipation in the Middle East."

Zakhura, *Mirat al-'asr*, I, insert before p. 457; III, 65–80.

———, *al-Suriyyun fi Misr*, 258–260.

Zaydan, Jurji, *Autobiography of Jurji Zaydan*.

———, *Mudhakkirat Jurji Zaydan*.

Zirikli, *al-A'lam*, II, 117.

al-Zayyat, Ahmad Hasan

(2 April 1885–12 June 1968)

Arabic teacher and scholar, writer, and editor of *al-Risala*. He was born to a peasant family in Kafr Damira, near Talkh (Daqahliyya). After attending his village *kuttab*, he was educated at al-Azhar and the Egyptian University, from which he earned a *license* in 1912. He later studied at the French Law School, earning his *license en droit* from Paris in 1925. Meanwhile, he taught Arabic at the École des Frères in Khoronfish, in a Muslim school founded by Shaykh JAWISH, and the American University in Cairo, whose Arabic Department he headed from 1922 to 1929. He wrote a history of Arabic literature, at first in abbreviated form for secondary school pupils, but he gradually expanded it until it became a general work on literary criticism, *Tarikh al-adab al-'arabi li al-madaris al-thanawiyya wa al-'ulya* [History of Arabic Literature for Secondary and Higher Schools]. The book was first published under that title in 1920 and reprinted more than twenty-five times. He turned down a teaching post at Cairo University in 1929, choosing instead to teach at the Teachers Training College in Baghdad, an experience that led him to reorient Egyptian public opinion toward Arab nationalism. Returning to Cairo in 1933, he founded the monthly literary magazine *al-Risala*, which soon became immensely popular in Egypt and other Arab countries. He translated works by Arnold Bennett, de Maupassant, and Goethe into Arabic. He was elected to membership in the Arabic Language Academy in 1949. After *al-Risala* ceased publication in 1953, Zayyat edited al-Azhar's monthly journal, *Majallat al-Azhar*, which became a major influence for its reform. He received state prizes for literature in 1953 and 1962 and was appointed to the Supreme Council for the Arts in 1963. His village's preparatory school was named for him after his death.

Bibliographic Sources

al-Ahram Archives, file 3103.

'Allam, "Ahmad Hasan al-Zayyat."

———, *Majma'iyyun*, 41–47.

'Alusi, *Ahmad Hasan al-Zayyat*.

Ayyad, "Ahmad Hasan al-Zayyat."

'Azzawi, *Ahmad Hasan al-Zayyat*.

Bayyumi, Muhammad Rajab, *Ahmad Hasan al-Zayyat*.

———, "Athar al-Zayyat fi al-yaqza al-'arabiyya."

Brugman, *Introduction*, 329–330, 382–386.

Daghir, *Masadir*, III, i, 507–510.

al-Dawha (Mar. 1982): 10–12.

Faqi, *Ahmad Hasan al-Zayyat*.

Fuad, Ni'mat Ahmad, in *al-Ahram*, 9 Apr. 1997.

———, *Qimam adabiyya*, 175–232.

Haykal, Ahmad, in *al-Ahram*, 3 June 1976.

Jindi, Anwar, *al-Muhafaza wa al-tajdid*, 655–667.

Khatib, 'Adnan, in *MMIA* 43 (1963): 676.

Muti'i, *Haula al-rijal min al-Azhar*, 49–64.

———, *Mawsu'a*, 232–239.

Ramadi, *Min a'lam al-adab*, 40–49.

Sayigh, *al-Fikra al-'arabiyya fi Misr*, 233–235.

Sharqawi, 'Abd al-Rahman, in *al-Jumhuriyya*, 19 June 1968.

Walker, "Contribution of Ahmad Hasan az-Zayyat."

Zirikli, *al-A'lam*, I, 113–114.

Ziwar, Ahmad
(14 November 1864–21 August 1945)

Lawyer, minister, senator, and premier. Born in Alexandria to a family of Circassian origin, he was educated at the Lazariyya College there, the Jesuit Collège St-Joseph in Beirut, and the School of Languages in Cairo. He earned his law degree at Aix-en-Provence University in France in 1887. After working for the *Niyaba* briefly, he moved over to the bench in 1899, serving as a judge and counselor in the National Court of Appeal for many years. He was governor of Alexandria, minister of *awqaf* (1917–1919), education (1919), communications (1919–1921, 1923), foreign affairs (1924–1926), and also interior (1925–1926). The Senate's first president under the 1923 Constitution, he succeeded SA'D ZAGHLUL as premier following Sir Lee Stack's assassination in November 1924. After the 1925 elections, in which the Wafd won a majority of the seats in the Chamber of Deputies, he formed a coalition cabinet of Constitutional Liberals, Ittihad partisans, and Independents. The newly elected chamber was dissolved when it elected Zaghlul as its speaker. Backed by King FUAD, Ziwar's coalition amended the electoral law to keep the Wafd out of power. His government increased controls over the Egyptian press, passed an associations law to curb the parties' political activities, ceded the Jaghbub oasis to Italian-ruled Libya, passed an electoral law raising the financial requirements and qualifications for both voters and candidates, and muzzled "Bolshevik" propagandists. His government was viewed as Palace-dominated and repressive. Its fall in January 1926 was ascribed to High Commissioner LLOYD's intrigues. Ziwar remained in the Chamber of Deputies until 1930 and was an appointed senator from 1931 to 1934. He then became King Fuad's *chef du cabinet* until he resigned in 1935. Tall, stout, lazy, and affable with foreigners, he ignored nationalistic attacks on his policies.

Bibliographic Sources
al-Ahram (22 Aug. 1945): 3.
Bishri, 'Abd al-'Aziz, *Fi al-mirat*, 7–14.

Fuad, Faraj Sulayman, *al-Kanz al-thamin*, 249–255.

Grafftey-Smith, *Bright Levant*, 98–99.

Mujahid, *al-A'lam al-sharqiyya*, I, 64–65.

The Near East 44 (9 May 1935): 562–563.

Sayyid-Marsot, *Egypt's Liberal Experiment*, 83–84.

Times (London) (23 Aug. 1945): 7c.

Wright, *Twentieth Century Impressions of Egypt*, 106.

Zakhura, *Mirat al-'asr*, II, 164–165.

Zirikli, *al-A'lam*, I, 130.

Ziyada, Mari Ilyas ["Mayy"]
(11 February 1886–20 October 1941)

Writer. Born in Nazareth to a Palestinian father and a Lebanese mother, she was educated in Catholic schools in Nazareth and 'Ayn Tura, then moved with her parents to Cairo, where her father edited *al-Mahrusa*, which would publish some of her earliest writings. She learned French, English, Italian, and German. An ardent reader of European and Arabic literature, she published her first book of poems, *Fleurs de rêve*, under the pseudonym Isis Copia in 1911. Soon afterward, she began a lengthy and platonic correspondence with Jubran Khalil Jubran [Khalil Gibran], whose work she admired. Drawn to feminist causes by MALAK HIFNI NASIF and HUDA SHA'RAWI, during World War I she became the first Arab woman to attend the Egyptian university. In the 1920s she became an intellectual leader, hosting a salon that attracted writers from many Arab countries, advocating women's access to education and employment, and writing for *al-Siyasa al-usbu'iyya* and *L'Égyptienne*. She delivered eulogies and wrote biographies of Malak Hifni Nasif and 'AISHA AL-TAYMURIYYA as well as numerous articles, especially for *al-Muqtataf*. She was the first woman contributor to *al-Ahram*. In the early 1930s the deaths of her parents, Khalil Jubran, and YA'QUB SARRUF aggravated her feelings of loneliness. Her later years were troubled, and her relatives sent her to a mental hospital in Beirut, but she was released and allowed to return to Cairo, where she died. Although Mayy is said to have been loved by many men, she kept them at a distance.

Bibliographic Sources
Abd al-Hakim, *Nisa*, 73–82.
al-Adib 1:1 (Jan. 1942), special issue.

al-Ahram, 17 Jan. 1938; 20 Oct. 1941; 5 Dec. 1941; 12 Feb. 1982.

Amin, Mustafa, *Shakhsiyyat*, II, 20–39.

Badran and Cooke, *Opening the Gates*, 238–243.

Becka, *DOL*, III, 200–201.

Booth, Marilyn, "Biography and Feminist Rhetoric."

Brockelmann, *GAL*, S III, 259–262.

Bushrui, "May Ziadeh."

Daghir, *Masadir*, II, i, 435–441.

Dimashqiyya, *Mayy fi Suriyya wa Lubnan*.

EAL, II, 826–827.

EI2, VI, 927–928, article by S. Moreh.

Fahmi, Mansur, *Mayy Ziyada wa raidat al-adab*.

———, *Muhadarat 'an Mayy*, 104 et passim.

Filastin, *Mayy: hayatuha wa salunuha wa ad-abuha*.

Ghurayyib, *Mayy Ziyadeh*.

Gibran, *Blue Flame*.

Haddad, Haroun, "Les amours de Mayy Ziyada."

Hafiz, 'Abd al-Salam Hashim, *al-Rafi'i wa Mayy*.

Hamada, Husayn 'Umar, *Ahadith 'an Mayy Ziyada*.

Hasan, Muhammad 'Abd al-Ghani, *Hayat Mayy*.

———, *Mayy adibat al-sharq wa al-'uruba*.

Jabr, Jamil, *Mayy fi hayatiha al-mudtaraba*.

———, *Mayy fi hayatiha wa-adabiha*.

———, *Mayy, silsilat al-manahil*.

———, *Mayy wa Jubran*.

Jundi, *A'lam al-adab*, II, 534–535.

Kahhala, *Mu'jam*, VIII, 165–166.

Khemiri and Kampffmeyer, *Leaders*, 24–27.

Kuzbari, *Mayy Ziyada*.

MMIA 30 (1950): 318–319.

Muhammad, Fathiyya, *Balaghat al-nisa*, II, 113–130.

al-Muqtataf 99:4 (Nov. 1941): 385–393.

Musa, Salama, "al-Anisa Mayy."

———, "Hadith 'an al-Anisa Mayy."

Radwan, Fathi, *'Asr wa rijal*, 239–368.

Ramadi, *Adab wa tarab*, 127–131.

Rossi, "Una scrittrice araba cattolica Mayy."

Sa'd, Amal Da'uq, *Fann al-murasala 'inda Mayy Ziyada*.

Sa'd, Faruq, *Baqat min hadaiq Mayy*.

Sakakini, *Mayy Ziyada fi hayatiha wa athariha*.

Sayigh, Salma, *al-Nasamat*, 140–142.

Sharara, 'Abd al-Latif, *Mayy Ziyada*.

Shinnawi, Kamil, *al-Ladhina ahabbu Mayy*.

Tanahi, Tahir, *Atyaf min hayat Mayy*.

Tuqan, Fadwa, in *al-Risala* 9:449 (15 Aug. 1941): 1497–1498.

UNESCO, *A'lam al-Lubnaniyyin*, 213.

Walili, *Mafakhir al-ajyal*, 108–110.

Ya'qub, *Mayy*.

Zahlawi, *Udaba mu'asirun*, 81–91.

Zayyat, Ahmad Hasan, in *al-Risala* 9:448 (8 Aug. 1941): 1473–1474.

Zeidan, *Arab Women Novelists*, 53–55, 74–77.

Zirikli, *al-A'lam*, V, 253–254.

ABBREVIATIONS AND ACRONYMS

The following abbreviations are used in the Bibliographic Sources and in the Bibliography:

AAS	*Asian and African Studies* (Haifa).	EI2	*Encyclopaedia of Islam.* 9 vols., 6 suppl. fascicles. 2nd ed. Leiden, 1960–.
AIEO	*Annales de l'Institut des Études Orientales* (Algiers, ?–1962; Paris, 1963–).		
		EMME	*Encyclopedia of the Modern Middle East.* Ed. Richard Bulliet, Reeva Simon, and Philip Mattar. 4 vols. New York, 1996.
AION	*Annali Instituto Orientale di Napoli* (Naples).		
BDME	*Biographical Dictionary of the Middle East.* Ed. Yaacov Shimoni. New York, 1991.	GAL	*Geschichte der arabischen literatur.* By Carl Brockelmann. 5 vols. Leiden, 1937–1949.
BEO	*Bulletin des études orientales* (Beirut).	IBLA	*[Revue de] l'Institut des belles lettres arabes* (Tunis).
BIE	*Bulletin de l'Institut Égyptien* (Cairo).	IC	*Islamic Culture* (Hyderabad).
BSOAS	*Bulletin of the School of Oriental and African Studies* (London).	IJMES	*International Journal of Middle East Studies* (Cambridge, UK).
CE	*Coptic Encyclopedia.* Ed. Aziz S. Atiya. 8 vols. New York, 1991.	IQ	*Islamic Quarterly* (London).
		IS	*Islamic Studies* (Islamabad).
CHAL	*The Cambridge History of Arabic Literature: Modern Arabic Literature.* Ed. M.M. Badawi. Cambridge, UK, 1992.	JAL	*Journal of Arabic Literature* (Leiden).
		JAOS	*Journal of the American Oriental Society* (New Haven).
CHE	*Cahiers d' histoire égyptien* (Cairo).	JARCE	*Journal of the American Research Center in Egypt* (Boston).
DBF	*Dictionnaire de biographie française.* Paris, 1929–.		
		JIS	*Journal of Islamic Studies* (Oxford, UK).
DNB	*Dictionary of National Biography.* London, 1885–1901 (with ten-year supplements).	JRCAS	*Journal of the Royal Central Asian Society* (name changed to *Asian Affairs* in 1970) (London).
DOL	*A Dictionary of Oriental Literature.* III. *West Asia and North Africa.* Ed. Jiri Becka. New York, 1974.	MEJ	*Middle East Journal* (Washington, D.C.)
EAL	*Encyclopedia of Arabic Literature.* Ed. Julie Scott Meisami and Paul Starkey. London and New York, 1998.	MES	*Middle Eastern Studies* (London).
		MIDEO	*Mélanges de l'Institut Dominicain des Études Orientales* (Cairo).
EI1	*Encyclopaedia of Islam.* Ed. M. Th. Houtsma. 1st ed. 5 vols. Leiden, 1910–1938.	MMIA	*Majallat al-Majma' al-'Ilmi al-'Arabi* (Damascus).
		MMLA	*Majallat Majma' al-Lugha al-'Arabiyya* (Cairo).

241

MTM	*al-Majalla al-tarikhiyya al-misriyya* (Cairo).		Dictionary]. Alexandria, 1995.
MW	*Muslim World* (Hartford, Conn.).	*REI*	*Revue des études islamiques* (Paris).
OEMIW	*Oxford Encyclopedia of the Modern Islamic World.* Ed. John L. Esposito. 4 vols. New York, 1995.	*TSAB*	*Turkish Studies Association Bulletin* (Bloomington, Ind.).
OM	*Oriente Moderno* (Rome).	*WI*	*Welt des Islams* (Leiden).
QTQ	*Qamus al-tarajim al-qibtiyya* [Egyptian Christian Biographical	*WWAW*	*Who's Who in the Arab World.* Beirut, 1964/65– (annual).

BIBLIOGRAPHY

Abaza, Faruq. *Fikri Abaza, faris al-mu'arada*. Cairo, 1980.
———. "Lamahat min hayati." *al-Ahram*, 11 Dec. 1992; 8, 15 Jan. 1993.
Abaza, Tharwat. "'Amid al-adab wa jiluhu." *al-Ahram* (1 Nov. 1981): 12.
———. *Dhikrayat la mudhakkirat*. Cairo, 1988.
———. *Shu'a' min Taha Husayn*. Cairo, 1974.
'Abbas, Rauf. *al-Nizam al-ijtima'i fi Misr fi zill al-milkiyya al-zira'iyya al-kabira*. Cairo, 1973.
'Abbas Hilmi. *'Ahdi: mudhakkirat 'Abbas Hilmi al-Thani, khidiw Misr al-akhir*. Trans. Jalal Yahya. Cairo, 1993.
Abbate Pacha. *Séance solemnelle pour Riaz Pacha*. Cairo, 1911.
'Abbud, Marun. "Adib Ishaq." *al-Kitab* (5 Feb. 1948): 271–283.
———. "Farah Antun." *al-Hilal* 31:1 (Oct. 1922): 65–67.
———. "Farah Antun." *al-Kitab* 4 (Nov. 1947): 1736–1747.
———. *Judud wa qudama*. Beirut, 1954.
———. *al-Ruus*. Beirut, 1959.
———. *Ruwwad al-nahda al-haditha*. Beirut, 1966.
'Abbud, Nazir. *Jurji Zaydan: hayatuhu, a'maluh*. Beirut, 1983.
'Abd al-'Al, Muhammad Mahmud. *Umm Kulthum: qasidat hubb la tunsa*. Cairo, 1975.
'Abd al-'Azim, 'Ali. *Mashyakhat al-Azhar mundhu inshaiha hatta al-an*. 2 vols. Cairo, 1978–1979.
'Abd al-'Aziz, Isma'il. *al-Milaff al-shakhsi li-Tawfiq al-Hakim*. Cairo, [1992?].
'Abd al-Birr, M. "al-Sanhuri." *al-'Arabi* 249 (Aug. 1979): 90–94.
'Abd al-Fattah, Ahmad. *al-Amir Ahmad Fuad wa nashat al-Jami'a al-Misriyya*. Cairo, 1950.
'Abd al-Fattah, Muhammad. *Ashhar mashahir udaba al-sharq*. 2 vols. Cairo, [1940s?].
'Abd al-Ghafur, Muhammad. *Abu Shadi fi al-mizan*. Cairo, 1933.
'Abd al-Ghani, Ahmad Zaki. "Mahmud Taymur." *Bustan* 1 (1960): 25–26.

'Abd al-Ghani, Mustafa. *Ahmad Baha al-Din: sira qawmiyya*. Cairo, 1996.
———. *I'tirafat 'Abd al-Rahman al-Sharqawi*. Cairo, 1996.
———. *al-Sharqawi mutamarridan*. Cairo, 1987.
———. *Taha Husayn wa al-siyasa*. Cairo, 1986.
'Abd al-Hadi, Ahmad. *al-Manfaluti: hayatuhu wa muallafatuhu*. Cairo, 1981.
'Abd al-Hadi, Amin. *al-Sihafa al-tahira*. Cairo, 1923.
'Abd al-Halim, Ahmad Zaki. *Nisa fawq al-qimma*. Cairo, 1987.
'Abd al-Hamid, Birlanti. *al-Mushir wa ana*. Cairo, 1993.
'Abd al-Hamid, Isma'il. *al-Udaba al-khamas*. Cairo, [1936?].
'Abd al-Hamid, Muhammad Muhyi al-Din. "Muhammad Mustafa al-Maraghi." *al-Kitab* 1 (Nov. 1945): 48–59.
'Abd al-Haqq, 'Abd al-Sattar. *'Abbas Mahmud al-'Aqqad*. Cairo, 1964.
'Abd al-Hayy, 'Abd al-Tawwab. *'Asir hayati*. Cairo, 1966.
'Abd al-'Izz, Ahmad 'Abd al-Wahhab. *Ithna 'ashr 'aman fi suhbat amir al-shu'ara Ahmad Shawqi*. Cairo, 1932.
'Abd al-Jawad, Muhammad. *Hayat mujawir fi al-Jami' al-Ahmadi*. Cairo, 1947.
———. *al-Shaykh al-Husayn ibn Ahmad al-Marsafi*. Cairo, 1952.
———. *Taqwim Dar al-'Ulum*, I. Cairo, 1952.
'Abd al-Jawad, Tawfiq. *'Amaliqat al-'imara fi al-qarn al-'ishrin*. Cairo, 1977.
'Abd al-Karim, Ahmad 'Izzat. *Tarikh al-ta'lim fi 'asr Muhammad 'Ali*. 3 vols. Cairo, 1945.
———. *Tarikh al-ta'lim fi Misr min nihayat hukm Muhammad 'Ali ila awail hukm Tawfiq, 1848–1882*. 3 vols. Cairo, 1945.
'Abd al-Karim, Ahmad 'Izzat, ed. *'Abd al-Rahman al-Jabarti—dirasat wa buhuth*. Cairo, 1976.
'Abd al-Karim, Lotus. *al-Malika Farida*. Cairo, 1993.
'Abd al-Karim, Muhammad. *'Ali Mubarak: hayatuhu wa maathiruhu*. Cairo, 1966.

'Abd Allah, 'Abd Allah Ahmad. *Safahat majhula 'an 'Abd al-Wahhab.* Cairo, 1992.

'Abd Allah, Sa'id 'Abd al-Raziq Yusuf. *Mahmud Fahmi al-Nuqrashi wa dawruhu fi al-siyasa al-misriyya.* Cairo, 1995.

'Abd Allah Nadim. Beirut, 1975.

'Abd al-Latif, Kamal. *Salama Musa wa ishkaliyyat al-nahda.* Casablanca, 1982.

'Abd al-Latif, Muhammad Fahmi. *Falasifa wa sa'alik.* Cairo, [1960s?], 1974.

———. "Mustafa Kamil wa Pierre Loti." *Akhbar al-Yawm,* 7 Oct. 1978.

'Abd al-Malik, Balsam. *Dhikra Bahithat al-Badiya.* Cairo, 1920.

'Abd al-Muttalib, 'Abd Allah. *Muwaylihi al-saghir, hayatuhu wa adabuh.* Cairo, 1985.

'Abd al-Muttalib, Rif'at Fawzi. *'Abqariyyat al-'Aqqad.* Cairo, 1969.

'Abd al-Nur, Fakhri. *Mudhakkirat Fakhri 'Abd al-Nur: Thawrat 1919.* Ed. Yunan Labib Rizq. Cairo, 1992.

'Abd al-Qadir, Muhammad Zaki. "Mudhakkirat." *al-Jil al-jadid,* 25 July 1960.

'Abd al-Rahman, 'Abd al-Ghaffar. *al-Imam Muhammad 'Abduh wa manhajuhu fi al-tafsir.* Cairo, 1980.

'Abd al-Rahman, 'Aisha. Introduction to *Hilyat al-tiraz,* by 'Aisha al-Taymuriyya. Cairo, 1302/1885, 3–31.

'Abd al-Rahman, Ibrahim Hilmi. "Mahmud al-Falaki." *Silsilat ahadith Kulliyyat al-'Ulum bi-Jami'at al-Qahira* 2 (1945).

'Abd al-Ra'uf, Kamal. *Dubabat hawl al-qasr.* Cairo, [1970s?].

'Abd al-Raziq, 'Ali. *Min athar Mustafa 'Abd al-Raziq.* Cairo, 1957.

———. "al-Shaykh Muhammad 'Abduh." *al-Hilal* 63:1 (Jan. 1955): 80–83.

'Abd al-Raziq, Mustafa. "Ali Bey Bahgat, 1858–1924: sa vie et ses oeuvres." *BIE* 6 (1924): 103–113.

———. *Muhammad 'Abduh.* Cairo, 1946.

'Abd al-Sabur, Salah. *Madha yabqa minhum li al-tarikh.* Cairo, 1968.

———. "al-Mazini sha'iran." *al-Katib,* no. 18 (Sept. 1960), republished in *Aswat al-'asr.*

———. *Rihla 'ala al-waraq.* Cairo, 1971.

'Abd al-Wahhab, Muhammad. *Mudhakkirat Muhammad 'Abd al-Wahhab.* Ed. Muhammad Rif'at. Beirut, n.d.

Abdel-Fadil, Mahmoud. *The Political Economy of Nasserism.* Cambridge, UK, 1980.

Abdel-Magued, Abdel Aziz. *The Modern Arabic Short Story.* Cairo, 1955.

Abdel-Malek, Anouar. *Idéologie et renaissance nationale: l'Égypte moderne.* Paris, 1963.

Abdel-Malek, Anouar, ed. *Contemporary Arab Political Thought.* Trans. Michael Pallis. London, 1983.

Abdel Mooti, Farouk. *Yahya Haqqi: al-adib sahib al-qandil.* Beirut, 1994.

Abdel Nasser, Walid. *The Islamic Movement in Egypt: Perceptions of International Relations, 1967–81.* London, 1994.

Abdel Wahab, Farouk. "The Sultan's Dilemma." In *Modern Egyptian Drama: An Anthology.* Minneapolis and Chicago, 1974.

'Abduh, Ibrahim. *Abu Nazzara.* Cairo, 1953.

———. *A'lam al-sihafa al-'arabiyya.* 2nd ed. Cairo, 1948.

———. *Ruz al-Yusuf: sira wa sahifa.* Cairo, 1961.

———. *Tal'at Harb.* Cairo, 1946.

———. "Tarikh al-Waq'i al-Misriyya." Cairo, 1942.

———. *Tarikh jaridat "al-Ahram," 1875–1945.* Cairo, 1948.

———. *Tatawwur al-sihafa al-misriyya.* 2nd ed. Cairo, 1945.

'Abduh, Ibrahim, and 'Ali 'Abd al-'Azim. *Tidhkar Muhammad Tal'at Harb.* Cairo, 1945.

'Abduh, Muhammad. "Mudhakkirat 'an al-thawra al-'urabiyya." Manuscript in Dar al-Kutub.

———. *al-Thair al-Islami Jamal al-Din al-Afghani.* Cairo, 1973.

'Abduh, Muhammad Amin. "Dhikra Dinshaway." *al-Shabab* 1:8 (6 Apr. 1936): 34–41.

———. "Hadithat al-Kamilin." *al-Shabab* 1:6 (23 Mar. 1936): 38–42.

'Abidin, 'Abd al-Majid. *Bayn sha'irayn mujaddidayn Ilya Abu Madi wa 'Ali Mahmud Taha al-muhandis.* Cairo, 1952.

Abou al-Kheir, Yasmine. "Old Wine New Bottles? Dialogue Finally Begins." *Middle East Times/Egypt* 12:27 (4–10 July 1994): 6.

Abou-Ghazi, Dia M. "Ahmad Kamal, 1849–1923." *Annales du Service des Antiquités de l'Egypte* 64 (1981): 1–5.

Abou-Ghazi, Dia M., and Gabriel Boctor. *Moukhtar ou le reveil de l'Égypte.* Cairo, 1949.

Aboushadi, Ahmad Zaki. "Shawqi, Hafiz, and Matran." *Middle Eastern Affairs* 3 (1952): 239–244.

Abu al-Anwar, Muhammad. *Mustafa Lutfi al-Manfaluti.* 2 vols. Cairo, 1981.

Abu al-Fath, Mahmud. *Ma'a al-Wafd al-Misri.* Cairo, [1920?].

———. *al-Masala al-misriyya wa al-Wafd.* Cairo, [1920?].

Abu al-Futuh, Amira. *Ihsan 'Abd al-Quddus yatadhakkir.* Cairo, 1982.

Abu al-Hasan, Muhammad. *Taha Husayn wa dimuqratiyat al-ta'lim.* Cairo, 1951.

Abu al-Ma'ali, Muhammad Rifa'at. *Shaykh al-shu'ara Isma'il Sabri Basha.* Cairo, 1936.

Abu al-Majd, Sabri. *Amin al-Rafi'i: munadil misri min ajl al-dustur wa hurriyyat al-ray: 1886–1927.* Cairo, 1971.

———. *Amin al-Rafi'i, raid sihafat al-ray fi Misr.* Cairo, 1987.

———. *Amin al-Rafi'i: shahid al-wataniyya al-misriyya.* Cairo, 1981.

———. *Ayyam Faruq.* Cairo, 1943.

———. *'Aziz 'Ali al-Misri wa suhbatuh.* Cairo, 1990.

———. *Fikri Abaza.* 2 vols. Cairo, 1986.

———. "Misr ma qabla al-thawra." *al-Musawwar,* nos. 2955–2957 (May–June 1981).

———. *Muhammad Farid: dhikrayatuhu wa mu-dhakkiratuhu.* Cairo, 1969.

———. *Muhammad Mahmud: safahat min tarikhihi al-qawmi.* Cairo, [1940s?].

———. "Qissat al-khilaf bayna Mustafa al-Nahhas wa Makram 'Ubayd." *al-Musawwar,* no. 2958–2959 (19–26 June 1981).

———. "Rajul al-shari' yaqul." *al-Kawakib,* 25 Oct., 15 Nov., 12 Dec. 1988.

———. *Sanawat ma qabla al-Thawra.* 4 vols. Cairo, 1988–1991.

———. *Zakariyya Ahmad.* Cairo, 1963.

Abu al-Su'ud, Fakhri. *al-Thawra al-'urabiyya: khulasa tarikhiyya wa makanuha min al-nahda al-qawmiyya al-misriyya.* Cairo, 1930.

Abu al-Su'ud, Su'ad. *Qissati ma'a Jihan al-Sadat.* Cairo, 1988.

Abu al-'Uyun, Mahmud. *al-Jami' al-Azhar: nubdha fi tarikhih.* Cairo, 1949.

Abu 'Arja, Taysir. "*al-Muqattam" : jaridat al-ihtilal al-baritani fi Misr, 1889–1952.* Cairo, 1997.

Abu Diyya, Sa'd. "al-Afkar al-Masuniyya fi majallat *al-Muqtataf.*" *al-Majalla al-tarikhiyya al-'arabiyya li al-dirasat al-'Uthmaniyya* 1–2 (Jan. 1990): 9–19.

Abu Ghazi, Badr al-Din. *al-Maththal Mukhtar.* Cairo, 1964.

———. *Mukhtar: hayatuhu wa fannuhu.* Cairo, 1988.

Abu Hadid, Muhammad Farid. *'Isamiyyun 'uzama min al-sharq wa al-gharb.* Cairo, 1954.

———. *Sirat al-Sayyid 'Umar Makram.* Cairo, 1937, 1949.

———. *Za'im Misr al-awwal al-Sayyid 'Umar Makram.* Cairo, 1951.

Abu Hamdan, Samir. *Rifa'a Rafi' al-Tahtawi, raid al-tahdith al-urubbi fi Misr.* Beirut, 1992.

Abu 'Izz al-Din, Sulayman. *Ibrahim Basha fi Suriya.* Beirut, 1929.

Abu Jaber, Kamal. "Salamah Musa: Precursor of Arab Socialism." *MEJ* 20 (1966): 196–206.

Abu Khalil, Shawqi. *Jurji Zaydan fi al-mizan.* Damascus, 1981, 1983.

Abu Lughod, Ibrahim. *Arab Rediscovery of Europe.* Princeton, 1963.

———. "The Transformation of the Egyptian Elite." *MEJ* 21 (1962): 342–344.

Abu-Rabi', Ibrahim M. "al-Azhar and Islamic Rationalism in Modern Egypt: The Philosophical Contributions of Mustafa 'Abd al-Raziq and 'Abd al-Halim Mahmud." *Islamic Studies* 27:2 (summer 1988): 129–159.

———. *Intellectual Origins of Islamic Resurgence in the Modern Arab World.* Albany, N.Y., 1996.

Abu Rayya, Mahmud. *Jamal al-Din al-Afghani.* Cairo, 1961, 1966.

———. *Min rasail al-Rafi'i.* Cairo, 1950.

Abu Ruwa', Muhammad Ibrahim. *al-Shahid Ahmad Mahir.* Cairo, 1946.

Abu Salim, Salah al-Din. *Mahmud Taymur al-adib wa al-insan.* Cairo, 1961.

Abu Sayf, Layla. *Najib al-Rihani.* Cairo, 1972.

Abu Shadi, Ahmad Zaki. "Muhammad Hafiz Ibrahim." *Apollo* 1:1 (Sept. 1932): 32–33.

———. *Shu'ara al-'arab al-mu'asirun.* Cairo, 1958.

———. *Yawmiyyat al-Duktur Ahmad Abu Shadi.* Amman, 1995.

Abyad, Su'ad. *Jurj Abyad: al-masrah al-misri fi miat 'am.* Cairo, 1970.

———. *Jurj Abyad: ayyam lan yusdal 'alayha al-sattar.* Cairo, 1991.

An Account of the Revolt of Aly Bey. London, 1783.

Adalian, Rouben. "The Armenian Colony of Egypt During the Reign of Muhammad 'Ali, 1805–1848." *Armenian Review* 33:2 (1980): 115–144.

Adam, Colin Forbes. *Life of Lord Lloyd.* London, 1948.

Adam, Juliette. *L'Angleterre en Égypte.* Paris, 1922.

Adams, C.C. *Islam and Modernism in Egypt.* London, 1933.

———. "Shaykh Mustafa 'Abd al-Razik." *MW* (July 1946): 246–247.

al-'Adawi, Ibrahim, *Rashid Rida: al-imam al-mujahid.* Cairo, 1964.

Addison, Herbert. "Thomas Waghorn and the Overland Route." *JRCAS* 45:2 (1958): 179–185.

Adham, Isma'il, and Ibrahim Naji. *Tawfiq al-Hakim.* Cairo, 1984.

Adham, Isma'il Ahmad. *Khalil Mutran, sha'ir al-'arabiyya al-ibda'i.* Cairo, 1939.

al-Afghani, Sa'id, and Muhammad Sa'id 'Abd al-Majid. *Nabighat al-sharq al-Sayyid Jamal al-Din al-Afghani.* Cairo, 1967.

Aflatun, Inji. *Mudhakkirat Inji Aflatun.* Ed. Sa'id al-Khayyal. Cairo, 1993; Kuwait, 1994.

Afro-Asian Peoples' Solidarity Organization. *Youssef El-Sibai: In Memoriam.* Cairo, 1978.

Aghion, M., and M. Poilay. "Excursion dans les grands domains—propriété de S.E. Riaz Pacha." *Bulletin de l'Union Syndicale des Agriculteurs d'-Egypte* 1:5 (Nov. 1901).

Agliette, B. "Mustafa Kamil, 1874–1908, fondatori del Partito Nationalista Egiziano." *OM* 22 (1942): 305–317.

Ahmad, 'Abd al-'Ati Muhammad. *al-Fikr al-siyasiyya li al-Imam Muhammad 'Abduh.* Cairo, 1978.

Ahmad, Ahmad Yusuf. *Fannan al-sha'b Mahmud Bayram al-Tunisi.* Cairo, 1962.

Ahmad, Anwar. "Muhakamat al-Shaykh 'Abd al-'Aziz Jawish." *al-Musawwar* (29 Oct. 1948): 34–35.

Ahmad, Muhammad Ali. *Mustafa al-Nahhas Basha.* Cairo, [1950?].

Ahmad, Muhammad Khalaf Allah. *Ma'alim 'ala tariq al-klasikiyya al-'arabiyya al-haditha: Taha Husayn wa Mahmud Taymur.* Cairo, 1977.

Ahmad 'Urabi. Beirut, 1976.

Ahmed, J.M. *The Intellectual Origins of Egyptian Nationalism.* London, 1960.

Ahmed, Leila. *Edward W. Lane: A Study of His Life and Works.* London and New York, 1978.

———. *Women and Gender in Islam: Historical Roots of a Modern Debate.* New Haven, 1992.

Ajami, Fouad. "The Sorrows of Egypt." *Foreign Affairs* 74:5 (Sept. 1995): 72–88.

'Ajlan, 'Abbas Bayyumi. *al-Islam fi adab al-Rafi'i.* Alexandria, 1982.

Akhavi, Shahrough. "Sayyid Qutb." In *Cultural Transitions in the Middle East,* ed. Serif Mardin. Leiden, 1994.

A'lam "al-Muqtataf," I. Cairo, 1925.

Alexander, J. *The Truth About Egypt.* London, 1911.

al-Alfi, Ahmad. "Dr. Sarruf wa fann al-zira'a." *al-Muqtataf* 74:1 (Jan. 1929): 110–112; 3 (Mar. 1929): 333–335; 4 (Apr. 1929): 450–452.

'Ali, Kamal Hasan. *Muhariban wa mufawidan.* Cairo, 1986.

'Ali, Kamal Muhammad. *Ihsan 'Abd al-Quddus fi arba'in 'aman, sira wa 'amal adabiyya.* Cairo, 1985.

Ali, Mohamed. *Souvenirs de jeunesse.* Cairo, 1951.

'Ali, Muhammad Kurd. "Hayat Hafiz Ibrahim." *MMIA* 13 (1933): 744–749.

al-'Alim, Mahmud Amin. *Taamulat fi 'alam Najib Mahfuz.* Cairo, 1970.

———. "Thawra fikriyya . . . wa lakin." *al-Musawwar,* no. 2191 (7 Oct. 1966): 32–33.

Alkhayat, Hamdi. *Gurgi Zaydan: Leben und Werk.* Cologne, 1976.

'Allam, [Muhammad] Mahdi. "Ahmad Hasan al-Zayyat." *Majallat Ma'had al-buhuth wa al-dirasat al-'arabiyya* 1 (Mar. 1969): 153–177.

———. *al-Majma'iyyun fi khamsin 'aman.* Cairo, 1986.

———. "Safahat min al-adab al-'arabi: *Hadith 'Isa ibn Hisham.*" *al-Siyasa al-usbu'iyya,* 13 Nov. 1943; 22 Jan. 1944.

'Allam, [Muhammad] Mahdi, and 'Abd al-Hamid Hasan. *Nathr Hifni Nasif.* Cairo, 1960.

Allen, Roger. *The Arabic Novel: An Historical and Critical Introduction.* Manchester, UK, 1982.

———. "The Artistry of Yusuf Idris." *World Literature Today* 55:1 (1981): 43–47.

———. *Critical Perspectives on Yusuf Idris.* Colorado Springs, 1994.

———. "Egyptian Drama After the Revolution." *Edebiyat* 4:1 (1979): 97–134.

———. "*Hadith 'Isa ibn Hisham* by Muhammad al-Muwaylihi: A Reconsideration." *JAL* 1 (1970).

———. "*Hadith 'Isa ibn Hisham*: The Excluded Passages." *WI,* N.S. 12 (1969): 74–89.

———. *A Period of Time.* Reading, UK, 1992.

———. "Poetry and Poetic Criticism at the Turn of the Century." In *Studies in Modern Arabic Literature,* ed. R.C. Ostle. Warminster, UK, 1975, 7–17.

———. "Some New al-Muwailihi Materials or the Unpublished *Hadith 'Isa ibn Hisham.*" *Humaniora Islamica* 2 (1974): 139–180.

———. "Some Recent Works of Najib Mahfuz: A Critical Analysis." *JARCE* 14 (1977): 101–110.

———. *A Study of "Hadith 'Isa ibn Hisham."* Albany, N.Y., 1954.

———. "Writings of the Members of the 'Nazli Circle.'" *Journal of the American Research Center in Egypt* 8 (1969–1970): 79–84.

Allen, Roger, ed. *Modern Arabic Literature: A Library of Literary Criticism.* New York, 1989.

'Alluba, Muhammad 'Ali. *Dhikrayat ijtima'iyya wa siyasiyya.* Ed. Ahmad Hamdi. Cairo, 1988.

———. "al-Hadith al-ladhi la ansah." *al-Hilal* 55:2 (Feb. 1947): 62–63.

———. *Mabadi al-siyasa al-misriyya.* Cairo, 1942, 1990.

Alterman, Jon. "American Aid to Egypt in the 1950s: From Hope to Hostility." *MEJ* 52:1 (winter 1998): 51–69.

Alterman, Jon, ed. *Sadat and His Legacy: Egypt and the World, 1977–1997.* Washington, D.C., 1998.

al-'Alusi, Jamal al-Din. *Ahmad Hasan al-Zayyat.* Baghdad, 1968.

———. *Taha Husayn bayn ansarihi wa khusumihi.* Baghdad, 1953.

'Alwan, Baha al-Din Muhammad. *'Abd al-Rahman al-Rafi'i: muarrikh Misr al-haditha.* Cairo, 1987.

Amer, Attia, *Lughat al-masrah al-'arabi.* Stockholm, 1967.

American National Biography. New York and Oxford, 1999.

Amin, Ahmad. "Bayna Qasim Amin wa Duq Darkur." *al-Thaqafa,* no. 173: 5; no. 175: 12; no. 177: 14 (1942).

———. *Fayd al-khatir.* 10 vols. Cairo, 1958–1974.

———. *Hayati.* Cairo, 1950. Eng. trans. Issa J. Boulatta. *My Life: The Autobiography of an Egyptian Scholar, Writer, and Cultural Leader.* Leiden, 1978.

———. *al-Sharq wa al-Gharb.* Cairo, 1955. Eng. trans. Wolfgang Behn. *Orient and Occident: An Egyptian's Quest for National Identity.* Berlin, 1984.

———. *Zu'ama al-islah fi al-'asr al-hadith.* Cairo, 1948.

Amin, Husayn Ahmad. *Fi bayt Ahmad Amin—wa maqalat ukhra.* 2nd ed. Cairo, 1989.

Amin, Mustafa. "Kitab majhul bi-qalam Sa'd Zaghlul." *al-Hilal* 70:3 (Mar. 1962): 22–28.

———. *al-Kitab al-mamnu'.* 2 vols. Cairo, 1974–1975.

———. *Li-kull maqal azma.* Cairo, 1979.

———. "Shakhsiyat la tunsa." *al-Akhbar,* 8 Mar. 1986.

———. *Shakhsiyyat la tunsa.* 2 vols. Cairo, 1988.

Amin, Osman. "Moustafa Abdel Raziq." *Revue du Caire,* special issue (1953): 120–126.

al-Amin, al-Sayyid Muhsin. *A'yan al-Shi'a*. 35 vols. Damascus, 1940.

Amin, 'Uthman. *Muhammad 'Abduh*. Cairo, 1944.

———. "Muhammad 'Abduh." *al-Kitab* 1 (Jan 1946): 332–338.

———. *Nazarat fi fikr al-'Aqqad*. Cairo, 1966.

———. *Ruwwad al-wa'y al-insani fi al-sharq al-islami*. Cairo, 1961.

Amir, Hasan. "Intihar am ightiyal al-Mushir Amir!" *Uktubir*, no. 390 (15 Apr. 1984): 32–33.

al-'Amiri, Muhammad Husni. *Nuzhat al-albab fi tarikh Misr wa shu'ara al-'asr wa murasalat al-ahbab*. Cairo, 1897.

Ampère, Jean-Jacques. *Voyage en Égypte et en Nubie*. Paris, 1881.

Anani, Muhammad. "Salah Jahin sha'iran." *al-Qahira* 59 (May 1986).

Anawati, G.C. "Une figure de proue: le Cheikh Mostafa Abd El-Raziq." *Bulletin de l'Institut Français d'Archéologie Orientale* (1960): 83–131.

———. "Shibli Shumayyil, Medical Philosopher and Scientist." In *The Islamic World, from Classical to Modern Times: Essays in Honor of Bernard Lewis*. Princeton, 1989, 637–650.

'Anbar, Muhammad Sadiq. *Dhikra faqid al-watan al-maghfur lahu Amin al-Rafi'i*. Cairo, 1928.

Anderson, Arthur. *Communications with India, China, etc*. London, 1843.

Andrews, Deborah, ed. *Annual Obituary 1989*. Chicago, 1990.

Anis, Muhammad. *4 Fibrayir 1942*. Beirut, 1973.

———. *al-Dawla al-'Uthmaniyya wa al-sharq al-'arabi*. Cairo, 1965.

———. *Dirasat fi wathaiq Thawrat 1919*. I, Cairo, 1963.

———. "Haqaiq 'an 'Abd al-Rahman al-Jabarti mustamadda min wathaiq al-mahkama al-shar'iyya." *MTM* 9–10 (1960–1962): 69–115.

———. *Madrasat al-tarikh al-misri fi al-'asr al-'uthmani*. Cairo, 1962.

———. *Safahat majhula min al-tarikh al-misri aw sanawat al-sira' al-'anif bayn Fuad wa 'Abbas*. Cairo, 1973.

———. *Safahat matwiya min tarikh al-za'im Mustafa Kamil*. Cairo, 1962.

———. "Thawrat 1919 wa Hizb al-'Ummal al-Baritani." *al-Hilal* 72:10 (Oct. 1965): 20–29.

Ansari, Hamied. "The Islamic Militants in Egyptian Politics." *IJMES* 16 (1984): 123–144.

———. "Mubarak's Egypt." *Current History* 84 (Jan. 1985): 21–24.

Antaki, Thabit. *al-Nujum al-zahr fi rusum a'yan Misr: dalil Misr wa al-Sudan li-sanat 1905*. Cairo, 1905.

Antonius, George. *The Arab Awakening*. London, 1939.

al-'Aqid, Yusuf. "I'tirafat mutaakhkhira li-Fathi Ghanim." *al-Musawwar*, no. 2996 (18 Mar. 1982): 42–45.

al-'Aqiqi, Najib. *al-Mustashriqun*. 3 vols. Cairo, 1965.

al-'Aqqad, 'Abbas Mahmud. "'Abd al-Rahman Shukri fi al-mizan." *al-Hilal* 67:2 (Feb. 1959): 23–27.

———. "Ahamm hadith fi majra hayati." *al-Hilal* 38:2 (Dec. 1929): 139.

———. In *Ana*, ed. Tahir al-Tanahi. Cairo, 1964.

———. "Farah Antun." *al-Balagh* (5 Mar. 1924).

———. "Khalil Mutran: kitab wahid bi-qalamih." *al-Kitab* 10 (Feb. 1951): 176–179.

———. "Mahmud Basha al-Falaki." *al-Kitab* 5 (July 1950): 587–590.

———. *Muhammad 'Abduh*. Cairo, 1962.

———. *Muraja'at fi al-adab wa al-funun*. Beirut, 1966.

———. "Mustafa 'Abd al-Raziq (1885–1947)." *al-Kitab* 3:6 (Apr. 1947): 887–893.

———. *Mutala'at fi al-kutub wa al-hayat*. Cairo, 1924.

———. *Rijal 'araftuhum*. Cairo, 1963.

———. *Sa'd Zaghlul, sira wa tahiyya*. Cairo, 1936.

———. "Sa'd Zaghlul ba'da 20 sana." *al-Hilal* 55:9 (Sept. 1947): 8–12.

———. *Shu'ara Misr wa biatuhum*. Cairo, 1937.

al-Aqqad, Amir. *Ahmad Amin: hayatuhu wa adabuhu*. Beirut, 1982.

———. *al-'Aqqad: ma'arikuhu fi al-siyasa wa al-adab*. Cairo, 1972.

———. *Gharamiyyat al-'Aqqad*. Cairo, 1971.

———. *Lamahat min hayat al-'Aqqad*. Cairo, 1970.

———. *Safahat min ma'arik al-'Aqqad al-siyasiyya*. Beirut, 1979.

Arabi, Oussama. "al-Sanhuri's Reconstruction of the Islamic Law of Contract Deficits." *JIS* 6:2 (July 1995): 153–172.

Arafa, Bahiga. *The Social Activities of the Egyptian Feminist Union*. Cairo, 1973.

Arberry, Arthur J. "Hafiz Ibrahim and Shawqi." *Journal of the Royal Asiatic Society* (Jan. 1937): 41–58.

———. *Oriental Essays: Portraits of Seven Scholars*. London, 1960.

Arbose, Jules. "Osman Ahmad Osman: Egypt's Private Sector Crusader." *International Management* (June 1983): 36–42.

Archarouni, Victoria. *Nubar Pacha: un grand serviteur d'Égypte*. Paris, [1950s?].

Armbrust, Walter. *Mass Culture and Modernism in Egypt*. Cairo, 1996.

Arslan, Shakib. *Rashid Rida aw ikha arba'in sana*. Cairo, 1937.

———. *Shawqi aw sadaqat arba'in sana*. Cairo, 1936.

Arthur, George. *Life of Lord Kitchener*. 3 vols. London, 1920.

Artin, Yacoub. *Artin Bey, ministre Mohammed Aly, 1800–1859*. Cairo, 1896.

al-'Arusi, Mahmud Kamil. *Ashhar qadaya al-ightiyalat al-siyasiyya*. Cairo, 1989.

———. *Muhakamat Sayyid Qutb: dirasa wathaiqiyya*. Shibbin al-Qanatir, 1995.

al-'Aryan, Muhammad Sa'id. *Hayat al-Rafi'i*. Cairo, 1939, 1955.

Asaf, Yusuf. *Dalil Misr*. Cairo, 1890.

al-'Ashmawi, 'Abd al-Rahman Salih. *Waqfa ma'a Jurji Zaydan*. Riyad, 1993.

al-'Ashri, J. *Thaqafatuna bayna al-asala wa al-mu'asara*. Cairo, 1971.

'Ashur, 'Abd al-Ghaffar, and 'Abd al-Hamid Fuad. *al-Muntakhab min shi'r Abi Shadi*. Cairo, 1926.

'Ashur, Nu'man. *Butulat misriyya min 'Umar Makram ila Bayram al-Tunisi*. Cairo, 1973.

———. *Suwar min al-butula wa al-abtal*. Cairo, 1964.

Assad, Thomas J. *Three Victorian Travelers: Burton, Blunt, Doughty*. London, 1964.

'Assaf, Mahmud. *Ma'a al-imam al-shahid Hasan al-Banna*. Cairo, 1993.

Assali, Bassam. *al-Marishal Allinbi, 1861–1936*. Beirut, 1983.

Ata, A.W. "The Impact of Westernising and Other Factors in the Changing Status of Muslim Women." *IQ* 31 (1987): 38–56.

'Ata, Muhammad Mustafa. *Khalil Mutran, 1872–1949*. Cairo, 1959.

'Ata Allah, Nasri. "Ahmad Zaki fi 'id miladihi al-thamanin." *al-Hilal* 82:12 (Dec. 1974): 132–136.

'Atawi, Fawzi. *Ahmad Shawqi amir al-shu'ara*. Beirut, 1969.

Atiya, Aziz Suryal. *A History of Eastern Christianity*. 2nd ed. Millwood, N.Y., 1980.

'Atiyah, Edward. *An Arab Tells His Story*. London, 1946.

'Atiyya, Ahmad 'Abd al-Halim. *Ahmad Amin arba'un 'aman 'ala al-rahil*. Cairo, 1994.

'Atiyya, Na'im. *Yahya Haqqi wa 'alamuhu al-qissas*. Cairo, 1978.

'Atiyyat Allah, Ahmad. *Silsilat al-a'lam: 'Abdallah Nadim*. Cairo, 1955.

al-Atrash, Farid. *Farid al-Atrash: Mudhakkirat, majmu'at aghanihi*. Beirut, 1975.

'Atri, Fawzi. *Khalil Mutran: sha'ir al-aqtar al-'arabiyya*. Cairo, 1974; Beirut, 1989.

'Awad, Ahmad Hafiz. "Ahamm hadith fi majra hayati." *al-Hilal* 38:2 (Dec. 1929): 141–142.

———. "Dhikrayat Ahmad Hafiz 'Awad." *al-Hilal* 39:8 (June 1931): 1143.

———. *Fath Misr al-hadith, aw Nabuliyun Bonaparte fi Misr*. Cairo, 1925.

———. In *al-Hilal* 38:8 (June 1931): 1143–1146.

——— "Khamas shakhsiyyat misriyya atharat fi hayati." *Akhir sa'a* (16 May 1944): 28.

'Awad, Jirjos Philuthawus. *Dhikra muslih 'azim, al-Anba Kirullus al-rabi', abi al-islah al-qibti*. Cairo, 1911.

'Awad, Louis. "Ahmad Lutfi al-Sayyid." In *Maqalat fi al-naqd wa al-adab,* ed. Mahmud 'Awad. Cairo, 1964.

———. *Aqni'at al-nasiriyya al-sab'a: munaqashat Tawfiq al-Hakim wa Muhammad Hasanayn Haykal*. Beirut, 1975.

———, *Awraq al-'umr: sanawat al-takwin*. Cairo, 1989.

———. *Dirasat fi adabina al-hadith*. Cairo, 1961.

———. *al-Hurriyya wa naqd al-hurriyya*. Cairo, 1971.

———. *The Literature of Ideas in Egypt*. Atlanta, 1986.

———. *Mudhakkirat talib ba'tha*. Cairo, 1965.

———. "Problems of the Egyptian Theatre." In *Studies in Modern Arabic Literature,* ed. R.C. Ostle.

———. *al-Thawra wa al-adab*. Cairo, 1971.

'Awad, Mahmud. *Sa'd Zaghlul: za'im al-umma*. Cairo, 1980.

———. *Umm Kulthum al-lati la ya'rifuha ahad*. Cairo, 1969; partial Eng. trans. in Fernea and Bezirgan, *Middle Eastern Muslim Women Speak*, 135–175.

'Awad, Ramses. *Tawfiq al-Hakim al-ladhi la ta'rifuhu*. Cairo, 1974.

'Awad, Yusuf. *al-Ru'ya al-hadariyya wa al-naqdiyya fi adab Taha Husayn*. Cairo, 1979.

'Awadayn, Ibrahim. "Bayram al-Tunisi wa al-muqawama al-ijtima'iyya." *al-Hilal* 73:3 (May 1984).

'Awda, Muhammad. *al-Basha wa al-thawra*. Cairo, 1977.

Ayalon, Ami. *The Press in the Arab Middle East: A History*. New York and Oxford, 1995.

Ayalon, David. "The Historian al-Jabarti." In *Historians of the Middle East*, ed. Bernard Lewis and P.M. Holt. London, 1962, 391–402.

———. "The Historian al-Jabarti and His Background." *BSOAS* 23 (1960): 217–249.

———. "Studies in al-Jabarti: Notes on the Transformation of Mamluk Society in Egypt Under the Ottomans." *Journal of the Economic and Social History of the Orient* 3:2–3 (1960): 148–174, 275–325.

Ayubi, Nazih. *Political Islam: Religion and Politics in the Arab World*. London, 1991.

Ayyad, Shukri Muhammad. "Ahmad Hasan al-Zayyat, 1885–1968." *al-Majalla* 12:139 (July 1968): 9–13.

Ayyub, Mahmud. "Islam and Christianity: A Study of Muhammad Abduh's View of the Two Religions." *Humaniora Islamica* 2 (1974): 121–137.

al-Ayyubi, Ilyas. *Tarikh Misr fi 'ahd al-Khidiwi Isma'il Basha*. 2 vols. Cairo, 1923.

'Aziz, Khayri. *Udaba 'ala tariq al-nidal al-siyasi*. Cairo, 1970.

al-'Azmeh, Aziz. *Islamic Law: Social and Historical Contexts*. London and New York, 1988.

'Azmi, Mahmud. "'Abbas Hilmi al-Thani." *al-Kitab* 1 (Dec. 1945): 177–181.

———. *al-Ayyam al-mia: 'ala hamish tarikh Misr al-hadith—'ahd wizarat 'Ali Mahir Basha, 3 Yanayir-9 Mayu 1936*. Cairo, n.d.

'Azzam, 'Abd al-'Aziz. *al-Islam wa al-fikr al-'alami*. Beirut, 1963.

'Azzam, 'Abd al-Wahhab. *al-Awabid: maqalat wa manzumat*. Cairo, 1942.

al-'Azzawi, Ni'ma Rahim. *Ahmad Hasan al-Zayyat katiban wa naqidan*. Cairo, 1987.

Badawi, 'Abd al-Rahman, ed. *Ila Taha Husayn fi 'id miladihi al-sab'in.* Cairo, 1959.

———. *Taha Husayn wa qadiyyat al-shi'r.* Cairo, 1975.

Badawi, Ahmad Ahmad. *Rifa'a al-Tahtawi.* Cairo, 1950, 1959.

Badawi, M.M. "al-Barudi: Precursor of the Modern Arabic Poetic Revival." *WI* 12 (1969): 228–244.

———. "al-Mazini the Novelist." *JAL* 4 (1973): 112–145; reprinted in Badawi, *Modern Arabic Literature,* 136–166.

———. *Critical Introduction to Modern Arabic Poetry.* New York and Cambridge, UK, 1975.

———. *Modern Arabic Drama in Egypt.* Cambridge, UK, 1987.

———. *Modern Arabic Literature and the West.* Ithaca, N.Y., 1985.

———. "Shukri the Poet: A Reconsideration." In *Studies in Modern Arabic Literature,* ed. R.C. Ostle, 18–33.

Badawi, Mustafa Bahjat. "al-Janib al-akhar li raid al-mustasharin." *al-Ahram,* 7 Aug. 1978.

Badawi, Zaki. *The Reformers of Egypt: A Critique of Afghani, Abduh, and Rida.* Slough, UK, 1976.

Badr, 'Abd al-Muhsin Taha. *Tatawwur al-riwaya al-'arabiyya al-haditha fi Misr.* Cairo, 1963.

Badran, Margot. "Dual Liberation: Feminism and Nationalism in Egypt, 1870–1928." *Feminist Issues* 8:1 (spring 1988): 15–34.

———. "Expressing Feminism and Nationalism in Autobiography: The Memoirs of a Woman Educator." In *De/Colonizing the Subject: The Politics of Gender in Women's Autobiography,* ed. Sidonie Smith and Julia Watson. Minneapolis, 1992.

———. "Feminist Politics." In *Problems,* ed. John Spagnolo, 27–48.

———. "The Feminist Vision in the Writings of Three Turn-of-the-Century Egyptian Women." *British Society of Middle East Studies Bulletin* 15:1–2 (1988): 11–20.

———. *Feminists, Islam, and Nation: Gender and the Making of Modern Egypt.* Princeton, 1995.

———. "From Consciousness to Activism." In *Problems,* ed. John Spagnolo, 27–48.

Badran, Margot, and Miriam Cooke, eds. *Opening the Gates: A Century of Arab Feminist Writing.* Bloomington, Ind., 1990.

Badrawi, Malak. *Isma'il Sidqi, 1875–1950.* London, 1996.

Badrawi, Sami, ed. *Awraq al-Barudi: al-majmu'a al-adabiyya.* Cairo, 1981.

al-Badri, Mustafa Mumin. *al-Imam Mustafa Sadiq al-Rafi'i.* Baghdad, 1968.

Baer, Gabriel. "Ali Mubarak's *Khitat* as a Source for the History of Modern Egypt." In *Political and Social Change,* ed. P.M. Holt, 13–27.

———. *A History of Landownership in Modern Egypt.* London, 1962.

———. *Studies in the Social History of Modern Egypt.* Chicago, 1969.

al-Baghdadi, 'Abd al-Latif, *Mudhakkirat 'Abd al-Latif al-Baghdadi.* 3 vols. Cairo, 1977.

Baha al-Din, Ahmad. *Ayyam laha tarikh.* Cairo, 1954.

Bahgat, Aly. "Acte de mariage du Général Menou avec la dame Zobaideh." *BIE,* ser. 2, no. 2 (Apr.–May 1898): 221–235.

al-Bahrawi, 'Ali Ibrahim. *'Ali Basha Mubarak awwal wazir li al-ma'arif.* Cairo, [1940s?].

Baignières, Paul de. *L'Égypte satirique: alboum d'Abou Naddara.* Paris, 1886.

Baker, Raymond William. *Egypt's Uncertain Revolution Under Nasser and Sadat.* Cambridge, Mass., 1978.

———. *Sadat and After: Struggles for Egypt's Political Soul.* Cambridge, Mass., 1990.

Bakhit, Muhammad. *Haqiqat "al-Islam wa usul al-hukm."* Cairo, 1925.

Bakr, 'Abd al-Wahhab. "al-'Alaqat al-sirriyya bayn al-Malik Fuad wa al-Khidiwi 'Abbas Hilmi." *MTM* 34 (1987): 113–144.

al-Bakri, Muhammad Tawfiq. *Bayt al-Siddiq.* Cairo, 1904.

al-Balihi, Ibrahim ibn 'Abd al-Rahman. *Sayyid Qutb wa turathuhu al-adabi wa al-fikri.* Riyadh, 1972.

Baljon, J.M.S. *Modern Koran Interpretation (1880–1960).* Leiden, 1961.

Ballas, Shim'on. "Italat 'ala manhaj Muhammad 'Uthman Jalal fi al-tarjama." *al-Karmil* 6 (1985): 6–36.

Balta, Paul, and Claudine Rulleau. *Nasser.* Paris, 1995.

al-Banna, Hasan, *Majmu'at rasail al-Imam al-shahid Hasan al-Banna.* Beirut, 1965.

al-Banna, Muhammad Kamil. *Bayram al-Tunisi kama 'araftuh.* Tripoli, 1980.

———. *Mahmud Bayram al-Tunisi: qitharat al-adab al-sha'bi.* Tunis, 1980.

al-Baqari, Ahmad Mahir. *al-'Aqqad wa al-mara.* Alexandria, [1976?].

———. *Ibrahim Naji min shi'rihi.* Alexandria, 1983.

Baqli, Muhammad Qandil. *Abtal al-muqawama al-sha'biyya li al-hamla al-firaniyya fi Misr.* Cairo, 1963.

Barakat, A. *Tatawwur al-milkiyya al-zira'iyya wa atharuhu 'ala al-haraka al-siyasiyya (1813–1914).* Cairo, 1978.

Barakat, Daud. "Ma 'araftuhu 'an Madam Taqla Basha." *al-Hilal* 33:1 (Oct. 1924): 78–83.

Barakat, [Muhammad] Bahi al-Din. "Abu al-Jami'a." *al-Hilal* 59:1 (Jan. 1951): 14–18.

———. *Safahat min al-tarikh.* Cairo, 1961.

Barbour, Nevill. "The Arabic Theatre in Egypt." *BSOAS* 8 (1935–1937): 173–187.

———. "'Audatu r-ruh—an Egyptian Novel." *IC* 9 (1935): 487–492.

———. "al-Manfaluti—an Egyptian Essayist." *IC* 7 (1933): 490–501; 8 (1934): 140–145, 222–236, 448–456, 621–630; 9 (1935): 359–367, 645–664; 10 (1936): 477–485.

Baron, Beth. "Nationalist Iconography: Egypt as a Woman." In *Rethinking Nationalism*, ed. Israel Gershoni and James Jankowski, 109–113.

———. *The Women's Awakening in Egypt: Culture, Society, and the Press.* New Haven, 1994.

Barrada, Muhammad. *Muhammad Mandur wa tanzir al-naqd al-'arabi.* Beirut, 1979.

al-Basyuni, Muhammad Rajab. "Insaf batal shadid." *al-Adib* 33:9 (1964): 5–8.

al-Batatuni, Muhammad Labib. *Tarikh al-Duktur Klut Bey.* Cairo, 1891.

Ba'thi, Ibrahim. *Shakhsiyyat islamiyya wa mu'asira.* Cairo, 1973.

al-Bayyumi, Muhammad Rajab. *Ahmad Hasan al-Zayyat bayn al-balagha wa al-naqd al-adabi.* Riyadh, 1985.

———. "Ahmad Taymur." *al-Kitab* 5 (Apr. 1948): 599–606.

———. "Athar al-Zayyat fi al-yaqza al-'arabiyya." *al-Adib* 43:5 (May 1984): 17–21.

———. *al-Azhar bayn al-siyasa wa hurriyyat al-fikr.* Cairo, 1983.

———. *Mustafa Sadiq al-Rafi'i: faris al-qalam taht rayat al-Quran.* Damascus, 1997.

Bayyumi, Zakariyya Sulayman. *al-Hizb al-Watani, 1912–1953.* Cairo, 1981.

———. *al-Tayyarat al-siyasiyya wa al-ijtima'iyya bayn al-mujaddidin wa al-muhafizin: dirasa tarikhiyya fi fikr al-Shaykh Muhammad 'Abduh.* Cairo, 1983.

al-Baz, Ni'am. *Thair taht al-imama.* Cairo, 1988.

Beaman, Ardern Hulme. *The Dethronement of the Khedive.* London, 1929.

Beard, Michael, and Adnan Haydar, eds. *Naguib Mahfouz: From Regional Fame to Global Recognition.* Syracuse, N.Y., 1993.

Beattie, Kirk. *Egypt During the Nasser Years.* Boulder, Colo., 1994.

Beatty, Charles. *Ferdinand de Lesseps: A Biographical Study.* London, 1956.

Beaucour, Fernand, Yves Laissus, and Chantal Orgogozo. *The Discovery of Egypt.* Trans. Bambi Ballard. Paris, 1990.

Beck, Lois, and Nikki Keddie, eds. *Women in the Muslim World.* Cambridge, Mass., 1978.

Beinin, Joel. *The Dispersion of Egyptian Jewry, Culture, Politics and the Formation of the Modern Diaspora.* Berkeley, 1998.

Beinin, Joel, and Zachary Lockman. *Workers on the Nile: Nationalism, Communism, Islam, and the Egyptian Working Class, 1882–1954.* Princeton, 1987.

Bell, C.F. Moberly. *Khedives and Pashas.* London, 1884.

Bellefonds, Y.L. de. "'Abd al-Razzak al-Sanhuri: Masadir al-haqq fi al-fiqh al-islami." *Revue internationale de droit comparé* 10 (1958): 476–479.

Bencheneb, Saadeddine. "Deux sources d'al-Manfaluti." *Revue Africaine* 85 (1941): 260–264.

———. "Edmond About et al-Muwaylihi." *Revue Africaine* 88 (1944): 270–273.

———. "Études de litterature arabe moderne: Muhammad al-Muwaylihi." *Revue Africaine* 83 (1939): 358–382; 84 (1940): 77–92.

Benoist-Mechin, Jacques Gabriel Paul Michel. *Bonaparte en Egypte ou le rêve inassouvi, 1797–1801.* Paris, 1978.

Bernard-Derosne, Jean. *Farouk: la déchéance d'un roi.* Paris, 1953.

Bernoyer, Francois. *Avec Bonaparte en Egypte et en Syrie: 1798–1800.* Ed. Christian Tortel. Abbeville, Fr., 1976.

———. *Bonaparte de Toulon au Caire: d'après 19 lettres de François Bernoyer.* Ed. Christian Tortel and Patricia Carlier. Montelimar, 1996.

Berque, Jacques. *Egypt: Imperialism and Revolution.* Trans. Jean Stewart. London, 1972.

———. "L'Islam vu par Taha Husayn." *BEO* 29 (1977): 65–72.

Berrah, Mouni, Jacques Levy, and Claude-Michel Cluny. *Les cinémas arabes.* Paris, 1987.

Bertrand, Émile. *Nubar Pacha, 1825–1899.* Cairo, 1904.

Bianchi, Robert. "Egypt: Drift at Home, Passivity Abroad." *Current History* 85 (fall 1986): 71–74.

"Bibliography of Taha Husayn." *JAL* 6 (1975): 141–145.

Bierbrier, M.L. "Auguste Mariette: The Founder of Egyptian Archaeology." In *Egypt: Ancient Culture, Modern Land,* ed. Jaromir Malek. Norman, Okla., 1993.

Bili, Ahmad. *'Adli Basha aw safha min tarikh al-zi'ama bi-Misr.* Cairo, 1922.

Bindari, Muhammad Thabit. *Za'im al-nahda Mustafa Kamil.* Cairo, [1945?].

Binder, Leonard. "Ali Abd al-Raziq and Islamic Liberalism." *AAS* 10 (Mar. 1982): 31–67.

———. *Islamic Liberalism.* Chicago, 1988.

Bint al-Shati. *'Ala al-jisr: usturat al-zaman.* Cairo, 1967.

———. *Sirr al-shati.* Cairo, 1952.

al-Bishri, 'Abd al-'Aziz. *Fi al-mirah.* Cairo, 1927.

———. *al-Mukhtar.* 2 vols. Cairo, 1935.

———. "Yawmiyyat." *al-Siyasa al-usbu'iyya* (2 Mar. 1929): 10.

al-Bishri, Tariq. *al-Haraka al-siyasiyya fi Misr, 1945–1952.* Cairo, 1972.

———. *al-Muslimun wa al-Aqbat fi itar al-jami'a al-watanyya.* Cairo, 1984.

———. *Sa'd Zaghlul yufawid al-isti'mar.* Cairo, 1977.

al-Bitar, 'Abd al-Raziq. *Hilyat al-bashr fi tarikh al-qarn al-thalith 'ashr.* Damascus, 1961.

al-Bitar, Muhammad Bahjat. "al-Musab al-'amm." *MMIA* 15:9–10 (Sept.–Oct. 1937): 365–374; 11–12 (Nov.–Dec.): 474–480.

Blunt, Wilfrid S. *Gordon at Khartoum.* London, 1911.

———. *My Diaries, Being a Personal Narrative of Events, 1882–1914* (1-vol. ed.). New York, 1932.

———. *Secret History of the English Occupation of Egypt.* London, 1907.

Bonin, Hubert. *Suez: du Canal à la finance, 1858–1987.* Paris, 1987.

Bonnet, Georges Edgar. *Ferdinand de Lesseps*, I. Paris, 1951.

Booth, Marilyn. *Bayram al-Tunisi's Egypt: Social Criticism and Narrative Strategies.* Exeter, UK, 1990.

———. "Biography and Feminist Rhetoric in Early Twentieth Century Egypt: Mayy Ziyada's *Stories of Three Women's Lives*." *Journal of Women's History* 3:2 (spring 1991): 38–64.

———. "Exemplary Lives, Feminist Aspirations: Zaynab Fawwaz and the Arabic Biographical Tradition." *JAL* 26 (1995): 120–146.

Boselli, Jules. "Edmé-François Jomard." *Revue d'Egypte* 4 (Jan.–Apr. 1897).

Bosseno, Christian, ed. "Youssef Chahine l'Alexandrin." *Cinémaction* 33 (1985), special issue.

Bosworth, C.E. "Henry Salt, Consul in Egypt 1816–1827 and Pioneer Egyptologist." *Bulletin of the John Rylands Library* 57 (1974–1975): 69–91.

———. "al-Jabarti and the Frankish Archaeologists." *IJMES* 8 (1977): 229–236.

Boudot-Lamotte, Antoine. *Ahmad Shawqi: l'homme et l'oeuvre.* Damascus, 1977.

Boulatta, Issa J. "The Early Schooling of Ahmad Amin and Marun Abbud." *MW* (April 1975): 93–100.

———. "Modern Quran Exegesis: A Study of Bint al-Shati's Method." *MW* 64 (1974): 103–113.

Boustany, Saladin, ed. *The Journals of Bonaparte in Egypt, 1798–1801.* 10 vols. Cairo, 1971.

Boutros-Ghali, Boutros. *Egypt's Journey to Jerusalem.* New York, 1997.

———. *Unvanquished: A U.S.-U.N. Saga.* New York, 1999.

Bouvier, Jean. *Les deux scandales de Panama.* Paris, 1964.

Bowie, Leland. "The Copts, the Wafd, and Religious Issues." *MW* 67:2 (Apr. 1977): 106–126.

Bowman, Humphrey. *Middle-East Window.* London, 1942.

Boyle, Clara [Asch]. *Boyle of Cairo: A Diplomatist's Adventures in the Middle East.* London, 1965.

———. *A Servant of the Empire.* London, 1938.

Brinton, Jasper Yeates. *The American Effort in Egypt.* Alexandria, 1972.

Broadley, A.M. *How We Defended Arabi and His Friends.* London, 1884.

Browne, Edward G. *The Persian Revolution of 1905–1909.* Cambridge, UK, 1910.

Browne, Haji Abdallah. *Bonaparte in Egypt and the Egyptians of Today.* New York, 1907.

Bruce, James. *Travels to Discover the Sources of the Nile.* London, 1790.

Brugman, J. *An Introduction to the History of Modern Arabic Literature in Egypt.* Leiden, 1984.

Buheiry, Marwan, ed. *Intellectual Life in the Arab East.* Beirut, 1981.

Buhuth Nadwat al-Ihtifal bi-Dhikra Murur Miat 'Am 'ala Wafat 'Abd Allah al-Nadim. Cairo, 1997.

Buqtur, Amir. "Sadiqi Taha Husayn." *al-Hilal* 45:8 (June 1937): 917–921.

Bushrui, Suhail B. "May Ziadeh." *al-Kulliyah* (spring 1972): 16–19.

Busool, Assad Nimer. "Development of Taha Husayn's Islamic Thought." *MW* 68 (1978): 259–283.

Busool, Assad Nimer. "Rashid Rida's Struggle to Establish a Modern Islamic State." *American Journal of Islamic Studies* 1 (1984): 83–99.

———. "Shaykh Muhammad Rashid Rida's Relations with Jamal al-Din al-Afghani and Muhammad 'Abduh." *MW* 66 (1976): 272–286.

al-Bustani, Ahmad Ifrad. *al-Ma'lum wa al-majhul: Wali al-Din Yakan.* 5th ed. Beirut, 1966.

al-Bustani, Butrus. *Udaba al-'arab.* 2nd ed. 3 vols. Beirut, 1934.

al-Bustani, Fuad Ifram. *Muqaddimat diwan Niqula al-Turk.* Beirut, 1970.

Butcher, Edith. *Story of the Church of Egypt.* 2 vols. London, 1897.

Butler, Alfred Joshua. *Court Life in Egypt.* London, 1897.

Butrus, Fikri. *A'lam al-musiqa wa al-ghina al-'arabi.* Cairo, 1976.

Butti, Rufa'il. *Sihr al-shi'r.* Cairo, 1922.

Buyers, Patricia, ed. *Annual Obituary, 1987.* London, 1990.

Cable, Boyd. *A Hundred Year History of the P and O.* London, 1937.

Cachia, Pierre. *Taha Husayn: His Place in the Egyptian Literary Renaissance.* London, 1956.

Cameron, Donald Andreas. *Egypt in the Nineteenth Century.* London, 1898.

Campagne de Mohamed Bey Farid. Brussels, [1910?].

Cantori, Louis J. "Egyptian Policy Under Mubarak." In *The Middle East After the Israeli Invasion of Lebanon,* ed. Robert O. Friedman. Syracuse, N.Y., 1986.

Carra de Vaux, Baron. *Les penseurs de l'Islam,* V. Paris. 1926.

Carré, Jean-Marie. *Voyageurs et écrivains français en Égypte.* 2 vols. Cairo, 1956.

Carré, Olivier. "Note sur la politique de Hasan al-Banna et celle de Sayyid Qutb d'après leurs écrits." *Mélanges de l'Université St Joseph* 50:2. Beirut, 1984.

Carré, Olivier, and Gérard Michaud. *Les Frères Musulmans, 1928–1982.* Paris, 1983.

Carter, B.L. *Copts in Egyptian Politics.* London, 1986.

Caspar, R. "Le renouveau du Mo'tazilisme." *MIDEO* 4 (1957): 178–184.

Cassar, George. *Kitchener: Architect of Victory.* London, 1977.

Castro, F. "'Abd al-Razzak Ahmad al-Sanhuri (1895–1971): primi appunti per una biografia." In *Studia in onore di Francesco Gabrieli nel suo ottantesimo compleano.* Rome, 1984, 173–210.

Cattaoui, René. *Mohamed-Aly et l'Europe.* Paris, 1950.

———. *La règne de Mohamed Aly après les archives russes en Égypte.* Cairo, 1931.

Chaillé-Long, Charles. *Three Prophets.* New York, 1884.

Chakroun, Abdallah. "Du conte dans la littérature arabe moderne: les frères Taymour." *BEA,* no. 23 (1945): 99–101.

Chaleur, Sylvestre. *Histoire des Coptes d'Egypte.* Paris, 1960.

Chaloner, W.H. "De Lesseps and the Suez Canal." *History Today* 6 (1956): 680–684.

Champollion-Figeac, Aimé. *Les deux Champollion: leur vie et leurs oeuvres.* Grenoble, 1887.

Chandler, David G. *The Campaigns of Napoleon.* New York, 1966.

———. *Dictionary of the Napoleonic Wars.* New York, 1979.

Charles-Roux, François. *Bonaparte: Governor of Egypt.* Trans. E. W. Dickes. London, 1937.

———. "Clot Bey et le consul-general Cochelet." *CHE* 2 (1949): 237–312.

———. *Edmé-François Jomard et la réforme de l'Égypte en 1839.* Cairo, 1955.

———. *Thiers et Méhémet-Ali.* Paris, 1951.

Charles-Roux, J. *L'Isthme et le Canal du Suez.* 2 vols. Paris, 1901.

Charmley, John. *Lord Lloyd and the Decline of the British Empire.* London, 1987.

Cheikho, Louis. "al-Adab al-'arabiyya." *al-Mashriq* 23:5 (May 1925): 377–379.

———. *al-Adab al-'arabiyya fi al-qarn al-tasi' 'ashr.* 2 vols. Beirut, 1924–1926.

———. *Tarikh al-adab al-'arabiyya fi al-rub' al-awwal min al-qarn al-'ishrin.* Beirut, 1926.

Choueiri, Youssef. *Islamic Fundamentalism.* London, 1990.

———. *Arab History and the Nation-State.* London and New York, 1989.

Chuquet, Arthur. *Quatre généraux de la Révolution . . . Kléber . . . . Lettres et notes inédites.* Paris, 1911–1926.

Clayton, Gilbert. *An Arabian Diary.* Berkeley and Los Angeles, 1969.

Cleveland, William. "The Role of Islam as Political Ideology in the First World War." In *National and International Politics in the Middle East,* ed. Edward Ingram. London, 1986, 84–88.

Clot-Bey, A.B. [Antoine Barthelemy]. *Aperçu général sur l'Égypte.* 2 vols. in 1. Paris, 1840.

——— *À Son Altesse Ismail-Pacha, vice-roi d'Égypte: trente années de service en Égypte.* Paris, n.d.

———. *Documents concernant le Dr. Clot-Bey dans ses rapports avec LL AA Mohammed-Ali, Abbas-Pacha, et Said Pacha.* Marseilles, 1862.

———. *Le Dr Clot-Bey et sa conduite en Egypte, depuis 1825 jusqu'en 1858.* Paris, 1862.

———. *Histoire de Mohammed-Ali, vice-roi d'Égypte.* Paris, 1860.

———. *Memoires.* Ed. Jacques Tagher. Cairo, 1949.

———. *Position officielle de Clot-Bey en Egypte.* Marseilles, n.d.

Cluny, Claude-Michel, ed. *Dictionnaire des nouveaux cinémas arabes.* Paris, 1978.

Cohen-Mor, D. *Yusuf Idris: Changing Visions.* Potomac, Md., 1992.

Colby, Vinetta. *World Authors 1980–1985.* New York, 1991.

Cole, Juan Ricardo. *Colonialism and Revolution in the Middle East: Social and Cultural Origins of Egypt's Urabi Movement.* Princeton, 1993.

———. "Feminism, Class, and Islam in Turn-of-the-Century Egypt," *IJMES* 13 (1981): 394–407.

———. "Rifa'a al-Tahtawi and the Revival of Practical Philosophy." *MW* 70 (1980): 29–46.

Coles Pasha. *Recollections and Reflections.* London, 1918.

Colombe, Marcel. *L'évolution de l'Égypte, 1924–1950.* Paris, 1951.

Colvin, Auckland. *The Making of Modern Egypt.* London, 1906, 1909.

Conermann, Stephan. *Mustafa Mahmud (geb. 1921) und der modifizierte islamische Diskurs im modernen Ägypten.* Berlin, 1996.

Connelly, Owen, ed. *Historical Dictionary of Napoleonic France, 1798–1915.* Westport, Conn., 1985.

Cooke, Miriam. *The Anatomy of an Egyptian Intellectual: Yahya Haqqi.* Washington, D.C., 1984.

———. "Zaynab al-Ghazali: Saint or Subversive?" *WI* 34:1 (Apr. 1994): 1–20.

Cooper, Mark N. *The Transformation of Egypt.* Baltimore, 1982.

Cordier, Henri. *Bibliographie de Gaston Maspéro.* Paris, 1922.

Cortambert, Richard. *Notice sur la vie et les oeuvres de M. Jomard.* Paris, 1863.

Counillon, P. "À propos d'une nouvelle d'al-Mazini." *Bulletin des Études Arabes* 5 (1942): 3–6.

Courau, Robert. *Ferdinand de Lesseps: de l'apothéose du Suez au scandale de Panama.* Paris, 1932.

Coury, Ralph M. "The Arab Nationalism of Makram 'Ubayd." *JIS* 6:1 (1995): 248–281, 459–479.

———. *The Making of an Arab Nationalist: The Early Years of Azzam Pasha, 1893–1936.* London, 1998.

———. "Who 'Invented' Egyptian Arab Nationalism?—II." *IJMES* 14 (1982): 248–281, 459–479.

Cox, Frederick J. "Arabi and Stone: Egypt's First Military Rebellion, 1882." *CHE* 8 (1956): 155–173.

Crabbs, Jack A., Jr. "Egyptian Intellectuals and the Revolution: The Case of 'Abd al-Rahman al-Rafi'i." In *Egypt from Monarchy to Republic,* ed. Shimon Shamir. Boulder, Colo., 1995, 250–266.

——. "Politics, History, and Culture in Nasser's Egypt." *IJMES* 6:4 (Oct. 1975): 386–420.

——. *The Writing of History in Nineteenth Century Egypt.* Detroit, 1984.

Crabites, Pierre. "Abdel Khalek Saroit Pasha." *MW* 19 (1929): 179–182.

——. *Americans in the Egyptian Army.* London, 1938.

——. *Ibrahim of Egypt.* London, 1935.

——. *Ismail: The Maligned Khedive.* London, 1933.

Cragg, Kenneth. "Then and Now in Egypt: The Reflections of Ahmad Amin, 1886–1954." *MEJ* 9 (1955): 28–40.

Cramer, Maria. *Das christlich-koptische Ägypten einst und heute.* Wiesbaden, 1959.

Crankshaw, Edward. *The Forsaken Idea: A Study of Viscount Milner.* London and New York, 1952; reprinted Westport, Conn., 1974.

Crecelius, Daniel. *The Roots of Modern Egypt.* Minneapolis and Chicago, 1981.

——. "The Waqfiyah of Muhammad Bey Abu al-Dhahab." *JARCE* 15 (1978): 83–105.

"The Crisis of the Intellectuals: Ihsan Abd el-Quddus." *Jerusalem Quarterly* 30 (winter 1984): 50–56.

Cromer, Lord [Sir Evelyn Baring]. *Abbas II.* London, 1915.

——. *Internal Administration of Egypt.* London, 1884.

——. *Memorandum on the Present Situation in Egypt.* London, 1882.

——. *Modern Egypt.* 2 vols. London, 1908.

——. *The Situation in Egypt: Address Delivered to the Eighty Club on December 15th, 1908.* London, 1908.

Crowther, James G. *Six Great Engineers.* London, 1959.

Cunningham, Alfred. *Today in Egypt.* London, 1912.

Cuno, Kenneth. "The Origins of Private Ownership of Land in Egypt: A Reappraisal." *IJMES* 12 (1980): 245–275.

Cuoq, J. "al-Jabarti: chroniqueur de l'expedition française en Égypte (1798–1901)." *IBLA* 42, no 142 (1979): 91–105.

Daghir, Yusuf As'ad. "'Abbas Mahmud al-'Aqqad." *al-Adib* 23:5 (May 1964): 39–41.

——. *Masadir al-dirasat al-adabiyya.* 4 vols. in 5. Sidon, 1950–1983.

al-Dahhan, Sami. *Sha'ir al-sha'b.* Cairo, 1953.

al-Dali, Wahid. *Asrar al-jami'a al-'arabiyya.* Cairo, 1982.

Daly, Martin W. *The Sirdar: Sir Reginald Wingate and the British Empire in the Middle East.* Philadelphia, 1997.

al-Danasuri, Fahim Hafiz. *Ahmad Amin wa atharuhu fi al-lugha wa al-naqd al-adabi.* Cairo, 1986.

Danielson, Virginia. "Artists and Entrepreneurs: Female Singers in Cairo During the 1920s." In *Women in Middle Eastern History: Shifting Boundaries,* ed. Beth Baron and Nikki Keddie. New Haven, 1991.

——. *Voice of Egypt: Umm Kulthum, Arabic Song, and Egyptian Society in the Twentieth Century.* Chicago, 1997.

Darwish, al-'Arabi Hasan. *Zaki Mubarak sha'iran.* Cairo, 1986.

Darwish, Darwish Muhammad. "Wali al-Din Yakan." *al-Kitab* 7 (May 1949): 709–718.

Darwish, Hasan. *Min ajl abi Sayyid Darwish.* Cairo, 1990.

Darwish, Mustafa. *Dream Makers on the Nile: A Portrait of Egyptian Cinema.* Cairo, 1998.

Daud, 'Abd al-Ghani. "Hasan Fathi: al-musiqar wa shi'r fi fann al-'imara." *al-Watan,* 15 Oct. 1989.

Daud, Anis. *'Abd al-Rahman Shukri, 1886–1958: nazarat fi shi'rihi.* Cairo, 1970.

Davidian, S. *Généalogie . . . Yacoub Artin Pacha.* Cairo, 1917.

Davis, Eric. *Challenging Colonialism: Bank Misr and Egyptian Industrialization, 1920–1941.* Princeton, 1983.

Dawn, C. Ernest. *From Ottomanism to Arabism.* Chicago, 1973.

Dawson, Warren R. *Who Was Who in Egyptology.* 1st ed. London, 1951; 2nd ed. London, 1972.

Dawwara, Fuad. *Muhammad Mandur.* Cairo, 1996.

——. *Najib Mahfuz min al-qawmiyya ila al-'alamiyya.* Cairo, 1989.

——. "Shaykh al-nuqqad yatahaddath." *al-Majalla,* no. 96 (Dec. 1964): 44–52; no. 98 (Feb. 1965): 58–71.

Dawwara, Muhammad Mahmud. *Sawt al-thawra aw qissat Sayyid Darwish.* Cairo, [1953?].

——. *Sayyid Darwish al-fannan wa al-insan.* Cairo, 1996.

Dayf, Shawqi. *al-Adab al-'arabi al-mu'asir fi Misr.* 1st ed. Cairo, 1957; 2nd ed. Cairo, 1961.

——. *al-Barudi: raid al-shi'r al-hadith.* Cairo, 1964.

——. *Dirasat fi al-shi'r al-'arabi al-mu'asir.* 2nd ed. Cairo, 1959.

——. *Ma'a al-'Aqqad.* Cairo, 1964.

——. *Shawqi sha'ir al-'asr al-hadith.* Cairo, 1953.

Deeb, Marius. "Bank Misr and the Emergence of the Local Bourgeoisie in Egypt." *MES* 12:3 (Oct. 1976): 69–86.

——. "Continuity in Modern Egyptian History." In *Problems,* ed. John Spagnolo.

——. *Party Politics in Egypt: The Wafd and Its Rivals, 1919–1939.* London, 1979.

Dehérain, Henri. *L'Égypte turque: pachas et mamlouks du XVIe et XVII siècle.* Paris, 1934.

——. *Le Soudan égyptien sous Mehemet Ali.* Paris, 1898.

Deighton, H.S. "The Impact of Egypt on Britain." In *Political and Social Change,* ed. P.M. Holt, 231–248.

De Jong, Frederick. "The Itinerary of Hasan al-'Attar (1766–1835): A Reconsideration and Its Implications." *Journal of Semitic Studies* 28 (1983): 99–128.

———. *Turuq and Turuq-Linked Institutions in 19th Century Egypt.* Leiden, 1978.

———. "The Works of Tantawi Jawhari (1862–1940): Some Bibliographical and Biographical Notes." *Bibliotheca orientalis* 34:3–4 (May–July 1977): 153–161.

Dekmejian, Richard. *Egypt Under Nasir: A Study in Political Dynamics.* Albany, N.Y., 1972.

Delanoue, Gilbert. "'Abd Allah Nadim (1845–1896): les idées politiques et morales d'un journaliste égyptien." *BEO* 17 (1961–1962): 75–119.

———. "Ahmad Lutfi al-Sayyid (1872–1963)." *REI* 31 (1963): 89–103.

———. *Moralistes et politiques musulmans dans l'Égypte du XIXe siècle.* 2 vols. Cairo, 1982.

De la Roquette, Jean-Bernard-Marie-Alexandre. "Notice sur la vie et les travaux de M. Jomard." *Bulletin de la Société de Géographie* (Feb. 1863): 81–101.

de Leon, Edwin. *Egypt Under Ismail Pasha.* London, 1882.

———. *The Khedive's Egypt.* New York, 1878.

de Moor, E. "Husayn Fawzi and 'The New School.'" *JAL* 25 (1994): 223–244.

De Moulinaere, Philippe. *Bibliographie raisonée des témoignages oculaires imprimés de l'expédition d'Égypte: 1798–1801.* Paris, 1993.

Dep, Arthur C. *The Egyptian Exiles in Ceylon—Sri Lanka.* Colombo, 1983.

DePopolo, Margaret, and Reinhard Goethert. *Hassan Fathy, Architect: An Exhibition of Selected Projects.* Cambridge, Mass., 1981.

Des Boves, J. Santerre. *Son excéllence Chérif Pacha.* Cairo, 1887.

Deseille, Ernest. *Auguste Mariette.* Boulogne-sur-Mer, 1882.

———. *Les debuts de Mariette-Pacha.* Boulogne-sur-Mer, 1881.

Des Michels, Baron Jules Alexis. *Souvenirs de carrière, 1855–1886.* Paris, 1901.

Desormeaux, C. "La renaissance arabe—l'oeuvre de George Zaidan." *Revue du Monde Musulman* 4 (1908): 837–845.

Dessouki, Ali E.H. [Hilal]. "The Primacy of Politics: The Politics of Continuity and Change." In *The Foreign Policies of the Arab States,* ed. Bahgat Korany and Ali E.H. Dessouki. Boulder, Colo., 1984.

———. "The Views of Salama Musa on Religion and Secularism." *Islam in the Modern Age* 4 (1973): 23–34.

Dewachter, Michel. *Champollion: un scribe pour l'Égypte.* Paris, 1991.

Dhikra al-maghfur lahu al-Amir 'Umar Tusun. Cairo, 1946.

Dhikra faqidat al-'uruba . . . Huda Hanim Sha'rawi. Cairo, 1948.

Dhuhni, Salah al-Din. *Misr bayn al-ihtilal wa al-thawra.* Cairo, 1939.

al-Dibs, Yusuf. *Tarikh Suriyya.* Beirut, 1893.

Dicey, Edward. *The Story of the Khedivate.* London, 1902.

Dickie, James. "Sayyid Darwish: A Biographical Note." *IQ* 18:1 (Jan. 1974): 8–10.

al-Didi, 'Abd al-Fattah. *'Abqariyyat al-'Aqqad.* Cairo, 1965.

———. *al-Falsafa wa al-ijtima' 'ind al-'Aqqad.* Cairo, 1969.

———. *al-Naqd wa al-jamal 'ind al-'Aqqad.* Cairo, 1968.

Dimashqiyya, Julia. *Mayy fi Suriyya wa Lubnan.* Beirut, 1924.

Dimirdash, Ahmad Sa'id. *Mahmud Hamdi al-Falaki.* Cairo, 1965.

al-Disuqi, 'Abd al-'Aziz. *Jama'at Apollo.* Cairo, 1960.

al-Disuqi, 'Umar. *Dirasat adabiyya.* Cairo, 1958.

———. *Mahmud Sami al-Barudi.* Beirut, 1953; Cairo, 1958.

———. *al-Manfaluti: dirasa naqdiyya tahliliyya.* Cairo, 1976.

———. "al-Shaykh 'Ali Yusuf." *al-Kitab* 6 (July 1948): 232–249.

Diyab, 'Abd al-Hayy. *'Abbas Mahmud al-'Aqqad naqidan.* Cairo, 1965.

———. *al-'Aqqad wa tatawwuruhu al-fikri.* Baghdad, 1969.

———. *al-Mara fi hayat al-'Aqqad.* Cairo, 1968.

———. *al-Nuzha al-insaniyya fi shi'r al-'Aqqad.* Cairo, 1969.

———. *Sha'iriyyat al-'Aqqad fi mizan al-naqd al-hadith.* Cairo, 1969.

Diyab, Muhammad Hafiz. *Sayyid Qutb: al-khitab wa al-idiyulugiyya.* 2nd ed. Beirut, 1988.

Dodwell, Henry. *The Founder of Modern Egypt.* Cambridge, UK, 1931.

Doriant, François. "Le bicentenaire de la naissance de Kléber." *CHE* 5 (1953): 77–81.

Douglas, William Solto. *Years of Command.* London, 1966.

Douin, Georges. *Histoire du règne du Khédive Ismail.* 3 vols. Rome and Cairo, 1931–1938.

———. *Mohamed Aly, pacha du Caire, 1805–1807.* Cairo, 1926.

———. *Mohamed Aly et l'expédition d'Alger (1829–1830).* Cairo, 1930.

Doumato, Lamia. *Hassan Fathy.* Monticello, Ill., 1987.

Dozier, Kimberly. "An Angry Old Man." *Middle East Times* 11:49 (6–12 Dec. 1993): 8.

Driault, Édouard. *La formation de l'empire de Mohamed Aly de l'Arabie au Soudan, 1814–1823.* Cairo, 1927.

———. *Mohamed Aly et Napoléon, 1807–1814.* Cairo, 1925.

Drioton, Étienne. "Le musée de Boulac." *CHE* 3 (1950): 1–12.

Drovetti, Bernardino. *Il corpo epistolare di Bernardino Drovetti ordinato et illustrato*, I. Rome, 1940.

Drozdik, L. "La conception linguistique de Mahmud Taymur." *AION*, N.S. 3 (1949): 473–486.

Du Bus, Ch. "E.F. Jomard et les origines du cabinet des cartes (1777–1868)." Congrès international de géographie. Comité des travaux historiques et scientifiques: *Bulletin de la Société de Géographie*, 46 (1931): 1–128.

Dunya, 'Abd al-'Aziz Hafiz. *Rasail tarikhiyya min Mustafa Kamil ila Fuad Salim al-Hijazi*. Cairo, 1969.

———. *al-Shahid Muhammad Karim*. Cairo, 1965.

Dunya, Sulayman. *al-Shaykh Muhammad 'Abduh bayn al-falsafa wa al-kalamiyyin*. 2 vols. Cairo, 1958.

Durand-Viel, Georges Edmond Just. *Les campagnes navales de Mohammed Aly et Ibrahim*. Paris, 1935–1937.

Durnayqa, Muhammad Ahmad. *al-Sayyid Rashid Rida, islahatuhu al-ijtima'iyya wa al-diniyya*. Tripoli-Beirut, 1986.

Durri [al-Hakim], Muhammad. *al-Nukhba al-durriyya fi maathir al-'aila al-Muhammadiyya al-'Alawiyya*. Bulaq, 1889.

Durri, Muhammad, ed. *Tarjamat hayat 'Ali Mubarak*. Cairo, 1894.

Dykstra, Darrell. "Pyramids, Prophets, and Progress: Ancient Egypt in the Writings of 'Ali Mubarak." *JAOS* 114 (1994): 54–65.

Early, Evelyn Allene. "Bahithat al-Badiya: Cairo Viewed from the Fayyum Oasis." *Journal of Near Eastern Studies* 40:4 (Oct. 1981): 339–341.

Eban, Aubrey S. "The Modern Literary Movement in Egypt." *International Affairs* (London) 20 (1944): 166–178.

Eccel, A. Chris. *Egypt, Islam, and Social Change*. Berlin, 1984.

Eckstein, Percy. *Ferdinand von Lesseps: Der Mann, der die Meere verband*. Vienna, 1947.

Egger, Vernon. *A Fabian in Egypt: Salamah Musa and the Rise of the Professional Classes in Egypt, 1900–1939*. Lanham, Md., 1986.

Egypt, Department of Antiquities. *Rapports sur la marche du Service des Antiquités de 1899 à 1910*. Cairo, 1912.

Egypt, Ministry of Information. *al-Mawsu'a al-qawmiyya li al-shakhsiyyat al-misriyya al-bariza*. 2nd ed. 2 vols. Cairo, 1992.

Egypt, National Courts. *al-Kitab al-dhahabi li al-mahakim al-ahliyya*. Bulaq, 1933.

Egypt, Niyabat Misr. *Muhakamat Taha Husayn*. Beirut, 1972.

Egypt, Supreme Council for the Preservation of Arts and Letters. *Dhikra Hafiz Ibrahim*. Cairo, 1958.

Egyptian Medical Society. "Takrim 'Ali Pasha Ibrahim." *Majmu'a min al-shi'r wa al-nathr*. Cairo, 1931.

Elad, A. *The Village Novel in Modern Egyptian Literature*. Berlin, 1994.

Elbarbary, Samir. "al-Aqqad's Hardy: Essays and Translations." *JAL* 22 (1991): 66–82.

Elbée, Jean d'. *Un conquistador de génie: Ferdinand de Lesseps*. Paris, 1943.

El-Enany, Rasheed. *Naguib Mahfouz: The Pursuit of Meaning*. London and New York, 1993.

Eliraz, Giora, "Egyptian Intellectuals and Women's Emancipation." *AAS* 16:1 (Mar. 1982).

El-Kholy, Samha. "Musical Life in Egypt." *Arts and the Islamic World* 2:2 (summer 1984): 64, 75.

Elon, Amos. *Flight into Egypt*. New York, 1981.

———. "Ideology and Structure in Fathi Ghanim's 'al-Jabal.'" *JAL* 20:2 (Sept. 1989): 168–196.

Ende, Werner. "Die Azhar, Saih Saltut und die Schia." *Deutscher Orientalistentag* 24 (Stuttgart, 1990): 308–318.

Erman, Johann P.A. "Die Entzifferung der Hieroglyphen." *Sitzungsbericht der Berlin Akademie*. Berlin, 1922.

Ernouf, Alfred Auguste. *Le général Kléber*. Paris, 1867.

Esposito, John L. *Islam and Politics*. Syracuse, N.Y., 1984.

Euzière, Jules Georges. *Petite histoire d'un grand homme, Clot Bey*. Montpellier, 1952.

Evans, Trefor E., ed. *The Killearn Diaries, 1934–1946*. London, 1972.

Evetts, B. "Un prélat reformateur, le patriarche copte Cyrille IV, 1854–1861." *Revue de l'orient chrétien*, 2e ser. VII (1912): 3–15.

Fadil, Muhammad. *Salama Hijazi*. Damanhur, 1932.

Fadl Allah, Mahdi. *Ma'a Sayyid Qutb fi fikrihi al-siyasi wa al-dini*. 2nd ed. Beirut, 1979.

Fahmi, 'Abd al-'Aziz, *Hadhihi hayati*. Cairo, 1963; based on *al-Musawwar*, 10 June–23 Dec. 1949.

Fahmi, Isma'il. *Negotiating for Peace in the Middle East*. Baltimore, 1983.

Fahmi, Mahir Hasan. *Muhammad Tawfiq al-Bakri*. Cairo, 1967.

———. *Qasim Amin*. Cairo, 1963.

———. *Shawqi: shi'ruhu al-islami*. Cairo, 1959.

Fahmi, Mahmud. *al-Bahr al-zakhir fi tarikh al-'alam wa akhbar al-awail wa al-awakhir*. Bulaq, A.H. 1312.

———. *Mudhakkirat Mahmud Basha Fahmi*. Cairo, 1976.

Fahmi, Mansur. "Ahamm hadith aththara fi majra hayati." *al-Hilal* 38 (Jan. 1930): 268–269.

———. "Limadha darastu al-falsafa." *al-Hadith* 6:1 (Jan. 1932): 25–28.

———. *Mayy Ziyada wa raidat al-adab al-'arabi al-hadith*. Cairo, 1954.

———. *Muhadarat 'an Mayy Ziyada*. Cairo, 1955.

———. "al-Ustadh Muhammad Shafiq Ghurbal." *MMLA* 14 (1962): 195–205.

Fahmi, Qallini. *al-Amir 'Umar Tusun: hayatuhu, atharuhu, a'maluhu*. Cairo[?], 1944.

———. *Mudhakkirat Qallini Fahmi.* 2 vols. Cairo, 1934.

Fahmi, Zaki. *Safwat al-'asr fi tarikh wa rusum akabir rijal Misr.* Cairo, 1926.

Fahmy, Khaled. *All the Pasha's Men: Mehmed Ali, His Army, and the Making of Modern Egypt.* Cambridge, UK, 1997.

Fairman, Ed. St. John. *Prince Halim Pacha of Egypt—A Freemason.* London, 1884.

Faiz, Ahmad. *Tariq al-da'wa fi zilal al-Quran.* 2 vols. Beirut, 1977–1978.

al-Fakhiri, Ja'far. *Awwal athar li-Muhammad 'Ali.* Alexandria, 1926.

Fakhri, Husayn. "Mudhakkirat Husayn Basha Fakhri." In *al-Kitab al-dhahabi.* Cairo, 1937–1938.

Fakhry, Majid. "Shibli Shumayyil." In *Quest for Understanding: Arabic and Islamic Studies in Memory of Malcolm Kerr*, ed. Samir Seikaly et al. Beirut, 1991, 51–70.

al-Falaki, Mustafa Kamil. *Batl al-istiqlal al-iqtisadi: Tal'at Harb.* Cairo, 1940.

al-Faqi, Muhammad Rajab. *Ahmad Hasan al-Zayyat wa majallat "al-Risala."* Cairo, 1981.

Faraj, Nabil. *Najib Mahfuz, hayatuhu wa adabuh.* Cairo, 1986.

———. *Salah 'Abd al-Sabur: al-hayat wa al-mawt.* Cairo, 1985.

Faraj, al-Sayyid. *Hurub Muhammad 'Ali.* Cairo, 1945.

Farès, Bichr. "Nécrologie: Ahmad Zaki Pacha." *REI* 8 (1934): 383–392.

Fargeon, Maurice. *Les juifs en Égypte.* Cairo, 1938.

Farhud, Muhammad al-Sa'di. *al-Ittijahat al-fanniyya fi shi'r 'Abd al-Rahman Shukri.* Cairo, 1961.

———. *Malhat al-shi'r Ahmad Shawqi.* Cairo, 1969.

———. *al-Tayyar al-fikri fi shi'r 'Abd al-Rahman Shukri.* Cairo, 1972.

Farid, 'Abdel Magid. *Nasser: The Final Years.* Reading, UK, 1994.

Farid, Muhammad. *The Memoirs and Diaries of Muhammad Farid, an Egyptian Nationalist Leader (1868–1919).* Trans. Arthur Goldschmidt, Jr. Lewiston, N.Y., 1992.

Farman, Elbert Eli. *Egypt and Its Betrayal.* New York, 1908.

Farnie, D.A. *East and West of Suez: The Suez Canal in History.* Oxford, 1969.

Farraj, Samir. *al-Malika Nazli.* Cairo, 1991.

Farrukh, 'Umar. *Ahmad Shawqi.* Beirut, 1950.

———. *Arba'a udaba mu'asirun.* Cairo, 1944.

———. *Kalima fi Ahmad Shawqi.* Beirut, 1942.

Fawwaz, Zaynab. *al-Durr al-manthur fi tabaqat ribat al-khudur.* Cairo, 1897.

———. *al-Rasail al-Zaynabiyya.* Cairo, 1906.

Fawzi, M. *Adab al-azafir al-tawila.* Cairo, 1987.

Fawzi, Mahmud. *Jihan al-Sadat, al-mara—al-lati hakamat Misr.* Cairo, 1993.

———. *Thuwwar Yulyu yatahaddathun.* Cairo, 1988.

Fawzi, Mufid. "Akhir hiwar ma'a Zaki Tulaymat." *Majallat al-Duha* (Feb. 1983): 80–82.

Fawzi, Muhammad. *Harb al-thalath sanawat, 1967–1970.* Beirut, 1983.

———. *'Umar 'Abd al-Rahman.* Cairo, n.d.

Fayid, Sayyid Ahmad. *'Abdallah al-Nadim al-nathir al-ladhi lam yastaslim.* Cairo, [1957?].

Fayza, Haykal. "Family Life in Modern Egypt." In *Egypt: Ancient Culture, Modern Land,* ed. Jaromir Malik. Norman, Okla., 1993.

Featherstone, Donald. *Tel El-Kebir 1882: Wolseley's Conquest of Egypt.* London, 1993.

Fernea, Elizabeth W., and Fatima Bezirgan, eds. *Middle Eastern Muslim Women Speak.* Austin, 1977.

Fikri, 'Abd Allah, and Amin Fikri. *Irshad al-alibba.* Cairo, 1889.

Fikri, 'Ali. *Subul al-najah.* 3 vols. Cairo, 1923.

Fikri, Amin. *al-Athar al-fikriyya.* Bulaq, 1897.

Filastin, Wadi'. *Ibrahim Naji: hayatuh wa ajmal ash'aruh.* Cairo, 1983.

Filastin, Wadi', ed. *Mayy: hayatuha wa salunuha wa adabuha.* Alexandria, 1981.

Finbert, Elian J. "Mohammed Naghi." *L'art vivant,* Jan. 1924.

Finch, Edith. *Wilfrid Scawen Blunt, 1840–1922.* London, 1922.

Finklestone, Joseph. *Anwar Sadat: Visionary Who Dared.* London, 1996.

al-Fiqi, Ahmad 'Abd al-Majid. *Qissat Ahmad 'Urabi.* Cairo, 1966.

al-Fiqi, 'Ali Muhammad. *Ibrahim Naji.* Cairo, 1977.

al-Fiqi, Mustafa. *al-Aqbat fi al-siyasa al-misriyya: Makram 'Ubayd wa dawruhu fi al-harakah al-wataniyah.* Cairo, 1985.

———. "Makram Ebeid: Politician of the Majority Party." In *Contemporary Egypt,* ed. Charles Tripp.

Fliedner, Stephan. *'Ali Mubarak und seine Hitat: kommentierte Übersetzung der Autobiographie und Werkbesprechung.* Berlin, 1990.

Fontaine, Jean. *Mortrésurrection, une lecture de Tawfiq al-Hakim.* Tunis, 1978.

Font-Réaulx, Hyacinthe de. *Le général Kléber.* Limoges, 1891.

Foreign Office List, 1909. London, 1909.

Foreign Office List, 1912. London, 1912.

Foreign Office List, 1917. London, 1917.

Foreign Office List, 1921. London, 1921.

Foreign Office List, 1928. London, 1928.

Foreign Office List, 1930. London, 1930.

Foreign Office List, 1962. London, 1962.

Forman, B., and Ramses Wissa Wassef. *Fleurs du Desert: tapisseries d'enfants égyptiens.* Prague, 1961.

———. *Tapestries from Egypt.* Trans. Jean Layton. London, 1962.

Forster, E.M. *Abinger Harvest.* London, 1936.

Fowler, Montague. *Christian Egypt: Past, Present, and Future.* London, 1961.

Francis, Raymond. *Aspects de la littérature arabe contemporaine.* Beirut, 1963.

———. *Taha Hussein romancier.* Cairo, 1945.

Frankel, Norman. "Interview with Isma'il Fahmy, Ashraf Ghorbal, and Mohamed Riad." *American Arab Affairs*, no. 31 (winter 1989–1990): 87–105.

Fuad, 'Atif Ahmad. "'Abd al-Rahman al-Jabarti: al-muarrikh al-misri—dirasa fi susyulujiya al-ma'rifa." *MTM* 25 (1978): 175–204.

Fuad, Faraj Sulayman. *al-Kanz al-thamin li-'uzama al-misriyyin*. Cairo, 1917.

Fuad, Ni'mat Ahmad. *'Abd al-Qadir al-Mazini*. 3rd ed. Cairo, 1978.

———. *Adab al-Mazini*. Cairo, 1954.

———. *Ahmad Rami: qissat sha'ir wa ughniya*. Cairo, 1979.

———. *Dirasa fi adab al-Rafi'i*. Cairo, 1953.

———. *al-Jamal wa al-hurriyya wa al-shakhsiyya al-insaniyya fi adab al-'Aqqad*. Cairo, 1975.

———. *Naji al-sha'ir*. Cairo, 1954.

———. *Qimam adabiyya: dirasat wa tarajim li-a'lam al-adab al-misri al-hadith*. Cairo, 1966.

———. *Shu'ara thalatha—Naji, al-Shabbi, al-Akhtal al-Saghir*. Cairo, 1987.

———. "al-Tabib al-sha'ir." *al-Ahram*, 14 May 1997.

———. *Umm Kulthum wa 'asr min al-fann*. Cairo, 1976.

Fuda, Hazim, *Nujum Shari' al-Sihafa*. Cairo, 1972.

Gabra, Sami. *À la mémoire de Champollion à l'occasion du 150e anniversaire du déchiffrement des hiéroglyphiques*. Cairo, 1973.

Gabrieli, Francesco. "Commemorazione di Ahmad Shawqi." *OM* 39 (1959): 486–497.

———. "La Napoli di Mahmud Taymur." *AION*, N.S. 14 (1964): 157–160.

———. "L'opera letteraria di Mahmud Taimur." *OM* 32:5–6 (1952): 142–152.

———. "Uno scritto di Mahmud Taimur." *OM* 19 (1939): 605–615.

Garçot, Maurice. *Kléber, 1753–1800, avec un portrait*. Paris, 1936.

Gardner, Brian. *Allenby of Arabia: Lawrence's General*. New York, 1965.

Garnot, Jean Sainte Fare. *Mélanges Mariette*. Cairo, 1961.

Garstin, William Edmund. *Reports on the Administration of the Irrigation Services in Egypt and the Sudan for the Year 1906*. Cairo, 1910.

Gendzier, Irene. *The Practical Visions of Ya'qub Sanu'*. Cambridge, Mass., 1966.

Gershoni, Israel. "Emergence of Pan-Nationalism in Egypt." *AAS* 16:1 (1982): 59–94.

———. "Imagining the East: Muhammad Husayn Haykal's Changing Representations of East-West Relations, 1928–1933." *AAS* 25:3 (Nov. 1991): 209–251.

———. "An Intellectual Source for the Revolution: Tawfiq al-Hakim's Influence on Nasser and His Generation." In *Egypt from Monarchy to Republic*, ed. Shimon Shamir. Boulder, Colo., 1995, 213–249.

Gershoni, Israel, and James Jankowski. *Redefining the Egyptian Nation, 1930–1945*. Cambridge, UK, 1995.

Gershoni, Israel, and James Jankowski, eds. *Rethinking Nationalism in the Arab Middle East*. New York, 1997.

al-Ghadban, 'Adil. "Khalil Mutran fi dhikrahi al-sanawiyya al-rabi'a." *al-Kitab* 13 (July 1953): 815–821.

Ghali, Ibrahim Amin. *L'Égypte nationaliste et libérale*. La Haye, 1969.

Ghali, Mirrit Boutros. Introduction to *Mémoires de Nubar Pacha*, by Nubar Nubarian, ix–xvii.

———. "Marcus Simaika Pacha, C.B.E., F.S.A., 1864–1944." *Bulletin de la Société d'Archéologie Copte* 10 (1944): 207–209.

al-Ghamrawi, Muhammad Ahmad. *al-Naqd al-tahlili li kitab "Fi al-adab al-jahili."* Cairo, 1970.

Ghandur, Muhammad. *Muhadarat 'an masrahiyyat Shawqi*. Cairo, 1955.

Ghanim, Bulus. "Daud Barakat: suratuhu wa hayatuh." *al-Muqtataf* 83:6 (Dec. 1933): 589–592.

Ghannam, Husayn al-Mahdi. *Hafiz Ibrahim: dirasa wa tahlil wa naqd*. Alexandria, 1936.

Gharaba, 'Abd al-Hamid. *Shakhsiyyat laha tarikh*. Cairo, 1962.

Gharib, Mamun. *Anis Mansur, hayatuhu wa adabuh*. Beirut, 1970.

Ghayth, Zaki Muhammad. "Shuyukh Jami' al-Azhar fi al-qarn al-thalith 'ashr al-hijri." *MTM* 2 (May 1949): 272–285.

al-Ghazali, Muhammad. *al-Sunna al-nabawiyya bayn ahl al-fiqh wa ahl al-hadith*. 10th ed. Cairo, 1991.

al-Ghazali, Zaynab. *Ayyam min hayati*. Cairo, 1982, 1995.

Ghiryani, Tal'at. *Fuad Siraj al-Din: ustura . . . akhir bashawat Misr*. Cairo, 1995.

al-Ghitani, Jamal. *Najib Mahfuz yatadhakkir*. Cairo, 1987.

Ghorbal, Shafik. *The Beginnings of the Egyptian Question and the Rise of Mehemet Ali*. London, 1928.

———. "Dr Bowring and Mohammed Ali." *BIE* 24 (1942): 107–112.

Ghunaym, 'Abd al-Hamid. *Sannu', raid al-masrah al-misri*. Cairo, 1966.

Ghunaym, Mahmud. *Hifni Nasif: butula fi mukhtalaf al-mayadin*. Cairo, 1965.

Ghurab, Ahmad 'Abd al-Hamid. *'Abd al-Rahman Shukri*. Cairo, 1977.

Ghurayyib, Ruz. *Mayy Ziadeh: al-tawahhuj wa al-uful*. Beirut and Washington, D.C., 1978.

Gibb, H.A.R. *Modern Trends in Islam*. Chicago, 1947.

———. *Studies on the Civilization of Islam*. Boston, 1962.

Gibran, Kahlil. *Blue Flame: The Unpublished Letters of Kahlil Gibran to May Ziadeh*. Ed. and trans. Suheil Bushrui and Salma Kuzbari. New York, 1983.

Gillespie, Charles C. "The Scientific Importance of Napoleon's Egyptian Campaign." *Scientific American* 271:3 (Sept. 1994): 78–85.

Godart de Soponay. "Notice nécrologique sur la vie et les travaux de M E.F. Jomard." *Bulletin de la Société d'Instruction élémentaire,* May 1863.

Goldschmidt, Arthur, "The Butrus Ghali Family." *JARCE* 30 (1993): 185–191.

———. "The Egyptian Nationalist Party, 1892–1919." In *Political and Social Change,* ed. P.M. Holt. London, 1968, 308–333.

———. *al-Hizb al-watani al-misri.* Trans. Fuad Dawwara. Cairo, 1983.

———. "The National Party from Spotlight to Shadow." *AAS* 16:1 (Mar. 1982): 11–30.

Goldziher, Ignaz. "'Ali Pascha Mubarak." *Wiener Zeitschrift für die Kunde des Morgenlandes* 14 (1890): 347–352.

———. *Die Richtungen der islamischen Koranauslegung.* Leiden, 1920.

Gollin, Alfred. *Proconsul in Politics: A Study of Lord Milner in Opposition and in Power.* London, 1964.

Gomaa, Ahmad M. *The Foundation of the League of Arab States.* London, 1977.

Goncourt, Edmond de, and Jules de Goncourt. *Portraits intimes du dix-huitième siècle.* Geneva, 1986.

Gordon, Haim. *Naguib Mahfouz's Egypt: Existential Themes in His Writings.* New York, 1990.

Gordon, Joel. *Nasser's Blessed Movement: Egypt's Free Officers and the July Revolution.* Oxford, 1991.

Gottheil, R.J.H. "Ahmad Taimur Pasha, Theodor Nöldecke, and Edward Sachau: An Appreciation." *JAOS* 51 (1931): 104–107.

Grafftey-Smith, Lawrence. *Bright Levant.* London, 1970.

Graham-Brown, Sarah. "Feminism in Egypt: A Conversation with Nawal Sadawi." *MERIP Reports* 95 (1981): 24–27.

Gran, Peter. *The Islamic Roots of Capitalism, 1760–1840.* Austin, Tex., and London, 1979.

———. "The Writing of Egyptian History: A Contribution to Today's Problems." *Newsletter of the American Research Center in Egypt* 160 (winter 1993): 1–6.

Gregory, Lady. *Ahmad Arabi and His Household.* London, 1882.

Greiss, K.A. "La crise de 1882 et le mouvement Orabi." *CHE* 5 (1953): 47–54.

Grünwald, Kurt. "On Cairo's Lombard Street." *Tradition* 1 (1972): 8–21.

Guemard, Gabriel. "Le tombeau et les armes parlantes de Soliman Pacha." *BIE* 9 (1926–1927): 67–81.

Guidi, M. "L'onoranzo al poeta egiziano Shawqi ed il loro significato politico." *OM* 7 (1927): 346–353.

Guigniant, Joseph-Daniel. *Funérailles de M. Jomard: discours prononcé le 26 septembre 1862.* Paris, 1862.

Guindi, G., and Jacques Tagher. *Ismail d'après des documents officiels.* Cairo, 1946. Arabic trans. Jurj

Jundi. *Isma'il kama tusawwiruhu al-wathaiq al-rasmiyya.* Cairo, 1947.

Habib, Tawfiq. *Abu Jilda wa akharun.* Cairo, [1930s?].

———. *Hawamish al-sihafi al-'ajuz.* Alexandria, 1934.

———. "Tarikh kashf 'an al-athar." *al-Hilal* 32:1 (Nov. 1923): 135–141.

Haddad, George M. "The Historical Work of Niqula al-Turk." *JAOS* 81 (1961): 247–251.

———. "Mustafa Kamil: A Self-Image from His Correspondence with Juliette Adam." *MW* 43:2 (Apr. 1973): 132–138.

Haddad, Haroun. "Les amours de Mayy Ziyada." In *Atti des terzo congresso di studi arabi e islamici.* Ravello, 1966, 373–384.

Haddad, Mahmoud. "Arab Religious Nationalism in the Colonial Era: Rereading Rashid Rida's Ideas on the Caliphate." *JAOS* 117 (1997): 253–277.

Haddad, Roza Antun, and Jabir Dumit. *Farah Antun: hayatuhu wa tabinuhu wa mukhtaratuhu.* Cairo, 1923.

Haddad, Yvonne Yazbeck. "The Quranic Justification for an Islamic Revolution: The View of Sayyid Qutb." *MEJ* 37:1 (winter 1983): 14–29.

———. "Sayyid Qutb: Ideologue of Islamic Revival." In *Voices of Resurgent Islam,* ed. John L. Esposito. New York, 1983, 67–98.

al-Hadidi, 'Ali. *'Abdallah Nadim khatib al-wataniyya.* Cairo, 1962, 1987.

———. *Mahmud Sami al-Barudi: sha'ir al-nahda.* Cairo, 1967.

El-Hadidy, Mohammed Alaa el-Din. "Mustafa al-Nahhas and Political Leadership." In *Contemporary Egypt Through Egyptian Eyes,* ed. Charles Tripp, 72–88.

Hafiz, 'Abbas. *Mustafa al-Nahhas, aw al-zi'ama wa al-za'im.* Cairo, 1936.

Hafiz, 'Abd al-Salam Hashim. *al-Rafi'i wa Mayy.* Cairo, 1964.

Hafiz, Ahmad. *Ayyam min shababihim.* Cairo, 1970.

Hafiz, Hasan. *al-Thawra al-'urabiyya fi al-mizan.* Cairo, 1962.

Hafiz, S. *The Genesis of Arabic Narrative Discourse.* London, 1993.

———. "The Maturation of a New Literary Genre." *IJMES* 16 (1984): 367–389.

Haim, Sylvia. "Salama Musa: An Appreciation of His Autobiography." *WI,* N.S. 2 (1953): 10–24.

Haim, Sylvia G. "Sayyid Qutb." *AAS* 16:1 (Mar. 1982): 147–156.

Hairi, A. "Afghani on the Decline of Islam." *WI* 13 (1971): 121–125.

al-Hajiri, Muhammad Taha. *Muhammad Farid Wajdi: hayatuhu wa atharuhu,* I. Cairo, 1970.

al-Hajj, Kamil Yusuf. *Mustafa Sadiq al-Rafi'i wa adabuhu.* Cairo, 1946.

al-Hajjaji, Ahmad Shams al-Din. *al-Adab wa fann al-masrah.* Cairo, 1975.

al-Hakim, Nazih. *Mahmud Taymur: raid al-qissa al-'arabiyya.* Cairo, 1944.

al-Hakim, Tawfiq. *Sijn al-'umr.* Cairo, 1964. Eng. trans. Pierre Cachia. *The Prison of Life: An Autobiographical Essay.* Cairo, 1992.

Hall, Trowbridge. *Egypt in Silhouette.* New York, 1928.

Halls, John James. *Life and Correspondence of Henry Salt.* 2 vols. London, 1834.

Halperin, Vladimir. *Lord Milner et l'évolution de l'impérialisme britannique.* Paris, 1950. Eng. trans. *Lord Milner and the Empire.* London, 1952.

al-Halwaji, 'Abd al-Sattar. *'Abbas Mahmud al-'Aqqad: nashra biblyughrafiyya bi-atharihi al-fikriyya.* Cairo, 1964.

———. *Ma' al-mallah al-taih 'Ali Mahmud Taha.* Cairo, 1970.

Hamada, 'Abd al-Mun'im. *al-Ustadh al-Imam Muhammad 'Abduh.* Cairo, 1945.

Hamada, Husayn 'Umar. *Ahadith 'an Mayy Ziyada.* Damascus, 1983.

Hamamsi, Jalal al-Din. *Hiwar wara al-aswar,* 4th ed. Cairo, 1976.

Hamid, Rauf 'Abbas. *The Japanese and the Egyptian Enlightenment: A Comparative Study of Fukuzawa Yukichi and Rifa'a al-Tahtawi.* Tokyo, 1990.

Hammad, Jamal. "Kayfa qarara Majlis al-Thawra tanhiyat Muhammad Najib." *Uktubir,* no. 828 (6 Sept. 1992).

———. "Kayfa takhallas Majlis al-Thawra min Khalid Muhyi al-Din." *Uktubir,* 30 Aug. 1992.

———. "Kayfa wajaha Muhammad Najib azmat Fibrayir 1954." *Uktubir,* 15 Nov. 1985.

Hammad, Muhammad Ali. *Sayyid Darwish: hayat wa naghm.* Cairo, 1970.

Hammond, Andrew. "Still Crazy After All These Years." *Middle East Times* (27 Nov.–3 Dec. 1994): 13.

Hammud, Majida Muhammad. *al-Mu'tadilun fi al-siyasa al-misriyya: dirasa fi dawr Muhammad Mahmud Basha.* Cairo, 1992.

Hamont, P.N. *L'Égypte sous Méhémet-Ali.* Paris, 1943.

Hamrush, Ahmad. "Dhikrayati 'an Muhammad Najib." *Ruz al-Yusuf,* 15 Oct. 1984.

———. *Qissat Thawrat Yulyu.* 5 vols. Cairo, 1983–1984.

Hamuda, 'Abd al-Wahhab. *al-Tajdid fi al-adab al-misri al-hadith.* Cairo, 1957.

Hamuda, 'Adil. *Ightiyal al-rais.* Cairo, [1985?].

———. *Sayyid Qutb min al-qarya ila al-mishnaqa.* Cairo, [1987?].

Hamza, 'Abd al-Latif. *Adab al-maqala al-suhufiyya fi Misr.* 9 vols. Cairo, 1952–1966, 1996–.

———. "Sahibat jalalat al-sihafa." *al-Hilal* 42:2 (Nov. 1933): 73–75.

Hanna, Milad. "Amina al-Sa'id: ustadhuna fi fann al-hayat." *al-Ahram,* 22 Aug. 1997.

Hanna, Sami. "Ahmad Shauqi: A Pioneer of Modern Arabic Drama." *American Journal of Arabic Studies* 1 (1973): 81–117.

Hanna, Sami, and G.H. Gardner. "Salama Musa, 1887–1958—A Pioneer of Arab Socialism." In *Arab Socialism: A Documentary Study.* Leiden, 1969, 64–79.

Hanna, Suhail ibn-Salim. "L'autobiographie chez Taha Husayn et Salama Musa." *IBLA* 129 (1972): 59–72.

Hanotaux, Gabriel. *Histoire de la nation égyptienne.* 7 vols. Paris, 1931–1940.

Haqqi, Mamduh. *al-Islam wa usul al-hukm: ba'th fi al-khilafa wa al-hukuma fi al-Islam: naqd wa ta'liq.* Beirut, 1966.

Haqqi, Nuha, ed. *Rasail Yahya Haqqi ila ibnatihi.* Cairo, 1997.

Haqqi, Yahya. *Un égyptien à Paris.* Trans. A. Abul Naga. Algiers, 1973.

———. *Fajr al-qissa al-misriyya.* Cairo, 1960.

———. *Khalliha ila Allah: al-sira al-dhatiyya.* Cairo, 1991.

———. *Qandil Umm Hashim ma'a sira dhatiyya li al-muallif.* Cairo, 1975.

———. *The Saint's Lamp and Other Stories.* Trans. M.M. Badawi. Leiden, 1973.

———. *Yahya Haqqi: dhikrayat matwiyya.* Kuwait, 1993.

Harb, Joseph. *Jurji Zaydan, rijal fi rajul.* Beirut, 1970.

Harb, Muhammad al-Ghazali. *'Ali al-Jarim bahithan wa adiban.* Cairo, [1988?].

Haroun, Georges. *Sibli Sumayyil: Une pensée évolutioniste arabe à l'époque d'an-Nahda.* Beirut, 1985.

Harris, Christina Phelps. *Nationalism and Revolution in Egypt: The Role of the Muslim Brotherhood.* Stanford, 1964.

Harris, Murray. *Egypt Under the Egyptians.* London, 1925.

Hartleben, Hermine. *Champollion, sein Leben und sein Werk.* 2 vols. Berlin, 1906.

———. *Lettres de Champollion.* 2 vols. Paris, 1909.

Hartmann, Martin. *The Arabic Press of Egypt.* London, 1899.

———. "Ein modernägyptischer Theolog und Naturfreund." *Beitrage zur Kenntnis des Orients* 13 (1916): 54–82.

Hasan, 'Abbas. *al-Mutanabbi wa Shawqi.* Cairo, 1951.

Hasan, Ilhami. *Muhammad Tal'at Harb: raid sina'at al-sinima al-misriyya.* Cairo, 1986.

Hasan, Muhammad 'Abd al-Ghani. *'Abd Allah Fikri.* Cairo, 1965.

———. *A'lam min al-sharq wa al-gharb.* Cairo, 1949.

———. *Hasan al-'Attar.* Cairo, 1968.

———. *Hayat Mayy.* Cairo, 1942.

———. "Husayn al-Marsafi." *al-Kitab* 7 (Feb. 1949): 253–260.

———. Introduction to *A'lam al-fikr al-islami,* by Ahmad Taymur.

———. *Jurji Zaydan.* Cairo, 1970.

———. *Mayy adibat al-sharq wa al-'uruba.* Cairo, 1964.

———. *Tarajim 'arabiyya.* Cairo, 1968.

Hasan, Muhammad 'Abd al-Ghani, and 'Abd al-'Aziz al-Disuqi. *"Rawdat al-Madaris."* Cairo, 1975.

Hasana, 'Umar. *Fiqh al-da'wa.* Qatar, 1988.

Hashim, Labiba. "al-Sayyida Zaynab Fawwaz." *Fatat al-Sharq* 1 (1907): 225–228.

Hatem, Mervat. "Aisha Taymur's Tears and the Critique of the Modernist and the Feminist Discourses on Nineteenth Century Egypt." In *Remaking Women: Feminism and Modernity in the Middle East,* ed. Lila Abu-Lughod. Princeton, 1998.

Hatim, Muhammad 'Abd al-Qadir. "Hadhihi qissatuna ma' al-shuyu'iyyin." *al-Hawadith,* 26 Aug. 1977.

al-Hawi, Ilya Salim. *Ahmad Shawqi.* Beirut, 1977.

al-Hawwal, Hamid 'Abduh. *al-Sukhriyya fi adab al-Mazini.* Cairo, 1972.

Hawwari, Ahmad Ibrahim. *Naqd al-mujtama' fi "Hadith 'Isa ibn Hisham" li al-Muwaylihi.* Cairo, 1981.

Haykal, Muhammad Hasanayn. *'Abd al-Nasir wa al-'alam.* Beirut, 1972.

———. *Bayn al-sihafa wa al-siyasa.* Cairo, 1984.

———. *The Cairo Documents.* New York and London, 1973.

Haykal, Muhammad Husayn. *al-Adab wa al-hayat al-misriyya.* Cairo, 1992.

———. *Fi awqat al-faragh: majmu'at rasail adabiyya tarikhiyya akhlaqiyya, falsafiyya.* Cairo, 1925.

———. *Mudhakkirat al-shabab.* Cairo, 1996.

———. *Mudhakkirat fi al-siyasa al-misriyya.* 3 vols. Cairo, 1951.

———. *Tarajim misriyya wa gharbiyya.* Cairo, 1928.

Haywood, John A. *Arabic Lexicography as History and Its Place in the General History of Lexicography.* 2nd ed. Leiden, 1965.

Headlam, Cecil, ed. *The Milner Papers.* London, 1931.

Heikal, Mohamed H. *Autumn of Fury: The Assassination of Sadat.* London, 1983.

Herold, Christopher. *Bonaparte in Egypt.* London, 1962.

Herrmann, Auguste Lebrecht. *Mehemet Aly: Pascha von Ägypten.* Leipzig, 1833.

Hesseltine, William B., and Hazel Wolf. *The Blue and the Gray on the Nile.* Chicago, 1963.

Heyworth-Dunne, J. "Education in Egypt and the Copts." *Bulletin de la Société Archéologique Copte* 6 [1940?]: 91–108.

———. *Introduction to the History of Education in Egypt.* London, 1939.

———. "Rifa'a Badawi Rafi' al-Tahtawi: The Egyptian Revivalist." *Bulletin of the School of Oriental Studies* 9 (1937–1939): 961–967; 10 (1939–1942): 399–415.

Heyworth-Dunne, Jamal al-Din. *Religious and Political Trends in Modern Egypt.* Washington, D.C., 1950.

Heyworth-Dunne, James. "Egypt Discovers Arabism: The Role of the Azzams." *Jewish Observer and Middle East Review* 14 (26 Mar. 1965).

———. "Society and Politics in Egyptian Literature." *MEJ* 2 (1948): 306–318.

al-Hifni, Mahmud Ahmad. *Sayyid Darwish: hayatuhu wa athar 'abqariyyatih.* Cairo, 1962, 1974.

———. *al-Shaykh Salama Hijazi, raid al-masrah al-'arabi.* Cairo, 1968.

al-Hifni, R. *Muhammad 'Abd al-Wahhab: hayatuh wa fannuh.* Cairo, 1991.

Hijazi, Ahmad 'Abd al-Mu'ti. *Haykal wa haula.* Cairo, 1971.

Hijazi, Anwar. *'Amaliqa wa ruwwad.* Cairo, 1965.

Hijazi, Muhammad Fahmi. *Usul al-fikr al-'arabi al-hadith 'ind al-Tahtawi.* Cairo, 1974.

Hilal [al-Dessouki], 'Ali al-Din. "al-Nubugh al-fardi wa al-'usur al-jama'i." *al-Ahram al-iqtisadi,* 24 Oct. 1988.

al-Hilal editors. *Jurji Zaydan, 1861–1914: tarjamat hayatihi . . . .* Cairo, 1915.

———. *al-Hilal fi arba'in sana.* Cairo, 1932.

al-Hilali, 'Abd al-Raziq. *Zaki Mubarak fi al-'Iraq.* Beirut, 1970.

Hilbawi, Ibrahim. "Ahamm hadith fi majra hayati." *al-Hilal* 38:2 (Dec. 1929): 138–142.

———. *Mudhakkirat Ibrahim Hilbawi.* Ed. 'Isam Diya al-Din. Cairo, 1995.

Hill, Enid. *'Abd al-Razzaq al-Sanhuri and Islamic Law.* Cairo, 1987.

———. "al-Sanhuri and Islamic Law." *Arab Law Quarterly* (1988): 33–64, 182–218.

Hilmi, Muhammad Mustafa. "Mustafa 'Abd al-Raziq raid al-madrasa al-islamiyya al-hadith." *al-Fikr al-mu'asir* (June 1965): 81–89.

Himada, 'Abd al-Mun'im. "'Umar Makram, 1755–1822." *al-Kitab* 2 (Oct. 1946): 915–924.

al-Hindawi, Khalil. *Hafiz Ibrahim sha'ir al-Nil.* Beirut, 1973.

Hinnebusch, Raymond A. *Egyptian Politics Under Sadat.* 2nd ed. Boulder, Colo., 1988.

Hirst, David, and Irene Beeson. *Sadat.* London, 1981.

Hirszowicz, L. "The Sultan and the Khedive, 1892–1908." *MES* 8 (1972): 287–311.

Hoffman, Valerie J. "An Islamic Activist: Zaynab al-Ghazali." In *Women and the Family in the Middle East: New Voices of Change,* ed. Elizabeth W. Fernea. Austin, Tex., 1985, 233–254.

Hoffman-Ladd, Valerie J. "Polemics on the Modesty and Segregation of Women." *IJMES* 19 (1987): 23–50.

Holod, Renata, and Carl Rastorfer. "Hassan Fathy, Chairman's Award." In *Architecture and Community Building in the Islamic World Today.* New York, 1983, 235–245.

Holt, Derek. *Egypt: Politics and Society, 1945–1990.* 3rd ed. London and New York, 1991.

Holt, P.M. "'The Cloud Catcher': Ali Bey the Great of Egypt." *History Today* 9:1 (Jan. 1959): 48–58.

———. "al-Jabarti's Introduction to the History of Ottoman Egypt." *BSOAS* 25 (1962): 38–51.

Holt, P.M., ed. *Political and Social Change in Modern Egypt.* London, 1968.

Holynski, Alexandre. *Nubar Pacha devant l'histoire.* Paris, 1886.

Horward, Donald, ed. *Napoleonic Military History: A Bibliography.* London, 1986.

Hoskins, Halford L. *British Routes to India.* London and Philadelphia, 1928; New York, 1966.

———. "Mohamed Ali and Modern Egypt." *Journal of Modern History* 4 (1932): 93–103.

Houghton, Richard Monckton Milnes. *Monographs Personal and Social.* London, 1873.

Hourani, Albert. *Arabic Thought in the Liberal Age, 1798–1939.* London, 1962.

———. *Europe and the Middle East.* Berkeley, 1980.

———. "Ottoman Reform and the Politics of Notables." In *Beginnings of Modernization in the Middle East,* ed. William R. Polk and Richard L. Chambers. Chicago, 1968, 41–68.

———. "Rashid Rida and the Sufi Orders: A Footnote to Laoust." *BEO* 29 (1977): 231–241.

Houth, Émile. "Jomard l'Égyptien." *BIE* 15 (1930–1933): 259–266.

al-Hufi, Ahmad. *al-Ittijah al-nafsi fi dirasat al-'Aqqad al-naqdiyya.* Cairo, 1967.

al-Hufi, Ahmad Muhammad. *al-Islam fi shi'r Shawqi.* Cairo, 1972.

———. *Wahy al-nasib fi shi'r Shawqi.* Cairo, 1934.

———. *Wataniyyat Shawqi: dirasa adabiyya tarikhiyya muqarana.* Cairo, 1978.

Hunayn, Édouard. *Shawqi 'ala al-masrah.* Beirut, 1936.

Hunter, F. Robert. *Egypt Under the Khedives.* Pittsburgh, 1984.

———. "The Making of a Notable Politician: Muhammad Sultan Pasha (1825–1884). *IJMES* 15 (1983): 537–544.

———. "Self-Image and Historical Truth: Nubar Pasha and the Making of Modern Egypt." *MES* 23:3 (July 1987): 263–275.

al-Husami, Munir. "Sayyid Darwish." *al-Kitab* 4 (May 1947): 1059–1068.

Husayn, Ahmad. *Imani.* Cairo, 1936, 1946.

———. *Mawsu'at tarikh Misr.* 5 vols. Cairo, 1972–1983.

Husayn, Muhammad Muhammad. *al-Ittijahat al-wataniyya fi al-adab al-mu'asir.* 2 vols. Cairo, 1954–1956.

Husayn, Mustafa Ibrahim. *Yahya Haqqi: mubdi'an wa naqidan.* Cairo, 1970.

Husayn, Qadriyya. *Shahirat al-nisa fi al-'alam al-islami.* Cairo, 1922.

Husayn, Suzan Taha. *Ma'ak.* Cairo, 1979. Trans. from *Avec Toi.* Paris, 1975.

Husayn, Taha. *al-Ayyam.* Eng trans., *The Days: His Autobiography in Three Parts.* Cairo, 1997.

———. *Hadith al-arba'a.* Cairo, 1926.

———. *Hafiz wa Shawqi.* Cairo, 1933, 1958.

———. Introduction to *Awham shu'ara al-'arab,* by Ahmad Taymur. Cairo, 1950.

———. "al-Marhum al-Duktur 'Abd al-Wahhab 'Azzam." *MMLA* 14 (1962): 241–245.

———. "Mustafa 'Abd al-Raziq." *al-Katib al-Misri* 5 (1947): 340–344.

———. "Tharwat wa *al-Shi'r al-jahili.*" *al-Muqtataf* 73:4 (Oct. 1928): 242–248; 5 (Nov.): 371–372; 6 (Dec.): 365–373.

———. "Zawjati." *al-Hilal* 43:1 (Nov. 1934): 12–16.

al-Husayni, Musa. *al-Ikhwan al-Muslimin.* Beirut, 1952. Eng. trans. by the author. *The Muslim Brethren.* Beirut, 1956.

al-Husry, Khaldun Sati. *Origins of Modern Arab Political Thought.* New York, 1980.

———. *Three Reformers.* Beirut, 1966.

Hutchins, William. *al-Mazini's Egypt.* Washington, 1983.

———. "The Theology of Tawfiq al-Hakim: An Exposition with Examples." *MW* 78:3–4 (July–Oct. 1988): 243–279.

'Ibada, 'Abd al-Fattah. "'Aisha al-Taymuriyya." *al-Hilal* 35:4 (Feb. 1927): 401–408.

Ibish, Yusuf. *Rihlat al-Imam Muhammad Rashid Rida.* Beirut, 1971.

Ibn al-Sharif, Mahmud. *Adab Mahmud Taymur li al-haqiqa wa al-tarikh.* Cairo, [1960s?].

Ibn Mas'ud, Dayf Allah Muhammad al-Akhdar. *Nathr Mustafa Sadiq al-Rafi'i.* Algiers, 1968.

Ibn al-Sharif, Mahmud. *Khalil Mutran: ustadh Shawqi wa Hafiz.* Cairo, [1950s?].

Ibrahim, 'Abd al-Fattah. *Shu'arauna al-dubbat.* Cairo, [1935?].

Ibrahim, Ibrahim A. "Salama Musa: an Essay in Cultural Alienation." *MES* 15 (1979): 346–357.

Ibrahim, Ibrahim I. "Taha Husayn: The Critical Spirit." In *Problems,* ed. John Spagnolo, 105–118.

Ibrahim, Muhammad. *al-Musiqar Sayyid Darwish.* Cairo, 1958.

Ibrahim, Muhammad 'Abd al-Fattah. *Ahmad Zaki Abu Shadi: al-insan al-muntij.* Cairo, 1955.

Ibrahim, Muhammad Hafiz. *Diwan Hafiz Ibrahim.* Cairo, 1937.

———. *Layali satih.* Cairo, 1959.

Ibrahim, Saad Eddin. "Anatomy of Egypt's Militant Islamic Groups." *IJMES* 12 (1980): 423–453.

Ibrahim, Shihata 'Isa. *'Uzama al-wataniyya fi Misr.* Cairo, 1977.

al-Ibyari, Fathi Husayn. *'Alam Taymur al-qasasi.* Cairo, 1976.

———. *Fann al-qissa 'inda Mahmud Taymur.* Cairo, 1964.

———. *Mahmud Taymur wa fann al-uqsusa al-'arabiyya.* Cairo, 1961.

'Id, Muhammad al-Sayyid. *Ahmad Amin.* Cairo, 1994.

'Id, Raja. *Dirasa fi adab Tawfiq al-Hakim.* Alexandria, 1977.

Idenogle, David W. "The Khedive's Cartographers." *Aramco World* 35:5 (Sept.–Oct. 1984): 16–23.

Ignatieff, Michael. "Alone with the Secretary General." *New Yorker* (14 Aug. 1995): 33–39.

Imam, 'Abd Allah. *'Abd al-Nasir wa al-Ikhwan.* Cairo, 1981.

———. *'Amir wa Birlanti.* Cairo, 1988.

———. *Jihan: sayyidat Misr al-ula wa al-akhira.* Cairo, 1985.

al-Imam, Salih. *Husayn al-Shafi'i wa asrar Thawrat Yulyu wa hukm al-Sadat.* Cairo, [1991?].

al-Imam al-shahid Hasan al-Banna bi-qalam waladihi wa akharin. Beirut, 1970.

'Imara, Muhammad. *'Ali Mubarak: mu'arrikh al-mujtama' wa muhandis al-'umran.* Beirut, 1984.

———. *al-Imam Muhammad 'Abduh: mujaddid al-dunya bi-tajdid al-din.* Beirut, 1985.

———. *Jamal al-Din al-Afghani al-muftara 'alayhi.* Beirut, 1984.

———. *al-Jami'a al-islamiyya wa al-fikra al-qawmiyya 'inda Mustafa Kamil.* Beirut, 1976.

———. *Ma'rakat "al-Islam wa usul al-hukm."* Cairo, 1989.

———. *Qasim Amin: "Tahrir al-mara" wa al-tamaddun al-islami.* 2nd ed. Cairo, 1988.

———. *Rifa'a al-Tahtawi: raid al-tanwir fi al-'asr al-hadith.* Cairo and Beirut, 1984.

———. *al-Shaykh Muhammad al-Ghazali: al-mawqi' al-fikri . . . wa al-ma'arik al-fikriyya.* Cairo, 1992.

al-'Imari, Ahmad Suwaylim. *Adab Shawqi fi al-siyasa wa al-ijtima.* Cairo, 1972, 1975.

———. *Mustafa Kamil ka-madrasa wataniyya wa siyasiyya.* Cairo, 1976.

al-'Imari, Muhammad 'Abd al-Qadir. *Muhakamat al-zaman aw Taha Husayn.* Cairo, 1942.

al-'Inani, 'Ali. *Dhikra Shawqi.* Cairo, 1932.

'Inani, Sayyid. *'Abd Allah Basha Fikri: hayatuhu wa atharahu wa makanatuhu al-adabiyya.* Cairo, 1946.

International Dictionary of Women's Biography. New York, 1982.

"Interview with Esmat Abdul Magid." *American Arab Affairs* 22 (fall 1997): 41–44.

al-'Iraqi, 'Atif. *al-Shaykh Muhammad 'Abduh, 1849–1905 M.* Cairo, 1995.

'Iryan, Muhammad Sa'id. *Hayat al-Rafi'i.* Cairo, 1939.

'Isa, Ahmad. *Mu'jam al-atibba min sanat 650 hijriyya ila yawmina hadha.* Cairo, 1942.

'Isa, Mamduh. "Mustafa Kamil fi al-madrasa." *al-Thaqafa* 11:529 (14 Feb. 1949): 11–14.

'Isa, Salah. *Muhakamat Fuad Siraj al-Din.* Cairo, 1983.

———. *al-Thawra al-'urabiyya.* Beirut, 1972.

Ishaq, 'Awni, ed. *al-Durar.* Beirut, 1909.

Iskandar, Rushdi. *Khamsun sana min al-fann.* Cairo, 1962.

Iskarus, Tawfiq. *Nawabigh al-aqbat wa mashahiruhum fi al-qarn al-tasi' 'ashar.* 4 vols. Cairo, 1910–1913.

Isma'il, Haydar Hajj. *al-Mujtama' wa al-din wa al-ishtirakiyya: Farah Antun.* Beirut, 1972.

Ivray, Jehan d'. *Un chef au service de l'Égypte.* Paris, 1940.

———. *La vie aventureuse du Général Menou (1938).* In *Les oeuvres libres,* vol. 201 (1948): 91–134.

'Izz al-Din, Amin. *Shakhsiyyat wa marahil 'ummaliyya.* Cairo, 1970.

al-Jabalawi, Muhammad Tahir. *Dhikrayati ma'a 'Abbas al-'Aqqad.* 2 vols. Giza, 1996.

———. *Jamal al-Din al-Afghani.* Cairo, 1971.

Jab Allah, Rashwan Mahmud. *'Ali Mahir.* Cairo, 1987.

Jabara, Abdeen, et al. "The Arab Image in American Film and Television." *Cineaste* 17:1 (1989).

al-Jabari, 'Abd al-Mut'al M. *al-Muslima al-'asriyya 'inda Bahithat al-Badiya Malak Hifni Nasif.* Cairo, 1976.

al-Jabarti, 'Abd al-Rahman. *'Ajaib al-athar fi al-tarajim wa al-akhbar.* 4 vols. Cairo, 1879.

———. *Napoleon in Egypt: al-Jabarti's Chronicle of the French Revolution, 1798.* Trans. Shmuel Moreh. Princeton, 1993.

al-Jabiri, Muhammad Salih. *Mahmud Bayram al-Tunisi fi al-manfa: hayatuh wa atharauh.* 2 vols. Beirut, 1987.

Jabr, Jamil. *Mayy fi hayatiha al-mudtaraba.* Beirut, 1953.

———. *Mayy fi hayatiha wa-adabiha.* Beirut, 1960.

———. *Mayy, silsilat al-manahil.* Beirut, 1954.

———. *Mayy wa Jubran.* Beirut, 1950.

Jabr, Mustafa al-Nahhas. *Mudhakkirat Sa'd Zaghlul: dirasa.* Cairo, 1973.

Jad, Ali. *Form and Technique in the Egyptian Novel.* Cairo, 1983.

Jadu, 'Abd al-'Aziz. *al-Shaykh Tantawi Jawhari: dirasa wa nusus.* Cairo, 1979.

Jahim, Sayyah. *Khalil Mutran al-sha'ir.* Damascus, 1990.

al-Jamal, Shawqi, ed. *Awraq Mustafa Kamil: al-murasalat.* Cairo, 1982.

Jamal al-Din, Najib. *Khalil Mutran: sha'ir al-'asr.* Beirut, 1949.

Jamasi, Muhammad 'Abd al-Ghani. *Mudhakkirat al-Jamasi: Harb Uktubir 1973.* Paris, 1990. Eng. trans. *The October War: Memoirs of Field Marshall El-Gamasy of Egypt.* Cairo, 1993.

al-Jambalati, 'Ali, and 'Abd al-Futuh al-Tunisi. *Fi al-dhikra al-khamsin li al-thair al-batal al-qawmi wa za'im al-sha'bi Ahmad 'Urabi.* Cairo, 1961.

James, Lawrence. *Imperial Warrior: The Life and Times of Field Marshal Viscount Allenby, 1861–1936.* London, 1993.

Jami'at al-Duwal al-'Arabiyya. *al-Fihris al-tamhidi li al-makhtutat al-musawwara.* Cairo, 1948.

al-Jami'i,'Abd al-Mun'im. *'Abdallah Nadim wa dawruhu fi al-haraka al-siyasiyya wa al-ijtima'iyya.* Cairo, 1980.

———. *al-Jami'a al-misriyya al-qadima.* Cairo, 1981.

———. *al-Jami'a al-misriyya wa al-mujtama'*, *1908–1940*. Cairo, 1983.

———. *al-Khidiwi 'Abbas Hilmi al-thani wa al-hizb al-watani, 1892–1914*. Cairo, 1982.

———. "Min qadaya al-'unf al-siyasi fi Misr: ightiyal Amin 'Uthman wa dalalatuhu al-siyasiyya." *MTM* 30–1 (1983–1984): 507–552.

———. "Mustafa Kamil wa tasis al-Hizb al-Watani." In *al-Mawsim al-shitan li al-Jam'iyya al-Tarikhiyya*. Cairo, 1983.

———. "al-Tanafus 'ala al-khidiwiyya al-misriyya bayn al-Amir Muhammad 'Abd al-Halim wa al-Khidiwi Tawfiq." *MTM* 28 (1981–1982): 359–372.

———. *Tarikh Misr al-iqtisadi wa al-ijtima'i fi 'asr Muhammad 'Ali*. Shubra, 1995.

———. *al-Thawra al-'Urabiyya fi daw al-wathaiq al-misriyya*. Cairo, 1982.

al-Jami'i, 'Abd al-Mun'im, ed. *Majallat "al-Ustadh."* Cairo, 1994.

———. *"al-Masamir."* Cairo, n.d.

al-Jam'iyya al-Khayriyya al-Islamiyya. *Sirat al-marhum 'Ali Mubarak Basha*. Cairo, 1904.

al-Jam'iyya al-Misriyya li al-dirasat al-Tarikhiyya. *Mustafa Kamil: buhuth ulqiyat fi al-nadwa al-lati 'aqadaha al-jam'iyya . . . bi-munasabat murur miat 'am 'ala mawlidihi, 1874–1974*. Cairo, 1976.

Jam'iyyat Asdiqa Musiqa al-Sayyid Darwish. *Fannan al-sha'b: Sayyid Darwish*. Alexandria, 1964.

al-Janbulati, 'Ali. *Fi dhikra Tantawi Jawhari*. Cairo, 1962.

Jankowski, James. "Arab Nationalism in 'Nasserism' and Egyptian State Policy, 1952–1958." In *Rethinking Nationalism*, ed. Israel Gershoni and James Jankowski, 150–167.

———. *Egypt's Young Rebels*. Stanford, 1974.

Jansen, J.J.G. *Interpretation of the Koran in Modern Egypt*. Leiden, 1974.

———. "A Little-Known Endorsement by Shaykh al-Sha'rawi." *Acts des XII Congreso de la U.E.A.I.* (Malaga, 1984): 379–389.

al-Jarim, 'Ali. "Sadiqi Ahmad Shawqi." *al-Hilal* 86:9 (Sept. 1948): 84.

———. *Salasil al-dhahab, al-a'mal al-nathiriyya al-kamila*. Cairo, 1989.

Jarvis, C.S. *Desert and Delta*. London, 1938.

al-Jawadi, Muhammad. *Mudhakkirat al-mara al-misriyya*. Cairo, 1995.

Jawadi, Muhammad Muhammad. *Musharrafa bayn al-dharra wa al-dhirwa*. Cairo, 1980.

Jawda, Ahmad Qasim. *Nawabigh al-shabab*. Cairo, 1938.

Jawdat, Salih. *Balabil min al-sharq: 10 shu'ara*. 1st ed. 1960; 2nd ed. Cairo, 1972.

———. *Naji: hayatuhu wa shi'ruhu*. Cairo, 1960; Beirut, 1977.

———. "Sahib al-Jundul fi wataniyyatihi." *al-Hilal* 76:1 (Jan. 1968): 72–76.

———. "Tal'at Harb." *al-Kitab* 7 (Mar. 1949): 403–409.

al-Jawhari, 'Abd al-Rahim. *'Umar al-Tilmisani mujahidan, mufakkiran, katiban*. Cairo, 1986.

al-Jawhari, Mahmud. "Kayfa kana Muhammad 'Ali yu'amil al-sha'b." *al-Hilal* 63:3 (Mar. 1955): 80–83.

Jawhari, Tantawi. *Kitab al-Arwah*. Cairo, 1916.

Jawish, Nasir. Introduction to *al-Islam din al-fitra*, by 'Abd al-'Aziz Jawish. Cairo, 1952.

Jayyar, Midhat. *Ma'rakat al-Mazini wa Hafiz: al-awraq al-kamila 1915–1918*. Cairo and Limassol, 1993.

Jayyusi, Salma Khadra. *Trends and Developments in Modern Arabic Poetry*. Leiden, 1977.

al-Jaziri, Muhammad Ibrahim. *Sa'd Zaghlul: dhikrayat tarikhiyya tarifa*. Cairo, 1954.

Jeffery, Arthur. "Three Cairo Modernists." *International Review of Missions* 21 (1932): 498–515.

Jerrold, Blanchard. *The Belgium of the East*. London, 1882.

———. *Egypt Under Ismail-Pacha*. London, 1879.

Jewish Agency for Palestine. *Documents Relating to the McMahon Letters*. London, 1939.

al-Jiddawi, Hasan Salih. *Nazarat naqdiyya fi al-shi'r Abi Shadi*. Cairo, 1925.

al-Jindi, 'Abd al-Halim. *Jaraim wa ightiyalat al-qarn al-'ishrin*. Cairo, n.d.

al-Jindi, 'Abd al-Hamid Sanad. *Hafiz Ibrahim: sha'ir al-Nil*. Cairo, 1959, 1968.

al-Jindi, Anwar. *'Abd al-'Aziz Jawish: min ruwwad al-tarbiya wa al-sihafa wa al-ijtima'*. Cairo, 1965.

———. *Adwa 'ala hayat al-udaba al-mu'asirin*. Cairo, 1968.

———. *Ahmad Zaki al-mulaqqab shaykh al-'uruba*. Cairo, 1964.

———. *A'lam lam yunsifhum jiluhum*. Cairo, [1962?].

———. *A'lam wa ashab aqlam*. Cairo, 1968.

———. *al-Imam al-Maraghi*. Cairo, 1952.

———. *Jurji Zaydan: munshi "al-Hilal."* Cairo, 1958.

———. *al-Kuttab al-mu'asirun: adwa 'ala hayatihim*. Cairo, 1955.

———. *Min a'lam al-hurriyya fi al-'alam al-arabi al-hadith*. Cairo, 1961.

———. *al-Muhafaza wa al-tajdid fi al-nathr al-'arabi al-mu'asir*. Cairo, 1961.

———. *Muhammad Farid Wajdi: raid al-tawfiq bayn al-'ilm wa al-din*. Cairo, 1974.

———. *Qissat Mahmud Taymur*. Cairo, 1957.

———. *al-Sharq fi fajr al-yaqza*. Cairo, 1966.

———. *al-Sihafa al-siyasiyya fi Misr min nashatiha ila al-Harb al-'Alamiyya al-Thaniya*. Cairo, 1962.

———. *Taha Husayn: hayatuhu wa fikruhu fi daw al-Islam*. Cairo, 1976.

———. *Tarikh al-sihafa al-islamiyya*, I: *"al-Manar."* Cairo, 1983; II. Cairo, 1986.

———. *Zaki Mubarak: hayatuhu wa adabuh*. Cairo, 1963.

Johansen, Baber. *Muhammad Husayn Haikal: Europa und der Orient im Weltbild eines Ägyptischen Liberalen.* Beirut, 1967.

Jomard, E.F. "L'École Égyptienne de Paris." *Nouveau journal asiatique* 2 (1828): 99, 104.

Jomier, Jacques. "Le Cheikh Tantawi Jawhari (1862–1940) et son commentaire du Coran." *MIDEO* 5 (1958): 115–174.

———. *La commentaire coranique du "Manar."* Paris, 1954.

———. "Les raisons d'adhésion du Sayyid Rashid Rida au nationalisme arabe." *BIE* 53–54 (1971–1973): 53–61.

———. "La vie l'une famille du Caire d'après trois romans de M. Naguib Mahfuz. *MIDEO* 4 (1957): 27–94.

Jones, Marsden, and Hamdi Sakkut. *A'lam al-adab al-mu'asir fi Misr: II. Ibrahim 'Abd al-Qadir al-Mazini.* Cairo, 1979.

Joynboll, J.G.H. "Ismail Ahmad Adham (1911–1940), the Atheist." *JAL* 3 (1972): 54–71.

Jum'a, Muhammad Lutfi. In *al-Balagh al-usbu'i,* no. 121 (6 July 1929).

Jum'a, Muhammad Kamil. *Hafiz Ibrahim: ma lahu wa ma 'alayhi.* Cairo, 1960.

Jumayyil, Antun. "Ahamm hadith fi majra hayati." *al-Hilal* 38:5 (Mar. 1930): 534–536.

———. *Shawqi.* Cairo, 1932.

———. "Wali al-Din Yakan." *al-Hilal* 29:8 (May 1921): 777–784.

Jumayyil, Zuhayr, and Karima Zaki Mubarak. *al-Fikr al-tarbawi 'inda Zaki Mubarak.* Cairo, [1992?].

al-Jundi, 'Abd al-Halim. *al-Imam Muhammad 'Abduh.* Cairo, 1979.

al-Jundi, Adham. *A'lam al-adab wa al-fann.* 2 vols. Damascus, 1958.

Kafafi, Husayn. *al-Khidiwi Isma'il wa ma'shuqatuh Misr.* Cairo, 1994.

Kahf, Mohja. "Huda Sha'rawi's *Mudhakkirati:* The Memoirs of the First Lady of Arab Modernity." *Arab Studies Quarterly* 20:1 (winter 1998): 53–82.

Kahhala, 'Umar Rida. *A'lam al-nisa fi 'alamay al-'arab wa al-Islam.* 2nd ed. 5 vols. Damascus, 1958–1959; 4th ed. Beirut, 1982.

———. *Mu'jam al-muallifin.* 20 vols. Damascus, 1957–1961.

Kamal, 'Abd Allah. *Nisa Anwar al-Sadat.* Cairo, 1995.

Kamal al-Din, Muhammad. "Muhammad 'Uthman Jalal wa al-masrah al-kumidi." *al-Masrah wa al-sinima,* no. 57 (Sept. 1968): 61–64.

———. *Ruwwad al-masrah al-misri.* Cairo, 1970.

Kamil, 'Ali Fahmi. *Mustafa Kamil Basha fi 34 rabi'an.* 9 vols. Cairo, 1908–1911.

Kamil, Mahmud. *Tazawwuq al-musiqa al-arabiyya.* Cairo, 1974.

Kamil, Mustafa. *Lettres égyptiennes françaises addressées à Mme Juliette Adam, 1895–1908.* Cairo, 1909.

Kamil, Raouf. *Waçif Ghali, l'écrivain.* Paris, 1960.

Kamil, Rashid. *Tal'at Harb: damir watan.* Cairo, 1993.

Kan'an, Muhammad Ahmad, and Zuhayr al-Shawish. *Mukhtasar tafsir "al-Manar."* 3 vols. Beirut-Damascus, 1984.

Karim, Samih. *Madha yabqa min Taha Husayn.* Cairo, 1973.

———. *Taha Husayn fi ma'arikihi al-adabiyya wa al-fikriyya.* Cairo, 1974.

Karim, Sayyid, "al-Tabi' al-qawmi wa al-'imara fi Misr." *al-'Imara* 5–6 (1940): 271–275.

Karkouti, Mustapha. "Egypt and the Arabs: Interview." *Middle East* 90 (Apr. 1982): 27–28.

Karnouk, Liliane. *Contemporary Egyptian Art.* Cairo, 1995.

———. *Modern Egyptian Art: The Emergence of a National Style.* Cairo, 1988.

Karrum, Hasanayn. *'Abd al-Nasir al-muftara 'alayh.* Cairo, 1985.

Katz, Ephraim, ed. *The Film Encyclopedia.* 2nd ed. New York, 1994.

Kawtharani, Wajih, ed. *al-Dawla wa al-khilafa fi al-khitab al-'arabi abana al-Thawra al-Kamaliyya fi Turkiya: Rashid Rida, 'Ali 'Abd al-Raziq, 'Abd al-Rahman Shabandar.* Beirut, 1996.

al-Kayyali, Sami. *Ma'a Taha Husayn.* Cairo, 1951, 1973.

———. *al-Rahilun.* Cairo, n.d.

———. *Wali al-Din Yakan.* Cairo, 1960.

al-Kayyali, Sami, ed. *Diwan Ibrahim Naji.* Beirut, 1973.

Kazim, Safinaz. "al-Raida Nabawiya Musa wa in'ash dhakirat al-umma." *al-Hilal* 73:1 (Jan. 1984): 116–119.

Keddie, Nikki. *An Islamic Response to Imperialism: Political and Religious Writings of Sayyid Jamal al-Din "al-Afghani."* 2nd ed. Berkeley, 1983.

———. *Sayyid Jamal al-Din "al-Afghani."* Berkeley and Los Angeles, 1972.

Kedourie, Elie. *Afghani and 'Abduh: An Essay on Religious Unbelief and Political Activism in Islam.* London, 1966.

———. *The Chatham House Version and Other Middle Eastern Studies.* London, 1970.

———. "The Death of Adib Ishaq." *MES* 9 (1973): 31–36.

———. *In the Anglo-Arab Labyrinth.* Cambridge, UK.

Kelidar, Abbas. "Shaykh Ali Yusuf: Egyptian Journalist and Islamic Nationalist." In *Intellectual Life,* ed. Marwan Buheiry, Beirut, 1981, 10–20.

Kenny, Dallas. "The Magic of Om Kalthoum: Her Star Still Shines." *Places in Egypt* (May–June 1991): 54–57.

Kenny, Lorne. "'Ali Mubarak: Nineteenth Century Educator and Administrator." *MEJ* 21:1 (1967): 35–51.

Kepel, Gilles. *Muslim Extremism in Egypt: The Prophet and Pharaoh.* Berkeley, 1986.

Kerr, Malcolm. *The Arab Cold War: Gamal Abd al-Nasir and His Rivals.* 3rd ed. London, 1971.

———. *Islamic Reform: The Political and Legal Theories of Muhammad 'Abduh and Rashid Rida.* Berkeley and Los Angeles, 1966.

Kettel, Jeannot. *Jean-François Champollion le Jeune: repertoire de bibliographie analytique 1806–1989.* Paris, 1990.

Khabbaz, Hanna. *Mukhtarat "al-Muqtataf."* Cairo, 1931.

Khadduri, Majid. *Arab Contemporaries: The Role of Personalities in Politics.* Baltimore, 1973.

———. "Aziz Ali al-Misri and the Arab Nationalist Movement." *St. Antony's Papers* 17. London, 1974.

———. *Political Trends in the Arab World: The Role of Ideas and Ideals in Politics.* Baltimore, 1970.

Khafaji, Muhammad 'Abd al-Mun'im. *'Abbas Mahmud al-'Aqqad bayn al-sihafa wa al-adab.* Cairo, 1985.

———. *al-Azhar fi alf 'am.* 2nd ed. 3 vols. Cairo, 1987–1988.

———. *Madhahib al-adab.* Cairo, 1953.

———. *Qisas min al-tarikh.* Cairo, 1954.

———. *Qissat al-adab fi Misr.* 4 vols. Cairo, 1956.

———. *Raid al-shi'r al-hadith, Ahmad Zaki Abu Shadi.* Cairo, 1955.

———. *Suwar min al-adab al-hadith.* Cairo, [1950s?].

al-Khafif, Mahmud. *Ahmad 'Urabi: al-za'im al-muftara 'alayhi.* Cairo, 1947, 1971, 1981.

Khaki, Ahmad. *Ahmad Amin: tarikh hayatihi al-fikri.* Cairo, 1973.

———. *Qasim Amin.* Cairo, 1945, 1973.

Khalaf, Fadil. *Zaki Mubarak bayna riyad al-adab wa al-fann.* Kuwait, [1968?].

Khalaf Allah, Muhammad Ahmad. *'Abdallah al-Nadim wa mudhakkiratuhu al-siyasiyya.* Cairo, 1956.

———. *'Ali Mubarak.* Cairo, 1957.

Khalafallah, Mohamed. "L'évolution de la langue et de la littérature arabe du XXe siècle." *Cahiers d'histoire mondiale* 1 (1960): 122–157.

Khalid, Detlev. "Ahmad Amin and the Legacy of Muhammad 'Abduh." *IS* 9 (1970): 1–32.

———. "Ahmad Amin: Modern Interpretations of Muslim Universalism." *IS* 8 (1969): 47–93.

———. "Some Aspects of Neo-Mu'tazilism." *IS* 8 (1969): 329–348.

al-Khalidi, Salah 'Abd al-Fattah. *Sayyid Qutb: al-shahid al-hayy.* Amman, 1981.

———. *Sayyid Qutb min al-milad ila al-istishhad.* Damascus-Beirut-Jiddah, 1991.

al-Khalili, Muhammad. *Mu'jam udaba al-atibba.* Najaf, 1946.

Khan, Mohamed. *An Introduction to Egyptian Cinema.* London, 1969.

Khashaba, Darini. "Shi'r Naji." *al-Risala* 12:566 (1944): 366–368.

Khater, Akram. "Egypt's Feminism: The Egyptian Feminist Movement Is Accused of Being Too Preoccupied with Intellectual Debate." *Middle East* (Feb. 1987): 17–18.

al-Khatib, Adnan. *Umm Kulthum: mu'jizat al-ghina al-'arabi.* Damascus, 1975.

al-Khatib, Muhibb al-Din. "Mudhakkirat . . . ." *al-Thaqafa* 2 (Aug.–Sept. 1973): 85–90.

Khatir, Muhammad 'Abd al-Mun'im. *'Ali al-Jarim.* Cairo, 1971.

Khattab, Diya Shit. *al-Maghfur lahu al-'allama 'Abd al-Razzaq Ahmad al-Sanhuri, 1895–1971.* Baghdad, [1972?].

Khattab, Sadiq Ibrahim. *al-Shi'r fi al-'asr al-hadir wa athr al-Barudi fihi.* Cairo, 1944.

Khayati, Khemais. *Cinémas arabes: topographe d'une image éclatée.* Paris and Montreal, 1996.

Khemiri, Tahir, and George Kampffmeyer. *Leaders in Contemporary Arabic Literature.* Leipzig, 1930.

Khidr, 'Abbas. *Muhammad Taymur: hayatuhu wa adabuhu.* Cairo, 1966.

———. *Suhufiyyun mu'asirun: lamahat min nashatihim wa kifahihim.* Cairo, 1967.

Khouri, Mounah A. "Lewis 'Awad: A Forgotten Pioneer of the Free Verse Movement." *JAL* 1 (1970): 137–144.

———. *Poetry and the Making of Modern Egypt.* Leiden, 1971.

Khoury, R.G. "Taha Husayn (1889–1973) et la France." *Arabica* 22:3 (Oct. 1975): 225–266.

Khoury, René. "Le mariage musulman du Général Abdallah Menou." *MTM* 25 (1978): 65–85.

al-Khozai, Ali. *The Development of Early Arabic Drama, 1947–1900.* London, 1984.

al-Khuli, Lutfi. "Taslim wa tasallum." *Ruz al-Yusuf,* 12 Dec. 1988.

Khurays, Husayn [Zaki Mubarak(?)]. *Jinayat Ahmad Amin 'ala al-adab al-'arabi.* Sidon, [1970s?].

Kiernan, Maureen. "Cultural Hegemony and National Film Language." *Alif: Journal of Comparative Poetics* 15 (1995): 130–152.

Kilani, Muhammad Sayyid. *'Abbas Hilmi al-Thani, aw 'asr al-taghalghul al-baritani fi Misr.* Cairo, 1991.

———. *al-Sultan Husayn Kamil: fitra muzlima fi tarikh Misr, 1914–1917.* Cairo, 1963.

Kilani, Sayyid. *Taha Husayn al-sha'ir al-katib.* Cairo, 1963.

Kilpatrick, Hilary. *The Modern Egyptian Novel.* London, 1974.

Kinross, Sir Patrick Balfour. *Between Two Seas: The Creation of the Suez Canal.* London, 1968.

Kinsey, David. "Egyptian Education Under Cromer." Ph.D. diss., Harvard, 1965.

Kishk, Muhammad Jalal. *Jahalat 'asr al-tanwir: qiraa fi fikr Qasim Amin wa 'Ali 'Abd al-Raziq.* Cairo, 1990.

———. *al-Shaykh Muhammad al-Ghazali bayn al-naqd al-'atib wa al-madh al-qamat.* Cairo, 1990.

al-Kitab al-dhahabi li-yubil "al-Muqtataf" al-kham-sin (1876–1926). Cairo, 1926.

Kooij, C. "Bint al-Shati: A Suitable Case for Biography." In *The Challenge of the Middle East,* ed. Ibrahim A.A. El-Sheikh et al. Amsterdam, 1982.

Krämer, Gudrün. *The Jews in Modern Egypt.* Seattle, 1989.

———. "The Rise and Decline of the Jewish Community of Cairo." *Pe'anim: Studies in the Cultural History of Oriental Jewry* 7 (1981): 4–30.

Kramer, Martin. *Islam Assembled: The Advent of the Muslim Congresses.* New York, 1986.

———. "Pen and Purse: Sabunji and Blunt." In *Essays in Honor of Bernard Lewis: The Islamic World from Classical to Modern Times,* ed. C.E. Bosworth, Charles Issawi, Roger Savory, and A.L. Udovitch. Princeton, 1988, 771–780.

Kramer, Walter. "Shaykh Maraghi's Mission to the Hijaz." *AAS* 16:1 (1982): 121–136.

Kratschkovsky, Ignaz Y. "Le roman historique dans la littérature arabe moderne." *WI* 12 (1930): 69–79.

Kudsi-Zadeh, A. Albert. "Afghani and Freemasonry in Egypt." *JAOS* 92 (1972): 25–35.

———. "Islamic Reform in Egypt: Some Observations on the Role of Afghani." *MW* 61 (1971): 1–12.

———. "Jamal al-Din al-Afghani and the National Awakening of Egypt: A Reassessment of his Role." *Actes du Ve Congrès International d'Arabisants et d'Islamisants* (1970): 297–305.

———. *Sayyid Jamal al-Din al-Afghani: An Annotated Bibliography.* Leiden, 1970.

Kuhnke, Laverne. *Lives at Risk.* Berkeley, 1990.

Kuppershoeck, P.M. *The Short Stories of Yusuf Idris: A Modern Egyptian Author.* Leiden, 1981.

Kurd 'Ali, Muhammad. "al-'Allama al-Maraghi Shaykh al-Azhar." *MMIA* 21 (July 1946): 289–305.

———. *al-Mu'asirun.* Damascus, 1980.

———. *al-Mudhakkirat.* 2 vols. Damascus, 1948–1951.

———. *al-Qadim wa al-hadith.* Cairo, 1925.

———. "Sadiqi Jurji Zaydan." *al-Hilal* 48:2 (Dec. 1939): 154–155.

Kurum, Hasanayn. *Mustaqbal al-quwwa al-siyasiyya fi Misr ba'da zuhur al-Wafd: radd 'ala Siraj al-Din.* Cairo, 1977.

Kusel, Baron de. *An Englishman's Recollections of Egypt, 1863 to 1887.* London, 1914.

Kushayk, Muhammad. "Rahil sha'ir kabir: Salah Jahin, 1930–1986." *al-Thaqafa al-jadida* 11 (July 1986).

al-Kuzbari, Salma H. *Mayy Ziyada: masat al-nubugh.* Beirut, 1982.

al-Labban, Sharif Darwish. *"Akhbar al-Yawm": masira suhufiyya fi nisf qarn.* Cairo, 1994.

Labib, Subhi. "The Copts in Egyptian Society." In *Islam, Nationalism, and Radicalism in Egypt and the Sudan,* ed. Gabriel Warburg. New York, 1983.

Laborde, Leon E.S.J. de. *Voyage de l'Arabie Pétrée,* reprint. Paris, 1994.

Lacouture, Jean. *Nasser.* New York, 1983.

LeCerf, J. "Chibli Chemayyel: métaphysicien et moraliste contemporain." *BEO* 1 (1931): 153–186.

LeGassick, Trevor, trans. and ed. *The Defense Statement of Ahmad Urabi the Egyptian.* London, 1982.

LaJonquière, C.E.L.M. *L'expédition en Égypte, 1798–1801.* Paris, 1897–1901.

Lampson, Miles. *Politics and Diplomacy in Egypt: The Diaries of Sir Miles Lampson, 1935-1937.* Ed. M.E. Yapp. London, 1997.

Landau, Jacob M. "Abu Naddara: A Jewish Egyptian Nationalist." *Journal of Jewish Studies* 3 (1952): 30–44; 5 (1954): 179–180.

———. "al-Afghani's pan-Islamic Project." *IC* 26 (1952): 50–54.

———. *The Jews in Nineteenth Century Egypt.* New York, 1969.

———. *Middle Eastern Themes: Papers in History and Politics.* London, 1973.

———. *Parliaments and Parties in Egypt.* Tel Aviv, 1953.

———. *Studies in the Arab Theater and Cinema.* Philadelphia, 1958.

Landes, David S. *Bankers and Pashas.* Cambridge, Mass., 1958.

Lane-Poole, Stanley. *Life of Edward William Lane.* London, 1877.

Laoust, Henri. *Le caliphat dans la doctrine de Rashid Rida.* Beirut, 1938.

———. "Le réformisme orthodoxe des 'salafiyya.'" *REI* 6 (1932): 175–224.

Lashin, 'Abd al-Khaliq. *Adwa 'ala mawqif wizarat 'Ali Mahir min al-harb al-'alamiyya al-thaniyya.* Cairo, 1977.

———. *al-Fikr al-siyasi 'inda 'Ali Mubarak.* Cairo, 1980.

———. *Sa'd Zaghlul wa dawruhu fi al-siyasa al-misriyya.* Beirut, 1975.

Laskier, Michael. *The Jews of Egypt, 1920–1970.* New York and London, 1971.

Laurens, Henry. *L'expédition d'Égypte: 1798–1801.* Paris, 1989.

———. *Kléber en Égypte, 1798–1800.* 4 vols. Cairo, 1988–1995.

———. *Les origines intellectuelles de l'expedition d'Egypte: l'orientalisme islamisant en France (1698–1798).* Istanbul, 1987.

Lawson, Fred H. *The Social Origins of Egyptian Expansionism During the Muhammad 'Ali Period.* New York, 1992.

Le Gassick, Trevor. "An Analysis of *al-Hubb tahta al-matar* (Love in the Rain)—a Novel by Najib Mahfuz." In *Studies in Modern Arabic Literature,* ed. R.C. Ostle, 140–151.

Lehmann, Joseph H. *All Sir Garnet: A Life of Field-Marshall Lord Wolseley.* London, 1964.

Lemke, Wolf-Dieter. *Mahmud Saltut (1893–1963) und die Reform der Azhar.* Frankfurt, 1980.

Lemsine, Aicha. "Outspoken Emissary for Peace." *Washington Report on Middle Eastern Affairs*, 1 Nov. 1992.

Lerner, Gerda. "Nawal el-Saadawi." *Progressive* 56 (Apr. 1992): 32–35.

Leslie, Shane. *Men Were Different*. London, 1937.

Lesseps, Ferdinand de. *History of the Suez Canal: A Personal Narrative*. Edinburgh, 1876.

———. *Le percement de l'Isthme de Suez: exposé et documents officiels*. 6 vols. Paris, 1855–1866.

Lester, J. "Stone of Egypt." *Aramco World* 23:1 (Jan.–Feb. 1972): 14–19.

Lévi, I.G. "La note de Sir William Brunyate, K.C.M.G., Conseiller financier P.I. sur le budget de 1918." *Egypte Contemporaine* 9 (1914): 411–420.

Lewis, Bernard. *The Muslim Discovery of Europe*. London, 1982.

Lia, Brynjar. *The Society of the Muslim Brothers in Egypt: The Rise of an Islamic Mass Movement 1928–1942*. Reading, UK, 1998.

Lieutenant Waghorn, R.N., Pioneer of the Overland Route to India. London, 1884.

Linant de Bellefonds, Louis Maurice Adolphe. *Journal d'un voyage à Merue dans les années 1821 et 1822*. Ed. Margaret Shinnie. Khartum, 1958.

Livingston, John W. "Ali Bey al-Kabir and the Mamluk Resurgence in Ottoman Egypt." Ph.D. diss., Princeton, 1968.

———. "Muhammad 'Abduh on Science." *MW* 85: 3–4 (July–Oct. 1995): 215–234.

———. "The Rise of Shaykh al-Balad Ali Bey al-Kabir: A Study in the Accuracy of the Chronicle of al-Jabarti." *BSOAS* 33 (1970): 283–294.

———. "Western Science and Educational Reform in the Thought of Shaykh Rifa'a al-Tahtawi." *IJMES* 28 (1996): 543–564.

Long, Richard. *Tawfiq al-Hakim, Playwright of Egypt*. London, 1979.

Longford, Elizabeth. *Pilgrimage of Passion*. London, 1979.

Loring, W.W. *A Confederate Soldier in Egypt*. New York, 1884.

Lott, Emmeline. *The Mohaddetyn in the Palace: Nights in the Harem*. 2 vols. London, 1867.

Louca, Anouar. "Le harem du khédive." *Kitabi* (July 1958): 9–51.

———. "Masrah Ya'qub Sannu'." *al-Majalla* 51 (Mar. 1961): 51–71.

———. "Les Parisiens dans le Miroir de Rifa'a." *Revue du Caire* (Dec. 1958).

———. "Taha Hussein and the West." *Cultures* 2:2 (1975): 115–139.

———. *Voyageurs et écrivains égyptiens en France*. Paris, 1970.

Luhayta, Muhammad Fahmi. *Tarikh Fuad al-awwal al-iqtisadi*. 3 vols. Cairo, 1943–1947.

Luqa, Nazmi. *Rayhanat al-shuhada Mahmud Fahmi al-Nuqrashi*. Cairo, 1949.

Lusignan, Sauveur K. *A History of the Revolt of Ali Bey Against the Ottoman Porte*. London, 1783–1786.

Lutfullah, Mirza. *Jamal al-Din al-Asad Abadi*. Trans. Sadiq Nashat and 'Abd al-Mun'im Hasanayn. Cairo, 1957.

Lüthi, Jean-Jacques. *Les français en Égypte*. Beirut, 1981.

———. *Introduction à la littérature d'expression française en Égypte*. Paris, 1979.

Lytton, Noel Anthony Scawen. *Wilfrid Scawen Blunt: A Memoir by His Grandson*. London, 1961.

Ma'ati, Salah al-Din. *Wasiyyat sahib al-qandil*. Cairo, 1995.

Mackesy, Piers. *British Victory in Egypt*. London and New York, 1995.

Madkur, Ibrahim. "Lutfi al-Sayyid bayn al-muslihin." *Hiwar* 4 (May–June 1963): 5–13.

Madkur, Ibrahim, and Muhammad Diyab. "al-Marhum al-Duktur Mansur Fahmi." *MMLA* 14 (1962): 353–365.

Madkur, Ibrahim Bayumi, et al. *al-Shaykh al-akbar Mustafa 'Abd al-Raziq mufakkiran wa adiban wa muslihan*. Cairo, 1982.

Madkur, Muhammad Salam. *al-Hakim al-thair Jamal al-Din al-Afghani*. Cairo, 1962.

al-Madlaji, Thabit. *al-Raid al-a'sar: Jamal al-Din al-Afghani*. Beirut, 1954.

al-Maghribi, 'Abd al-Qadir. *Jamal al-Din al-Afghani: dhikrayat wa ahadith*. Cairo, 1948, 1967.

Magnus, Philip M. *Kitchener: Portrait of an Imperialist*. London, 1958.

Mahallawi, Hanafi. *al-Malika Nazli bayn sijn al-harim wa kursi al-'arsh*. Cairo, 1994.

———. *Layali al-Qahira fi 'asr Badi'a: al-raqisa al-lati hakamat bashawat Misr wa sa'alik 'Imad al-Din*. Damascus, 1997.

———. *Sayyidatan min Misr: Umm Kulthum wa Jihan al-Sadat*. Agouza, 1994.

al-Mahasini, Zaki. *'Abd al-Wahhab 'Azzam*. Cairo, 1968.

———. *Muhadarat 'an Ahmad Amin*. Cairo, 1962/1963.

Mahdavi, Asghar, and Iraj Afshar, eds. *Documents inédits concernant Seyyed Jamal al-Din al-Afghani*. Tehran, 1963.

Mahfuz, Ahmad. *Hayat Hafiz Ibrahim*. Cairo, 1957.

———. *Hayat Shawqi*. Cairo, 1955.

Mahfuz, Najib. *Atahaddath ilaykum*. Beirut, 1977.

Mahmud, 'Ali 'Abd al-Hamid. *Mustafa Sadiq al-Rafi'i wa al-ittijahat al-islamiyya fi adabihi*. Riyadh, 1975.

Mahmud, Fatima al-Zahra Muhammad. *al-Ramziyya fi adab Najib Mahfuz*. Beirut, 1981.

Mahmud, Hafiz. "al-'Amaliqa al-sitta." *al-Hilal* 81:9 (Sept. 1973): 106–116.

———. *Asrar al-madi min 1907 ila 1952*. Cairo, 1973.

———. "Ibrahim 'Abd al-Hadi." *al-Jumhuriyya*, 20 Feb. 1981.

Mahmud, Muhammad. *al-Shi'r al-nisai al'asri wa shahirat nujumih.* Cairo, 1929.

Mahna, Jurji. *Sirr najah al-mujahid al-kabir al-ustadh Makram 'Ubayd.* Cairo, n.d.

Mahran, Rashida. *Taha Husayn bayn al-sira wa al-tarjama al-dhatiyya.* Cairo, 1979.

Mahrez, Samia. *Egyptian Writers Between History and Fiction.* Cairo, 1994.

Majdi, [Muhammad] Salih. *Diwan al-Sayyid Salih Majdi Bey.* Bulaq, 1894.

———. *Hilyat al-zaman bi-manaqib khadim al-watan.* Ed. Jamal al-Din al-Shayyal. Cairo, 1958.

Majed, Jaafer. *La presse littéraire en Tunisie de 1904 à 1955.* Tunis, 1979.

Makariyus, Shahin. *Tarikh al-Israiliyyin.* Cairo, 1904.

Makhawif, Muhammad. *Shajarat al-nur al-zakiyya fi tabaqat al-malikiyya.* Cairo, 1349/50.

Makhluf, Hasanayn Hasan. *Mustafa Sadiq al-Rafi'i: hayatuhu wa adabuh.* Cairo, 1976.

Makhluf, N. *Nubar Basha wa ma tamma 'ala yadihi.* Cairo, n.d.

Makhzanji, Ahmad. *Nazra tahliliyya fi kitabat D. Muhammad Husayn Haykal.* Cairo, 1987.

al-Makhzumi, Muhammad. *Khatirat Jamal al-Din al-Afghani.* Beirut, 1931.

al-Malaika, Nazik. *Muhadarat fi shi'r 'Ali Mahmud Taha.* Cairo, 1965.

al-Malaika, Sadiq. *Dhawu al-fuqaha fi al-tarikh.* Baghdad, 1948.

Malet, Edward. *Egypt, 1879–1883.* London, 1909.

———. *Shifting Scenes or Memories of Many Men in Many Lands.* London, 1901.

Maliji, Musharrafa. *'Abd al-Khaliq Tharwat.* Cairo, 1989.

al-Mallakh, Kamal. *al-Hakim bakhilan.* Cairo, 1973.

———. "Hikayati ma'a al-markab." *al-Musawwar,* no. 2998 (26 Mar. 1982): 62–63.

———. *Qahir al-zalam, Duktur Taha Husayn.* Cairo, 1973.

Malortie, Ernst von. *Egypt: Native Rulers and Foreign Interference.* London, 1882.

Malti-Douglas, Fedwa. *Blindness and Autobiography: "al-Ayyam" of Taha Husayn.* Princeton, 1988.

———. *Men, Women, and Gods: Nawal El Saadawi and Arab Feminist Politics.* Berkeley, 1995.

———. *Women's Body, Women's Word: Gender and Discourse in Arabo-Islamic Literature.* Princeton, 1991.

al-Ma'luf, 'Isa Iskandar. "Ahmad Zaki Basha." *MMIA* 13:9–10 (Sept.–Oct. 1935): 394–399.

———. *Dawani al-qatuf fi sirat Bani Ma'luf.* Ba'abda, 1907.

Manaf, 'Abd al-'Azim, ed. *al-Thawra al-'urabiyya, miat 'am, 1881–1981.* Cairo, 1981.

Mandur, Muhammad. "al-Adab surat al-nafs." *al-Thaqafa* 2 (1940): 74–78.

———. *A'lam al-shi'r al-'arabi al-hadith.* Beirut, 1970.

———. *Khalil Mutran.* Cairo, 1972.

———. *al-Masrah.* Cairo, 1963.

———. *Masrah Tawfiq al-Hakim.* 2nd ed. Cairo, 1966.

———. *Muhadarat 'an Ibrahim al-Mazini.* Cairo, 1954.

———. *Muhadarat 'an Isma'il Sabri.* Cairo, 1956.

———. *Muhadarat 'an Wali al-Din Yakan.* Cairo, 1955.

———. *al-Naqd wa al-nuqqad al-mu'asirun.* Cairo, [1963?].

———. *al-Shi'r fi Misr ba'd Shawqi.* Cairo, 1944.

al-Manfaluti, Mustafa Lutfi. *al-Nazarat.* Cairo, 1910.

al-Mansi, Ahmad Abu al-Khidr. *Farah Antun.* Cairo, 1923.

———. *Wali al-Din katiban wa sha'iran.* Cairo, 1921.

Mansur, Anis. "Wa lakinnana dahikna akthar." *Uktubir,* no. 576 (8 Nov. 1987).

Mansur, Sa'id Husayn. *al-Tajdid fi shi'r Khalil Mutran.* 2nd ed. Alexandria, 1977.

Manzalawi, Mahmoud. *Arabic Writing Today: Drama.* Cairo, 1977.

Maqalih, 'Abd al-'Aziz. *'Amaliqa 'inda matla' al-qarn.* Cairo, 1984; Beirut, 1988.

al-Maqdisi, Anis. *al-Funun al-adabiyya wa a'lamuhu fi al-nahda al-'arabiyya al-haditha.* Beirut, 1963.

al-Maraghi, Mahmud. "Ayyam laha tarikh." *Sabah al-khayr* (5 Sept. 1996): 25–29.

Mardam, Khalil. *A'yan al-qarn al-thalith 'ashr fi al-fikr wa al-siyasa wa al-ijtima'.* Beirut, 1971.

Marel, J. "Contribution à l'étude de l'Association des Frères musulmans: une brochure du Cheikh El-Banna: 'Vers la lumière.'" *Orient* 1:4 (1957): 37–62.

Mar'i, Sayyid. *Awraq siyasiyya.* 3 vols. Cairo, 1978–1979.

Mariette, Édouard. *Mariette Pacha: lettres et souvenirs personnels.* Paris, 1904.

Marlowe, John. *Cromer in Egypt.* London, 1970.

———. *The Making of the Suez Canal.* London, 1964.

———. *Milner: Apostle of Empire.* London, 1976.

———. *Perfidious Albion: The Origins of Anglo-French Rivalry in the Levant.* London, 1970.

———. *Spoiling the Egyptians.* New York and London, 1975.

al-Marrakushi, Muhammad Salih. *Tafkir Muhammad Rashid Rida min khilal majallat "al-Manar."* Tunis-Algiers, 1985.

Marro, Giovanni. *La personalita di Bernardino Drovetti nel suo archivo inedito.* Rome, 1951.

Marshall, J.E. *The Egyptian Enigma, 1890–1928.* London, 1928.

Marsot, Afaf Lutfi al-Sayyid. "The Porte and Ismail Pasha's Quest for Autonomy." *JARCE* 12 (1975): 89–96.

Marzuq, 'Abd al-Sabur. *al-Khataba al-siyasiyya fi Misr.* Cairo, 1966, 89–109.

Masabni, Badi'a. *Mudhakkirat Badi'a Masabni.* Ed. Nazik Basila. Beirut, n.d.

Masiha, Rufail. *Hafiz Ibrahim, al-sha'ir al-siyasi.* Cairo, 1947.

Maskuni, Yusuf Ya'qub. *Min abqariyyat nisa al-qarn al-tasi' 'ashr*. 2nd ed. Baghdad, 1947.

Maspéro, Gaston. *Bibliothèque Égyptologique*. XVIII. Paris, 1893–1895.

———. "Éloge de Mahmoud Pacha al-Falaki." *BIE*, 2e série, no. 6 (1885): 403.

Mas'ud, Jubran. *Wali al-Din Yakan*. Cairo, 1960.

Matar, Fuad. *Bi-saraha 'an 'Abd al-Nasir: hiwar ma'a Muhammad Hasanayn Haykal*. Beirut, 1975.

Matthee, Rudi. "Jamal al-Din al-Afghani and the Egyptian National Debate." *IJMES* 21 (1989): 151–169.

Maurice, J. *Military History of the Campaign of 1882 in Egypt*. London, 1887.

Mayer, Thomas. *The Changing Past: Egyptian Historiography of the Urabi Revolt, 1882–1983*. Gainesville, Fla., 1988.

Mazhar, Isma'il. *Mu'addat al-madaniyya al-haditha*. Cairo, 1928.

———. "Shibli Shumayyil." *al-Kitab* 3 (Nov. 1946): 126–135.

Mazini, Ahmad Fathi. *al-Qudat wa al-muhafizun*. Cairo, 1944.

al-Mazini, Ibrahim 'Abd al-Qadir. "Ahamm hadith fi majra hayati." *al-Hilal* 38:5 (Mar. 1930): 532–533.

———. "Asatidhati." *al-Hilal* 55:5 (May 1947): 85–88.

———. *Diwan*. II. Cairo, 1915–1917.

———. *Qissat hayah*. Cairo, 1943.

———. *Shi'r Hafiz Ibrahim*. Cairo, 1915.

———. "Ummi." *al-Hilal* 43:1 (Nov. 1934): 17–20.

Mazuel, J. *L'oeuvre géographique de Linant de Bellefonds*. Cairo, 1937.

Mazyad, Ali Mahmud Hasan. *Ahmad Amin: Advocate of Social and Literary Reform in Egypt*. Leiden, 1963.

McBride, Barrie St. Clair. *Farouk of Egypt: A Biography*. London, 1967.

McCoan, J.C. *Egypt*. London and New York, 1898.

McIntyre, John D. *Boycott of the Milner Mission: A Study in Egyptian Nationalism*. New York, 1985.

McLeave, Hugh. *The Last Pharaoh*. London, 1970.

McNaught, Lewis. *Henry Salt: His Contribution to the Collections of Egyptian Sculpture in the British Museum*. London, 1978.

Meier, Olivier. *"al-Muqtataf" et le débat sur le Darwinisme: Beyrouth, 1876–1885*. Cairo, 1996.

Meinardus, Otto. *Christian Egypt: Faith and Life*. Cairo, 1970.

Mellini, Peter. *Sir Eldon Gorst: The Overshadowed Proconsul*. Stanford, 1977.

Mengin, Felix. *Histoire de l'Égypte sous le gouvernement de Mohammed Aly*. 2 vols. Paris, 1823–1824.

Mera, Édouard. *Une page de politique coloniale: Lord Cromer en Égypte: 1883–1907*. Paris, 1913.

Merriam, John G. "Egypt After Sadat." *Current History* 81 (Jan. 1982): 5–8, 38–39; 82 (Jan. 1983): 24–27, 36–37.

Merruau, Paul. *L'Égypte contemporaine de Méhémet Ali à Said Pacha*. Paris, 1858.

Michel, B., and Mustafa Abdel-Raziq. *Risalat al-tawhid*. Paris, 1925.

Miéville, Walter. *Under Queen and Khedive*. London, 1884.

Mikhail, Mona. *Images of Arab Women: Fact and Fiction*. Washington, D.C., 1978.

———. "Shawqi: The Poet as Playwright." *Arab Perspectives* (Dec. 1984): 24–26.

———. *Studies in the Short Fiction of Mahfouz and Idris*. New York and London, 1992.

Mikhail, Sa'd. *Adab al-'asr fi shu'ara al-Sham wa al-'Iraq wa Misr*. Cairo, 1922.

Miller, Judith. "Mubarak's Venture in Democracy." *New York Times Magazine* (27 May 1984): 30–31ff.

Milner, Alfred. *England in Egypt*. London, 1892.

Milson, Menahem. "The Elusive Jamal al-Din al-Afghani." *MW* 58 (1968): 295–307.

———. "Najib Mahfuz and Jamal 'Abd al-Nasir: The Writer as Political Critic." *AAS* 23:1 (Mar. 1989): 1–22.

———. *Najib Mahfuz: The Novelist-Philosopher of Cairo*. London, 1998.

———. "Reality, Allegory, and Myth in the Work of Najib Mahfuz." *AAS* 11:2 (autumn 1976): 157–179.

Miot, Jacques. *Memories of My Service in the French Expedition to Egypt and Syria*. Tyne and Wear, 1997.

Mirsami, Janet Scott, and Paul Starkey, eds. *Encyclopedia of Arabic Literature*. London and New York, 1998.

al-Misri, 'Abd al-Sami'. *Sha'ira al-'uruba: Shawqi wa Hafiz*. Cairo, 1948.

al-Misri, Ibrahim. "Sha'iriyyat Abi Shadi." In *Atyaf al-rabi'*, by Ahmad Zaki Abu Shadi. Cairo, 1933.

Misri, Nashat. *Salah 'Abd al-Sabur*. Cairo, 1980.

Mitchell, Richard. *The Society of the Muslim Brothers*. Princeton, 1969.

Mizrahi, Maurice. *L'Égypte et ses juifs*. Lausanne, 1977.

———. "The Role of Jews in Economic Development." In *The Jews of Egypt: A Mediterranean Society in Modern Times*, ed. Shimon Shamir. Boulder, Colo., 1987.

Moazzam, A. "Jamal al-Din al-Afghani: Views on Individual and Society." *IC* 56 (July 1982): 213–232.

Moftah, Ragheb. "Coptic Music." *Bulletin de l'Institut des études coptes* (1958): 42–53.

———. "Coptic Music." In *Saint Mark and the Coptic Church*, ed. Coptic Church. Cairo, 1968.

Mohamed, Duse. *In the Land of the Pharaohs*. London, 1911.

Mohammed Naghi Retrospective Exhibition Catalogue. Prague, 1958.

Moosa, Matti. *The Early Novels of Naguib Mahfouz: Images of Modern Egypt*. Gainesville, Fla., 1994.

———. "Ya'qub Sanu' and the Rise of Arab Drama in Egypt." *IJMES* 5 (1974): 401–433.

Morabia, A. "Des rapports entre religion et état selon un théologien égyptien d'al-Azhar." *Orient* 32–33 (1964–1965): 257–303.

Moreh, Shmuel. "Free Verse (*al-shi'r al-hurr*) in Modern Arabic Literature: Abu Shadi and His School." *BSOAS* 30:1 (1968): 28–51.

———. *Modern Arabic Poetry, 1800–1970.* London, 1976.

Moreh, Shmuel, and Menahem Milson. *Modern Arabic Literature: A Research Bibliography, 1800–1980.* Jerusalem, 1993.

Morineau, R. "Artisinat égyptien: La tapisserie sauvage." *L'Estampille* 59 (1974): 28–31.

Morpain, Adrian. *Kléber: documents inédits sur la vie du Général Kléber.* Strasbourg, 1865.

Morris, James. *Pax Britannica.* London, 1968.

Morsi, Laila. "Britain's Wartime Policy in Egypt." *MES* 25:1 (1989): 64–94.

———. "Farouk in British Policy." *MES* 20:4 (1984): 193–211.

———. "Indicative Cases of Britain's Wartime Policy in Egypt." *MES* 30:1 (1994): 91–122.

Moseley, Sydney A. *With Kitchener in Cairo.* London, 1917.

el Mouelhy, Ibrahim. "Les Mouelhy en Égypte: II. Mohammad el Mouelhi Bey." *CHE* 5 (1953): 168–179.

———. "Ibrahim el-Mouelhy Pacha." *CHE* 2 (1949): 313–328.

———. "Mohammad Ali et l'éducation de ses enfants." *CHE* 2 (1949): 67–71.

———. "Le wali Mohammed Ali et son divan, 1220–1226 (1805–1811)." *CHE* 2 (1949): 61–66.

Moussalli, Ahmad. *Radical Islamic Fundamentalism: The Ideological and Political Discourse of Sayyid Qutb.* Beirut, 1992.

Mubarak, 'Ali. *al-Khitat al-tawfiqiyya al-jadida.* 20 vols. in 4. Cairo, 1886–1889.

Mubarak, Karima Zaki. *Zaki Mubarak wa naqd al-shi'r.* Cairo, 1987.

Mubarak, Zaki. "'Aduwi Taha Husayn." *al-Hilal* 45:8 (June 1937): 921–923.

———. *Ahmad Shawqi,* ed. Karima Zaki Mubarak. Cairo, 1977.

———. *Hafiz Ibrahim,* ed. Karima Zaki Mubarak. Cairo, 1978.

———. *al-Muwazana bayn al-shu'ara.* Cairo, 1926.

———. "Ruh al-Shaykh Rashid Rida." *al-Risala* 11 (2 Aug. 1943): 604–605.

———. *Zaki Mubarak naqidan.* Cairo, 1978.

Mughith, Kamal Hamid. *Taha Husayn: masadiruhu al-fikriyya.* Cairo, 1997.

Muhammad, Fathiyya. *Balaghat al-nisa fi al-qarn al-'ishrin.* 2 vols. Cairo, 1925.

Muhammad, Muhammad Sayyid. *Haykal wa "al-Siyasa al-Usbu'iyya."* Cairo, 1996.

Muhammad, Muhsin. *Man qatala Hasan al-Banna?* Cairo, 1987.

———. *Sa'd Zaghlul: muwallid thawra bi al-wathaiq al-britaniyya wa al-amrikiyya.* Cairo, 1988.

Muhammad Naji al-fannan al-tathiri al-misri. Cairo, 1988.

Muhammad Tal'at Harb fi ba'd khutubihi wa maqalatihi wa muhadaratihi ma'a lamha min tarikh hayatihi wa a'malihi. Cairo, 1957.

Muhyi al-Din, Fuad. "'Ashar sanawat ma'a al-Sadat." *al-Musawwar,* no. 2953 (15 May 1981): 10–11.

Mujahid, Zaki Muhammad. *al-A'lam al-sharqiyya fi al-mia al-rabi'a 'ashara al-hijyriyya.* 2nd ed. 3 vols. Beirut, 1994.

Mukhtar, Muhammad Jamal al-Din. "Ahmad Kamal al-athari al-awwal fi Misr." *MTM* 12 (1964–1965): 43–57.

———. "Salim Hasan." *MTM* 19 (1972): 73–87.

Mumin, al-Makki Habib, and 'Ali 'Ujayl Manhal. *Min Talai' yaqzat al-umma al-'arabiyya.* Baghdad, 1981.

al-Muntasir, Salah. "Tawfiq al-Hakim wa ara lam tasbiq nashruhu." *al-Ahram,* 23, 30 Aug. 1996; 6 Sept. 1996.

Muqbil, Fahmi Tawfiq. *Ruwwad al-islah fi al-'asr al-hadith: al-Afghani, 'Abduh, al-Kawakibi, Rida.* Beirut, 1995.

Murad, Mahmud. *Tawfiq al-Hakim wa al-thawra al-misriyya.* Sidon, 1974.

Murqus, Yuwaqim Labib. *Sihafat al-Hizb al-Watani, 1907–1952.* Cairo, 1985.

Murqus, Yuwaqim Labib, ed. *Maqalat Mustafa Kamil.* Cairo, 1986.

al-Murshidi, Muhammad 'Isam. *al-Thawra al-'urabiyya wa atharuha fi tatawwur al-sha'b wa hadatihi.* Cairo, 1958.

Mursi, A. "Ustadh al-asatidha." In *al-'Id al-miawi li-Kulliyyat al-Huquq.* Cairo, 1980.

Muruwwa, Husayn. "Adib Ishaq." *al-Thaqafa al-wataniyya* (Beirut) (Oct.–Nov. 1959): 59–62.

Musa, 'Ayda al-'Azab, ed. *Tis'in sana 'ala al-thawra al-'urabiyya.* Cairo, 1971.

Musa, Nabawiyya. "Dhikrayati." *Majallat al-fatat,* 5 May 1938–2 Aug. 1942.

Musa, Salama. "'Abbas Mahmud al-'Aqqad." *al-Hilal* 32:3 (Dec. 1923): 291–295.

———. "Ahmad Shawqi Bek." *al-Hilal* 32 (July 1924): 1068–1071.

———. "al-Anisa Mayy." *al-Hilal* 32:7 (Apr. 1924): 747–750.

———. "Hadith 'an al-Anisa Mayy." *al-Hilal* 36:1 (Apr. 1928): 658–661.

——— [S]. "Hadith ma'a Ahmad Zaki Basha." *al-Hilal* 35:5 (Mar. 1927): 522–526.

——— [S]. "Hadith ma'a al-Amir Muhammad 'Ali." *al-Hilal* 35:4 (Feb. 1927): 394–397.

———. "Hafiz Ibrahim Bey." *al-Hilal* 32:6 (Mar. 1924): 631–634.

———. "Mustafa Lutfi al-Manfaluti." *al-Hilal* 32:1–2 (Nov. 1923): 154–159.

——— [S]. "Sa'a ma'a Ahmad Hasanayn Bey." *al-Hilal* 37:5 (Mar. 1929): 526–531.

——— [S]. "Sa'a ma'a al-Duktur Taha Husayn." *al-Hilal* 36:1 (Nov. 1927): 32–33.

——— [S]. "Sa'a ma'a al-Shaykh 'Ali 'Abd al-Raziq." *al-Hilal* 37:1 (June 1928): 20–22.

——— [S]. "Sa'a ma'a al-Shaykh Mustafa 'Abd al-Raziq." *al-Hilal* 37:10 (Aug. 1929): 1162–1166.

——— [S]. "Sa'a ma'a al-ustadh al-akbar Shaykh Jami' al-Azhar." *al-Hilal* 37:9 (July 1929): 1034–1038.

——— [S]. "Sa'a ma'a Hafiz Ibrahim Bey." *al-Hilal* 36:9 (June 1928): 906–910.

——— [S]. "Sa'a ma'a shaykh al-sihafa." *al-Hilal* 36:4 (Jan. 1928): 272–276.

——— [S]. "Sa'a ma'a Tal'at Harb Bey." *al-Hilal* 36:8 (May 1928): 778–781.

———. *Tarbiyat Salama Musa.* Cairo, 1947. Eng. trans. L.O. Schuman. *The Education of Salama Musa.* Leiden, 1960.

———. "al-'Uzama al-khamsa fi Misr al-yawm." *al-Hilal* 36:6 (Apr. 1928): 651–653.

Musallam, A.A. "Prelude to Islamic Commitment: Sayyid Qutb's Literary and Spiritual Orientation, 1932–1938." *MW* (1990): 176–179.

———. "Sayyid Qutb and Social Justice, 1945–1948." *JIS* 4:1 (1993): 52–70.

Mussad, Hani William. "Muslim Debate on the Adoption of the Shari'a and Its Implications for the Church." Ph.D. diss., Fuller Theological Seminary," 1996.

Mustafa, Ahmad 'Abd al-Rahim. "'Abd al-Rahman al-Rafi'i, 1889–1966." *al-Hilal* 75:1 (Jan. 1967).

———. "Afkar Jamal al-Din al-Afghani." *MTM* 9–10 (1962): 215–239.

———. *'Alaqat Misr bi-Turkiya fi 'ahd al-Khidiwi Isma'il.* Cairo, 1968.

———. "Nazra jadida ila Jamal al-Din al-Afghani." *MTM* 23 (1976): 397–404.

———. "Shafiq Ghurbal muarrikhan." *MTM* 11 (1963): 255–278.

———. *Tawfiq al-Hakim: afkaruhu, atharuhu.* Cairo, 1952.

———. *al-Thawra al-'urabiyya.* Cairo, 1961.

Mustafa, Ismail, and M. Mukhtar. *Notice nécrologique de S.E. Mahmoud P., l'astronome.* Cairo, 1886.

Mustafa, Kamal. *'Ali Mahir Basha.* Cairo, 1938.

Mustafa, Zaki. *Umm Kulthum: ma'bad al-hubb.* Cairo, 1975.

Mustafa Kamil muqiz al-wataniyya. Beirut, 1975.

al-Mu'tasim Billah, Ahmad. *Naji: sha'ir al-wijdan al-dhati.* Cairo, [1963?].

Mutawalli, Mahmud. *Dirasat fi tarikh Misr al-siyasi wa al-iqtisadi wa al-ijtima'i.* Cairo, 1985.

———. "Shakhsiyyat rasmaliyya." *al-Katib,* no. 142 (1973).

al-Muti'i, Lam'i. *Haula al-rijal min al-Azhar.* Cairo, 1989.

———. *Haula al-rijal min Misr.* 3 vols. Cairo, 1987–1993.

———. *Mawsu'at hadha al-rajul min Misr.* Cairo, 1997.

Mutran, Khalil. "Ahamm hadith fi majra hayati." *al-Hilal* 38:3 (Jan. 1930): 269.

———. *Bishara Taqla Basha.* Cairo, 1902.

———. "al-Musiqa al-sharqiyya wa 'Abduh al-Hamuli." *al-Muqtataf* 88 (1936): 305–311.

———. *Suda al-ritha fi Salim Bey Sidnawi.* Cairo, 1908.

Naddaf, Sandra. "Mirrored Image: Rifa'ah al-Tahtawi and the West: Introduction and Translation." *Alif,* no. 6 (Sept. 1986): 16–83.

Nadi Dar al-'Ulum. *al-Majmu'a al-thaniyya.* Cairo, [1908?].

al-Nadim, 'Abd al-Fattah. *Sulafat al-Nadim.* 2 vols. Cairo, 1914.

Nadwat Amin al-Khuli. *al-Asala wa al-tajdid.* Cairo, 1996.

Nahhas, Yusuf. *Dhikrayat: Sa'd, 'Abd al-'Aziz, Mahir wa ruffaquhu.* Cairo, 1952.

Naji, 'Iffat, et al. *Muhammad Naji (1888–1956).* Cairo, 1989.

Naji, Najib. *al-Nuzu' ila al-'alimiyya: nashat al-waqi'iyya al-hissiyya.* Beirut, 1995.

Najib, Mustafa. *Mawsu'at a'lam Misr fi al-qarn al-'ishrin.* Cairo, 1996.

al-Najjar, Husayn Fawzi. "'Abd al-Rahman al-Rafi'i wa tarikh Misr al-qawmi." *al-Fikr al-mu'asir* (Feb. 1967): 79–86.

———. *Ahmad Lutfi al-Sayyid: Ustadh al-jil.* Cairo, 1965, 1975.

———. *Ahmad 'Urabi Basha: Misr li al-Misriyyin.* Cairo, 1992.

———. *'Ali Mubarak abu al-ta'lim.* Cairo, 1967, 1987.

———. *al-Duktur Haykal wa tarikh jil.* Cairo, 1988.

———. *Lutfi al-Sayyid wa al-shakhsiyya al-misriyya.* Cairo, 1963.

———. *Mustafa Kamil raid al-wataniyya.* Cairo, 1994.

———. *Rifa'a al-Tahtawi raid fikr wa imam nahda.* Cairo, 1966, 1987.

———. *Sa'd Zaghlul: al-za'ama wa al-za'im.* Cairo, 1986.

Najm, Muhammad Yusuf. *al-Masrahiyya fi al-adab al-'arabi al-hadith.* Beirut, 1956.

———. *Muhammad 'Uthman Jalal: ikhtiyar wa taqdim.* Beirut, 1965.

———. "al-Silat al-thaqafiyya bayna Misr wa Lubnan fi al-nahda al-haditha." *al-Adab* 10:6 (June 1962): 1–3, 66–69.

———. *Ya'qub Sannu'.* Beirut, n.d.

al-Najmi, Kamal. "Fann al-dumu'," *al-Ghina al-misri.* Cairo, 1966.

Nakhla, R. Yusuf. *Tarikh al-umma al-qibtiyya.* Cairo, 1899.

Nallino, Maria. "Notizie biobibliografiche su Taha Husein Bey." *OM* 30 (1950): 83–87.

al-Naqqash, Raja. *Lughz Umm Kulthum.* Cairo, 1978.

———. *Maq'ad saghir amam al-sitar.* Cairo, 1971.

———. *Udaba mu'asirun.* Cairo, 1971.

al-Naqqash, Salim Khalil. *Misr li al-misriyyin.* Alexandria, 1884.

al-Nashashibi, Muhammad Is'af. *al-'Arabiyya wa sha'iruha al-akbar Ahmad Shawqi.* Cairo, 1928.

———. *al-Batl al-khalid Salah al-Din wa al-sha'ir al-khalid Shawqi.* Jerusalem, 1932.

Nashat, Kamal. *Abu Shadi wa harakat al-tajdid di al-shi'r al-'arabi al-hadith.* Cairo, 1967.

———. *Mustafa Sadiq al-Rafi'i.* Cairo, 1967.

Nasif, 'Ali al-Najdi. *al-Din wa al-akhlaq fi shi'r Shawqi.* Cairo, 1948.

Nasif, Majd al-Din. *Athar Bahithat al-Badiya Malak Hifni Nasif: 1886–1918.* Cairo, 1962.

———. *Shi'r Hifni Nasif.* Cairo, 1957.

———. *Tahrir al-mara fi al-Islam.* Cairo, 1924.

Nasif, Mustafa. *Ramz al-tifl: dirasa fi adab al-Mazini.* Cairo, 1965.

Nasir, Munir. *Press, Politics, and Power: Egypt's Haykal and "al-Ahram."* Ames, Iowa, 1978.

Nasr, Marlene. *al-Tasawwur al-qawmi al-'arabi fi fikr Jamal 'Abd al-Nasir, 1952–1970.* Beirut, 1982.

Nasr, Muhammad. *Safahat min hayatihim.* Cairo, 1968.

Nasr, Nasim. "Adib Ishaq: fata al-inbi'ath al-shamal fi al-adab al-'arabi." *al-Adib* 9:5 (May 1950): 42.

———. *Shawqi wa mirat adabihi.* Beirut, 1940.

Nasr Allah, Hasan. *Khalil Mutran bayn al-taqlid wa al-tajdid.* Beirut, 1993.

Nassar, Husayn. *Dirasat hawl Taha Husayn.* Beirut, 1981.

Nassar, Siham. *al-Yahud al-misriyyin bayn al-misriyya wa al-yahudiyya.* Beirut, 1980.

Nasser, Gamal Abdel. *The Philosophy of the Revolution.* Washington, D.C., 1956.

Nawfal, 'Abdallah Habib. *Tarajim 'ulama Tarablus wa udabaiha.* Tripoli, 1929.

Nawfal, Yusuf Hasan. "Taha Husayn sha'iran." *al-Hilal* 84:2 (Feb. 1976): 80–87.

Neguib, Mohamed. *Egypt's Destiny.* New York, 1955.

Nelson, Cynthia. *Doria Shafik: Egyptian Feminist: A Woman Apart.* Gainesville, Fla., 1996.

Network of Egyptian Professional Women. *Egyptian Women in Social Development: A Resource Guide.* Cairo, 1988.

Newell-Smith, Geoffrey, ed. *The Oxford History of the World Cinema.* Oxford, 1996.

Newhouse, John. "Letter from Cairo." *New Yorker* 60 (30 July 1984): 68–83.

———. "Diplomatic Round." *New Yorker* 60 (2 July 1984): 84–95.

Nimnim, Hilmi. *al-Raida al-majhula: Zaynab Fawwaz, 1960–1914.* Cairo, 1998.

Nimock, Walter. *Milner's Young Men: The Kindergarten in Edwardian Imperial Affairs.* Durham, N.C., 1968.

Ninet, John. *Arabi Pacha.* Berne, 1884.

Nouvelle biographie générale. XXVI. Paris, 1861.

Nu'ayma, Mikhail. *al-Ghurbal.* Beirut, 1964.

Nubarian, Nubar. *Mémoires de Nubar Pacha.* Ed. Mirrit Boutros Ghali. Beirut, 1983.

Nusseibeh, Hazem Zaki. *The Ideas of Arab Nationalism.* Ithaca, 1956.

Nutting, Anthony. *Nasser.* London, 1972.

O'Brien, Terence H. *Milner.* London, 1979.

Omrani, Faruq. "Les tournants de la critique arabe chez Muhammad Mandur." *IBLA* 143 (1979): 25–50.

Ostle, R.C. "Khalil Mutran: The Precursor of Lyrical Poetry in Modern Arabic." *JAL* 2 (1971).

Ostle, R.C., ed. *Studies in Modern Arabic Literature.* Warminster, UK, 1975.

Ostle, Robin C. "Modern Egyptian Renaissance Man." *BSOAS* 57:1 (1994): 184–192.

Owen, E.R.J. *Cotton and the Egyptian Economy, 1820–1914.* Oxford, 1969.

———. "The Influence of Lord Cromer's Indian Experience on British Policy in Egypt, 1883–1907." *St. Antony's Papers,* no. 17. Oxford, 1965.

Pajol, Charles P.V. *Kléber: sa vie, sa correspondance.* Paris, 1877.

Pakdaman, Homa *Djamal al-Din Assad Abadi dit Afghani.* Paris, 1969.

Palmer, Alan, ed. *Encyclopedia of Napoleon's Europe.* New York, 1984.

Paret, R. *Zur Frauenfrage in der arabisch-islamischen Welt.* Stuttgart, 1934.

Parker, Barrett, ed. *Famous British Generals.* London, 1951.

Parkinson, Sir Cosmo. "The Rt. Hon. Lord Lloyd of Dolobran." *JRCAS* 28:2 (Apr. 1941): 120–123.

Peled, Matityahu. *al-Aqsusa al-taymuriyya fi marhalatayn.* Tel Aviv, 1977.

———. *Religion, My Own: The Literary Works of Najib Mahfuz.* New Brunswick, N.J., 1983.

Pérès, Henri. "Ahmad Sawqi, années de jeunesse et de formation intellectuelle en Égypte en et France." *AIEO* 2 (1936): 313–340.

———. *L'Espagne vue par les voyageurs musulmans de 1610 à 1930.* Paris, 1937.

———. "Essai sur les éditions successives de *Hadit Isa Ibn Hisam.*" *Mélanges Louis Massignon* III. Damascus, 1958.

———. "L'Institut d'Égypte et l'oeuvre de Bonaparte jugé par deux historiens arabes contemporains." *Arabica* 4 (1957): 120–129.

———. "Les origines d'un roman célèbre de la littérature arabe moderne: *Hadith Isa ibn Hisham* de Mohamed al-Muwailihi." *BEO* 10 (1944): 101–118.

———. "Le roman arabe dans le premier tiers du XXème siècle: al-Manfaluti wa Haykal." *AIEO* 17 (1959): 145–168.

———. "Le roman dans la littérature arabe moderne." *AEIO* 5 (1939–1941): 167–186.

———. "Le roman historique dans la littérature arabe." *AIEO* 15 (1957): 23–33.

Perlmann, Moshe. "The Education of Salama Musa." *MEA* 2 (1951): 279–285.

Pernot, Maurice. *Sur la route de l'Inde.* Paris, 1927.

Pesloüan, J.M.L. [pseud. Jean Lucas-Dubreton]. *Kléber, 1753–1800.* Paris, 1937.

Peyre, Henri, ed. *Connaissance de l'étranger.* Paris, 1964.

Philipp, Thomas. "Class, Community, and Arab Historiography in the Early 19th Century." *IJMES* 16 (1984): 161–175.

———. "Feminism and Nationalist Politics in Egypt." In *Women,* ed. Lois Beck and Nikki Keddie, 277–294.

———. "The French and the French Revolution in the Works of al-Jabarti." In *Eighteenth Century Egypt: The Arabic Sources,* ed. Daniel Crecelius. Claremont, Calif., 1990.

———. *Gurgi Zaydan: His Life and Thought.* Wiesbaden and Beirut, 1979.

———. "Language, History, and Arab National Consciousness in the Thought of Jurji Zaydan (1861–1914)." *IJMES* 4 (1973): 3–22.

Philipp, Thomas, ed. *'Abd al-Rahman al-Jabarti's History of Egypt.* 3 vols. Stuttgart, 1994.

Philips, Daisy Griggs. "The Growth of the Feminist Movement in Egypt." *MW* 21 (1926): 277–285.

Pictorial Records of the English in Egypt. London, [1885?].

Plauchot, Edmond. *L'Égypte et l'occupation anglaise.* Paris, 1889.

Podell, Janet, ed. *Annual Obituary 1981.* New York, 1982.

Politis, Athananios G. *Le conflit turco-égyptien de 1838–1841.* Cairo, 1931.

Poole, Sophia. *The Englishwoman in Egypt: Letters from Cairo.* 3 vols. London, 1844–1846.

Porath, Yehoshua. *In Search of Arab Unity, 1930–1945.* London, 1986.

Porterfield, Todd. *The Allure of Empire: Art in the Service of French Imperialism, 1798–1836.* Princeton, N.J., 1998.

Pourpoint, Madeleine. *Champollion et l'énigme égyptienne.* Paris, 1963.

Puryear, Vernon John. *Kléber and Menou: Egypt Enters World Politics.* Davis, Calif., 1968.

al-Qabbani, 'Abd al-'Alim. *Mahmud Bayram al-Tunisi.* Cairo, 1969.

al-Qadi, Shukri. *Khamsun shakhsiyya misriyya wa shakhsiyya.* Cairo, 1989.

———. *Miat shakhsiyya wa shakhsiyya.* Cairo, 1987.

al-Qadi, Wadad. "East and West in Mubarak's *'Alam al-Din.*" In *Intellectual Life,* ed. Marwan Buheiry, 21–37.

al-Qal'aji, Qadri. *Jamal al-Din al-Afghani, hakim al-sharq.* Beirut, 1947.

———. *Ma'a Tawfiq al-Hakim min "'awdat al-ruh" ila "'awdat al-wa'y."* Cairo, 1974.

———. *Muhammad 'Abduh.* Beirut, 1948.

———. *Sa'd Zaghlul raid al-kifah al-watani fi al-sharq al-'arabi.* Beirut, 1946, 1957.

al-Qalamawi, Suhayr. *Dhikra Taha Husayn.* Cairo, 1974.

———. *My Grandmother's Cactus: Stories by Egyptian Women.* Trans. Marilyn Booth. London, 1991.

Qallini, Rawhiyya. *Sha'irat 'arabiyyat.* Cairo, 1964.

Qandil, Fuad. *Shaykh al-nuqqad Muhammad Mandur.* Cairo, [1980s?].

al-Qaradawi, Yusuf. *al-Shaykh al-Ghazali kama 'araftuh.* Cairo, 1995.

Qarni, 'Izzat. "al-'Adala wa al-hurriyya 'inda Jamal al-Din al-Afghani." *MTM* 26 (1979): 103–139.

Qasim, Mahmud. *Jamal al-Din al-Afghani: hayatuhu wa falsafatuhu.* Cairo, 1958.

———. *Mawsu'at mamaththili al-sinima al-misri.* Cairo, 1998.

Qattan, Muna. *Ayyam ma'a Salah Jahin: al-tadakhul wa nazif al-zaman.* Cairo, 1987.

al-Qulali, Muhammad Mustafa. "Kalimat al-Duktur Muhammad Mustafa al-Qulali." *MMLA* 29 (1972): 269–282.

Qultah, Kamal. *Taha Husayn wa athar al-thaqafa al-fransiyya fi adabihi.* Cairo, 1973.

Qumayha, Jabir. *Sawt al-Islam fi shi'r Hafiz Ibrahim.* Cairo, 1987.

Qunaybir, Salim 'Abd al-Nabi. *al-Ittijahat al-siyasiyya wa al-fikriyya wa al-ijtima'iyya fi al-adab al-'arabi al-mu'asir: 'Abd al-'Aziz Jawish.* Benghazi, 1968.

Qurra'ah, Saniyya. *Nimr al-siyasay al-misriyya.* Cairo, 1952.

al-Qusi, Ihsan. *Lamha tarikhiyya 'an al-nahda al-niswiyya al-misriyya.* Cairo, 1930.

Qutb, Muhammad Ali. *Sayyid Qutb aw thawrat al-fikr al-islami.* Beirut, 1967.

Qutb, Sayyid. "Ayna anta, ya Mustafa Kamil." *al-Risala* 13:648 (3 Dec. 1945): 1309–1310.

———. *Tifl min al-qarya.* Beirut, 1946, 1973.

al-Quwaysni, Nirmin. *Ihsan 'Abd al-Quddus ams wa al-yawm wa ghadan.* Cairo, 1991.

Raafat, Samir. "Dynasty: The House of Yacoub Cattaui. *al-Ahram Weekly,* 2 Apr. 1994.

———. "The House of Cicurel." *al-Ahram Weekly,* 15 Dec. 1994.

Rachad, Ahmad. "Rifaa Rafée el Tahtaoui." *CHE* 1:2 (1948): 175–185.

Radi, Nawal 'Abd al-'Aziz. *Sidqi wa al-Ikhwan wa Wafd al-Sudan, 'am 1946 M.* Cairo, 1988.

Radwan, 'Abd al-Rahman Mustafa. *'Ali Mahir, shakhsiyat al-jil.* Cairo, 1939.

Radwan, Fathi. *Afkar al-kibar.* Cairo, 1978.

———. *'Asr wa rijal.* Cairo, 1967.

———. *Dawr al-'amaim fi tarikh Misr al-hadith.* Cairo, 1986.

———. *72 shahran ma'a 'Abd al-Nasir.* Cairo, 1985.

———. *Mashhurun munsiyyun.* Cairo, 1970.

———. *Mustafa Kamil.* Cairo, 1946, 1974.

———. *Tal'at Harb: bahth fi al-'azama.* Cairo, 1970.

Radwan, Lutfi. *Muhammad 'Abd al-Wahhab: sira dhatiyya.* Cairo, 1992.

Radwan, Muhammad Mahmud. *Safahat majhula min hayat Zaki Mubarak.* Cairo, 1974.

Rae, W. Fraser. *Egypt Today: From the First to the Third Khedive.* London, 1892.

Rafful, Emile. *al-Tariq ila al-i'rab.* Beirut, [1974?].

al-Rafi'i, 'Abd al-Rahman. *'Asr Isma'il.* 2 vols. Cairo, 1932.

———. *'Asr Muhammad 'Ali.* 3rd ed. Cairo, 1951.

―――. "Durus li al-shabab fi hayat Muhammad Farid." *al-Hilal* 75:12 (Dec. 1967): 262–267.

―――. *Fi a'qab al-Thawra al-Misriyya*. 3 vols. Cairo, 1951.

―――. *Jamal al-Din al-Afghani: ba'ith nahdat al-sharq*. Cairo, 1967.

―――. *Muhammad Farid ramz al-ikhlas wa al-tadhiya*. 2nd ed. Cairo, 1948.

―――. "Mustafa Kamil." *al-Kitab* 5 (Mar. 1948): 434–441.

―――. *Mustafa Kamil ba'ith al-haraka al-wataniyya*. 3rd ed. Cairo, 1950.

―――. *Shu'ara al-wataniyya*. Cairo, 1954, 1966.

―――. *Tarikh al-haraka al-qawmiyya*. 5th ed. 2 vols. Cairo, 1961.

―――. *al-Thawra al-'urabiyya wa al-ihtilal al-inglizi*. Cairo, 1949.

―――. *Thawrat sanat 1919*. 2nd ed. 2 vols. Cairo, 1955.

al-Rafi'i, Mustafa Sadiq. "al-Kutub al-lati afadatni." *al-Hilal* 35:3 (Jan. 1927): 285–286.

―――. "Shi'r al-Barudi." *al-Muqtataf* 30:3 (Mar. 1905): 189–194.

Ragai [Shafiq], Doria. *La femme et le droit religieux de l'Égypte contemporaine*. Paris, 1940.

Raghib, Nabil. *A'lam al-tanwir al-mu'asir*. Cairo, 1989.

―――. *Huda Sha'rawi wa 'asr al-tanwir*. Cairo, 1988.

Rahma, Muhammad Ahmad. *Kawkab al-sharq Umm Kulthum*. Khartum, 1969.

Rahman, Fazlur. *Islam and Modernity*. Chicago, 1982.

al-Ra'i, 'Ali. *Dirasat fi al-riwaya al-misriyya*. Cairo, n.d.

―――. *Tawfiq al-Hakim fannan al-furja wa fannan al-fikr*. Cairo, 1969.

al-Rajabi, Khalil ibn Ahmad. *Tarikh al-wazir Muhammad 'Ali Basha*. Cairo, 1997.

Ramadan, 'Abd al-'Azim. *'Abd al-Nasir wa azmat Mars*. Cairo, 1976.

―――. "Jaysh Isma'il fi daw wathiqa lam tunshar." *MTM* 26 (1979): 85–102.

―――. *Mustafa Kamil fi mahkamat al-tarikh*. Cairo, 1987.

―――. *al-Sira' al-ijtima'i wa al-siyasi fi 'ahd Husni Mubarak*. 7 vols. Cairo, 1993–1995.

―――. *al-Sira' bayn al-Wafd wa al-'arsh 1936–1939*. Beirut, 1979.

Ramadan, Muhammad Hafiz. *Safha siyasiyya*. Cairo, 1923.

Ramadan, Muhammad Rif'at. *'Ali Bey al-Kabir*. Cairo, 1950.

Ramadan, Tal'at Isma'il. *Muhammad Sharif Pasha wa dawruhu fi al-siyasa al-misriyya*. Cairo, 1983.

al-Ramadi, Muhammad Jamal al-Din. *Adab wa tarab*. Cairo, 1962.

―――. *'Abd al-'Aziz al-Bishri*. Cairo, 1964.

―――. *Khalil Mutran: sha'ir al-aqtar al-'arabiyya*. Cairo, [1965?], 1972.

―――. *Min a'lam al-adab al-mu'asir*. Cairo, 1965.

―――. *Sha'ir al-sharq al-'arabi: Khalil al-Nil*. Cairo, [1963?].

―――. *Sihafat al-fukaha wa sani'uha*. Cairo, 1963.

Rami, Ahmad, *Mudhakkirat Ahmad Rami wa qissat hubbihi li-Umm Kulthum*. Sidon, 1979.

―――. "Umm Kulthum." *al-Hilal* 55:11 (Nov. 1947): 57–59.

Ramitch, Yusuf. *Usrat al-Muwaylihi fi al-adab al-'arabi al-hadith*. Cairo, 1980.

al-Ramli, Fathi. *al-Burkan al-thair: Jamal al-Din al-Afghani*. Cairo, 1966.

―――. *Thawrat 'Urabi fi al-manhaj al-ishtiraki*. Cairo, 1982.

Ramsay, G. *The Novels of an Egyptian Romanticist: Yusuf al-Siba'i*. Edsbruk, 1996.

Ramzi, Kamal. *Nujum al-sinima al-misriyya*. Cairo, 1997.

Rashad, Ahmad. *Mustafa Kamil: hayatuhu wa kifahuhu*. Cairo, 1958.

Rathmann, Lothar. "Ägypten in Exil (1914–1918): Patrioten oder Kollaborature des deutschen Imperialismus?" In *Asien in Vergangenheit und Gegenwart*. Berlin, 1974.

―――. "Mustafa Kamil: politisches Denken und Handeln eines ägyptischen Patrioten." *Zeitschrift für Geschichtswissenschaft* 9 (1961): supp. vol., 101–122.

―――. *Neue Aspekte des Arabi-Aufstandes: 1879 bis 1882 in Ägypten*. Berlin, 1968.

Raymond, André. *Égyptiens et français au Caire, 1798–1801*. Cairo, 1998.

Recueil d'études égyptologiques dédiés à la mémoire de Jean-François Champollion. Paris, 1922.

Reich, Bernard, ed. *Political Leaders of the Contemporary Middle East and North Africa: A Biographical Dictionary*. New York, 1990.

Reid, Donald M. "Archaeology, Social Reform, and Modern Identity Among the Copts." In *Entre reforme social*, ed. Alain Roussillon, 311–335.

―――. *Cairo University and the Making of Modern Egypt*. Cambridge, UK, 1990.

―――. "Cromer and the Classics: Imperialism, Nationalism, and the Greek and Roman Past in Modern Egypt." *MES* 32 (1996): 1–29.

―――. "Cultural Nationalism and Imperialism: The Struggle to Define and Control the Heritage of Arab Art in Egypt." *IJMES* 24 (1992): 57–76.

―――. "Fuad Siraj al-Din and the Egyptian Wafd." *Journal of Contemporary History* 15 (1980): 721–744.

―――. "Indigenous Egyptology." *JAOS* 105 (1985): 233–246.

―――. *Lawyers and Politics in the Arab World, 1880–1960*. Minneapolis and Chicago, 1981.

―――. "The National Bar Association and Egyptian Politics, 1912–1954." *International Journal of Middle East Studies* 7 (Cambridge, UK) (1974): 608–646.

——. "Nationalizing the Pharaonic Past." In *Rethinking Nationalism,* ed. Israel Gershoni and James Jankowski.

——. *The Odyssey of Farah Antun: A Syrian Christian's Quest for Secularism.* Minneapolis, 1975.

——. "Return of the Egyptian Wafd." *International Journal of African Historical Studies* (Boston) 13:3 (1979): 389–415.

——. "The Syrian Christians and Early Socialism in the Arab World." *IJMES* 5 (1974): 177–193.

Reimer, Michael. "Contradiction and Consciousness in 'Ali Mubarak's Description of al-Azhar." *IJMES* 29 (1997): 53–69.

Rejwan, Nissim. *Nasserist Ideology.* New York, 1974.

——. "Taha Hussein, 1889–1973: The Checkered Fortunes of a Westernizer." *New Outlook* (Feb. 1974): 36–45.

Renouf, P. Le Page. "Young and Champollion." *Proceedings of the Society of Biblical Archaeology* 19 (1897): 188–209.

Riad [Riyad], Mahmud. *Mudhakkirat Mahmud Riyad (1948–1978).* 3 vols. Cairo, 1981–1986.

——. *The Struggle for Peace in the Middle East.* London, 1981.

Richards, J.M. *Hassan Fathy.* Singapore, 1985.

Rida, Muhammad Rashid. *Tarikh al-Ustadh al-Imam.* 3 vols. Cairo, 1906–1931.

Rida, Muhyi al-Din. *Abtal al-wataniyya.* Cairo, 1923.

Ridley, Ronald T. *Napoleon's Proconsul in Egypt: The Life and Times of Bernardino Drovetti.* London, 1998.

Rifa'i, 'Abd al-'Aziz. *Ahmad Shafiq al-muarrikh: hayatuhu wa atharuhu.* Cairo, 1965.

——. *Muhammad Sultan amam al-tarikh.* Cairo, 1958.

al-Rifa'i, 'Abd al-Hakim. "Abd al-Hamid Badawi." *Misr al-Mu'asira* (Oct. 1965): 1–4.

al-Rifa'i, Husayn 'Ali. *Bank Misr fi khamsat 'ashr 'aman.* Cairo, 1935.

Rifa'i, Muhammad 'Ali. *Rijal wa mawaqif.* 2 vols. Cairo, 1974–1977.

Rigault, Georges. *Le Général Abdallah Menou et la dernière phase de l'expédition d'Égypte (1799–1801).* Paris, 1911.

Rivlin, Helen. *Agricultural Policy of Muhammad Ali in Egypt.* Cambridge, Mass., 1961.

Riyad, Henry. *Muhammad Mandur raid al-adab al-ishtiraki.* Khartum, 1956; Beirut, 1983.

Riyad, Muhammad. "Muhammad Najib al-muftara 'alayh." *al-Wafd,* 11 Jan. 1985.

Rizq, Fathi. *Khamsa wa sab'una najman fi balat sahib al-jalala.* Cairo, 1991.

Rizq, Qustandi. *al-Musiqa al-sharqiyya wa ghina al-'arabi wa hayat 'Abduh al-Hamuli.* Cairo, [1937?].

Rizq, Yunan Labib. *al-Azhab al-siyasiyya fi Misr, 1907–1984.* Cairo, 1984.

——. *Tarikh al-wizarat al-misriyya, 1878–1953.* Cairo, 1975.

——. *al-Wafd wa "al-Kitab al-Aswad."* Cairo, 1978.

Rizzitano, Umberto. "Lo scrittore arabo-agiziano Ahmad Amin." *OM* 35 (1955): 76–89.

Rooke, Tetz. *In My Childhood: A Study of Arabic Autobiography.* Stockholm, 1997.

Roosevelt, Selwa. "The Fascinating Women of Egypt." *Town and Country,* Nov. 1978.

Rosenthal, E.I.J. *Islam in the Modern Nation State.* Cambridge, UK, 1965.

Rossi, Ettore. "Una scrittrice araba cattolica Mayy." *OM* 5:11 (1925): 604–613.

Rothstein, Theodore. *Egypt's Ruin.* London, 1910.

Roussillon, Alain, ed. *Entre réforme sociale et mouvement national: identité et modernisation en Égypte: 1882–1962.* Cairo, 1995.

——. *Sayyid Qutb: al-mujtama' al-misri.* Cairo, 1995.

Royle, Trevor. *The Kitchener Enigma.* London, 1985.

Rubinacci, R. "'Magnun Laila' di Ahmad Sawqi." *Annali Instituto Orientale di Napoli* N.S. 7 (1957): 9–66.

Rushdi, Fatima. *Kifahi fi al-masrah wa al-sinima.* Cairo, 1971.

Russell, Sir Thomas. *Egyptian Service, 1902–1946.* London, 1949.

Russell, W.H. "Why Did We Depose Ismail?" *Contemporary Review* 48 (1885): 305–325.

Rustum, Asad. *Hurub Ibrahim Pasha al-misri fi Suriya wa al-Anadul.* Cairo, 1927.

——. *The Royal Archives of Egypt and the Disturbances in Palestine, 1834.* Beirut, 1938.

——. *The Royal Archives of Egypt and the Origins of the Egyptian Expedition to Syria 1831–1841.* Beirut, 1936.

——. "Syria Under Mehemet Ali." *American Journal of Semitic Languages* 41 (1924–1925): 34–57, 183–191.

Saad El Din, Morsy, ed. *Gazbia Sirri: Lust for Color.* Cairo, 1998.

Saadé, Nicolas. *Halil Mutran héritier du romantisme française et pionnier de la poésie arabe contemporaine.* Paris, 1979.

Sa'b, Hasan. *Shakhsiyyat 'araftuha wa ahbabtuha.* Beirut, 1990.

Sabah, Su'ad. *Mawsu'at Tharwat 'Ukasha.* Cairo, [1998?].

Sabet, Adel. *A King Betrayed.* London, 1989.

Sabri, 'Abd al-Qadir. *Amir al-naghm Riyad al-Sumbati.* Cairo, 1985.

Sabri, 'Ali Baligh, *'Ali Sabri yatadhakkir.* Beirut, 1988.

Sabri, Muhammad [Sabry, M.]. *Adab wa tarikh.* 2nd ed. Cairo, 1927.

——. *Isma'il Sabri: hayatuhu wa shi'ruhu.* Cairo, 1923.

——. *Khalil Mutran: arwa' ma kutiba.* Cairo, 1960.

——. *Mahmud Sami al-Barudi: bahth adabi tarikhi fi hayat wa shi'r al-marhum . . . .* Cairo, 1923.

——. *al-Shawqiyyat al-majhula.* Cairo, 1961.

———. *Shu'ara al-'asr.* 2 vols. Cairo, 1910.

Sabry, M. [Sabri, Muhammad] *La Genèse de l'esprit national égyptien (1863–1882).* Paris, 1924.

———. *L'Empire égyptien sous Mohamed-Ali.* Paris, 1930.

———. *Episode de la question d'Afrique: l'Empire égyptien sous Ismail et l'ingérence anglo-française.* Paris, 1933.

———. *Mémoire d'Arabi Pacha à ses avocats.* Paris, 1924.

Sacré, Amadé, and Louis Outrebon. *L'Egypte et Ismail Pacha.* Paris, 1865.

Sa'd, Ahmad Sadiq. *Safahat min al-Yasar al-Misri fi a'qab al-Harb al-'Alamiyya al-Thaniyya, 1945–1946.* Cairo, 1976.

Sa'd, Amal Da'uq. *Fann al-murasala 'inda Mayy Ziyada.* Beirut, 1982.

Sa'd, Faruq. *Baqat min hadaiq Mayy.* Beirut, 1973.

Sa'd, Saib. *Khalil Mutran.* Damascus, 1990.

Sa'd al-Din, Muhammad. *Za'im Misr al-khalid Mustafa al-Nahhas.* Cairo, 1977.

Sadat, Anwar. *Revolt on the Nile.* New York, 1957.

Sadat, Jihan. *A Woman of Egypt.* New York, 1987.

al-Sa'dawi, Nawal. *Awraqi hayati.* Cairo, 1995.

———. *The Nawal El Saadawi Reader.* London and New York, 1997.

Sadgrove, P.C. *Egyptian Theatre in the Nineteenth Century.* Reading, UK, 1996.

Sadoul, Georges. *Dictionary of Film Makers.* Ed. and trans. Peter Morris. Berkeley and Los Angeles, 1972.

Sadoul, Georges, ed. *Cinema in the Arab Countries.* Beirut, 1986.

Sa'fan, Kamil. *Amin al-Khuli.* Cairo, 1982.

Safran, Nadav. *Egypt in Search of Political Community.* Cambridge, Mass., 1961.

al-Saghir, 'Isam Diya al-Din al-Sayyid 'Ali. *al-Hizb al-Watani wa al-nidal al-sirri 1907–1915.* Cairo, 1987.

al-Saharti, Ahmad 'Abd al-Hamid. *al-Manfaluti.* Cairo, 1930.

al-Saharti, Mustafa 'Abd al-Latif. *Adab al-tabi'a.* Alexandria, 1937.

———. *Khalil Mutran al-rajul wa al-sha'ir.* Cairo, 1949.

———. *al-Shi'r al-mu'asir 'ala daw al-naqd al-hadith.* Cairo, 1948.

Sahhab, Victor. *al-Sab'a al-kibar fi al-musiqa al-'arabiyya al-mu'asira.* Beirut, 1987.

Saiah, Y. *Oum Kalsoum, l'étoile de l'Orient.* Paris, 1985.

Said, Hamed. *Contemporary Art in Egypt.* Cairo, 1964.

Sa'id, Amina. "Min yawmiyyat taliba." *al-Hilal* 75:12 (Dec. 1967): 244–253.

Sa'id, Naffusa Zakariyya. *'Abdallah Nadim bayn al-fusha wa al-'amiyya.* Alexandria, 1966.

al-Sa'id, Rif'at. *Ahmad Husayn, kalimat wa mawaqif.* Cairo, 1979.

———. *al-Asas al-ijtima'i li al-thawra al-'urabiyya.* Cairo, 1967.

———. "al-Fikr al-ishtiraki al-misri fi matla' al-qarn al-'ishrin." *al-Tali'a* 4:10 (Oct. 1968): 62–63.

———. *Hasan al-Banna: mata, kayfa, wa limadha?* Cairo, 1977.

———. *Muhammad Farid: al-mawqif wa al-masat.* Cairo, 1978.

———. *Mustafa al-Nahhas: al-siyasi wa al-za'im wa al-munadil.* Beirut, 1976.

———. *Sa'd Zaghlul bayn al-yamin wa al-yasar.* Beirut, 1976.

———. *al-Sihafa al-yasariyya fi Misr.* Cairo, 1977.

———. *Thalathat Lubnaniyyin fi al-Qahira.* Beirut, 1973.

Sa'idi, 'Abd al-Mut'al. *al-Mujaddidun fi al-Islam.* Cairo, 1954.

Sakakini, Wadad. *Mayy Ziyada fi hayatiha wa athariha.* Cairo, 1969.

———. *Qasim Amin.* Cairo, 1965.

Sakkut, Hamdi. *'Abbas Mahmud al-'Aqqad.* 2 vols. Cairo, 1983.

———. *'Abd al-Rahman Shukri.* Cairo, 1980.

———. *The Egyptian Novel and Its Main Trends, 1913–1952.* Cairo, 1971.

———. "Najib Mahfuz's Short Stories." In *Studies in Modern Arabic Literature,* ed. R.C. Ostle, 114–125.

———. "Udaba Misr fi al-qarn al-'ishrin." *Sabah al-khayr,* 20 Oct. 1988.

al-Sakkut, Hamdi, and Marsden Jones. *Ahmad Amin.* Cairo, [1981?].

———. *A'lam al-adab al-mu'asir fi Misr: I, Taha Husayn.* Cairo, 1975.

Sakr, Tarek Mohamed Refaat. *Early Twentieth Century Islamic Architecture in Cairo.* Cairo, 1993.

Salah, Mahmud. *Muhakamat za'im: awraq al-qadiyya al-asliyya li-muhakamat Ahmad 'Urabi.* Cairo, 1996.

Salama, Jirjis. *Athar al-ihtilal al-baritani fi al-ta'lim al-qawmi fi Misr.* Cairo, 1966.

Salama, Yusri Muhammad. *Sha'ir al-wijdan 'Abd al-Rahman Shukri.* Cairo, 1964.

Salih, 'Izz al-Din. *Mahmud Sami al-Barudi.* Alexandria, 1911.

Salih, Sulayman. *al-Shaykh 'Ali Yusuf wa jaridat "al-Muayyad."* Cairo, 1990.

Salim, 'Abd al-Hamid. *al-Malik Fuad al-Awwal.* Alexandria[?], 1936.

Salim, Jamal. *Qiraa jadida li-hadith 4 Fibrayir.* Cairo, 1975.

Salim, Latifa Muhammad. "The Changing Position of the Egyptian Woman, 1919–1945." *MTM* 34 (1987): 13–25.

———. *Faruq.* Cairo, 1989, 1998.

———. *al-Quwwa al-ijtima'iyya fi al-thawra al-'urabiyya.* Cairo, 1981.

———. *'Urabi wa ruffaquhu fi Jannat Adam, 1883–1901.* Cairo, 1987.

Salim, Muhammad Khalil. *Azmat al-Wafd al-kubra: Sa'd wa 'Adli.* Cairo, 1976.

———. *Sira' Sa'd fi Urubba.* Cairo, 1975.

———. *Thawrat 1919 kama 'ishtuha wa 'araftuha.* Cairo, 1975.

Sallam, Hilmi. *Ayyamuhu al-akhira: qissat malik ba'a nafsahu li al-Shaytan.* Cairo, 1972.

al-Samakuri, Sami. *Asrar hukm al-qusur, yarwiha: Salah al-Shahid.* Cairo, 1990.

al-Samarrai, Hasib. *Rashid Rida al-mufassir.* Baghdad, 1977.

Sami, Amin. *al-Ta'lim fi Misr.* Cairo, 1917.

———. *Taqwim al-Nil.* 3 vols. in 6. Cairo, 1915–1936.

Sammarco, Angelo. "I documenti diplomatici concernanti il regno di Mohammed Ali egli archivi di stati italiani." *OM* 4 (1929): 287–296.

———. *Le règne du Khédive Ismail.* Cairo, 1937.

———. *Les règnes de Abbas, de Said, et d'Ismail, 1848–1879.* Rome, 1935.

Sanderson, Thomas Henry. "Evelyn Earl of Cromer: A Memoir." *Proceedings of the British Academy* 8 (1917).

al-Sandubi, Hasan. *A'yan al-bayan fi subh al-qarn al-thalith 'ashr ila al-yawm.* Cairo, 1914.

———. *al-Shu'ara al-thalatha: Shawqi, Mutran, Hafiz.* Cairo, 1923.

al-Sanhuri, 'Abd al-Razzaq. "al-Marhum al-Duktur 'Abd al-Hamid Badawi." *MMLA* 21 (1966): 159–174.

al-Sanhuri, Nadia, and T. al-Shawi. *'Abd al-Razzaq al-Sanhuri: minkhilal awraqihi al-shakhsiyya.* Cairo, 1988.

Sankey, Marjorie. *"Care of Mr. Waghorn": A Biography.* Petworth, UK, 1964.

Saqr, Muhammad 'Abd al-Wahhab, and Fawzi Sa'id Ibrahim. *'Abdallah Nadim.* Cairo, [1950s?].

Sarahan, 'Abd al-'Aziz. *Musahamat al-qadi 'Abd al-Hamid Badawi fi fiqh al-qanun al-duwali.* Cairo, 1967.

Sarkis, Yusuf Ilyas. *Mu'jam al-matbu'at al-'arabiyya wa al-mu'arraba.* 2 vols. Cairo, 1928.

Sarruf, Fuad. *Ya'qub Sarruf al-'alim wa al-insan.* Beirut, 1960.

Saussey, E. "Ibrahim al-Mazini et son 'Roman d'Ibrahim.'" *BEO* 2 (1932): 145–178.

al-Sawadi, Muhammad. *Aqtab Misr bayn al-thawratayn.* Cairo, 1976.

al-Sawi, Muhammad. *Sinima Yusuf Shahin: rihla idiyulujiyya.* Alexandria and Beirut, 1990.

———. *'Umar al-Sharif fi al-sinima al-misriyya.* Beirut, [1995?].

Sayf, Muhammad. *Salah Jahin wa 'alamuhu al-shi'ri.* Cairo, 1986.

Sayigh, Anis. *al-Fikra al-'arabiyya fi Misr.* Beirut, 1959.

Sayigh, Salma. *al-Nasamat.* Ed. Jurji Niqula Baz. Beirut, 1980.

al-Sayrafi, Hasan Kamil. *Hafiz wa Shawqi.* Cairo, 1943.

———. "Shawqi wa Hafiz wa Mutran." *al-Hilal* 76:11 (Nov. 1968): 90–101.

al-Sayyid, Afaf Lutfi. *Egypt and Cromer: A Study in Anglo-Egyptian Relations.* London, 1968.

———. "Lutfi al-Sayyid al-insan." *Hiwar* 4 (May–June 1963): 14–21.

al-Sayyid, Ahmad Lutfi. *Dhikra Ahmad Lutfi al-Sayyid.* Cairo, 1965.

———. *Taammulat.* Cairo, 1946.

al-Sayyid, Ahmad Lutfi, ed. *al-Duktur Muhammad Husayn Haykal.* Cairo, 1958.

Sayyid, 'Isam Diya al-Din. *Hadith 17 yunyu 1940 fi al-tarikh al-misri al-hadith.* Cairo, 1991.

al-Sayyid, Jalal. "Lutfi al-Sayyid: madrasa fikriyya fi tarikhina." *al-Katib* 25 (Apr. 1963): 131–138.

Sayyid-Ahmad, Ahmad Ahmad. *Rifa'a Rafi' al-Tahtawi fi al-Sudan.* Cairo, 1973.

Sayyid-Ahmad, Rif'at. *al-Islambuli: ruya jadida li-tanzim al-jihad.* Cairo, 1989.

Sayyid-Ahmad, al-Sayyid Taqi al-Din. *'Ali Mahmud Taha: hayatuhu wa shi'ruhu.* Cairo, 1964.

al-Sayyid-Marsot, Afaf. *Egypt in the Reign of Muhammad 'Ali.* Cambridge, UK, 1984.

———. *Egypt's Liberal Experiment.* Berkeley, 1977.

Schacht, Joseph. "Ahmad Pascha Taymur, ein Nachruf." *Zeitschrift der deutschen morgenländischen Gesellschaft* N.F. 8:84 (1930): 255–258.

Schaede, A. "Ahmad Taymur Pasa und die arabische Renaissance. *Orientalische Literaturzeitung* 33 (1920): 854–859.

Schleifer, Abdullah. "Hassan Fathi: A Voyage to New Mexico." *Arts and the Islamic World* (winter 1982–1983): 31.

Schnepp, B., ed. *Mémoires ou travaux présentés à l'Institut Égyptien.* Paris, 1862.

Schofield, G. "An Autograph Manuscript of 'Urabi Pasha." *BSOAS* 24 (1961): 139–141.

Schölch, Alexander. *Egypt for the Egyptians!* London, 1981.

Schom, Alan. *Napoleon Bonaparte.* New York, 1997.

Schonfield, Hugh J. *Ferdinand de Lesseps.* London, 1937.

———. *The Suez Canal in Peace and War, 1869–1969.* Coral Gables, Fla., 1969.

Schoonover, K. "Contemporary Egyptian Authors: II, Taha Husayn." *MW* 45 (1955): 359–370.

———. "Contemporary Egyptian Authors: Tawfiq al-Hakim and al-'Aqqad." *MW* 45 (1955): 26–32.

———. "Contemporary Egyptian Authors: Mahmud Taymur." *MW* 47 (1957): 36–45.

Schulze, R. *Die Rebellion der ägyptischen Fallahin 1919.* Berlin, 1981.

Segev, David. *Fundamentalism and Intellectuals in Egypt, 1973–1993.* London, 1995.

Seikaly, Samir. "Coptic Communal Reform, 1860–1914." *MES* 6:3 (Oct. 1970): 248–265.

———. "Prime Minister and Assassin: Butrus Ghali and Wardani." *MES* 13:1 (1977): 112–122.

Semah, David, ed. *Four Egyptian Literary Critics.* Leiden, 1974.

————. "Muhammad Mandur and the 'New Poetry.'" *JAL* 2 (1971): 143–153.

Seth, Ronald. *Russell Pasha.* London, 1966.

Shaarawi, Huda. *Harem Years: The Memoirs of an Egyptian Feminist.* Trans., ed., and introduced by Margot Badran. New York, 1987.

Shafiq, Ahmad. *Mudhakkirati fi nisf qarn.* 3 vols. in 4. Cairo, 1934.

al-Shadhili, Muhammad. "Man huwa Salah Jahin?" *al-Musawwar,* no. 3211 (25 Apr. 1986).

Shah, Iqbal Ali. *King Fuad of Egypt.* London, 1936.

Shahid,'Irfan. *al-'Awda ila Shawqi ba'd khamsin 'am.* Beirut, 1986.

al-Shahid, Salih. *Dhikrayati fi 'ahdayn.* Cairo, 1976.

Shahin, Emad Eldin. "Muhammad Rashid Rida's Perspectives on the West as Reflected in *al-Manar.*" *MW* 79 (1989): 113–132.

Shaikh, M.N. *Memoirs of Hassan al-Banna Shaheed.* Karachi, 1981.

al-Shak'a, Mustafa. *Mustafa Sadiq al-Rafi'i katiban 'arabiyyan wa mufakkiran islamiyyan.* Beirut, 1970, 1978.

Shaked, Haim. "The Biographies of 'Ulama in Mubarak's *Khitat* as a Source for the History of 'Ulama in 19th Century Egypt." *AAS* 7 (1971): 41–76.

Shakir, Ahmad Muhammad. "Ustadhuna al-imam hujjat al-Islam Muhammad Rashid Rida." *al-Muqtataf* 87:3 (Mar. 1935): 318–323.

Shal, Mahmud al-Nabawi. *Mahmud Mukhtar: raid fann al-naht al-mu'asir fi Misr.* Cairo, 1991.

Shalabi, 'Ali 'Atiya. *Dhikrayat min hayat al-marhum al-Sayyid 'Ali Yusuf.* Cairo, n.d.

Shalabi, Muhammad. *Hasan al-Banna imam wa qaid.* Cairo[?], 1989.

————. *Ma'a ruwwad al-fikr wa al-fann.* Cairo, 1982.

————. *Mustafa Lutfi al-Manfaluti al-adib al-ishtiraki.* Cairo, [1962?].

————. *al-Shaykh al-Ghazali wa ma'rakat al-suhuf fi al-'alam al-islami.* Cairo, 1987.

Shalabi, Rauf. *al-Shaykh Hasan al-Banna wa madrasatuhu "al-Ikhwan al-Muslimin."* Cairo, 1978.

Shalash, 'Ali. *Taha Husayn: matlub hayyan wa mayyitan.* Cairo, 1993.

————. *The Unknown Works of Mustapha Lutfi al-Manfaluti.* London, 1987.

Shamis, 'Abd al-Mun'im. *Safir Allah: Jamal al-Din al-Afghani.* Cairo, 1969.

————. "Shakhsiyyat fi hayat Shawqi." *al-Katib* (Dec. 1978): 50–65.

————. "Shakhsiyyat fi hayat Shawqi: VII. Dr. Muhammad Husayn Haykal." *al-Katib* (Sept. 1978): 8–19.

————. *'Uzama min Misr.* Cairo, 1985.

Shanuda, Emile Fahmi Hanna. *Sa'd Zaghlul nazir al-ma'arif.* Cairo, 1977.

al-Sharabasi, Ahmad al-Sharbini Jum'a. *Rashid Rida sahib "al-Manar."* Cairo, 1970.

Sharabi, Hisham. *Arab Intellectuals and the West.* Baltimore, 1970.

Sharaf, 'Abd al-'Aziz. *'Asr al-'Aqqad: safahat matwiyamin hayat al-'Aqqad al-suhufiyya.* Cairo, 1989.

————. *Fann al-maqal al-suhufi fi adab Muhammad Husayn Haykal.* Cairo, 1989.

————. *Muhammad Husayn Haykal fi dhikrahi.* Cairo, 1978.

————. *Muhammad Husayn Haykal wa al-fikr al-qawmi al-misri.* Beirut, 1992.

————. *Mukhtarat al-zuhm: qasaid li-kibar al-shu'ara: dirasa 'an al-mukhtarat al-shi'riyya bayna Khalil Mutran wa Antun Jumayyil.* Beirut, 1990.

————. *Taha Husayn wa zawal al-mujtama' al-taqlidi.* Cairo, 1977.

Sharaf, Sami. *'Abd al-Nasir: kayfa hakam Misr.* Cairo, [1996?].

Sharara, 'Abd al-Latif. *Hafiz: dirasa tahliliyya.* Beirut, 1961.

————. *Khalil Mutran.* Beirut, 1964.

————. *Mayy Ziyada: dirasa tahliliyya.* Beirut, 1968.

Sha'rawi, Huda. *Mudhakkirat raida al-'arabiyya al-haditha Huda Sha'rawi.* Ed. 'Abd al-Hamid Mursi. Cairo, 1981. Eng. trans. *Harem Years: The Memoirs of an Egyptian Feminist.* Ed. Margot Badran. New York, 1987.

Sharif, Mian Mohammad, ed. *A History of Muslim Philosophy.* 2 vols. Wiesbaden, 1966.

Sharif, Omar. *The Eternal Male.* Trans. Martin Sokolinsky. Garden City, N.Y., 1977.

al-Sharqawi, Mahmud. *'Ali Mubarak.* Cairo, 1962.

————. *Dirasat fi tarikh al-Jabarti.* 3 vols. Cairo, 1955–1957.

————. *Masabih 'ala al-tariq.* Cairo, 1963.

————. *Misr fi al-qarn al-thamin 'ashr.* Cairo, 1957.

————. *Salama Musa: al-mufakkir wa al-insan.* Cairo, 1968.

Sharubim, Mikhail. *al-Kafi fi tarikh Misr al-qadim wa al-hadith.* 4 vols. Bulaq. 1898–1900.

Sharuni, Salih. *'Abd al-Hadi al-Jazzar: fannan al-asatir wa 'alam al-fada.* Cairo, 1966.

Sharuni, Yusuf. *Sab'un sham'a fi hayat Yahya Haqqi.* Cairo, 1975.

al-Sharuni, Yusuf, ed. *al-Layla al-thaniya ba'da al-alf: mukhtarat min al-qissa al-nisaiyya fi Misr.* Cairo, 1975.

al-Shatti, 'Abd al-Fattah 'Abd al-Munsin. *'Abd al-Rahman Shukri shar'iran.* Cairo, 1995.

al-Shawabika, Ahmad Fahd Barakat. *Muhammad Rashid Rida wa dawruhu fi al-hayat al-fikyiyya wa al-siyasiyya.* Amman, 1989.

Shawi, Yahya 'Abd al-Amir. *Hafiz Ibrahim: hayatuhu wa shi'ruhu.* Beirut, 1995.

Shawkat, Mahmud Hamid. *al-Fann al-qasasi fi Misr.* Cairo, [1963?].

————. *al-Masrahiyya fi shi'r Shawqi.* Cairo, 1947.

Shawqi, Ahmad. "Ahammu hadith fi majra hayati." *al-Hilal* 38:1 (Nov. 1929): 19–20.

Shawqi, Husayn. *Abi Shawqi.* Cairo, 1947.

Shawrib, al-Sa'id Hamid. *Ahmad Rami.* Cairo, 1985.

Shaybub, Khalil. *'Abd al-Rahman al-Jabarti.* Cairo, 1948.

Shaybub, Siddiq. *Shakhsiyyat 'arabiyya.* Alexandria, 1965.

al-Shayib, Ahmad. *Ahmad Shawqi: 'asruhu, hayatuhu, adabuhu, manziluhu fi tarikh al-shi'r al-'arabi.* Cairo, 1950.

———. *al-Jarim al-sha'ir: 'asruhu, hayatuhu, shi'ruhu.* Cairo, 1967.

———. *Muhammad 'Abduh.* Alexandria, 1929; Cairo, 1932.

al-Shaykh al-Imam Muhammad Mutawalli al-Sha'rawi fi al-hukm wa al-siyasa. Cairo, 1990.

al-Shaykh al-Sha'rawi bayn al-Islam wa al-siyasa. Cairo, 1990.

al-Shaykh al-Sha'rawi min al-qarya ila al-qimma. Cairo, 1992.

al-Shaykha, Hasan. *'Abd al-'Aziz Jawish.* Cairo, 1961.

———. *Aqlam thaira.* Cairo, 1963.

al-Shayyal, Jamal al-Din. "'Abd Allah Nadim, 1845–1896." *al-Kitab* 7 (Jan. 1949): 78–91.

———. *A'lam al-Iskandariyya fi al-'asr al-islami.* Cairo, 1965.

———. *Rifa'a al-Tahtawi.* Alexandria, 1945; Cairo, 1958.

———. *al-Tarikh wa al-muarrikhun fi Misr.* Cairo, 1958.

Shazly [Shadhili], Sa'd al-Din. *The Crossing of the Suez.* San Francisco, 1980.

Sheehan, Edward R.F. "The Most Powerful Journalist in the World." In *The Cairo Documents.* Garden City, N.Y., 1973.

———. "The Second Most Important Man in Egypt." *New York Times Magazine* (22 Aug. 1971): 12ff.

Shepard, William. "The Dilemma of a Liberal: Some Political Implications in the Writings of the Egyptian Scholar Ahmad Amin." *MES* 16 (May 1980): 84–97.

———. *The Faith of a Modern Muslim Intellectual: The Religious Aspects and Implications of the Writings of Ahmad Amin.* New Delhi, 1983.

———. "A Modernist View of Islam and Other Religions." *MW* 65 (Apr. 1975): 79–92.

———. *Sayyid Qutb and Islamic Activism.* Leiden, 1996.

Shihabi, M. "'Abbas Mahmud al-'Aqqad (1889–1964)." *MMIA* 44 (1964): 343–352.

al-Shiliq, Ahmad Zakariyya. *Hizb al-ahrar al-dusturiyyin 1922–1953.* Cairo, 1982.

———. *Ruya fi tahdith al-fikr al-misri: Ahmad Fathi Zaghlul wa qadiyyat al-taghrib.* Cairo, 1987.

Shinnawi, 'Abd al-'Aziz Muhammad. *'Umar Makram batal al-muqawama al-sha'biyya.* Cairo, 1967.

al-Shinnawi, Kamil. *al-Ladhina ahabbu Mayy.* Cairo, 1972.

al-Shinnawi, Mahmud, and 'Abdallah al-'Ashd. *Ali Mubarak, hayatuhu wa da'watuhu wa atharuhu.* Cairo, 1962.

Shiri, Keith. *Directory of African Film-Makers and Films.* Westport, Conn., 1992.

Shukri, Ghali. "Hawl al-minbar al-dawli li-jaizat al-Nubil." *al-Ahram,* 2 Nov. 1988.

———. *Madha yabqa min Taha Husayn.* Beirut, 1974.

———. *Muhammad Mandur al-naqid wa al-manhaj.* Beirut, 1981.

———. *al-Muntami: dirasa fi adab Najib Mahfuz.* Cairo, 1964, 1969, 1982, 1988.

———. *Najib Mahfuz: min al-Jammaliyya ila Nubil.* Cairo, 1988.

———. *Salama Musa wa azmat al-damir al-'arabi.* Cairo, 1962; Sidon and Beirut, 1965.

———. *Thawrat al-fikr fi adabina al-hadith.* Cairo, 1965.

———. *Thawrat al-mu'tazil: dirasa fi adab Tawfiq al-Hakim.* Cairo, 1966, 1973.

Shukri, Muhammad Fuad. *'Abd Allah Jak Minu wa khuruj al-firansawiyyin min Misr.* Cairo, 1952.

———. *Bina dawlat Misr Muhammad 'Ali: al-siyasa al-dawliyya.* Cairo, 1948.

———. *al-Hamla al-firansiyya wa zuhur Muhammad 'Ali.* Cairo, 1942.

[Shukri] Shukry, Muhammad Fuad. *The Khedive Ismail and Slavery in the Sudan, 1863–1879.* Cairo, 1937.

Shumayyil, Shibli. "Isma'il wa Riyad." *al-Hilal* 33:2 (Nov. 1924): 137–142.

Shusha, Muhammad al-Sayyid. *Ahmad Rami sha'ir al-shabab al-daim.* Cairo, 1981.

———. *Asrar 'Ali Amin wa Mustafa Amin.* Cairo, n.d.

———. *Umm Kulthum: hayat naghm.* Cairo, 1976.

al-Siba'i, Muhammad. *Abtal Misr.* Cairo, 1922.

Sidebottom, John K. *The Overland Mail: A Postal Historical Study of the Mail Route to India.* London, 1948.

Sidqi, 'Abd al-Rahman. "al-'Aqqad kama 'araftuh." *al-Hilal* 68:3 (Mar. 1960): 80–87.

Sidqi, Isma'il, *Mudhakkirati.* Cairo, 1950.

Silvera, Alain. "Edmé-François Jomard and the Egyptian Reforms in 1839." *MES* 7 (1971): 301–306.

Siraj al-Din, Fuad. *Limadha al-hizb al-jadid.* Cairo, 1977.

Sirhan, Samir. *Yusuf Idris. 1927–1991.* Cairo, 1991.

Sivan, Emmanuel. *Radical Islam.* 2nd ed. New Haven, 1985.

Skelton, Barbara. *Tears Before Bedtime.* London, 1987, 1989, 1993.

Smith, Charles D. "The 'Crisis of Orientation': The Shift of Egyptian Intellectuals to Islamic Subjects in the 1930s." *IJMES* 4 (1973): 382–410.

———. "4 February 1942: Its Causes and Its Influence on Egyptian Politics and on the Future of Anglo-Egyptian Relations, 1937–1945." *IJMES* 10 (1979): 453–479.

———. "*Hakadha khuliqat*: The Triumph of the Irrational in the Fiction of Muhammad Husayn Haykal." *Edebiyat* 1:2 (1976): 177–197.

————. *Islam and the Search for Social Order in Modern Egypt.* Albany, N.Y., 1983.

————. "Love, Passion, and Class in the Fiction of Muhammad Husayn Haykal." *JAOS* 99 (1979): 249–261.

Smith, Wilfrid Cantwell. *Islam in Modern History.* Princeton, 1957.

Snir, Reuven. "Human Existence According to Kafka and Salah 'Abd al-Sabbur." *Jusur* 5 (1989): 34–39.

Solecki, John. *Hosni Mubarak.* London, 1991.

Somekh, Sasson. *The Changing Rhythm: A Study of Najib Mahfuz's Novels.* Leiden, 1983.

————. "The Function of Sound in the Stories of Yusuf Idris." *JAL* 16 (1985): 95–104.

————. "Husayn Fawzi: An Egyptian Intellectual." *Bulletin of the Israeli Academic Center in Cairo* 16 (May 1992): 21–23.

————. "Language and Theme in the Short Stories of Yusuf Idris." *JAL* 6 (1975): 89–100.

Sonbol, Amira. "Egypt." In *The Politics of Islamic Revivalism,* ed. Shireen Hunter. Bloomington, Ind., 1988.

————. "Hassan al-Banna." *Encyclopedia of World Biographies,* 20th Century Supplement. New York, 1997, 25–27.

Sorokine, Dimitri. *Champollion et les secrets de l'Égypte.* Paris, 1967.

Spagnolo, John, ed. *Problems of the Modern Middle East in Historical Perspective.* Reading, UK, 1996.

Spencer, Samia. "A Francophone at the Helm: Boutros Boutros-Ghali." *Contemporary French Civilization* 17 (winter 1993): 84–101.

Springborg, Robert. *Family, Power, and Politics in Egypt.* Philadelphia, 1982.

————. *Mubarak's Egypt: Fragmentation of the Political Order.* Boulder, Colo., 1989.

Stadiem, William. *Too Rich: The Life and High Times of King Farouk.* New York, 1991.

Starkey, Paul. *From the Ivory Tower.* London, 1987.

————. "Tawfiq al-Hakim: Leading Playwright of the Arab World." *Journal of Theater and Cinema of the Modern World* 3:6 (spring 1989): 21–30.

Steele, James. *Architecture for the People: The Complete Works of Hassan Fathy.* Cairo, 1997.

————. *Hassan Fathy.* New York, 1988.

Steele, James, comp. *The Hassan Fathy Collection.* Geneva, 1989.

Stephens, Robert. *Nasser: A Political Biography.* London, 1971.

Steppat, Fritz. *Nationalismus und Islam bei Mustafa Kamil.* Leiden, 1956.

Stewart, Desmond. *Middle East: Temple of Janus.* London, 1972.

————. "The Rise and Fall of Muhammad Haykal." *Encounter* 42 (June 1974): 87–93.

St. John, Robert. *The Boss: The Story of Gamal Abdel Nasser.* New York, 1960.

Stock, Raymond. "Preserving Pharaoh's Psalms for Christ." *Egypt Today* 18:4 (Apr. 1997): 76–83.

————. "They Say It's His Birthday: Naguib Mahfouz Turns 85." *Egypt Today* (Dec. 1996): 88–95.

Storrs, Ronald. *Orientations.* London, 1937.

Stowasser, Karl. *Ein Muslim entdeckt Europa: Rifa'a al-Tahtawis Bericht über seinen Aufenthalt in Paris, 1826–1831.* Munich, 1988.

Strika, V. "Filosofia a religione in 'Abbas Mahmud al-'Aqqad." *OM* 52 (1972): 329–339.

Strothmann, R. *Die koptische Kirche in der Neuzeit.* Tübingen, 1932.

Subayh, Muhammad. *Batl la nansahu.* Beirut and Sidon, [1971?].

Subki, Amal. *al-Haraka al-nisaiyya fi Misr bayna Thawratay 1919 wa 1952.* Cairo, 1986.

————. *Sa'd Zaghlul wa al-kifah al-sirri.* Cairo, 1989.

al-Sudani, Salih 'Ali 'Isa. *al-Asrar al-siyasiyya li-abtal al-thawra al-misriyya.* Cairo, [1945?].

Sulayman, 'Abd al-Jawad. *al-Shaykh Muhammad 'Abduh.* Cairo, 1951.

Sulayman, Muhammad. *Rasail sair.* Cairo, 1948.

Sullivan, Denis J. *Private Voluntary Organizations in Egypt: Islamic Development, Private Initiative, and State Control.* Gainesville, Fla., 1994.

Sullivan, Earl L. *Women in Egyptian Public Life.* Syracuse, 1986.

Sultan, Mahmud. *'Abd al-Wahhab, mujiza al-zaman fi al-fann al-musiqi wa al-ghinai.* Cairo, 1986.

al-Suruji, Muhammad Mahmud. *al-Jaysh al-misri fi al-qarn al-tasi' 'ashr.* Cairo, 1967.

al-Sutuhi, 'Abd al-Sattar 'Ali. *al-Janib al-islami fi adab Mustafa Sadiq al-Rafi'i.* Qatar, 1971.

Tabarak, Muhammad. *Dhikrayat 'ashiq: Rami wa Umm Kulthum.* Cairo, 1990.

al-Tabi'i, Muhammad. *Min asrar al-sasa wa al-siyasa: Misr ma qabla al-Thawra.* Cairo, 1970.

Taboulet, G. "Ferdinand De Lesseps et l'Égypte avant le canal (1803–1854)." *Revue française d'histoire d'outre-mer* 60 (1973): 143–171, 364–407.

Tadrus, Ramzi. *al-Aqbat fi al-qarn al-'ishrin.* 4 vols. Cairo, 1910.

al-Tafahum, 'Abd. "A Cairo Debate on Islam and Some Christian Implications." *MW* 44 (1954): 236–252.

Tagher, Jacques. "Bibliographie analytique et critique de publications françaises et anglaises relatives à l'histoire du règne de Mohammad Ali." *CHE* 2 (1949): 128–235.

————. "Mohamed Aly et les anglais." *CHE* 2 (1950): 447–492.

————. "Mohamed Aly étudiait l'histoire et rédigeait ses mémoires." *CHE* 2 (1949): 72–75.

————. "La naissance et le développement du journal al-Ahram." *CHE* 4 (1951): 236–248.

———— [J.T.] "Nubar Pacha et la réforme judicaire." *CHE* 1:5 (1948): 373–412.

————. "Portrait psychologique de Nubar Pacha." *CHE* 1:5 (1948): 353–372.

Taha, M. "Taha Husayn, trahison ou universalisme." *IBLA* 142 (1978): 271–283.

Taha, Samir Muhammad. *Ahmad 'Urabi wa dawruhu fi al-hayat al-siyasiyya al-misriyya.* Cairo, 1986.

———. *Muhammad Sultan bayn al-wataniyya wa al-tab'iyya.* Cairo, 1979.

Tahar, Meftah. *Taha Hussein: sa critique littéraire et ses sources françaises.* Tunis, 1976.

Tahir, Ahmad. *Muhadarat 'an Hafiz Ibrahim.* Cairo, 1934.

El-Tahtawi, Fathy Rifaah. *Petit aperçu historique de la vie et de l'oeuvre de Rifaah Badawi el-Tahtawi.* Cairo, 1958.

Tajir, Jak. *Harakat al-tarjama bi-Misr khilal al-qarn al-tasi' 'ashr.* Cairo, 1945.

al-Tamawi, Ahmad Husayn. *'Abd al-Rahman Shukri.* Cairo, 1968.

———. *"al-Hilal" miat 'am min tarikh.* Cairo, 1992.

———. *Jurji Zaydan.* Cairo, 1992.

———. *Sabri al-Surbuni.* Cairo, 1986.

al-Tanahi, Tahir Ahmad. *'Ala firash al-mawt.* Cairo, 1939.

———. *Atyaf min hayat Mayy.* Cairo, 1974.

———. *Faruq al-awwal.* Cairo, 1936.

———. "Hal al-sihafi adib?" *al-Hilal* 42:5 (Mar. 1934): 561–562.

———. *Hayat Mutran.* Cairo, 1965.

———. "al-Hubb al-ruhi . . . bayn al-Anisa Mayy wa Antun al-Jumayyil." *al-Hilal* 56:5 (May 1948): 69–76.

———. "al-Manfaluti al-sha'ir." *al-Hilal* 41:3 (Dec. 1932): 222–226.

———. "Mashahir al-'alam fi tufulatihim." *al-Hilal* 62:9 (Sept. 1954): 26–30.

———. "Sa'a ma'a al-Ustadh al-Akbar shaykh Jami' al-Azhar." *al-Hilal* 43:8 (June 1935): 893–898.

———. "al-Sayyid Mustafa Lutfi al-Manfaluti." *al-Hilal* 39:2 (Nov. 1930): 20–26.

———. *Suwar wa zilal min hayat Shawqi wa Hafiz.* Cairo, 1967.

Tantawi, Salah. *Sayyid Darwish.* Cairo, 1966, 1978.

Taqi al-Din, al-Sayyid. *Taha Husayn, atharuhu wa afkaruhu.* 2 vols. Cairo, 1978.

Tarabay, Edouard. "Des causes du progrès de l'Europe et du retard de l'Orient." *l'Orient,* no. 16 (1960): 99–114.

Tarabishi, Georges. *Lu'bat al-hulw wa al-waqi': dirasa fi adab Tawfiq al-Hakim.* Beirut, 1972.

———. *Untha didda al-unutha: dirasa fi adab Nawal al-Sa'dawi 'ala daw al-tahlil al-nafsi.* Beirut, 1984.

al-Tarabishi, Mata'. *Ahmad Amin min khilal "Fayd al-Khatir."* Damascus, 1954–1955.

al-Tarabulsi, Muhammad al-Hadi. *Khasais al-uslub fi "al-Shawqiyyat."* Tunis, 1981.

Tarrazi, Philippe de. *Tarikh al-sihafa al-'arabiyya.* 4 vols. Beirut, 1913–1933.

Tattawi, 'Abd Allah. *al-Turath wa al-mu'arada 'inda Shawqi.* Cairo, 1987.

Tauber, R. "Rashid Rida as Pan-Arabist Before World War I." *MW* 79 (1989): 102–112.

Tawfiq, 'Awad, and Hasan Sabri. *Wuzara al-ta'lim fi Misr.* Cairo, 1980.

Tawfiq, Najib. *'Abdallah al-Nadim, 1845–1896: khatib al-thawra al-'urabiyya.* Cairo, 1970.

———. *Ashhar al-usrat al-adabiyya fi Misr.* Cairo, 1995.

———. *Isma'il Sabri: shaykh al-shu'ara, hayatuhu wa atharuhu fi al-adab.* Cairo, 1985.

———. *Mustafa Kamil: adwa jadida 'ala hayatihi.* Cairo, 1981.

———. *al-Thair al-azim 'Abdallah Nadim.* Cairo, 1957.

———. *al-Za'im al-khalid Sa'd Zaghlul Basha.* Cairo, 1996.

Tawfiq, Sa'd al-Din. *Salah Abu Sayf, fannan al-sha'b.* Cairo, 1969.

al-Tawil, 'Abd al-Qadir Rizq. *al-Maqala fi adab al-'Aqqad.* Cairo, 1987.

Taymur, Ahmad. *A'lam al-fikr al-islami fi al-'asr al-hadith.* Cairo, 1967.

———. *Dhikra Ahmad Taymur.* Cairo, 1954.

———. *Tarajim a'yan al-qarn al-thalith 'ashr.* Cairo, 1940.

———. *Tarikh al-usra al-taymuriyya.* Cairo, 1948.

Taymur, Mahmud. "Antun al-Jumayyil." *al-Kitab* 5 (Feb. 1948): 239–243.

———. *al-Barqiyyat li al-risala wa al-maqala.* Cairo, n.d.

———. *Hayatuna al-tamthiliyya.* Cairo, 1922.

———. Introduction to *Muallifat Muhammad Taymur: Wamid al-ruh.* Cairo, 1971.

———. *Ittijahat al-adab al-'arabi fi al-sinin al-mia al-akhira.* Cairo, 1970.

———. "Lutfi al-Sayyid." *al-Hilal* 58:6 (June 1947): 80–83.

———. *Malamih wa ghudun.* Cairo, 1950.

———. *Marathi al-Marhum Muhammad Taymur.* Cairo, 1922.

———. *Ma tarahu al-u'yun.* Cairo, 1927.

———. *al-Shakhsiyyat al-'ishrun.* Cairo, 1969.

———. *Talai' al-masrah al-'arabi.* Cairo, 1966.

Terry, Janice Joles. *The Wafd, 1919–1952: Cornerstone of Egyptian Political Power.* London, 1982.

Tewfiq, Antoinette. *Nouvelles/Mahmoud Teymour: biographie et traduction.* Cairo, 1975.

Textes et langues de l'Égypte pharaonique: cent cinquante années de recherches, 1822–1972. Cairo, 1972.

Thabit, Karim. "Kayfa habat al-Shaykh Jawish Misr fajatan." *Kull shay wa al-'alam,* no. 169 (4 Feb. 1929).

———. *al-Malik Fuad, malik al-nahda.* Cairo, 1944.

———. *Sa'd fi hayatihi al-khassa.* Cairo, 1929.

———. "Tawfiq Nasim Basha." *al-Hilal* 38:7 (May 1930): 778–781.

———. "Ziyara li al-amir al-sha'ir." *al-Hilal* 37:6 (Apr. 1929): 650–654.

———. "Ziyara li al-Amir 'Umar Tusun." *al-Hilal* 37:5 (Mar. 1929): 522–525.

Thabit, Munira. *Thawra fi al-burj al-'aji: mudhikkirat fi 'ishrin 'am.* Cairo, 1946.

Thiers, Henri. *Le Docteur Clot Bey: sa vie et ses travaux en Égypte.* Paris, 1869.

Thomas, Nicholas, ed. *International Directory of Films and Filmmakers.* 2nd ed. 5 vols. Chicago, 1990–1994.

Thompson, Jason. "Edward William Lane as an Artist." *Gainsborough's House Review* (1993–1994): 33–42.

———. "Edward William Lane as Egyptologist." *Minerva* 6 (fall 1995): 12–17.

———. "Edward William Lane in Egypt." *JARCE* 34 (1997): 243–261.

———. "Edward William Lane's 'Description of Egypt.'" *IJMES* 28 (1996): 565–583.

———. "'I Felt Like an Eastern Bridegroom': Edward William Lane's First Trip to Egypt, 1825–1828." *TSAB* 17 (1993): 138–141.

———. "'Of the Osmanlees, or Turks': An Unpublished Chapter from Edward William Lane's *Manners and Customs of the Modern Egyptians*." *TSAB* 19 (1995): 19–39.

———. "Reassessment of Edward William Lane." *Newsletter of the American Research Center in Egypt* 166 (1994–1995): 1–5.

Thoraval, Yves. *Regards sur le cinéma égyptien.* Beirut, 1975.

Tidrick, K. *Heart-Beguiling Araby.* Cambridge, UK, 1981.

Tignor, Robert L. "Bank Misr and Foreign Capitalism." *IJMES* 8 (1977): 161–181.

———. "The Egyptian Revolution of 1919." *MES* 12 (1976): 51–58.

———. *Modernization and British Colonial Rule in Egypt, 1882–1914.* Princeton, 1968.

———. "Muhammad Ali: Modernizer of Egypt." *Tarikh* 1 (1967): 4–14.

———. "New Directions in Egyptian Modernization: Ismail, Khedive of Egypt, 1863–1879." *Tarikh* 2 (1968): 64–71.

———. "Some Materials for the Study of the Arabi Rebellion: A Bibliographical Survey." *MEJ* 16 (1962): 239–248.

al-Tilmisani, 'Umar. *Dhikrayat la mudhakkirat.* Cairo, 1985.

Tincq, Henri. "Siege Mentality Grips the Copts of Egypt." *Guardian* (21 Feb. 1988): 15–16.

Toledano, Ehud R. "Mehmet Ali Pasa or Muhammad 'Ali Basha?" *MES* 21:4 (Oct. 1985): 141–159.

———. *State and Society in Mid-Nineteenth-Century Egypt.* Cambridge, UK, 1990.

Tomiche, Nada. "Taha Hussein: à la recherche d'un monde perdu." *Arabica* 28:1 (Feb. 1981): 107–110.

Toubiana, S. "Entretien avec Youssef Chahine." *Cahiers du Cinéma* 431–432 (May 1990): 48–50ff.

Trefzger, Marc. *Die nationale Bewegung Ägyptens vor 1928 im Spiegel der schweizerischen Offentlichkeit.* Basel and Stuttgart, 1970.

Tripp, Charles. "Ali Mahir and the Politics of the Egyptian Army, 1936–1942." *Contemporary Egypt*, 45–71.

Tripp, Charles, ed. *Contemporary Egypt Through Egyptian Eyes: Essays in Honour of P.J. Vatikiotis.* London, 1993.

Tucker, Judith. *Women in Nineteenth Century Egypt.* Cambridge, UK, 1985.

Tugay, Emine Foat. *Three Centuries.* London, 1963.

Tulard, Jean, Jean-François Fayard, and Alfred Fierro. *Histoire et dictionnaire de la Révolution Française 1789–1799.* Paris, 1987.

Tulaymat, Zaki. *Dhikrayat wa wujuh.* Cairo, 1981.

———. "Drama in Egypt." In *Egypt in 1945*, ed. M.L. Roy Choudhuri. Calcutta, 1946, 207–217.

———. Introduction to *Hayatuna al-tamthiliyya*, by Muhammad Taymur. Cairo, 1922.

———. "Jurj Abyad al-raid wa al-fannan." *al-Hilal* 67:7 (July 1959): 44–51.

———. *al-Kitab al-dhahabi li-mahrijan Khalil Mutran.* Cairo, 1948.

al-Tunisi, Khalifa. *Fusul min al-naqd 'ind al-'Aqqad.* Cairo, n.d.

Tusun, 'Umar. *al-Ba'that al-'ilmiyya fi 'ahd Muhammad 'Ali.* Alexandria, 1934.

———. *al-Jaysh al-misri fi Harb al-Krim.* Alexandria, 1936.

———. *Safha min tarikh Misr fi 'ahd Muhammad 'Ali.* Cairo, 1940.

———. *al-Sana'i' wa al-madaris al-harbiyah fi 'ahd Muhammad 'Ali Basha.* Alexandria, 1932.

Tutungi, Gilbert. *Tawfiq al-Hakim and the West.* Bloomington, Ind., 1966.

Tweedy, Owen. "Sa'd Pasha Zaghlul." *Fortnightly Review* N.S. 122 (1927): 492–503.

———. "Sa'd Zaghlul Pasha." *Fortnightly Review* N.S. 120 (1926): 110–118.

UAR, Supreme Council for the Protection of Arts and Letters. *Mahrajan Ahmad Shawqi.* Cairo, 1958.

———. *Mahrajan Mahmud Sami al-Barudi.* Cairo, 1958.

UAR, Supreme Council for the Protection of Arts, Letters, and Social Sciences. *Mahrajan Khalil Mutran.* Cairo, 1960.

———. *Mahrajan Rifa'a Rafi' al-Tahtawi.* Cairo, 1960.

'Ubayd, Ahmad. *Dhikra al-sha'irayn: sha'ir al-Nil wa amir al-shu'ara.* Damascus, 1933.

———. *Kalimat al-Manfaluti.* Damascus, 1942.

———. *Mashahir shu'ara al-'asr.* Damascus, 1922.

'Ubayd, Muna Makram, ed. *Makram 'Ubayd, 1889–1989: kalimat wa mawaqif.* Cairo, 1990.

'Ubayd, William Makram. *Makramiyyat.* Cairo, 1945.

———. "al-Siyasa 'allamatni." *al-Hilal* 55:10 (Oct. 1947): 15.

Uhiba, al-Sadiq 'Ali. *Manhaj al-Maraghi fi al-tafsir.* Rabat, 1996.

'Ukasha, Tharwat, *Mudhakkirati fi al-siyasa wa al-thaqafa.* 2 vols. Cairo, 1987.

'Umar, Mahmud Fathi. *Abtal al-hurriyya fi Misr wa Amrika.* Cairo, [1940s?].

'Umar, Najah. *Taha Husayn: ayyam wa ma'arik.* Beirut, [1970s?].

Umm Kulthum. "Ahmad Rami." *al-Hilal* 56:1 (Jan. 1948): 32–33.

Umm Kulthum qitharat al-'arab. Beirut, 1975.

'Urabi, Hazim. *Ahmad 'Urabi rahib al-layl wa faris al-nahar.* Cairo, 1973.

'Uruq, Muhammad. *Qiraa fi awraq 'Ali Sabri.* Cairo, [1992?].

'Usfur, Jabir. *al-Maraya al-mutajawira: dirasa fi naqd Taha Husayn.* Cairo, 1983.

'Usfur, Jabir, and Nabil Faraj. *Muhammad Husayn Haykal fi u'yun mu'asirihi.* Cairo, 1996.

'Uthman, 'Abd al-Fattah. *al-Uslub al-qisasi 'inda Yahya Haqqi.* Cairo, 1990.

'Uthman, Ahmad. "Fi dhikra al-rabi'a: Taha Husayn wa Mustaqbil al-thaqafa al-klasikiyya fi Misr." *al-Katib* (Oct. 1977): 22–32.

'Uthman, Muhammad Fathi. *Sharh al-Burda li al-Busiri wa nahj al-Burda li-Shawqi.* Cairo, 1973.

'Uthman, Muhammad Salih. *al-'Aqqad fi nadwatihi.* Cairo, 1965.

'Uthman, 'Uthman Ahmad. *Safahat min tajribati.* Cairo, 1981.

'Uwayda, Kamil Muhammad Muhammad. *Ahmad Amin, al-mufakkir al-islami al-kabir.* Beirut, 1995.

'Uwayda, Kamil Muhammad Muhammad. *Ahmad Rami: sha'ir al-hubb al-dafi'.* Beirut, 1995.

———. *Ahmad Zaki Abu Shadi: al-sha'ir al-namudhaji.* Beirut, 1994.

———. *Khalil Mutran: sha'ir al-qutrayn.* Beirut, 1994.

Vansittart, Robert G. *The Mist Procession.* 1958.

Vásquez, E. Gálvez. *El Cairo de Mahmud Taymur—Personajes literarios.* Seville, 1974.

Vatikiotis, P.J. *The Middle East from the End of Empire to the End of the Cold War.* London and New York, 1997.

———. *Nasser and His Generation.* New York, 1978.

Vatikiotis, P.J., ed. *Egypt Since the Revolution.* New York, 1968.

Vaucher, Georges. *Gamal Abdel Nasser et son équipe.* Paris, 1959.

Vial, C. "al-'Aqqad (1888–1964)." *Arabica* 11 (1964): 213–216.

———. "Rifa'a al-Tahtawi . . . precursor du feminisme en Egypte." *Maghreb-Machrek* 87 (Jan.–Mar. 1980): 35–48.

———. "Contribution à l'étude du roman et de la nouvelle en Égypte des origines à 1960." *Revue de l'Occident Musulman et de la Mediterranée* 4:2 (1967): 133–174.

Vidal, Fina Gued. *Safiyya Zaghlul.* Cairo, [1946?].

Vingtrinier, Aimé. *Soliman-pacha, Colonel Sève, généralisme des armées égyptiennes.* Paris, 1886.

Vitalis, Robert. "On the Theory and Practice of Compradors: The Role of 'Abbud Pasha in the Egyptian Political Economy." *IJMES* 22:3 (1990): 291–315.

Vivielle, J. "Cerisy Bey." *BIE* 8 (1926): 71–91.

Volait, Mercedes. *La Revue Imara (1939–1962): L'architecture moderne en Égypte et la revue "al-'Imara."* Cairo, 1988.

Voll, John O. "Fundamentalism in the Sunni Arab World." In *Fundamentalisms Observed*, I, ed. M.E. Marty and Scott Appleby. Chicago, 1991, 345–402.

Volney, C.F. *Voyage en Égypte et en Syrie pendant les années 1783, 1784, et 1785.* Paris, 1787.

Waddy, Charis. *Women in Muslim History.* New York and London, 1980.

Wadi, Taha 'Imran. *al-Duktur Muhammad Husayn Haykal: hayatuhu wa turathuhu al-adabi.* Cairo, 1969.

———. *Shi'r Naji al-mawqif wa al-'adat.* Cairo, 1976, 1981.

Wahba, Sa'd al-Din. *al-Nahr al-khalid: Muhammad 'Abd al-Wahhab fi hiwar ma'a Sa'd al-Din Wahba.* Cairo, 1992.

al-Wahhabi. *Maraji' tarajim udaba al-'arab.* 5 vols. Baghdad, 1956–1972.

Wahid, 'Ala al-Din. *'Ashiq al-hurriyya: Wali al-Din Yakan.* Cairo, 1987.

———. *Masrah Muhammad Taymur.* Cairo, 1975.

———. *Yusuf al-Siba'i bayna al-ayyam wa al-layali.* Cairo, 1979.

Wajdi, Muhammad Farid. "Ahamm hadith fi majra hayati." *al-Hilal* 38:1 (Nov. 1929): 20–21.

———. "Wafat al-ustadh al-imam." *Majallat al-Azhar* 16:7 (Rajab 1364): 334–336.

———. *al-Wajdiyyat.* Cairo, 1928; ed. Muhammad 'Abd al-Mun'im Khafaji. Beirut, 1982.

Wakeman, John, ed. *World Film Directors.* 2 vols. New York, 1987–1988.

al-Wakil, al-'Awadi. *al-'Aqqad wa al-tajdid fi al-shi'r.* Cairo, 1967.

———. *Qadiyyat al-saffud bayn al-'Aqqad wa khusumihi.* Cairo, 1971.

al-Wakil, Mukhtar. "Ibrahim Naji." *al-Kitab* 13 (May 1953): 599–603.

———. *Khalil Mutran wa madrasatuhu.* Cairo, 1947.

———. *Ruwwad al-shi'r al-hadith fi Misr.* Cairo, 1934.

Wakin, Edward. *A Lonely Minority: The Story of Egypt's Copts.* New York, 1963.

al-Walili, Ibrahim Mustafa. *Mafakhir al-ajyal fi siyar a'azim al-rijal.* Cairo, 1934.

Walker, Dennis. "Egypt's Liberal Arabism: The Contribution of Ahmad Hasan az-Zayyat." *Rocznik orientalistyczny* T.L.Z. 1 (1995): 61–98.

Wallon, H. *Notice sur la vie et les travaux de F.A.F. Mariette.* Paris, 1883.

Warburg, Gabriel. "Lampson's Ultimatum to Faruq." *MES* 11:1 (1975): 24–32.

———. *The Sudan Under Wingate.* London, 1971.

Ware, Lewis B. "Women's Emancipation in the Middle East: Jurji Zaydan's View." *Journal of South Asian and Middle Eastern Studies* 2:4 (1979): 38–55.

Warner, Philip. *Kitchener: The Man Behind the Legend.* London, 1985.

Wasfi, Huda. "Molière et le théâtre égyptien: affinités satiriques." *Le miroir égyptien.* Marseilles, 1984.

———. "al-Shaykh Matluf bayn Mulyir wa Muhammad 'Uthman Jalal." *al-Masrah* 1 (Jan. 1964): 29–31.

Waterbury, John. *The Egypt of Nasser and Sadat.* Princeton, 1983.

Waterfield, Gordon. *Professional Diplomat: Sir Percy Loraine of Kirkbride, Bt.* London, 1973.

Wavell, Archibald. *Allenby: A Study in Greatness.* New York and London, 1941.

———. *Allenby in Egypt.* London, 1943. Arabic trans. Ali Ibrahim al-Aqtash and Mustafa Kamil Fuda. *Allinbi fi Misr.* Cairo, 1945.

Weaver, Mary Anne. "The Trail of the Sheikh." *New Yorker* (12 Apr. 1993): 71–89.

Weinthal, Leo. *Anglo-African Who's Who.* London, 1910.

Weizman, Ezer. *The Battle for Peace.* New York, 1983.

Wendell, Charles. "Ahmad Lutfi al-Sayyid: In Memoriam." *Middle Eastern Affairs* 14 (June 1963): 169–172.

———. *Evolution of the Egyptian National Image.* Berkeley, 1972.

Wendell, Charles, ed. and trans. *Five Tracts of Hasan al-Banna (1906–1949).* Berkeley and Los Angeles, 1978.

Wentworth, Lady [Judith Blunt]. *The Authentic Arabian Horse and His Descendants.* 3rd ed. Canaan, N.Y., 1979.

Wessels, Antonie. *A Modern Arabic Biography of Muhammad.* Leiden, 1972.

———. "Nagib Mahfuz and Secular Man." *Humaniora Islamica* 2 (1974): 105–119.

Weygand, Maxime. *Histoire militaire de Mohamed Aly et de ses fils.* 2 vols. Paris, 1936.

Wheelock, Keith. *Nasser's New Egypt.* New York, 1960.

Who's Who in Egypt and the Near East. 19th ed. Cairo, 1953.

Widmer, Gottfried. "Ibrahim al-Muwailihi: Der Spiegel der Welt." *WI*, NS 3 (1954): 57–126.

———. "Übertragungen aus des neuarabischen Literatur: 1. Mahmud Taymur." *WI* 13 (1932): 1–103.

Wielandt, Rotraud. *Das Bild der Europäer in der modernen arabischen Erzähl—und Theaterliteratur.* Beirut, 1980.

———. *Das erzählerische Frühwerk Mahmud Taymurs.* Beirut, 1983.

———. *Offenbarung und Geschichte im Denke moderner Muslime.* Wiesbaden, 1971.

Wiet, Gaston. "L'agonie de la domination ottomane en Egypte." *CHE* 2:4 (1949–1950): 496–497.

———. "Les déplacements de Mohammed Ali." *CHE* 2 (1949): 86–120.

———. *Fihris ajaib al-athar.* Cairo, 1954.

———. *Mohammed Ali et les beaux-arts.* Cairo, 1949.

Wilbour, Charles Edwin. *Travels in Egypt, December 1880 to May 1891.* Brooklyn, 1936.

Willcocks, William. "In Egypt During the Forty Years of British Occupation." *BIE* 8 (1925–1926): 19–37.

———. *Sixty Years in the East.* Edinburgh and London, 1935.

Wills, Walter H., and R.J. Barrett. *Anglo-African Who's Who and Biographical Sketchbook.* London, 1905.

Wilson, Arnold T. *The Suez Canal: Its Past, Present, and Future.* London, 1933.

Wilson, C. R. *Chapters from My Official Life.* London, 1916.

Wilson, Colin, ed. *Encyclopedia of Modern Murder, 1962–1982.* New York, 1985.

Wilson, John. *Signs and Wonders upon Pharaoh.* Chicago, 1974.

Wingate, Ronald. *Wingate of the Sudan.* London, 1955; Westport, Conn., 1975.

Winslow, H. "The Child Weavers of Egypt." *Craft Horizons* (Jan. 1958): 30–33.

Wissa, Hanna F. *Assiout: The Saga of an Egyptian Family.* Sussex, UK, 1994.

Wood, H.F. *Egypt Under the British.* London, 1896.

Woodsmall, Ruth. *Muslim Women Enter a New World.* London, 1936.

Woodward, Peter. *Nasser.* London and New York, 1992.

Wrench, Evelyn. *Alfred, Lord Milner: The Man with No Illusions, 1854–1925.* London, 1958.

Wright, Arnold. *Twentieth Century Impressions of Egypt.* London, 1909.

Yaghi, 'Abd al-Rahman. *Fi al-juhud al-riwaiyya min Salim al-Bustani ila Najib Mahfuz.* 2nd ed. Beirut, 1981.

Ya'qub, Lusi. *Ihsan 'Abd al-Quddus wa al-hubb.* Cairo, 1996.

———. *Mayy: usturat hubb wa al-'alam.* Cairo, 1998.

Yarid, Nazik Saba. *Ahmad Shawqi: lahn al-mujtama' wa al-watan.* Beirut, 1970.

——— [Yared, Nazik Saba]. *Arab Travellers and Western Civilization.* London, 1996.

Yeghen, Foulad. *L'Égypte sous le regne de Fouad Ier.* Cairo, 1929.

Yunis, Mahmud. *Idarat Qanat al-Suways qabl al-tamim wa ba'dah.* Cairo, 1962.

al-Yusuf, Fatima. *Dhikrayat.* Cairo, 1953.

Yusuf, Hasan. *al-Qasr wa dawruhu fi al-siyasa al-mis-riyya, 1922–1952.* Cairo, 1982.

Yusuf, Majid. In *Majallat al-Kuwayt,* no. 61 (Sept. 1987): 73–78.

Yusuf, Mustafa al-Nahhas Jabr. *Siyasat al-ihtilal tujah al-haraka al-wataniyya, 1906–1914.* Cairo, 1975.

Yusuf, Niqula. *A'lam min al-Iskandariyya.* Alexandria, 1969.

———. Introduction to *Diwan 'Abd al-Rahman Shukri.* Alexandria, 1960, I, 2–15.

Yusuf, al-Sayyid. *al-Ikhwan al-Muslimun: hal hiya sahwa islamiyya?* Vols. I– (Ma'adi, 1994–).

Zaghlul, Muhammad, and [Isma'il] Sirri. *Hawla mashru'at al-rayy al-kubra: al-munaqasha al-fan-niyya allati darat bayna . . . Muhammad Zaghlul Basha wa Isma'il Sirri Basha.* Cairo, 1928.

al-Zahlawi, Habib. *Udaba mu'asirun.* Cairo, 1935.

Zakhura, Ilyas. *Mirat al-'asr fi akabir al-rijal bi-Misr.* 3 vols. Cairo, 1897–1916.

———. *al-Suriyyun fi Misr.* Cairo, 1927.

Zaki, 'Abd al-Hamid Tawfiq. *A'lam al-musiqa al-mis-riyya 'abra 150 sana.* Cairo, 1990.

———. *al-Mu'asirun min ruwwad al-musiqa al-'ara-biyya.* Cairo, 1993.

Zaki, 'Abd al-Rahman. *A'lam al-jaysh wa al-bahriyya.* Cairo, 1947.

———. *Ibrahim Pasha: 1789–1848.* Cairo, 1948.

———. "Le journal manuscrit d'Abbas Bey." *CHE* 6 (1954): 229–232.

———. *Muhammad 'Ali wa 'asruhu.* Cairo, [1940s?].

———. "Taqrir Amir al-Bahr Muharram Bey 'an sa-far al-ustul al-misri ila al-Mura." *MTM* 2:1 (May 1949): 139–203.

———. *al-Tarikh al-harbi fi 'asr Muhammad 'Ali al-kabir.* Cairo, 1950.

Zaki, Ahmad. *Un mot sur Riaz Pacha, homme d'état égyptien.* Cairo[?], 1911.

———. *al-Safr ila al-mutamar.* Cairo, 1894.

———. *Tarjamat hayat al-'alim al-fadil al-maghfur lahu Isma'il Pasha al-Falaki.* Cairo, n.d.

Zaki, Ahmad Kamal. *al-Naqd al-adabi al-hadith.* Cairo, 1972.

Zaki, Muhammad Amin. *Mashahir al-Kurd wa Kur-distan fi al-'asr al-islami.* 2 vols. Cairo, 1947.

Zaki, Muhammad Shawqi. *al-Ikhwan al-Muslimin wa al-mujtama' al-misri.* Cairo, 1954.

Zaki al-Din, Muhammad Muhammad. *al-Kuttab al-thalatha: Wali al-Din, al-Manfaluti, al-'Aqqad.* Cairo, 1924.

———. *al-Manfaluti.* Cairo, 1942.

Zalat, 'Abd al-Salam Mahmud. *al-Janib al-insani fi shi'r Shawqi wa Hafiz.* Alexandria, 1988.

Zalat, Ahmad. *al-Duktur Muhammad Husayn Haykal: bayna al-hadaratayn al-islamiyya wa al-ghar-biyya.* Cairo, 1988.

Zalata, 'Abd Allah. *Ali Amin: shakhsiyya–madrasa.* Cairo, 1986.

Zananiri, Gaston. *Le Khédive Ismail et l'Égypte.* Alexandria, 1923.

Zand, Mustafa. *al-Qawl al-haqiqi fi ritha wa tarikh al-khidiwi al-maghfur lahu Muhammad Tawfiq.* Cairo, 1892.

Zarruq, Hasan al-Tahir. *Muwahhidat al-'arab al-Sayyida Umm Kulthum.* Khartum, 1969.

al-Zawahiri, Fakhr al-Din al-Ahmadi. *al-Siyasa wa al-Azhar.* Cairo, 1945.

al-Zawi, Ahmad Tahir. *Jihad al-abtal fi Tarabulus al-Gharb.* Beirut, 1970.

Zaydan, Jurji. *The Autobiography of Jurji Zaydan, In-cluding Four Letters to His Son.* Ed. Thomas Philipp. Washington, 1990.

———. *Bunat al-nahda al-'arabiyya.* Cairo, 1957.

———. *Mudhakkirat Jurji Zaydan.* Ed. Salah al-Din al-Munajjid. Beirut, 1968.

———. *Tarajim mashahir al-sharq fi al-qarn al-tasi' 'ashr.* 2 vols. Cairo, 1902, 1910.

———. *Tarikh adab al-lugha al-'arabiyya.* 4 vols. Beirut, 1900.

Zaydan, Yusuf. *Fihris makhtutat Rifa'a Rafi' al-Tahtawi.* Cairo, 1996.

Zayid, Mahmud. "Nashat Hizb al-Wafd, 1918–1924." *al-Abhath* 15:2 (1962): 242–280.

Zayid, Sa'id. *'Ali Mubarak wa a'maluhu.* Cairo, 1958.

al-Zayn, Ahmad, ed. *Diwan Sabri.* Cairo, 1938.

Zayn al-Din, Isma'il Muhammad. *al-Ajanib wa dawruhum fi al-idara al-misriyya, 1820–1882.* Cairo, 1990.

Zayn al-Din, Muhammad Amin. *Ma'a al-Duktur Ah-mad Amin fi hadith al-Mahdi wa al-mahdawiyya.* Beirut, 1990.

Zayyan, Bahi al-Din. *Mustafa Kamil bi-munasabat murur khamsin 'aman 'ala wafatihi.* Cairo, 1958.

al-Zayyat, Ahmad Hasan. "al-Imam al-akbar al-Shaykh Mahmud al-Shaltut." *Majallat al-Azhar* 35 (Jan. 1964): 641–643.

———. "al-Marhum al-Ustadh Muhammad Farid Abu Hadid." *MMLA* 23 (1968): 115–126.

———. *Sa'd Zaghlul min aqdiyatihi.* Cairo, 1932; Beirut, 1974.

———. *Wahy "al Risala."* 3 vols. Cairo, 1949–1950.

al-Zayyat, Muhammad Hasan. *Ma ba'da "al-Ayyam."* Cairo, 1986; earlier version in *al-Musawwar,* nos. 2987–3007 (8 Jan.–28 May 1982).

el-Zayyat, Mohamed Hasan. "Taha Hussein and the Arab World." *Cultures* 2:2 (1975): 101–114.

al-Zayyati, Sulayman Rasd al-Hanafi. *Kanz al-jawhar fi tarikh al-Azhar.* Cairo, 1903.

Zebiri, Kate. *Mahmud Shaltut and Islamic Mod-ernism.* Oxford, 1993.

Zeidan, Joseph T. *Arab Women Novelists: The Forma-tive Years and Beyond.* Albany, N.Y., 1995.

Zeine, Zeine. *Emergence of Arab Nationalism.* Beirut, 1976.

Zetland, Lawrence, Marquis of. *Lord Cromer.* London, 1932.

Ziadeh, Farhat. *Lawyers, the Rule of Law, and Liber-alism in Modern Egypt.* Stanford, 1970.

Zincke, Foster Barham. *Egypt of the Pharaohs and the Khedive*. London, 1871; Boston, 1977.

al-Zirikli, Khayr al-Din. *al-A'lam: qamus tarajim li-ashhar al-rijal wa al-nisa min al-'arab wa al-musta'ribin wa al-mustashriqin*. 8 vols. 4th ed. Beirut, 1980.

Ziyada, Ahmad. *Salah Jahin, 1930–1986*. Cairo, 1996.

Ziyada, Mayy. *'Aisha Taymur: sha'irat al-tali'a*. Cairo, 1926; Beirut, 1975.

―――. *Bahithat al-Badiya aw Malak Hifni Nasif: bahth intiqadi*. Cairo, 1920; Beirut, 1993.

―――. *al-Sahaif*. Cairo, 1924.

Zolondek, Leon. "*al-Ahram* and Westernization: Socio-Political Thought of Bisharah Taqla." *WI*, N.S. 12:4 (1969): 182–195.

―――. "al-Tahtawi and Political Freedom." *MW* 54:2 (1964): 90–97.

az-Zubaydi, Abd al-Mun'im K. "The Diwan School." *JAL* 1 (1970): 36–48.

Zuhayri, K. "Mudhakkirat 'an Taha Husayn." *al-'Arabi* 253 (Dec. 1979): 12–17.

Zuhur, Sherifa. *Revealing Reveiling: Islamist Gender Ideology in Contemporary Egypt*. Albany, N.Y., 1992.

INDEX

Abaza, 'Aziz, 1
Abaza, [Muhammad] Fikri, 1
Abaza, Ibrahim Disuqi, 1
Abaza, Tharwat, 1–2
'Abbas Hilmi I, 2, 33, 43, 168
'Abbas Hilmi II, 2–3, 5, 136; aide-de-camp to, 59;
    al-Bakri and, 33; Cromer and, 51; entourage of,
    49; Fakhri and, 52; opposition to, 183;
    opposition to British, 230; 'Urabi Revolution,
    219; veiled protectorate, 44
al-Abbasi, Shaykh Muhammad al-Mahdi, 4
'Abbud, [Muhammad] Ahmad, 4
'Abd al-Hadi, Ibrahim, 4
'Abd al-Halim, Muhammad, 5
'Abd al-Majid, Dr. Ahmad 'Ismat, 5
'Abd al-Nur, Fakhri, 5–6
'Abd al-Quddus, Ihsan, 6, 231
'Abd al-Rahman, Dr. 'Aisha, 6–7, 106
'Abd al-Rahman, Shaykh 'Umar [Ahmad], 7
'Abd al-Raziq, 'Ali, 7–8, 33
'Abd al-Raziq, Shaykh Mustafa, 8, 115
'Abd al-Sabur, Salah, 9
'Abd al-Wahhab, Muhammad, 9–10, 115, 205
'Abduh, Shaykh Muhammad, 8, 10, 22, 33, 34,
    106, 110, 153, 166, 168, 183
Abu al-Dhahab, Muhammad, 11–12, 18
Abu al-Fath, Mahmud, 12
Abu Hadid, Muhammad Farid, 12
Abu Naddara Zarqa monthly magazine, 182
Abu Sayf, Salah, 6, 13
Abu Shadi, Dr. Ahmad Zaki, 13–14, 149
Abu Zayd, Dr. Hikmat, 14
Abyad, Jurj, 14, 23, 47, 77, 115, 126, 167, 214,
    231
Accession Day fete, 27
activism, 22; anti-British, 15, 44; anti-caliphate, 8;
    anti-Islamist, 26; anti-Zionist, 45; Islamic, 119,
    177; in the media, 21–22; political, 7, 226
actors and actresses, 93–94; Cairo troupes, 115;
    comic, 167; film, 26–27, 67, 69–70, 187–188,
    192, 224; musical, 9–10; stage, 14, 125–126,
    224, 231; touring troupes, 77
al-Afghani, Jamal al-Din, 15, 89, 146, 181

'Afifi, Dr. Hafiz, 16
al-Afkar journal, 12
Aflatun, Inji, 17
Afro-Asian Peoples' Solidarity Organization, 32,
    137, 192, 196
al-Ahali newspaper, 137
Ahli Sporting Club, 1
Ahmad, Zakariyya, 17
al-Ahram newspaper, 141, 161; anti-British
    writers, 1; cartoons, 93; competitors to, 169,
    230; editors of, 9, 12, 21, 35, 75, 98, 197;
    entertainment column, 121; first woman
    contributor, 239; founders of, 207; managers of,
    6; rival papers, 182; translators, 123; women
    writers, 7, 213; women's education and, 139
al-Akhbar al-Yawm newspaper, 6, 21, 22, 32, 35,
    74, 127, 137, 164
Akhir sa'a magazine, 22, 63, 74, 196
al-'Alam newspaper, 212
Alfi Bey, 17–18, 36
'Ali, Kamal Hasan, 18–19
'Ali Bey al-Kabir, 18
Allenby, Edmund Henry, Viscount, 19, 42, 226,
    234
'Alluba, Muhammad 'Ali, 19–20
al-Amal periodical, 212
ambassadors and diplomats, 5, 61, 62; to Britain,
    57–58, 185–186; British, 39, 42, 65, 109, 120;
    Egyptian, 185–186; French, 110; to Pakistan,
    19–20; to U.S., 79–80
Amin, Ahmad, 12, 20
Amin, 'Ali, 21
Amin, Muhammad, 4
Amin, Mustafa, 21–22
Amin, Qasim, 10, 22
'Amir, 'Abd al-Hakim, 23
Anglo-Egyptian Treaty (1936): Faruq and, 54;
    negotiators of, 16, 62, 118, 148, 189, 199;
    opposition to, 177; signing of, 109
Anglo-Egyptian Treaty (1954), 58
Anglo-Ottoman trade agreement, 134
antiquities collectors, 47
Antun, Farah, 23–24, 139

287

ABOUT THE BOOK

Scholars and writers often encounter problems when conducting research on Asian and African countries because of the scarcity or inaccessibility of information about the lives of significant historical figures. Responding to that lacunae in the coverage of Egypt, this desk reference provides biodata, biographical sketches, and source material for approximately four hundred men and women who have played a major role in Egypt's national life.

Arthur Goldschmidt is professor of Middle East history at Pennsylvania State University. His publications include *Modern Egypt: The Formation of a Nation-State*, *A Historical Dictionary of Egypt*, and *A Concise History of the Middle East* (now in its sixth edition).